Footprint Nicaragua

Richard Arghiris & Richard Leonardi
3rd edition

"The immense green lamp lights the faces
of those who gather beneath it with their simple lives"

Pablo Antonio Cuadra

❶ Ometepe
Rustic dual volcano island with pre-Columbian remains, cloud forests and inspiring organic farms, page 139.

❷ Pacific Coast
Pounding surf, golden beaches and turtle nesting sites, page 153.

❸ Isla Zapatera
Extinct volcano, national park and important pre-Columbian site, page 128.

❹ Laguna de Apoyo
Nicaragua's most beautiful crater lake with thermally heated waters, page 94.

❺ Granada
Handsome colonial city in the shadow of a volcano, page 110.

❻ Masaya
Visit the famous craft market and meet the talented artisans, page 84.

❼ Volcán Masaya
Active volcano with good hiking around a smoking crater, page 91.

❽ Managua
Nicaragua's anarchic heart has the best restaurants, nightlife and galleries, page 42.

❾ León
Lively student city with colonial architecture and access to a volcano chain, page 194.

Nicaragua Highlights

See colour maps at back of book

⑩ UCA Miraflor
Community tourism project in an enchanting nature reserve, page 252.

⑪ Coffee culture
Jinotega and Matagalpa are key coffee-growing towns, full of political history, pages 243 and 234.

⑫ Bosawás Biosphere Reserve
The largest national park and greatest wilderness in Central America, page 291.

⑬ Miskito heartland
Dense rainforests, mighty rivers and isolated indigenous communities, page 288.

⑭ Pearl Lagoon
Fascinating villages set in mangroves, savannah and rainforests, page 280.

⑮ Corn Islands
White-sand beaches, vibrant coral reefs and Caribbean culture, page 270.

⑯ Reserva Biológica Indio-Maíz
More species of birds, trees and insects than in all of Europe, page 182.

⑰ Río San Juan
Follow the river through rainforest reserves all the way to the Caribbean Sea, page 177.

⑱ Archipiélago Solentiname
Full of bird life, liberation theology and exceptional artists, page 171.

Contents

Río Indio, navigating inside the spectacular Indio-Maíz Biological Reserve, Central America's finest lowland tropical forest reserve.

1

2

4

5

7

8

10

11

1 Over 150 folkloric dance groups – mostly made up of children – perform regularly in and around Masaya. ▸▸ *See page 310.*

2 Granada's historic centre is ideal for long strolls through adobe passageways that lead back 480 years. ▸▸ *See page 110.*

3 The rugged lunar landscape of Volcán Masaya National Park is eerily beautiful. ▸▸ *See page 91.*

4 San Juan del Sur, on Nicaragua's Pacific Coast, has managed to hold onto its small town, fishing village feel. ▸▸ *See page 153.*

5 Volcán Concepción rises above the waters of Lake Nicaragua on Isla de Ometepe; the cone is a magnet for adventurous hikers. ▸▸ *See page 143.*

6 The chestnut-mandibled toucan is one of Nicaragua's 700+ species of bird; it's common in the rainforest of the Río San Juan. ▸▸ *See page 177.*

7 Pre-Columbian petroglyphs, outside the town of Boaco. Nicaragua is one of the world's richest countries for ancient rock art. ▸▸ *See page 14.*

8 León's cathedral, the largest temple in Central America, bathes in the afternoon light of Nicaragua's old colonial capital. ▸▸ *See page 197.*

9 Playa San Diego on Nicaragua's central Pacific Coast offers good surfing breaks without the ever-growing crowds of the southern coast. ▸▸ *See page 73.*

10 The noisy, pungent chaos of Granada's central market contrasts with the relative order of its well-tended tourist drags. ▸▸ *See page 124.*

11 Olive ridley sea turtle hatchlings make a run for the water at the La Flor Wildlife Refuge. ▸▸ *See page 156.*

12 Bringing home the cows and leña*; more than half of Nicaragua's population cooks on an open fire fuelled by burning wood.* ▸▸ *See page 320.*

Oasis of Peace
Fishermen mend their nets on the shores of the Isla de Ometepe.

A foot in the door

Few countries can boast such an authentic character as Nicaragua. Its universally negative image has worked in its favour to preserve it from the pressures of mass tourism: only the most jaded traveller could ignore the hospitality of its people, who greet foreigners openly and warmly despite years of economic and political problems. The culture revels in unique forms of dance, music and festivals, but most of all, Nicaragua breathes poetry, the unrivalled national passion, which has produced some of the most important poets in the history of the Spanish language. This creativity is fuelled by Nicaragua's kitchen, amongst the finest in Latin America, which puts a premium on fresh ingredients and generous servings. The tropical fruits, grilled meats and fresh fish are complemented by home-made cheeses, vine-ripened vegetables, handmade tortillas and Nicaragua's famously smooth rum.

Nicaragua's natural beauty has for years been a jealously guarded secret, but with more than 10% of the planet's biodiversity, Nicaragua is being discovered as a land of great parks. The two largest rainforest reserves in Central America are to be found here, forming part of 83 national protected areas that cover nearly 20% of its landmass. The reserves display a diverse portfolio of ecosystems and stunning geography, most distinct in the Pacific Basin, marked by numerous lakes, rivers and more than 50 volcanoes.
The thorny spine of volcanoes that run from Nicaragua's northwest Pacific shores into Lake Nicaragua and the dual-volcano island of Ometepe include many beautiful cones for hiking, seven which are active and 14 filled with crystal-clear crater lakes. On the coast, washed by two warm oceans, few can resist Nicaragua's beaches, whether it be the deep blue Pacific Coast or the turquoise Caribbean Sea.

Land of warriors and poets

Nicaragua's culture and tragic political history reflect a society of vibrant contrasts, a national psyche that is a blend of its two greatest national heroes, poet Rubén Darío and rebel general Augusto C Sandino. Darío and Sandino's qualities recall the two dominant Indian chiefs encountered at the time of the Spanish conquest; the philosophical and highly educated Chief Niqueragua and the clever and brave warrior Chief Diriangén. The mixture of Spanish and indigenous elements in the 480 years since the conquest of Diriangén and Niqueragua has created a nearly homogenous society: hardworking, talented and playful. It is a culture that enjoys life to its fullest, bends under pressure until breaking point and then snaps into rebellion. Numerous battles between internal rival political groups and repeated foreign government interventions from Europe, the US and Central American neighbours wreaked havoc on Nicaragua for much of the last two centuries. The popular insurrection and overthrow of the final Somoza dictatorship led by both poets and warriors was finally achieved in 1979. Subsequent unrest in rural Nicaragua, aided by the economic and military pressure from the United States that included the infamous Contra War, spelt defeat for the Sandinistas in 1990 elections and peace for Nicaragua. Since peace was won, a rapid modernization has been taking place and Nicaragua has been creeping into the international mainstream, for better or worse, while economically struggling back to its feet. Ironically, Nicaragua's international image continues to wallow in the mire, branded unstable since the war years, despite the fact that today it is the least violent nation in Central America.

Irrepressibly creative under pressure

Nicaragua's culture and self-pride bloomed in the 1980s during the troubled years of Sandinista rule. Poet and rebel-priest Ernesto Cardenal ran a brilliantly successful Ministry of Culture during a time of horrible suffering and war. The positive cultural effects of those years can still be felt today. Since the international fame of the immortal Rubén Darío, Nicaraguan poets have remained on centre stage, and the Spanish language and poetry has such a broad appeal that it is often said that "everyone in Nicaragua is a poet until proven otherwise". Along with poetry and the irrepressible and daily reinvention of the Spanish language, Nicaraguans boast an ironic self-mocking sense of humour and a love for food considered unrivalled in Central America. Visitors can rest assured that despite the growing pressures of globalization after 15 years of political stability, Nicaragua's idiosyncrasies are still fully in place.

Essentials

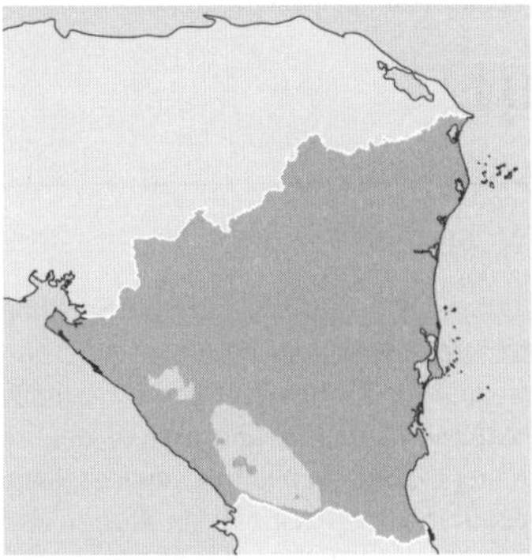

Footprint features

Planning your trip

Where to go

With some notable exceptions like Granada, Ometepe, the Corn Islands and San Juan del Sur, most of Nicaragua is well off the beaten track, with large nature reserves and small villages devoid of travellers and commercialization. However, there are many sights of interest within easy reach of the capital, Managua, and a great deal of ground can be covered in a matter of days using express public bus services, local tour operators or hired taxis. Road communication in the Pacific Basin is good and most areas of interest are less than 200 km from the capital. Travel between the two coasts and to the rainforest areas on the east side of the great lakes is more difficult and involves marathon bus rides or journeys by boat and/or small aircraft.

Managua and Masaya

Since it is the nation's capital and the main point of arrival in Nicaragua, most people will want to visit the sights of Managua before moving on to the more attractive countryside, colonial cities and villages. A couple of days in **Managua** are enough for most: beyond its importance as the country's business centre, the best part of the city is its nightlife and access to international services. Even those short on time can make it to **Masaya**'s famous craft market and to the national volcano park (where you can see inside an active crater), both less than 30 km south of the capital. Other viable day trips include the nearby Pacific beaches of **Montelimar** and **Pochomil**, or east of the great lakes to the cowboy towns of **Boaco** and **Juigalpa**. Managua is also the jumping-off point for trips to the **Río San Juan** rainforest reserves, the **Corn Islands**, **Bilwi**, **Bluefields** and other destinations best reached via light aircraft from the capital.

Colonial cities and villages

A seven- to 10-day stay on the Pacific Coast allows most travellers to get a good taste of the twin colonial cities of **Granada** and **León** and some of the easy-access ecological sites in the western region of the country. As the colonial capital and an intellectual and artistic centre, León is a must. A couple of days will be enough to visit the surrounding attractions such as **Las Peñitas** beach and the **Maribios** volcanic range. Around Masaya are the charming and hard-working villages called **Los Pueblos**, which are famous throughout the region for their festivals and handmade crafts. Granada, just south of Masaya, has a relaxed air and a good variety of lodging in one of the continent's oldest European settlements. Nearby are the **Mombacho Volcano Cloud Forest Reserve** and the archipelago of **Las Isletas** in Lake Nicaragua (see below).

Lake Nicaragua

Arrival in Granada marks the beginning of the great Lake Nicaragua. It would be easy to spend several weeks exploring this tropical body of water and its islands. One week on the lake will provide a chance to visit **Ometepe**, a dual volcano island that is a hiker's paradise with two forest reserves as well as many attractions of cultural interest. A week visiting Ometepe combines well with a trip to the southern Nicaraguan Pacific Coast with its wildlife reserves, like the **La Flor** turtle nesting site, and the bay of **San Juan del Sur**. In the **Archipiélago Las Isletas**, near Granada, it is possible to sleep on one of the 354 tiny islands of a water-bound community. From there or its mainland docks you can travel one hour south by fast boat to the country's most renowned archaeological sites on the **Archipiélago Zapatera**.

How big is your footprint?

Even small groups of travellers can have a big impact on the environment and local communities, especially where local people may be unused to their conventions or lifestyles and natural environments may be sensitive. Here are a few tips:

- Where possible choose a destination, tour operator or hotel with a proven ethical and environmental commitment; if in doubt ask.
- Spend money on locally produced (rather than imported) goods and services. Use common sense when bargaining – your few dollars saved may be a week's salary.
- Use water and electricity carefully – travellers may receive preferential supply while the needs of local communities are overlooked.
- Rather than giving money or sweets to children some visitors prefer to donate to a project, charity or school.

Learn about local etiquette and culture, consider local norms and behaviour, dress appropriately for local cultures and situations.

- Protect wildlife and other natural resources – don't buy souvenirs or goods made from wildlife unless they are clearly sustainably produced and are not protected under CITES legislation.
- Always ask before taking photographs or videos of people.
- Stay in local, rather than foreign owned, accommodation. The economic benefits for host communities are far greater and there are more opportunities to learn about local culture.
- Community tourism is growing in Nicaragua, offering the chance to participate in, and directly contribute to, rural communities. For more information, see the Guía Turismo Rural Comunitario, available in Granada or León, www.guiaturismocomunitario-nicaragua.com.

Río San Juan

Lovers of rainforest vegetation and wildlife will find the southeastern part of Lake Nicaragua and its Caribbean drainage, the Río San Juan, the most exciting part of the country. One week travelling in this region will reveal the country's two finest wildlife reserves, both of which have decent tourism infrastructure: the wetlands and gallery forest of the **Los Guatuzos Wildlife Refuge**; and the massive rainforest of the **Indio-Maíz Biological Reserve**, which houses Central America's best-preserved lowland tropical forest. The pristine **Archipiélago Solentiname** in Lake Nicaragua is also home to rich bird life and a very interesting school of rural artists and artisans. Travel to the river, lake, reserves and islands begins in Managua by bus or air and Granada by boat arriving at the jungle capital of **San Carlos**, after which boat travel is the only option.

Northern mountains

An interesting four- to six-day extension will take you back in time to the relatively cool highlands north of Managua. This region is different from the rest of Nicaragua because of its rugged mountains and pine forests. **Matagalpa** and **Jinotega** are key coffee-growing regions, full of political history and some precious cloud forest reserves. Across the northern range is **Estelí**, the home of Nicaraguan cigars and starting point for visits to many quaint northern villages in the region with historic churches, ancient traditions and indigenous crafts.

Caribbean Coast

One or two weeks can be spent experiencing the 'other Nicaragua': its eastern seaboard. Most people opt for a three- to four-day stay on the **Corn Islands** to enjoy the white-sand beaches and coral reefs. But with an additional three or four days, you can also visit **Bluefields** and the majestic **Pearl Lagoon**, or head north deep into Miskito country and **Bilwi** – cultural odysseys that include a good dose of tropical nature. Around both Bluefields and Bilwi you will find remote forests, lagoons and villages; most are challenging to reach, but worth the effort for those who want to really explore.

When to go

Most people prefer to visit western and northern Nicaragua during the rainy season or shortly after the rains have ended. During the dry season the Pacific Basin receives practically no rain at all and from mid-February until the rains arrive in late May the region is very hot and dry. During the rainy season the Pacific Basin is bright green and freshened daily by the rains, which normally last for less than two hours in the afternoon before clearing and then falling again during the night. December is an extraordinarily beautiful time to visit the Nicaraguan Pacific, with all the landscape in bloom, the air still fresh and visibility excellent across the volcanic ranges.

Nicaraguans consider the dry season (Dec-May) summer and the rainy season (Jun-Nov) winter, which can lead to confusion considering the country lies well north (11-16°) of the equator.

The dry season becomes shorter the further east you travel, and in the Caribbean Basin it can rain at any time of year. For snorkelling, March to mid-May and late September to October offer the best chances of finding calm waters with great visibility. For birdwatching in the rainforest areas of the Río San Juan, the dry season is best as you'll have the chance to see the many migratory species and nesting birds.

During Easter week and between Christmas and New Year all of Nicaragua rushes to the beach, lake and riverfront areas to swim, drink and dance; avoid these dates if you don't want to encounter massive crowds and fully booked hotels.

Activities and tours

Nicaragua has a number of options for independent and organized special-interest travel. Many activities, like whitewater rafting, free climbing or windsurfing, provide good opportunities for the experienced adventure traveller who wants to explore without tourist infrastructure or a safety net. Those listed below are onebs which have been developed by local tour operators and are accessible to independent travellers. Further details are available in the relevant chapters.

Archaeology and architecture

Although the archaeology is not as inspiring as the Mayan temples further north, Nicaragua's pre-Columbian history is fascinating. Around the country, museums display artefacts that have been discovered in each region; the best are at the **Palacio Nacional de la Cultura** in Managua (page 47), the **Museo Antiguo Convento de San Francisco** in Granada (page 118) and the **Museo Arqueológico** in Juigalpa (page 77). In Lake Nicaragua, there are some remains on the islands of **Zapatera** (page 128) and **Ometepe** (page 142), where you can see some large basalt statues. Petroglyphs are also present on many islands in Lake Nicaragua as well as numerous sites around the mainland. Colonial archaeology can be examined in the UNESCO World Heritage

Site of **León Viejo** (page 214). A guide is recommended since English language books on Nicaragua's archaeological heritage are virtually non-existent.

Colonial-era architecture is best in **León** (page 197) and **Granada** (page 113) and there are some fine examples in small villages all around the countryside, particularly in the highlands of Masaya (page 97) and Granada and in the northern provinces of **Nueva Segovia** (page 261) and **Madriz** (page 258).

Birdwatching

According to the latest count Nicaragua is home to over 700 species of bird, including boat-billed flycatcher, collared aracari, black-headed trogon, wood stork, roseate spoonbill, long-tailed manikin and osprey. The national bird is the turquoise-browed mot mot, beautiful and common in the highlands of Managua. The sheer number of birds in Nicaragua is amazing. **Reserva Biológica Indio-Maíz** (page 182) in Río San Juan area has primary rainforest with the scarlet macaw still filling the sky with red plumage. The **Refugio de Vida Silvestre Los Guatuzos** (page 173) has gallery forest and ample wetlands teeming with birds. The **Archipiélago Solentiname** (page 171) has two islands that are massive nesting sites. In the northern mountains of **Jinotega** (page 243) and **Matagalpa** (page 234) the cloud forests are home to many prize bird species like the quetzal. The **Montibelli Private Nature Reserve** (page 70), **Laguna de Apoyo** (page 94) and the **Reserva Natural El Chocoyero** (page 71) located just outside the capital, also offer a chance to see many interesting species including 1000 or so nesting parakeets.

Climbing

Guided climbs are non-technical in nature. There is potential for technical climbing, but routes are undeveloped and you need to have to your own gear as there are no climbing outfitters or stores. The most popular location is the **Maribios** volcanic range (page 210), set on a broad plain just 20-30 miles inland from the Pacific Ocean and made up of more than 20 volcanoes, five of which are active. Another key spot is the island of **Ometepe** (page 139) which has two cones affording sparkling lake views. While the Pacific volcanoes are no higher than 1700 m, the climbs are not as easy as they might seem. Most routes start just above sea level and are steep with difficult conditions including sharp rocks, sand and loose terrain, combined with serious heat. Further details can be found in the regional chapters, along with details of tour operators offering climbing and trekking.

Diving and snorkelling

There are professional dive operators on both of the **Corn Islands** (page 270). To find any depth a boat trip is needed, but the reefs lining both islands are beautiful and the marine life is rich. Snorkelling in the waters that wash the Corn Islands is world class and a real joy. Though scuba gear can be rented for diving, snorkellers would be wise to bring their own gear as most equipment available outside the dive operations is of poor quality. Snorkelling is also good around the **Pearl Cays** (page 280), but access is by expensive charter boat. The Pacific Coast, beaten by waves, is usually too rough for diving or snorkelling. **Laguna de Apoyo** (page 94) offers diving opportunities for those interested in taking part in scientific research.

Fishing

Nicaragua is a fisherman's paradise, with its wide selection of rivers, lakes and seas. Deep-sea fishing can be arranged in **San Juan del Sur** (page 153) or **Marina Puesta del Sol** (page 223) in the Pacific and bonefishing is possible on the **Corn Islands** (page 270). Lake Nicaragua is great for bass fishing. The island of **Zapatera** (page 128) and its archipelago are home to Central America's biggest annual freshwater tournament. In **Pearl Lagoon** (page 280) on the Caribbean side and on the **Río San Juan** (page 190) tarpon and snook fishing is very good.

Spectator sports

Baseball

Baseball is the national sport in Nicaragua. The first league games were organized over

100 years ago and there is a very hard-fought national championship for the first division and many minor divisions. Nicaraguans follow the major leagues in the United States with more fervour than many Americans. The regular season begins in Nov and runs until the championships in Feb. Games are played all over the country during the dry season on Sun in stadiums that are in themselves a cultural experience. Nicaragua has put several players into the North American professional league and usually finishes in the top five in the world championships. You can see a game anywhere in the country on a Sun in dry season.

Boxing

Another big passion for Nicaraguans is boxing, with five world champions in the lighter categories to be proud of. Though most fights of importance take place outside Nicaragua, it may be possible to watch low-level Nicaraguan fights as well as quality boxers in training at the **Alexis Argüello gymnasium**, Barrio San José Oriental, de la Clínica Santa María, 2 c sur, 1 c arriba, Managua.

Bullfighting

Bullfighting in Nicaragua is a strange hybrid of bullfighting and bull rodeo. The bull is not killed or injured, just intensely annoyed. The beast is brought inside the ring roped by a few mounted cowboys and tied to a bare tree in the centre. Someone mounts its back using a leather strap to hold on and the angry bull is released from the tree. The rider tries to stay on top and a few others show the animal some red capes for as long as they dare, before running off just before (in most cases) being impaled. When the bull gets too tired, a fresh one is brought in, mounted and shown more capes. Every patron saint festival has a bullfight. One of the most famous takes place at the Santa Ana festival in La Orilla, see page 131.

Cockfighting

Cock fights are legal and take place every Sun all over the country. The biggest time for the fights (*pelea de gallo*) is during the patron saint festival of each town. To find the fight rings you will need to ask around (they do not have signs). The fight ring in Estelí is one of the most serious, with bets of over US$3000 being waged.

Football

The standard of Nicaraguan *fútbol* is among the poorest in Latin America. The passion for baseball is mainly to blame. The most notable teams in the country come from the central plateau, northern mountains and coastal areas. Games can be watched on Sun in stadiums, such as Estelí, Somoto and Diriamba.

Surfing

Nicaragua's Pacific Coast is home to countless beautiful breaks, many of which are only just starting to become popular. Most surfing is done along the coast of Rivas, using **San Juan del Sur** (page 153) as a jumping-off point to reach breaks to the north and south. The country's biggest and most famous break is at **Popoyo** (page 158) in northern Rivas. It is possible to rent boards in San Juan del Sur, but in most cases you will need to bring everything with you, as even wax can be hard to find at times. Many used to rave at the tube rides and point breaks that lie empty all year round, but recent complaints include surf operators converging on breaks with a boat full of clients.

Trekking

Most of Nicaragua's Pacific Basin is great walking country. You will need to speak some Spanish to get by, but once outside the city a whole world of beautiful landscapes and friendly people awaits you. Fences outside cities in Nicaragua are for animals, not people, and if you respect the privacy and rights of the local residents you need not worry about trespassing. Local guides are helpful and you should ask around each village to see who can accompany you and how far. Accommodation will be in hammocks (see Camping, page 24). Due to wild driving habits, avoid walking along the road wherever possible and use the volcanoes as landmarks. It is possible to trek the **Maribios** volcano range (page 210) in northwestern Nicaragua, starting at the extinct lake-filled crater of **Volcán Cosigüina**, which is the most westerly point of Nicaragua, and taking in all 21 cones, five of which are active. The route passes through many ranches and farms, where you can ask for directions if you need to. Another great place for trekking is the island of **Ometepe** (page 139) with its breathtaking beauty, friendly people and many dirt trails; it is essential to use local guides here.

Getting there and away

Air

Managua and Granada are Nicaragua's international airports, the former for commercial jets and the latter for light aircraft from northern Costa Rica. There are no direct flights from the UK to Managua. **British Airways,** www.british-airways.com, uses Miami as a hub to connect with Central American carriers. Another option is to travel via Madrid from where **Iberia** fly direct to Costa Rica or Guatemala and then a use a local carrier to Managua (around US$600-900 in addition to the cost of getting to Madrid from your home city). The most direct flights are from Gatwick on **Continental Airlines,** www.continental.com, with a stop in Houston. Prices range from US$900-1200.

Two US carriers fly direct to Managua. **American Airlines** flies from Miami twice a day and **Continental Airlines** flies once a day from Houston. **TACA,** www.taca.com, the Central American group airline, also flies daily from Miami direct to Managua and has a direct flight twice a week from Los Angeles. **COPA,** www.copaair.com, the national carrier of Panama has twice-weekly flights from Houston. Flights from Miami cost US$350-500; from Houston or Los Angeles US$450-750; and upwards of US$700 from Canada. From Montreal, cheap charter flights are available from November to March.

The most efficient route to Nicaragua from Australia, at a cost of around US$1800, is direct from Sydney with **Qantas,** www.qantas.com.au, to Los Angeles, then to Houston with **Continental Airlines** for a direct flight from Houston to Managua or a **TACA** flight to Managua via El Salvador. From Auckland with the same connections and routes the fare comes to about US$1600.

TACA flies to Managua from all countries in Central America several times daily, as does the Panamanian carrier **COPA,** with superior in-flight service to Managua from Guatemala, Costa Rica and Panama, although connections are less frequent. Return flights to Managua normally cost around US$260 from Guatemala or Panama and US$220 from Costa Rica.

Discount travel agents

Nicaragua deals are hard to come by due to shortage of flights. UK residents can try www.traveljungle.co.uk. In the US there is company that specializes in Latin American flight tickets, www.exitotravel.com. Generally speaking local carriers TACA and COPA are less expensive from the US, Central and South America than US and European carriers, although code sharing means you can often combine the two from Europe.

UK and Ireland

STA Travel, 52 Grosvenor Gardens, Victoria, London SW1W 0AG, T020-7881 1299, www.statravel. co.uk. Specialists in low-cost student/youth flights and tours, also good for student IDs and insurance.
Trailfinders, 48 Earl's Court Rd, London, W8 6FT T0845-058 5858.

North America

Air Brokers International, 323 Geary St, Suite 411, San Francisco, CA94102, T01-800-883 3273, www.airbrokers.com. Consolidator and specialist in RTW and Circle Pacific tickets.
Discount Airfares Worldwide On-Line, www.etn.nl/discount.htm. A hub of consolidator and discount agent links.
International Travel Network/Airlines of the Web, www.itn.net/airlines. Online air travel information and reservations.
STA Travel, 5900 Wilshire Blvd, Suite 2110, Los Angeles, CA90036, T1-800-777 0112, www.sta-travel.com. With branches in New York, San Francisco, Boston, Miami, Chicago, Seattle and Washington DC.
Travel CUTS, 187 College St, Toronto, ON, M5T 1P7, T1-800-667 2887, www.travelcuts.com. Specialist in student discount fares, IDs and other travel services.

Australia and New Zealand
Flight Centres, 82 Elizabeth St, Sydney, T13-1600; 205 Queen St, Auckland, T09-309 6171. Also branches in other towns and cities.
STA Travel, T1300-360960, www.sta travelaus. com.au; 702 Harris St, Ultimo, Sydney, and 256 Flinders St, Melbourne. In NZ: 10 High St, Auckland, T09-366 6673. Also in major towns and university campuses.
www.travel.com.au, 80 Clarence St, Sydney, T02-929 01500.

Arriving in Nicaragua overland

There are three land crossings into Nicaragua from Honduras. Via Tegucigalpa, the most direct is the **Las Manos** crossing, entering just north of Ocotal. See page 259 for more details on Las Manos and El Espino crossings. The most travelled route into Nicaragua is via the lowlands adjacent to the Golfo de Fonseca using the crossing at **El Guasaule**, north of Chinandega (see page 225), south from Choluteca, Honduras. This entrance is also the nearest crossing for those coming from El Salvador via Honduras. An alternative from Choluteca is **El Espino**, which enters via the northern mountains and passes Estelí en route to Managua. The only road crossing that connects Nicaragua to Costa Rica and unites Central America via road is at **Peñas Blancas** (see page 160), 144 km south of Managua. Motorists and motorcyclists must pay US$20 in cash on arrival at the border (cyclists pay US$2, and up to US$9 at weekends, although this tends to vary from one customs post to the next). For motorcyclists crash helmets are compulsory. Several cyclists have said that you should take a 'proof of purchase' of your cycle or suggest typing out a phoney 'cycle ownership' document to help at border crossings. Motorists also pay the same entry tax per person as other overland arrivals. Make sure you get all the correct stamps on arrival, or you will encounter all sorts of problems once inside the country. Do not lose the receipts, they have to be produced when you leave; without them you will have to pay again. Up to four hours of formalities are possible when entering Nicaragua with a vehicle. On leaving, motorists pay five córdobas, as well as the usual exit tax.

International buses are a cheap and efficient way to travel between Nicaragua and other Central American countries. Buses are available to and from Honduras, El Salvador and Guatemala in the north, Costa Rica and Panama to the south. When leaving Managua you will need to check in one hour in advance with your passport and ticket. Three good companies operate the international routes to and from Managua. **Ticabus** ⓘ *de Cine Dorado, 2 c arriba, T222-6094, www.ticabus.com*, and **King Quality** ⓘ *at the end of 27 de Mayo street opposite Plaza Inter, T228-1454, www.king qualityca.com, both arrive at Barrio Martha Quezada*; and **Transnica** ⓘ *T277-2104, www.transnica.com*, located between the Catedral Nueva and Laguna de Tiscapa. The buses all have air conditioning, toilet and reclining seats; most have television screens and offer snacks. See box, opposite page for major routes into Nicaragua and one-way costs.

Arriving by boat

The water crossing into Nicaragua from Costa Rica is via **Los Chiles** using the Río Frío. There is road access to Los Chiles from La Fortuna, Costa Rica. Exit stamps and taxes must be paid in Los Chiles before boarding public boats for the journey down the Río Frío to San Carlos for immigration and customs for Nicaragua (see page 170).

Getting around

A decent road system covers the west of Nicaragua and the country's small size makes car or bus travel practical and fairly simple. Buses run between all Pacific and central cities and villages on a daily basis and fares are very cheap. A 4WD is needed

International bus routes

To/from Costa Rica
Ticabus leaves Managua at 0600, 0700, 1200 and San José at 0600, 0730 and 1230, US$15, 8½ hrs.
King Quality leaves Managua at 1330 and San José at 0300 US$21, 8½ hrs.
Transnica leaves Managua at 0530, 0700, 1000, 1200 (executive) 1500 and San José at 0400, 0530, 0700, 0900, 1200 (executive), US$20, Executive Service US$40, 8½ hrs.

To/from El Salvador
Ticabus leaves Managua at 0500 and San Salvador at 0500, US$30, 12 hrs.
King Quality leaves Managua at 0330 ('Quality class'), 0530 ('Cruceros Class'), 1100 ('King Class'), and San Salvador at 0530 ('Cruceros Class') and 1130 ('Quality Class'), 'Cruceros class', US$25, 'Quality Class' US$35, 'King Class' US$51, 11 hrs.
Transnica leaves Managua at 0500, 1230 and San Salvador at 0500, 0800, US$50, 11 hrs.

To/from Guatemala
Ticabus leaves Managua at 0500 and Guatemala City at 1300, US$46, 30 hrs including an overnight stay in El Salvador.
King Quality leaves Managua at 0230 ('Cruceros Class'), 1530 ('Quality Class') and Guatmela City at 0400 ('Cruceros Class') and 0630 ('Quality Class'), 'Cruceros class' US$52, 'Quality Class' US$62, 'King Class' US$86, 15 hrs.

To/from Honduras
Ticabus leaves Managua at 0500 (continues to San Pedro Sula, US$37, 14 hrs) and Tegucigalpa at 0915, US$23, 8 hrs (departs San Pedro Sula at 0500).
King Quality leaves Managua at 0330 ('King Class'), 1130 ('Quality Class'), and Tegucigalpa at 0600 ('King Class') and 1400 ('Quality Class'), 'Quality Class' US$30, 'King Class' US$42, 8½ hrs.
Transnica leaves Managua at 1400 and Tegucigalpa at 0700, US$40, 8 hrs.

To/from Mexico
Ticabus leaves Managua at 0500 and Tapachula at 0700, US$63, 36 hrs including overnight stay in El Salvador.
King Quality also has daily services between Managua and Tapachula, 'Quality Class' US$74, 'King Class' US$96.

To/from Panama
Ticabus leaves Managua at 0600, 0700, 1200 and Panama City at 1100, US$44, 28-32 hrs, including a 2- to 6-hr stopover in Costa Rica.

to get off the beaten path in all parts of the country. Boat and plane are the only options for long-distance travel on the Caribbean Coast and in the rainforest areas of the north and south where roads are horrible to non-existent.

Air

Domestic return flights should always be reconfirmed immediately on arrival to a destination. There is a 9 kg hand luggage limit. Stowed luggage maximum 20 kg on most flights. Domestic departure tax is US$2. **La Costeña** ① *T263-1228*, operates internal air services to Bluefields, Corn Island, Las Minas (Bonanza/Siuna/Rosita), Bilwi (previously known as Puerto Cabezas), San Carlos and Waspám (see text for details). **Atlantic Airlines** ① *T222-3037*, *www.atlanticairlines.com.ni*, provides coverage to Bluefields, Corn Island and Bilwi with connections to Tegucigalpa and other cities in Honduras. Flights are often booked full and early arrival is important as no seat assignments are given on most flights. All flights leave from Managua, so hopping from place to place by plane will mean a lot of returns to Managua.

 The exception is a **La Costeña** flight between Bilwi and Bluefields and Las Minas and Bilwi. All flights to Corn Islands stop in Bluefields.

Bus

This is how most Nicaraguans get around and, outside Managua, the bus drivers are usually friendly and helpful. Route schedules are pretty reliable except on Sundays. It is best to arrive early for all long-distance buses, especially if it is an express bus or for a route that only runs once or twice a day. On routes that leave every hour or half-hour you only need to check the destination above the front window of the bus and grab a seat. You can flag down most buses that are not marked 'Express'. Fares are collected as you board city buses or en route in the case of intercity buses. For express buses, you need to purchase your ticket in advance at the terminal or from the driver; some buses have reserved seating. Most Nicaraguan buses are 'retired' school buses from the United States and have very limited legroom. Sitting behind the driver may alleviate this problem for tall passengers and is a good idea if you plan to get off before the final destination. Buses often fill up to the roof and can be very hot and bumpy, but they are a great way to meet and get to know the Nicaraguan people. Most major destinations have an express service, which makes fewer stops and travels faster; for longer journeys an express bus could mean cutting travel times in half. For services between Granada, Jinotepe, Masaya, León and several other destinations the express bus may also be a 12- or 24-seat minibus and charge up to double the normal rate.

Car

The road network has been greatly extended and improved in recent years. The Pan-American Highway from Honduras to Costa Rica is paved the whole way (384 km), as is the shorter international road to the Honduran frontier via Chinandega. The road between Managua and Rama (for boat access to Bluefields) is paved, but not in good condition. Around 80% of Nicaragua's roads are unpaved with lots of mud bogs in the wet season and dusty washboard and stone-filled paths in the dry season so be flexible with your schedules. Petrol stations are very rare in the countryside; it's best to fill up the tank (unleaded, premium grade fuel and diesel are available everywhere) if going into the interior. There are 24-hour petrol stations in the major cities, elsewhere they close at 1800. 4WD drive for cities or travel within the Pacific Basin is not necessary, although it does give you dramatically more flexibility across the country and is standard equipment in mountain and jungle territory. It is obligatory to wear a seatbelt. If you are involved in a car accident where someone is injured, you may be held for up to two days, guilty or not, while blame is assessed. Hiring a driver covers this potentially disastrous liability. Be careful when driving at night, few roads are lit and there are many people, animals and holes in the road.

Car hire Renting a vehicle costs around US$45 a day for a basic car, rising to US$85 for a 4WD. Weekly discount rates are significant and if you want to cover a lot of sites quickly it can work out to be worthwhile. A minimum deposit of US$500 is required in addition to an international drivers' licence or a licence from your country of origin. Insurance is US$10-25 depending on cover. Before signing up check the insurance and what it covers and also ask about mileage allowance. Most agents have an office at the international airport and offices in other parts of Managua.

Cycling

A mountain bike is strongly recommended. If you hire one, look for a good-quality, rugged bike with low gear ratios for difficult terrain, wide tyres with plenty of tread for good road-holding, cantilever brakes and a low centre of gravity for improved stability. Imported bike parts are impossible to find in Nicaragua so buy everything you need before you leave home. Most towns have a bicycle shop of some

Road warrior – driving and surviving in Nicaragua

Anyone familiar with driving in Latin America will be aware to some extent of the challenge that lies ahead, although there are some specific Nicaraguan variations on the theme. Three delectable kinds of driving experiences await you in this tropical state of motoring madness.

City In the Managua battle-zone the visiting gladiator must steer clear of axle-breaking holes, and city buses – smoking beasts, filled to the ceiling with sweating commuters and professional thieves and manned by some of the most aggressive men on earth. The crazed and ruthless bus driver mounts his challenge, horn wailing, sharpened metal spikes spinning from chromed wheels. The bus driver will never slow down, yield or even acknowledge anyone, except a boarding or disembarking passenger. That poor paying customer will be lifted onto or tossed off the still-moving bus by a hyperactive screaming assistant, whose task it is to collect money. He hangs out of the open door, his flailing arms and legs signalling the next life-threatening lane change. Here is where the guest gladiator must yield, brake or just get the heck out of the way, as any counter-challenge will result in sure death. Taxi drivers too must be respected for what they are; rogue messengers from planet anarchy, routinely breaking every rule of legal driving in ways previously unimaginable. Don't be surprised by the crash-the-red-light-by-driving-into-oncoming-traffic-to-overtake-waiting-cars-at-the-intersection manoeuvre or their maniacally obsessive horn usage.

The open road Out of the confines of Managua you can breathe deep, relax and run free, but you still need grand prix reaction time to avoid ox and horse carts, people sitting on the road shoulder, potholes as deep as the 12th circle of hell and your fellow road warriors blissfully passing on blind corners and hills. There is no speed limit, just a limit on common sense, patience and judgement. The open-road Nicaraguan driver does, however, give ample room to the oncoming car, the overtaker and the undertaker. No matter how conservative you set out to be, you will be forced into aggressive overtaking. Be sure to use your horn to warn the vehicle you are passing in the daytime and your headlights at night. Be decisive and give space to the other gladiators, they will return the favour.

Off road The real fun of driving in Nicaragua lies beyond the limits of its paved universe. Rock-filled and river-sliced passages lead to places forgotten by earth and roadside services. Driving here is more akin to an off-road endurance test with mud bogs and raging rivers to be forged in the rainy season and relentless banging over rocky dust roads in the dry. The pace is slower and when you are not busy coating well-dressed women and children with thick layers of billowing dirt or sheepishly asking for an ox cart to pull you out of a bog, friends can be made and rides offered – even if a horse really would have been a better choice.

description, but it is best to do your own repairs and adjustments whenever possible. Take care to avoid dehydration by drinking regularly. In hot, dry areas with limited water supplies, be sure to carry an ample supply on the bike. For food, carry the staples and supplement these with whatever local foods can be found in the markets. Give your bicycle a thorough daily check for loose nuts or bolts or bearings.

 Always see that your bicycle is secure (most hotels will allow bikes to be kept in rooms). Carry a stick or some small stones to frighten off dogs, most of which are more bark than bite. Because of traffic it is usually more rewarding to keep to the smaller roads or to paths. Watch for oncoming, overtaking vehicles, protruding or unstable loads on trucks. Make yourself conspicuous by wearing bright clothing and a helmet. Recent reports suggest that bringing a bike into Nicaragua is full of customs red tape (see Arriving in Nicaragua overland, above). If you are charged, ask to speak to the superior and be sure to have proof that it is your bike. This will be easier if the bike doesn't look too new (throw some mud on it before you get to the border).

Hitchhiking

Hitchhiking is a common way to travel in the countryside, less so in the cities. Men will find it significantly more difficult to get a ride if they do not have a female companion. Pick-up trucks are the best bet, you should offer to help pay for fuel. Picking up hitchhikers is a great way to make friends, but not advisable if there is more than one man, unaccompanied by at least one woman. In the deep countryside it is considered quite rude not to offer a ride if you have room, particularly for women with babies.

Truck

In many rural areas and some cities, flat-bed trucks – usually covered with a tarpaulin and often with bench seating – are used for getting to places inaccessible by bus or to fill in routes where no buses are available. The trucks charge a fixed fare and, apart from eating a bowlful of dust in the dry season or getting soaked in the wet, they can be a great way to see the country. Communication with the driver can be difficult, so make sure you know more or less where you are going; other passengers will be able to tell you where to jump off. Banging the roof of the driver's cabin is often necessary to tell the driver he has arrived at your destination.

Sea

In a country with two oceans, two great lakes and numerous lagoons, estuaries and rivers, a boat is never far away and is often the only means of travel. The main Pacific ports are Corinto, San Juan del Sur and Puerto Sandino. The two main Atlantic ports are Bilwi and Bluefields. Public river boats are often slow but are a good way to meet local people; private boats can be hired if you are short on time or want to make stops along the way. There are regular services between the two Corn Islands and a big boat runs from Bluefields to Big Corn three times a week. Apart from the Bluefields route, boat travel along the Pacific and Caribbean coasts is difficult, and often the only option is to hire a boat or convince the fishermen to take you out. Fishermen are also an option in Lake Managua where there is no regular service. In Lake Nicaragua you can choose between big ferries and old wooden *African Queen* models or you can hire a private motor boat. There is a weekly service connecting Granada, Ometepe Island and San Carlos. The rivers and coastal lagoons are home to regular commuter boats, which are long, thin, covered boats with outboards or cargo boats, which are extremely slow. Private motor boats are very expensive to hire but are useful for both wildlife exploration and touring.

Maps

Detailed road maps are yet to be adopted in Nicaragua, but the government tourism board's map shows major routes. Since road signage is weak at best, it is important to have a map and some basic Spanish to get even a little way off the main highway. Stop by INTUR's main office in Managua, one block south and one block west from the Crowne Plaza Hotel, to get a country map. The only decent map made internationally is *Nicaragua – An International Travel Map*, published by International Travel Maps in Vancouver. Despite some errors, it is far better than other foreign attempts.

Hotel price codes explained

Unless otherwise stated, prices are for double rooms, including taxes and service charges.

LL over US$200
L US$151-200
AL US$101-150
A US$66-100
B US$46-65
C US$31-45
D US$21-30
E US$12-20
F US$7-11
G US$6 and under

Detailed maps (1:50,000) can be bought at the government geological survey office, **INETER** ⓘ *across from the Nicaraguan Immigration main office in Managua, T249-3590*. Some maps are sold out and waiting for funding to reprint, but those that remain are useful if you are planning to escape the beaten track and/or go trekking. Good regional maps are available for around US$6 each. See also page 37.

Sleeping

Nicaragua has a rapidly expanding portfolio of lodging options, from million-dollar private ecolodges to backpacker hostels. Quality lodging is limited to the Pacific Basin and other select areas, but there is an increasing trend in offering country farms (mostly coffee haciendas) as a rural option. Most beach hotels raise their rates for Holy Week and almost all hotels charge higher prices for the Christmas holiday season with sell-outs common months in advance.

Nicaraguan hotels are not a reason to visit the country, but there are some very charming lodges in beautiful locations. In Managua you can either pay more than you would expect for a Latin American hotel or put up with some fairly unpleasant sleeping conditions. Outside Managua the hotels in the **D-E** range are usually pleasant and some good deals are to be found. In some rural areas there will be only one option, although hanging your hammock in someone's home is always possible, if your language skills are up to the task. A room with private bath usually costs over US$25 per night in the city and US$15 in the country, while air-conditioning and running hot water will push you above US$40 in most cases. In remote areas, meals are often included in the price and electricity is produced by a diesel generator that runs for only a few hours after sunset. Water is sometimes scarce outside Managua, particularly at the end of the dry season in the northern mountains and in Bluefields. You should be aware that establishments calling themselves 'autohotel' or 'motel' or displaying 'open 24 hours' signs serve a purpose other than just providing a bed for the night (see box).

Always ask to see the room in advance. Below the **D** bracket, quality can vary radically. In the more costly **A-C** range, a slight price hike could mean a room overlooking the park instead of the laundry area. Budget travellers should bring a padlock, toilet paper, soap, insecticide, mosquito net and a decent towel. **G** bracket travellers should remember to shake out the sheets, if there are any. Many hotels on the outskirts of cities will lock up and go to bed early; if you are heading out for a night on the town, make sure you can get back in and that you know who has the key. Do not put toilet paper or any non-organic material in any toilet in the country; you will find a little wastebasket for that purpose. Electric showers are common below the **C** category and, if poorly wired, decidedly more effective than Nicaraguan coffee at getting the blood pumping in the morning. The shocks are not fatal, but it is wise to set the shower head on *caliente* (hot) with your feet in the dry and then turn on the

Love shack – automotels in Nicaragua

Many first time visitors are confused. What is an 'autohotel' or 'automotel'? Why all the romantic imagery on their signs? In reality, the 'auto' reference is a clue, a subtle indicator that the establishment will hide your car, as well as your love partner. Autohotels are for making love; they serve no other purpose. Rooms are sold in two- or three-hour blocks and include fresh towels, sheets and a condom. The customers pull quickly into an open parking stall connected to a private hotel room. Whoosh! A big curtain is closed immediately behind their car, effectively hiding the identity of the couple and their vehicle. Each room also has a little blind-box door for the discreet staff to pass ordered beers or soft drinks through.

These hotels are part of the Nicaraguan culture. They are used for illicit affairs and by impatient courting couples – most Nicaraguan women must live at home until they are married. Some of them look very inviting from the outside, a lot nicer than many a budget traveller's *hospedaje*. On occasion, weary travellers have stumbled into an autohotel, looking for a simple night's rest. The hotel staff, confused, perhaps at a loss for what to do, will rent them a room for the night. However, if those unsuspecting travellers are not paired off – three men travelling together, for example – the staff might shake their head a bit, mumbling as they shut the privacy curtain, "whatever happened to tradition?".

water with your body outside the shower stream; do not touch anything metal or the shower head until you are outside the shower and dry again.

Among the many ugly species of cockroaches there are two principal types: indoor and outdoor. Indoor ones are small, run fast and have a million cousins, while the outdoor ones are usually quite big, a little slow and much crunchier. The presence of indoor cockroaches means the hotel is dirty and/or rarely sprayed. The outdoor ones can come into any hotel at night, from budget to five-star, and are not necessarily a sign of dirtiness, just a reminder that you are in the tropics.

It is wise to pull the bed away from the wall in the tropics so whatever is crawling on the wall does not see your head as a logical progression.

Camping

In the heat of Nicaragua the thought of putting yourself inside a tent – or worse, inside a sleeping bag inside a tent – can be unpleasant. However, relief from the heat can be found in the northern mountains or on the slopes of the volcanoes. In more remote areas you can usually find a roof to hang your hammock under (ask for permission first). A mosquito net, which you should bring from home, will keep off the vampire bats as well as the insects. (Hammocks are found in markets all over the country, though the best quality ones are made in Masaya and can be bought at the market there or in Managua at an average cost of US$20.) Some black plastic sheeting (sold by the metre in any city market) will keep the rain off if there's no roof handy. If camping in the rainforest, mark the boundary of your campsite with your urine to discourage jaguars and other uninvited night guests. The urine should be collected in empty water bottles in the morning (when it is strongest), then spread around the campsite at night before turning in.

Eating

Nicaragua has a great selection of traditional dishes that are usually prepared with fresh ingredients and in generous portions. The midday heat dictates that you get out and tour early with a light breakfast, head for shelter and enjoy a long lunch and rest, then finish with an early dinner.

Food

A typical Nicaraguan breakfast is coffee with *gallo pinto* or *nacatamales*. *Gallo pinto*, the dish that keeps most of Nicaragua alive, is a mixture of fried white rice and kidney beans, which are boiled apart and then fried together with onions and sweet pepper, served with handmade corn tortillas. This can be breakfast, lunch and dinner for much of the population at home and for this reason is not found in most restaurants. *Nacatamales* consist of cornmeal, pork or chicken, rice, *achote* (similar to paprika), peppers, peppermint leaves, potatoes, onions and cooking oil, all wrapped in a big green banana leaf and boiled. Lunch is the biggest meal of the day and dinner is usually lighter unless it's a special occasion. A normal lunch includes a cabbage and tomato salad, white rice, beans, tortilla, onions, fried or boiled plantain and a meat or fish serving. *Asado* or *a la plancha* are key words for most foreigners. *Asado* is grilled meat or fish, which often comes with a chilli sauce. *Carne asada*, grilled beef, is popular street food. *Pollo asado* or *cerdo asado* (grilled chicken or pork) are very good and usually fresh. *A la plancha* means the food is cooked on a sizzling plate or flat grill, and at the more expensive restaurants your beef, chicken or pork will be brought to the table still cooking on its own hotplate. At the coast, fresh *pargo rojo* or *pargo blanco* (red or white snapper) is almost always on the menu, and is best fried whole with a tomato, sweet pepper and onion sauce. *Curvina* (sea bass) is also very good, though often served filleted, which means it may have been frozen first. Lobster – the tail only variety – is good on the Caribbean side but is getting smaller and smaller on the Pacific Coast. Shrimp is good too, especially grilled or sautéed in garlic butter. In the lake or river regions there are good lake fish and *camarones de río* (freshwater prawns) which are prevalent in the Río San Juan region and very tasty in *ajillo* (garlic butter). The lake fish includes *guapote* (a local large-mouthed bass) and the smaller *mojarra* as well as *robalo* (snook) and the introduced African *tilapia*. They are all best fried whole and drenched in a tomato, sweet pepper and onion sauce. In the countryside *cuajada* is a must. It is a soft feta cheese made daily in people's homes, lightly salted and excellent in a hot tortilla. There are other white cheeses: *queso seco* is a slightly bitter dry cheese and *queso crema* a moist bland cheese that is excellent fried. If there is any room left, there are three traditional desserts that are well worth trying: *tres leches*, which is a very sweet cake made with three different kinds of milk; *Pío V*, named after Pope Pius (though no one seems to know why), is a corn cake topped with light cream and bathed in rum sauce; and if these are too heavy, there is the ubiquitous *cajeta*, which is milk mixed with cane sugar or endless varieties of blended or candied fruit. Look out, too, for *piñonate*, thinly sliced strips of candied green papaya. Other regional dishes are described in the local chapters.

> *Nicaragua's strongest cultural marker may be its cuisine, and its most successful export is its food.*

Drink

Since Nicaragua is the land of a thousand fruits, the best drink is the *refresco* or *fresco*, fruit juices or grains and spices mixed with water and sugar. *Jugo* means pure fruit juice, but is almost impossible to find in Nicaragua. If you ask the waiter what fresh drinks they have to offer (*¿qué frescos hay?*), you will receive a few suggestions or in some cases a mind-boggling list of choices which may include pineapple, carrot, passion fruit, beetroot, orange, mandarin, lemonade, grenadine, tamarind, mango,

Restaurant price codes explained

Prices refer to the cost of a meal for one person with a drink, not including service charge.

TTT	over US$12
TT	US$6-12
T	under US$6

star-fruit, papaya, and more. Two favourites are *cacao* and *pithaya*. *Cacao*, the raw cocoa bean, is ground and mixed with milk, rice, cinnamon, vanilla, ice and sugar and is refreshingly cold and filling. *Pithaya* is a cactus fruit, which is blended with lime and sugar and has a lovely, sensual deep purple colour and seedy pulp. The usual fizzy **soft drinks** are also available and called *gaseosas*. For **beer** lovers there are four national brands (all lagers), the strongest being *Cerveza Victoria*, with *Toña* a softer choice and *Premium* and *Búfalo* watery versions. Nicaragua is best known for its **rum**. *Flor de Caña* has been called the finest rum in the world and its factory – more than 100 years old – is a national institution producing seven different flavours, which mature for between four and 21 years. Nicaraguans often spend a night round the table with a bottle of *Flor de Caña*, served up with a bucket of ice, a plate of limes and a steady flow of mixers (Coca-Cola or soda water). Although Nicaraguan **coffee** is recognized as one of the world's finest, most Nicaraguans are unable to pay for the expensive roasts on a daily basis and this is reflected in the restaurants' selection of coffee grinds. City Nicaraguans like to drink instant coffee; *Café Presto* is a Nicaraguan company with international success. In the cities ask for *café percolado*, which is often quite good if it's available. In the countryside most prefer home-roasted coffee, *café de palo*. Finding an espresso coffee or cappuccino outside the main cities is difficult, if not impossible and hot **tea** is rare too, so bring your own teabags.

Water is safe to drink in Managua, Granada, León and other major towns. Bottled water is available throughout the country and is recommended as a simple precaution, but in the cities it is fine to drink frescos and drinks with ice cubes made with from local tap water.

Eating out

Anyone looking for international cuisine will be disappointed as choices and quality tend to be poor. However, if you focus on authentic Nicaraguan food, it can be very rewarding, especially for those with a more open-minded palette. The most expensive dish is not always the best, but a crowded mid-range restaurant is a good indication of a particularly successful kitchen. High turnover is the best guarantee of fresh ingredients. Many restaurants offer *comida corriente* (also called *comida casera*), a set menu that works out far cheaper than ordering à la carte. If travelling on the cheap and tired of street food, ask at a restaurant if they have *comida corriente*. Generally speaking, *fritanga* (street food), costs about US$1.50 and is best for the cast-iron stomach crowd, while the US$2-3 *comida corriente* is often much better, though a bit salty and/or oily; the good eating starts at US$4 and runs up to US$12 a dish in most places. To get the best out of a restaurant, take account of the region you are in and the sort of food that is available locally. Make sure that any fish you order has been freshly caught that day.

Bars and clubs

The favoured entertainment when not eating out is to drink and dance. All cities and most big villages have a *discoteca* and if you can bear music played at deafening volumes the dancing is very unpretentious and surprisingly varied. Bars range from upmarket business chat rooms in Managua to rough cowboy bars in the countryside and are an excellent place to take the pulse of the local population. Political discussion is a common thread, though in the countryside and villages leaving early might be in order at the weekends to avoid fist fights and the town drunk wrapping his arms around you and explaining his life story. Note that pool halls are designed for men only and a woman visitor will draw a great deal of attention.

Eating precautions

Don't let culinary paranoia ruin your trip or you will miss out on one of the best eating experiences in Central America. Simply stick to a few basic rules. Washing your hands thoroughly before eating is the best way to avoid stomach problems. Portable hand-wash bottles (consisting mostly of alcohol) are a good way to clean up if there's nothing else available. To err on the safe side, avoid shell fish and lettuce. Also avoid fried street food as the oil, which has probably been used many times before, may cause stomach upsets. The street grills are okay, as long as the meat has been well cooked, but don't eat salads or pre-peeled fruits off the street or market stands. Common traveller's diarrhoea is difficult to avoid, for it is as much a product of travel stress or a radically new diet as it is of unclean food. In rural areas try to eat in the best restaurants you can afford, and in the cities avoid food from markets or street stalls.

Shopping

Nicaragua is one of the richest countries in the region for handmade crafts, though many of them, like the wicker furniture, are difficult to take back home. Variety, quality and prices are favourable. Every city and town has its market. Usually the meats, fruits and vegetables are inside the market, while the non-perishable goods are sold around the outside. Some kind of handmade crafts or products of local workmanship can be found in most markets around the country. It may take some digging to find some markets as Nicaragua is not a mainstream tourist destination and the markets are not adapted to the visitor. The major exceptions are the craft market in Masaya, which is dedicated solely to the talents of the local and national craftsmen, and the central market in Managua, Roberto Huembes, which has a big section dedicated to crafts from all over the country. Crafts sold at hotels tend to be significantly more expensive.

Nicaraguan custom dictates that all music is played at full volume, so that speakers distort and blow apart – a perfect excuse to go out and buy bigger and louder ones.

What to buy

Items to look out for include: cotton hammocks and embroidered handmade clothing from Masaya; earthenware ceramics from San Juan de Oriente, Condega, Somoto, Mozonte, Matagalpa and Jinotega; wooden tableware from Masaya; wooden rocking chairs from Masatepe; wicker furniture from Granada; jícaro cups from Rivas; *agave* Panama hats from Camoapa; leather goods from León and Masaya; home-made sweets from Diriomo; *agave* rope decor from Somoto; coconut and seashell jewellery from the Caribbean Coast and islands; paintings and sculptures from Managua; balsa wood carvings and primitivist paintings from the Solentiname archipelago.

Tips/trends

Shoppers will find visits to artisan workshops interesting and buying direct from the artisan is often rewarding. Prices in the Nicaraguan markets are not marked up in anticipation of bargaining or negotiation. A discount of 5-10% can be obtained if requested, but the prices quoted are what the merchant or artisan hopes to get.

Festivals and events

1 January, **New Year's Day**. The week leading up to Easter Sunday is **Semana Santa** (Holy Week), with massive celebrations countrywide, religious processions starting

on Palm Sunday and ending on Easter. All rivers, lakes and beachfronts are full of holiday-makers, most businesses close at 1200 on Wednesday and don't reopen until the Monday following Easter. 1 May, **Labour Day**. 30 May, **Mother's Day**, many businesses close after 1200. 19 July, **anniversary of the 1979 Revolution**, most offices close. 14 September, **Battle of San Jacinto** (first victory against William Walker), and 15 September, for Nicaragua's **Independence from Spain**, are nationwide celebrations, all businesses close and there are school parades. 2 November, **Día de los Difuntos** (Day of the Dead), families visit grave sites to remember and decorate their tombs with flowers and fresh paint, most businesses close after 1200. 7 and 8 December, **La Purísima**, is a celebration of the Immaculate Conception of Virgin Mary and the most Nicaraguan of all celebrations. It's celebrated countrywide with home altars being visited by singers after 1800 on the 7th and massive fireworks. Most businesses close at 1200 on 7 December and don't reopen until 9 December. 24 and 25 December, **Christmas**, is celebrated with the family on the evening of the 24, most businesses close at 1200 on 24 December and reopen on 26 December, although some stay closed from 23 December to 2 January. 31 December, **New Year's Eve**, is normally spent with family members, or at parties for Managuans, most businesses close at 1200.

Local celebrations of each town's patron saint are listed throughout the book.

A to Z

Accident and emergency

Police: 118. **Fire**: 115. **Ambulance**: 128.
In case of emergency, contact the relevant emergency service and your embassy (see page 68) and make sure that you obtain police/medical reports in order to file insurance claims. See also listings in the directories throughout the guide for local services. If you are in trouble with the police your embassy can recommend the services of a Nicaraguan lawyer.

Begging

Begging has been practised since pre-Columbian times in the area, when most of the indigenous people were willing to lend a hand to people who had fallen on tough times, and therefore, in proportion to the economic situation of most Nicaraguans, begging is not a problem. Most of it will be encountered in Managua and in the central parks of Granada and León. A small gift of some use (such as pens, pencils, small notebooks) may be an alternative to money.

Children

Nicaragua is not a difficult country to travel in with children and the Nicaraguan people, renowned for their kindness and openness, are even friendlier if you have kids in tow. However, the lack of sophisticated medical services in rural Nicaragua can make travelling with babies less attractive. Travel outside Managua, León and Granada is not recommended for people with children under two. Children over the age of five will find much of interest, not least Nicaraguan children of their own age. Many of the luxuries taken for granted (e.g. snacks) will be unavailable and children should be prepared mentally for this change as it can be a major sore point for children travelling in Nicaragua. Parents with small children should expect that Nicaraguans will want to hold their baby. This is normal social behaviour and not obliging could be taken as an insult, unless the request comes from a complete stranger. Most Nicaraguans love babies so much that they must hold them, pat them and grab their little cheeks. Hotels do not charge for children under two and offer a discount rate for 2-11 year olds; those aged 12 and above are charged as adults. Very small children sitting on their parent's lap should travel free on public buses and boats. On internal flights children under the age of two pay 10% the normal fare; 2-11 year olds pay 50% and anyone aged 12 or older pays the adult fares.

The website **www.babygoes2.com** has useful advice about travelling with children.

Customs and duty free

Duty free import of 500 g of tobacco products, three litres of alcoholic drinks and one large bottle (or three small bottles) of perfume is permitted. If you are bringing in large quantities of film or other items that could, in theory, be resold, it is wise to take them out of their original packages to avoid being charged. Nicaraguan customs agents are reasonable and you only need to convince them that what you have brought is for personal use. Avoid buying products made from snakeskin, crocodile skin, black coral or other protected species on sale in some Nicaraguan markets; apart from the fact that they may be derived from endangered species, there may be laws in your home country outlawing their import. Note that taking pre-Columbian or early colonial pieces out of Nicaragua is illegal and could result in two years in prison.

Disabled travellers

Nicaragua is not an ideal place for disabled travellers. The country has very little in the way of conveniences for disabled people, despite the fact that many Nicaraguans were left permanently disabled by the war years of the late 1970s and 1980s. Outside of Managua Nicaraguans are warm, helpful people and sympathetic to disabilities. Emotional solidarity may not compensate, however, for lack of wheelchair ramps, user-friendly bathrooms and hotel rooms designed for the disabled. There are elevators in the international airport and hotels such as the Holiday Inn and Crowne Plaza; the Hotel Seminole Plaza has special rooms for the disabled on its first floor at a slightly higher cost. Nicaraguan public buses are not designed for disabled people, but most long-haul bus attendants will be helpful with travellers who need extra help – if you arrive early. The local airline La Costeña has small Cessna aircraft that use a drop-down door ladder, but they are also very helpful with passengers in need of assistance. If using a tour operator it would be wise to book a private tour to assure proper flexibility. For wildlife viewing the Solentiname and Río San Juan areas are ideal as there is a great deal of nature to be seen by boat throughout the region, though private transportation on the river and lake is essential. If you fancy a challenge, Ometepe Expeditions, ometepexpeditions@hotmail.com, T664-6910, recently made history by guiding a disabled group to the summit Volcán Concepción; an impressive feat televized by the BBC.

Drugs

Recreational drugs of any kind are illegal in Nicaragua and are sure to bring big problems for the user. It is wise to leave any drugs behind and not go looking for them in Nicaragua. To be offered drugs is uncommon and could be a trap. Nicaraguan society puts marijuana in the same category as heroin and prosecutes accordingly. Men with long hair and earrings may arouse more suspicion in local police and run a greater risk of being considered drug users; not a problem as long as they are not.

Electricity

Voltage is 110 volts AC, 60 cycles, and US-style plugs are used throughout the country.

Embassies and consulates

Belgium, 55 Av de Wolvendael, 1180 Brussels, T375-6500.
Canada, see Embassy in USA.
Costa Rica, Av Central No 2540, Barrio La California, opposite Pizza Hut, San José, T223-2924.
El Salvador, Calle El Mirador y 93 Av Norte, No 4814, Col Escalón, San Salvador, T263-2486.
France, 34 Av Bugeaud, 75116, Paris, T4405-9042.
Germany, Joachim-Karnatz-Allee 45 (Ecke Paulstr), 10557, Berlin, T206-4380.
Honduras, Col Tepeyac, Bloque M-1, No 1130, DC, T239-5225.
Italy, Via Brescia 16, 00198 Roma, T841-4693.
Japan, Kowa Bldg 38, Rm 903, 4-12-24, Nishi-Azabu, Minato-Ku, Tokyo 106, T3499-0400.
Mexico, Prado Norte No. 470, Col Lomas de Chapultepec, T5520-6961.
Spain, Paseo de la Castellana 127, 10-B, 28046, Madrid, T555-5510.

Sweden, Sandhamnasgatan 40, 6 tr, 11528, Estocolmo, T667-1857.
UK, Vicarage House, 58-60 Kensington Church St, London, W8 4DB, T020-79382373.
USA, 1627 New Hampshire Av NW Washington DC, 20009, T202-939-6570.

Gay and lesbian

Nicaragua is as *machista* (in this context homophobic) as any Latin American country, although the Sandinista regime of the 1980s resulted in a more liberal attitude in terms of accepting gay and lesbian lifestyles. Public display of gay affection will be greeted by loud (and normally) mocking response in Managua, León and Granada. In smaller towns and the countryside this response could turn hostile and many locals will be very offended. It may be wise to consider cultural sensitivity the better part of discretion in Nicaragua and respect local views as much in Nicaragua as you expect yours to be respected in your home country. The website, **www.purpleroofs.com/centralamerica/nicaragua.html** specializes in gay-owned or gay-friendly establishments. For more general information, try the **International Gay and Lesbian Travel Association**, www.iglta.com. There are some gay bars and clubs in Managua including: **Discoteca Medianoche**, Linda Vista, T266-6443; **Pacu's**, Puente el Eden, 1 c lago, 1 c arriba; and **Somos**, near Gonzales Pasos 1.

Health

Health risks

No vaccinations are specifically required to enter Nicaragua, however, it is recommended that you are up to date with basic immunization. The major risks posed are those caused by insect disease carriers such as mosquitoes and sandflies, especially during the wet season and along Nicaragua's Caribbean Coast. The key parasitic and viral diseases are malaria, South American tyrpanosomiasis (Chagas disease) and dengue fever. You are always at risk from these and dengue fever is particularly hard to protect against as the mosquitoes can bite throughout the day as well as at night (unlike those that carry malaria and Chagas disease); try to wear clothes that cover arms and legs and also use effective mosquito repellent. Mosquito nets dipped in permethrin provide a good physical and chemical barrier at night. Some form of diarrhoea or intestinal upset is almost inevitable, the standard advice is to be careful with drinking water and ice; if you have any doubts about the water then boil it or filter and treat it. In a restaurant buy bottled water or ask where the water has come from. Food can also pose a problem, be wary of salads if you dont know whether they have been washed or not. There is a constant threat of tuberculosis (TB) and although the BCG vaccine is available, it is still not guaranteed protection. It is best to avoid unpasteurized dairy products and try not to let people cough and splutter all over you.

Further information

www.btha.org British Travel Health Association.
www.cdc.gov US government site that gives excellent advice on travel health and details of disease outbreaks.
www.fco.gov.uk British Foreign and Commonwealth Office travel site has useful information on each country, people, climate and a list of UK embassies/consulates.
www.fitfortravel.scot.nhs.uk A-Z of vaccine/health advice for each country.
www.numberonehealth.co.uk Travel screening services, vaccine and travel health advice, email/SMS text vaccine reminders and screens returned travellers for tropical diseases.

Insurance

Always take out travel insurance before you set off and read the small print carefully. Check that the policy covers the activities you intend or may end up doing. Also check exactly what your medical cover includes (eg ambulance, helicopter rescue or emergency flights back home). Also check the payment protocol. You may have to cough up first before the insurance company reimburses you. To be safe, it is always best to dig out all the receipts for expensive personal effects like jewellery or cameras. Take photos of these items and note down all serial numbers. You are advised to shop around.

Internet

Since most Nicaraguans can't afford computers there is no shortage of internet cafés offering full computer services. Many internet cafés also offer low rate international telephone services through their hook-ups. Apart from contacting friends and family at home and on the road, it can also be useful for checking out destinations and booking hotels. However, response time in Nicaragua is slow and often indifferent, even at some of the more expensive establishments, so do as much of this type of computer work as possible before you arrive. Internet cafés are prevalent throughout the country in cities and bigger villages.

Language

Spanish is the official language although understanding Nicaraguan dialect can be difficult for many non-fluent Spanish speakers. If you look lost people are usually helpful and happy to repeat themselves. English will generally only be spoken in the more upmarket hotels in Managua, Granada and León, as well as at tour operators and car rental agencies. Afro-Caribbean 'Creole' English is widely spoken on the Atlantic Coast. On the Caribbean Coast Spanish, Creole English, Mayagna, Rama and Miskito are all spoken – many locals are able to converse in 3 languages. Efforts to communicate are appreciated. See also the language section in Footnotes, page 326. **Amerispan**, PO Box 58129, 1334 Walnut St, 6th floor, Philadelphia, PA 19107, T+1-800-879-6640, www.amerispan.com. Offer Spanish immersion programmes, educational tours, volunteer and internship postitions throughout Latin America.

Media

One of the great advantages of being able to read or understand Spanish is the chance to tune into the local media. Nicaragua's press is aggressive, contradictory, often sensationalist and does not pull any punches. It mainly focuses on the high profile political issues and characters, but it also manages to report on the plight of the average man with great compassion.

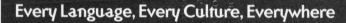

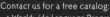

Newspapers and magazines

All daily newspapers cost five córdobas and are published in Managua, but are available in most of the country. They are sold at traffic lights and in many shops in Managua and in select stores in outlying cities. The country's oldest and most influential daily is **La Prensa**, centre-right in leaning; though normally anti-Sandinista they are willing to criticize all politicians. It was the murder of **La Prensa**'s director Pedro Joaquín Chamorro that sparked the Revolution of 1978-1979 into a struggle of all social classes and political viewpoints. His widow, Violeta Barrios de Chamorro, was president of Nicaragua from 1990-1996. The family maintains control of the newspaper, which is one of the most influential voices in the country. The other major daily is centre-left **El Nuevo Diario** which, despite a tendency to be sensationalist and focus on crime news, does have some very good provincial news coverage and is more willing to criticize the right, but also left parties. The three weeklies are more difficult to find outside the city (supermarkets and petrol station stores are the best sources): they are **Tempos del Mundo**, based in Argentina with good coverage of Latin America and in-depth stories on Nicaragua; **7 Días**, a populist magazine with light news and filler; and **Confidential**, an investigative news magazine edited by the country's finest journalist, Carlos Fernando Chamorro, son of the assassinated **La Prensa** director. The only English-language publication, **Between the Waves**, is a free quarterly magazine whose focus seems to be Nicaraguan real estate for Americans but offers occasionally interesting coverage on Nicaraguan destinations and history. **Decenio, Revisita Centro Americana de Cultura**, published in Managua, is an excellent bi-monthly magazine that deals mainly with Nicaraguan art and culture, though other Central American literature and art are represented too. You'll find it in Managua's Hispamer, La Colonia supermarkets and Casa de Café where you can also find the monthly **Envio**, a left-leaning journal of the Universidad Centro Americana (La UCA) that publishes essays and reports on local and regional economics, cultural and political themes.

Radio

If your Spanish is up to it you can hear all kinds of other relevant and irrelevant news programmes up and down the AM dial, the lifeblood of the countryside and still remarkably popular in these days of TV and internet. Since the volatile days leading up to the success of the Revolution, when the mobile station Radio Sandino kept the rebels and population up to date on the fighting and where to attack next, radio has been an essential means of transmitting the latest in events to Nicaraguans. **Radio Sandino** (AM 740) has long since been above-ground and can be found just north of the Mirador Tiscapa restaurant in Managua, though the populist voice of the FSLN, **Radio Ya** (AM 600), is the number one rated. The polar opposite to the Sandinista radio stations has always been **Radio Corporation** (AM 540), Nicaragua's oldest station, which holds the Liberal Party line. The most noteworthy of the AM shows is **Poncho Madrigal** a continuing 40-year tradition of radio theatre that (outside occasional political stumping) is a free entrance into the collective consciousness of the non-urban Nicaraguan. The 30-minute programme, laced with distinctly Nicaraguan humour, language and morals, airs daily at 0500, 1300 and 2100 at AM 540. The music stations on FM radio take a very eclectic approach to programming, though there are stations that define their programming, specializing in dance music FM 95.1, progressive FM 99.9, classical FM 101.1, Mexican FM 93.9, English language FM 103.9 or romantic FM 95.5 and FM 98.7.

Television

Visitors are quite often amazed at the penetration of television in Nicaragua. The most out-of-the-way, humble of homes are wired-up and tuned in nightly to the collective passion of after-dark viewing, the **telenovela**, or soaps, produced mostly in Mexico, Colombia, Brazil, Venezuela and Argentina. The other most important element of Nicaraguan television, and all stations devote extensive time and effort to it, is news coverage. The most influential is **Canal 2** which has good nightly news broadcasts (1830 and 2200 weekdays). It also has a great Saturday afternoon cultural programme (1630) hosted by folk singer Carlos Mejía

Godoy; an excellent human-interest programme at 1800 on Sun called **Vidas y Confesiones**; and the best weekly news summary, **Esta Semana**, hosted by the son of legendary *La Prensa* publisher Carlos Fernando Chamorro at 2000 every Sun night. The Sandinista **Canal 4** has news broadcasts weekdays at 1830 and **Canal 8** has the most bloody of the sensationalist newscasts that are sweeping Nicaragua television at 1800 nightly. When cable is available, **BBC World** usually can be found at Channel 67, **TV5** from Paris at 69, **DW** from Berlin at 68, **RAI** from Rome at 66, **TVE** from Madrid at 65 and **CNN** International at 58.

Money

Currency

The unit of currency is the **córdoba** (C$), divided into 100 centavos. The exchange rate as of March 2008 was C$19 to US$1. Notes are used for 10, 20, 50, 100 and 500 córdobas and coins for one and five córdobas and 5, 10, 25 and 50 centavos. 100 córdoba notes can be a problem to change for small purchases, buses and taxis, so use them at supermarkets as well as in restaurants and hotels and hang on to the smaller notes for other purchases. For money exchange, US dollars are the currency of choice and identification is required. You can pay for almost anything in US dollars as well, but the exchange rate will be unfavourable, change will be given in córdobas and anything larger than a US$5 note will trigger a change crisis. Avoid 500 córdoba notes as no-one will have change for one. Costa Rican and Honduran currencies can only be changed at the respective borders. Travellers entering the country with more than US$10,000 will need to declare the amount to customs upon arrival in Nicaragua.

Exchange

Credit cards are a far wiser alternative to traveller's cheques (TCs) in Nicaragua. You will avoid paying commission and they are accepted all over the country (provided there are telephones available) in hotels, restaurants and most shops. Travellers' cheques are a nuisance in Nicaragua, with only two banks and one *casa de cambio* willing to cash them. **VISA**, **MasterCard** and **American Express** are widely accepted with VISA being the most prevalent. ATM machines are increasingly prevalent, easily found in Managua and other major cities. Debit cards using the Cirrus and MasterCard credit systems work with the 'Red Total' or 'Credomatic' which can be found in shopping malls, **Banco de América Central** (BAC) and Texaco, Shell and Esso station stores. However, it would be unwise to rely too heavily on debit/credit cards; if there are communication problems with the outside world, which is not uncommon, Nicaraguan ATMs will not approve the transaction and you will have to try again later. For this reason, never allow your cash to run out, especially when travelling between places. Take all the cash you need (and some more) when visiting the Atlantic departments and Río San Juan region, which have limited or no ATM facilities at all. Details of banks are provided in the directory section of the listings for each chapter.

Cost of living and travelling

Most visitors to Nicaragua are surprised to find prices higher than expected. The problem stems mainly from the hyperinflation of the 1980s and the córdoba being adjusted to the US dollar in 1990. The cost of public transport, however, ranges from reasonable to very cheap. A normal taxi fare is US$1-2 with buses costing less than a dollar in almost all domestic cases. The cost of local flights is rising with oil prices, starting at around US$120 for a round-trip from Managua. Car rental is comparable with other countries around the world. Food can be cheap depending on the quality: dishes from street vendors cost from US$1-2; moderate restaurants have marginally more healthy fare that ranges from US$3-5; and quality restaurants charge US$5-10 per dish. As a rule, hotels in Nicaragua are not good value and those in Managua tend to be overpriced; anything under US$30 in the capital usually means very poor quality. Outside Managua, hotels are more reasonable and you can find some very good deals in all price brackets.

Nicaraguans often use the generic term 'pesos' *to describe the córdoba.* 'Cinco reales' *means 50 centavos. On the Caribbean Coast* 'bucks' *means córdobas.*

Million dollar Coke – hyperinflation in the 1980s

At the end of the 1980s and beginning of the 1990s, Nicaraguans would say in an ironic tone that "We are a country of millionaires". Everyone had millions and millions of córdobas, but it was barely enough for a taxi ride or to buy a can of Coke. The phenomenon, known as hyperinflation, began in 1989, when agricultural exports dropped at the same time as the country was suffering the effects of a prolonged rebel war and an economic embargo imposed by the United States. To make things worse, the Soviet Bloc, Nicaragua's biggest supporter, went into crisis in this same year. These factors contributed to a rise in the official exchange rate from 2000 córdobas to US$1 in January 1989, to 38,150 córdobas to US$1 in December 1989. The following year, the exchange rate shot up to 3 million córdobas to US$1 – a 12 oz bottle of Coke cost more than 1 million córdobas. To eat out at a restaurant clients had to show up with backpacks full of money. The government could not print new money fast enough to keep up with the hyperinflation so they re-stamped notes with dramatically higher denominations. The 100 córdoba note was rubber stamped to a value of 100,000 córdobas and the 1000 córdoba note became 1,000,000 córdobas, the highest denomination. At the beginning of the 1990s, the re-stamped bills of the Sandinista government were recalled and new paper money was issued. The notes were bought back by the government at an exchange rate of 5 million córdobas for US$1. Today Nicaragua's córdoba is devalued on a controlled plan that has kept inflation hovering around 7% per annum.

Opening hours

Generally 0800-1700. **Banks** open Mon-Fri 0830-1600; Sat 0830-1200 (or 1300). **Churches** are usually open daily during the daytime but be aware of services that may be taking place and be respectful of entering during them if you only want to look around. **Government offices** open Mon-Fri 0800-1700.

Packing

Travelling light is recommended. Your specific list will depend greatly on what kind of travelling you plan to do. Cotton clothes are versatile and suitable for most situations. A hat, sun lotion and sunglasses will protect you from the instant grilling that the Nicaragua sun could cause. A light sweater or very light jacket is useful for those heading into the highlands or rainforest. English-language books are very rare in Nicaragua, so bring reading material with you. Contact-lens wearers and people with special medical needs must bring all prescription medicines and lens-cleaning products. If you intend to hike in the volcanoes you will need very sturdy, hard-soled trekking shoes, which should also ideally be lightweight and very breathable. A lightweight pack filled with energy bars and a flask is useful. Take mosquito netting if travelling on the cheap or to the jungle or Caribbean coastal regions. Wellington boots, worn by the locals in the countryside, will allow you to tackle any rainforest trail with comfort and protection. Insect repellent is a must in these areas. Rain poncho, zip-lock bags and heavy-duty bin liners/trash bags (for backpacks) are highly recommended for rainforest travel. A fairly powerful torch is useful all over Nicaragua's countryside as electric power is either irregular or non-existent. A penknife and a roll of duct tape are the traveller's indispensable, all-purpose items.

Police and the law

You may well be asked for identification at any time, and if you cannot produce it you will be jailed. In the event of a vehicle accident in which anyone is injured, all drivers involved are automatically detained until blame has been established, and this does not usually take less than 2 weeks. You may also be stopped on a routine check and the law states that all cars must carry an emergency triangle reflector and fire extinguisher. Note that in Nicaragua you must hold your lane for 30 m before and after a signal. If turning into a lane not designated left or right, you will be pulled over and your license will be taken until you pay a fine at a police station. It's best to carry an international driver's license to avoid losing your normal one. Never offer a bribe unless you are fully conversant with the customs of the country. Do not assume that an official who accepts a bribe is prepared to do anything else that is illegal. If an official suggests that a bribe must be paid before you can proceed on your way, be patient (assuming you have the time) and they may relent. Note that Nicaraguan police pride themselves on being the least corrupt in Latin America, and as such, they generally do not ask for bribes.

Post

Correos de Nicaragua is very slow but reliable. The average time for a letter to the USA is 18 days while European letters normally take 7-10 days. The cost of mailing normal-sized letters is: US$0.80 to Europe, US$0.55 to North America and just over US$1 to Australia and Asia. Parcels should be left open to be inspected and sealed at the post office. Courier services from Nicaragua, available from companies like DHL and UPS, are expensive, with a three-day letter to the USA averaging US$45 or US$55 to the UK, with mainland Europe just a bit more. For details on Correos de Nicaragua offices see regional chapters.

Safety

Crime is not a major issue for visitors to Nicaragua as long as sensible precautions are taken. Due to the fact that traveller's cheques are difficult to change and ATM machines are less reliable outside Managua, visitors will find themselves with a lot of cash to carry. Money belts and leg pouches are useful, but keep small amounts of cash in your pocket to avoid opening money belts and pouches in public. Spreading money and credit cards around different parts of your body and bags is a good idea.

Don't try to mount Managua's overflowing buses with luggage or rucksacks. Once settled in a hotel, the best way to get around town is by bus or taxi duing the daytime and by taxi at night. Avoid dark areas and places that are not full of people. Bus stops are notorious hotspots for pickpockets. Outside Managua Nicaragua is very safe, but there are theives in Granada and Estelí and pickpockets throughout the country. Public buses in the north central and northeastern extremes of Nicaragua are subject to hold-ups by thieves. Most country bars should be avoided on Sun when fights often break out. See specific chapters for relevant warnings. Rape is not a big threat for travellers in Nicaragua, although 'date rape' is not uncommon so take the normal precautions. See also, 'Women', below.

In hotels hide valuables away in cases or in safe deposit boxes. Budget travellers should bring locks for doors and luggage. If something goes missing ask the hotel manager to investigate and then ask them to call the police if nothing can be resolved.

Women

A lone female walking down the street is a sight to behold for Nicaraguan men: horns will sound, words of romance (and in Managua some less than romantic phrases) will be proffered and in general you may well feel as if you are on stage. Nicaraguan men consider the verbal romance of an unacquainted woman to be an art form and take pride in their creativity in getting her to notice them. Attitudes to foreign women are more reserved, although this is changing rapidly. Touching a woman, Nicaraguan or foreign, is not socially acceptable and normally greeted with a hearty slap or a swift kick. The best advice is to dress for the amount of attention you desire; it is not necessary to travel clothed as a nun, but any suggestive clothing will bring double its weight in suggestions. In Managua it is dangerous to walk alone at night for either gender; there is more risk of robbery than rape, but it should be avoided. Two women walking together are less likely to be targeted by thieves. For more advice, see www.journeywoman.com.

Student travellers

If you are in full-time education you will be entitled to an **International Student Identity Card** (ISIC), www.isic.org, which is distributed by student travel offices and travel agencies in 77 countries. The ISIC gives you discounted prices on all forms of public transport and access to a variety of other concessions and services.

Working in Nicaragua

Finding paid work in Nicaragua is a monumental challenge for Nicaraguans and even more so for visitors who hope to get by in the country by working for a short period. It is a good idea to research your own country's aid programmes to Nicaragua and to make contact well in advance of arrival. The sister-city programmes that most countries have with Nicaragua are good examples. Finding English teaching work may be possible although rents are high and survival on a teaching salary will be difficult. It is best to go through an organization that will help with any legal documentation and accommodation. There are numerous opportunities for volunteer work. The following list is a selection of organizations, although it is by no means exhaustive:

The Nicaragua Solidarity Campaign, www.nicaraguasc.org.uk, can arrange volunteer work within rural communities.
Habitat for Humanity, www.habitat.org, is involved with housing projects in the northern highlands.
El Porvenir, www.elporvenir.org, is an outgrowth of Habitat for Humanity and deals with water, reforestation and sanitation projects.
Global Exchange, www.globalexchange.org, is an interesting, socially aware organization involved with human rights.
Quetzaltrekkers, www.quetzaltrekkers.com, need volunteers to get involved with their tour agency in León.
Witness for Peace, www.witnessforpeace.org, is dedicated to peace, economic justice and social development.
The Miraflor Foundation, www.miraflor-foundation.org, needs teachers to work in Miraflor nature reserve, Spanish speakers and 6-month commitment is preferred.

Tax

There is an arrival tax of US$5 payable at immigration when you enter Nicaragua and an exit tax of US$32 payable at the airline check-in counter when you leave (although it's sometimes be included in the price of your ticket). All hotels, restaurants and shops charge a 15% IVA tax.

Telephone

The Nicaraguan telephone company, **ENITEL**, has offices in all cities and most towns; their telephone is often the only telephone in a small village. Calls can be placed to local or international destinations with pre-payment for an allotted amount of time. To make a reverse-charge (collect) call to any country in the world you will need to name the country in Spanish and say '*una llamada para cobrar*'. The average rate for direct calls to Europe or the USA is about US$3 for the first minute and then US$1 a minute thereafter; collect calls cost more. **Operators**: dial 171 for Sprint, 174 for AT&T and 166 for MCI. European operators: for Germany dial 169; Belgium 172; Canada 168; Spain 162; The Netherlands 177; and the UK 175. Public phones accept phonecards, which are available for purchase in petrol station convenience stores. Phone numbers in Nicaragua have seven digits. To make international calls from Nicaragua, dial 00 and then the country code. To call into Nicaragua, dial your international access then 505 and the number, minus the first zero.

Time

The official time is 6 hrs behind GMT (7 hrs during daylight saving). Note that a European or North American sense of punctuality is an incomprehensible concept for most Nicaraguans. Television shows might start at 1914, instead of 1900 as programmed, radio stations often come on the air late or sign off early, 1-hr meetings can run the entire afternoon, ferries may leave early from the dock and *ya viene* (it's coming now) could mean that the plane is hours away from arrival. In the countryside you may ask how far it is to walk to a given place and receive the answer *una vuelta* (just around the corner) when in fact you may be in for a good 5-hr hike. Be sure when you ask how long or far you are from somewhere to mention your mode of transport (how long walking? how long by bus?) and arrive early, armed with ample patience, to all appointments.

Tipping

The 10% service charge often included in restaurant bills is not mandatory, although most people choose to pay it. This charge usually goes to the owners, so if you want to tip a waiter or waitress it's best to give it to them directly. For porters at the airport or in an upmarket hotel the normal tip is US$0.50 per bag. Taxi drivers do not expect tips unless hired out on an hourly or daily basis. About US$0.20 is usual for people who offer to look after your car (usually unnecessary, but a way to make a living). The going rate for local guides at national parks is US$5 or more, while kids in the market who help you with translations expect about US$3-5. Salaries in Nicaragua are among the lowest in the northern hemisphere, so any extra sum will be very much appreciated. A tip of anything lower than five córdobas will likely be considered an insult.

Tourist information

Useful websites

Information on Nicaragua is still hard to come by in comparison with most countries and most websites are in Spanish and often poorly researched and inaccurate. However, there are a few reliable ones worth checking before boarding your flight.

www.babelfish.altavista.com Very useful translating engine for English-only speakers who want to understand the Spanish language sites.

www.cdc.gov/travel/destination Nicaragua.aspx Useful for health information and other travel recommendations.

www.groups.yahoo.com/group/ NicaraguaLiving Internet forum, a way to chat to people in the country and travellers.

www.guegue.com A very good portal, with lots of links to NGOs, Nicaraguan press and cultural sites.

www.sjordi.com/volcanoes/default.htm Photographs of the country including some of the volcanoes.

www.intur.gob.ni The government tourist board is a good place to start.

www.laprensa.com.ni The country's best newspaper, a good source for information on what is happening in Nicaragua.

www.manfut.org A comprehensive compilation of newspaper stories about Nicaragua, in Spanish.

www.timeanddate.com/worldclock Useful site for sunset and sunrise data and other information.

www1.lanic.utexas.edu/la/ca/Nicaragua A good general portal from the Latin American Network Information Center.

www.marena.gob.ni Nicaragua's official ministry for the environment with information on national parks and reserves.

www.nicaliving.com Community based website with lots of news articles and discussion forums.

www.nicanet.org The latest activist issues.

www.nicaragua.com General English language website that gives a good overview of the country.

www.vianica.com A very handy website that has good travel information including bus schedules and descriptions of popular attractions.

Online maps

www.eaai.com.ni/english/turismo/ nic.shtml The Nicaraguan airport authority has a good map for free download.

www.maps.com The best internationally produced map of the country, enter Nicaragua in their search engine.

See also Maps, page 22.

Tour operators

Many tour operators specializing in Latin American travel will arrange trips to Nicaragua if requested, although sadly few of them know the country well. To find someone who is knowledgeable about Nicaragua, you may need to speak to the product manager. Recommended tour operators are listed below. For tour operators in Managua, see page 64.

UK

Condor Journeys and Adventures, 2 Ferry Bank, Colintraive, Argyll, PA22 3AR, T01700-841318, www.condorjourneys-adventures.com.

Exodus Travels, Grange Mills, Weir Rd, London SW12 0NE, T0845-863 9600, www.exodus.co.uk.
Geodyssey, 116 Tollington Park, London, N4 3RB, T020-7281 7788, www.geodyssey.co.uk.
Journey Latin America, 12 and 13 Heathfield Terr, Chiswick, London, W4 4JE, T020-8747 8315, www.journeylatinamerica.co.uk.
Pura Aventura, 18 Bond St, Brighton, BN1 1RD, T01273-676712, www.pura-aventura.com.
South American Experience, Welby House, 96 Wilton Rd, London SW1V 1DW, T0845-277 3366, www.southamericanexperience.co.uk.
Steppes Travel, 51 Castle St, Cirencester, Gloucestershire, GL7 1QD, T01285-880980, www.steppeslatinamerica.co.uk.
Trips Worldwide, 14 Frederick Pl, Clifton, Bristol, BS8 1AS, T0117-311 4400, www.tripsworldwide.co.uk.

Rest of Europe

Sawadee Reizen, Holland, T020-4202220, www.sawadee.nl.
Rese Konsulterna, Sweden, T463-1101275, www.resek.se.
Tropical Tours, Greece, T210-324 9504, tropical@ath.forthnet.gr.
Nuove Esperienze, Italy, T06-39725999, www.nuove-esperienze.it.

North America

Destination by Design, Inc, T186-63927865, www.destinationbydesign.com.
Unique Travel Concepts, T800-8798635, www.uniquetravelconcepts.com.
Latin American Escapes, T800-5105999, www.latinamericanescapes.com.
Big Five Tours & Expeditions, T800-2443483, www.bigfive.com.

Australia and New Zealand

World Expeditions, Australia, T1300-720 000, www.worldexpeditions.com.au.
World Expeditions, New Zealand, T09-2684161, www.worldexpeditions.co.nz.

Visas and immigration

Visitors to Nicaragua must have a passport with a minimum validity of 6 months. In rare cases you may be asked to show proof of an onward ticket or some cash. Most visitors who do not require visas (see below) will simply pay the tourist card fee (US$5 at the airport and between US$5-8 at land and river immigration checkpoints); see individual chapters for details. An entrance visa is required only for citizens of the following countries: Afghanistan, Albania, Angola, Armenia, Bosnia, Cameroon, Colombia, Cuba, Ecuador, Egypt, Ghana, Haiti, India, Iraq, Iran, Jordan, Kenya, Lebanon, Libya, Mali, Mozambique, Nepal, Nigeria, Pakistan, Palestine, Peru, Dominican Republic, China, North Korea, Romania, Sierra Leone, Syria, Sri Lanka, Sudan, Somalia, Ukraine, Vietnam, Yemen and former Yugoslavian countries. The requirements for visa application can be found on the website of the Nicaraguan foreign ministry **www.cancilleria.gob.ni**. Visa application at the border is not recommended as approval can be very slow. If you need an extension beyond the standard 30 days you receive upon entering the country, you will have to visit the **Dirección de Migración y Extranjería**, Semáforo Tenderí, 1½ c norte, Managua, T244-3989 ext 3, Immigration Mon-Fri 0800-1500. Direct questions (in Spanish) to dgm@migracion.gob.ni. Take your passport to the information department, preferably in the early morning, and ask for an extension form; the current rate for a 30- to 60-day extension is US$20. The whole procedure should not take more than 2 hrs, unless queues are unusually long. Another option would be to leave the country for 3 days or more before returning, although this if you do this more than once, the authorities will not be too pleased. Note that citizens of Colombia, Cuba, Ecuador, Bangladesh, China and India may have difficulties acquiring an extension.

Weights and measures

The metric system is the official one in Nicaragua but in practice a mixture of metric, imperial and old Spanish measurements (including the *vara*, which is equivalent to about 1 m and the *manzana* which is 1.73 acres) is used. Petrol in gallons, speed in kph, fabric in yards, height in centimetres and metres, weight in pounds and temperature in Celsius.

Managua & around

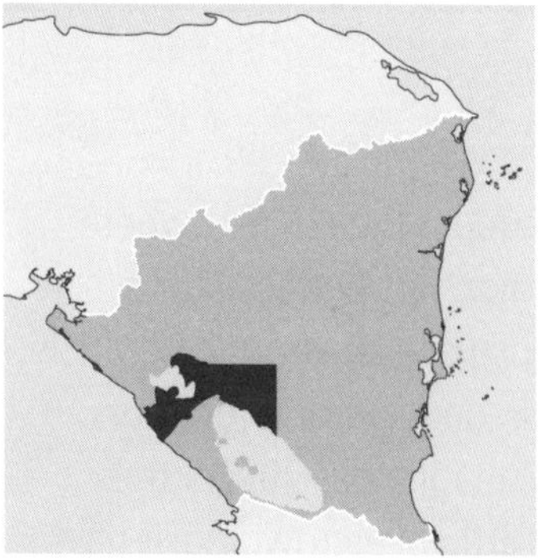

Footprint features

Introduction

If, as the local saying goes, Nicaragua is the country where 'lead floats and cork sinks', Managua is its perfect capital. It's certainly hard to make any sense of a lakefront city which ignores its lake and where you can drive around for hours without ever seeing any water. Managua has 20% of the country's population, yet there is little overcrowding; it has no centre and lots of trees (from the air you can see more trees than buildings); and this is a place where parks are concrete, not green, spaces – there are too many of those already – and where, when directions are given, they refer to buildings that haven't existed for over 30 years. Managua is the capital without a city, a massive suburb of over a million people (there was a downtown once but it was swept away in the 1972 earthquake). And yet despite having no centre, no skyline and no logic, Managua is still a good place to start your visit. It is full of energy, and it is the heartbeat of the Nicaraguan economy and psyche.

The extinct volcanoes and crater lakes within and surrounding the city provide a dramatic setting, and the rugged central mountains, the warm Pacific waters and Managua's Sierra mountain forests all lie an hour or less away in opposite directions: to the east are the cowboy departments of Boaco and Chontales, famous for their great cheese, sprawling cattle ranches and pre-Columbian remains; to the west is the wave-swept Pacific Coast, which has everything from rustic fishing villages to expensive vacation homes and five-star resorts; and to the south are the rich tropical vegetation and wildlife of the Managua Sierra nature reserves of Chocoyero and Montibelli.

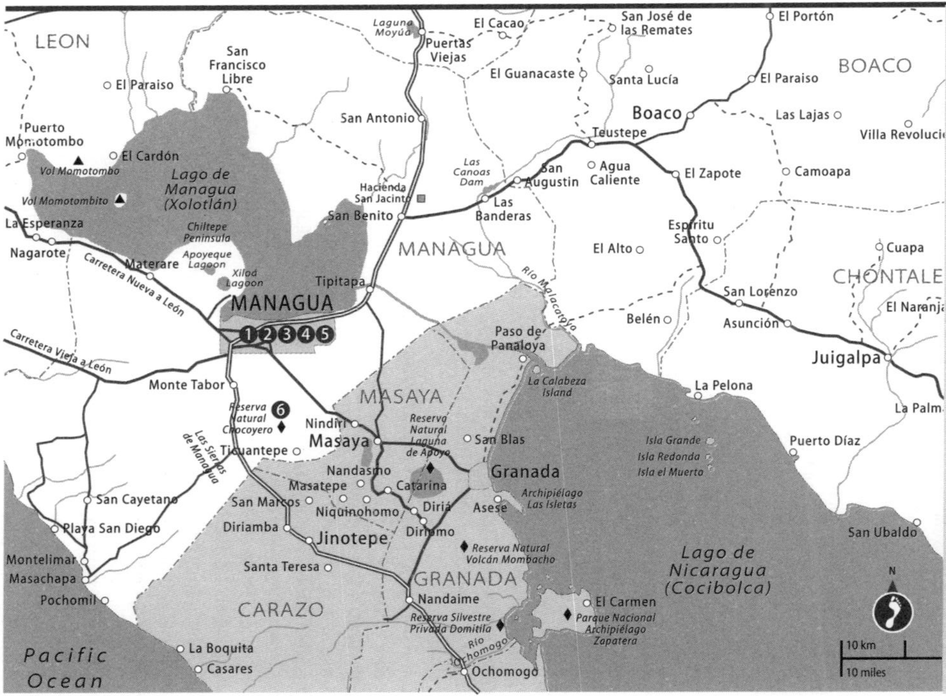

★ Don't miss …

1 **Swan song** Managua's old cathedral is a sad and beautiful symbol of the city before and after the great earthquake, page 48.

2 **Buried history** The stark Peace Park memorial is the last resting place of weapons from the Contra war, page 48.

3 **Ancient steps** The prehistoric footprints at Museo Las Huellas de Acahualinca provide an enigmatic glimpse of life in Managua in 4000 BC, page 49.

4 **300º in the shade** Parque Nacional de la Loma de Tiscapa offers a stunning view of the city and its volcanoes, page 50.

5 **Join the club** Meet Managua's emerging moneyed class in the country's most happening discos and night clubs, page 60.

6 **The Birds** The lush forest of the narrow canyon of Chocoyero Nature Reserve is teeming with monkeys and thousands of noisy parakeets, page 71.

Managua

It is safe to say that Managua is an acquired taste, and one that few tourists will ever acquire. The city overwhelms most first-time visitors with its haphazard semi-urban development, ample evidence of poverty and lack of a focal point. However, there are some interesting sites, sweeping views, great opportunities for eating out and dancing and, most of all, it is the transport hub of the country with all but one internal flight originating here and an extensive network of bus services that cover all the paved, and a great deal of the unpaved, road system of Nicaragua. ⏩ *For Sleeping, Eating and other listings, see pages 53-69.*

Ins and outs → *Population: 1,328,695. Altitude: 40-200 m. Colour map 3, B3.*

Getting there

Air **Managua International Airport** (see page 17 for details on getting to Managua from abroad), on the eastern outskirts of Managua, is small and manageable. Upon landing you will need to pay US$5 at the immigration counter, before retrieving your bags and passing through customs. If you want to rent a car, there are counters through the sliding glass doors on your left after the customs point. Taxis to Metrocentro, Bolonia or Martha Quezada should cost US$15 (less if you speak Spanish, take one from the highway outside the airport, and know exactly where you are going), journey time is 20-30 minutes in good traffic. The taxis that wait along the Carretera Norte just 100 m from the building will normally charge half the price of those at the terminal. Be sure to have precise directions in Spanish to your desired destination. When returning to the airport from the capital, a taxi hailed on the street will charge US$5-6. If leaving early, a radio-taxi costing US$10 is safer and will not make stops along the way.

Like most capitals Managua suffers from a healthy criminal population, so be sure to take all the usual precautions. See page 44 for more on safety.

Bus International bus companies provide comfortable transportation from all capitals of Central America. The three main ones are **Transnica**, near Metrocentro; **King Quality** and **Ticabus**, both in Martha Quezada district. Taxis wait at the bus stations; transfers to central hotels are normally around US$4-5.

Car From the south, the Carretera a Masaya leads directly to Managua's new centre, Metrocentro, and a range of good restaurants and accommodation; try to avoid arriving from this direction from 0700-0900 when the entrance to the city is heavily congested. The Pan-American Highway (Carretera Panamericana) enters Managua at the international airport, skirting the eastern shores of Lake Managua. Stay on this highway until you reach the old centre before attempting to turn south in search of the new one. The Avenida Bolívar runs south from the old centre past the Plaza Inter shopping centre and into the heart of new Managua; turn east onto the Pista de la Resistencia to reach the Metrocentro shopping mall. If arriving from León and the northwest you need to head east from Km 7 of Carretera Sur to find new Managua. ⏩ *For further transport details, see page 64.*

Getting around

On foot Managua has nothing that even remotely resembles a city grid or urban planning and walking is a challenge and unsafe for those who are not familiar with the city's 600 barrios. The best bet is to get to Martha Quezada or Metrocentro and not travel more than 10 blocks on foot.

Directions in Managua and beyond

How do you find anything in a country without street names or numbers? Sometimes visitors feel as if they are going round in circles, quite literally in the case of Managua with its epidemic of dizzying *rotondas* (roundabouts). The Nicaraguan system is foolproof – as long as you know every landmark that exists, or used to exist, in the city which means that, more often than not, foreigners spend most of their time completely lost.

In Managua, directions are based around the lake, so it is essential to know where the lake is and keep a bird's eye view of the city in your mind. With the location of Lake Managua you have north (*al lago*); away from the lake is south (*al sur*). Then you need to use basic Spanish and the sun. Where the sun comes up (*arriba*) is east and where it goes down (*abajo*) is west. City blocks are *cuadras* (abbreviated in this book as 'c'), and metres are better known here by their old Spanish approximation – *varas* (vrs). The key element once you fix your compass is the landmark from which directions begin, which can be a hotel, park, pharmacy, factory or, in worst-case scenarios, where a factory used to be before the earthquake in 1972! Once you find the landmark, getting to your ultimate destination is simple. For example, take Bar Changó, Plaza Inter, 2 c sur, 15 varas abajo (see page 60): to sip Nicaraguan rum here first you need to locate Plaza Inter, then go two blocks south and continue 15 m west.

Outside Managua you may also hear the standard orientation points of *norte*, *sur*, *oeste* and *este*. In Granada, *al lago* refers to the east; on the Pacific Coast *al mar* refers to the west, on the Caribbean side it means east. In mountainous areas, *arriba* and *abajo* may also indicate the rise and fall of the land, so it can get confusing. In smaller towns, many directions are given from the Parque Central or Iglesia (central church). It is useful to remember that nearly all the façades of Catholic churches in Nicaragua face west; so when stepping out of the church the north is to your right, south to the left, etc. If the worst comes to worst, hire a taxi, give the driver the coordinates and let him figure it out.

Bus Local bus routes are confusing as they snake around the city and you must know where you need to get off so you can whistle or holler when the destination grows near. It's best to avoid rush hours and sit near to the driver. Major routes include the 119 which passes the Centroamérica roundabout, travels through the heart of Metrocentro and past Plaza España. Route 110 takes you from the northbound bus terminal of Mercado Mayoreo to La UCA where Express buses leave southwards.

Taxi This is the preferred method of transport for newcomers and although some drivers are grumpy or looking to make a week's pay in one journey, most Managua *taxistas* are very helpful and happy to share the city's hidden attractions. Hiring a Managua taxi is not as straightforward as you might hope, but once mastered it is an efficient and inexpensive way to explore Managua (see box, page 67).

Best time to visit

Managua's searing heat never abates, though October through to early January tends to have cooler nights. Daytime highs of 30-32°C are nearly guaranteed year round. The city's patron saint festival for Santo Domingo (1-10 August) is one of the least interesting in Nicaragua, but the Purísima celebrations for the Virgin (7 December) are

24 hours in Managua

Early birds can watch the heavy tropical sun rise over muddy Lake Managua before setting off on the popular morning jogging circuit (3 km) around Laguna de Tiscapa which has fine views. A well-earned breakfast at the Casa de Café in the Metrocentro area (see page 59), with a stiff café Nicaragüense, will set you up for a morning of museums before the real heat sets in: the 6000-year-old footprints at Museo las Huellas de Acahualinca can be followed by the fine pre-Columbian collection at the Museo Nacional.

For some lunch and people-watching, drop into the noisy Metrocentro food court and *El Guapinol* (page 59) to dine on grilled meat or a good veggie dish. After lunch browse the Roberto Huembes central market for the best crafts in Managua, and everything else you may need from a haircut to shoe repair. Afterwards pay a visit to some of the Bolonia galleries to see the very latest in Nicaraguan art trends.

In the early evening, catch the sunset at the Catedral Nueva (New Cathedral) bathed in golden light before washing down an octopus cocktail and grilled dorado at El Muelle (page 58) with a cold Victoria beer. With the night now in full swing check out some folk music at La Casa de los Mejía Godoy (page 60), a very intimate concert setting and an opportunity to take in the humorous lyric and ethnic instrumentation of Nicaragua's greatest musical heroes. After this work up more of a sweat at the dance disco XS Excess (page 61) and then cool down afterwards with a few buckets of ice, cut limes, sodas and Flor de Caña rum at the *Bar Changó* (page 60).

Before long you will hear the happy squeal of Managua's most vocal bird, the great-tailed grackle, calling forth the new dawn and hopefully you will have packed your jogging shoes ...

very festive in Managua. If you are into revolutionary history, the 19 July celebrations in the old centre at the *malecón* are interesting. The worst time to visit is at the end of the dry season from March to mid-May when blowing dust and smoke from surrounding farmlands combine with 36-38°C heat.

Tourist information

The Nicaraguan Institute of Tourism, **INTUR** ⓘ *T254-5191, www.intur.gob.ni, Mon-Fri 0800-1200, 1400-1700,* is one block south and one block west of the Crowne Plaza Hotel (the old Intercontinental). They sell a good map and provide free brochures in English. The airport INTUR is just past the immigration check and has similar documents to the main office, though staff are more knowledgeable at the city office. Information on nature reserves and parks can be found at the Ministerio de Medio Ambiente y Recursos Naturales, **MARENA** ⓘ *Km 12.5, Carretera Norte, T263-2617, www.marena.gob.ni.*

Safety

With over 600 barrios, a definitive breakdown of Managua safety is a book in itself. As a general rule, at night don't ever walk more than a few blocks anywhere in Managua. There are almost no police during the night time and with no centre there are few places where the streets will be busy. The Metrocentro area is safer, but it's still best not to walk alone. The only place that lends itself to walking is the *malecón* and central park area of old Managua, but do not walk here at night under any circumstances. Even during the daytime take precautions, don't carry any more than

Arriving at night

Barring delays, there are usually no flight arrivals between 0100 and 0530. There are no money-changing facilities for flights arriving before and after business hours. Most rental car agencies stay open until 2000. Taxis are available on the highway outside the airport if none are available on a late or early arrival (very rare). Buses do not run after 2000, although some Managua hotels will have shuttles waiting with signs outside customs. The only hotel nearby is Best Western Las Mercedes which is directly across the street; you should book in advance if arriving late. The airport is safe, but exercise caution on the highway in front of the airport. Avoid late night/early morning transfers between Granada and the airport via Tipitapa highway. Robberies have been reported here in the past; it's better to use the slightly longer alternative route through Managua and Carretera a Masaya.

you need and avoid walking alone. Be careful when visiting the Catedral Nueva, which is next to a barrio with many thieves. Having said all of this, in comparison with other Central American capitals Managua is safe for the visitor, although theft is common at bus stations and outside the more affluent neighbourhoods. Using the inexpensive city taxis is a great way to avoid risk, but make sure you agree on the price in clear Spanish. Some drivers have been known to feign communication problems for short fares at night, looking for a healthy profit. If you are staying in Managua for some time, stick with a friendly and honest driver once you've found one (nearly all have mobile telephones). It will cost a bit more than finding one on the street, but it's worth it to enjoy the city at very low risk.

Background

The southern shore of Lake Managua has been inhabited for at least 6000 years and was once an area of major volcanic activity with four cones, all of which are now extinct. Managua means 'place of the big man' or 'chief' in the Mangue language of the Chorotega Indians who inhabited Managua at the arrival of the Spanish. At that time it was a large village that extended for many kilometres along the shores of Lake Managua (whose indigenous name is Ayagualpa or Xolotlán). When the Spaniards first arrived Managua was reported to have 40,000 inhabitants, but shortly after the conquest, the population dropped to about 1000, partly due to a brutal battle waged by the Chorotegas against Spanish colony founder Francisco Hernández de Córdoba in 1524. Managua remained a stopping-off point on the road between León and Granada, and so avoided some of the intercity wars that plagued the country after Independence. In 1852 it was declared the capital of Nicaragua as a compromise between the forever bickering parties of León and Granada, even though its population was still only 24,000. Today it remains the centre of all branches of government and it often seems that life outside Managua is little noticed by the media and political leaders.

The land under Managua is very unstable and the city experiences a big earthquake every 40 years or so, with those of 1931 and 1972 generating widespread damage and erasing a city centre populated by 400,000 residents. Managua's crippled infrastructure was further damaged by the looting of international relief aid in 1972 and aerial bombing in 1979 by the last Somoza and his National Guard troops. Following the troubled years of the 1980s and the resulting waves of migrations from the countryside, the capital now has an inflated population of over one million. Since 1990 the city has been rebuilding and trying to catch up with its rapid population growth. Investment has intensified in the early 21st century, solidifying Managua as the economic heart of the country.

Sights

Attractions for the visitor in Managua are not as plentiful as you might expect but there are two good museums, two very different and interesting cathedrals, a nice park and an entertaining market. The city also has many private art galleries which provide the only available glimpse of modern Nicaraguan painting and sculpture. Performances in the national theatre are usually good, if you are lucky enough to be in town when there is a show on.

Lakefront and the old centre

The only place in the city to see Lake Managua is around the small *malécon* (waterfront) in what used to be the city centre. From the *malécon*, Avenida Bolívar runs south away from the lake past the main tourist attractions of Managua (Teatro Nacional, Casa Presidencial, Catedral Vieja and Palacio Nacional de la Cultura). The boulevard then crosses the Carretera Norte past the revolutionary statue to the workers, to the park-like area that surrounds the parliament building.

Malécon

The *malecón*, or what remains of it after Hurricane Mitch in 1998 when most of it was lost to the rising lake, is a popular place to spend a Sunday afternoon with plenty of

Managua

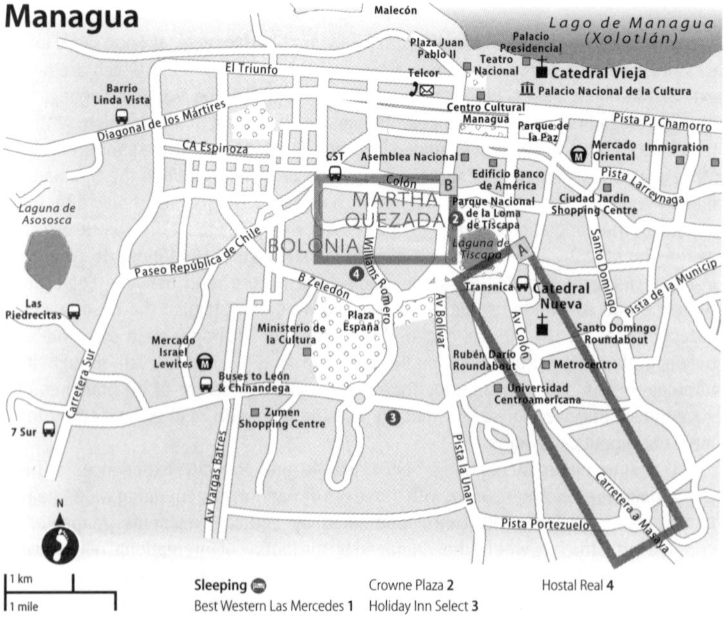

Sleeping
Best Western Las Mercedes **1**
Crowne Plaza **2**
Holiday Inn Select **3**
Hostal Real **4**

cheap food and drinks available in the establishments that line the lakeside. The **Península Chiltepe** can be seen jutting out into the lake and is part of the ancient volcanic complex that includes two beautiful crater lakes, Apoyeque and Xiloá. The stage with the giant acoustic shell next to the *malecón* is used for concerts as well as political speeches and rallies. The area in front of the stage, **El Parque Juan Pablo II**, has been turned into a monument and park in honour of Pope John Paul II who preached here in 1996.

Teatro Nacional

ⓘ *US$1.50-US$20, depending on show, most programmes Thu-Sun.*

Past the statue of Simón Bolívar is the 35-year-old Teatro Rubén Darío or Teatro Nacional, a project of the last Somoza's wife, which survived the earthquake of 1972 and provides the only quality stage in Managua for plays, concerts and dance productions. There are occasionally temporary art exhibitions in the theatre so, in the day, ask at the window to view the exhibit and you can probably look inside the auditorium as well.

Parque Rubén Darío

Just south of the theatre is the Parque Rubén Darío, a small park with one of the most famous monuments in Nicaragua. Sculpted from Italian marble in 1933 by Nicaraguan architect Mario Favilli and restored in 1997, it is said to be the aesthetic symbol of modernism, the poetry movement which Darío founded. Passages from some of his most famous poems are reproduced on the monument.

Parque Central and around

In front of the Darío statue is the Parque Central. Now central to almost nothing, it was once surrounded by three- to five-storey buildings and narrow streets that made up the pre-1972 Managua. The **Templo de la Música** erected in 1939 is at the centre of the park and there's a monument above the burial site of the revolutionary Sandinista ideologue, Carlos Fonseca. Next to the park is a dancing, musical fountain complete with its own bleachers. Around the fountain are two of Managua's most historic buildings, the Palacio National and old Cathedral, as well as the garish **Casa Presidencial**, with its own 'oval office' facing the lake that has been described (generously) as 'post-modernist eclectic'.

Palacio Nacional de la Cultura

Directly across from the presidential office is the attractive neoclassical Palacio Nacional de la Cultura. Finished in 1935 after the original had been destroyed in an earthquake in 1931, the cultural palace was once the seat of the Nicaraguan Congress and the site of Edén Pastora's (Comandante Cero) famous August 1978 revolutionary raid and hostage taking (see page 302). The elegant interior houses two gardens and the **Museo Nacional de Nicaragua**

 ⓘ *T222-4105, Mon-Fri 0800-1700, Sun 0900-1600, closed Sat, US$2 (guided tour only, sometimes available in English), US$2.50 extra charge to photograph*, as well as the national archive and national library. The National Museum has a fine pre-Columbian collection, some of which is on permanent display in the Pacific and Northern archaeology display halls; there's also a statue exhibit from the islands of Ometepe and Zapatera, as well as a natural history hall. The museum has temporary exhibits and several murals, including a very dramatic one depicting the history of Managua and the earthquake (upstairs at the south end of the Salon Azul).

Catedral Vieja

Next to the Palacio de la Cultura is the Old Cathedral. Baptized as La Iglesia Catedral Santiago de Los Caballeros de Managua, it is now known simply as La Catedral Vieja. The church was almost finished when it was shaken by the big earthquake of 1931, and when the earth moved again in 1972 it was partially destroyed. It has been tastefully restored; only the roof of narrow steel girders and side-window support bars were added to keep it standing. There is something romantic about this old and sad cathedral in ruins; a monument to what Managua might have been. Recent tremors have closed the old church indefinitely, though the Mexican government has promised funds to restore it.

Centro Cultural Managua

ⓘ *On the south side of the Palacio de la Cultura, T222-5921.*

The Centro Cultural Managua was built out of the ruins of the Gran Hotel de Managua, the best hotel in town from the 1940s to 1960s. Now, as a cultural centre, it has a selection of before-and-after photos of quake-struck Managua in 1972 and small artists' studios upstairs. The centre is also home to the national art school and the national music school. There are art exhibits downstairs in the galleries and temporary antique and craft shops. The central area is used for performances (check the Thursday newspapers or ask entrance staff to see what is coming up). On the first Saturday of every month an artisans' fair gives craftsmen from outside Managua a chance to show and sell their wares.

Parque de la Paz

Across the Carretera Norte from the Centro Cultural Managua, the Peace Park is a graveyard for a few dozen truckloads of AK-47s and other weapons which are buried here; some can be seen sticking out of the cement. The park was built as a monument to the end of the Contra conflict, with a big lighthouse, a mini-amphitheatre and a tank with a palm tree growing out of it. The plaques on the northern wall include names of most of the big players in the conflict and its resolution.

Asemblea Nacional

Heading south from the old centre down the Avenida Bolívar is the Asemblea Nacional (parliamentary building), a square red-roofed building. The complex is marked by a white 16-storey building, a true giant in Managua and by far the tallest in Nicaragua. It served as the Bank of America before the Revolution and is now an office building for the *diputados* (parliamentary members). Just south of the government administrative offices that accompany the congress is the **Arboretum Nacional**, which houses 180 species of plants including Nicaragua's national flower, the *sacuanjoche* (*Plumeria rubra*) of which there are five varieties. The most common species has delicate flowers with five white petals and yellow centres at the end of the dry season. The national tree, the *madroño* (*Calycophyllum candidissimumx*), also has tiny white flowers, used in Purísima celebrations, at the end of the rainy season.

Museo Las Huellas de Acahualinca

Few think of little 'New World' countries like Nicaragua when looking for mankind's ancient footprints. Yet most scholars agree that the Americas were populated somewhere between 9000 and 50,000 years ago by waves of migrants that crossed over the Bering Strait. Virtually nothing is known about these ancient peoples. However, in 1874, during digging for quarry stone near the shores of Lake Managua, one of the oldest known evidences of human presence in Central America was found: footprints of men, women and children left in petrified volcanic mud, 4 m beneath the topsoil. *Las Huellas de Acahualinca* ('footprints in the land of sunflowers') were radiocarbon-dated to 4000 BC. Archaeologists from around the world have come to examine the site and in 1941 another site was found, with prints made by the same prehistoric people as well as tracks made by birds, deer and racoons.

The tracks and footprints were imprinted in fresh volcanic mud, the product of a burning cloud eruption, characterized by a discharge of ashes, gases, water and volcanic fragments. Such clouds destroy vegetation upon descent and form mud capes, which may take days or months to harden.

What were these ancient ancestors doing when they made these perfectly preserved footprints? After numerous theories, some of which involved dramatic images of natives fleeing a volcanic eruption, the Nicaraguan National Police made an anthropometric study of the footprints. They determined that they had been made by 10 different people, with an average height of 140-150 cm, walking upright, some weighed down, perhaps with children or supplies. The volcanic mud was most likely from one of Managua's now-extinct volcanic cones. The footprints were undoubtedly covered in volcanic sand shortly afterwards, preserving an ancient passage and a modern enigma.

West of the old centre

Museo Las Huellas de Acahualinca

ⓘ *Along the lake, 2 km due west of the Museo Nacional, T266-5774, Mon-Fri 0800-1700, Sat 0800-1600, US$2 with an additional US$2 charged to take photographs and US$3 to use video cameras. Taxi recommended as it is hard to find.*
This museum has been created around the original site where ancient footprints (see box, above) were unearthed at a stone quarry. The 6000-year-old footprints have been left exactly as they were found in excavation and represent some of the oldest evidence of human occupation in Nicaragua. The museum also has a small display of ceramic artefacts found at the site (the oldest ceramics date from 1000 BC, 3000 years later than the footprints) and an illustration of the estimated height of the people who made the footprints. This little museum is a must for lovers of archaeology and indigenous history.

Barrio Martha Quezada to Plaza España

Two blocks south of the government offices is the historic pyramid-shaped Intercontinental building, now home to the Crowne Plaza, and its newer shopping centre (see Metrocentro, below). Directly west from the old Intercontinental, is Barrio

Martha Quezada, home to budget accommodation and two of the international bus stations. Avenida Bolívar runs up the hill from the Intercontinental and down to a traffic signal which is the road that runs west to Plaza España or east for Carretera a Masaya and Metrocentro. Plaza España, marked by the grass mound and Indian statues of Rotonda El Güegüence, is a series of small shops, banks, airline offices and a big supermarket. Just to the north of Plaza España and west of Martha Quezada is Managua's gallery district (see box, page 52), which provides some more comfortable accommodation as well.

Laguna de Tiscapa and Metrocentro

On the south side of the Tiscapa crater lake is the Carretera a Masaya, which runs through the closest thing Managua has to a centre. The bizarre New Cathedral stands on the north side of the big fountains of Rotunda Rubén Darío, which marks Metrocentro. To the south is the Metrocentro shopping complex and a new Intercontinental Hotel. The Carretera a Masaya runs south past single-storey shops and restaurants and the monstrous new headquarters of Casa Pellas to the plain grass roundabout of Rotonda Centroamérica, and further south past the Camino de Oriente shopping centre.

Parque Nacional de la Loma de Tiscapa

① *Tue-Sun 0900-1730, US$2 admission for cars.*

The Parque Nacional de la Loma de Tiscapa has a fabulous panoramic view of Managua and is great for photographing the city and trying to figure out its layout. It is reached by the small road that runs directly behind the Crowne Plaza Hotel, passing a Second World War-period monument to Franklin D Roosevelt and up the hill to the summit.

Martha Quezada & Bolonia

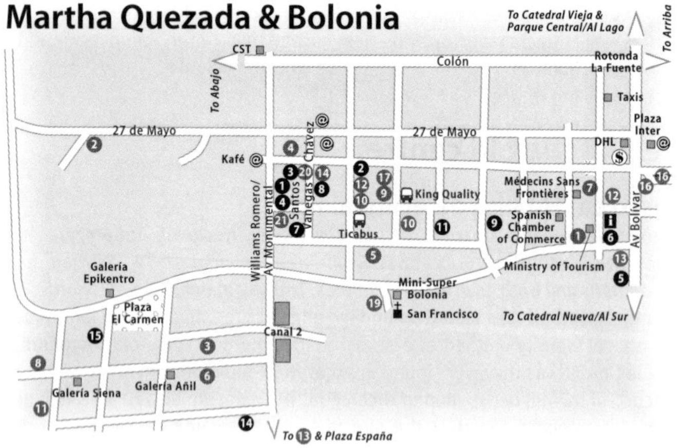

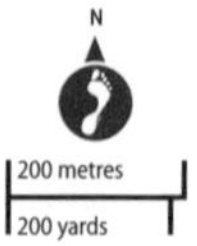

Sleeping
Casa de Huéspedes Santos **4**
Casa Gabrinma **5**
Clay **8**
Crowne Plaza **16**
El Conquistador **7**
El Hotelito **9**
El Molinito **10**
Europeo **6**
Estancia La Casona **3**
Hospedaje Carlos **12**
Hospedaje Quintana **14**
Hostal Real **13**
Jardín de Italia **17**
La Posada del Angel **19**
Los Cisneros **20**
Los Felipes **21**
Mansión Teodolinda **1**
María La Gorda **2**
Posadita de Bolonia **11**

Eating
Aderezo **11**
A La Vista Buffet **15**
Cocinarte **6**
Comida a la Vista Buffet **4**
Corono de Oro **5**
El Buen Sabor **2**
El Cantonés **14**
Las Cazuelas **3**
Mirna's **7**
Panadería Norma **1**
Panadería Tonalli **9**
Típicos Doña Pilar **8**

Bars & clubs
Changó **13**
Grillo **12**
La Curva **16**
Shannon Irlandés **10**

What lies beneath

In 1972 the Tiscapa fault ruptured, less than 5 km beneath the lakefront, sending forth a 6.6 earthquake that rocked the city and crumbled (and later burned) all that could be considered downtown. The quake came cruelly just after midnight on Saturday, 23 December, a day before Christmas. Most of Managua was inside, enjoying big parties; many were never found. Half the population (then 200,000) was left homeless, and at least 5000 Nicaraguans were killed.

There are plenty of reasons not to rebuild the high-rises that once constituted the city's downtown. In fact, 14 good reasons, and that is counting only the principal seismic fault lines that run underneath greater Managua. As a consequence, today's 21st-century Managua is one of the greenest capitals in the world, wide open spaces in every direction, with sprawling barrios and a couple of new low-rise office and hotel buildings looking very much out of place. Much of what was downtown became a sort of monument valley, home to a confused garden of statues, concrete parks and a few new government buildings. With a proper sense of Nicaraguan irony, the new presidential office was built directly over the epicentre of the 1972 quake.

At the top, a giant black silhouette of Augusto C Sandino (see page 101) stands looking out over the city and the crater lake, **Laguna de Tiscapa**, on the south side of the hill. The perfectly round lake has been polluted by years of street run-off but is undergoing an intense clean-up and is home to many turtles as well as the occasional caiman. This park is also the site of the former presidential palace (ruined by the earthquake in 1972) and has much historical significance. Sandino signed a peace treaty here in 1933 and, after dining here with the then President Sacasa one year later, was abducted and shot under orders of the first Somoza who would later push Sacasa out of office in 1936 and found a 43-year family dynasty. Both father and son dictators used part of the palace to hold and torture dissidents. The old torture cells can be seen from the eastern part of the park near the drop-off to the crater lake. Next to the statue of Sandino are two tanks, one said to have been a gift to the first Somoza from Mussolini and the other taken from the National Guard during the Sandinista battle for León in 1979. The graffiti on the tank was written by rebels in memory of a fallen female revolutionary named Aracely. The remains of the presidential palace are used for temporary exhibits; the park is popular with families on Sundays.

The **Tiscapa Canopy Tour** ⓘ *T893-5017, Tue-Sun 0900-1730, US$14*, is a breathtaking zip-line ride that is operated from the park using three long metal cables and four huts with platforms to traverse the lake clipped to a harness and at times more than 70 m in the air. The tour finishes at the bottom of the lake (which is sadly polluted and unfit for swimming) and an old bread truck is used to bring participants back to the summit. Down inside the crater there is a nature walk that is interesting only during the rainy season. Avoid taking photographs until you're at the top of the hill, as the access road to the park passes Nicaragua's national military headquarters which are located next to the Crowne Plaza Hotel.

Catedral Nueva

ⓘ *Access for pedestrians is from the Metrocentro junction and for cars from the east side entrance. Avoid flash photography and entering during Mass via the side doors.*

Some 500 m south of the Laguna de Tiscapa is the Catedral Metropolitana de la Purísima Concepción de María, designed by the Mexican architect Ricardo Legorreta,

Gallery tour

Hiring a taxi for 3-4 hours (US$10 per hour) should allow enough time to do a complete gallery circuit.
Once outside Managua there is little in the way of art galleries, so take advantage of the opportunity while you are in the capital to see something of Nicaragua's art scene. Since Nicaragua lacks a modern art museum, most of the private galleries fill that void with both permanent collections and temporary exhibitions. The highest concentration of galleries is in the Bolonia neighbourhood, a burgeoning 'Gallery District', west of Barrio Martha Quezada and north of Plaza España.

In Bolonia, **Galería Praxis** ⓘ *Plaza España, 2 c norte, 1 c abajo, ½ c norte, T266-3563, Mon-Fri 0900-1900, Sat 0900-1400*, is an artists' co-operative founded by some of Nicaragua's finest 20th-century painters, the legendary Grupo Praxis. Their gallery has a small café and exhibits of works by member and visiting artists. Nearby **Museo-Galería Josefina** ⓘ *Embajada de Japón, ½ c abajo, T268-5809, Mon-Fri 0800-1730, Sat 0800-1600*, has permanent displays and changing exhibits in an airy attractive space. They also have an annual exhibit (every Christmas holiday season) of works on the theme of the Virgin Mary. Also in Bolonia is the **Epikentro Gallery** ⓘ *opposite Plaza El Carmen, T266-2200, Mon-Fri 0800-1730, Sat 0800-1300*, with its emphasis on aggressively modern styles of visual arts, as well as regular poetry readings and book presentations. Just two blocks south of Epikentro is the beautiful space of the **Añil, Galería de Artes Visuales** ⓘ *Canal 2, 1 c abajo, 5 vrs sur, T266-5445, anil@cablenet.com.ni, Mon-Fri 1300- 800, Sat 0900-1800*, featuring an impressive list of artists, including all the Nicaraguan greats, artisan works, sculpture and photography. This could be Nicaragua's best private gallery with works ranging in price from US$25-4000. Next to Añil is the gallery and studio of Nicaragua's greatest sculptor, **Miguel Abarca** ⓘ *T266-3551*. If you speak Spanish call for an appointment (at least 2 hours in advance) to see his sublime works which use a staggering array of materials. Nearby is the **Galería Siena** ⓘ *Canal 2, 3 c abajo, T266-0884, Mon-Sat 0900-1900*, which has permanent exhibitions and visiting shows like the art of Nicaragua's Caribbean and the work of art students who study at the gallery.

The Metrocentro area also has galleries, the most famous is **Galería CodIce** ⓘ *Colonial Los Robles, Hotel Colón, 1 c sur, 2½ c arriba, No 15, T267-2635, www.galeriacodice.com, Mon-Sat 0900-1830*, with art from Nicaragua and the other parts of Latin America and a very impressive display of Nicaraguan artisan works from all over the country which are for sale. Also in Los Robles, on the other side of Carretera a Masaya, is the gallery of the famous poet/sculptor/priest/politician Ernesto Cardenal, **Galería Casa de los Tres Mundos** ⓘ *Restaurante La Marseillaise, 2½ c norte, T267-0304, Mon-Fri 0800-1700*, with primitivista paintings from Solentiname, crafts from the islands, a tiny but very progressive book store and some works of the controversial padre himself. Another gallery specializing in Solentiname art and artisan works is **Galería Solentiname** ⓘ *Altamira, opposite la Vicky, T270-1773, Mon-Fri 0800-1730, Sat 0800-1600*. On the Carretera Masaya is the **Galería Pléyades** ⓘ *bottom floor of the Edificio Pellas, T274-4114, Mon-Fri 0900-1730, Sat 0900-1200*, which has some of the most expensive works of Nicaragua's well-known painters and a corporate clientele.

who has said his inspiration was found in an ancient temple in Cholula, Mexico. Begun in 1991 and finished in September 1993, it is popularly known as La Catedral Nueva (the New Cathedral). This mosque-like Catholic church faces south-north, instead of the usual west-east, and is basically a squat, anti-seismic box with a beehive roof. Each of the roof's 63 domes has a small window, which lets heat out and light in. In addition, a row of massive side doors that are opened for Mass allow the east to west trade winds to ventilate the church. The stark concrete interior has a post-nuclear feel with a modern altar reminiscent of a UN Security Council setting. Many visitors are fascinated by the Sangre de Cristo room, which vaguely recalls a Turkish bath and holds a life-size, bleeding Christ icon encased in a glass and steel dome, illuminated by a domed roof with hundreds of holes for the sun to filter through. At night, the dome sparkles with the glow of light bulbs in the holes. The bell tower holds the old bells from the ruins of the Catedral Vieja. The church has capacity for 1500 worshippers at any one time, but is filled well beyond that every Sunday at 1100, for what is the most popular Mass in the capital.

Bolonia

With its quiet tree-lined streets, Bolonia is inner Managua's finest residential neighbourhood, and home to all of Nicaragua's major television networks, most of its embassies, some art galleries well worth visiting (see opposite page) and several good eating and sleeping options. The area is bordered by Plaza España to the south, Martha Quezada to the north, Laguna Tiscapa to the east and the sprawling barrios that run to Mercado Israel Lewites to the west.

East of Metrocentro

Mercado Roberto Huembes

For shopping, the Roberto Huembes market or Mercado Central is the best place in the capital. It is an interesting visit just for the fruit, vegetable and meat sections, which are found inside the structure proper, along with flowers and other goods. At the northwest corner of the market is a very big craft section with goods from all over the country. While the market in Masaya is more famous and more pleasant to shop at, the artisan section of Huembes is in some ways more complete, if more jumbled and difficult to move about. The market is a few kilometres north of the Centroamérica roundabout and the shopping entrance is next to the fire station. The market is also used for buses to Masaya, Granada, Rivas and the frontier with Costa Rica.

Sleeping

If you are going to splash out on a fancy hotel during your visit to Nicaragua, this is the place to do it, as the hotels below the **E** category are in areas that are not very safe or attractive. See box, page 43, for directions and addresses.

Martha Quezada *p49, map p50*

This area is becoming less safe every year, particularly the area around Ticabus that has most of the **D** and below lodging.

LL-AL Hotel Crowne Plaza, 'el viejo Hotel Inter', in front of the Plaza Inter shopping centre, T228-3530, www.crowneplaza.com. This is one of the most historic buildings in Managua, home to the foreign press for more than a decade, Howard Hughes when he was already off the deep end, and the new Sandinista government briefly in the early 1980s. Some rooms have lake views, but are generally small for the price.

For an explanation of the sleeping and eating price codes used in this guide, see inside the front cover. Other relevant information is found in Essentials, see pages 23-27.

Hotel Crowne Plaza – revolution and chocolate bars

Built in 1969, Managua's pyramid-shaped Crowne Plaza was originally called the Hotel Intercontinental and has a richer history than your average business hotel. Best known to the world's international press corps, which used the hotel as a base while covering the Revolution and, later, the Contra War, the pyramid has also served as a hostel for an eccentric millionaire and two Nicaraguan governments.

Despite the fact that it was built right on the Tiscapa fault, the hotel was one of the few buildings that withstood the great earthquake that devastated Managua in 1972. At the time of the earthquake, the paranoid North American billionaire Howard Hughes and his many employees occupied the entire seventh and eighth floors of the hotel. Hughes had come to do business with the last Somoza dictator, but spent most of his days sitting naked on his favourite high-backed leather chair engrossed in films. The respected hotel chief was given the heavy responsibility of keeping the sophisticated palate of 'The Aviator' happy, a delicate practice that consisted of heating an endless supply of canned Campbell soups, Hughes' daily diet, which were then sent upstairs on a silver tray with a Hershey chocolate bar. When the 1972 earthquake hit, the millionaire dashed downstairs to his car, and was driven directly to the airport where his private plane was already warmed up and ready for take-off, his jet circled once over the horror of the ruined city, alight in flames, never to return to Nicaragua again.

On 17 July 1979, after Somoza Debayle resigned from power and fled to the United States, the Nicaraguan legislature met on the top floor of the hotel and chose Francisco Urcuyo as the new provisional President. He would rule for 43 hours. For several weeks after the Sandinista victory on 19 July, the eight-storey 200-room building became the offices for the Junta del Gobierno de Reconstrucción Nacional, which had taken control of a country in ruins. At the hotel Nicaragua's new authorities carried out government business, received foreign visitors and diplomats, and held emergency cabinet meetings.

Today the hotel is Nicaragua's Hotel Crowne Plaza, offering rooms with a view of Managua's past and future.

A El Conquistador, Plaza Inter, 1 c al sur, 1 c abajo, T222-4789, www.hotelelconquistador.com. 11 airy rooms with a/c, hot water, cable TV, telephone and Wi-Fi. There's a pleasant courtyard patio, and a range of services including tours, business centre and laundry.

A Mansión Teodolinda, INTUR, 1 c al sur, ½ c abajo, T228-1060, www.teodolinda.com.ni. This hotel, popular with business people, has good quality, unpretentious rooms, all with private bath, hot water, kitchenette, cable TV, telephone. There's also a pool, bar, restaurant and laundry service.

C (per person) **Jardín de Italia**, Ticabus, 1 c arriba, ½ c lago, T222-7967, www.jardindeitalia.com. Well-known hotel with 8 rooms. Each has private bath, a/c and cable TV. There's a garden, and services include tours, airport transfer and parking. Mixed reports – take care of your belongings.

C Los Cisneros, Ticabus, 1c al norte, 1½ c abajo, T222-3535, www.hotelloscisneros.com. Apartments and rooms, with hot water, cable TV and Wi-Fi, overlook a lush garden with hammock space. They can organize transit to the airport, serve breakfast, and speak English. Cheaper with fan (**D**). Recommended.

C María La Gorda, Iglesia El Carmen, 1 c al sur, ½ c arriba, ½ c al sur, T268-2455. 8 simple, secure rooms with a/c, private bath, hot water and cable TV. There's internet, laundry services, airport transit, breakfast included and free local calls. Just west of Martha Quezada, good value.

D El Hotelito, Ticabus, 1 c arriba, T222-5100. Simple rooms with private bath, a/c and cable TV. There's bar service, internet and laundry. Tours in Spanish or English are offered.

D (per person) **El Molinito**, Ticabus, ½ c lago, T222-2013. 14 small, basic rooms with private bath and fan. Good value, simple, clean and hot during day.

D Hospedaje Carlos, Ticabus, ½ c al lago, T222-2554. Secure, family-run place with 8 clean, good value rooms, some with private bath. Rooms on left at the back are better than those on the right.

D Los Felipes, Ticabus, 1½ c abajo, T222-6501, www.hotellosfelipe.com.ni. This pleasant hotel has a lovely garden and a plethora of brightly coloured parrots. The 28 rooms have private bath, cable TV, Wi-Fi and telephone. There's a pool and staff are friendly. Cheaper (**E**) with fan.

E Casa Gabrinma, Ticabus 1 c al sur, ½ c arriba, opposite radio *La Primerísima*, T222-6650. This family hotel has 4 basic rooms with fan and cable TV. Cheap food, group discounts, friendly and quiet.

E Hospedaje Quintana, Ticabus, 1 c lago, ½ c abajo, T254-5487. Clean, dark, windowless rooms with shared, cold shower. Family-run and friendly. Recommended for longer stays or groups. Internet services available.

F Casa de Huéspedes Santos, Ticabus, 1 c al lago, 1½ c abajo, T222-3713. Ramshackle cheapie with interesting courtyard space and basic rooms. Some have bath, others have washbasins outside. Breakfast is served and internet available. Friendly, popular, and a good place to meet travellers.

Metrocentro *p50, map p56*

LL-L Hilton Princess Managua, Km 4.5, Carretera a Masaya, T255-5777, www.managua.hilton.com. Classy decor and a plethora of facilities including bar, laundry, secretary and internet. Ask for a room facing the pool. The restaurant is good, if expensive.

LL-AL Real Intercontinental Metrocentro, Metrocentro shopping plaza, T278-4545, www.realhotelsandresorts.com. Nicaragua's finest international hotel, popular with business travellers. It has 157 rooms with hot water, a/c, telephone and cable TV. Facilities include pool, restaurant, bar and secretary service. Special weekend and multi-day rates with some tour operators. Certain rooms can be noisy on weekend nights. Recommended.

L-AL Holiday Inn Select, Rotonda Rubén Darío, 1 km abajo, T270-4515, www.holidayinn.com.ni. Comfortable, if inconveniently located, with 155 rooms. All have private bath with hot water, a/c, telephone, cable TV. Facilities include pool, gym, high speed internet connections and business centre. Ask about room packages and special deals with rental cars.

AL Hotel Los Robles, Restaurante La Marseillaise, 30 vrs al sur, T267-3008, www.hotellosrobles.com. Managua's best B&B offers comfortable rooms with classy furnishings, cable TV, a/c, hot water, Wi-Fi and luxurious bath tubs. The beautiful colonial interior is complimented by a lush, cool garden, complete with bubbling fountain. It's often full, so book in advance. Recommended.

AL Hotel Seminole Plaza, Intercontinental Metrocentro, 1 c abajo, 1 c al sur, T270-0061, www.seminoleplaza.com. Somewhat generic, if comfortable, rooms with private bath, hot water, cable TV, a/c, telephone. There's a small pool, restaurant and bar, and 1st floor rooms are accessible for disabled people. Pleasant location within walking distance of numerous bars and restaurants, rooms on the pool side are quieter. Good value, recommended.

A Casa Real, Rotonda Rubén Darío, 2 c al sur, ½ c arriba, T278-3838, www.hcasareal.com. This business and NGO hotel has a quiet, central location. Spacious, relaxing rooms have private bath, hot water, a/c, telephone, cable TV. French, German and English spoken.

A Hotel Colón, Lacmiel, 2 c arriba, T278- 2490, hcolon@ibw.com.ni. Bright, comfortable, clean rooms with a/c, cable TV and hot water. Close to good restaurants. Pleasant and tidy, if slightly pricey. Breakfast included.

A Hotel Ritzo, Lacmiel, 3 c arriba, 25 vrs al sur, T277-5616, www.hotelritzo.net. 10 sparse, comfortable rooms, decorated with Nicaraguan art. There's 24 hour room service, cable TV, internet, hot water and a/c. Good coffee and close to restaurants.

B Casa San Juan, Reparto San Juan, Calle Esperanza 560, T278-3220, www.hotelcasasanjuan.com. Rooms in this friendly, family-run hotel are clean, fresh and comfortable. They have a/c, bath and cable TV. Other services include internet, airport transfer, vehicle rental, laundry and ticket reservation.

Metrocentro

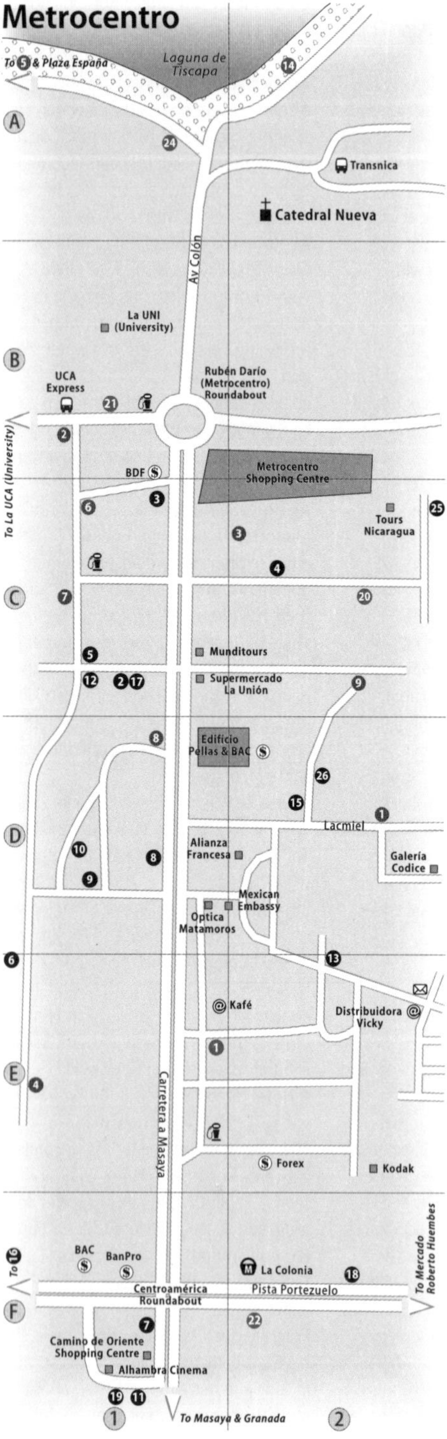

Sleeping
Casa Real **6** *C1*
Casa San Juan **5** *A1*
Colón **1** *D2*
El Almendro **2** *B1*
Hilton Princess Managua **8** *D1*
Los Robles **4** *E1*
Real Intercontinental Metrocentro **3** *C2*
Ritzo **9** *C2*
Seminole Plaza **7** *C1*

Eating
Don Pan **26** *D2*
El Cartel **3** *C1*
El Muelle **4** *C2*
Hippos Tavern & Grill **5** *C1*
La Ballena que Cayó del Cielo **7** *F1*
La Casa de Los Mejía Godoy **25** *C2*
La Casa del Pomodoro **8** *D1*
La Cocina de Doña Haydée **9** *D1*
La Marseillaise **6** *E1*
Las Brasas **11** *F1*
Marea Alta **12** *C1*
María Bonita **13** *E2*
Ola Verde **10** *D1*
Pizza Valenti **15** *D2*
Rock 'n Grill **17** *C1*
Rostipollo **16** *F1*
Scampi International **2** *C1*
Tacos Charros **18** *F2*
Topkapi **19** *F1*

Bars & clubs
Chamán **20** *C2*
El Parnaso **21** *B1*
El Quetzal **22** *F2*
Mirador Tiscapa **14** *A2*
Rhumba & Z Bar **24** *A1*
XS Excess **1** *E1*

B Hotel El Almendro, Rotonda Rubén Darío, 2 c abajo, ½ c sur (behind big wall, ring bell), T270-1260, www.hotelelalmendro.com. 2 blocks from La UCA university, this private and secure hotel has good quality, good value rooms with hot water, a/c, cable TV, telephone, internet access, kitchenette, cooking facilities and utensils. It's a decent choice, if University students aren't in annual protest (normally Nov-Dec).

B Royal Inn Bed & Breakfast, Reparto San Juan, Calle Esperanza, No 553, T278-1414, www.hroyalinn.com/en/. This intimate hotel has cosy rooms and good attention to detail. Services include hot water, a/c, cable TV, radio, internet, garden, breakfast and very good coffee. The Nicaraguan touch.

Bolonia *p53, map p50*

A Hostal Real, opposite German Embassy, T266-8133, www.hostalreal.com.ni. A very interesting and unusual hotel laden with exuberant antiques and art. Rooms vary greatly, and some of the interiors are exceptionally beautiful, particularly near the reception area. Very popular so book in advance.

A La Posada del Angel, opposite Iglesia San Francisco, T268-7228, www.hotelposada delangel.com.ni. This hotel, filled with interesting art work and antique furniture, has lots of personality. Good, clean rooms have private bath, hot water, cable TV, a/c, minibar, Wi-Fi and telephone. There's a pool and laundry service. Book in advance.

B Estancia La Casona, Canal 2, 1 c lago, ½ c abajo, T266-1685, www.estancialacasona.com. Located on a quiet street close to galleries, this family-run hotel has 9 rooms with private bath, hot water, a/c, cable TV. Breakfast is included, English and French are spoken, and internet services available.

B Hotel Europeo, Canal 2, 75 vrs abajo, T268-2130, www.hoteleuropeo.com.ni. Each room is different, and some have interesting furnishings. The rooms out back are best. Features include a/c, private bath with hot water, cable TV. There's a restaurant, bar, fax, secure parking, laundry service, free internet in lobby and pool. Price includes continental breakfast. Staff are friendly and helpful. A quiet location.

B Posadita de Bolonia, Canal 2, 3 c abajo, 75 m al sur, casa 12, T268-6692, www.posaditade bolonia.com.ni. This intimate hotel has 8 rooms with private bath, cable TV, internet. It's in a quiet area, close to several galleries. Friendly owner speaks English and is helpful. Complete breakfast included.

F Hotel Clay, Canal 2, 3½ c abajo, T268-1277. A very basic hotel that doubles up as a love motel (3-hr rental). It's in a quiet and safe location, and the girls at the desk are friendly. Some rooms are much nicer than others.

Managua Airport

A Best Western Las Mercedes, Km 11 Carretera Norte, directly across from international terminal of airport, T263-1011, www.lasmercedes.com.ni. Conveniently located for flight connections, with large, tree-filled grounds, tennis court, pool and barber shop. Rooms are predictably comfortable, but check before accepting one. There can be noise and fumes from the airport during peak hours. Local phone calls can be made here when airport office is shut; the outdoor café is the best place to kill time while waiting for a plane.

Eating

With the exception of the street vendors and lunch buffets almost all establishments accept Visa cards and many accept MasterCard and American Express.

The Metrocentro shopping centre has several good ¥ restaurants in its food court on the bottom level of shopping centre. Along with US standards and Nicaraguan chains like **Rostipollo**, **Tip-Top** and **Quick Burger**, it has cheaper versions of good Nicaraguan restaurants like **Doña Haydée**, **Marea Alta** and **María Bonita**. Most restaurants will make a big salad or a rice and bean dish (*plátano*) for veggie lovers. Nicaraguan lunch buffets are not all-you-can-eat: rather, you are charged for what you ask to be put on your plate, but this is still the most economical way to eat a big meal in Managua. Most Nicaraguans drink coffee like water so it is hard for them to comprehend a special place set aside just to enjoy a little black brew. The closest thing to a café in Managua are the many pastry shops.

Martha Quezada *p49, map p50*

¥¥ Anada, Estatua de Montoya 10 vrs arriba, T228-4140. Daily 0700-2100. Nicaragua's original non-meat eatery and still one of the best. They serve wholesome vegetarian food, juices, smoothies, breakfasts and soups.

¥¥ **Cocinarte**, INTUR, 1 c sur. Closed Sun. International and vegetarian cuisine in a rancho-style setting.

¥¥ **Corona de Oro**, INTUR, 1 c arriba, 2 c sur. Chinese cuisine, for the jaded international traveller in search of flavour.

¥¥-¥ **Rancho Tiscapa**, gate at Military Hospital, 300 vrs sur, T268-4290. Laid-back ranch-style eatery and bar. They serve traditional dishes like *indio viejo*, *gallo pinto* and *cuajada con tortilla*. Good food and a great, breezy view of new Managua and Las Sierras. Recommended.

¥ **Aderezo**, Ticabus 2 c arriba, ½ c sur. Clean, pleasant little place serving home-cooked *comida típica*.

¥ **Comida a la Vista Buffet**, Ticabus, 2 c abajo. Often packed out at lunchtime. Cheap buffet food.

¥ **El Buen Sabor**, Ticabus, 1 c lago, T222-3573. Cheap lunch buffet, frequented by locals. Mon-Sat 1130-1500.

¥ **Las Cazuelas**, CST, 2 c sur, 1 c arriba, opposite Casa de Huéspedes Santos, T228-6090. Always music on here. They do great value breakfasts (US$1.50) with big portions, lunch and dinner too.

¥ **Mirna's**, near Pensión Norma, 0700-1500. Good value breakfasts and *comidas*, lunch buffet 1200-1500 popular with travellers and Nicaraguans, friendly service. Recommended.

¥ **Típicos Doña Pilar**, ½ c from Santos on Santos Vargas Chávez. Cheap buffet-style Nicaraguan food, very good, from 1700.

Cafés and bakeries

Café y Té Jordan, 1st floor Plaza Inter, T222-3525. Although the atmosphere and decor is very hotel-like, they do have a salad bar, *café veneciano*, and are unique in that they offer Earl Grey tea.

Panadería Norma, Ticabus, 2 c abajo, ½ al lago. Unpretentious café-bakery serving rolls, sweet breads and hot black coffee.

Panadería Tonalli, Ticabus, 3 c arriba, ½ c al sur. Pleasant little bakery serving nutritious wholemeal breads, cakes, cookies and coffee. Proceeds go to social projects.

Metrocentro *p50, map p56*

¥¥¥ **La Marseillaise**, Calle Principal Los Robles, T277-0224. Closed Sun. Classy (although there have been mixed reviews in the past) and expensive French restaurant with a good wine list and a sophisticated array of gastronomic offerings including salmon and lobster.

¥¥¥ **Lo Stradivari**, Lacmiel, ½ c abajo, T277-2277. Low-key, no-frills ambience at this Italian restaurant. Excellent home-made pastas, good salads, outdoor seating and good wine sauces. Recommended.

¥¥¥ **Marea Alta**, Colonial los Robles 75, T278-2459. Daily 1200-2200. Has good fresh fish, including sushi. Skip the shellfish but try the grilled dorado fish or tuna. There's outdoor seating and a relaxed ambience.

¥¥¥ **María Bonita**, Altamira, la Vicky, 1½ c abajo, T270-4326. Mexican and Nicaraguan food, including a lunchtime buffet during the week. However, it's most popular on weekend nights, with live music and a noisy, happy crowd. Nice ambience and friendly staff.

¥¥¥ **Rock 'n Grill**, next to Marea Alta, T278-6906. Filled with rock memorabilia, this fun restaurant serves steaks, ribs, burgers and shrimps. Music on Thu night. Popular with Nicaraguans and foreigners.

¥¥¥ **Scampi International**, ALKE 1 ½ c abajo, T270-6013. Big, club-like space that attracts a mostly young clientele. They serve sushi and lobster, and keep live fish in a giant tank near the entrance. The seafood is as fresh as it gets.

¥¥¥ **Sharky's**, Colonial los Robles, Hotel Princess, 25 vrs abajo, T278-0814. This pleasant, relaxed restaurant offers a good selection of seafood including shrimp *quesadillas*, fish sandwiches, fillets and lobster.

¥¥¥ **Tre Fratelli**, Colonial los Robles, Hotel Princess, 20 vrs abajo, T278-3334. Service is reportedly excellent at this classic Italian restaurant, but has had mixed reviews regarding the food; avoid the white cream sauces. Happy hour on the deck outside.

¥¥ **El Cartel**, across Carretera a Masaya from Metrocentro shopping centre, T277-2619. Traditional Nicaraguan fare and reasonable lunch specials, including a buffet. Nice setting, popular with Miami crowd, outdoor seating.

¥¥ **El Muelle**, Intercontinental Metrocentro, 1½ c arriba, T278-0056. Managua's best seafood. There's excellent *pargo al vapor* (steamed red snapper), *dorado a la parilla*, *cocktail de pulpo* (octopus), and great *ceviche*. It's a crowded, informal setting with outdoor seating. Highly recommended.

¥¥ **Hippos Tavern and Grill**, Colonial los Robles, ½ c al sur, T267-1346. Tavern-style place serving grilled food and good salads. Nice ambience and music. A popular spot for people-watching and after-work cocktails.

¥¥ **La Ballena que Cayó del Cielo**, next to Camino de Oriente, T277-3055. Good hamburgers, good grilled chicken, all in a laid-back open-air seating.

¥¥ **La Casa del Pomodoro**, Km 4.5, Carretera a Masaya. Italian place that does average pasta and pizza but very good *calzone*. Outdoor seating.

¥¥ **La Cocina de Doña Haydée**, opposite Pastelería Aurami, Planes de Altamira, T270-6100, www.lacocina.com.ni. Mon-Sun 0730-2230. Once a popular family kitchen eatery that has gone upscale. They serve traditional Nicaraguan food – try the *surtido* dish for 2, the *nacatamales* and traditional *Pio V* dessert, a sumptuous rum cake. Popular with foreign residents.

¥¥ **La Hora del Taco**, Monte de los Olivos, 1 c al lago, on Calle Los Robles. Good Mexican dishes including *fajitas* and *burritos*. A warm, relaxed atmosphere.

¥¥ **Las Brasas**, in front of Cine Alhambra, Camino Oriente. This restaurant is the best value in town, serving decent, traditional Nicaraguan fare in an outdoor setting. It's a good place to come with friends and order a half bottle of rum; it comes with ice, limes, coke and 2 plates of food. Great atmosphere.

¥¥ **Ola Verde**, Doña Haydée, 1 c abajo, ½ c lago, T270-3048, www.olaverde.info. All organic menu of mostly veggie food, but some organic meat dishes too. Servings can be small and service mediocre, but there's a good store with organic coffee to keep you busy while you wait.

¥¥ **Rostipollo**, just west of Centroamérica roundabout, next to McDonald's inside the Metrocentro food court, T277-1968. Headquarters for Nicaraguan chain that is, quite impressively, franchised right across Central America and Mexico. They do great chicken cooked over a wood fire, Caesar salad, lunch specials and combo dishes.

¥ **El Guapinol**, Metrocentro. The best of the food-court eateries with very good grilled meat dishes, chicken, fish and a hearty veggie dish (US$5). Try *Copinol* dish with grilled beef, avocado, fried cheese, salad, tortilla and *gallo pinto* US$4, from 1100 daily.

¥ **La Casa de Los Mejía Godoy**, Plaza el Sol, 2 c sur, T270-4928. This famous, terraced restaurant regularly hosts nationally renowned live music acts. They serve Nicaraguan cuisine, and good, cheap lunch buffets. Very popular and recommended.

¥ **Pizza Valenti**, Colonial Los Robles, T278-7474. Best cheap pizza in town, packed on Sun nights – national 'eating out with the family' night. They do home delivery.

¥ **Tacos Charros**, Plaza el Café, 1 c abajo. The place for cold beer and tasty *tacos*. Check out the great photos of Pancho Villa, Mexico's enigmatic revolutionary hero.

¥ **Topkapi**, Camino de Oriente, across from Alhambra cinema. This locals' haunt serves pizza, *tacos* and Nicaraguan food. Good people-watching from the outdoor seating.

Cafés

Café Jardín, Galería Códice, Colonial Los Robles, Hotel Colón, 1 c sur, 2½ c arriba, No 15, T267-2635. Mon-Sat 0900. Here you can sip espresso in the confines of an art gallery, and eat sandwiches and salads.

Café Kafé, Edificio Pellas next to Galería Pléyades, T274-4025. Mon-Sat 1030-2000. This is the closest thing you will find to a hot corporate cappuccino anywhere in Nicaragua, people actually wearing ties and simultaneously sipping good espresso.

Casa de Café, Lacmiel, 1 c arriba, 1½ c sur, T278-0605. Mon-Sun 0700-2200. The mother of all cafés in Managua, with airy upstairs seating area that makes the average coffee taste much better. Good turkey sandwiches, desserts, pies and *empanadas*. There's another branch on the 2nd level of the Metrocentro shopping plaza, but it lacks the charm and fresh air. Popular and recommended.

Bolonia *p53, map p50*

¥¥¥ **El Churrasco**, Rotonda El Güegüence. This is where the Nicaraguan president and parliamentary members decide the country's future over a big steak. Try the restaurant's namesake which is an Argentine-style cut with garlic and parsley sauce. Recommended.

¥¥ **Santa Fe**, across from Plaza Bolonia, T268-9344. Tex-Mex style with walls covered in stuffed animal heads. They do a pretty good beef grill and *taco* salad, but bad *burritos*. Noisy and festive at lunchtime.

A La Vista Buffet, Canal 2, 2 c abajo, ½ c lago (next to Pulpería América). Lunch only 1130-1430. Nicaragua's best lunch buffet. They do a staggering and inexpensive variety of pork, chicken, beef, rice dishes, salads and vegetable mixers, plantains, potato crêpes and fruit drinks. Popular with local television crews and reporters. Highly recommended.

El Cantonés, Canal 2, 1 c sur, 20 vrs abajo, T266-9811. Acceptable Chinese food, quality varies from dish to dish.Try the rice with shrimp and egg rolls (*tacos chinos*). Service is friendly; eat in or take out.

Rincón Cuscalteco, behind Plaza Bolonia, T266-4209. Daily 1200-2200. Good, cheap *pupusas salvadoreñas*, as well as *vigorón* and *quesillos*. Cheap beer and very relaxed.

Managua suburbs

La Plancha, Montoya, 3 c sur and various other locations, T278-2999. Good value, very generous portions of tender flat-grilled beef, very popular, 1 serving of *lomo a la plancha* can feed 2 people.

Las Delicias del Bosque, Colegio Centroamérica, 5 km sur, T883-0071 (no public transport; have the taxi driver wait or return). Daily 1200-2400. Charming old coffee hacienda with forest and lots of flowers, decent food and service, but most come for the beautiful day and night time views of Managua. Visit the little chapel where the coffee workers used to pray. Past the fountain below the main patio is an improbable bar with stools that look out on the forest and capital beyond.

Habibi's, Km 7, Carretera a Masaya, Plaza Familiar, T270-0746. Good Middle Eastern and Mediterranean cuisine, lunch specials.

Rincón Salvadoreño, la UCA, 2 c abajo, 2 c lago, T0886-7584. *Pupusas*, *tamales* and *quesadillas*, very cheap, the original in Managua, simple food in a plant-filled hut.

Cafés

Don Pan, Km 4, Carretera Norte, across from *El Nuevo Diario*, T249-0191. Mon-Sat 0700-1900. Right across from the country's 2 biggest newspapers. This is the place to go to share the morning news buzz with the country's finest hacks. There is another branch behind the Edificio Pellas.

Bars and clubs

Bars

Bar Chamán, Colonial Los Robles, US$2 entrance. This place for lots of dancing and sweating, with a young, wild crowd and salsa, rock and disco on tape.

Bar Changó, Plaza Inter, 2 c sur, 15 vrs abajo, T268-6230. Tue-Sat 1900-dawn. Where a hip crowd enjoys salsa, reggae, Brazilian, hip-hop, rock, pop-rock, jazz and more world music. Nice setting under a huge tree.

Bar Grillo, next to INTUR, near Crowne Plaza Hotel. Live and recorded music in a rustic, colourfully painted gazebo. They serve snacks like *tostones con queso*. Informal young crowd.

El Parnaso, la UCA, 1 c arriba, 1 c lago. Bohemian crowd, live music Thu-Sat, bookshop across from la UCA.

El Quelite, Enitel Villa Fontana, 5 c abajo, near University roundabout. Daily 1400-0200. A very Nicaraguan place with a spacious, open-air dance floor, unpretentious crowd, and entire families on weekends. They serve very good sea bass and play live music Thu-Sun.

El Quetzal, Centro América roundabout, 1 c arriba, opposite Shell. Thu-Fri after 1800. Fun crowd who fill the big dance floor and dance non-stop. No entrance fee, loud live music, *ranchera*, salsa, merengue.

Island Taste, Km 6, Carretera Norte, T240-0010. Wed-Sun 1800-0400. Garífuna, socca and reggae music from Nicaragua's Caribbean; the only authentic bar of its kind in Managua. Not a nice area, use caution and a radio taxi.

La Casa de los Mejía Godoy, Plaza El Sol, 2 c sur, T278-4913, www.losmejiagodoy.org. Thu-Sat from 2100. This is a chance to see two of Nicaragua's favourite sons and most famous folk singers. A very intimate setting, check with programme to make sure either Carlos or Luis Enrique is playing. Fri is a good bet, entrance US$10.

La Cavanga, trendy bar inside Centro Cultural Managua. Live jazz and folk music weekends, but don't walk at night here.

La Curva, Plaza Inter, 2 c sur, behind Crowne Plaza, T222-6876. This thatched roof bar is low- key most of the week and has live music on weekends with a US$2 entrance. Try the star-fruit (*melocotón* in Nicaragua) and *pitahaya* margaritas, keep track of your bar tab or it may grow.

La Ruta Maya, Montoya, 150 m arriba. Entrance US$5. Good bands play Thu-Sun, with reggae often on Thu, fine folk concerts and political satirists.
Mirador Tiscapa, Laguna de Tiscapa. Daily 1700-0200. Open-air restaurant and bar with a dance floor and live band on weekends. It's overpriced and service is slow, but the setting above the crater lake is lovely.
Rhumba and Z Bar, Km 3.5, Carretera a Masaya, opposite Galería Simón, T278-1733. Very popular with singles, lots of dancing here, weekends only.
Shannon Bar Irlandés, Ticabus, 1 c arriba, 1 c sur. Fabled Irish pub serving fast food, whisky and expensive Guinness. Popular with an international crowd.
Toro Huaco Parrillas Bar, la Vicky, 1 c abajo, 20 vrs sur. Folkloric dance and music performances on Tue nights at 1630. Entrance (US$20) includes drink and buffet, there's also happy hour at 0200 on Sat.

Clubs

The biggest rage in Nicaragua dancing is *reggaeton*, a Spanish language rap-reggae. Dancing is an integral part of Nicaraguan life, at any age, and the line between *el bar* and *la discoteca* is not very well defined. Generally, people over 30 dance at bars and the discos are for 18-30 years. Part of this may be due to the music being played at a deafening volume in discos. If your ears can take the pain, the party is always good and, as long as there is music, Nicaraguans will take to the floor. Most discos play a variety of dance music, though hip-hop and *reggaeton* are omnipresent. Most of the establishments in the bar section above offer dancing.
Arriba, upstairs from **Bróder** (see below). Live music, dancing after 2000 on weekends only.
Bar Chamán, on street behind Metrocentro Intercontinental. US$3 entrance which includes US$1.50 drink coupon. A young, devout dancing crowd sweats it out to salsa, rock and *reggaeton* on tape.
Bróder, Plaza Coconut Grove, la Vicky, 1 c abajo, 2 c sur. Wed-Sat, from 2000 until you drop, Thu ladies free. The place for cocktails like *pantera rosa* (Pink Panther). A young crowd, *reggaeton* and rock.
Dallas Karaoke Discotheque, Camino de Oriente, formerly Boleraza, 50 vrs sur. 1800-dawn. Mexican food and US themes. Plenty of dancing, singing, and cocktails like the 'blue Dallas': triple sec, lime juice and blue curaçao.
Hipa Hipa, Carretera Masaya, Plaza Familiar. Dress smartly for this popular disco, a favourite among Managua's rich kids. The best action is on Wed, Fri and Sat night, cover includes a few beverages.
Island's Taste, Km 6, Carretera Norte, T240-0010. Wed-Sun 1800-0400. Reggae, Garífuna music, the only place to dance to Nicaraguan Caribbean music this side of Bluefields.
Mango's, Km 5.5, Carretera a Masaya, Edificio Delta, T278-1944. Wed-Sat from 2000, US$6 entrance, ladies free on Thu. Very lively crowd with great variety of music, 'every kind of music except *ranchera*'. Recommended.
Matrix, Km 4 ½ Carretera Masaya. Often packed out with well-to-do revellers, this is a good club to dance in until the early hours. The bar is on the pricey side.
Moods, Galería Santo Domingo, Modulo 1, www.moodsmanagua.com. Smart, sexy disco with beautiful people, DJs and dry ice. Dress well.
XS Excess Bar & Grill, Km 5, Carretera a Masaya, T277-3086. Wed-Sat after 2000, entry US$6. One of the most popular discos in Managua, with pumping techno, trance, *reggaeton* and hip-hop.

Entertainment

Cinema

If possible, see a comedy; the unrestrained laughter of the Nicaraguan audience is sure to make the movie much funnier.
Alianza Francesa, Altamira, Mexican Embassy, 1 c norte. French films every Wed and Sat at 2000, free admission, art exhibits during the day.
Cinemas Inter, Plaza Inter, T222-5122. 8 screens showing American films, subtitles in Spanish, buy weekend tickets in advance .
Cines Alhambra, 3 screens, Camino de Oriente, T270-3835. Mostly US films with Spanish subtitles, occasional Spanish and Italian films, US$3, icy a/c.
Metrocentro Cinemark, Metrocentro. T271-9037. 6 screens, small theatres with steep seating, very crowded so arrive early, impossible to see well from front rows, US$4. Flyers with film schedules are free at supermarkets and petrol station mini-markets.

Dance and theatre

Managua has no regular dance and theatre performances so it will take a bit of research to time your visit to coincide with a live show. To find out what's on the cultural and musical calendar for the weekend in Managua, Granada and León, check the *La Prensa* supplement *Viernes Chiquito* every Thu. **Ballet Tepenahuatl**, one of many folkloric dance companies in Managua, gives regular performances in the **Centro Cultural Managua** as well as the **Teatro Nacional Rubén Darío**. Performances as well as folkloric, salsa and merengue dance classes take place at the **Escuela de Danza**, across from main entrance of La UNI University near La UCA. **Teatro Nacional Rubén Darío** also has plays in the main theatre and a small one downstairs. You could call the country's best-known theatrical group, **Comedia Nacional**, T244-1268 to see what's on. The **Centro Cultural Managua** also has regular weekend performances.

Festivals and events

Jul **19 de Julio** is the anniversary of the fall of the last Somoza in 1979, a big Sandinista party in front of the stage with the big acoustic shell at the *malecón*. The party atracts around 100,000 plus from all over the country; don't forget to wear black and red.
Aug **Santo Domingo** is the patron saint of Managua and his festival is from 1-10 Aug. On 1 Aug a statue of Nicaragua's most diminutive saint is brought from his hilltop church in Santo Domingo in the southern outskirts of Managua, in a crowded and heavily guarded (by riot police) procession, to central Managua. With party animals outnumbering the devotees, this may be the least religious and least interesting of any of the Nicaraguan patron saint festivals. Domingo must be the smallest saint celebrated in Nicaragua, too, about the size of a Barbie doll and reported to be a replica, with the original in a safe box. On the final day, there is the country's biggest *hípica*, a huge parade of very fine horses and very well lubricated (drunk) riders from all over the country, while the saint is marched back up to the Iglesia Santo Domingo.
Dec **La Purísima**, celebrating the purity of the Virgin occurs every 7 Dec countrywide and is particularly well celebrated in Managua in the more than 600 barrios of the city. Private altars are erected to the Mary and food gifts are given to those who arrive to sing to the altars, with some families serving up as many as 5000 *nacatamales* in a night. Considering the truly difficult economic circumstances of the Managuans, this outpouring of faith exhibited in generosity to the general public is all the more moving. The festival runs from 1800-2100 with massive fireworks echoing throughout the city (making walking rather hazardous) at 1800 and 2400.

Shopping

Books

If you can't read Spanish, shop for books before you arrive in Nicaragua. Most *librerías* in Nicaragua sell school and office supplies, not books, which few people can afford. **Hispamer**, La UCA, 1 c arriba, 1 c sur, 1 c arriba, www.hispamer.com.ni, is the best bookstore in the country, with a great selection of Nicaraguan authors and informative books. A good little bookstore is inside Centro Commercial Managua, near the Rotunda Centroamérica in modulo 54-B, called **Nuevos Libros**, T278-7163. **La Colonia** in Plaza España has a fine selection of books and some magazines. **Casa de Café** (see Cafés) also has books, as does **La Galería de los Tres Mundos** (see galleries, page 52), which has the poetry of Ernesto Cardenal and many other selections hard to find elsewhere. **Librería El Parnaso** in front of the entrance to La UCA, T270-5178, has many good books about Nicaragua, including its revolutionary history. Religious books can be found next to the New Cathedral at **Librería Catedral**, T278-2077.

Handicrafts

The best place for handicrafts in Managua is the **Mercado Central**, Roberto Huembes, where there's an ample selection from most of the country artisans. On the 1st Sat of every month there is a craft fair at the **Centro Cultural Managua**, which gives some more unusual crafts a chance to be seen and sold. **Mamá Delfina**, in Reparto San Juan next to IBW Internet in a beautiful colonial style home, has a very interesting selection of artisan crafts and antiques, probably the most beautiful store in Managua. For pottery try **Cerámica por la paz**, Km 9.5, Carretera a León,

T269-1388, even if you don't find the perfect earthenware piece they have great T-shirts. Across from La Casa de Mejía Godoy is the upmarket artisan shop **Tiempo Azul**, which sells some very original designs you won't find elsewhere but at a healthy mark-up. The most complete of the non-market artisan shops is **Galería Codice** (see galleries), which has a great selection of crafts from most of Nicaragua including rarely found items like rosewood carvings from the Caribbean Coast and ceramic dolls from Somoto. Note that all the markets have some crafts, but avoid the **Mercado Oriental**. Possibly the biggest informal market in Latin America, this is the heart of darkness in Managua, the centre for black market items. Travelling the labyrinth of its bowels is for hard-core adventure travel and survival television programmes, but not worth the risk for simple shopping. If you can't resist, strip off all valuables, bring a photocopy of your passport and a local who knows the market well.

Photography/laptop repair shops

For digital and video gear, bring a spare of everything you may need.

Mecánica Fotográfica de Róger Bermudez, near Mercado Huembes, Foto Castillo, ½ c sur, 1 c abajo, E-185, Villa Don Bosco, T249-0871. Mon-Fri 0800-1700. Camera repairs, good for mechanical problems (not electric) with still photography equipment and video gear.

Abdul Zarruk, T885-4279, azarruk@yahoo.com. Speaks English. Computer repairs, great with both software/hardware problems – if he can't bring your laptop back from the dead, it's over.

Shopping malls

The two big shopping malls are the **Plaza Inter** and **Metrocentro**, always full on weekends and a good place to people-watch. The Plaza Inter has better deals, with some low-price stores and good cinemas. They often programme events on the patio to the east of the mall. The Metrocentro is bigger and broader and attracts a more affluent crowd, which prices reflect. The cinemas are better in Plaza Inter, but the food court is much better in Metrocentro, where several good Nicaraguan restaurants offer good prices and quick service. Metrocentro also has a little area of banks underneath the southern escalator; some of these are open late on Sat. The other main shopping area is **Centro Commercial Managua** in the Centroamérica barrio, good prices and selection, the best place to get a watch fixed or pick up some inexpensive clothing without visiting an outdoor market.

Supermarkets

Three big chains are represented in Managua, **Supermercado La Colonia** being the best. It is located in Plaza España and at the roundabout in the Centroamérica neighbourhood. Both branches have a salad bar with some cheap cafeteria-style dishes for lunch, and a good selection of Nicaraguan books and magazines. **Supermercado La Unión** on Carretera a Masaya, is similar to La Colonia, also a few blocks east of the Plaza Inter and several blocks west of Plaza España. **Supermercados Pali**, brnaches of which can be found scattered around the city, is the cheapest, with goods still in their shipping boxes and no bags supplied at the checkout counter. Supermarkets have good prices for coffee and rum if you are thinking of taking some home, and they are great for finding imported goods such as tea.

Activities and tours

Baseball

The national sport and passion is baseball, which has been established in Nicaragua for more than 100 years. Games in Managua are on Sun mornings at the national stadium, **Estadio Denis Martínez**, just north of the Barrio Martha Quezada. It was in front of this stadium that one of the most symbolic scenes of the 1978-1979 Revolution occurred – the destruction of the statue of Somoza on horseback. The pedestal remains empty in front of the stadium while the remains of the horse can be seen at Loma de Tiscapa. Check the local newspapers for the game schedule. Seats range from US$1-5 per person.

Canopy Tour

Tiscapa Canopy Tour, T893-5017. Tue-Sun 0900-1630, US$14. A breathtaking zip-line ride that is operated from the park using 3 long metal cables and 4 huts with platforms to traverse the lake clipped to a harness at times more than 70 m in the air. The tour finishes at the bottom of the lake and an old bread truck is used to bring participants back to the summit. Down inside the crater there is a nature walk that is interesting only during the rainy season. Kayak rentals are planned for the near future.

Language schools

Universidad Centroamericana, better known as La UCA, T278-3923 and T267-0352, www.uca.edu.ni, runs Spanish courses that are cheaper than some private institutions, but with larger classes. The best school in Managua is the **Academia Europeo**, Hotel Princess, 1 c abajo, ½ c sur, T278-0829, with structured classes of varying lengths and qualified instructors.

Tour operators

See also local tour operators in Granada, Ometepe, León, Matagalpa, the Corn Islands and Pearl Lagoon.

Careli Tours, Edificio Invercasa, Villa Fontana, T278-6919, www.carelitours.com. One of Nicaragua's oldest tour operators with a professional service, very good English speaking guides and traditional tours to all parts of Nicaragua.

Gray Line Tours, Rotonda Güegüence, 250 vrs sur, T268-2412, www.graylinenicaragua.com. Good, professional company with a range of tours including good-value 1-day tours, night tours of Managua and folkloric performances. Manager Marlon speaks French and English.

Munditur Tours, Km 4.5, Carretera a Masaya, T267-0047, www.munditur.com.ni. Fishing programmes, bus rental and traditional tours are availble. Always humorous and helpful owner Adán Gaitán speaks English.

Nicarao Lake Tours, Bancentro Bolonia, 120 m arriba, T266-1694, www.nicaraolake.com.ni. Owner of several hotels and tourist properties, including a nice hotel in Las Isletas de Granada; fishing, inexpensive day tours to León and Granada departing from their office in Managua.

Solentiname Tours, Apartado Postal 1388 Eco-friendly tours of the lake, Caribbean Coast, colonial cities and Río San Juan. Spanish, English, German, French and Russian spoken.

Tours Nicaragua, Shell Plaza El Sol, 1 c al sur, 120 vrs abajo, Sasa 110, T252-4035, www.toursnicaragua.com. One of the best, offering captivating tours with a cultural, historical or ecological emphasis. Guides, transfers, accommodation and admission costs are included in the price. English-speaking, helpful, professional and highly recommended.

Transport

Air

Domestic flights The 50-min flight in the **La Costeña**, T263-2142, 12-seat Cessna Caravan 208B from Managua to **San Carlos** is a beautiful adventure, with great views over Lake Nicaragua. The gravel and mud landing strip in San Carlos has been described as 'an Irish country road' but what has been said about the alternative, a treacherous 9-hr bus ride, is unprintable. All **La Costeña** flights are in single-prop Cessna Caravans or 2-prop Short 360s. In the Cessna there is no room for overhead lockers, so pack light and check in all you can. For checked luggage on all flights there is a 15-kg (30-lb) weight limit per person for 1-way flight, 25 kg (55 lb) for round-trip tickets. US$2 exit tax on domestic flights.

The Caribbean Coast destinations of the **Corn Islands**, **Bluefields** and **Bilwi** are served by **La Costeña** (see above) and **Atlantic Airlines**, T270-5355, www.atlanticairlinesint.com; both have flights daily.

Tickets can be bought at the domestic terminal, which is located just west of the exit for arriving international passengers, or from city travel agents or tour operators.

Fuel and ticket prices are rising, and schedules are subject to change at any time. To **Bilwi**, **La Costeña**, 0630, 1030, 1430, US$148 return, 1½ hrs. To **Bluefields**, **La Costeña**, 0600, 0630, 1000, 1400, US$128 return, 1 hr; **Atlantic Airlines**, 0645, 1410. To **Corn Islands**, **La Costeña**, 0630, 1400, US$165 return, 1½ hrs; **Atlantic Airlines**, 0645, 1410. To **Minas**, **La Costeña**, 0900, US$139 return, 1 hr. To **San Carlos**, **La Costeña**, 0925, 1425, US$120 return, 1 hr. To **Waspam**, **La Costeña**, 1000, US$155 return, 1½ hrs. For return times see individual destinations.

International flights You should reconfirm your flight out of Nicaragua 48 hrs in advance by calling the local airline office during business hours Mon-Sat. Most good hotels will provide this service. There's a US$32 exit tax on all international flights, sometimes included in the price of your ticket.

"" The flight to San Carlos is a beautiful adventure despite the landing strip there being described as 'an Irish country road'. What has been said about the alternative, nine-hour bus ride from Managua, however, is unprintable.

You'll find some souvenir shops, fast food outlets and cafés inside, with better options before security and immigration. There are also ATMs and money-changing facilities.The X-ray machines at the security checkpoint are not recommended for film above 200 ASA (pass film around the machine).

Airlines Taca Airline, Edificio Barcelona, Plaza España, T266-3136, www.taca.com. AeroMéxico, Óptica Visión, 75 vrs arriba, 25 vrs al lago, T266-6997, www.aeromexico.com. American Airlines, Rotunda El Güegünse 300 vrs al sur, T255-9090, www.aa.com. Continental Airlines, Edificio Ofiplaza, segundo piso edificio 5, T278-7033, www.continental.com. Copa Airlines, Carretera a Masaya Km 4 ½ edificio CAR 6, T233-1624, www.copaair.com. Spirit Airlines, airport, T233-2884, www.spirit air.com. Delta Airlines, Rotonda El Güegüense 100 m al este, T254-8130, www.delta.com.

Bus

City bus City buses are usually run-down and very full and try not to come to a full stop if only 1 or 2 people are getting on or off; they slow down and the assistant yanks you on or tosses you off. City buses in Managua charge US$0.30 per ride; pay when you get on. They run every 10 mins 0530-1800, and every 15 mins 1800-2200; buses are frequent but their routes are difficult to fathom. Beware of pickpockets on the crowded urban buses. Crime is prevalent at bus stops and on city buses, if there are no seats available (which is often) you are at more risk – avoid peak hours 0700-0930 and 1600-1830. The main bus routes are: **101** from Las Brisas, passing CST, Mercado Oriental, then on to Mercados San Miguel and Mayoreo; **103** from 7 Sur to Mercado Lewites, Plaza 19 de Julio, Metrocentro, Mercado San Miguel and Villa Libertad; **109** from Teatro Darío to the Bolívar/Buitrago junction just before Plaza Inter, turns east, then southeast to Mercado Huembes/bus station; **110** from 7 Sur to Villa San Jacinto passing en route Mercado Lewites, Plaza 19 de Julio, Metrocentro, Mercado Huembes/bus station and Mercado San Miguel; **119** from Plaza España to Mercado Huembes/bus station via Plaza 19 de Julio; **123** from Mercado Lewites via 7 Sur and Linda Vista to near Palacio Nacional de Cultura and Nuevo Diario.

Intercity buses *'Bus Expresos'* are dramatically faster than regular routes. Check with terminal to confirm when the next express will leave. Payment is required in advance and seat reservations are becoming more common. There are also microbuses serving some of the major destinations. These are comparatively speedy and as comfortable as it gets. However, there's little space for luggage, and you may have to pay extra to stash large objects.

La UCA serves just a few destinations. The express and microbuses are cheap, fast and recommended if travelling to Granada or Masaya. To **Granada**, every 15 mins or when full, 0530-2200, US$1.10, 1 hr. To **Jinotepe**, 0530-1800, every 20 mins or when full, US$1.10, 1 hr. To **León**, every ½ hr, 0730-2100, US$1.75, 1 ½ hrs, To **Masaya**, every 15 mins or when full, 0530-2000, US$0.60, 40 mins.

Mercado Roberto Huembes, also called Mercado Central, is used for destinations southwest. To **Granada**, every 15 mins, 0520-2200, Sun 0610-2100, US$0.80, 1½ hrs. To **Masaya**, every 20 mins, 0625-1930, Sun until 1600, US$0.50, 50 mins. To **Peñas**

Blancas, express bus, 0400, US$4, 3½ hrs; or go to Rivas for connections. To **Rivas**, every 30 mins, 0400-1800, US$2, 2½ hrs; express buses, US$2.50, 2 hrs; microbuses, US$3, 1½ hrs. To **San Juan del Sur**, express bus, 0900, 1600, US$3.25, 2½ hrs; or go to Rivas for connections.

Mercado Mayoreo, for destinations east and then north or south. To **Boaco**, every 30 mins, 0500-1800, US$2, 2 hrs. To **Camoapa**, 8 daily, 0630-1700, US$2.25, 3 hrs. To **El Rama**, 8 daily, 0500-2200, US$8, 9 hrs; express bus 1400, 1800, 2200, US$9.50, 6 hrs. To **Estelí**, every 30 mins, 0400-1800, US$3, 3½ hrs; express buses, 12 daily, US$3.50, 2½ hrs. To **Jinotega**, express buses, 11 daily, 0400-1730, US$4.50, 3 ½ hrs. To **Juigalpa**, every 20 mins, 0500-1730, US$3, 2½ hrs. To **Matagalpa** every 30 mins, 0330-1800, US$2.50, 2½ hrs; express buses, 12 daily, US$3, 2 hrs. To **Ocotal**, express buses, 12 daily, 0545-1745, US$4.50, 3½ hrs. To **San Rafael del Norte**, express bus, 1500, US$5, 4 hrs. To **San Carlos**, 0500, 0600, 0700, US$9, 9½ hrs. To **Somoto**, express buses, Mon-Sat 0715, 0945, 1245, 1345, 1545, 1645, Sun no express after 1345, US$4.50, 3½ hrs.

Mercado Israel Lewites, also called Mercado Boer, for destinations west and northwest. Microbuses leave from here, particularly recommended for journeys to León. To **Chinandega**, express buses, every 30 mins, 0600-1915, US$2.50, 2½ hrs. To **Corinto**, every hr, 0500-1715, US$3.50, 3 hrs. To **Diriamba**, every 20 mins, 0530-1930, US$1.25, 1 hr 15 mins. To **El Sauce**, express buses, 0745, 1445, US$3.25, 3½ hrs. To **Guasaule**, 0430, 0530, 1530, US$3.25, 4 hrs. To **Jinotepe**, every 20 mins, 0530-1930, US$1.25, 1 hr 30 mins. To **León**, every 30 mins, 0545-1645, US$1.25, 2½ hrs; express buses, every 30 mins, 0500-1645, US$1.50, 2 hrs; microbuses, every 30 mins or when full, 0600-1700, US$1.50, 1½ hrs. To **Pochomil**, every 20 mins, 0600-1920, US$1, 2 hrs.

International buses If time isn't a critical issue, international buses are a cheap and efficient way to travel between Nicaragua and other Central American countries. Buses are available to and from **Honduras**, **El Salvador** and **Guatemala** in the north, **Costa Rica** and Panama to the south. When leaving Managua you will need to check in 1 hr in advance with passport and ticket. Four companies operate the international routes to and from Managua. The buses all have a/c, toilet, reclining seats; most have television screens and offer some sort of snacks. See Essentials, page 19, for examples of routes in and out of Managua.

Car

Car hire All agencies have rental desks at the international airport arrivals terminal. There are more than 15 car rental agencies in Managua. The rates are all very similar, though vehicles from the more successful agencies tend to be in much better condition. It is not a good idea to rent a car for getting around Managua, as it is a confusing city and fender benders are common and an accident could see you end up in jail (even if you are not at fault) until blame is determined. Outside the capital, however, main roads are better marked and a rental car means you can get around more freely. (Taxis can also be hired by the hour or by the day, see below.)
For good service and 24-hr roadside assistance, the best rental agency is **Budget**, with rental cars at the airport, T263-1222, and **Holiday Inn**, T270-9669. Their main office is just off Carretera Sur at Montoya, 1 c abajo, 1 c sur, T255-9000. Average cost of a small Toyota is US$50 per day while a 4WD (a good idea if exploring) is around US$100 per day with insurance and 200 km a day included; 4WD weekly rental rates range from US$600-750. Check website for details: www.budget.com.ni. Also at the airport are **Avis**, T233-3011, www.avis.com.ni and **Hertz**, T266-8399 (also at Hotel Seminole Plaza, T270-5896, and at Hotel Crowne Plaza, T262-2531), www.hertz.com. Another reliable agency is **Toyota Rent a Car**, www.toyotarentacar.com, which has cars to match its name at the airport, T266-3620, the Hotel Princess, T270-4937, and the Camino Real, T263-2358.

Taxis

Taxis without red licence plates are '*piratas*' (unregistered); avoid them. The Managua *taxista* has an unparalleled knowledge of the city. Taxis can be flagged down in the street. They also cruise the bus stations and markets looking for passengers. Find out the fare before you board the vehicle. Fares are always per person, not per car. For tips on the art of taxi hire in Managua see box, page 67. Have the telephone number of your hotel with you.

The art of taxi hire

Despite the Managua taxi driver's liberal interpretation of Nicaraguan driving laws, his knowledge of the city is second to none and taxis are often the best way to get around the city. The main point to understand is that the taxi hailed on the street is really a *colectivo*, with all seats inside available for hire to the similar destinations or places en route. After flagging down a taxi in the street, lean into the passenger window and state your desired destination (veiling your accent as best possible to try and keep the rates down). If the driver nods in acceptance, ask him how much – *¿por cuánto me lleva?* There are no set rates so, unless his quote is outrageously high (see guide lines below), get in. It is normal for most drivers to quote the going rate plus 5 to 20 córdobas extra for foreigners. When you reach your destination pay the driver with the most exact money possible (they never have change, an effective built-in tip technique).

The minimum charge is 15 córdobas per person (there will be a slight discount for two people riding together); within the same general area the fare should be about 20 córdobas; halfway across town no more than 30 córdobas; and all the way across town 50 córdobas, to the airport 100 córdobas. Radio taxis do not stop for other passengers and charge double for short prebooked trips and from the airport into the city (US$15, US$10 return). For an early morning or late night journey it is wise to call a radio taxi, they are private, safer and in most cases in better condition than the other taxis.

Street names and numbers are not universal in the city and the taxi driver may not recognize the name. Make sure you know the coordinates if you are heading for a private residence. If you are going to Barrio Martha Quezada, ask for the Ticabus terminal if you do not know your exact destination.

Radio taxis pick you up and do not stop for other passengers, they are much more secure for this reason and cost twice as much: **Cooperativa 25 de Febrero**, T222-5218; **Cooperativa 2 de Agosto**, T263-1512; **Cooperativa René Chávez**, T222-3293; **Cooperativa Mario Lizano**, T268-7669. Get a quote on the phone and reconfirm agreed cost when the taxi arrives.

Taxis can also be hired by the hour or by the day for use inside Managua and for trips anywhere in the country. This should be done with a radio taxi company, negotiating the fare per hour, per day or per journey. Some guidelines are: US$10 per hr inside Managua; US$50 per day inside Managua; a trip to Volcán Masaya, US$50, Granada US$65; León US$75, Estelí US$100, border with Honduras US$150. Some good *taxistas* are **León Germán Hernández**, T249-9416, T883-3703 (mob); **Dionisio Ríos Torres**, T263-1838; and **Freddy Danilo Obando**, T777-8578.

Directory

Banks

The best bank for foreigners is **Banco de América Central** (BAC) since they accept all credit cards and TCs. BAC offers credit card advances, uses the Cirrus debit system and changes all TCs with a 3% commission. Any other bank can be used for changing dollars to córdobas or vice versa. See page 33 for more details on ATMs. BAC's slick new office headquarters is at Edificio Pellas, Km 4 Carretera a Masaya, T277-3624. There is a BAC in Plaza España, T266-7062, and at Metrocentro, T278-5510.

Doctors

Dr Enrique Sánchez Delgado, T278-1031; Dr Mauricio Barrios, T255-6900. **Gynaecologist**, Dr Edwin Mendieta, T266-5855. **Ophthalmologist**, Dr Milton Eugarrios, T278-6306. **Paediatricians**, Dr Alejandro Ayón, T276-2142; Dr César Gutiérrez Quant, T278-3902, T278-5465 (home).

Dentists

Dr Claudia Bendaña, T277-1842; and **Dr Mario Sánchez Ramos**, T278-1409, T278-5588 (home).

Embassies and consulates

Austria, Rotonda El Guenguense, 1 c al norte, T266-3316. **Argentina**, Semáforos de Villa Fontana, 2 c abajo, 1 c sur, 1 c abajo, No 133, T270-2343. **Canada**, Bolonia Los Pipitos, 2 c abajo, T264-2723. Mon-Thu 0900-1200. **Costa Rica**, Los Robles, Tip Top, 25 vrs abajo, T270-3799. 0900-1500. **Denmark**, Bolonia Salud Integral, 2 c al lago, 50 vrs abajo, T254-5059. **Finland**, Hospital Militar, 1 c north, 1½ c abajo, T264-1137. 0800-1200, 1300-1500. **France**, Iglesia El Carmen, 1½ c abajo, T222-6210, 0800-1600. **Germany**, Plaza España, 200 m lago, T266-3917. Mon-Fri 0900-1200. **Guatemala**, just after Km 11 on Carretera a Masaya, T279-9834. Fast service, 0900-1200 only. **Honduras**, Las Colinas No. 298, T276-2406. **Italy**, Rotonda El Güegüence, 1 c lago, T266-6486. 0900-1200. **Mexico**, Km 4.5, Carretera a Masaya, 1 c arriba, T277-5886. **Panamá**, Col Mantica, el Cuartel General de Bomberos, 1 c abajo, No 93, T/F266-8633. 0830-1300, visa on the spot, valid 3 months for a 30-day stay, US$10, maps and information on the Canal. **Spain**, Las Colinas Ave, Central No. 13, T276-0968. **Sweden**, Plaza España, 1 c abajo, 2 c lago, ½ c abajo, Apdo Postal 2307, T266-0085. 0800-1200. **Switzerland**, Banpro Las Palmas, 1 c abajo, T266-3010. **UK**, La Fise, 40 vrs abajo, T278-0014. 0900-1200. **USA**, Km 4.5, Carretera del Sur, T266-6010. 0730-0900. **Venezuela**, Km 10.5, Carretera a Masaya, T276-0267.

Hospitals

The best are **Hospital Bautista**, near Mercado Oriental, T249-7070; **Hospital Militar**, T222-2763 (go south from Hotel Crowne Plaza and take 2nd turn on left); and **Hospital Alemán-Nicaragüense**, Km 6 Carretera Norte Siemens, 3 blocks south, 249-0701, operated with German aid, mostly Nicaraguan staff. Make an appointment by phone in advance if possible. Private clinics are an alternative. **Policlínica Nicaragüense**, in Bolonia across from AGFA, consultation US$30. **Med-Lab**, 300 m south of Plaza España, is recommended for tests on stool samples, the director speaks English.

Internet

Internet cafés are spread all over Managua. At Plaza Inter, there is a small stand on the top floor, next to the food court, and an internet café, phone and mail service on the bottom floor at the parking entrance. There are several cybercafés in Martha Quezada on the main road from CST south. In Bolonia next to the UHISPAM is **Cybercafé San Antonio** with cheap international calls and internet. Metrocentro shopping centre has a very good cybercafé, with a direct satellite connection: **IBW Cybercafé** across from the Casa de Café some English spoken, daily 0930-2000, T271-9417. At La UCA next to the *portón de salida* is **Cyberworld**, with international calls, internet and cheap food, T277-5088. In Managua cybercafés come and go with the seasons, ask at your hotel for the nearest paid hook-up if you don't see one.

Laundry

There are no public launderettes in Nicaragua. Ask your hotel or *hospedaje* to arrange laundry or dry cleaning. In Bolonia, **Dryclean USA**, Plaza Bolonia, 1 c arriba, T266-4070; and **American Dry Cleaners**, Rotonda El Güegüence, 2 c sur, T268-0710.

Libraries

Managua's main universities have big libraries although the texts are all in Spanish. The following university websites have more information: **www.uca.edu.ni**, **www.unica.edu.ni**, **www.uni.edu.ni**, **www.unicit.edu.ni**, **www.aum.edu.ni**. The country's finest library is next to the Nicaraguan Central Bank, Km 7, Carretera Sur, 150 m arriba, T265-0131. They also publish many important books on Nicaragua's history, culture and economy.

Post office

Correos de Nicaragua, www.correros.com.ni, is at 21 locations around Managua. The main office is Palacio de Communicación, Parque Central, 1 c abajo. The tall building was a survivor of the 1972 earthquake, but is looking the worse for wear.

Telephone

Inside the Palacio de Communicación, **Enitel** has telephone, fax and internet services, as well as a postal service and stamps for collectors, T222-4149. There is also a small office just before the security check at the international airport. **Enitel**, T278-4444, telephone offices are spread around Managua; most are next to or near the Correos office. Courier and express mail **Correos de Nicaragua** is slow so you may want to use an express courier. **DHL**, Rotunda Metrocentro, 600 vrs arriba, T255-8700, delivers letters to the USA and Europe, US$35-50. A little cheaper is **UPS** across from the German Embassy in Bolonia at Rotonda El Güegüence, 2 c norte, T254-4887.

Travel agents

Turismo Joven, Km. 5 1/2 Carretera a Masaya, Frente al Colegio Teresiano, T278-3788, www.otecviajes.com, travel agency, representative for ISIC, affiliated to YHA. **El Viajero**, Plaza España, 2 c abajo, No 3, T268-3815, helpful manager, cheap flights to all parts. In the Plaza España area are: **Aeromundo**, T266-8725, www.aeromundo cwt.com.ni; **Atlantida**, T266-8720, www.viajesatlantida.com; and **Capital Express**, T266-5043, capital@ibw.com.ni.

Useful numbers

Fire Dial 115 if an emergency; the central number is T265-0162. **Police** Dial 118 in an emergency. The local police station number will depend on what *distrito* you are in. Start with the Metrocentro area number, T265-0651. **Red Cross** Dial 128 in an emergency; to give blood call, T265-1517.

South of Managua

West and south of Managua are two dramatically different regions that make attractive one- to three-day trips. To the west is the Pacific Ocean and the wave-swept beaches of Nicaragua's central coast with everything from surfer ecolodges to luxury resorts. South of Managua is the surprisingly biodiverse area of Las Sierras, with broad swathes of tropical dry forest, mild climates and a great diversity of wildlife and vegetation. ▸▸ *For Sleeping, Eating and other listings, see pages 73-74.*

Las Sierras de Managua ▸▸ *p73.*

Behind the suburban sprawl that is Managua, Las Sierras rise 950 m above sea level into a broad area of forest and mountains. Considering it is less than 30 km from a city of more than a million people, the diversity of wildlife and vegetation that can be found here is remarkable. Accommodation is extremely limited but the area can be visited as a day trip from Managua or Granada. There are two entrances to the Sierras, from the Carretera Sur and the Carretera a Masaya, the former offering brilliant views of crater lakes, the great lake basin and numerous volcanoes, the latter with access to the excellent nature reserves of Montibelli and El Chocoyero.

Ins and outs

Getting there To get to Las Sierras, take a bus heading for Diriamba and Jinotepe from the Mercado Israel Lewites, just west of the alcaldía in Managua. Alight just after Las Nubes (the towers on the summit of the Carretera Sur) and walk up from the Carretera Sur on the tower road to see the fantastic views. To visit Montibelli or El Chocoyero, take a bus from Mercado Israel Lewites (or La UCA, Managua's University bus terminal) to La Concepción or San Marcos. Tell the driver you want to get off at the entrance; it is then a long dusty or muddy walk depending on the season, though you will meet lots of people along the way. Taxis can be hired for the trip. Agree in advance on the cost and how long you wish to stay. Expect to pay US$40-60 if you want the taxi to wait while you spend time walking. In the rainy season you will need to hire a 4WD. See Managua, page 66, for more information.

Getting around Buses pass regularly on both the Carretera a Ticuantepe and Carretera Sur. Once off the main roads walking or driving are the options. You might get a transfer from the Belli family if you book Montibelli in advance, see page 70.

Best time to visit Most prefer the lushness of the rainy season (June to November), but the bare (and blooming) trees in the tropical dry forest during the dry months make it easier to spot wildlife and migratory birds arrive after the rains stop. Visibility from Las Nubes is best after a clearing shower and November is the ideal month to see an eagle's nest view of the central Pacific slope.

Along the Carretera Sur

The Carretera Sur is one of the most dramatic roads in Nicaragua, with expansive views and several crater lakes to be seen as it rises up into the mountainous region of Las Sierras de Managua. At Km 6 is the little park **Las Piedrecitas**, which fills up at weekends with children, families and couples and has a cheap café serving bad hamburgers. The park has a great view of **Laguna de Asososca** ('blue waters' in Náhuatl), the principal reservoir of drinking water for Managua. It is a pretty lake and the view extends to Lake Managua and the Chiltepe Peninsula where two more crater lakes are hidden. At Km 9 is another crater lake, **Laguna de Nejapa** ('ash waters'), in the wooded crater of an old volcano that is almost dry during the summer. The highway continues south and turns right at a traffic signal 1 km past the final petrol station. From there the road rises gradually past some of the wealthiest homes in Nicaragua.

The section of road from Km 19 to Km 21 has no development, perhaps a coincidence, but some might tell you otherwise, as there is a **haunted house** at Km 20 (see box). Past the haunted house the highway twists and climbs to the summit, with its transmitter towers known as **Las Nubes**. You can turn left at the summit, just beyond the towers, and take a narrow road that runs along the ridge. Close to the end of the paved road, a small turning leads to a spectacular view of the valley of Lake Managua, Peninsula Chiltepe, the Pacific Ocean and the northern volcanic chain, Los Maribios, that runs from the province of León and into Chinandega.

Montibelli Private Nature Reserve

ⓘ *Km 19, Carretera a Ticuantepe, turn right at the sign for the reserve and follow signs for 2½ km, by reservation 3 days in advance only, T270-2487, www.montibelli.com.*

Montibelli Private Nature Reserve is a family-owned nature park in greater Managua and one of the Pacific Basin's best forest reserves for birdwatching. Montibelli protects 162 ha of forest at an altitude of 360-720 m. The combination of its forest and elevation allow a more comfortable climate than Managua, with temperatures ranging from 18-26°C. The sandy Sierras' soil is super-fertile, but also very susceptible to erosion, making projects like Montibelli all the more valuable for their preservation of the mountain wildlife and vegetation. The property once had three separate shade-coffee haciendas; today only 22 ha are dedicated to coffee production and another 8 ha to fruit cultivation, the rest is set aside as forest reserve. The tropical dry forest has three principal nature walks, 1-3 km in length, which you can combine up to 7 km. The forest is home to 115 species of trees, and there are more than 100 species of bird including toucans, parrots, mot-mots, trogons, manikins and hummingbirds. There are also an impressive 40 species of butterfly as well as wild boar, agouti and howler monkeys. The old coffee hacienda house acts as a small museum and on the back patio meals are served by prior arrangement. Birdwatching or a butterfly tour with a local guide is US$45 per person with breakfast. The reserve also offers guided trekking for US$15 per person (minimum of two). Every Sunday there are group nature walks that finish with a farm style *parillada* of grilled meats and the Belli family's excellent organic coffee.

La Casa Embrujada – a legend?

The Pan-American Highway twists its way up into the fresh forested highlands south of Managua, past many luxurious residences, the big walled-in homes of wealthy Nicaraguans and foreign dignitaries. Yes it seems strange that, suddenly, on one of the most beautiful stretches of the highway, the luxurious residences give way to the green goodness of Mother Nature. Then out of the blue, at Km 20, the road passes *La Casa Embrujada* ('the haunted house'), the ragged ruins of a two-storey house which, it is said, is not just haunted, but possessed.

Some 35 years ago the owner of this hilltop house killed everyone in his family and then took his own life. According to his will all the bodies were buried around the house. This house – now a monument to insanity and murder – stood empty for years. It was used again, at the time of the Revolution in the late 1970s, by Somoza's National Guard, who took Sandinista rebels to the empty house to be executed. Later, the Sandinistas got their revenge by taking captured members of the National Guard up the hill to the house to be shot and left to the vultures. The Devil could not have written a better script himself. The house was not torn down, nor was it rebuilt: it remained there in full view, a monument to man's darker side. People talked about it, its ghosts, the strange cries, and the danger of going inside, especially at night.

In the 1980s the Sandinista government was not amused by this nonsensical ghost talk, they sent 200 soldiers to the concrete red and white skeleton of a home. Their aim was to make a point to the Nicaraguan people: have no fear; we are in control. Darkness fell and the soldiers all found a spot to settle down for the night. The nervous chatter and laughter died out. One by one they fell into a deep sleep.

In the early morning the first soldier woke to a smell of tarmac and the deafening noise of an angry bus horn. Startled, he jumped to his feet, the smoking bus idling inches from his resting place. He suddenly realized he had been sleeping right in the middle of the Pan-American Highway. He felt a chill, he had no idea how he got there. He looked down the road and, to his befuddled amazement, saw the other 199 soldiers waking from a deep sleep – all in the middle of the highway.

Reserva Natural El Chocoyero

ⓘ *Km 21.5, Carretera a Ticuantepe, turn right at the sign for the reserve and then follow signs for 7 km, T278-3772, www.marena.gob.ni/comap. There is a park ranger station at the entrance, US$4, the rangers act as guides.*

The park's 184 ha houses 154 species of flora and 217 species of fauna and there are 2½ km of trails, the best one being Sendero El Congo for its howler monkeys. It is also easy to see agouti, hummingbirds, butterflies and coral snakes, but the big attraction here are parakeets (the park's name comes from the ubiquitous Chocoyo, Nicaraguan for parakeet). Pacific parakeets (*Aratinga strenua*) nest here in staggering numbers – there are around 700-900 couples. The best place to see them is at the El Chocoyero waterfall where the cliffs are dotted with tiny holes that they use for nesting. Arriving in the early afternoon allows time to explore the park and see them coming home to nest – a glorious racket. **Camping** is possible in the park, but bring plenty of insect repellent.

Managua's Pacific Coast » pp73-74.

The province of Managua has swathes of empty beaches and some tourist infrastructure exists in a few places, including Pochomíl, Masachapa, the resort Montelimar and the ecolodge of Los Cardones. All the beaches in this region are washed by strong waves and currents and there are excellent conditions for surfing near the settlement of San Diego. The beaches themselves are not terribly attractive with greyish sand and a good deal of litter near population centres but the ocean is warm and the sun shines for more than 300 days of the year and the beaches immediately in front of hotels are cleaned daily.

Ins and outs

Getting there Buses to Masachapa and Pochomíl (60 km from Managua) leave from the Mercado Israel Lewites in Managua. To visit Montelimar or Los Cardones you will need a private car or taxi or ask your hotel to pick you up. A taxi to the coast from Managua should cost no more than US$40 (less if you are sharing a ride), though if you want them to wait expect to pay US$60.

Getting around Walking along the beach is the best way to get around the area and from one beach town to the other, though passing Masachapa at high tide can be tricky as there are many rocks, and access to Montelimar is blocked by a rocky bluff from the south.

Best time to visit The dry season means bigger crowds and often stronger winds; the rainy season brings with it more mosquitoes. Avoid Montelimar from November to March when charter flights from Montreal fill the resort. For surfing, March to November is best.

Along the Carretera a Masachapa

At Km 32 on the Carretera Nueva a León is the turning to the Carretera a Masachapa – a long stretch of forest-lined highway paved with smooth cement cobblestones that runs through 25 km of pasture, forest and sugar cane. When the road ends, turn right and you will come to Masachapa. The first exit to the right is for the private beaches of the Montelimar Beach Resort; continue straight on for the little fishing village of Masachapa, or turn left and continue 1 km for the entrance to the broad public beaches of Pochomíl.

Pochomil and Masachapa beaches

The tourist centre of Pochomil (US$1.50 per car, free if you come by bus) has countless restaurants, mostly poor value, and a main beach that is not very clean. Further south the beach is cleaner, the sand lighter in colour and more attractive. The huge, garishly painted presidential summer house is here. Along a rocky break at high tide are natural saltwater waterfalls, created by waves crashing over a neat shelf of rocks, great for cooling off. Further south is a cove with more very expensive homes and beyond **Pochomil Viejo** is another long beach. At low tide it is possible to drive in a 4WD for almost an hour along this stretch of sand from Masachapa south to just short of **La Boquita** in Carazo.

North of the tourist centre is the rocky shore of **Masachapa**, which has many tidal pools at low tide. The surf here is strong and swimming is a considerable risk. If you are up early, head to the centre of Masachapa beach where the fishermen roll their boats on logs up the beach with the morning's catch. If the fishing has been good it is a very happy and busy time – fishing is the lifeblood of the village, aside from tourism.

Montelimar and Playa San Diego

North of Masachapa, reached by a slightly inland road, is the infamous beach house of the last Somoza dictator which was turned into **Montelimar Beach Resort** by 1980s Minister of Tourism Herty Lewites. Further north of Montelimar, the beaches become increasingly deserted, until you arrive at a small lodge at **Playa San Diego**, called Los Cardones. It was built by an Israeli/French couple around a small coastal estuary and backed by tropical dry forest; it's a great place for surfing and relaxing.

Sleeping

Montibelli Nature Reserve *p70*

C Montibelli Nature Reserve, T270-2487, www.montibelli.com. Simple cedar and stone cabins each with a deck that look out onto the forest reserve, private baths, with good beds, recommended. Meals are US$4-10 per dish.

Pochomil *p72*

AL Vistamar, Petronic, 600 m sur, turn right at sign, then 400 m on sandy road, T269-0431, www.vistamarhotel.com. This seafront hotel has 17 attractive cabins with ocean views, private bath, a/c and hammocks; some have kitchenettes. The beautiful grounds have 3 swimming pools and many different varieties of hibiscus. The restaurant TTT does good seafood soup.

B Ticomo Mar, just south of the presidential beach house on a good stretch of beach, T265-0210. Simple rooms at a pleasant location, they come with a/c and bath. Parking available.

C Villas del Mar, just north of Pochomil centre, T269-0426. There's a fun party atmosphere at the crowded, overpriced restaurant, and the rooms have private bath and a/c. Use of pool is US$5 per person.

D Alta Mar, 50 m south of bus station, T269-9204. Situated on a bluff with a great view of the ocean, but the rooms are generally poor value and suffocating, with dirty shared baths. The restaurant, however, is very good TT, and serves fish at the tables on the sand. Popular with backpackers largely because of a lack of choice.

Masachapa *p72*

L-AL Montelimar Beach Resort, 3 km north of Masachapa, T269-6769, www.barcelo montelimarbeach.com. Price includes all meals and national drinks. Most of the rooms are in bungalows surrounded by towering palms. Rooms have a/c, minibar, cable TV, private bathroom, a giant swimming pool, 4 restaurants, several bars, disco, fitness centre, shops, BAC bank to change TCs, laundry, tennis, casino (US$50 per person for use of all facilities for 6-hr day, including buffet lunch). This hotel is part of Nicaraguan history. It was once the sugar plantation of German immigrants. During the Second World War the first General Somoza confiscated the land. His son made the estate into the family's favourite beach house, built an airstrip and turned the sugar plantation into one of the best in the country. The Sandinista government then took over and after the Revolution turned it into an attractive beach resort. After the Sandinistas lost the elections in 1990, new President Violeta Barrios de Chamorro sold the resort to the Spanish hotel chain Barceló, which runs it today. It is set along an impressive beach with 3 km of uninterrupted sand. The beach is good for swimming with a very gradual shelf and (relatively) weak current. The resort is normally full with Canadian tourists between Nov and Mar.

B Ecológico, Petronic, 300 m south, T887-5144. 10 rooms with private bath, a/c, swimming pool, TV. Only comes alive during holidays.

C La Bahía, behind Petronic, T222-4821. Attractive little rooms with private bath a/c, TV, parking, swimming pool, friendly staff, bar and restaurant. Not a great location.

Montelimar and Playa San Diego *p73*

AL Finca Río Frío, Km 45, Carretera a Masachapa, T266-2709, rzq@ibw.com.ni. A lovely farmhouse and ranch inland from the ocean along the highway. The farm has a charming log cabin with 4 rooms with 1 bed in each, shared toilets and showers,

For an explanation of the sleeping and eating price codes used in this guide, see inside the front cover. Other relevant information is found in Essentials, see pages 23-27.

swimming pool, sun deck and a big thatched-roof dining area. This is the farm and rural tourism project of Rodrigo Zapata, son of Nicaragua's legendary musical artist Camilo Zapata, the father of Nicaraguan folk music (see page 315). Rodrigo rents the entire farm to visitors who can relax around the pool, plant trees, milk cows, horse ride and swim in the river that passes through the property and gives the farm its name. Guests can use the kitchen or receive 3 meals a day for US$20 per person, advance reservations only. Transfers round-trip to the farm in van are US$40 total.

AL Los Cardones Ecolodge, Km 49, Carretera a Masachapa, then 15 km to the coast, follow signs, T618-7314, www.loscardones.com. This upmarket surfers' lodge has simple bungalows with brick walls, tile floors and thatched roofs. The little complex, not easy to find, lies on a beautiful and wild stretch of beach next to the tiny coastal settlement of San Diego and backed by 7 ha of greenery. Owners Izic and Anne-Laure are surfers and they direct guests to a variety of waves from little sand bottom breaks to a harrowing shallow rock reef tube ride called 'Haemorrhoids'. Food is served by the owners and includes pizza and the original *nacatamal de pescado*. Horse rental and other tours offered.

Transport

Pochomil *p72*

Buses to **Managua**, every 20 mins, 0400-1745, US$1, 2 hrs. This can be a tedious ride with many stops.

East of Managua

East of the great lake basin of Lago de Managua and Lago de Nicaragua, the land rises and breaks into a mountainous region of dramatic peaks bridged by wide, gentle plains to form the departments of Boaco and Chontales. The region was heavily populated before the conquest and it remains rich in pre-Columbian archaeology, which is on display in Juigalpa. When the Spanish arrived they quickly recognized it as prime cattle grazing land and it has now been one of Central America's richest cattle and dairy lands for more than two centuries. Few foreign visitors bother to explore these provinces with their wide open spaces and traditional toughened cowboys, some of whom still ride with holstered guns. Accommodation is sparse due to the lack of tourism, but the region is worth visiting for anyone who wants to see real Nicaraguan cowboy culture, buy an authentic Nicaraguan woven sombrero or learn more about Nicaragua's Chontal indigenous culture. Travellers might also want to check out Cuapa, the site of pilgrimage after repeated appearances of the Virgin Mary to a humble local man during the Contra war of the 1980s. ▸▸ *For Sleeping, Eating and other listings, see pages 78-79.*

Ins and outs

Getting there and around Buses to all towns and cities in the region leave from the Mercado Mayoreo in Managua. Either provincial capital can be visited in a day trip from Managua or Matagalpa, though an overnight stop allows for better exploration. If short on time, getting around is easiest by taxi or a hired car. Bus connections between attractions are frequent but slow.

Best time to visit During the dry season, the region can feel a bit depressing. The wonderful pasture turns brown and the smoke from the fields, which the farmers burn while waiting for the rains, mixes with the dust. Though this region receives more rainfall than the Pacific Basin (and it normally rains earlier in the afternoon) most showers are strong and brief.

The road to Boaco and Chontales » pp78-79.

Leaving Managua on the Pan-American Highway, the road leads north to the small town of **San Benito** (Km 35). To the north lie the Northern Highlands and to the east begins the Carretera a Rama highway that leads eventually to the town of **El Rama** (270 km away) and the Río Escondido that drains into Bluefields Bay. A very good paved highway leads past the **Las Canoas** lake, created by damming the Río Malacatoya that drains into Lake Nicaragua. The water is used to irrigate thousands of hectares of sugar cane and rice that is cultivated south of the highway and runs all the way to Lake Nicaragua's shoreline. There are several places to eat a tasty lake bass (*guapote*) fried whole, including **Restaurante El Viajero**, where a plate of fried *guapote* is US$3, with rice and cabbage salad. At Km 74 the road forks: to the left is the highway to Boaco, which is paved as far as Muy Muy and then continues to the Caribbean town of Bilwi – more than 400 km of unpaved adventure and the only road link from the Pacific to the Caribbean. At Km 88 is the pleasant hilltop town of Boaco, capital of the department of the same name.

Boaco

Surrounded by mountains and perched on a two-tiered hill, Boaco's setting is impressive and its high-low division gives it the nickname *Ciudad de Dos Pisos* ('the two-storey city'). The relaxed cowboy atmosphere is reminiscent of some northern mountain towns, but the city is actually a commercial meeting place for the workers and owners of the sprawling cattle ranches that make up the department. Boaco has the history of a frontier town, having passed centuries on the edge of western and eastern Nicaragua. It has been moved west twice: in 1749 as a result of attacks from indigenous groups, then again in 1772 due to a harsh outbreak of cholera.

Ask if you can watch cheese being made at the factory by the entrance to Boaco, next to the open-air saddle workshop; they start at 1100 daily. Boaco is also a good place to buy cowboy boots.

The original location is now called **Boaco Viejo** and is more scenic and laid back than modern Boaco. Inside its 250-year-old church there are pre-Columbian statues from the region. This is also the site of some interesting dances during the festival of Santiago celebrated from 22-31 July – the 25th being its most important day with a ritual dance and mock fights between *'Moros'* and *'Cristianos'* recalling Spanish history of more than 500 years ago. Thirteen dancers represent each warring party, though the 'Moors' invariably end up being baptized year after year.

The streets of the upper level are pleasant to walk around. Above the church is a lookout point with an improbable lighthouse and a fabulous view of the town and the surrounding hills.

Camoapa

The pleasant town of Camoapa is 20 km past Boaco on a rough rocky road that passes through the outskirts of Boaco Viejo, which lies to the north of the highway. This is one of the prettiest regions in Boaco and the friendly locals are curious to see foreigners. Situated at 520 m above sea level Camoapa has a good climate and is known around Nicaragua for its *agave* hats, similar to the 'Panama' hat of southern Ecuador, though not quite as fine a weave. People of Camoapa also make purses and other items out of the fibre known as *pita*. Just down from the central park is Elsa Guevara Arróliga's very good artisan shop, **Artesanías Palmata** ① *Cooperativa Camoapa 20 vrs abajo, T549-2338*, with 50 years of family experience. They will explain the delicate process of preparing *pita* to be woven into hats and bags. It's a good place to pick up a local sombrero (the finer ones require three months of work), which are excellent in the heat of Nicaragua for their breathability.

There is a charming church in the centre of town, the **Iglesia San Francisco de Asís**, which dates from 1789 and enjoys protection as a national monument. The interior has been completely remodelled, but the façade is original and the biggest of the three icons representing San Francisco was carved in Spain and dates from the late 1600s. If staying in Camoapa you can organize an excursion to the **Río Caña Brava**, 25 minutes from the town; the river here is great for swimming and lined with forest. Few locals would hesitate to mention the pride of rural Camoapa, a 128-m *puente colgante* (hanging bridge) that passes 30 m above a particularly dangerous part of the river, 40 minutes by 4WD from the village. The festival for Camoapa in the name of San Francisco de Asís is on 24 June.

San Lorenzo

South past the Empalme de Boaco (the intersection in the highway) the road passes a paved turning to the left at Km 88 which leads to San Lorenzo, one of the most attractive villages in the region. Nestled in a narrow mountain pass, surrounded by lush green hills, this little village of 1400 people has a pleasant air; its cleanliness and beauty make it well worth a stop if you have your own transport. The locals are friendly and welcoming and often quite surprised to see foreigners. The central park is halfway up the cobblestone ridge and there is a small church, remodelled in 1977, with a white-tiled floor that contrasts with its dark wood ceiling. You can get some extremely crunchy but excellent *rosquillas* in the village, see page 78. The feast day of San Lorenzo is 10 August, when there is a rodeo at the entrance to the village.

Cuapa

Continuing along the highway to Juigalpa and on to El Rama, the striking, extraterrestrial-looking 600-m monolith of **Cerro Cuisaltepe** ('eagle mountain') appears to the east, beyond Km 91, believed to be part of an ancient volcano. This region is geologically one of the oldest in Nicaragua and volcanic activity ceased millions of years ago. The highway passes a prison and, later, a large slaughterhouse before reaching the dirt road turning to the small but famous village of Cuapa, marked by a little monument to the Virgin Mary.

Continuing east, the highway passes through pleasant countryside and at Km 134 another impressive monolith becomes visible to the south. **Piedra de Cuapa** is reminiscent of Cerro Cuisaltepe and is equally mysterious in form and appearance. At Km 149, there is a monument to more than 70 Sandinista government troops who died in an ambush by the Contras in 1985. The words, written by Chilean poet Pablo Neruda, are a reminder that this area was heavily contested during the war years.

At Km 152, another statue of the Virgin marks the entrance to an access road to a monument and open-air church at the spot where the Virgin appeared to a priest helper, Bernardo Martínez (known as Bernardo de Cuapa), on 8 May 1983. At the time Nicaragua was suffering from Contra rebel attacks against the Sandinista military and personal liberties were vanishing rapidly all over the country. The Virgin, known as **La Virgen de Cuapa**, appeared on a cedar tree and told Bernardo that the Nicaraguan people must unite their families and pray for peace. "Nicaragua has suffered much since the earthquake," she said. "It is in danger of suffering even more. You can be sure that you all will suffer more if you don't change." Bernardo told of his experience publicly and there was a media frenzy. In Nicaragua everything becomes political, and Bernardo's vision was no exception. The Sandinista administration, dealing with Contra attacks in an area that was unsympathetic to its cause, saw the Virgin's message as anti-Sandinista and denounced Bernardo as a counter-revolutionary. The experience changed his life and he went on to become a priest until his death in 2000. An elaborate monument stands on the beautiful hillside where the Virgin appeared in 1983; the only noise is the wind rustling the trees and parrots squawking in the distant forest. Even an atheist would find the setting special. On 8 May every year, some 5000 pilgrims celebrate the happening with mass, prayers and confessions, in the hope of seeing her again. During her life Mother Teresa of Calcutta visited the site twice. The village itself just 1 km down the main road is sleepy and uninteresting, though pleasant enough. The local church holds the official icon representing the Virgen de Cuapa, which is brought to the site of her appearance every 8 May.

Juigalpa

A hot and sprawling rural capital, Juigalpa is not terribly attractive, but its setting is beautiful and it is a great base for exploring the Sierra de Amerrisque mountain range, which lies to the east. Nineteenth-century naturalist Thomas Belt lived in the valley to the east and wrote about this area in his book *The Naturalist in Nicaragua* (see page 323). You'll get a great view of the Río Mayale, the Valle de Pauus and the Amerrisque range if you go to the east end of the street on which the museum (see below) stands. There, up on the left, is the lookout park, Parque Palo Solo, 'one tree park', which has an endless view of the mountains and valley.

On Parque Central, the very modern **Catedral de Nuestra Señora de la Asunción**, constructed in 1966 to replace the crumbling church built in 1648, appears starkly modern for Nicaragua with its two giant grooved bell towers. The cathedral has an interesting stained-glass treatment on the façade that is indecipherable from the outside; from inside the images appear to represent cowboys, women and Christ. Juigalpa has a raucous patron saint **festival** on 14-15 August, when the image of the Virgin is taken from the hospital (where she stays all year long to help with healing) to the cathedral at the head of a procession of cowboys and about 30 bulls. As in the rest of the country the bulls are mounted and brave young men run around in front of them with capes. As with most towns in this region, Juigalpa also has a brightly painted, very well-kept and attractive cemetery, on the main highway.

The town's claim to fame, and rightly so, however, is its superb **Museo Gregorio Aguilar Barea** or **Museo Arqueológico** ⓘ *bus station ½ c sur, ½ c arriba, T512-0784, Mon-Fri 0800-1130, 1400-1630, Sat 0800-1130, US$2*. Founded in 1952, the museum has more than 100 pre-Columbian statues, of all different sizes, and with varying reliefs, but always in the same cylindrical form. Many are in excellent condition, despite being carved out of relatively soft rock and having been exposed to the rain and sun for more than 600 years. The works date from AD 800-1200 and include one which, at over 4 m in height, is believed to be the tallest statue of its kind in Nicaragua and perhaps in Central America. Their smooth cylindrical form differentiates these statues from pieces found on the other side of Lake Nicaragua and its islands. They are sublime works, depicting men, women, priests, gods and warriors. The warriors hold knives; others hold hatchets or, if idle, their hands are crossed. The effort made to amass this collection and protect it in this private museum is staggering considering its limited funds. The curator, Carlos Villanueva, is a young, enthusiastic and sincere champion of national heritage, who knows the surrounding hills and their pre-Columbian treasures better than anyone in Chontales. It was Carlos who discovered the biggest ceremonial *metate* (used to crush corn for tortillas) encountered anywhere in Nicaragua (87 cm long and 46 cm tall). It is on display at the museum, along with many others. He has also recently discovered a previously unknown ceremonial site with eight statues. The museum also holds some colonial relics, taxidermy of native species and historic photography. One of the most beautiful statues – *La Chinita*, also known as the Mona Lisa Chontaleña (Mona Lisa of Chontales) – has now returned after a three year loan to the Louvre in Paris.

Carlos Villanueva will take visitors on archaeological expeditions (including camping and two to three days on horseback). Contact him at the museum or T512-0511 at home. The nearest archaeological site is just a few kilometres outside Juigalpa at the entrance to the highway to Cuapa, where numerous burial mounds and the ruins of some ancient homes lie behind a small school.

Sleeping

Boaco *p75*

F Hotel Alma, southeast corner of Parque Central, T542-2620. Basic rooms with fan and shared bath. Friendly and a good location.
F Hotel Boaco, across from Cooperativa San Carlos, T842-2434. This clean and friendly hotel has 22 tiny rooms with tired beds; some have private bath. Parking available.
F Sobalvarro, Parque Central. This well located hotel has a nice front patio and 15 very basic rooms with shared bath.

Camoapa *p75*

F Hotel Las Estrellas, Parmalat, 1 c norte, 1½ c arriba, T549-2240. The best in town has 17 small, no frills rooms with private bath, hot water, cable TV. The attached restaurant serves beef.
F Hotel Taisiwa, Puente entrada de Managua, 50 vrs arriba, T549-2158. Basic rooms with shared or private bath.

Juigalpa *p77*

E Hotel Casa Country, across from Parque Palo Solo, T512-4163. This attractive 2-storey house has 5 good value rooms with a/c, private bath and cable TV; some have good views. The best in town, recommended.
E Hotel La Quinta, across from the hospital on the highway at Km 141, T512-2574. 38 rooms with private bath, hot water, a/c, TV. There is also a ¶¶ restaurant, which is not very popular with the locals, but serves moderately priced steak dishes and good soups. The La Quinta disco charges US$2 entry for dancing, with a pleasant upper-view deck, complete with stuffed bulls' heads and wagon wheels. It's very noisy here on weekend nights thanks to the disco throbbing away.
F Hotel Rubio, cemetery on highway, 2½ c sur, T512-0630. Clean and basic rooms with private bath and fan. Grumpy staff, parking available.
G Hospedaje Angelita, Parque Central, ½ c abajo, T512-2408. Small, airless rooms with mosquito netting, shared bath and outhouse toilets. They are nice people, the grandmother makes some interesting crafts.

Eating

Boaco *p75*

There are lots of little places to eat, beef is the main dish.
¶¶-¶ La Casona, next to Texaco, T542-2421. Daily 0800-2200. Serves surf 'n' turf, traditional dishes, grilled chicken, good, moderate prices.
¶ Alpino, Iglesia Santiago, 1½ c arriba, T542-2270. Daily 0800-2100. Hamburgers, good *churrasco*, good value. Recommended.

Camoapa *p75*

¶¶-¶ Restaurante & Disco Atenas, Iglesia, 1 c arriba, T549-2300. Mon-Thu 1000-2400, Fri-Sat 1000-0200. Good beef and pork dishes, dancing to recorded music on weekend evenings after 2000.

San Lorenzo *p76*

¶ El Taurete, across from the church. Serves cheap *carne asada* and *tacos*.
¶ Restaurante El Mirador, down the hill, 50 m from Parque Central. Very cheap chicken and *taco* dishes, very friendly owners and lukewarm beer. There is a lookout point with little benches across from the eatery.

Juigalpa *p77*

¶ Comedor Quintanilla, just past the cemetery opposite Hotel Rubio. Serves the best cheap meal in town, wildly popular at lunch with locals, 3 meals a day, all less than US$2, with big servings, fruit juices, *sopa huevos de toro* (bull's balls soup).
¶¶ Restaurante Palo Solo, at the park by the same name, up from the museum. Has a great view of the valley and mountains and serves good fruit juices, fruit salad and *plancha palo solo*, a *carne asada* served with onions. For spice lovers, try *pollo a la diabla* (devil's chicken).

For an explanation of the sleeping and eating price codes used in this guide, see inside the front cover. Other relevant information is found in Essentials, see pages 23-27.

Transport

Boaco *p75*
Buses leave from the central market to **Managua**, every 30 mins, 0330-1715, US$2, 2 hrs.

Camoapa *p75*
Buses to **Managua**, 7 daily, US$2.50, 3 hrs. Express buses once daily to **Managua**, 0610, US$3, 2 hrs.

Juigalpa *p77*
From the terminal, buses to **Managua**, every hour from 0330-1700, US$2.50, 3 hrs. If you are staying on the highway and don't want to go into town to catch the bus you can wait at Esso petrol station on the highway exit to Managua.

Directory

Boaco *p75*
Bank Bancentro, next to Asociación de Ganaderos, T542-1568. **Fire** T542-1471. **Hospital** José Nieborowski on exit to Managua, T542-2301. **Police** T542-2274. **Red Cross** T542-2200.

Camoapa *p75*
Bank Bancentro, north side of the church, T549-2687. **Police** T549-2210. **Red Cross** T549-2118.

Juigalpa *p77*
Banks Bancentro, T512-1502; and BDF, T512-2467, both on Parque Central. **Fire** T512-2387. **Hospital** Asunción, T512-2332. **Police** T512-2727. **Red Cross** T512-2233.

Masaya & Los Pueblos

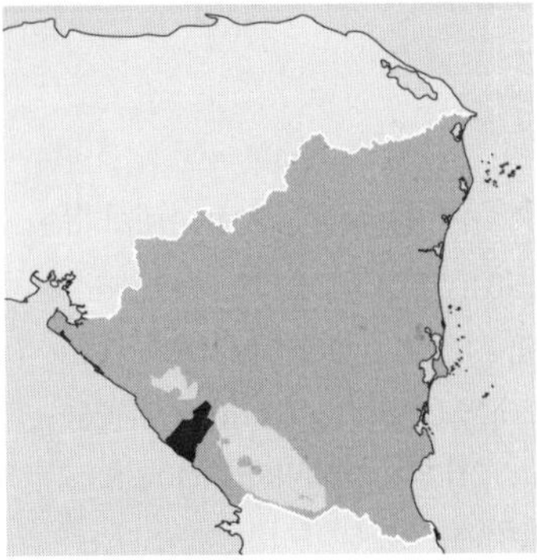

Footprint features

Introduction

Archaic folklore, vibrant craftwork and a vivid ceremonial life are some of the distinguishing features of Masaya and the surrounding *pueblos de la meseta*, a region deeply rooted in its indigenous past. Irresistibly sleepy until fiesta time, these ancient settlements are home to workshops, Nicaragua's best artesanía markets and intriguing communities whose inhabitants are warm, welcoming and directly descended from the ancient Chorotega peoples. Among their inherited gifts is a fierce indomitable spirit, roused time and again during difficult periods. It was here that the legendary chief Dirangén fought against the Spaniards, here that bloody rebellions erupted against Somoza, and here that the nation made a final stand against US invader William Walker. It is no surprise that the region also spawned Augusto Sandino, Nicaragua's most celebrated revolutionary.

Dramatic geographical features compliment the region's rich cultural assets with an intensely sulphuric and other-worldly volcano complex. Perpetually smoking, the tempestuous Santiago Crater has been threatening cataclysm for centuries. Hiking trails snake up and around the angry giant, promising unforgettable olfactory encounters, stirring views and vivid natural spectacles. Infinitely more sedate, Laguna Apoyo is the country's most attractive crater lake, with eternally warm, soothing waters heated by underwater vents. This is a special, peaceful place that is largely unspoiled although increasingly threatened by human activities. West of the *meseta*, the Pacific Coast is sparsely settled with wealthy vacation homes and sleepy fishing villages. It's an appropriately wild stretch, washed by strong surf and violent currents. The *mesa* of the highland villages, known as Los Pueblos de la Meseta, with their historic churche and interesting festivals, extends all the way from Laguna de Apoyo to the Pacific Coast.

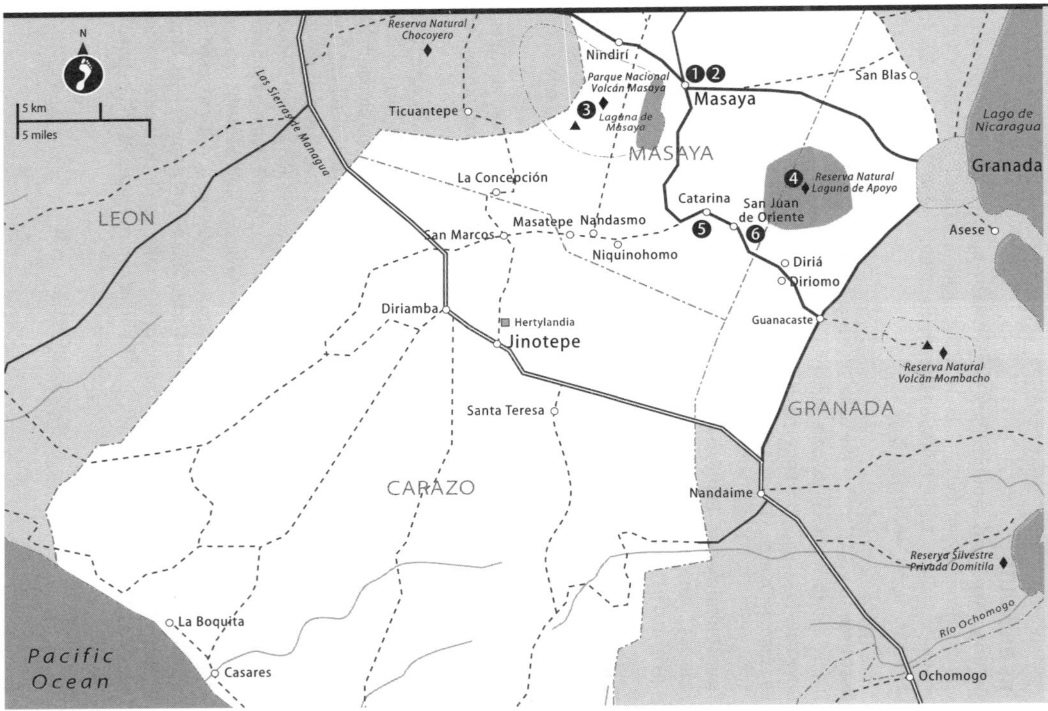

★ Don't miss ...

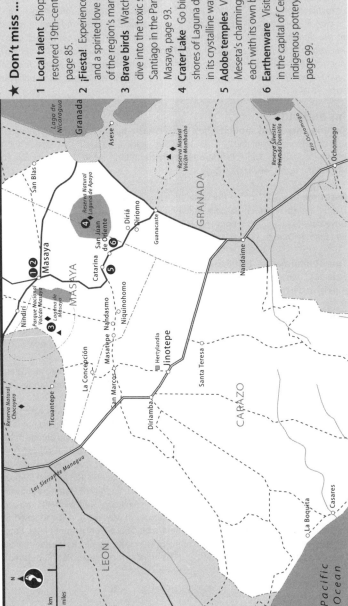

1. **Local talent** Shop for crafts in Masaya's restored 19th-century artistan market, page 85.
2. **¡Fiesta!** Experience processions, dances, and a spirited love of firecrackers in one of the region's many festivals, page 86.
3. **Brave birds** Watch squawking parakeets dive into the toxic smoke-filled crater of Santiago in the Parque Nacional Volcán Masaya, page 93.
4. **Crater Lake** Go birdwatching on the shores of Laguna de Apoyo then cool off in its crystalline waters, page 94.
5. **Adobe temples** Visit Los Pueblos de la Meseta's charming colonial churches, each with its own beauty, page 97.
6. **Earthenware** Visit an artisan's workshop in the capital of Central American indigenous pottery, San Juan de Oriente, page 99.

Ciudad de Masaya

→ *Population: 140,000. Altitude: 234 m. Colour map 3, B3.*

Masaya has long been a vibrant centre for Nicaraguan culture and is home to several beautiful churches. Shaken by an earthquake in 2000, this attractive town suffered damage to around 80 houses and most of its churches. However, some attractive homes remain and the city is full of bicycles and traditional horse-drawn carriages, the latter used as taxis by the local population. Protected from lava flows of the Santiago Crater by the Laguna de Masaya, the city is renowned across Nicaragua for its folklore and its craft tradition. The indigenous barrio of Monimbó is possibly the richest artisan centre on the isthmus with many of its handmade goods being offered for sale across Central America. » *For Sleeping, Eating and other listings, see pages 89-90.*

Ins and outs

Getting there and around There are frequent bus services from Managua's Roberto Huembes market and La UCA bus station, as well as Granada's bus terminals. Taxis are available in Masaya, both the motorized and horse-drawn variety. » *For further details, see Transport, page 90.*

Best time to visit Most of the region remains green year round, though Masaya, Nindirí and the national park are much more enjoyable in the rainy season. From November to January, the upper rim villages of Laguna de Apoyo, like Catarina and San Juan de Oriente, can be chilly by Nicaraguan standards.

Tourist information **INTUR** ⓘ *Banpro, ½ c sur, just south of the artisans' market, T522-7651, masaya@intur.gob.ni*, has a branch office in Masaya. They have maps of the city and information on events.

Background

Masaya has always been home to very hard-working and skilled craftsmen. The first tribute assessments of 1548 for the Spanish crown stipulated that Masaya was to produce hammocks and *alpargatas* (cloth shoes). Around 300 years later, when US diplomat and amateur archaeologist EG Squier visited Masaya, he noted that, along with Sutiava (León), Masaya was a thriving centre of native handicraft production. Composed of at least three pre-Columbian villages – Masaya, Diriega and Monimbó – Masaya was briefly the colonial capital of Nicaragua when Granada rose up in rebellion, and it has always been involved in major political events in Nicaragua. In November 1856, William Walker's occupying troops lost a critical and bloody battle here to combined Central American forces, triggering his eventual retreat from Granada and Nicaragua. In September 1912, Masaya was the scene of battles between Liberal army forces and the US Marines. The insurrection against Somoza was particularly intense here, with the indigenous community of Monimbó showing legendary bravery during popular rebellions in February and September 1978. Finally in June 1979, the Revolution took control of Masaya and it was used by retreating Managuan rebels as a refuge before the final victory a month later. Since the war years, Masaya has returned to making fine crafts, serving as the commercial centre for Los Pueblos de la Meseta and the heart of Nicaragua's Pacific culture.

Sights

Mercado Nacional de Artesanías

Most people come to Masaya to shop, and the country's best craft market is here in the 19th-century Mercado Nacional de Artesanías, one block east of the south side of Parque Central. The late Gothic walls of the original market were damaged by shelling and the inside of the market burned during the Revolution of 1978-1979. Work to repair the walls began in 1992 and the interior was also restored for its grand opening in May 1997. After two decades of sitting in ruin it was reopened and is now dedicated exclusively to handmade crafts. Masaya and its surrounding villages house an abundance of talent, which is clearly evident here. There are 80 exhibition booths and several restaurants inside the market and it's a great place to shop without the cramped conditions or hard sell of a normal Latin American market. Every Thursday night from 1900 to 2200 there is a live performance on the stage in the market. These usually include one of Masaya's more than 100 folkloric dance groups with beautifully costumed performers and live marimba music accompaniment, mixed with a more modern music ensemble.

Ciudad de Masaya

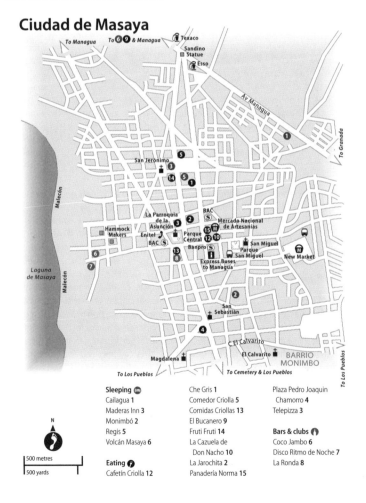

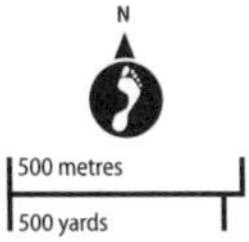

Sleeping
Cailagua 1
Maderas Inn 3
Monimbó 2
Regis 5
Volcán Masaya 6

Eating
Cafetín Criolla 12
Che Gris 1
Comedor Criolla 5
Comidas Criollas 13
El Bucanero 9
Fruti Fruti 14
La Cazuela de Don Nacho 10
La Jarochita 2
Panadería Norma 15
Plaza Pedro Joaquin Chamorro 4
Telepizza 3

Bars & clubs
Coco Jambo 6
Disco Ritmo de Noche 7
La Ronda 8

Masaya festivals

The festivals of Masaya and the *pueblos de la meseta* are some of the richest, most evocative and staunchly celebrated in Nicaragua.

2-8 February, **Virgen de la Candelaria, Diriomo** Festival for the patron saint, brought from Huehuetenango, Guatemala in 1720. Processions run from 21 January to 9 February with 2 February being her main feast day. On 2 February, a pilgrimage leaves from La Iglesia Guadalupe in Granada and arrives in Diriomo at 1000 to join the festivities. Dancing is performed by both children and adults, wearing masks and traditional costume. The dancers lead the procession up to the icon of La Virgen.

16 March, **La Virgen de la Asunción, Masaya** Also known as the festival of the cross, commemorating how the icon miraculously diverted lava flows during the 1772 volcanic eruption.

3 April, **Jesús del Rescate, Masaya** A procession of oxcarts travel from Masaya to San Jorge.

24 April, **Tope de las imágenes de San Marcos, San Marcos** This is the famous meeting of the icons of the four main saints of the region: San Sebastián (from Diriamba), Santiago (from Jinotepe), the black Virgen de Montserrat (from La Concepción) and San Marcos himself. They are paraded around in pairs until they all finally meet at El Mojón (on the highway between Diriamba and Jinotepe). It is a huge party with traditional dancing. The next day there is more dancing in the Parque Central and the four saints come out of the church together to tremendous fireworks, confetti and processions.

Week before Palm Sunday, San Lázaro, **Masaya** A fun, if highly surreal, celebration in which dogs are dressed up in costumes.

Mid-May, **Santísma Trinidad, Masatepe** This festival for the patron saint lasts over a month from mid-May and includes famous horse parades.

17-29 June, **San Pedro, Diría** This festival for the patron saint culminates

The market sells local leather, wood, ceramic, stone and fabric goods, as well as some crafts from around Nicaragua. Although most vendors try to keep a broad variety to guarantee steady income, there are some stalls that specialize. One of them is **Grupo Raíces** ⓘ *Módulo H-6, T552-6033*, which has a fine selection of ceramics from Condega, San Juan de Oriente and Jinotega, as well as soapstone sculptures from San Juan de Limay. They are located in the south wing of the market. Nearby, on the outside of the southern block of stalls, is a stall that has the finest examples of *primitivista* paintings from Solentiname and Masaya artists, as well as a good selection of books. Just north of the main entrance is a special stall that has a great selection of festival **masks** and **costumes**; these are not made for tourists but festival participants. Boys will greet you at the market with the handful of English words; they can help you find what you are looking for and will translate with the merchants for a tip of US$1-2.

There is a DHL office open daily 1000-1700, inside the market in case you end up buying more than you can carry.

Masaya's most famous craft is its cotton **hammocks**, which are perhaps the finest in the world and a tradition that pre-dates the arrival of the Spanish. The density of weave and quality of materials help determine the hammock's quality; stretching the hammock will reveal the density of the weave. You can visit the hammock weavers (normally in very cramped conditions) in their homes; the highest concentration is one block east from the stadium on the *malecón* and one block north of the *viejo hospital*. With a deposit and 48-hours' notice, you can also custom-order a hammock in the workshops. If you have no intention of buying a hammock it is better not to visit the workshops.

on the 29 June. Festivities include bullfights and violent ritualized fighting with cured wooden palettes.

24 June, **San Juan Bautista, San Juan de Oriente** An often wild festival for the patron saint with ritual fighting in the streets between believers and lots of *chichero* music (brass and drum ensembles).

24-26 July, **San Santiago, Jinotepe** Festival for the local patron saint.

26 July, **Santa Ana, Niquinohomo** Patron saint festival with folkloric dancing and fireworks.

15 August, **Día de la Virgen de la Asunción, Masaya** Monimbó festival honouring Mary Magdalene.

17-27 September, **San Sebastián, Diriamba** The legendary *Güegüence* is performed by masked dancers in bright costumes accompanied by music played with indigenous and mestizo instruments, which together have come to represent the very identity of Pacific Nicaraguan mestizo culture.

30 September – early December, **San Jerónimo, Masaya** 80 days of festivities, making it one of the longest parties in Latin America. Celebrations include processions and dances performed to the driving music of marimbas, such as *El Baile de las Inditas* and *Baile de las Negras* (Sundays throughout October and November), *Baile de los Diablitos* (last Sunday of November) and, most famous for its brutally humorous mocking of Nicaragua's public figures and policies, *El Toro Venado* (last Sunday in October and third Sunday in November).

Last Friday in October, **Noche de Agüizotes, Masaya** A festival commemorating bad omens, in which participants dress up like ghouls and monsters.

26 November, **Santa Catalina de Alejandría, Catarina** Patron saint festival.

31 December – 1 January, San Silvestre, Catarina The big fiesta in Catarina, with flower-festooned parades.

Laguna de Masaya and el Malecón

The best view of the deep blue 27 sq km Laguna de Masaya and the Masaya volcanic complex is from the *malecón*, or waterfront, usually populated with romantic couples. There is also a **baseball stadium**, named after the Puerto Rican baseball star Roberto Clemente, who died in a flying accident in Florida while en route to Nicaragua with earthquake relief aid in 1972. The lake is 300 m below, down a steep wall. Before the pump was installed in the late 19th century, all of the town's water was brought up from the lake in ceramic vases on women's heads – a 24-hour-a-day activity according to British naturalist Thomas Belt who marvelled at the ease with which the Masaya women dropped down into the crater and glided back out with a full load of water. The lake has suffered from city run-off for the last few decades and the city is looking for funding to clean its waters, which are not good for swimming at the moment. There are more than 200 petroglyphs on the walls of the descent to the lake that can also be seen reproduced in the Museo Nacional in Managua (see page 47). There are no official guides to take you to the petroglyph sites, but you can try the INTUR office near the market, or ask around locally.

La Parroquia de Nuestra Señora de la Asunción

Nearly every barrio in Masaya has its own little church, but two dominate the city. In Masaya's leafy Parque Central is La Parroquia de Nuestra Señora de la Asunción, a late-baroque church that dates from 1750. It was modified in 1830 and has undergone a complete restoration with financial help from Spain. The clean lines and simple elegance of its interior make it one of the most attractive churches in Nicaragua and well worth a visit. There is a subtle balance to its design, particularly inside, and its extensive use of precious woods and native tile floor add to its charm.

Iglesia de San Jerónimo

San Jerónimo, though not on Parque Central, is the spiritual heart of Masaya. This attractive domed church, visible from kilometres around, is home to the city's patron Saint Jerome (whose translation of the bible was the standard for more than a millennium) and a focal point for his more than two-month long festival. The celebration begins on 30 September and continues until early December, making it by far the longest patron saint festival in Nicaragua and perhaps in Latin America (see box, page 86). The church of San Jerónimo was badly damaged by the earthquake in 2000. The walls survive with four sets of temporary exterior supports, however it is awaiting proper funding to restore it.

Comunidad Indígena de Monimbó

The famous indigenous barrio of Monimbó is the heart and soul of Masaya. During Spanish rule the Spanish and Indian sections of major cities were clearly defined. Today, nearly all the lines have now been blurred, yet in Monimbó (and in the León barrio of Sutiava) the traditions and indigenous way of life have been maintained to some extent. The Council of Elders, a surviving form of native government, still exists here and the beating of drums of deerskin stretched over an avocado trunk still calls people to festival and meetings and, in times of trouble, to war. In 1978, the people of Monimbó rebelled against Somoza's repressive Guardia Nacional. They achieved this entirely on their own, holding the barrio for one week using home-made contact bombs and other revolutionary handicrafts to hold off what was then a mighty army of modern weapons and tanks.

Today the crafts of Monimbó are decidedly more aesthetic and the people of the southern barrio are masters of all kinds of domestic and decorative crafts. This neighbourhood should be the most famous artisan barrio in Central America, yet curiously commerce dictates otherwise. A visit to some of the workshops around Monimbó will quickly reveal why: here you will see leather goods with 'Honduras' written on them, flowery embroidered dresses that say 'Panama' and ceramics with 'Costa Rica' painted in bright letters are everywhere. Even Guatemala, which has perhaps the finest native textiles in the western hemisphere, imports crafts from Monimbó – of course with their country's name on it. It is possible to do an artisan workshop tour independently, though hiring a local guide will make it much easier. The highest concentrations of workshops are located between the unattractive Iglesia Magdalena and the cemetery. You can start from the Iglesia San Sebastián on Avenida Real de Monimbó, go two blocks away from the centre of town and then turn right.

Fortaleza de Coyotepe

ⓘ *Daily 0900-1600, US$2. Bring a torch/flashlight, or offer the guide US$2 to show you the cells below. The access road is a steep but short climb from the Carretera a Masaya, parking U$1.*

Just outside Masaya city limits is the extinct volcanic cone of Coyotepe (coyote hill) and a post-colonial fortress. The fort was built in 1893 by the Liberal president José Santos Zelaya to defend his control of Masaya and Managua from the Conservatives of Granada. In 1912, it saw action as the Liberals battled the US Marines (allied with the Conservatives) and lost the fortress. During the battle Liberal General Benjamín Zeledón was killed; his death would inspire future rebel leader Augusto C Sandino and give status to Zeledón as a martyred hero. Though donated to the Boy Scouts of Masaya during the 1960s, the fortress was used by the second General Somoza as a political prison. His National Guard used it to shell rebel-held civilian neighbourhoods in Masaya in 1979. When the Sandinistas took power Coyotepe remained a political prison. In 1990 it was finally returned to the boy scouts after the Sandinista electoral defeat. There are 43 cells below on two floors that can be visited; people have reported feeling a heavy vibe in the cells, or hearing the distant echo of screams. The top deck offers a splendid 360° view of Masaya, Laguna de Masaya and the Masaya volcanoes and on to Granada and its Volcán Mombacho.

Sleeping

Quality lodging in Masaya is very limited, due to its proximity to Managua and Granada.

C Hotel Monimbó, Iglesia San Sebastian, 1 c arriba, 1½ c norte, T522-6867, hotelmonimbo 04@hotmail.com. 7 good quality rooms with private bath, hot water, a/c and cable TV. There's a pleasant patio space and services include internet and transportation.

C Hotel Volcán Masaya, Km 23, Carretera a Masaya, T522-7114. Great location in front of the volcano park, with spectacular views from the shared patio. Rooms have private bath, a/c, fridge and cable TV. The lobby area is good for relaxing.

C Maderas Inn, Bomberos, 2 c sur, T522-5825. Small rooms with private bath, a/c, cable TV and continental breakfast included in the price. Cheaper without breakfast and a/c (**D**). Internet, tours, laundry service and airport transfer available.

D Cailagua, Km 30, T522-4435. Comfortable hotel with 22 rooms, secured parking, private bath, a/c, cable TV, swimming pool, restaurant. Noisy location, far from centre; for the exhausted driver.

F Hotel Regis, La Parroquia, 3½ c norte, T522-2300. Very friendly and helpful owner. Rooms are clean, with shared bath and fan. The best budget option.

Eating

₸₸ El Bucanero, Km 26.5, Carretera a Masaya. A Cuban-owned favourite with sweeping views of Laguna Masaya and a loud, party atmosphere. There's a constantly changing menu of international and Nicaraguan dishes, including good beef. Worth it for the views.

₸₸ La Cazuela de Don Nacho, inside artisan market, northeast side of stage, T522-7731. Fri-Wed 1000-1800, Thu 1000-0000. There's a jaunty atmosphere at this pleasant market-place eaterie, usually buzzing with diners. They serve *comida típica* and à la carte food like shrimps, *filet mignon*, *filete de pollo* and *churrasco* steak.

₸₸ La Jarochita, La Parroquia, 75 vrs norte, T522-4831. Daily 1100-2200. The best Mexican in Nicaragua; some drive from Managua just to eat here. Try *sopa de tortilla*, and chicken *enchilada* in *mole* sauce, *chimichangas* and Mexican beer. Recommended.

₸₸ Restaurante Che Gris, Hotel Regis, ½ c sur. Very good food in huge portions, including excellent *comida típica*, *comida corriente* and *à la carte* dishes like steaks, chicken and pork. They have another branch at the southeast corner of the market.

₸₸-₸ Telepizza, Parque Central, ½ c norte, T522-0170. Good wholesome pizza, thick or thin based. Delivery service.

₸ Cafetín Criolla, southwest corner of the artisan market. Cheap, filling, greasy food, popular with the locals and often bustling.

₸ Comedor Criolla, northeast corner of Parque Central, 5 c norte. Popular locals' haunt serving cheap Nica fare, buffet food, breakfasts and lunch.

₸ Comidas Criollas, Parque Central, south side. Yet another local eaterie with the 'criolla' namesake. This large, clean, buffet restaurant serves up healthy portions of Nica fare.

₸ Plaza Pedro Joaquin Chamorro, also known as Tiangue de Monimbó, in front of Iglesia San Sebastian in Monimbó. Good *fritangas* with grilled meats, *gallo pinto* and other traditional Masaya food, very cheap.

Cafés, juice bars and bakeries

Fruti Fruti, northeast corner of Parque Central, 3½ c norte. Tasty, sweet, fresh fruit

For an explanation of the sleeping and eating price codes used in this guide, see inside the front cover. Other relevant information is found in Essentials, see pages 23-27.

smoothies, including delicious *piña coladas*. **Panadería Norma**, northwest corner of the artisan market, ½ c norte. Good, fresh-brewed coffee, bread, cakes and pastries.

Bars and clubs

La Ronda, south side of Parque Central, T522-3310. Tue-Thu 1100-2400, Fri-Sun 1100-0200. Music and drinks, beautiful building with a young festive crowd.
Coco Jambo, next to the *malecón*, T522-6141. Fri-Sun from 1900. US$2, very popular disco, mixed music, lots of fun.
Disco Bar Ritmo de Noche, next to Coco Jambo, T522-5856. Fri-Sun 1900-0100. Open-air dance bar, also fun.

Shopping

There is a **Palí** supermarket next to Enitel on west side of Parque Central.

Transport

Bus

The regular market or Mercado Viejo is where most buses leave from, it is 4 blocks east of the south side of the artisan market. Express bus to **Managua**, every 20 mins, 0500-1800, US$0.60, 50 mins. To **Jinotepe**, every 30 mins, 0500-1800, US$0.50, 1½ hrs. To **Granada**, every 30 mins, 0600-1800, US$0.50, 45 mins. To **Matagalpa**, 0600, 0700, US$2.75, 4 hrs.

From Parque San Miguelito, between the artisan and regular markets on Calle San Miguel, express buses leave for La UCA in **Managua**, every 30 mins, 0400-2100, US$0.80, 40 mins. You can also board any bus on the Carretera a Masaya to **Managua** or towards **Granada**. Note the sign above front windshield for destination and flag it down. For **Parque Nacional Volcán Masaya** take any Managua bus and ask to step down at park entrance. Buses to **Valle de Apoyo** leave twice daily, 1000, 1530, 45 mins, US0.70, then walk down the road that drops into the crater.

International bus North and southbound **Transnica** and **King Quality** buses stop at the Texaco staion on the highway. **Ticabus**, agency opposite the fire station, T522-3697, stops at the Esso.

Taxi

Fares around town are US$0.40-1. Approximate taxi fares to: **Granada** US$15, **Laguna de Apoyo**, US$7, **Managua** US$20, **airport** US$25. Horse-drawn carriages (*coches*) are for local transport inside Masaya, US$0.50.

Directory

Banks All banks will change dollars. The BAC, opposite the northwest corner of the artisan market, has an ATM; as does **Banpro**, opposite the southwest corner. There's a **Bancentro** on the west side of the plaza with a Visa ATM. You'll also find street changers around the plaza. **Fire** T522-2313. **Hospital** T522-4166. **Internet** Several around town including **Cyber Pro**, southeast corner of artisan market, 1 c arriba; and **Cyber Space**, Plaza Miguelito, ½ c arriba. **Police** T522-4222. **Post office** Correos de Nicaragua is 1 block north of police station, T522-2631. **Red Cross** T522-2131. **Telephone** **Enitel** is on the west side of Parque Central, T522-2891.

Around Masaya

The city of Masaya is set among some spectacular geography that includes the Laguna de Apoyo crater lake nature reserve and the Volcán Masaya National Park. Both sites are within half an hour of the city and offer unique nature experiences. Masaya's tiny sister city is Nindirí, a truly ancient settlement with a charming colonial church, rich culture and a relaxed pace of life. » *For Sleeping, Eating and other listings, see pages 96-97.*

Parque Nacional Volcán Masaya

ⓘ *Daily 0900-1700, US$4, including entrance to the museum. The visitors' centre (the Centro de Interpretación Ambiental) is 1½ km up the hill from the entrance, T522-5415.* The heavily smoking Santiago crater of the Volcán Masaya complex is one of the most unusual volcanoes in the Americas and reported to be one of only four on earth that maintain a constant pool of lava (neither receding nor discharging) in its open crater. Just 30 minutes from the Metrocentro in Managua, with a 5-km paved road that reaches the edge of its active crater, this is undoubtedly one of the most accessible active volcanoes in the world. What the park protects is a massive caldera with more than half a dozen cones that have risen up inside it over the last seven millenniums. It is a place of eerie beauty, the rugged lunar landscape punctuated by delicate plant life, remarkably resilient animal life and a panorama view of the great lake valley. The main attraction, the smoking cone, seems almost peaceful – until one recalls that it is an open vent to the centre of the earth and prone to sudden acts of geological violence.

If you are hiking, bring plenty of water, sunscreen and a hat. Watch out for any significant change in smoke colour from the crater or persistent rumbling, which may indicate a pending eruption.

Ins and outs

Getting there Any bus that runs between Masaya and Managua can drop you at the park entrance, Km 23, Carretera a Masaya, though the long, hot walk without shade make a hired taxi, tour company or private car a valuable asset. Hitching is possible, as are guided hikes, US$0.70-3 per person payable at the museum before you set out. At the summit parking lot (Plaza de Oviedo) there are soft drinks for sale. There is a picnic area with *asadores* (barbecues) opposite the museum.

Background

At first glance it's not obvious that the park is actually located inside a massive extinct crater, Ventarrón (10 km by 5 km), which includes all the park's cones and the crater lake. From the summit of the active cone, you can see the ancient walls of the Ventarrón *caldera* sweeping around the outside of the park. Ventarrón is believed to have erupted in 4550 BC in a massive explosion. Since then, successive lava flows have filled in the cauldron and mountains have risen in its centre, the lake being the last remaining part of the original crater that has not been filled with rock and earth.

The current active complex was called Popogatepe ('burning mountain') by the Chorotega Indians. In 1529, the Spanish chronicler Gonzalo Fernández de Oviedo y Valdés (known simply as Oviedo) visited the volcano. He wrote that there were many ceremonies at the base of the mountain, with the Chorotegas supposedly sacrificing young women and boys to appease Chacitutique, the goddess of fire. In the adjacent village of Nindirí, Chief Tenderí of the Chorotegas told Oviedo that they would go down into the crater to visit a magical fortune-teller who lived there. She was a very ugly old woman, naked, with black teeth, wrinkled skin and tangled hair (there is a beautiful rendition of her in the park's museum painted by the Nicaraguan master Rodrigo Peñalba). The old fortune-teller predicted eruptions, earthquakes, the quality of the coming harvest, wars and victories; she even told the chief that he should go to war with the Christians (the Spaniards). Oviedo became convinced that she was the Devil. After visiting the volcano, he commented that any Christian who believed in Hell would surely fear the crater and be repentant for his sins. Around the same time Friar Francisco de Bobadilla hiked to the summit to perform an exorcism and place a large wooden cross above the lava pool to keep the door to Hell (the lava pool) shut. A cross still stands in its original place above the crater, though it has been replaced several times. Another friar, less religious perhaps, or at least more capitalistic – Friar

Blas de Castillo – organized an expedition into the west crater. Armed with a cross and a flask of wine and wearing a conquistador's helmet, Friar Blas descended into the crater to extract what he was sure was pure gold. With the help of his assistants and a metal bowl dangling on a long chain, he managed to extract some molten lava, which, to his profound disappointment, turned into worthless black rock when exposed to cool air.

The final eruption of the Nindirí crater occurred in 1670 and the lava flow can still be seen on the left side of the access road when climbing the hill to the summit. Volcán Masaya burst forth on 16 March 1772 with a major lava flow that lasted eight days. The eruption threatened to destroy the town of Nindirí, but the lava flow was supposedly stopped in its path by the **Cristo del Volcán**, a church icon, and diverted into the Laguna de Masaya, thus saving the city. A colourful mural depicting the event can be seen inside the park museum. Another violent eruption occurred in 1853, creating the Santiago crater as it stands today, some 500 m in circumference and 250 m deep. The crater erupted again in 1858 and fell silent until the 20th century, when it erupted in 1902, 1918, 1921, 1924, 1925, 1947, 1953, and 1965, before collapsing in 1985. The resulting pall of sulphurous smoke made a broad belt of land to the Pacific uncultivatable. From 1996 to 2000 the crater gave increasing signs of life, with sulphur output rising from 150 to over 400 tonnes per day and a noticeable increase in seismic activity. Since 1997, the increasingly unstable land under the lookout from the west side means the lava pool can no longer be seen from there. (The photographs you see on posters and brochures of the magma pool were taken from that side of the crater.) In early 2001 the crater's gaseous output came almost to a complete stop and on 23 April 2001 the resulting pressure created a minor eruption. Debris pelted the parking area at the summit (during visiting hours) with hundreds of flaming rocks at 1427 in the afternoon, and exactly 10 minutes later the crater shot some tubes of lava on to the hillside just east of the parking area, setting it ablaze. Miraculously there were only minor injuries but several vehicles were badly damaged by falling stones.

Volcán Masaya

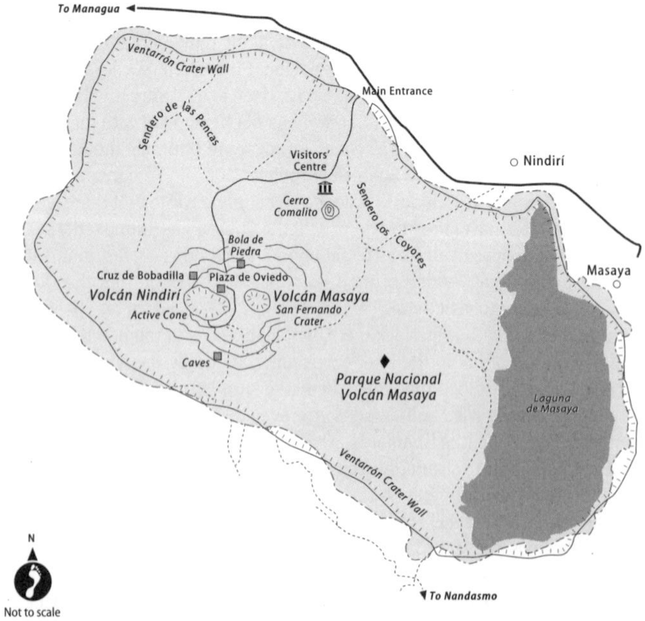

Sights and trails

The park boasts 20 km of trails that meander around this intense volcanic complex. This area includes *fumaroles* at the base of **Comalito**, a small extinct cone; the crater lake of **Laguna de Masaya**; and two extinct craters, **Masaya** and **Nindirí**, whose cones support the active crater of **Santiago**, along with three smaller extinct cones. The park is beautiful, a surreal moonscape punctuated by orchids and flowers such as the sacuanjoche (*Plumeria rubra*), Jesus flower (*Laelia rubescens*) and many species of small lizards. Racoons, deer and coyote share the rockscape, and mot-mots, woodpeckers and magpie jays nest in hillsides and trees. The real heroes of the park, however, are the bright green parakeets, that nest in the truly toxic environment of the active Santiago crater. The bird is known as the *Chocoyo coludo* in Nicaragua, its popular name in English is the Nicaraguan Green Conure (*Aratinga strenua*). The Chocoyos can be spotted late in the afternoon returning to their nests in the interior walls of Santiago, soaring happily through suffocating clouds of hydrochloric acid and sulphur dioxide, chattering away as they enter their cliff dwellings. The holes are tunnels which have a chamber at the end and can be as deep as 3 m inside the mountain. In July they lay two to four eggs. Most scientists attribute protection for the eggs as motivation for the Chocoyos' adaptation to the lethal environs of the crater.

A short path from the visitors' centre leads up to **Cerro El Comalito** and the *fumaroles* there, with good views of Mombacho, the lakes and the park's extraordinary volcanic landscapes. **Sendero Los Coyotes** is a 5½-km trail that accesses Laguna de Masaya. **Sendero de las Pencas** is a hike through lava flows that is interesting in the dry season because of the flowers to be found in the area. The **San Fernando crater**, straight up the hill from the summit parking area (Plaza de Oviedo), offers great views of Santiago and the valley below, as well as the interior of the forested crater. For a view of Masaya city and Laguna de Masaya, you need to make a 20-minute hike around the crater to its narrow east rim, where there are dozens of vultures nesting. Beware of **snakes** on this trail in the rainy season when the grass is tall. The hike up the 184 stairs to the **Cruz de Bobadilla** has been closed indefinitely for fear that the hillside beneath it may collapse. The **Cueva Tzinancostoc** is a gaseous cave formed by lava and full of bats.

Los Coyotes, Comalito and La Cueva can only be visited with a park ranger and all tickets must be bought at the museum (before you get to the summit), US$0.70 per person. The rangers there can tell you what is open, which depends on activity in the crater, their current staff size and fire hazards. If you want a good look at the red hot lava simmering beneath the earth's surface, a **night tour** is presently your best chance. They depart daily, 1700, US$3, five person minimum. You'll observe flocks of parakeets returning to roost, swarms of bats departing to feed, various rock tunnels, and a newly formed crater opening, glowing red and emitting pungent, sulphurous clouds.

Nindirí

» *pp96-97.*

At Km 25 on the east side of the Carretera a Masaya near the volcano park is the historic village of Nindirí. A cemetery marks the first entrance; the third or southernmost entrance leads directly to Parque Central. Inhabited continually for the last 3000 years, this attractive, well-kept village is built in one of Central America's richest areas for pre-Columbian ceramics. A quiet place, Nindirí makes quite a contrast from the hustle and bustle of Masaya just down the road. The leafy and colourful Parque Central is marked by a tall monument to **Tenderí**, the legendary Chorotega chief who was in charge of this area when the Spanish arrived in 1526. In 1528 Diego Machuca laid the plans of the town, which was not officially named a city until over 400 years later. The town church **La Iglesia Parroquial** is a charming primitive baroque structure that was first built in 1529, restored in 1798 and once again in 2004. It is a lovely church with tile floors, adobe walls and a traditional tile roof. It has a slightly indigenous feel to it and is home to the patron saint Santa Ana as well as the famous **Cristo del Volcán**, credited with stopping the lava flow of 1772 from annihilating the village (see page 92). The central park is well tended and the site of a performance celebrating the passion of Christ on the Wednesday evening before Easter during Semana Santa.

The **Museo Tenderí** ⓘ *corner house, Biblioteca Rubén Darío, Parque Central, 1 c norte, Mon-Fri 0800-1600, donation requested*, is so overflowing with relics that it is difficult to distinguish one piece from another. It's home to more than 1500 pre-Columbian pieces and a few very interesting colonial period artefacts. The elderly woman who owns the museum will show you around and may be coaxed into playing an ancient Indian flute that represents three different animals. Her deceased husband accumulated the collection. If she is not around ask the neighbours to help you find her.

Reserva Natural Laguna de Apoyo » *96-97.*

One of Nicaragua's most beautiful sites, this stunning crater lake is drawing increased attention with its tranquil, Mediterranean-blue waters, unique fish species and mysterious healing properties. Heated by thermal vents deep below the surface, the water is clean, clear and comfortably warm. Its light sulphur content makes it a fine skin tonic and a highly effective mosquito repellent. Swimming here is a rejuvenating experience, but many come just to gaze at the hypnotic waters that turn azure when directly illuminated by the sun. Others choose to hike through the thickly forested surroundings, observing birds and other prolific wildlife.

Ins and outs

Getting there Access to the inside of the crater, its forest and lake shores is from two cobbled roads, one that starts near Monimbó and the other from the Carretera a Granada at Km 37.5. Both end in a tiny settlement called Valle de Apoyo that sits at the edge of the crater's north rim. From there, a steep road slices down the northern wall of the crater to the lake shore. It's easiest to go by car, but infrequent buses do run to the inside of the crater. There are daily buses to Valle de Apoyo from Masaya, or regular buses between Masaya and Granada; get off at Km 37.5 and walk down the 5-km access road. Hitchhiking is possible though traffic is sparse on weekdays. **Hostal Oasis** in Granada offer transfers to Apoyo twice daily; the **Beaded Monkey,** also in Granada, runs shuttles three times a week. The other alternative is a taxi from Granada or Masaya (US$7-US$15) or Managua (US$35-40).

Getting around Once you reach lake level, a left turn takes you to the Spanish school, ecological station, **Crater's Edge** hostel and **Monkey Hut**. To the right are **Hotel Norome, San Simian,** the best nature walks, and tracks to Mirador de Catarina and Mirador de Diriá. Walking is the best way to enjoy the lake shore and nature.

Best time to visit Thanks to the relatively good condition of the tropical dry forest inside the crater it is still very attractive in the dry season, but to feel the lushness of the tropics and experience the total beauty of the reserve the rainy season is recommended. Birdwatching is best from December to March.

Background

Created by a massive volcanic explosion some 23,000 years ago, the drop from the extinct crater's highest point to the lake is more than 400 m, and the lake itself is 6 km in diameter. The maximum depth of the water is yet to be discovered, but it is known to be at least 200 m deep (more than 70 m below sea level), making it the

Ecological mysteries under threat

As yet relatively unspoiled, Laguna de Apoyo is Nicaragua's most beautiful crater lake and a true ecological jewel. Declared a nature reserve in 1991, the lake's surrounding tropical dry forests are home to a rich array of mammals including opposums, anteaters, pacas, jaguarondis, howler monkeys, white-headed capuchins, armadillos and agoutis. Bird life is equally prolific, with oropendolas, falcons and humming-birds among the 171 species.

The **Proyecto Ecológico**, located on the northern shores of the lake, has spent many years observing and documenting this diverse wildlife. Founded in 1996 and managed by Dr Jeffrey McCrary, the project's most fascinating discovery is three new species of fish, unique to lake and as yet unnamed. These exciting finds could change the way that scientists think about evolution, as the lake itself is a relatively young phenomena and only 23,000 years old. Dr McCrary also thinks there are other endemic species waiting to be discovered.

But the lake's fragile ecosystem faces serious threats. Pollution from motorboats, leaking septic tanks, forest fires, deliberately introduced foreign species and illegal wood cutting are among them. But the most serious dangers come from a handful of foreign investors. Having acquired large tracts of land very cheaply, these developers are deforesting it, dividing it and selling it on, piece by piece.

Some speculate that this de-forestation has contributed to the problem of the lake's rapidly diminishing water supply. The water level has dropped by 10 m in the last seven years and continues to drop 30 cm per year. Deforestation of the area around the Pueblos Blancos has been particularly detrimental, where rainfall filters down to the subterranean rivers that feed the lagoon. Water levels are also being effected by human extraction, and some speculate that new cracks were formed by an earthquake in 2000, and these are also draining the lagoon.

Protecting the lagoon for future generations will be a real challenge. Part of the problem is a disunited approach to managing the reserve, which falls under the jurisdiction of several districts who haven't agreed a plan. Some foreigners have taken advantage of this lack of co-ordination by building properties illegally, often on unsafe land. Meanwhile, the sheer ruthlessness of some developers, who boast about their ability to 'buy ministers', mean conservationists are in for a tough fight. Dr McCrary has even received death threats for his attempts to hamper the environmental destruction.

If developments continue, Laguna de Apoyo's unique evolutionary arc will be permanently and disastrously interrupted. Like Laguna de Masaya and Tiscapa, it will become little more than a dead crater lake, a dumping ground for human waste. Whilst environmentalists like Dr McCrary and groups like AMICTLAN (Asociación de Municipios Integrados por la Cuenca y Territorios de la Laguna de Apoyo) are working to raise awareness, it will require real political will to ensure the lake's long-term survival.

But the struggles of Laguna de Apoyo merely mirror wider national struggles for sustainable development and ecological harmony. Only time will tell whether tourism delivers its promise of redemption. For now it remains as beautiful and pristine as ever … almost.

If you would like to learn more, or contribute to reforestation projects in the area, contact the Proyecto Ecológico, north shore of lake, T882-3992, www.gaianicaragua.org.

 lowest point in Central America. When the Spanish arrived, Laguna de Apoyo was a central point for the Chorotega indigenous tribes, whose capital is thought to have been at Diriá, along the south upper rim of the crater above the lake. The basalt used for many of their ceremonial statues came from inside the crater. Today the reserve's only indigenous remains are petroglyphs submerged on the lower walls of the crater lake which can be seen using diving gear. The crater has seen some increased development in recent years, but at least half of it still consists of thick tropical dry forest.

Sleeping

Nindirí *p93*

B Hotel Besa Flor, Km 19.8 Carretera a Masaya, 200 m sur, 500 m oeste, T279-9845, www.hotel-besa-flor.de. Lovely hotel located close to Volcán Masaya national park. 5 rooms have private bath with hot water, Wi-Fi and free local calls. There's also a lush garden. Spanish, English and German are spoken.

Reserva Natural Laguna de Apoyo *p94*

L-A Norome Resort and Villas, on the western shores of the lake, T270-7154, www.noromevillas.com. 66 high-quality villas set back from the lake. Rooms have a/c, private bath and all amenities. On the lakeshore there is a bar, restaurant, swimming pool, jacuzzi, and dock. This is a controversial project due to environmental impacts on lake water.

B San Simian, south of Norome Resort, T813-6866, www.sansimian.com. A peaceful spot with 5 great cabañas with outdoor bathtubs – perfect for a soak under the starry sky. Facilities include restaurant, bar, hammocks, kayaks and a catamaran (US$15 per hour). Day use US$5. Recommended.

D-F Crater's Edge, foot of the access road, 500 m north, T860-8689, www.craters-edge.com. A friendly and hospitable hostel with dorm beds (**F**), private rooms (**D**) and plenty of facilities including kayaks, restaurant-bar, Wi-Fi, book exchange and a floating platform. Day use US$7. Daily transport to/from Oasis Hostel in Granada. Recommended.

D-F Monkey Hut, foot of the access road, 100 m north, T887-3546, www.thebeardedmonkey.com. Dorms (**F**), single and double rooms (**D**), and a lovely *cabaña* in front of the lake. Breakfast and dinner included. Can be booked with transfer from Granada. Canoe, kayak and sailing boat rentals and you can use facilities for US$7 if not a guest. A beautiful property with excellent views and a young backpacking clientele.

E Apoyo Proyecto Ecológico, north shore of lake, follow signs for Apoyo Spanish School, T882-3992, www.gaianicaragua.org. Lakefront forest location with dorms, small basic cabins and a great nature deck. Home cooked meals and reforestation projects, Spanish school, diving, kayaking and birdwatching available.

Eating

Nindirí *p93*

₸₸-₸ Restaurante La Llamarada, Iglesia, ½ c norte, T522-4110. Daily 0900-2000. Attractive setting in the village, try the *lomo relleno*.

₸₸-₸ Restaurante La Quinta, alcaldía, ½ c norte. Mon-Fri 1000-2400, Sat-Sun 1000-0200. Great *plato típico* that includes pork, fried pork skin, beans and cream, fried cheese, fried plantains, grilled beef and tortilla.

Activities and tours

Reserva Natural Laguna de Apoyo *p94*

Diving

Apoyo Proyecto Ecológico, north shore, T882-3992, www.gaianicaragua.org. Visibility is generally good, and native species include rainbow bass, freshwater turtles and various unique species (see box, page 95). A 2-tank dive with the research project costs US$55.

Transport

Reserva Natural Laguna de Apoyo *p94*

Buses to **Masaya**, 0630, 1130, 1630, 1 hr, US$0.50. To **Granada**, take a Masaya bus,

For an explanation of the sleeping and eating price codes used in this guide, see inside the front cover. Other relevant information is found in Essentials, see pages 23-27.

exit on the highway and catch a Granada-bound bus.

Shuttles to **Granada** depart daily from the Crater's Edge Hostel, 1100, 1730, ½ hr, US$2; and Mon, Wed and Fri from the Monkey Hut, 1800, ½ hr, US$2.

Taxi to **Granada** costs US$10-15, to **Masaya** US$7-10.

Nindirí *p93*

Buses to **Granada**, **Masaya** and **Managua** pass every 15 mins along the Carretera.

Directory

Reserva Natural Laguna de Apoyo *p94*

Language schools

Apoyo Intensive Spanish School, inside Proyecto Ecológico Research Centre, T882-3992, www.gaianicaragua.org. Small group instruction with complete immersion, 1 week US$220, 2 weeks US$430, 3 weeks US$630 and US$710 for 4 weeks, private lessons slightly more; all rates include meals and lodging, native instructors and 3 excursions per week. Recommended.

Los Pueblos de la Meseta

The Carretera a Los Pueblos runs south from Masaya and upon leaving the city rises to an average 500 m above sea level. Due to its elevation, it is one of the most agreeable areas in Nicaragua. The mesa is cooler than the lake valley where León, Managua and Granada sweat out the afternoon sun and most of it remains green throughout the dry season. Los Pueblos are shared politically by the separate provinces of Masaya, Granada and Carazo, but they are really one continuous settlement. This area, like Monimbó and Nindirí, is the land of the Chorotegas. Although you will not hear local languages nor see a particular style of dress (as in the Guatemalan highlands, for example), most of the people of Los Pueblos are of Chorotega ancestry. The Chorotega Empire stretched from the Gulf of Fonseca in Honduras to what is today the Nicoya Peninsula of Costa Rica. Made up of 28 chiefdoms, the capital for this large, remarkably democratic empire was here in the highlands of La Meseta. It is believed that the chiefs from all 28 local governments came to meet here every seven years to elect a new leader. Today the local people have a very quiet but firm pride in their pre-Conquest history and culture. ▸▸ *For Sleeping, Eating and other listings, see pages 104-106.*

Ins and outs

Getting there and around Los Pueblos de la Meseta have a very fluid network of buses in between towns and to Masaya and Managua; less so to Granada. A hired taxi from Managua is not too expensive due to relatively short distances involved with most villages less than 50 km from the capital. Outside Masaya there are limited taxis, but bicycle rickshaws can usually be found within a village. At the entrance to Catarina is a highway that cuts across the Meseta from east to west passing through the outskirts of Niquinohomo, Masatepe, Jinotepe and Diriamba and continuing to the Pacific Coast.

Catarina

This attractive hillside colonial-period village has a simple church built in 1778 and an obvious love of potted plants. From the highway, the town climbs up the extinct cone of the Apoyo volcano until its highest point overlooking the majestic deep blue crater lake of Laguna de Apoyo. Between the highway and the lookout point are numerous horticultural nurseries and Nicaraguans come here from around the country to buy their houseplants. There are also a number of artisans who specialize in heavy carved wooden furniture, bamboo furniture and baskets. The lookout point above the crater lake, **Mirador de Catarina**,

There are several small shops selling jewellery and crafts from neighbouring San Juan de Oriente in the town's car park.

Iguana soup

Hungover? Love life not what it used to be? What you need is a good soup, one that picks you up and rejuvenates the body. For a few dollars you can be a new person. Iguana is a traditional dish in Nicaragua and the soft and tender meat is prepared in all kinds of imaginative ways. The joke goes that when asked to describe what chicken tastes like, a Nicaraguan will say "hmm, you could say it tastes a bit like iguana".

First you must choose your species; most iguanas in Nicaragua are black or green. The black ones (*garrobos*) have meat that is higher in protein thanks to a diet that includes many insects; however, this also means they are more prone to parasites. The preferred meat is that of the green iguana (called simply *iguana*), which is vegetarian and has bigger eggs. Iguana eggs can be removed and cooked, and are said to be better than chicken eggs (really); perfect for that relaxing Sunday morning coffee, with toast and a Jurassic omelette.

The most traditional dish is *iguana en pinol*, which is a delicious reptile bathed in cornmeal and then fried. The lizard can also be grilled over a wood fire and smothered in tomatoes and onions. A two year old Iguana, is about 3-5 lbs and will normally feed a hungry couple or a small family, but a five year old reptile could weigh up to 8-15 lbs and feed a big family for a couple of days. The iguana is always cooked whole, only the fingers and mouth are removed, as the claws and teeth are considered unsanitary. Most men are interested in the soup, known as *sopa levanta muerto* (return from the dead soup). The name refers to a miraculously quick recovery from a long night of drinking or love making. Making iguana soup is simple: boil water and add salt, onions, sweet pepper, garlic,yucca and peppermint. Then add the iguana, boil until tender and serve ... *¡Buen provecho!*

has an entrance fee of US$0.80 if you come by car. On the rim of the Mirador there is a row of restaurants that share the magnificent view across the lake. From the lookout you can see the dormant Mombacho Volcano and its cloud forest as well as the city of Granada, Lake Nicaragua and part of the Las Isletas archipelago. This area is crowded on Sundays with families and young couples, quiet during the week. Due to its perch-like position it is breezy all year round but in the dry season the wind can be a bit strong. The walk down into the crater is easy, with spectacular views; the hike back up is quite strenuous – it's only about 500 m, but a very steady climb. Ask at the *mirador* for the trailhead and then keep asking on the way down as it's easy to get lost (see also Laguna de Apoyo, page 94). Catarina's patron saint, Santa Catalina, is celebrated on 26 November, but the town's big fiesta is for San Silvestre, on 31 December and 1 January (see box, page 86).

San Juan de Oriente

Across the highway from Catarina and just south is the traditional Chorotega village of San Juan de Oriente, which has gained international recognition for its elegant ceramic earthenware. Local clay has been used here to make hand-shaped pottery for at least 1000 years. Until about 25 years ago, all the houses in the village were made of adobe, however these have been replaced by stone-block constructions.

The last clay house in San Juan was demolished in 2001 by a local boy who crashed into it while learning how to drive.

Today, the distinguishing feature of the village is the tremendous creativity and dexterity of its population.

After the Spanish conquest, much of the ornamental expertise evident in pre-Columbian ceramics was lost, but the tradition continued until the 20th century. For many years, the village was known as San Juan de los Platos, because of the rustic ceramic plates it produced. In addition to plates, the villagers continue to make clay pots for plants and storing water (*la tinaja*), which are still used today throughout the Nicaraguan countryside.

In 1978, the Nicaraguan Ministry of Culture and the country's Central Bank initiated a programme of training scholarships. Eleven people from the village learned how to use a potter's kick-wheel for the first time, how to balance the mixture of the native clay with sand for added strength, and how to polish and paint pieces in the pre-Columbian style that had been lost in the centuries since the conquest. These 11 artists formed the **Artesanos Unidos**, the town's first co-operative. After the success of the Revolution, the Sandinista administration helped to support and promote the co-operative's work and the influx of foreigners provided a more affluent clientele.

In true Nicaraguan fashion, the skills and knowledge have been unselfishly passed on to other members of the community. Today at least 80% of the villagers who are old enough are involved in some aspect of pottery production and sales. The creativity of their designs and the quality of their work is excellent and their products can be found in many markets and shops across Central America. To buy direct from the source or to see the artisans at work, you can visit the artisans' co-operative, **Cooperativa Quetzal-Coatl** ⓘ *25 m inside the 1st entrance to the town, daily 0800-1700*.

The ceramic artists sell direct from their home workshops and may invite you in to see the process, these include: **Francisco Calero** ⓘ *Taller Escuela de Cerámica, ½ c arriba, T558-0300*; **Róger Calero** ⓘ *Iglesia, 2 c sur, T558-0007*; **Juan Paulino Martínez** ⓘ *across from Restaurante Quilite, T558-0025*; and **Duilio Jiménez** ⓘ *opposite los juzgados, next to the women's co-operative*, who is very welcoming. The most acclaimed of the ceramic artists is **Helio Gutiérrez** ⓘ *2nd entrance, 1 c abajo, 300 m sur, T558-0338*.

San Juan's small and precious early 17th-century church was badly shaken by the Laguna de Apoyo earthquake in 2000, which was followed a week later by the earthquake in Masaya. It has now been restored.

Diriá

Heading south towards the Mombacho Volcano on the highway that separates Catarina and San Juan de Oriente, there is another set of historic twin villages: Diriá and Diriomo. Diriá, in historical terms, is the most important of all Los Pueblos de la Meseta. It was here that the Chorotega elders met to elect new officials and from where the fierce Chorotega chief Diriangén ruled when the Spanish arrived to impose their dominance. Today it is one of the sleepiest of the highland *pueblos*, only really coming to life during festivals. **La Parroquia de San Pedro** church was first erected in 1650, damaged and rebuilt after an earthquake in 1739 and restored once again in 2003. It is a charming, simple construction in the Spanish colonial style with the bell tower a safe distance from the church in this highly seismic zone.

Diriá occupies part of the shoreline and upper rim of the Laguna de Apoyo. In some ways the lookout point here is more spectacular than the more developed complex at Catarina. There are several simple bars and eateries and a small Virgin Mary that stares out across the lake-filled crater. Access to the Diriá *mirador* is from the south of the church due east past the baseball diamond and the seminary. The people of Diriá are fond of statues and their central park has three interesting ones. On the north side is Moses with his Ten Commandments and on the south side is King Solomon. In the shaded part of the park is Chief Diriangén ready for battle and surrounded by idols. At the exit of the town is a mother nursing her child, the focal point for many festivals.

Diriomo

This farming centre is a charming town with a friendly populace that seems more open and relaxed than its twin, Diriá. Sorcery and folk healing is widely practised in Diriomo, a likely centre for magical activity prior to the Spanish conquest. Charms, potions, spells, incantations and readings are available from the various *brujos* and *curanderos* that work in town. If you're in the market for such spiritual remedies, or would simply like to know more, ask around for personal recommendations or enquire at the *alcaldía* to find a reputable practitioner.

Nicaragua's traditional sweets, known as *cajetas*, are an art form in Diriomo. The most famous of the sweet houses is **La Casa de las Cajetas** ① *Parque Central, opposite the church, T557-0015, cajeta@datatex.com.ni, tours available, call ahead*, founded in 1908 by the grandmother of the aging Socorro, who oversees operations today with the help of her grandchildren. The sweets are a combination of sugar, rice and various fruits; the most unusual is the *cajeta de zapoyol* which is made from the seed of the zapote fruit. Another, slightly less sophisticated, sweet house is that of **Hortensia González** ① *Enitel, 2 c norte*, whose family has 60 years of experience in making *cajetas*. They make an excellent *cajeta de leche* (milk sweet).

The **Iglesia Santuario de Nuestra Señora de Candelaria**, home of the town's patron saint, is a very attractive church but suffered some damage in the earthquakes of 2000. The church was built over the course of over 100 years from 1795 using a mixture of stone and brick, each stone being carried from a hill more than 1 km away. The church's cupola is said to have been inspired by the architecture of Tuscany while the façade combines baroque and neoclassical design – a result of its long period of construction. The roof is supported by 12 solid posts of cedar, each 12 m in height. This is one of the most visually pleasing structures in Nicaragua and deserves to receive funding to repair its damage.

Niquinohomo

This quiet colonial-period village founded in 1548 by the Spanish is best known for its famous son, the nationalist rebel General Augusto C Sandino (perhaps the only Nicaraguan who claims more attention is the León poet Rubén Darío). Tellingly, the name Niquinohomo is Chorotega for 'Valley of the Warriors'.

The town's entrance is marked by a small church and a statue of Sandino, a bronze relief of the nationalist warrior in memory of his legendary determination and integrity. The rebel General's childhood home is today the **public library** ① *Parque Central, opposite the gigantic cross that guards the church, Mon-Fri 0900-1200 and 1400-1800*, and houses a small display on the life of Sandino (see box, page 94).

The pride of the village is the town's stately church, finished in 1689. Both the classic exterior and clean simple interior of this long and elegant colonial church are pleasing to the eye, despite an unfortunate cement cross at the front. For the most part, the village is pleasant, if a bit lacking in energy. The Niquinohomo cemetery, on the far west side of the town, is well kept, brightly painted and pretty.

The village is also known for its original bamboo lamps, shaped mostly as pineapples, seen throughout Nicaragua. You can visit the artisan, Juan Norori, at his shop **Artesanías Pueblos Blancos** ① *Empalme de Niquinohomo, 1 km norte, T607-1278*.

Nandasmo

Nandasmo is several kilometres west of Niquinohomo and borders the south side of the beautiful Laguna de Masaya. The village itself feels neglected; it is a place few outsiders see and foreigners are greeted with wide eyes. However, it has a pleasant climate and a steady breeze from the lake. From the highway it is a 5-km walk to the Laguna de Masaya, where the views of the volcanoes and the city of Masaya are spectacular. It is possible to walk to Masaya from here although you will have to rely on local farmers to keep you on the right path. Past the entrance to Nandasmo, the

General Augusto C Sandino

The man from whom the revolutionary Sandinistas took their name has become a Nicaraguan and international symbol for armed opposition to external and internal domination. His shadow looms large over the Nicaraguan political landscape, as the giant silhouette of his statue looms above the Laguna de Tiscapa in Managua.

Sandino was born the illegitimate son of a white middle-class landowner and his Indian housekeeper in Los Pueblos de la Meseta in Niquinohomo in 1895. He spent his first 11 years living with his mother until his father agreed to accept him into the family house, where he was treated like a second-class citizen, eating at the servants' table. He grilled his father on life and equality. His father replied, "If I don't exploit, I will be exploited." Sandino would dedicate the rest of his life to a search for justice, defending the exploited while trying not to become the exploiter.

From 1923-1926 Sandino learned about the conflict between big business and revolutionary ideas while working for a US-owned oil company in Mexico, where anarchist, socialist and communist ideas were frequently discussed. The Mexican Revolution had also created a strong society of Freemasons. In 1926 Sandino returned to Nicaragua with new ideas and in time for the Liberal Party revolt against Conservative Party ruler Emiliano Chamorro. The Nicaraguan Liberals shared many ideals with the Mexican Liberal Party and nationalism was one of its strongest elements. When Sandino showed up at Liberal Party headquarters asking for arms from Liberal General Moncada and Anastasio Somoza García, they were suspicious of his ideologies. Somoza García, particularly, pointed to Sandino's use of the anarchistic phrase 'property is theft'. Despite the difficulties with Moncada and Somoza, Sandino managed to get an army together to fight the Conservative regime under the Liberal Party command. Later the US Marines intervened, pressured Emiliano Chamorro to resign and installed their ever-faithful president, Adolfo Díaz. The US threatened war against the Liberals unless they agreed to their appointment and terms. All of the Liberal generals capitulated, except Augusto Sandino. From 1927 to 1933 Sandino fought a war of anti-occupation from Nicaragua's northern mountains, first against the puppet government of Adolfo Díaz and the US Marines, then, with the election of General Moncada in 1928, against the US occupation. The Marines who enlisted the help of the newly formed Nicaraguan National Guard could not defeat Sandino's forces and their mountain guerrilla tactics. When the US Marines left Nicaragua in 1933 they left the National Guard in control of Nicaraguan security and Somoza García (who was also born in La Meseta, in San Marcos) as the National Guard commander. Sandino signed a peace treaty with the Nicaraguan government in 1933 and one year later he was abducted and shot on the order of Somoza García who would rule Nicaragua with his son Somoza Debayle until the Sandinista victory in 1979.

Much has been written about Sandino's religious and political theories. The truth seems to be that he was eclectic in his beliefs, combining bits and pieces of numerous theories, from socialism to Freemasonry. One thing everyone does agree on, however, is that Sandino was a nationalist, he never sold out his principles and today he is a national hero.

 highway leads to Masatepe and becomes an endless roadside market, with furniture makers displaying their wares in front of their workshop-homes. The village comes to life – in a big way – for its patron saint festival on 26 July.

Masatepe

This colonial-period village and ancient Chorotega Indian settlement is now the furniture capital of Nicaragua; its production dwarfs the rest of the nation's shops combined. Dining room sets, wicker baby cribs, hardwood bed frames and dressers, and the wonderful rocking chairs that are found in almost every house in Nicaragua, are made here in every style and type of wood imaginable. This is when many travellers wish they were going home on a boat rather than a plane. In addition to the countless roadside workshops that sell their products, there is a big store at the entrance to the town, in the old railway station. The town itself is warmer than most of the other *pueblos* of the region. Rickshaw taxis wait at the entrance and the Carretera to take visitors on a small tour of the village for US$3 and although the church **Iglesia San Juan Bautista de Masatepe** is not particularly interesting, it has a views of the smoking Masaya Volcano. The pueblo is famous also for its *cajeta* sweets, said to be among the best in Nicaragua, and it is the home of one of Nicaragua's favourite dishes, the *sopa de mondongo* (tripe soup).

San Marcos

Eight kilometres west of Masatepe, the *pueblos* highway enters the scenic coffee-growing department of Carazo and the university town of San Marcos, home to Central America's only US accredited English-speaking university, with courses given mostly by North American professors. **Ave María College of the Americas** ⓘ *T535-2339, www.avemaria.edu.ni*, is in the south of the town, its large student population (mostly well-off Central Americans) adding a vibrant atmosphere quite different to the rest of the *mesa*.

In 2005, the oldest evidence of organized settlement was unearthed in San Marcos in an archaeological excavation by the National Museum. The ceramic and human remains date from 2500 BC making San Marcos older than the two previously most ancient organized settlements in Managua and Los Angeles, Ometepe. The Spanish did not place much importance in the town, suggesting that it was not densely populated at the time of their arrival, and it remained a big ranch until the mid-19th century. Today, the town is clean and pleasant with a lively Parque Central, especially during the patron saint festival for San Marcos, which culminates on 24 April in the **Tope de las imágenes de San Marcos** (see box, page 86). The rather plain-looking church is colourful inside with a series of murals on the aqua ceiling. Above the altar is a fresco of Saint Mark in the tropics, complete with volcanoes in the distance. San Marcos is also the birthplace of Anastasio Somoza García (the first of the two rulers), whose mother owned a bakery in town and whose father had a coffee farm just outside the village. Somoza's home town is just a few kilometres down the road from Niquinohomo, the birthplace of his nemesis, Augusto C Sandino.

South from San Marcos is the highway to the Carazo department's two principal towns, **Jinotepe** and **Diriamba**. One kilometre before Jinotepe is the Nicaraguan version of Disneyland, a Herty Lewites-inspired theme park called **Hertylandia** ⓘ *T532-2155, Wed-Sun 0900-1800, US$5 entry to both sections, US$2 entry to amusement section only, additional charges for each ride US$0.50-2*. Herty Lewites, ex-rebel gunrunner, Minister of Tourism and Mayor of Managua from 2000-2004, tried to mount a bid for president in 2006 but died of a heart attack four months before the election. Hertylandia is a very simple amusement park in a green and spacious setting. The rides are specifically aimed at children. There are two separate sections, one with a big swimming pool and water slide and the other with mechanical rides.

El Güegüence: comedy and identity

In Nicaragua the name is omnipresent. The play *El Güegüence* is about humour, it is about corruption, the power of language and the clever art of revenge and it defines the very essence of what it means to be Nicaraguan.

Although the play's author is anonymous, it was almost certainly first written down between 1683-1710 in a mixture of Náhuatl and Spanish. The author was a master of languages and colonial law and had a sharp sense of humour. The play is both hilarious and profound in its use of language and comic timing. It is laced with double meanings, many to insult the Spanish colonial ruler who plays the sucker. The humour is often vulgar and all the characters in the play are targets. The great José Martí called it a "master comedy" and León's vanguard poet, Salomón de la Selva, said it was, "as good as or better than what we know of Greek comedy before Aristophanes". The work has been analysed by just about every Nicaraguan intellectual of any note who all have their own conception of the play's deeper meaning. However, they agree it to be a master play of American indigenous theatre, a source of cultural pride for Nicaragua.

The plot is simple. *El Güegüence* is an Indian trader in goods, some contraband, all of great variety, some of high value. He is called in by the local colonial chief of police for a bribe. He first plays semi-deaf, then stupid to avoid the subject of payment in a very funny "who's on first?" type of skit. Eventually he is brought in to meet with the governor and he befriends him with his cleverness, his humour and brilliantly funny lies. *El Güegüence* then manages to marry off one of his boys to the daughter of the governor by changing his reality from that of abject poverty (to avoid the bribe) to feigning immense wealth.

El Güegüence is the need of the Nicaraguan sense of humour to maintain pride, combat state corruption, salvage a seemingly hopeless situation with wit and break the chains of class structure. The use of laughter and irony to face difficult situations and the capacity to laugh at oneself are essential to the Nicaraguan character.

Jinotepe

ⓘ *INTUR office, Kodak, ½ c sur, T532-0298, carazo@intur.gob.ni, Fabio Sanchez has information on the region and maps.*

Another pleasant highland colonial town built on top of a Chorotega village, Jinotepe has a coffee- and agriculture-based economy and some pretty, older homes. The town prides itself on being the cleanest of the *pueblos*, although conditions at the bus station do little to support that theory. On the whole, though, it is clean and attractive. The city has a fine neoclassical church with some modern stained-glass windows, **La Iglesia Parroquial de Santiago** (1878), that almost appears to be a scale model of the Cathedral of León.

Diriamba

In comparison with many other *pueblos* on the *mesa*, Diriamba is a slightly grungy, disorganized place. Here the locals are a bit different from the rest. The bicycle-powered taxis have been modified to use little motors and the population tends to hang out more in the streets. The town's people are famously good-looking, open and friendly. Diriamba was one of the most important Chorotega settlements in

 Nicaragua when the Spanish first arrived in 1523 and it has been heavily populated for over a millennium. A statue of Chorotega Chief Diriangén, Nicaragua's oldest symbol of resistance, stands proudly over Parque Central, although the spear is now missing from his outstretched hand. It was at Diriamba that the late 17th century anti-establishment comedy and focal point of Nicaraguan culture, *El Güegüence*, is thought to have originated, and is performed during the town's patron saint festival for San Sebatián (see box, page 86).

One of the grandest of the *pueblos'* churches can be found in front of Diriamba's tired-looking Parque Central. Most of the buildings around the park were destroyed by the National Guard as the populace rebelled against Somoza in the 1978 Revolution, but the church stands proud with an elegant domed interior flooded with ambient light and sporting much fine woodwork. The **Museo Ecológico Trópico Seco** ⓘ *ENEL, 4 c abajo, T534-2129, museoeco@ibw.com.ni, Mon-Fri 0800-1200, 1400-1700, Sat 0800-1200*, provides an interesting ecological and geographical overview of the region and deals with conservation issues such as the effect of agriculture on local ecosystems.

The Pacific Coast of La Meseta » pp104-106.

La Boquita

The department of Carazo has 40 km of Pacific Ocean coastline with crashing waves and light grey sand. La Boquita, 25 km on rough paved highway from Diriamba, is a popular beach during the dry season and particularly Semana Santa (Easter week), which can be a raucous occasion here. For the rest of the year it is a fairly quiet, slightly artificial tourist centre that is popular with Nicaraguan families. It's not a spectacular spot, but pleasant enough and there are many little ranch-style restaurants that serve fresh fish against the background of the sound of the sea. If you are driving, there is a US$1.50 entrance fee to the parking area. Do not swim in the estuary in the dry season when it becomes polluted.

Casares

South of La Boquita, where the Río Casares drains into the Pacific, is the small, authentic and friendly fishing village of Casares. At the northern part of the beach are the homes of wealthy Managuans. There is little tourist infrastructure here, little shade, and a few very cheap places to eat. Fishing is done in little fibreglass boats with outboards. The ocean has strong currents here and it is not unusual for bathers to get caught out, even when close to the shore. Travel further south is possible by 4WD only and even they are known to get stuck attempting the river crossings. If you're heading south, the best access is from the Santa Teresa exit of the Pan-American Highway.

Sleeping

San Marcos *p102*

C Hotel Casa Blanca, across from the Baptist church, T535-2717, www.hotelcasablanca.com.ni. A very friendly, pleasant hotel with 16 clean rooms; some have a/c. There's Wi-Fi, hammocks, relaxing garden and breakfast included in the price.

C Hotel and Restaurante Lagos y Volcanes, La Concepción, San Marcos, 4 km sur, Instituto Guillermo Ampie, 1½ km arriba, lagosyvolcanes@hotmail.com. Surrounded by citrus trees and offering great views of Laguna Masaya, this hotel has 15 attractive rooms with good beds, cable TV, bath and hot water. Facilities include a good restaurant and pool.

For an explanation of the sleeping and eating price codes used in this guide, see inside the front cover. Other relevant information is found in Essentials, see pages 23-27.

Jinotepe *p103*
Jinotepe has the region's best accommodation, making it a good base for exploring the other *pueblos*.
C Casa Mateo, BDF, 1½ c abajo, T532-3284, www.hotelcasamateo.com. Formerly Hotel Casa Grande, this comfortable 3-storey hotel has 40 good rooms, some with a/c (**B**). There's a decent restaurant attached serving breakfasts and *comida típica*. Excellent central location and the best place in town.

Diriamba *p103*
F Diriangén, Shell station, 1 c arriba, ½ c sur, T534-2428. 11 simple rooms with private bath, fan, parking. A friendly, family-run place.

La Boquita *p104*
C Palmas del Mar, T552-8716. 25 rooms with private bath and a/c, tiny swimming pool. Palmas is at the heart of the tourist centre, which means it can be noisy at night, not least because of its own disco. Lovely patio on the beach.

Casares *p104*
C Hotel Lupita, Cruz Verde, 800 m sur, T552-8708, lupita41@ibw.com.ni. 16 rooms on Casares Beach with private bath, a/c, cable TV, swimming pool, steps to the beach, clean and pretty with nice views.

Eating

Catarina *p97*
ΨΨ El Túnel, at the Mirador de Catarina on the far north side of the wooden deck, T558-0303. 0700-2000. Order *a la plancha*, which comes as a sizzling plate of meat served with fried plantains, fried cheese, rice and salad, US$7.

Diriá *p99*
Ψ Cafetería La Plaza, north side of the church, T557-0207. Simple, open-air place offering good *comida corriente*.

Diriomo *p100*
Ψ El Aguacate, on the Carretera from the petrol station at town entrance 150 vrs al norte. Wild game dishes like *cuzuco* (armadillo) and *guardatinaja* (paca), traditional dishes are also excellent, good value.

Masatepe *p102*
ΨΨ-Ψ Mi Terruño Masatepino, Km 54, Carretera a Masatepe, T887-4949. Daily 0900-2100. Traditional dishes like *indio viejo* and Masatepe's own *sopa de mondongo*. *Cuajada* with tortilla is great here, as is the *sopa de albóndiga*, a popular soup that has meatballs made of chicken, eggs, garlic and corn meal. *Sopa de iguana* can often be found here. Most meals are US$3-5. A very big dish of assorted traditional foods is US$10, but feeds 2. Also try one of Nicaragua's grainy local drinks like *posol* and *tiste* served in an original *jícaro* gourd cup. Great coffee produced locally and roasted at home. This is the pueblos' most authentic eating experience and well worth a visit. The sign outside says simply *platos típicos*.

San Marcos *p102*
Ψ La Casona Coffee Shop, ENITEL, 1 c norte. 'Where cool people hang out', according to their own publicity material. A very fine eatery, popular with students and serving good coffee, cakes, pastas and salads. Recommended.

Jinotepe *p103*
ΨΨ Bar y Restaurante Sardina, Km 49.5 Carretera Sur, T889-4261. Outdoor dining and drinking under a ranch-style thatched roof. Good seafood and beef dishes, pleasant atmosphere and service.
ΨΨ Buen Provecho, next to Colisseo, T532-1145. Sun-Fri 1100-1500. Try the baked chicken or beef in asparagus.
ΨΨ-Ψ Pizzería Colisseo, Parque Central, 1 c norte, T532-2150, colisseo@ibw.com.ni. Tue-Sun 1200-2200. The most famous pizzas in Nicaragua. Some customers drive from Managua to eat here. They serve pasta too.
Ψ Casa Blanca, Cruz Lorena, 1 c arriba, T532-2379. Daily 1000-2200. Something different – Chinese food.

Diriamba *p103*
ΨΨ Mi Bohio, Museo, 1 c arriba, T534-2437. Founded in 1972, a good, clean restaurant serving chicken in wine sauce, soups and *ceviche* among other dishes.

La Boquita *p104*
At least one good restaurant serving excellent seafood.

Transport

Catarina and San Juan de Oriente *p97 and p98*
Buses pass through Catarina every 15 mins to **Masaya**, **San Marcos** or **Rivas**. Buses to **Granada** are less frequent; take a bus towards Masaya and get off on the highway to Granada for a connecting bus.

Diriá and Diriomo *p99*
Buses run along the highway nearby. For **Granada** take any bus heading east, get off at Empalme de Guanacaste and take bus heading north. For **Masaya** and **Managua** buses pass every 20 mins.

Niquinohomo and Masatepe *p100 and p102*
Buses pass on the highway between **Catarina** and **San Marcos** every 15 mins. Express bus to **Managua**, every 30 mins, 0500-1700, US$1.50, 1 hr 15 mins.

San Marcos *p102*
Buses run to **Managua** via La Concepción highway and to **Jinotepe** and **Rivas** (south) and **Masatepe** (east). Buses west connect with the Carretera Sur (Carretera Panamericana), from where buses can be caught south to **Diriamba** or north to **Managua**. To **Managua** every 20 mins, 0600-2000, US$1, 1 hr.

Jinotepe *p103*
As the capital of the western *pueblos* region, Jinotepe has good bus connections with many express options to **Managua**, some of which go to the centrally located La UCA (University stop) next to Metrocentro. The rest use Mercado Israel Lewites (also called Mercado Boer). To **Managua**, every 20 mins, 0530-1800, US$1.10, 1 hr 15 mins to Mercado Lewites. Express bus to **Managua**, every 15 mins, 0600-2000, US$1.10, 1 hr 25 mins to la UCA. To **Rivas**, express buses every 30 mins, 0540-1710, US$1.50, 1 hr 45 mins; and 9 regular buses daily. To **Granada**, express buses hourly, 0600-1600, US$1.10, 1 hr 25 mins; and 6 regular buses daily. To **Masaya**, express buses every 15 mins, 0500-1800, US$0.55, 1 hr 15 mins.

Diriamba *p103*
Buses run to central terminal at **Jinotepe** every 15 mins, US$0.25. To **Managua**, every 20 mins, 0530-1800, US$1, 1 hr 15 mins.

Directory

San Marcos *p102*
Bank BAC, next to Ave María College, T535-2339, cash from credit cards and TCs.
Police Parque Central, T535-2296.

Jinotepe *p103*
Bank Bancentro, north side of the church, T532-1432, can change Amex TCs.
Fire T532-2241. **Hospital** T532-2611.
Police T532-2510. **Red Cross** T532-2500.

Granada & around

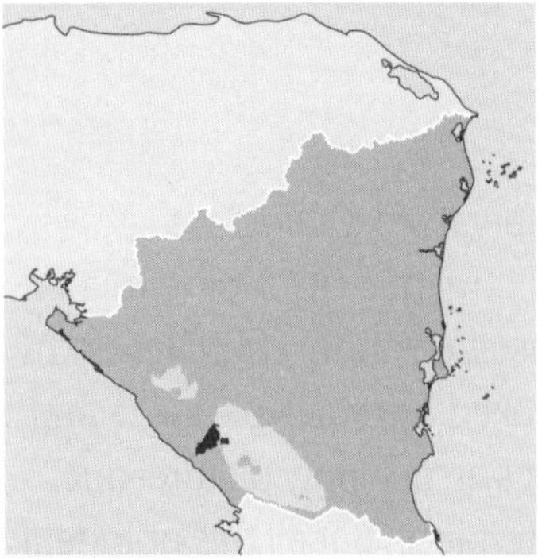

Footprint features

Introduction

A bastion of old money and conservatism, Granada is Nicaragua's most handsome and romantic city. Home to a wealth of grandiose Spanish houses, colourful churches and thronging public squares, overlooked by regal volcanoes and plied by horse-drawn carriages, it's an achingly picturesque, perfectly preserved colonial masterpiece. But all this grandeur is mere artifice. Repeatedly sacked by pirates and burned to the ground by marauding North Americans, few original features remain and today tourism is undermining Granada's backward-looking obsession with authenticity, threatening its very identity. Some visitors will delight in the well-developed infrastructure of reputable hotels and restaurants; others will despair at the sham of foreign-owned establishments, hordes of camera-toting tourists and profusion of shameless real estate agents. But through all this, Granada remains very much a Nicaraguan city – one full of history and character.

And beyond Granada's fine restaurant scene and disarming aesthetic charms, there is much else to entice you. Scattered over the waters of Lake Nicaragua, Las Isletas are an archipelago of over 300 jewel-like islands forged by an ancient volcanic eruption. Best experienced by kayak at dawn, they are now occupied by fishing and farming communities, wealthy vacation homes and prolific wildlife. Isla Zapatera, the second largest island, is a fascinating excursion for more intrepid travellers. Once host to an ancient, deeply religious culture, mysterious statues and petroglyphs now litter the island's forest-swathed slopes. Then there's Volcán Mombacho, looming darkly to the south. This is Nicaragua's best-managed wildlife reserve, with well-tended trails that snake through other-worldly cloud forests. The volcano's lower reaches are home to zip-lines, for those seeking more high-speed encounters with the arboreal canopy.

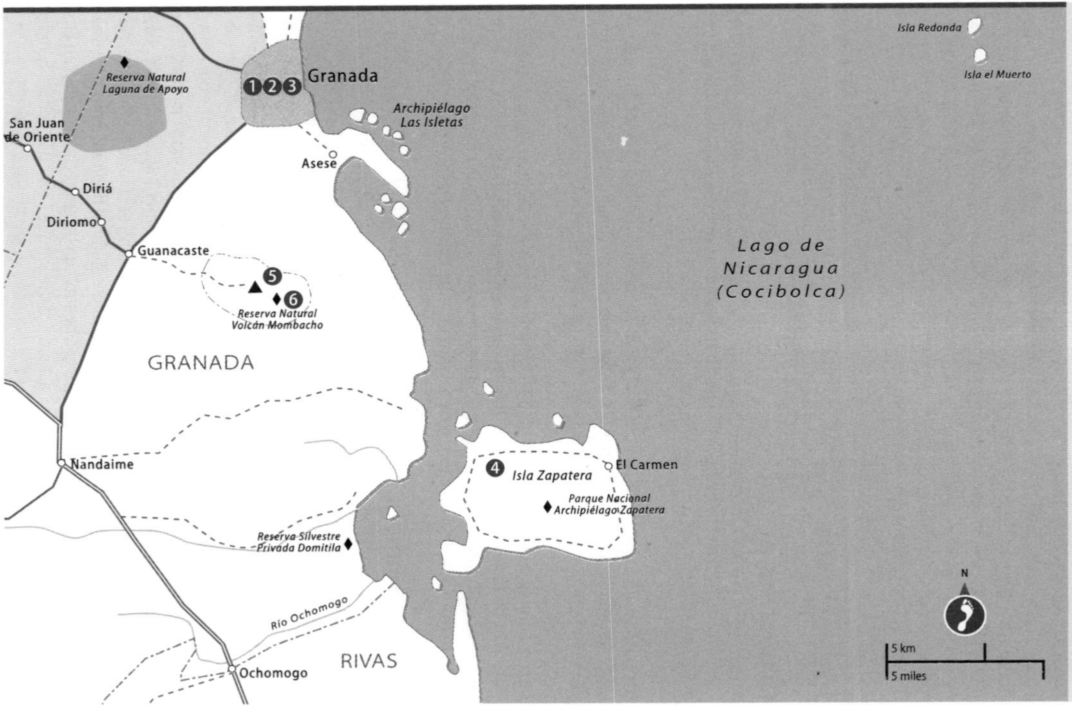

★ Don't miss ...

1 **Paddle early** Kayak the warm waters of Lake Nicaragua at dawn to salute the fishermen and birds, page 118.

2 **Pagan convent** Admire the pre-Christian idols from Isla Zapatera in the Museo Antiguo Convento de San Francisco, page 118.

3 **Fine dining** Thai, Italian and Mexican are among Granada's eclectic dining options, page 120.

4 **Sacrificial ground** Brave the choppy crossing to explore the remote islands of the Archipiélago Zapatera, page 128.

5 **Orchid trails** Hike the well-kept cloud forest trails in the Volcán Mombacho reserve, page 129.

6 **High-speed encounters** Soar like a bird on a world-class canopy tour of Mombacho's forests, page 130.

Granada

→ *Population: 111,500. Altitude: 60 m. Colour map 3, B4.*

Granada's burgeoning tourist trade has forged a very visible disparity between the locals and foreigners. The parque central is the hub of the city's social life and often thronging with activity: strolling families, hawkers, street kids, scavenging dogs, canoodling lovers and tourists with telephoto lenses and khaki combat trousers. The city's centre is prettified and endlessly photogenic, but real estate prices have soared here, making it unaffordable for the average Nicaraguan. Slowly, surely, it is becoming a city of foreigners, like Guatemala's Antigua, whose very soul has been devoured by the intensity of outside interest. But for now, Granada remains fascinating: between the carefully crafted colonial façades, there is still plenty of local colour – often supplied by the inhabitants of the city's impoverished and ramshackle barrios, places where gringos fear to tread. And even in the centre, many colonial houses remain the property of families who have been here for generations. It's hard not to steal glances through the open doors of those high-ceilinged homes, catching intimate glimpses of everyday Granadino life. The challenge of the future is a balancing act between authenticity and pretence, substance and form, progress and identity. The current King of Spain summed it up during a visit here, "don't touch anything," he remarked. ▸▸ *For Sleeping, Eating and other listings, see pages 119-126.*

Ins and outs

Getting there

Boat There is a ferry service from San Carlos, a challenging 12-14 hour journey across Lake Nicaragua that connects with river boats from Río San Juan and Los Chiles, Costa Rica. En route it stops at Altagracia, Isla Ometepe.

Bus There are express buses from Managua's Roberto Huembes market as well as La UCA. International bus companies **Transnica,** King Quality and **Ticabus** stop in Granada on some of their routes north from Costa Rica.

Car If coming from the north, take the Carretera a Masaya, turn right at the Esso station upon entering the city and then left up Calle Real towards the centre. If coming from the south, use the Carretera a Granada. You will enter at the cemetery; continue north to the Calle Real and turn east towards the lake to reach the centre.

Getting around

Granada's city centre is small and manageable on foot. Parque Central is the best reference point and the cathedral is visible from most of the city. There are three main streets: leading from the Fortaleza de La Pólvora, at the western extreme of the old centre, **Calle Real** runs east (*al lago*) past several churches to the central square. The road continues as Calle El Calmito east of the park past the city's two Spanish restaurants and on to the lake. Running perpendicular is **Calle Atravesada**, one block west of Parque Central, behind the Hotel Alhambra. This street runs from the old railway station in the north of the city past Parque Central and south to Granada market. It has most of the cheap eating and night entertainment. The other important route, **Calle Calzada**, starts at the big cross on Parque Central and runs east towards the lake, past many beautiful homes, colourful restaurants and small *hospedajes*, ending at Lake Nicaragua and the city port. Much of the city's beauty can be appreciated within an area of five blocks around the centre. The east side of the Parque Central is generally much quieter with far fewer cars and trucks. ▸▸ *For further details, see Transport, page 125.*

Community tourism around Granada

Granada may well be the country's most conventional destination for tourists, but it offers the chance for reassuringly alternative experiences too. Founded in 1984, UCA *'Tierra y Agua'* (Unión de Cooperativas Agropecuarias 'Earth and Water') is a union of nine co-operatives, one women's association and more than 150 families who supplement their farming-based income with touristic services. If you've ever wondered about work, culture and daily life in rural Nicaragua, then contact this excellent organization, which arranges tours and homestays in four different communities. Your money will directly contribute to their upkeep.

At the base of Mombacho volcano, **La Granadilla** and **Nicaragua Libre** are farming communities offering guided hikes in the cloud forest reserve, horse riding, cycling and tours of the plantations. Your guide will explain the many responsibilities of agricultural life, and if you wish, introduce you to members of the community. **Sonzapote**, on mysterious Isla Zapatera, promises the unique chance to explore the island's pre-Columbian relics, practice traditional fishing and hike the mountains for exceptional views. At **Agua Agrias** you can hike within an attractive nature reserve and bathe in freshwater streams and lakes. Economical and often delicious meals are available at all four communities.

The best way to learn about Nicaraguan life is to live it. A home-stay with a Nicaraguan family, no matter how brief, will afford you a priceless opportunity to observe the daily rhythms of life. And if you roll up your sleeves and muck in, all the better. Rustic homestays are available La Granadilla and Sonzapote for US$3 per person per night. There's a comfortable hostel at Nicaragua Libre, US$5 per person per night.

For more information and help planning your visit, contact **UCA 'Tierra y Agua'** ⓘ *Shell Palmira 75 vrs abajo, Mon, Wed, Fri 0830-1400, T552-0238, www.ucatierrayagua.org.*

Best time to visit

Granada is hot year round but due to it lakefront location it does not suffer from as much dust and smoke during the dry season as some other towns. If planning a trip on the lake avoid the windy months from November to March; the prettiest time of year is the rainy season from June to October. The main day of Granada's patron saint festival is 15 August with horse parades, bulls in the streets and processions (see page 123). Holy Week celebrations in Las Isletas include interesting boat processions.

Tourist office

INTUR ⓘ *Iglesia San Fransisco, opposite the southwest corner, on Calle Arsenal, T552-6858*. Possibly the best INTUR office in the country, with a healthy supply of brochures, maps and English-speaking staff.

Security

The centre of Granada is generally safe, but can become very empty after 2100 and some thefts have been reported. Police presence is almost non-existent on week nights so always be careful to take precautions. Avoid walking alone at night, avoid the barrios outside the centre. Take care along the waterfront at any time of day and avoid it completely after dark.

Background

The Chorotega population encountered by the first Spanish explorer, Captain Gil González Dávila, inhabited important settlements on both north and south sides of the Volcán Mombacho. Nochari, on the south side of the volcano, was later moved further southeast and became modern-day Nandaime (see page 130). Today's Granada was in the northern Lake Nicaragua Chorotega province of Nequecheri, and was dominated by the heavily populated settlement of Xalteva. Granada was founded by Captain Francisco Hernández de Córdoba around 21 April 1524 (the same year as León, and Nicaraguan historians have been arguing ever since to establish which was the first city of Nicaragua). The original wall, which divided the Spanish and Indian sectors of Granada, can be seen today just southeast of the Xalteva church. In 1585, a French chronicler described a religious procession in the city as rich in gold and emeralds, with Indian dances that lasted for the duration of the procession and a line of very well-dressed Spaniards, although the total Spanish population was estimated at only 200. Granada became a major commercial centre and when the Irish friar Thomas Gage visited in 1633 he marvelled at the city's wealth, most of which came from trade with Peru, Guatemala and Colombia.

Thanks to the lake and San Juan's river's access to the Atlantic, Granada flourished as an inter-oceanic port and trading centre, soon becoming one of the wealthiest, most opulent cities in the New World. But it was not long before reports of Granadino wealth began to reach the ears of English pirates occupying the recently acquired possession of Jamaica, which they wrested from Spain in 1665. Edward Davis and Henry Morgan sailed up the Río San Juan and took the city by surprise on 29 June 1665 at 0200 in the morning. With a group of 40 men they sacked the churches and houses before escaping to Las Isletas. In 1670 another band of pirates led by Gallardillo visited Granada via the same route. After destroying the fort at San Carlos, they sacked Granada and took with them men and women hostages.

In 1685, a force of 345 British and French pirates, led by the accomplished French pirate William Dampier, came from the Pacific, entering near where the Chacocente wildlife refuge is today (see page 158). The local population were armed and waiting to fight off the pirates but were easily overwhelmed by the size of the pirate army. They had, however, taken the precaution of hiding all their valuables on Isla Zapatera. The pirates burned the Iglesia San Francisco and 18 big houses, then retreated to the Pacific with the loss of only three men.

Granada saw even more burning and destruction in what were the biggest nationalist uprisings for Independence from Spain in 1811-1812 and during persistent post-Independence battles between León and Granada. When León's Liberal Party suffered defeat in 1854 they invited the North American filibuster William Walker (see box, page 117) to fight the Conservatives, thus initiating the darkest days of Granada's post-colonial history. Walker declared himself president of Nicaragua with the *cede* in Granada, but after losing his grip on power (which was regional at best) he absconded to Lake Nicaragua, giving orders to burn Granada, which once again went up in flames.

Since the days of William Walker, Granada has lost its importance as a commercial centre for inter-oceanic shipment of goods, but its Conservative Party supplied the country with presidents from 1869-1893 who brought modernization to the city with public lighting (1872), telephones (1879), running water (1880) and train travel (1886). The 20th century saw little action for the city other than continued economic growth for its landed aristocracy. In 1929 US journalist Carlton Beals described Granada as a town that "drowses in forgotten isolation". The old

Granada claims to be the oldest continuously inhabited city (in its original location) on mainland America.

A time of dreams and roses: Granada's poetry festival

I want to express my anguish in verses that speak of my vanished youth, a time of dreams and roses …
Rubén Darío (1867–1916)

Each February, Granada's elegant colonial courtyards, historic houses, public squares and churches reverberate to the sounds of poetic verse. Since 2005, an annual festival of poetry has been attracting over 100 scribes and thousands of spectators from around the world. Concerts, art exhibits, theatrical performances and impassioned debates accompany the lyrical occasion, but it is recitals from some of the world's finest poets, both Nicaraguan and international, that make it such an important event. Attended with all the vigour of a Catholic mass, these recitals are a rousing testament to Nicaragua's long-standing infatuation with poetic form.

Granada's poetic roots reach back to the Vanguardia movement of the late 1920s, an alliance of formidable wordsmiths like José Coronel Urtecho, Joaquín Pasos and Pablo Antonio Cuadra, who would meet in the city's public spaces to exchange ideas. Radical and confrontational, the Vanguardia's contributions were important and lasting, and marked a significant departure from Rubén Darío's *modernismo*.

Today, escaping the enduring shadow of this great 'Father of Modernism' is once again the challenge of Nicaragua's newest generation of poets, who are striving to define themselves in a political climate that is largely unsympathetic to creative endeavour. The closure of UCA humanities programmes, the rising cost of books, falling literacy rates and the growing popularity of television mean that they have their work cut out for them. Still, Granada's annual poetry festival, organized and funded privately, is a sign of impending cultural revitalization. The attending crowds of mainly ordinary working class Nicaraguans demonstrate that public enthusiasm for literature has not abated, even if government support has. And the themes of Nicaraguan poetry – poverty, war, identity and nature – are as eternal as words themselves. Conceivably, Nicaragua's love of verse will last forever.

For more information, see www.festivaldepoesiadegranada.com (Spanish only).

city was spared significant damage during the Revolution of 1978-1979, but Granada has undergone many facelifts in recent years. It is rapidly becoming an international city with its numerous foreign residents having a profound effect on the city's economy and culture.

Sights

Despite the repeated ransackings and burnings, Granada has maintained an unmistakable colonial charm. The architectural style has been described as a mixture of Nicaraguan baroque and neoclassical. Having been rebuilt on a number of occasions, the city has a fascinating visual mix of Spanish adobe tile roof structures and Italian-inspired neoclassical homes with some ornate ceiling work and balconies. Italian architects like Andrés Zapatta were contracted by the Granada elite to reconstruct the city after the many foreign-led assaults. The 20th-century writer Carlton

 Beals described Granada as "a haphazard picturesque little place, faintly reminiscent of Italian towns." However, most of the houses maintain the southern Spanish trademark interior gardens and large, airy corridors. It is interesting to compare the architecture of Granada with that of León, which was spared much of the looting and burning that the wealthier city of Granada suffered over the centuries.

Catedral Nuestra Señora de la Asunción

As a result of Granada's troubled history, its churches have all been rebuilt several times. Sadly, most have not retained much in the way of architectural interest or beauty. Last rebuilt and extended after William Walker's flaming departure in November 1856, the Catedral de Granada on Parque Central has become a symbol for Granada. The original church was erected in 1583 and rebuilt in 1633 and 1751. After Walker was shot and buried in Honduras in 1860, reconstruction began again on the cathedral, but was held up by lack of funds in 1891. The work in progress was later demolished and restarted to become today's church, finally opened in 1915. The cathedral has neoclassic and gothic touches and its impressive size and towers make it a beautiful backdrop to the city, but the interior is plain. An icon of the Virgin, much-loved patron saint of Granada, is housed over the main altar. Mary has been proclaimed several times by the Nicaraguan government as the supreme ruler of Nicaragua's armed forces, responsible for defending the city against numerous attacks.

Parque Central

Parque Central is officially called Parque Colón (Columbus Park), though no one uses that name. Its tall trees and benches make it a good place to while away some time. There are food stalls selling the famous and tremendously popular Granada dish *vigorón*, which consists of a big banana leaf filled with cabbage salad, fried pork skins, yucca, tomato, hot chilli and lemon juice.

Granada

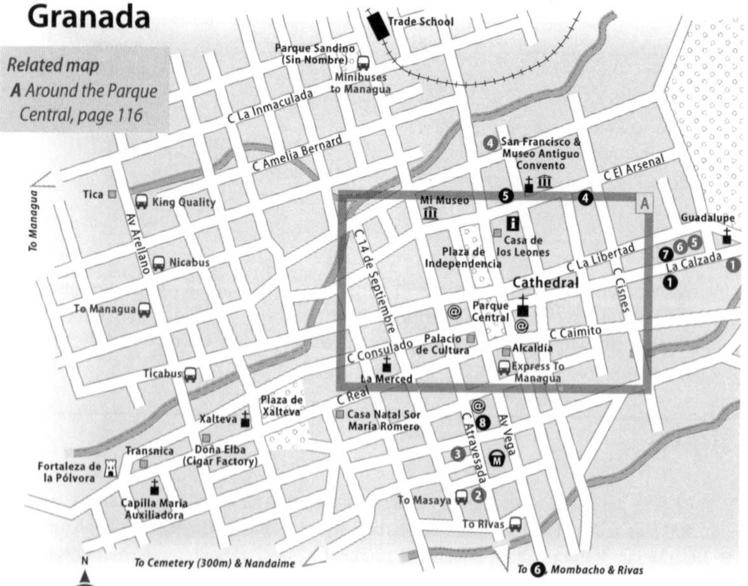

Sleeping
Casa San Francisco **4**
Granada **1**
Hospedaje El Maltese **7**
Hostal Esfinge **2**
Hostal Oasis Granada **3**
Italiano **5**
La Calzada **6**

Eating
Café Chavalos **4**
Casa Macondo **1**
Kathy's Waffle House **5**

Next to the cathedral is a big cross, erected in 1899, with a time capsule buried underneath. It was hoped that by burying common artefacts and personal belongings from the 19th century, it might ensure a peaceful 20th century. Despite the fairly violent period that followed, Granada did enjoy a reasonable amount of peace.

Calle Real

The most attractive of the Granada churches is **Iglesia La Merced**, which can be seen as part of a very nice walk from Parque Central down the Calle Real to the old Spanish Fortaleza de la Pólvora (see below). La Merced, built between 1751 and 1781 and also damaged by William Walker, has maintained much of its colonial charm and part of the original bell towers and façade. The pretty interior, painted an unusual tropical green colour, has an attractive altar and a painting of the Virgin on its north side. In front of the church is a cross constructed in 1999 as a symbol of hope for peace in the 21st century.

You can ascend the bell tower of La Merced for great views of the city's tiled rooftops, Cocibolca and Volcán Mombacho, particularly striking at dusk, US$1.

Further down the street is **Plaza de Xalteva**, which has unusual stone lanterns and walls, said to be a tribute to ancient Indian constructions. Unlike León and Masaya, Granada no longer has an Indian barrio of any kind, yet you can see the remains of the walls from the colonial period that separated the Spanish and indigenous sectors marked by a small tile plaque. The church on the plaza, **Iglesia Xalteva**, was yet another victim of William Walker. It was rebuilt at the end of the 19th century and is reminiscent of a New England church – a bit lacking in flair.

Just off the Calle Real, in between La Merced and Xalteva is the **Casa Natal Sor María Romero** ① *Tue-Sun 0800-1200, 1400-1700, free,* a small chapel and humble collection of artefacts and books from the life of María Romero Meneses (born in Granada 1902, died in Las Peñitas, León 1977). María was a local girl who became a Salesian nun at 28 and spent the rest of her life caring for the poor and ill, founding both a heathcare centre for the poor and a home for street children in Costa Rica. She is said to have assisted in various miracles and may become the first saint in the history of Central America – her beatification was approved in Rome on 14 April 2002 by Pope John Paul II.

Further west along the Calle Real is the charming little **Capilla María Auxiliadora**. This church has some interesting features on its façade and some lovely detail work inside and is worth a visit. At the end of the street is the 18th-century fort and ammunitions hold, **Fortaleza de la Pólvora** ① *open during daylight hours, US$1-2 donation to the caretaker*. The fort was built in 1749 and used primarily as an ammunitions hold, then as a military base and finally a prison. You can climb up inside the southeastern turret on a flimsy ladder to have a good view down the Calle Real.

Calle Atravesada

There are a few sights of interest along the Calle Atravesada. Dating from 1886 and beautifully restored, the **old train**

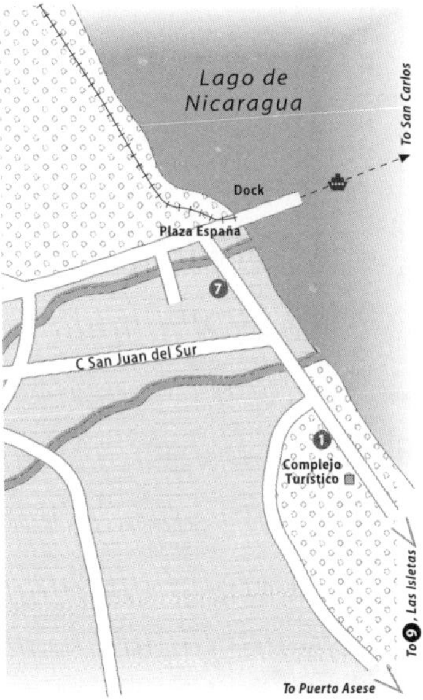

Las Colinas del Sur **6**
Monna Lisa **7**
Querube's **8**
La Terrazza La Playa **9**

Bars & clubs
César **1**

 station, is now a trade school. Next to it is the 'Parque Sin Nombre' (park with no name). This little park was called Parque Somoza until the Revolution, when it was changed to **Parque Sandino**. When the Sandinistas lost in the 1990 elections, the park once again needed a new name. Some wise locals have since decided it best to allow the park to remain anonymous, though Parque Sandino remains its official name. Several blocks south and opposite Calle Arsenal is **Mi Museo** ⓘ *Mon-Fri, 0800-1200, 1330-1700*. This new museum has an array of well-presented archaeological relics, including many rotund funerary pots that were once 'pregnant' with lovingly prepared human remains. Past Parque Central on the same street towards the volcano is the bustle and hustle of Granada's **market**. A visit here is a must, if only to compare the noisy, pungent chaos with the relative order of the more well-tended tourist drags.

Plaza de Independencia and around

Next to Parque Central is Plaza de Independencia, which has a movie-set quality to it. The bishop of Granada lives in the red house, at one time the presidential palace for William Walker. The telephone office is next door and just a few doors down is the historic **Casa de Los Leones** (its NGO name is **Casa de Los Tres Mundos**) ⓘ *www.c3mundos.org, daytime exhibitions free; admission charged for live concerts on weekend nights,* with its 17th-century Moorish stone door frame that survived all the burning. The building was once the municipal theatre, then a private house where poet/priest Ernesto Cardenal was born. Now it is a cultural centre, with exhibits, music and occasional poetry readings and it's a good place to see the inside of a traditional Granada house. The Plaza de Independencia is occasionally home to folkloric performances on weekend nights.

One block east from the northeast corner of Plaza de la Independencia is the bright blue **Iglesia San Francisco** (1524), Nicaragua's oldest standing church with

Around the Parque Central

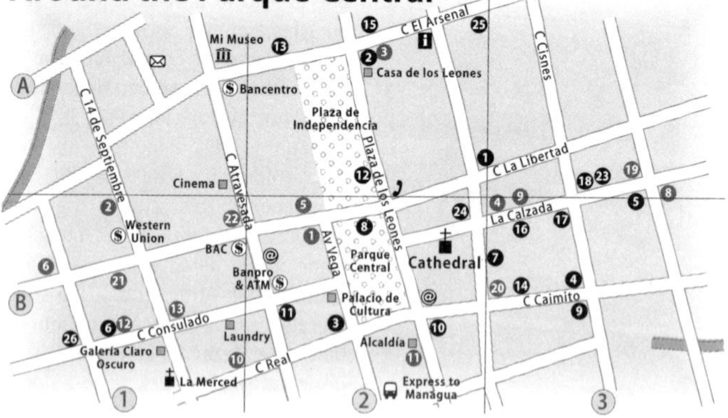

N

100 metres
100 yards

Sleeping
Alhambra **1** *B2*
Bearded Monkey **2** *B1*
Casa San Martín **4** *B3*
Colonial **5** *B2*
Darío **9** *B3*
El Club **6** *B1*
El Dorado Hostel **10** *B1*
Hospedaje Cocibolca **8** *A3*
La Casona de los Estrada **3** *A2*
La Gran Francia **11** *B2*
Nuestra Casa **12** *B1*
Posada Don Alfredo **13** *B1*

Eating
Asia Latina **23** *A3*
Café Dec Arte **24** *B2*
Café Mail **2** *A2*
Don Luca's **5** *B3*
Don Simón **3** *B2*
Doña Conchi's **4** *B3*
El Tercer Ojo **25** *A2*
El Zaguán **7** *B3*
Garden Café **1** *A2*
Jardín de Orión **26** *B1*
Jimmy Three Fingers **6** *B1*
Kiosko La Gata **8** *B2*
La Gran Francia **10** *B2*
La Jarochita **9** *B3*
Los Bocaditos **11** *B2*
Los Portales **12** *A2*
Maverick Reading Lounge **13** *A2*
Mediterráneo **14** *B3*
Nuevo Central **16** *B3*
Rainbow Juice Bar **17** *B3*
Roadhouse **18** *A3*
TelePizza **15** *A2*

Bars & clubs
Café Nuit **21** *B1*
El Quijote **20** *B3*
Safari Lounge **22** *B1*
Zoom **19** *A3*

William Walker – the paradox of a villain

It is a name that is a complete mystery to most first-time visitors to Central America. Yet for Nicaraguans, North American William Walker is the epitome of foreign intervention, the model of the evil invader. Had Walker been successful, the history of the isthmus and the United States would be radically different, for it was his plan that Nicaragua should become a new US state to relieve anti-slavery pressure on mid-19th century US plantation owners. History, however, did not favour slave masters; on 12 September 1860, Walker was put against an adobe wall and shot by firing squad in Honduras and seven months later the US Civil War began.

Walker not only brought the bickering states of Central America together against a common enemy, but he was also a fascinating and paradoxical character. Young Billy Walker, the son of a banker from Scotland, spent much of his early childhood taking care of his ill mother, reading Byron and history books. His friends at school were unimpressed and called him 'missy'. He may not have been overly macho, but neither was he slow. By the age of 16 he had earned a graduate degree in Classics from the University of Tennessee.

At the age of 19 he received his doctorate in medicine from the University of Pennsylvania and travelled to Europe to pursue advanced medical studies. For a short time he lived in the Latin quarter of Paris. By the age of 22, Walker had become fluent in Spanish, French and Italian and had a good knowledge of Greek and Latin. He had also found time to study US law and pass the bar exam. Walker found work as an editor at *The New Orleans Delta* (where an unknown poet named Walt Whitman worked under him) and his editorials demonstrated a pacifist, anti-slavery and anti-interventionist stance. His newspaper even exposed a plot to take over Cuba and make it a slave state, foiling the project. In New Orleans, Walker had met the love of his life, Ellen Martin, an upper-class girl who was witty, beautiful, mute and deaf. Walker learned sign language and got engaged, but both Ellen and Walker's mother died shortly afterwards from cholera.

Now alone, Walker moved to California during the gold rush and become hardened by the turn of events in his life. Indian massacres in California perpetrated by gold prospectors and land grabbers were commonplace, and as their defence lawyer, Walker became acquainted with selective law – with murderers getting off free. Love was gone from his life and Walker was now a proponent of slavery and expansionism, and soon he would become its leader. Poorly planned and executed military attempts by Walker at setting up colonies in Northern Mexico and Baja California failed. Yet Walker returned to the US more popular than ever. In Nicaragua the Liberals of León were unable to defeat the Conservatives of Granada and the Liberal leader looked to the north for help. The job was given to William Walker, setting the stage for the bloody invasion. What the Liberals did not know was Walker's detailed plan to legalize slavery in Nicaragua and annex it to the US. Every year Nicaraguans celebrate his failure.

Lake Nicaragua – El Mar Dulce

A lake so vast the Spanish conquistadors dubbed it the 'freshwater sea' (*mar dulce*), Lago de Nicaragua, also known as Cocibolca, covers 8264 sq km. In a little country like Nicaragua, this truly is massive. The lake is fed by numerous rivers in Nicaragua and northern Costa Rica and its waters drain into the Caribbean Sea, via the Río San Juan. Lago de Nicaragua is punctuated by more than 450 volcanic islands: this is the earth as it was being formed millions of years ago, for Cocibolca is actually a 160 km by 65 km flood plain with the earth rising up around it and inside it. Its average depth is 20 m with some deep sections near Ometepe at 60 m. The two continents were finally connected on the lake's west coast, some four or five million years ago, blocking off the Caribbean from the Pacific and forming a land bridge that allowed the wildlife and vegetation of the two great continents to mix.

For an estimated 30,000 years, the bridge has been used by people too. The indigenous name for the lake was Ayagualo and some of its islands were important religious sites, places of organized worship, human sacrifice and ritual cannibalism. Indeed, getting to the islands in canoes must have been a religious experience in itself: due to its shallow floor, Cocibolca's waves change by the hour and the lake surfaace can change from calm to rough in no time at all.

Lake Nicaragua is unique in its freshwater sawtooth fish, sharks, sardines and the prehistoric gar fish and a trip to Nicaragua without visiting its freshwater sea is like touring Egypt without visiting the pyramids. And yet it is still free of big resorts, pleasure yachts, and commercial fishing boats. Latin America's second biggest lake, remains as it has been for thousands of years: a place of volcanoes, mysteries and murmurs from the past; a huge body of clean, fresh water, teeming with fish, asleep under an endless sky.

original steps. It was burnt down in 1685 by the group of pirates led by William Dampier, rebuilt, then modified in 1836 before being reduced to flames in 1856 on Walker's departure. It was finally rebuilt in 1868 with a fine restoration of the interior and a controversial decoration of the façade – some complain that it now looks like a birthday cake. The legendary human rights priest Fray Bartolomé de las Casas preached here while visiting Granada in the 1530s.

Connected to the church is the mustard yellow **Museo Antiguo Convento de San Francisco** ⓘ *T552-5535, daily 0830-1730, US$2, US$2.50 extra to photograph.* Originally founded as a convent in 1529, it was also burnt down in 1685 by Dampier. In 1836, after the religious orders of Central America had been forced to leave by the Central American Federation, it became a university, and then, in 1856, it was used as a garrison by William Walker, who burned it down once again before leaving the country. The old convent was rebuilt and became the most important secondary school in town, the Colegio de Granada, which later became the Instituto Nacional de Oriente until it closed in 1975. Restoration began in 1989 with help from the Swedish government. There is a mural in the entrance that leads to a small shop and café. The interior garden is dominated by towering 100-year-old palms, often full of squawking parakeets. In the east wing of the building is one of the country's most interesting pre-Columbian museums, housing large religious sculptures from the island of

Zapatera in Lake Nicaragua (see page 119). The sculptures date from AD 800-1200; of particular note are the double standing or seated figures bearing huge animals, or doubles, on their heads and shoulders. The museum also has temporary exhibitions, historic photographs of Granada, some colonial period religious art and a gallery of Solentiname naïve painting.

Calle Calzada

East from the Parque Central, the brightly coloured and well-manicured Calle Calzada contains the city's highest concentration of restaurants and foreign tourists. This is the place for people-watching and enjoying a cold beer. The parade of gringo eateries peters out about half-way towards the lake, where you'll find the **Iglesia Guadalupe**. This church has seen plenty of action, thanks to its location near the water. Walker's forces used it as a final stronghold before escaping to the lake where Walker was keeping well away from the fighting, on a steamship. Originally constructed in 1626, its exterior has a melancholy, rustic charm, although the post-Walker interior lacks character. Beyond the church you'll pass the red cross and a baseball field before arriving at the lake and ferry port. Head south along the shore and you'll reach the fortress-like gates of the **complejo turístico**, a large recreation area of restaurants, discos and cafés, popular with the locals, particularly over Christmas and New Year.

Sleeping

Granada *p110, maps p114 and p116*

AL Hotel Darío, Calle La Calzada, de la Catedral, 150 vrs al lago, T552 3400, www.hoteldario.com. Right in the heart of town and housed by the smart, green and white neoclassical building you can't fail to notice. The interior is handsome, with comfortable rooms and beautiful grounds. There's a gym and a kidney shaped swimming pool for cooling off.

AL La Gran Francia, southeast corner of Parque Central, T552-6000, www.lagranfrancia.com. This traditional colonial building has handsome rooms with private bath, hot water, cable TV, a/c, minibar and internet access. Standard rooms are dark and face a wall, junior suites (**L**) have big wooden doors that lead on to small balcony with a lovely view and lots of light; worth the extra money. There's a pool, hotel staff are friendly and the rates include a stingy breakfast.

AL-A Hotel Alhambra, Parque Central, T552-4486, www.alhambra.com.ni. Granada's landmark hotel has a stunning location on the plaza. Rooms vary dramatically in quality and price. They include 'classic rooms' (**A**) with a/c, cable TV and hot water; 'superior rooms' (**A**) with king or queen size beds and minibar; and luxury 'suites' (**AL**). The ones overlooking the park are best. There's a pool and terrace for drinks, and a restaurant – not owned by the hotel – that receives a lot of criticism for poor service. Often full with groups.

A Hotel Colonial, Calle La Libertad, Parque Central, 25 vrs al norte, T552-7581, www.hotelcolonialgranada.com. This centrally located, colonial-style hotel has a range of pleasant, comfortable lodgings, including heavily decorated rooms with 4-poster beds and 10 luxury suites with jacuzzi (**A**); all have hot water, a/c, cable TV and Wi-Fi. There are 2 pools, and the restaurant serves breakfast only.

A La Casona de los Estrada, Iglesia San Francisco, 1/2 c abajo, T552-7393, www.casonalosestrada.com.ni. Decorated with fine furnishings, this small, homely hotel has 6 pleasant, well-lit rooms with private bath, hot water, a/c and cable TV. There's a pleasant plant-filled courtyard, English and French are spoken, and prices include breakfast.

B Casa San Francisco, Corrales 207, T552-8235, www.casasanfrancisco.com. This attractive, tranquil hotel comprises 2 colonial houses with 13 lodgings that vary greatly. One house has 2 suites and 2 comfortable rooms with private bath, cable TV, a/c, pool and a modern kitchen. The other has 8 rooms and 1 suite, a pool and restaurant. The friendly and helpful staff speak English.

B Casa San Martín, Calle La Calzada, catedral, 1 c lago, T552-6185, javier_sanchez_a@yahoo.com. 7 rooms in beautiful colonial home, with cable TV, private bath, a/c or fan. Nice decor and garden terrace, very authentic Granadino feel. Staff speak English.

B El Club, Parque Central, 3 c abajo, T552-4245, www.elclub-nicaragua.com. This Dutch-owned hotel has 10 small, modern rooms with private bath, a/c, cable TV and Wi-Fi. There's a restaurant and bar downstairs, which can be noisy at times. The staff are friendly and helpful.

C Hotel Granada, opposite Iglesia Guadalupe, T552-2974, www.hotelgranadanicaragua.com. This recently renovated hotel has smart, clean, comfortable rooms with cable TV, Wi-Fi, a/c and hot water. A pool is being constructed, and there's a lovely view from the balcony and restaurant.

C Italiano, next to Iglesia Guadalupe, T552-7047, italianriky@latinmail.com. Bath and a/c, nice patio, drinks available, good value, Italian spoken.

C Hospedaje El Maltese, Plaza España, 50 m sur, opposite *malecón* in Complejo Turístico, T552-7641, www.nicatour.net. 8 very clean rooms with private bath, nice furnishings, Italian spoken, restaurant La Corte Del Maltese, Mon-Fri 1600-2200. Don't walk here at night alone.

D Posada Don Alfredo, La Merced, 1 c norte, T552-4455, alfredpaulbaganz@hotmail.com. This interesting old hotel is housed in an historic building with many original features like high, wooden ceilings and slatted windows. The rooms are dark and simple, some with a/c and hot water (**C**). The German management is hospitable and friendly.

D-G El Dorado Hostel, southwest corner of Parque Central, 1½ c abajo, T552-6932, www.hostaldorado.com. Housed in a lovely colonial building, this new hostel has a relaxing patio, free Wi-Fi and DVDs. Lodgings include single (**E**) and double rooms (**D**), and dormitories (**F**) of various sizes, cheaper with shared bath (**G**).

E Hospedaje Cocibolca, Calle La Cazada, T552-7223, www.hospedajecocibolca.com. A friendly, family house with 24 clean, simple rooms. There's a kitchen and internet access.

E Hostal Esfinge, opposite market, T552-4826, esfingegra@hotmail.com.ni. Lots of character at this friendly old hotel near the market. Rooms in the newer building are smaller, but some have bath and cable TV. Friendly and clean, with motorcycle parking in the lobby.

E Nuestra Casa, La Merced, 1 c al norte, ½ abajo, T552-8115, www.hotelnuestracasa.com. Simple rooms with and without bath, cable TV and a/c. There's a pleasant honeymoon suite and the owner, an ordained Minister in the Universal Life Church, does marriages on request. There's a popular bar and restaurant attached.

E-G Bearded Monkey, Calle 14 de Septiembre, near the fire station, T552-4028, www.thebeardedmonkey.com. A sociable, popular hostel with dormitories (**G**), private rooms (**E**), and hammocks for seriously impoverished backpackers. There's a plethora of services to keep you entertained including restaurant, bar, cable TV, internet access, cheap calls, evening films, bike rentals, and free tea and coffee. Use lockers, as everybody is free to walk in and out. Runs trips to Laguna de Apoyo, see page 94.

E-G Hostal Oasis Granada, Calle Estrada 109, south of the centre, T552-8006, www.nicaraguahostel.com. Mix of dormitory, shared and private rooms (**E** or **C** with all mod-cons), with food available, laundry service and washing facilities. Full range of entertainment from book exchange and swimming pool, through to free internet (and internet calls to Canada and USA) and DVDs – popular, gets good reports. Daily transit to Laguna Apoyo.

F La Calzada, near Iglesia Guadalupe, T475-9229, guesthouselacalzada@yahoo.com. This family-run guesthouse has 8 big, simple rooms with fan and private bath; cheaper with shared bath.

Eating

Granada *p110, maps p114 and 116*

TTT El Jardín de Orión, northwest corner of Parque Central, 4 c abajo, ½ c al sur, T552-1220. This buzzing French restaurant has a fabulous garden terrace and a changing menu of sophisticated European cuisine. Great atmosphere and friendly service.

TTT La Gran Francia, corner of Parque Central. Daily 1100-2300. This beautiful restaurant is the epitome of colonial grandeur, with high ceilinged dining rooms and a plethora of elegant, antique furniture. They serve expensive French- Nicaraguan cuisine, with pleasant views from the upper floor balcony.

TTT Mediterráneo, Calle Caimito, T552-6764. Daily 0800-2300. Mediterranean cuisine served in a Spanish-owned colonial house with an attractive and tranquil garden setting. Mixed reviews; good seafood but bad paella. Popular with foreigners.

TTT-TT Doña Conchi's, Calle Caimito, T552-7376. Wed-Mon 1100-2300. A very beautiful restaurant, completely illuminated by candles and adorned with rustic decorations. They serve quality dishes like grilled salmon, seabass and lobster. There's also an interesting artesanía shop attached. Recommended.

TTT-TT El Zaguán, on road behind cathedral, T552-2522. Mon-Fri 1200-1500 and 1800-2200, Sat and Sun 1200-2200. Incredible, succulent grilled meats and steaks, cooked on a wood fire and served impeccably. Undoubtedly the best beef cuts in Granada, if not Nicaragua. Highly recommended.

TT Asia Latina, Calle La Calzada, 2 ½ c al lago. Thai and Asian fusion, with a touch of Latin. They do great curries and vegetarian dishes, served in a friendly, atmospheric setting.

TT Café Chavalos, corner of calle Arsenal and Matirio, T852-0210, www.cafechavalos.com. An interesting training programme for would-be gang members who, under supervision of chef Sergio, now learn to prepare international cuisine. Best to book in advance. Recommended.

TT Casa Macondo, Calle La Calzada, 3½ c al lago, T680-6420. This Spanish restaurant serves paella, tapas and the strongest Sangría in Granada. There's a happy hour from 1700-2000, a musical ambience, dance classes and exhibitions. Closed Mon.

TT Charly's Bar, Petronic, 5c abajo, 25 vrs al sur, T552-2942, www.charlysbar.com. Mon-Fri 1100-1500, 1800-2300, Sat-Sun 1100-2300, closed Tue. Great BBQ food under a relaxed, beach bar-style palapa. Dishes include juicy kebabs and German sausages. Good, but a bit out of town.

TT Don Luca's, Calle La Calzada, catedral, 2 c al lago, T552-7822. Excellent wood oven pizza, *calzone*, and pasta. Nice setting.

TT El Tercer Ojo, Calle El Arsenal, south corner of the Convento San Francisco, T552-6451. Tue-Sun 1000-2400. This lounge restaurant has interesting, exotic decor, reminiscent of some far eastern locale. They serve fairly decent, if unimaginative, international cuisine. Relaxed and pleasant, with weekly specials like sushi night (Tue).

TT Jimmy Three Fingers, La Merced, 1 c al norte, ½ abajo, T552-8115, www.jimmythreefingers.com. Famous rib-shack serving lovingly prepared, slow-cooked baby back ribs, seafood, Italian cuisine, gourmet soups and comfort food for Granada's homesick expats. Celebrated and reassuringly creative. Also a live music bar (see below).

TT La Jarochita, alcaldía, 2 c al lago, T552-8304. Quite possibly Nicaragua's finest Mexican restaurant, serving *tacos*, *burritos* and *quesadillas con mole*, among other national staples. Colourful and friendly. They have a branch in Masaya too.

TT Las Colinas del Sur, Shell Palmira, 1 c sur, T552-3492. Daily 1200-2200, Tue lunch only 1200-1500. Seafood specialities, excellent lake fish, try the *guapote* fried whole, boneless fillets, avocado salad, far from centre, but worth it, take a taxi, recommended.

TT La Terrazza La Playa, Complejo Turístico. Great *cerdo asado* and *filete de guapote*.

TT Los Chocoyos, Calle Corrales, north corner of the Convent, inside Casa San Fransisco, T552-8235. Daily 1200-2300. A range of tasty international cuisine including Mexican, Italian and French, served in a colonial setting.

TT Monna Lisa, Calle La Calzada, 3½ c al lago, T552-8187. Undoubtedly the best pizzas in Granada; stone-baked, tasty and authentic. Recommended.

TT Roadhouse, Calle La Calzada, 2 c al lago. Popular with Nicaraguans, this rocking American-style restaurant serves a range of wholesome burgers. Their fries, flavoured with cajun spices, are the real stand-out dish though.

TT-T Los Bocaditos, Calle el Comercio. Mon-Sat 0800-2200, Sun 0800-1600. A bustling, but clean locals' joint with buffet from 1100-1500, breakfast and dinner menu.

TT-T Los Portales, opposite Cafemail on Plaza de los Leones, T552-4115. Daily 0700-2200. Simple Mexican food, sometimes overpriced but there are good people-watching opportunities to make up for it.

₸₸-₸ **Nuevo Central**, Calle La Calzada, 1½ c al lago. An unassuming little place, and just one of many terraced restaurants along this stretch. They do unpretentious, cheapish chicken and meat dishes with enormous portions. Popular with locals.

₸ **Kiosko La Gata**, Parque Central. Daily 1000-1900. Offers traditional Nica drinks like *chicha* and *cacao con leche*.

₸ **Restaurant Querube's**, Calle el Comercio, opposite Tiangue 1. Clean and popular locals' joint near the market. They serve Nicaraugan and Chinese fare from a buffet, and do set lunches and breakfasts.

₸ **TelePizza**, Bancentro, 1½ c al lago, T552-4219. Daily 1000-2200. Good, tasty pizzas; but not outstanding. Popular with Nicaraguan families, if you've had enough of the gringo places. They deliver too.

Cafés

Café Dec Arte, Calle Calzada, near cathedral, T552-6461. Tue-Sun 1100-2200. This charming café hosts exhibitions of local artists and the desserts are to die for. Recommended.

Café Isabella, 108 Calle Corrales, Bancentro, 1 c norte, ½ c abajo. Open for breakfast and lunch, this café has a large covered balcony and interior garden. They serve some vegetarian dishes.

Café Mail, next to Casa de Tres Mundos, T552-6847. Daily 0700-2200. Check your email while sipping a cappucino; they do breakfasts and light meals too. Nice patio outside.

Don Simón, Parque Central, T884-1393. Daily 0700-2100. Great views over the plaza. They serve simple breakfasts, good pastries, coffee, espresso, cappuccino, sandwiches.

Garden Café, Enitel, 1 c al lago. A very relaxed, breezey café with a lovely leafy garden and patio space. They do good breakfasts, sandwiches, coffees, muffins and cookies. Friendly and pleasant. Recommended.

Kathy's Waffle House, opposite Iglesia San Francisco. 0730-1400. Kathy does the best breakfasts in Granada, and it's always busy here in the morning. You'll find everything from waffles to pancakes to *huevos rancheros*, all with free coffee refills. Highly recommended.

Maverick Reading Lounge, Telepizza, 1 c abajo. Fair trade gourmet coffee, hot tea, good selection of magazines in English and Spanish, second-hand books, cigars.

Rainbow Juice Bar, Calle La Calzade, 2 c al lago. Sweet, tasty juices and *licuados* – great for a nutrient boost.

Bars and clubs

Granada *p110, maps p114 and 116*

Café Nuit, northwest corner of Parque Central, 2½ c abajo. Wed-Mon 1900-0200. Great live music venue, with acts on Fri and Sat performing inside a pleasant colonial courtyard. Very cool and popular.

César, on waterfront (Complejo Turístico). Fri and Sat only. Recommended for dancing and drinking, very popular, inexpensive bar with merengue and salsa music.

El Club, northwest corner of parque central, 3 c abajo. Mon-Thu until 2400, Fri-Sun until 0200. Clean, modern bar with European ambience, dance music and a mixture of locals and foreigners. Stylish and a cut above the rest.

El Quijote, southeast corner of parque central, 1 c al lago. Loud, boozey pub with a fun, foreign and mostly beer swilling crowd.

Jimmy Three Fingers (see Eating, above). Fri-Sun 1800-0200. A renowned expat bar, also popular with Nicas and the local Harley Davidson chapter. The boss is an interesting and entertaining character. Live music and good, cold beer.

Safari Lounge, northwest corner of parque central, 1 c abajo. Complete with mock zebra-skin upholstery, this modern bar is popular with foreigners and a great spot for people-watching over a rum. The bar upstairs is more of a local affair.

Zoom Bar, Calle Calzada, Parque Central, 3 c lago, across from Hospedaje Cocibolca. A very North American sports bar with a big-screen TV and American football memorabilia. Very popular with beer-soaked gringos and expats. The burgers, contrary to the sign outside, are only just average.

Cacao from Nandaime was used by the local population as a monetary unit for a thousand years or so and later came to be known in Europe as the 'food of the gods'.

Entertainment

Granada *p110, maps p114 and p116*

Cinema

Cine Karawala, Calle Atravezada, behind Hotel Alhambra, T552-2442. Good, modern, 2 screens.

Festivals and events

Granada *p110, maps p114 and p116*

Feb **Poetry Festival**, a new and popular literary festival that draws national and international crowds (see box, page 113), check website for dates, www.festivaldepoesiadegranada.com.

Mar **Folklore, Artesanía and Food Festival** for 3 days in Mar (check locally for dates).

Aug (14-30 Aug), **Assumption of the Virgin**. 1st weekend in August is **El Tope de los Toros** with bulls released and then caught one at a time, much tamer than Pamplona, though occasionally the bulls get away sending everyone running for cover.

Dec Celebrations for the **Virgin Mary** on 7 Dec and **Christmas**.

Shopping

Granada *p110, maps p114 and p116*

Antiques and artisan crafts

Granada is the best place to hunt for antiques in Nicaragua. Keep in mind that pre-Columbian pieces cannot be taken out of the country and colonial-period relics may also be considered national patrimony and subject to the same laws.

There are not many good places to buy artisan crafts, most are marked-up, but if you are not planning to visit Masaya and Los Pueblos de la Meseta, this might be the only chance. **La Piedra Bocona**, Iglesia La Merced, 2 c norte, English spoken. **Mercedes Morales**, La Merced, 1½ c sur, for appointment phone T887-1488. **Casa de Antiguedades Felicia**, Calle El Beso, Casa 114, T552-4677, religious relics, furniture, Nicaraguan art, owner Felicia Sandino also offers to take care of shipping. **Casa Elena**, Iglesia Xalteva, 2 c sur, ½ c abajo, Casa 215, T552-6242, Tue-Sun 1000-1800, crafts from Mexico and Nicaragua.

There are usually artesanías on sale in the Parque Central and inside Restaurant Doña Conchi. There's primitivist art inside the centro comercial near the BAC.

Granada is famous for its high quality rattan (*mimbre*) furniture, which is better here than anywhere else in Nicaragua. They are not cheap, but these handmade pieces are made to last at least 50 years. The most famous workshop is at the entrance to Granada, on the Carretera between Masaya and Granada. Call in advance if you want to visit: **Muebles de Mimbre Auxiliadora**, at Km 45, and its sister shop **Muebles de Mimbre Granada**, at Km 45.5, both reached on T522-2217. **Muebles de Mimbre El Hogar**, catedral, ½ c lago, La Calzada 409, T522-2366. **Mimbre y Ratán Kauffmann**, Parque Sandino, 4 c sur, ½ c arriba, T552-2773.

Bali Bagus, Xalteva, 1 ½ c al lago, T552-2844, www.balibagusnicaragua.com, deals in exotic furniture with an Eastern flavour.

Galleries

Casa de los Tres Mundos, Plaza de Independencia, T552-4176, www.3mundos.org, has changing exhibits in a gorgeous space. **Claro Oscuro**, north side of Iglesia La Merced, T871-0627, galeria_claroscuro@hotmail.com, is a multi-room space, with very good exhibits of Nicaraguan artists from all styles, also black and white photography. **Galería Paseo de Arte**, catedral, ½ c lago, shows modern art from Nicaraguan painters and other mediums. **Casa Sacuanjoche**, southeast corner of parque central, 1 c al lago, 1 ½ c sur, T552 6151, www.galeria.casasacuanjoche.com, has paintings by local artist Alvaro Berroteran. **Galería Isthmo arte and diseño**, Calle Altravesada, opposite BanCentro, www.galeriaistmo.com, is a new gallery with mostly modern art by local and Latin talent.

Books

Mavericks Reading Lounge, Calle Arsenal, behind Hotel Colonial. Second-hand books and English-language magazines. **Mockingbird Books**, next to Café Euro, northwest corner of Parque Central. Has a selection of second-hand books including novels and travel guides.

Cigars

There is some rolling done in Granada although the wrap and filler are brought down from Estelí where the best cigars are made outside Cuba (see Estelí page 249). You can ask to enter the factory, or just pick up some *puros*. **Doña Elba Cigars**, Calle Real, Iglesia Xalteva, 1 c abajo, T552-3217, and **Sultan Cigars**, Parque Central, next to Hotel Alhambra, T655-0136, eddyreyes@yahoo.es.

Markets

El Mercado de Granada, Parque Central, 1 c abajo, then south on Calle Atravesada, is a large green building surrounded by many street stalls. It's dark, dirty and packed and there have been plans to move it for years but for now it remains in its claustrophobic location. Just south of the market is **Supermercado Palí**, also dark and dirty, with a selection of low-price goods.

Activities and tours

Granada *p110, maps p114 and p116*

Baseball

During the baseball season between Jan-Apr you can check out the **Granada Sharks** who play in a stadium at the edge of town, heading towards Masaya, US$1-5.

Canopy tours

See also page 130.

Mombacho Canopy Tour, T888-2566 (book at least 24 hours in advance), Tue-Sun 0830-1730, is located on the road up to the Mombacho cloud forest reserve. US$30, US$10 student discount. It combines well with a visit to the cloud forest reserve which is on this side of the volcano.

Mombotour, Centro Comercial Granada No2, next to BAC, T552-4548, www.mombotour.com. US$38 per person. Cost includes transfers by 4WD up and down the mountain from Granada; transfers normally leave at 0900 and 1300 daily and you must book in advance.

Cultural and community tourism

UCA Tierra y Agua, Shell Palmira, 75 vrs abajo, T552-0238, www.ucatierrayagua.org. Mon, Wed, Fri, 0830-1400. This organization will help you organize a visit to rural communities around Granada including Isla Sonzapote, La Granadilla, Nicaragua Libre and Aguas Agrias (see box, page 111). Very interesting and highly recommended for a perspective on local life and the land.

Horse riding

Blue Mountain, southwest corner of Parque Central, 1 ½ c abajo, T552-5323, www.bluemountainnicaragua.com. They do daily cowboy-style tours of the region, with birdwatching, swimming and fishing options. You can bottle-feed some calves too, before they're made into burgers.

Kayaking

Inuit Kayaks, entrance to the touristic centre, 400 m sur on the lake, T608-3646, www.inuitkayak.com. They offer kayak rental, sales and tours of the Isletas. Sailing, catamarans and windsurfing too.

Mombotour, Centro Comercial Granada No2, next to BAC, T552-4548, www.mombotour.com. Having acquired the reputable 'Island Kayaks' agency, Mombotour offer kayak lessons and guided tours of the Isletas, which can be combined with longer birding expeditions.

Massage

Seeing Hands, inside EuroCafe, off the northwest corner of Parque Central. This excellent organization offers blind people an opportunity to earn a living as masseurs. A range of effective, professional massages are available, from a 15-min back, neck and shoulder massage, US$2.50, to a 1-hr table massage, US$12.50.

Sailing

Puerto Asese, www.aseselasisletas.com. 3 km from Granada, this low-key dock is the place to find transport to Las Isletas or Zapatera.

Marina Cocibolca, www.marinacocibolca.net. Check the Marina's administrative offices for information on costs and schedules for visits to the Isletas, Zapatera, and nearby private reserves.

Zapatera Tours, Calle Palmira contiguo a la Cancha, T842-2587, www.zapatera tours.com. This company specializes in lake tours with trips to las Isletas, Zapatera, Ometepe and the Solentiname archipelago. They also offer biking, hiking and windsurfing.

Tour operators

JB Fun Tours, on Parque Central inside artisan shop at cultural centre, T552-6732, www.jbfuntours.com. Lots of options including fishing, manager Christian Quintanilla speaks English and is a good guide.

Oro Travel, Convento San Francisco, ½ c norte, T552-4568, www.orotravel.com. Granada's best tour operator offers quality, specialized tours and trips, many including transfers and hotels. Owner Pascal speaks French, English and German. Friendly and helpful.

Tierra Tour, Calle la Calzada, catedral, 2 c lago, T0862-9580, www.tierratour.com. This well-established Dutch-Nicaraguan agency offers a wide range of services including good-value trips to Las Isletas, cloud forest tours, birding expeditions and shuttles. Helpful and friendly.

Va Pues, Parque Central, blue house next to the cathedral, T552-8291, www.vapues.com. This award-winning agency offers canopy tours, turtle expeditions, car rental, domestic flights and a 'romantic getaway' tour to a private island.

Transport

Granada *p110, maps p114 and p116*

Bus

Intercity bus For the border with **Costa Rica** use **Rivas** bus to connect to **Peñas Blancas** service or use international buses.

Express minibuses to La UCA in **Managua** from a small lot just south of Parque Central on Calle Vega, every 20 mins, 0500-2000, 45 mins, US$1.10. They can drop you on the highway exit to **Masaya**, US$0.60, from where it's a 20-min walk or 5-min taxi ride to the centre. Buses tc Mercado Roberto Huembes, Managua, also leave from a station near the old hospital in Granada, west of centre, but they're slower and only marginally cheaper.

Leaving from the Shell station, Mercado, 1 c al lago: to **Rivas**, 7 daily, 0540-1510, 1½ hrs, US$1.50; to Nandaime, every 20 mins, 0500-1800, 20 mins, US0.70; to **Niquinohomo**, every 20 mins, 0550-1800, 45 mins, US$1, use this bus for visits to **Diriá**, **Diriomo**, **San Juan de Oriente**, **Catarina**; to **Jinotepe**, 0550, 0610, 0830, 1110, 1210 and 1710, 1½ hrs, US$1, for visits to **Los Pueblos**, including **Masatepe** and **San Marcos**. There's a second terminal nearby, Shell station, 1 c abajo, 1 c norte, serving **Masaya**, every 30 mins, 0500-1800, 40 mins, US$0.50.

International bus To **San José**, Costa Rica, daily. See individual offices for schedules: **King Quality**, Shell Guapinol, 1½ c al sur, opposite Ticabus, www.kingqualityca.com; **Ticabus**, Shell Guapinol, 1½ c al Sur, T552-2899, www.ticabus.com; **Transnica**, Calle Xalteva, Frente de Iglesia Auxiliadora, T552-6619, www.transnica.com.

Shuttles to **Laguna Apoyo**, leave twice daily from Hostal Oasis, Calle Estrada 109, south of the centre to Crater's Edge hostel at the lake, 1000, 1600, ½ hr, US$2. They return at 1100 and 1700.

Paxeos, Parque Central, blue house next to cathedral, T552-8291, www.paxeos.com. Daily shuttles to **Managua airport**, **León**, **San Juan del Sur** and **San Jorge**.

Car hire

Budget Rent a Car, at the Shell station near the north city entrance, T552-2323, provides very good service. If you rent a car in Managua you can leave it here, or you can hire it in Granada and drop it off in Managua or other northern destinations. However, cheaper rates can be found in Managua with other companies.

Ferry

Schedules are subject to change. The ferry to **San Carlos** leaves the main dock on Mon and Thu at 1400, and stops at **Altagracia**, **Ometepe** after 4 hrs (US$4 1st class, US$2 2nd class), **Morrito** (8 hrs, US$5 1st class, US$3, 2nd class), **San Miguelito** (10 hrs, US$5.50 1st class, US$3 2nd class) and finally **San Carlos** (14 hrs, US$8 1st class, US$4 2nd class). This journey is tedious, take your own food and water, and a hammock, if you have one. The ferry returns from San Carlos on Tue and Fri following the same route. For **Altagracia** you can also take a cargo boat with passenger seats on Wed and Sat (1200, 4½ hrs, US$2). It is faster to go overland to **San Jorge** and catch a 1-hr ferry to **Ometepe**, see San Jorge, page 136, for more details.

Horse-drawn carriages

Coches are for hire and are used as taxis here, as in Masaya, Rivas and Chinandega. Normal rate for a trip to the market or bus station should be no more than US$1.50. The drivers are also happy to take foreigners around the city and actually make very good and willing guides if you can decipher their Spanish. Rates are normally US$5 for 30 mins, US$10 for 1 hr. You can see most of the city's sights in a ½-hr rental unless you want to enter the fort, churches and museum. A good carriage ride starts from La Pólvora and continues down Calle Real, past La Capilla María Auxiliadora, La Jalteva, and La Merced to Parque Central. From the cathedral you can then continue to La Virgen de Guadalupe and to the lakefront along the La Calzada, returning via a visit to the Iglesia San Francisco.

Taxis

Granada taxi drivers are useful for finding places away from the centre, fares to anywhere within the city are US$0.50 during the day, US$1 at night. To **Managua** US$25, but check taxi looks strong enough to make the journey.

Directory

Granada *p110, maps p114 and p116*

Banks Banco de Centro América (BAC) Parque Central, 1 c abajo, on Calle La Libertad, has an ATM and will change TCs and US dollars. ATM at Esso Station (15-min walk from town centre) accepts Cirrus, Maestro, MasterCard as well. **Banpro**, BAC, 1 c al sur, has a less reliable ATM and money changing facilities. **Bancentro**, BAC, 1 c al norte, has a Visa ATM. **Western Union**, fire station, ½ c sur, Mon-Sat 0800-1300, 1400-1700.
Doctors Dr Francisco Martínez Blanco, Clínica de Especialidades Piedra Bocona, Cine Karawala, ½ c abajo, T552-5989, general practitioner, speaks good English, consultation US$10. **Fire** T552-4440. **Hospital** T552-2719. **Internet** Internet cafés can be found all over town, while most hostels and hotels also offer internet access as well as international calls. **Language schools** Granada is becoming a hot-bed for Spanish schools, with many rising and falling with the city's increasing popularity. The se ones are well-established and proven. **Casa Xalteva**, Iglesia Xalteva, ½ c al norte, T552-2436, www.casaxalteva.com. Small Spanish classes for beginners and advanced students, 1 week to several months. Homestays arranged, and voluntary work with children. Recommended. **APC Spanish School**, west side of Parque Central, T552-4203, www.spanish granada.com. Flexible immersion classes in this centrally located language school. There are volunteer opportunities with local NGOs. **Nicaragua Mia Spanish School**, inside Maverick's reading lounge, Calle Arsenal, behind Hotel Colonial, T552-2755, www.nicaragua-mia-spanishschool.com. An established and professional language school with various learning options, from hourly to weekly tuition. They take an ethical approach and contribute to local causes. **One on One**, Calle La Calzada 450, T552-6771, www.1on1tutoring.net. One on One uses a unique teaching system where each student has four different tutors, thus encouraging greater aural comprehension. Instruction is flexible, by the hour or week, with homestay and activities available. There's an evening restaurant too, where you can practise your Spanish with locals. Recommended. **Laundry** Parque Central, 1½ c abajo, around US$3 for a medium-sized load, daily 0700-1900. **Police** T552-2929. **Post office** Fire station, ½ c al lago, ½ c norte; also for express mail, **DHL**, next to Casa de los Tres Mundos, T552-6847. **Red Cross** T552-2711. **Telephone Enitel** on northeast corner of Parque Central.

Around Granada

Despite Granada's five centuries of European settlement, there remains plenty of pristine nature close to the old city. The shores of Lake Nicaragua offer access to the well populated archipelago of Las Isletas and the mysterious and largely unvisited indigenous ceremonial sites of Parque Nacional Archipiélago Zapatera. On the mainland it is hard to miss the sulking mountain of Mombacho, its cloud forest draped in mist most of the year, but nevertheless great for hiking in and canopy touring. On the south side of the volcano there are expansive tropical dry forests including the private nature reserve of Domitila. Past the trees are vast plains of sugar cane, rice and cattle pasture that lead to the tough cowboy town of Nandaime, a distant echo of Granada's colonial sister city, lost forever in a 16th-century Mombacho landslide. ▸▸ *For Sleeping, Eating and other listings see pages 131-131.*

Archipiélago Las Isletas ▸▸ *pp131-131.*

Just five minutes outside Granada, in the warm waters of Lake Nicaragua, is the chain of 354 islands called Las Isletas. The islands are big piles of basalt rock covered in lush vegetation growing in the fertile soil that fills in the islands' rocky surface. The number of mango trees on the archipelago is staggering (the abundance of fruit in general is an important part of the local diet along with fish) and magnificent giant ceiba and guanacaste trees dominate the landscape. Bird life is rich, with plenty of egrets, cormorants, ospreys, magpie jays, kingfishers, Montezuma oropendulas and various species of swallows, flycatchers, parrots and parakeets, as well as the occasional mot-mot. A great way to appreciate the bird life is to head out for a dawn kayaking expedition with **Iniuit Kayaks** or **Mombotour**, see page 124 for further details.

The islands were created by a massive eruption of the Mombacho volcano that watches over the lake and islands to the west. You can see from the tranquillity of Las Isletas' waters how much of the mountain was blown into the water during the eruption. The islands' population consists mainly of humble fishermen and boatmen, though many of the islands are now privately owned by wealthy Nicaraguans and a handful of foreigners who build second homes and use them for weekend and holiday escapes. The school, cemetery, restaurants and bars are all on different islands and the locals commute mostly by rowing boat or by hitching rides from the tour boats that circulate in the calm waters. Fishing is the main source of income and you may well see the fishermen in the water laying nets for the lake's delicious *guapote* or *mojarra*. Many also find work building walls or caretaking on the islands owned by the weekenders.

The peninsula that jets out between the islands has small docks and restaurants on both sides. The immediate (north) side of the islands is accessed by the road that runs through the tourist centre of Granada and finishes at the docks. This is the more popular side of the archipelago and boat rides around the islands are cheaper from here (US$13 per hour per boat). In addition to the many luxurious homes on this part of the islands, is the tiny, late 17th-century Spanish fort, **San Pablo**, on the extreme northeast of the chain; it can be visited from the north side of the peninsula. Real estate companies have moved into this side of the archipelago and it is not unusual to see 'For Sale' signs in English.

> *Las Isletas are often frequented by groups of foreign tourists in noisy motor boats, making it less than ideal for wildlife watching. Rising early and setting out with a kayak should remedy this.*

There is a turning before the road ends with big signs for **Puerto Asese** ⓘ *T552-2269, www.aseselasisletas.com*, which is a larger, more luxurious marina with a big restaurant. The boats from Puerto Asese also offer one-hour rides around the islands. Despite the fact that there are fewer canals you will have a better chance to see normal island life since this part southern part of the archipelago is populated by more locals, some of them quite impoverished. An hour on this side is normally US$15 with both sides charging US$1.50 for parking. A taxi or horse-drawn carriage to the docks costs US$4 or less. You will also be able to find transport to Las Isletas from nearby **Marina Cocibolca** ⓘ *T228-1223, www.marinacocibolca.net*, which has public boat schedules at its administrative office.

Parque Nacional Archipiélago Zapatera

Although most important relics have been taken to museums, this archipelago of 11 islands remains one of the country's most interesting pre-Columbian sites. Isla Zapatera, the centrepiece and Lake Nicaragua's second largest island, is a very old and extinct volcano that has been eroded over the centuries and covered in forest.

Ins and outs

Getting there The island system is 40 km south of Granada. The journey to the islands takes one hour from Granada by *panga* (skiff), more if there are lake swells. The passage between the protected waters of Las Isletas and Zapatera can be especially rough. Public boats depart irregularly from Puerto Assese and the average cost of hiring a private boat is US$100-150. Several Granada tour companies offer one-day trips that include lunch, boat and guide, including **Oro Travel**, see page 128. **Tours Nicaragua** in Managua offer a visit to Zapatera as part of a sophisticated week-long archaeological trip guided by a National Museum archaeologist. Alternatively, **UCA Tierra y Agua** in Granada organizes rustic lodging, transport and tours of the island (see box, page 111). There have been some isolated reports of park rangers turning away visitors who do not have permission from MARENA, so it is best to use a tour operator to avoid being disappointed. All hiking on Zapatera is guided. Beyond a single simple restaurant and rustic lodgings, there are no facilities on the island or shops of any size. Bring all the supplies you need, including food and water.

Sights

Isla Zapatera has both tropical dry and wet forest ecosystems depending on elevation, which reaches a maximum height of 625 m. It is a beautiful island for hiking, with varied wildlife and an accessible crater lake, close to the northwest shore of the island. The main island is best known for what must have been an enormous religious infrastructure when the Spanish arrived, though many of the artefacts were not 'discovered' until the mid-19th century. There are conflicting reports on the island's indigenous name, ranging from *Xomotename* (duck village) to *Mazagalpan* (the houses with nets). Archaeological evidence dating from 500 BC to AD 1515 has been documented from more than 20 sites on the island. Massive basalt images attributed to the Chorotega Indians were found at three of these sites and some can be seen in the Museo Convento San Francisco in Granada and the Museo Nacional in Managua. US diplomat and amateur archaeologist Ephraim George Squier, on his visit to the island in 1849, uncovered 15 statues, some of which he had shipped to the US where they are in a collection at the Smithsonian Museum in Washington, DC. Another 25 statues were found by the Swedish naturalist Carl Bovallius in 1883, in what is the most interesting site, Zonzapote, which appears to have been part of an ancient ritual amphitheatre. In 1926, the US archaeologist Samuel Kirkland Lothrop theorized that Bovallius had uncovered a Chorotega temple consisting of several sacred buildings each with a separate entrance, idols and sacrificial mounds. But the evidence is not conclusive and further studies are needed.

Equally impressive is the broad, flat rock that sits on the highest point of a small island to the north, **Isla el Muerto**. This 100 m x 25 m rock is one of the most interesting of Nicaragua's hundreds of petroglyph sites. The extraordinary range of rock drawings is believed to have been part of a very important burial site (hence the name 'Death Island').

Isla Zapatera has several hundred inhabitants who arrived during the 1980s from the northern extremes of Nicaragua to escape the violence of the Contra War. They are not legally allowed on the island, which enjoys national park status, so they may appear shy or suspicious. However, you can visit and stay at their community at Sonzapote through **UCA Tierra y Agua** in Granada (see box, page 111), from where you can also hire guides to visit the petroglyphs or surrounding forests. Trails lead up Banderas Hill with great views of Ometepe and the lake, but the most demanding trail ascends Zapatera Hill (also known as Cerro Grande), the island's highest peak, for which you should allow six hours.

Reserva Natural Volcán Mombacho

Just 10 km outside Granada is one of only two cloud forests found in Nicaragua's Pacific lowlands. As well as the forest reserve, the volcano is home to coffee plantations and some ranches. The summit has five craters: four small ones – three covered in vegetation and one along the trails of the nature park – and one large one that lost one of its walls in a tragic mudslide in 1570 (see Nandaime, below).

Ins and outs

Getting there Take a bus between Nandaime or Rivas and Granada or Masaya. Get off at the Empalme Guanacaste and walk (or take a taxi) 1 km to the car park. From here you can take a truck to the top of the volcano (great view), 25 minutes; they leave every couple of hours from the parking area. The last trip is at 1500, although if there are enough people they will make another trip. It is also possible to walk the 5½ km to the top using the steep cobblestone road (see below). Bring water, hiking shoes and a light sweater or better still a rain jacket or poncho.

Admission and information Park administration is in Granada T552-5858, www.mombacho.org. Thu-Sun, 0830-1700, US$9 adult, US$3.25 children, which includes transfer to the reserve from the parking area and the aid of a park guide. Tickets are sold at the parking area at the base, along with purified water and snacks.

Sights

The nature reserve is administered by the non-profit Cocibolca Foundation and is one of the best organized in Nicaragua. It's home to many species of butterfly and the famous Mombacho salamander (*Bolitoglossa mombachoensis*) which is found nowhere else in the world. Among other resident fauna, the biologists have counted some 60 species of mammals, 28 species of reptiles, 10 species of amphibians, 119 species of birds and a further 49 species that are migratory visitors. More than 30,000 insect species are thought to exist, though only 300 have been identified to date. The volcano has terrific views of extinct craters and, if cloud cover permits, of Granada, Lake Nicaragua and Las Isletas. The cloud often clears for a few hours in the after- noon, 1400-1530 being your best bet for a good view.

There's a small but pretty butterfly sanctuary and orchid house near the park entrance at the foot of the volcano.

Paths are excellently maintained and labelled. For those who want to see a pristine, protected cloud forest the easy way, this is the perfect place. Most visitors opt for a one or two-hour stroll along the **Sendero Cráter**, an easy trail that leads through magnificent cloud forest full of ferns, bromeliads and orchids (752 species of flora have been documented so far), has various lookout points and a micro-desert on the cone where you'll encounter steaming *fumaroles* and a stunning view of Cocibolca, Granada, Laguna de Apoyo and Volcán Masaya. An optional guide costs US$5 per group. Hardcore hikers may be disappointed by this relatively tame and well-tended trail, but there is an opportunity for a more challenging excursion too. The **Sendero El Puma** is only 4 km in length but takes around four hours to cover because of the elevation changes. This is the best walk for seeing wildlife, which can be very elusive during the daytime. A guide is obligatory, some speak English and they cost US$15 per group.

The main beauty of the park is its vegetation; if you wish to examine the amphibian, reptile and bird life of the reserve, you will have to sleep in the research station itself and go hiking at night and in the early morning. They have one big room with several beds, shared baths, kitchen and an outhouse. Cost per person with meals and a night tour is US$30. The research station offers simple, cheap sandwiches and drinks to visitors and has a good model of the volcano and historical explanations.

Canopy tours

Canopy tours are not designed for nature watching, but to give you a bit of a rush and a sense of what it's like to live like the birds and monkeys up in the trees. Most people find it takes a long time for their smile to wear off. Mombacho has two canopy tours. On the forest reserve (west face) is the **Mombacho Canopy Tour** (see page 124), which includes lessons on a practice cable at ground level, assistance of one of the company guides, and all gear, and has 15 platforms from which you can buzz along a cable from platform to platform, high up in the trees and a suspended 1500-m long bridge. The Mombacho tour is over coffee plants and has some very big trees and the service includes refreshments in a little viewpoint overlooking the valley after your adventure. The views are not as spectacular as the Mombotour (below), but fun, and cheaper. The operating company, unrelated to the park administration, will pick you up at the same parking area as the truck for the forest reserve, but if you want to see both you will have to pay admission to the reserve. The other canopy tour is on the east face of the mountain and is run by **Mombotour** (see page 124). This is a world-class canopy tour designed by the inventor of the sport, with 17 platforms 3-20 m above the ground on the lake side of Volcán Mombacho. The tour concludes with a pants-wetting vertical descent on a rappel line.

South from Granada

Nandaime

Travelling south from Granada, the highway joins the Pan-American Highway, which travels north to Los Pueblos and on to Managua. To the south, the highway continues to the departments of Granada and Rivas and on to the border with Costa Rica (buses leave from the Shell station terminal in Granada to Rivas at regular intervals). A few kilometres south of the junction is the ranching town of Nandaime, which lies just west of the highway.

Nandaime (which translates roughly as 'well-irrigated lands') has an interesting history. Little is known about the original settlement, which was near the shores of the lake opposite the Zapatera Archipelago and was visited by the Spanish explorer Gil González Dávila. It was the most important town for the Chorotega southern federation and could have been responsible for administering the religious sites on Isla Zapatera. The city was then moved for unknown reasons to a second location further west along the base of the Mombacho volcano and could have grown to be a sister city to Granada – had it survived. It was reported to have been a town with the same classic colonial design as Granada, home to a "formal and solid Catholic church". However, in 1570 an earthquake caused the rim of the Volcán Mombacho crater lake to collapse and the village was annihilated in a massive landslide. A third settlement was established at Nandaime's current position.

At the time of the Spanish arrival, it was a place for cultivation of the cacao fruit, the raw ingredient from which chocolate is made. During the 19th century much of the cacao was destined for the chocolate factories of Menier in France and the area became known as Valle de Menier. Today the area is home to big ranches and sugar cane and rice farms.

Nandaime has two pretty churches, **El Calvario** and **La Parroquia** (1859-1872). It is a peaceful cowboy town for most of the year, but becomes a raucous party town for the patron saint festival of Santa Ana in the last week of July (the most important day is 26 July). The festival includes the dance of the *Diablos de al Orilla*, which is a colourful, spectacular display of more than 40 men, who accompany the saint on an annual pilgrimage to the tiny settlement of **La Orilla**, closer to the southern face of Volcán Mombacho. There is a bullfight in La Orilla and much dancing and drinking, and the following days in Nandaime include more dancing in colonial period costume, cross-dressing, more drinking and some parading around on horseback.

Reserva Silvestre Privada Domitila

ⓘ *María José Mejía (the owner), Calle Amelia Benard, Casa Dr Francisco Barbarena, Granada, T881-1786, www.domitila.org or Amigo Tours, Hotel Colonial, Granada, T552-4080, who act as agent, arrange reservations. To get to Domitila you will need to hire a taxi or car, though a 4WD is needed in the rainy season. Entrance to the park is US$5 and guides cost from US$10-40. Reservations to stay or visit the reserve must be made at least three days in advance. Prices are overvalued so negotiate. The forest is quite bare at the end of the dry season; ideal months to visit would be Nov-Jan.*

Five kilometres south of Nandaime is the turning to an 8-km unpaved road that heads towards the lake and private nature reserve of Domitila. Just south of this turning, the Pan-American Highway passes over the region's most important river, Río Ochomogo, the ancient border between the worlds of the Chorotega and that of the indigenous Nicaraguans to the south. Today it marks the end of Granada and the beginning of the isthmus department of Rivas (see page 136). Most of the pristine low-altitude tropical dry forest that has not been cut for grazing is located at the back of the Mombacho volcano. However, further south there is a small swatch of it at this private wildlife reserve. Entry to the reserve is expensive, but it is home to more than 100 howler monkeys and 165 birds, 65 mammal and 62 butterfly species have been documented on their land. Due the small size of the reserve, nature watching is a more rewarding experience.

Lodging is available in eco-friendly rustic and attractive thatched huts at US$65 per person with three meals included, although food is average at best. The reserve management also offers **horse riding** and **sailing** excursions (US$15). Best to arrange visits in advance.

Sleeping

Archipiélago las Isletas *p119*

A Nicarao Lake Resort, on the island of La Ceiba in Las Isletas, T266-1694, www.nicarao lake.com.ni. Includes all meals, a/c, part-time generator and fresh lake fish. Can visit for the day to use their facilities and have lunch

Eating

Archipiélago las Isletas *p127*

TT Restaurante Puerto Assese, at the dock of Assese in Las Isletas, T552-2269. Tue-Sun, 1100-1800. Good value fish specialities, relaxed service, great views.

Rivas Isthmus & Ometepe Island

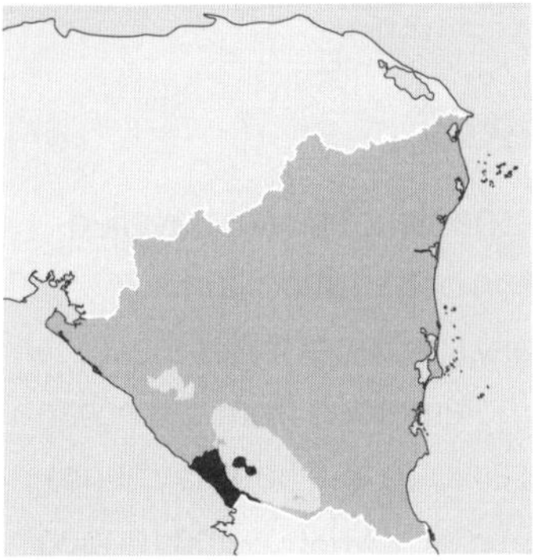

Footprint features

Introduction

Bordering Costa Rica to the south, the slender, well-travelled isthmus of Rivas is an exciting region of transition and international activity. Geographically speaking, this is the youngest part of the country, having emerged from the ocean four or five million years ago to fuse North and South America into a single continent. Here, ultra-fertile lowlands and rugged hills separate the Pacific Ocean from expansive Lake Nicaragua. Its east coast comprises 110 km of black-sand shores and sprawling ranches. The west coast is rugged and wave-swept, with low mountains and more than 130 km of Pacific beaches.

Rising from the waters of Lake Nicaragua with perfectly symmetrical twin cones, Isla de Ometepe is both a national emblem and an archetype of volcanic beauty. It's also home to a growing community of organic farmers who are transforming the island into a bastion of ecological soundness. There is an enchanted, other-worldly feel to Ometepe; her forests and slopes hide mystical secrets, ancient relics that whisper of magical power and long-lost jaguar cults. Although you can hike, swim, cycle and kayak here, much of the island's pleasure comes from simply lazing in a hammock.

Home to two of the world's most important turtle nesting sites, the entrancing beauty of the Pacific Coast is complemented by one of nature's most vivid spectacles. But the region's rugged splendour has not been overlooked by international developers, who are constructing a host of beachfront retirement homes and grotesque gated communities around San Juan del Sur. Once a quiet fishing town it's now swollen with foreign prospectors, surfers and party-goers. Still, the sunsets are immense, development is in its early stages, and a poor infrastructure means much of the coast has been spared, for now.

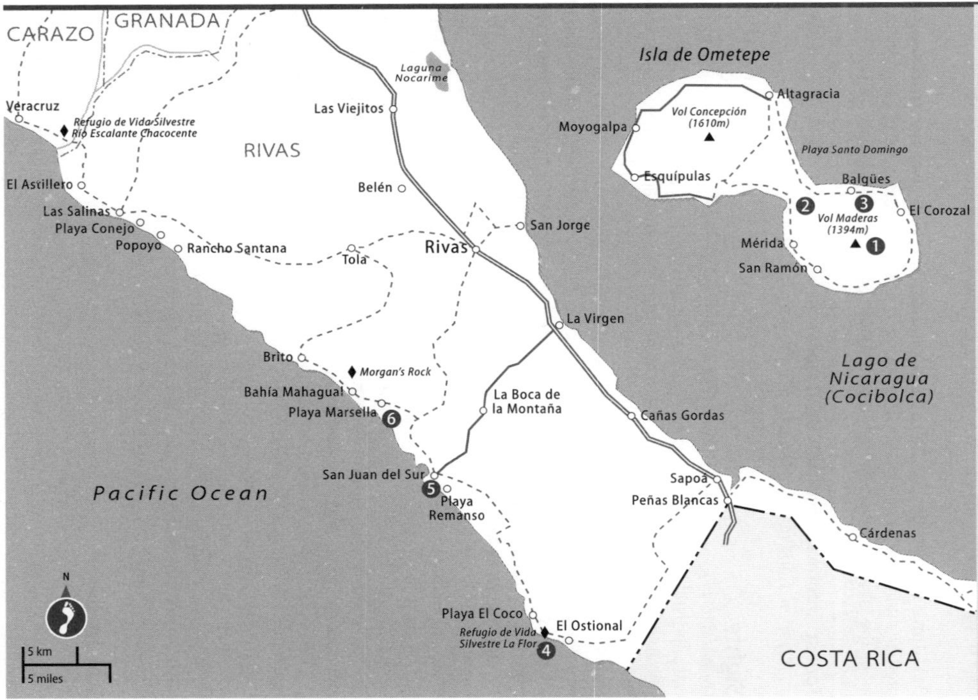

★ Don't miss ...

1 **A summit trip** Climb in the misty cloud forest of the Maderas Volcano and listen to the calls of howler monkeys, page 142.

2 **Stone art** Journey on horseback through Ometepe's ruggedly spectacular scenery to see one of the island's many pre-Columbian petroglyph sites, page 143.

3 **Muck and mulch** Work the land at one of Ometepe's organic farms, the place to learn about permaculture and sustainable agriculture, page 144.

4 **An amphibious landing** Watch the sea turtles arriving to lay their eggs at Playa La Flor or Chacocente, pages 156 and 158.

5 **Catch of the day** Dine on fresh snapper, octopus or lobster in San Juan del Sur, a burgeoning beach town with an international crowd, page 162.

6 **Surf's up** Experience the awesome power of the Pacific Ocean at a host of hard-to-reach, lesserknown surfing spots, page 164.

Rivas

→ *Population: 41,764. Altitude: 139 m. Colour map 3, B4.*

The capital of the department that carries its name, Rivas is a pleasant city with two beautiful churches, a happy, friendly population and lots of horse-drawn carriages with car tyres, particular to this area. It carries the nickname 'city of mangos' for the trees that grow seemingly everywhere around the city. Sadly, few travellers bother to visit this town, preferring to head straight for San Jorge along the route that leads to Isla de Ometepe. ⏩ *For Sleeping, Eating and other listings, see pages 137-139.*

Ins and outs

Getting there and around Rivas is a transport hub and there are frequent bus services from Managua, Granada, San Juan del Sur and the border with Costa Rica at Peñas Blancas. Taxis can be hired from either San Juan del Sur or Granada, or you can try an ungainly looking horse-drawn carriage. Bicycle rickshaws are also popular for short trips around town. Connections between Rivas and the dock at San Jorge are best by taxi, which is inexpensive. ⏩ *For further details, see Transport, page 138.*

Best time to visit During the dry season everything is brown; the area is much prettier during the rainy season. The strong winds from November to February can make the lake crossing from San Jorge to Ometepe Island quite rough.

Tourist information INTUR de Texaco ⓘ *½ c abajo, T563-4914, rivas@intur.gob.ni*. Good maps of Nicaragua and general information.

Sights

Founded in 1720 and named after a high-level Spanish diplomat in Guatemala, Rivas was, and still is, a ranching centre. For the filibuster William Walker (see page 117), who fought and lost three battles here, it was never a very happy place. The **Templo Parroquial de San Pedro** on Parque Central dates from 1863 and is the city's principal church, with a design reminiscent of the cathedral in León. Inside there is a famous fresco depicting the heroic forces of Catholicism defeating a withered Communism in a rather one-sided looking sea battle. There is also the gaily painted **Iglesia San Francisco** to the west of the park, which is the older of the two churches.

The **Museo de Antropología e Historia** ⓘ *Escuela International de Agricultura, 1½ c norte, Mon-Fri 0900-1200, 1400-1700, Sat 0900-1200*, US$1, is the region's best museum. It has a dwindling, poorly labelled, but precious, collection of archaeological pieces as well as taxidermic displays and some ecological information. The main attraction is the beautiful old **Hacienda Santa Ursula** in which the museum is housed. The hacienda is said to have been built in the late 18th century and its charming corridors and views make it well worth a visit.

Rivas is famous throughout Nicaragua for the production of finely crafted indigenous drinking cups called *jícaras*, made from the dried, hard case of the fruit that grows on the native *jícaro* tree. The *jícaro* fruit is oval in shape like a very big egg and they have been used as drinking cups since long before the arrival of the Spanish. Each cup has its own base or can be hung on a cup rack. Archaeological digs have found that early ceramic cups had similar characteristics. In Monimbó, in Masaya (see page 88), the *jícaro* is used to make maracas.

San Jorge

It may seem like an extension of Rivas, but San Jorge is actually a separate town, one that most visitors see only on their way to the ferry for Ometepe. To catch the **ferry**, head east from the roundabout on the highway towards the lake, as far as the Parque Central.

Chief Niqueragua and Conquistador Gil González

The image is forever engrained in the minds of the Nicaraguan people. It adorns murals, plaques, paintings and postage stamps: the first meeting of the European explorers and the Nicaragua natives in what is now San Jorge on 12 April 1523. The conquistador Gil González holds out a linen shirt as an offering to the most powerful chief of the land, Niqueragua, who looks on, somewhat suspicious, yet welcoming. It is said that González traded his shirt, a silk jacket and a red hat for 18,506 gold pesos. The pillage of Nicaragua had begun, with one of the worst trades in modern history.

Yet Chief Niqueragua lives on as a symbol of nobility and intelligence. He welcomed the Spaniard peacefully and he sat for one week with González in philosophical discussion. With the help of an interpreter, Niqueragua grilled the Spaniard thoroughly on all subjects, from astronomy and geology to philosophy and religion. González later admitted sheepishly that Chief Niqueragua was a "linguistic engineer" and that he did not have the rhetorical capacity to debate with the great Chief, excusing himself with "I'm just a soldier". Yet destiny was on the side of greed, not reason.

Not only was trade with Chief Niqueragua good for the Spanish, but his land was also a treasure. The chronicler Oviedo described the land of Niqueragua just after the Conquest: "its healthful and soothing climate, its fine waters and fisheries and its abundance of hunting and game, there is nothing in all the Americas, that feature for feature, surpasses it."

Further north, Gil González would come across real trouble with the less philosophical Chief Diriangén of the Chorotega Indians. The first bricks, however, had been laid for the destruction of the indigenous world of Nicaragua.

Here you will pass the **Iglesia de San Jorge**, a little Gothic-Mudéjar (a mixture of Christian and Muslim architecture from Spain) church, with the ruins of an ancient convent behind. From the church it is two blocks north, then east again all the way to *el muelle* (the dock). The cross over the road between the highway and the church is known as **La Cruz de España** and, together with a small mural painting and a few plaques, commemorates the fateful arrival of the Spanish. The cross marks the assumed spot where the Spanish explorer Gil González Dávila met Chief Niqueragua, the leader of the most developed indigenous society in the region when San Jorge was still known as *Nicaraocalli*. The town celebrates its patron saint's day (St George) on 23 April.

The waterfront area of town is not safe at night.

Sleeping

Rivas *p136*

B Nicarao Inn Hotel, Parque Central, 2 c oeste, T563-3836, www.hotelnicaroinn.com.ni. The finest hotel in Rivas has 18 tastefully decorated, comfortable rooms, all with a/c, cable TV, hot water and Wi-Fi. Services include conference centre, restaurant and bar. Breakfast included.

D Español, across from the southeast corner of Iglesia San Pedro, T563-0006. 5 basic rooms with bath and fan. Restaurant attached.

E El Coco, on highway near where bus from the border stops. Noisy, basic, small rooms, some with private bath. Interesting bar, *comedor* with vegetarian food and a nice garden.

For an explanation of the sleeping and eating price codes used in this guide, see inside the front cover. Other relevant information is found in Essentials, see pages 23-27.

E Hospedaje Lidia, Texaco, ½ c abajo, near bus stop, T563-3477. 12 rooms, clean, family atmosphere, some with private bath, noisy, helpful. Recommended.

G Hospedaje Hilmor, across from the northeast corner of Iglesia San Pedro. Ultra-cheap, ultra-basic lodgings. Consider it only if you're stuck or impoverished.

San Jorge *p136*

There are a few ultra-cheap *hospedajes* scattered around the port, otherwise most lodgings in San Jorge start at around US$20.

C Hotel Dalinky, el puerto, 200 vrs abajo, T563-4990. Large, clean double rooms with a/c, cable TV and bath. Breakfast included and parking available. There's a handful of cheaper rooms too (**E**).

C Hotel Hamacas, el puerto, 100 vrs abajo, 25 vrs sur, T563-1709. As the name suggests, lots of hammocks, mostly slung across porches. The rooms are large and clean with a/c and cable TV. Breakfast included. Cheaper with fan (**D**).

D Hotel California, el puerto, 200 vrs abajo, T563-1659, hotelcalifornia@budweiser.com. North American-owned, motel-style place. Clean, comfortable rooms with cable TV, a/c and private bath.

Eating

Rivas *p136*

₸₸ El Mesón, Iglesia San Francisco, ½ c abajo, T563-4535. Mon-Sat 1100-1500. Very good, try *pollo a la plancha* or *bistec encebollado*.

₸₸ La Lucha, Km 118.5, south of Rivas on lake side of highway, wild game menu and traditional dishes, *guardatinaja asada* (grilled paca), *cuzuco en salsa* (armadillo in tomato sauce), *huevo de toro asado* (grilled bulls' balls), *garrobo en caldillo* (black iguana soup) or *boa en salsa* (boa constrictor in tomato sauce), good service, big seating area, friendly.

₸₸ Rancho Coctelera Mariscazo, Estadio de Rivas, 800 vrs sur, on the Carretera Panamercicana. One of the best seafood restaurants in Nicaragua, with great fish dishes *a la plancha*, excellent *sopa de mariscos* (seafood soup). Simple decor, friendly service, very good value. Highly recommended.

₸₸ Restaurante El Ranchito, near Hotel El Coco. Friendly place serves delicious *churrasco*.

₸ Chop Suey, southwest corner of the plaza, T563-3235. Daily 1000-2100. Chinese food at Nicaraguan prices, for those intent on a change.

₸ El Padrino, BDF, ½ c abajo. T802-5924. Locals' joint serving *comida típica* and wholesome buffet fare.

₸ Pizza Hot, north side of the plaza, T563-4662. Fast food including burgers, fried chicken and fairly good pizza.

₸ Rayuela, across from police station, T563-3221. Prices here are a steal with very cheap tacos, *repochetas* and sandwiches.

San Jorge *p136*

Plenty of cheap places around the dock area.

₸₸-₸ El Gran Diamante, San Jorge Plaza, 300 vrs sur, 800 vrs arriba. Seafood restaurant perched on the lake, with panoramic views of Ometepe's volcanoes.

₸₸-₸ El Refugio, Portuaria, 200 vrs sur, T563-4631. Daily 0900-2200. Overlooking the water and specializing in seafood. The beef is reportedly good.

₸ Restaurante Ivania, alcaldía Municipal, 1 c abajo, 2½ c sur, T563-4764. Daily 0600-2300. Good fish soup or shrimp *ceviche*.

Cafés

Soda Café Exquisito, el puerto, 600 vrs oeste. A nice little café serving cappuccinos, lattes, americanos, and a host of sweet, home-made cakes and brownies. Good for refuelling before or after a ferry trip.

Activities and tours

San Jorge *p136*

Boat trips

Ometepe Tours, T563-4779, in San Jorge at the dock. For boats to the island, hotel reservations, rent-a-car, tours on the island, student groups, information.

Transport

Rivas *p136*

Bus

To **Managua**, every ½ hr, 0630-1700, US$2, 2½ hrs; express buses, US$2.50, 2 hrs; microbuses, US$3, 1½ hrs. To **Granada**, every 45 mins, 0530-1625, US$1.50, 1¾ hrs. To **Jinotepe**, every ½ hr, 0540-1710, US$1.50, 1¾ hrs. To **San Juan del Sur**, every ½ hr, 0600-1830, US$1, 45 mins. To

Peñas Blancas, every ½ hr, 0500-1600, US$0.75, 1 hr.
International buses Ticabus, T848-8622, www.ticabus.com, and **Transnica**, T563-5469, www.transnica.com,have buses bound for Costa Rica and Honduras stopping at the Texaco station on the highway.

Taxi

Taxi from centre of Rivas to the dock at **San Jorge**, US$1.50. To **San Juan del Sur**, US$5 colectivo. To **Peñas Blancas**, US$10 colectivo. Beware overcharging.

San Jorge *p136*

For a timetable of boats and ferries to Moyogalpa, see page 141. There's a motorboat or *lancha*, the *Mozorola*, that goes to Altagracia Tue, Wed, Fri, Sat, 1410, 2½ hrs, US$2.

There are 7 daily buses to **Managua**, 0830-1630, US$2.50, 2½ hrs. A **taxi** direct from/to **San Juan del Sur** costs US$15; colectivo US$5. Taxi to **Rivas** terminal US$1.50.

Directory

Rivas *p136*

Banks The plaza has 2 banks: a **Banpro** on the west side, and a **Banco Procredit** with a Visa ATM on the northwest corner. There's also a **BAC** ATM, plaza, 2 c oeste. **Fire** T563-3511. **Hospital** T563-3301. **Police** T563-3732. **Post office** Correos de Nicaragua, Gimnasio Humberto Méndez, ½ c abajo, T563-3600. **Red Cross** T563-3415. **Telephone** Enitel, Parque Central, west side, T563-0003.

Isla de Ometepe

→ *Population: 37,000. Colour map 3, B4.*

The ancient Nahuas of Mexico were delivered to Ometepe by a dream, so the legend goes, after many years of fruitless wandering. Rising from the waters like a numinous vision, a long-promised sanctuary of goodness and tranquility, it seems as though little has changed since then. Two ethereal volcanoes comprise this mysterious realm: Concepción is larger, active and periodically spews ash; Maderas is smaller, extinct and swathed in cloud forest. Each evening at dusk, their green slopes erupt with the chattering of exotic birds. Ometepe's pre-Columbian heritage survives in the form of bizarre petroglyphs and a statuary that is testament to a shamanic reverence for animal spirits. The island's inhabitants, descended from these cultures, are mostly fishing and farming communities, and some of Nicaragua's kindest people. This is a fine place for volunteering or learning about organic farming. The rich volcanic soil means agriculture here has always been organic, but a wave of foreigners are introducing more sophisticated, ecologically aware permaculture techniques. Thus far, tourist development has kept within the style and scale of the island, although there are now murmurings of larger, less sympathetic construction projects. ►► *For Sleeping, Eating and other listings, see pages 149-153.*

Ins and outs

Getting there Boat connections from Granada and San Carlos are possible, but the most user-friendly are the one-hour boats and ferries from San Jorge to Moyogalpa, running almost hourly throughout the day, with reduced services on Sunday (see box for the timetable). The best choice is the ferry, which has three levels, a toilet, snack bar, television (with *telenovelas* blasted through concert speakers over the noise of the motors) and room for six cars. It's worth timing your crossing to use it, both for its facilities and for the great viewing deck, which offers a panoramic view of the lake and islands. If it's a clear day, the Zapatera archipelago is visible to the north, with Volcán Mombacho rising up behind it; on really clear days you'll see the smoke surging out of Volcán Masaya. A *lancha* called the *Mozorola* travels between Altagracia and San

Jorge four times a week. If you are prone to seasickness buy Nausil from the farmacía before the crossing.

Car If you have a high-clearance 4WD you may want to take it across on the ferry (US$20 each way). Arrive at least one hour before the ferry departure to reserve a spot (if possible call the day before, T278-8190 to make an initial reservation). You will need to fill out some paperwork and buy a boarding ticket for each person travelling. Make sure you reserve your spot as close to the ferry ramp as possible, but leave room for trucks and cars coming off the ferry.

Getting around Taxis (vans and pick-ups) wait for the boat arrivals, as do buses. Most of the island is linked by a bus service, otherwise trucks are used. Walking, cycling or horse riding are the best ways to see the island; however, it can be dusty in the dry season.

Best time to visit The dry season is normally less harsh here, but after February everything is brown. The end of May is a happy, optimistic time, especially for farmers, but there can be a lot of gnats in the air. The rainy season is much prettier as the countryside becomes lush and green. The windy season from November to February can make the ferry crossing unsettling.

Tourist information **Ometepe Expeditions** ⓘ *20 m from the port in Moyogalpa*, are the island's best tour operator and a good source of information. There's usually someone there who speaks English.

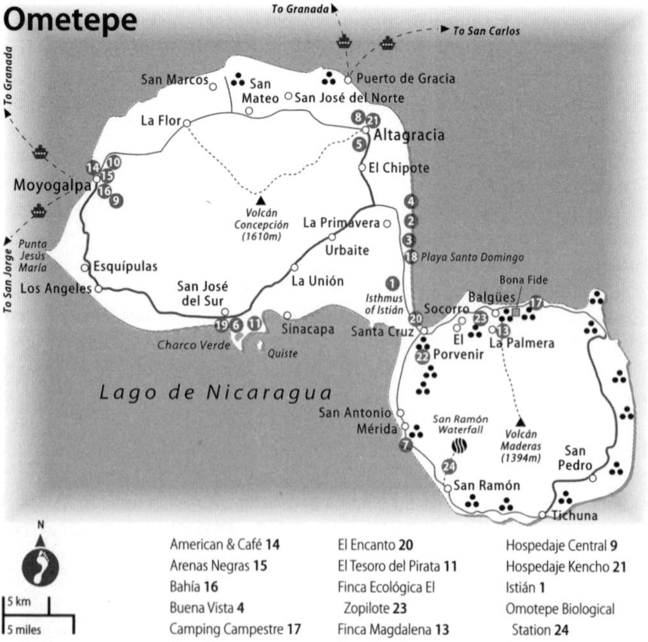

Sleeping 🛏
Albergue Ecológico Porvenir **22**
American & Café **14**
Arenas Negras **15**
Bahía **16**
Buena Vista **4**
Camping Campestre **17**
Central **5**
Charco Verde Inn **6**
Chico Largo Hostel **19**
Costa Azul **18**
El Encanto **20**
El Tesoro del Pirata **11**
Finca Ecológica El Zopilote **23**
Finca Magdalena **13**
Finca Playa Venecia **6**
Finca Santo Domingo **2**
Hacienda Mérida **7**
Hospedaje Castillo **8**
Hospedaje Central **9**
Hospedaje Kencho **21**
Istián **1**
Omotepe Biological Station **24**
Ometepetl **10**
Villa Paraíso **3**

Petroglyphs ⁂

Ferry timetable

The ferry is US$2 per person each way, other boats cost US$1.50.

San Jorge – Moyogalpa		Moyogalpa – San Jorge	
0730	Ferry	0530	Boat
0900	Boat	0600	Ferry
0930	Boat	0630	Boat
1030	Ferry	0700	Boat
1130	Boat	0800	Boat
1230	Boat	0900	Ferry
1330	Boat	1100	Boat
1430	Ferry	1130	Boat
1530	Boat	1230	Ferry
1630	Boat	1330	Boat
1730	Boat	1500	Boat
1830	Ferry	1600	Ferry

Background

Ceramic evidence shows that the island has been inhabited for at least 3500 years, although some believe this figure could be 12,000 years or more. Little is known about the pre-Conquest cultures of the island. From ceramic analysis carried out by US archaeologist Frederick W Lange (published in 1992), it appears the people of 1500 BC came from South America as part of a northern immigration that continued to Mexico. They lived in a settlement in what is today the town of Los Angeles and were followed by waves of settlement to both the western and eastern sides of the island.

Mystery also surrounds the people who inhabited the island at the time of the Conquest. A visiting priest reported in 1586 that the natives of the island spoke a language different from any of those spoken on the mainland. Yet the large basalt statues found on Ometepe appear to be of the same school as the ones found on Zapatera and attributed to the Chorotegas. Dr J F Bransford, a medical officer for a US Navy, came to Nicaragua in 1872 as part of an inter-oceanic exploratory team. His observations (published in 1881 by the Smithsonian Institute) remain one of the few sources of information about this mysterious place. During his digs in 1876 and 1877, near Moyogalpa, he noted that the Concepción volcano was forested to the top and 'extinct' (it would become very much alive five years later) and that the isthmus between the two volcanoes was passable by canoe during the rainy season. The island's population was estimated at 3000, with most living in Altagracia and some 500 others scattered around the island. Most people he described fitted the description of an Ometepino today – basically Chorotega in appearance; however, on the very sparsely populated Maderas side of the island lived a tall people – many of the men were over 6 ft – with decidedly unusual facial features. These people were more suspicious by nature and reluctant to talk or share the location of the big basalt idols of the islands. From this, Bransford concluded that they still worshipped the gods represented in the statues (by contrast, the other inhabitants of the island had happily revealed the location of their statues). There is little evidence of these people

Despite the mystery surrounding the pre-Conquest history of Ometepe, the population remains mostly indigenous: this was that last place on the Pacific where the indigenous lingua franca *of Náhuatl was spoken, until finally disappearing in the late 19th century.*

today, but their religious statues can be found next to the church in Altagracia and in the National Museum in Managua.

During the colonial period, Ometepe was used as a refuge for pirates, en route to or returning from a pillaging raid on Granada. The bandits would steal food supplies, livestock or even women, forcing some of the population to move inland. During William Walker's occupation of Granada, Moyogalpa was used as a temporary medical field hospital for retreating troops and would-be colonizers, until the local population attacked and they were forced to escape in canoes to the mainland.

In the 1870s the indigenous population rioted against a pact between Conservative and Liberal politicians during local elections. More problems arose in 1908 when *mestizo* migrants from Chontales fought to appropriate 4653 acres of indigenous communal lands that stretched from Urbaite to Maderas. The mainlanders eventually succeeded, but not without a long struggle that was still being fought in 1942, when the indigenous community rioted against the National Guard removing Indians from their land. The riot killed 23 indigenous and three soldiers. However, the island was spared involvement in the bloody battles of the Revolution and the Contra War and for this reason the Ometepinos call their island the 'Oasis of Peace'.

Sights

Geology, vegetation and wildlife

Ometepe's two volcanoes rising up out of Lake Nicaragua appear prehistoric and almost other-worldly. The two cones are nature reserves and they are connected by a 5-km wide lava-flow isthmus. The island is always in the shadow of one of its two Olympian volcanic cones. The dominant mountain, one of the most symmetrical cones in the world and covered by 2200 ha of protected forest, is **Volcán Concepción** (1610 m high, 36½-km wide). It is an active volcano that last blew ash in February 2007 and had its most recent major lava flow in 1957. The volcano was inactive for many years before it burst into life in 1883 with a series of eruptions continuing until 1887. Concepción also erupted from 1908 until 1910, with further significant activity in 1921 and 1948-1972. Thanks to its hot lava outbursts, one of the cone's indigenous names was *Mestlitepe* (mountain that menstruates). The other well-known name is *Choncotecihuatepe* (brother of the moon); an evening moonrise above the volcano is an unforgettable sight.

Climbing is good on both volcanoes. The vegetation and wildlife of Maderas is superior in both quantity and diversity, but there are more hikers to scare off animals. See box, opposite for more details.

Volcán Maderas (1394 m high, 24½ km maximal diameter) last erupted about 800 years ago and is now believed to be extinct. The mountain is wrapped in thick forest and is home to the only cloud forest in Nicaragua's Pacific Basin other than Volcán Mombacho. The Nicaraguans called the mountain *Coatlán* (land of the sun). The 400 m by 150 m cold, misty crater lake, **Laguna de Maderas**, was only discovered by the non-indigenous population in 1930 and has a lovely waterfall on the western face of the cone. Maderas has 4100 ha of forest set aside and protected in a reserve.

Both cones have monkey populations, with the Maderas residents being almost impossible to miss on a full-day hike on the cone. The forest of Maderas also has a great diversity of butterfly and flower species, as well as a dwarf forest and the island is home to numerous parrots and magpie jays; the latter are almost as common as the pigeons in the squares of European cities. The **Isthmus of Istián**, the centre of the island's figure-of-eight shape and a fertile lowland finger that connects the two volcanoes' round bases, has several lagoons and creeks that are good for birdwatching. Off the northeast side of the isthmus are a couple of islands that also shelter rich bird life, in addition to the legendary **Charco Verde** on the southern coast of Concepción (see page 146).

Climbing the volcanoes

Volcán Concepción

There are two main trails leading up to the summit. One of the paths is best accessed from Moyogalpa, where there is lots of accommodation. The other is from Altagracia. Climbing the volcano without a local guide is not advised under any circumstances and can be very dangerous: a climber died here in 2004 after falling into a ravine. Ask your hotel about recommended tour guides; many of the locals know the trail well but that does not make them reliable guides and use extreme caution if contacting a guide not recommened by a tour operator or well-known hotel. See page 152 for recommended guides. The view from Concepción is breathtaking. The cone is very steep near the summit and loose footing and high winds are common. Follow the guide's advice if winds are deemed too strong for the summit. From **Moyogalpa** the trail begins near the village of La Flor and the north side of the active cone. You should allow eight hours for the climb. Bring plenty of water and breathable, strong and flexible hiking shoes. From **Altagracia** the hike starts 2 km away and travels through a cinder gully, between forested slopes and a lava flow. The ascent takes five hours, 3½ hours if you are very fit. Take water and sunscreen. Tropical dry and wet forest, heat from the crater and howler monkeys are added attractions.

Volcán Maderas

Three trails ascend Maderas. One departs from Hotel La Omaja near **Mérida**, another from Finca El Porvenir near **Santa Cruz**, and the last from Finca Magdalena near **Balgües**. Presently, the trail from Finca Magdelena is the only one fit enough to follow, but check locally. You should allow five hours up and three hours down, though relatively dry trail conditions could cut down hiking time considerably. Expect to get very muddy in any case. Ropes are necessary if you want to climb down into the Laguna de Maderas after reaching the summit. Swimming in the laguna is not recommended, as a tourist got stuck in the mud after jumping in. Rather farcically, she had to be pulled out with a rope made of the tour group's trousers. Hiking Maderas can no longer be done without a guide, following the deaths of British and American hikers who apparently either got lost or tried to descend the west face of the volcano and fell. While some hikers still seem offended to have to pay a local guide, it is a cheap life insurance policy and helps the very humble local economy. Guides are also useful in pointing out animals and petroglyphs that outsiders may miss. There is an entrance fee of US$2 to climb Maderas. The trail leads through farms, fences and gets steeper and rockier with elevation. The forest changes with altitude from tropical dry, to tropical wet and finally cloud forest, with howler monkeys accompanying your journey. Guides can be found for this climb in Moyogalpa, Altagracia and Santo Domingo or at Finca Magdelena where the hike begins.

Petroglyph sites

Ometepe has much to offer the culturally curious as well, with numerous pre-Columbian sites. A six-year survey in the mid-1990s revealed 73 sites with 1700 petroglyph panels and that is just the tip of the iceberg. A guided visit is recommended to one of the petroglyph sites, which are known according to the name of the farm they are found on. To list but a few: **San Marcos** has an eagle with

¡Viva la Revolución Verde! Principles of permaculture

Ometepe's rich volcanic soil means organic methods have always prevailed here. But now a new wave of foreign settlers are bringing sophisticated permaculture techniques and the promise of an even greener island.

But what exactly *is* permaculture? In short, it is a holistic design method for creating sustainable human habitats. The word itself, coined by Dr Bill Mollison and David Holmgren in the 1970s, embodies two ideas: permanent agriculture and permanent culture. So in addressing the challenge of sustainable living, permaculture deals with both agrarian production and human activity.

At the heart of permaculture philosophy are three core values: earthcare, peoplecare and fairshare. **Earthcare** is the idea of the earth as living entity from which all life springs, including our own. We are part of it, not apart from it. **Peoplecare** embodies the notion of social responsibility. We should help each other develop healthier and more sustainable ways of living. **Fairshare** addresses the problem of limited resources, which we should use fairly and wisely.

If pre-industrial agriculture is labour intensive and industrial agriculture is petroleum intensive, then permaculture is design and information intensive. It draws many ideas from ecology, examining the inter-relationships of elements within a dynamic system. Specifically, each element is analysed in terms of properties, needs and outputs. They are then arranged so each output feeds the needs of an adjacent element. In this manner, intelligent and interconnected webs evolve. Such is the basis of nature's ecosystems.

In this type of design, it can be said that nature is the great teacher, as well as the great provider. All pesticides, fertilizers and energy are supplied by the natural world. Dead leaves become fertile mulch for seeds, birds become controllers of pests, goats become

outstretched wings; **Hacienda San Antonio** has geometric figures; **Altagracia**, in the house of Domingo Gutiérrez, shows a rock with an 'x' and a cross used to make sacrifices to the cult of the sun; **Hacienda La Primavera** has various images; **La Cigueña** shows the southern cross and various animals; and **El Porvenir** has a sundial and what some believe to be an alien being and a representation of the god of death. **La Palmera, Magdalena, San Ramón** and **Mérida** all have interesting petroglyph sites and **Socorro** has some sun calendars.

Moyogalpa

Moyogalpa is the port of entry for arrivals from San Jorge. It is a bustling town of commerce and travel, with a decidedly less indigenous population than the rest of the island. There is little of cultural or natural interest here but because it's a port it does have a lot of hotels. You may decide to spend the night if leaving on an early boat or if climbing Concepción from the western route, otherwise Altagracia, Santo Domingo and San Ramón are all more attractive options.

One interesting excursion (dry season only) is to walk or rent a bicycle to visit **Punta Jesús María,** 4-5 km away. It is well signposted from the road: just before Esquipulas head straight towards the lake. Jesús María has a good beach, a panoramic view of the island and a small café. In the mornings you can watch the fishermen on the long sandbar that extends into the lake. During the end of the dry season there are temporary places to eat and drink.

There is a small museum, cybercafé and artisan store called **Museo Ometepe** ① *up the street that runs from the dock to the church, ½ block from the Pro Credit* lawnmowers and manure becomes the very foundation of life. In this way, problems are seen as possibilities and perma- culture becomes a truly radical system for dealing with – and living in – the world.

But a permaculture design mimics nature in some other more specific ways. Polyculture, multiple crops in the same space, is an attempt to replicate the biodiversity of a naturally occurring ecosystem. This is seen as more desirable than traditional monoculture – typically a large field with a single crop – which tends to erode soil and discourage wildlife. Polyculture techniques include *layering*, which imitates the complex system of canopies in a woodland, with seven consecutive layers planted from tree canopy down to a vertical layer of climbers and vines.

Permaculture also makes frequent use of *guilds*; groups of plants that compliment each other. 'The Sisters of Maize' is a guild well known to the ancient indigenous peoples of the Americas. Climbing beans, which contribute high quantities of nitrogen to the soil, are planted alongside maize stalks which they use for growing support. Together, they provide shelter for squash plants trailing on the ground below, which in turn keep the earth damp and free from weeds. These three plants encourage and strengthen each other when grown together.

By its nature, permaculture is extremely clean and energy efficient. In a perfect permaculture design there is no waste, no wasted energy – just like a mature ecosystem. Or to put it another way, in permaculture, waste and pollution are merely energy in the wrong place. As our earth accelerates towards environmental catastrophe, energy crises and conflicts over resources, perhaps permaculture holds the promise of a more sustainable life for all. At the very least, it is delivering creative new interpretations of our world, and a greener life for some.

office, T569-4225, daily 0800-2000. The artisan crafts available here are hard to find anywhere else in Nicaragua. There are plantain rope hats from Pul, *jícaras* from La Concepción, oil paintings by local artists from Esquipulas and Moyogalpa, seed necklaces from Moyogalpa, wood sculptures from Altagracia and pottery from San Marcos. You can also buy beautiful all-natural canteens known as a *calabazos* – a big round *jícaro* fruit, hollowed and smartly decorated, with a rope strap attached and drinking hole plugged with a corn cob.

Moyogalpa to Altagracia

Most transport uses the southern route to Altagracia as it is faster and in much better condition. The northern route is very rough but is more natural and scenic; it runs east from Moyogalpa along the north shores through the tiny villages of **La Concepción, La Flor** and **San Mateo**. There are commanding views of the volcano with its forests and 1957 lava flow visible beyond rock-strewn pasture and highland banana plantations. To the north lies the deep blue of Lake Nicaragua. A fork to the left leads to the coast and the small, indigenous settlement of **San Marcos**; to the right it leads to **Altagracia**, past a baseball field (matches on Sundays) and a school. A tiny chapel marks your arrival in Altagracia. The town entrance is just southeast of the cemetery, and is perhaps the most scenic in all Nicaragua with its backdrop of Volcán Concepción.

Moyogalpa translates as the 'place of mosquitoes', but there aren't really any more here than elsewhere in the region.

The southern route, which is more heavily populated and completely paved with cement cobblestones, is the quickest route to Altagracia, Playa Santo Domingo and the Maderas side of Ometepe. The road passes the town of **Esquipulas**, where it is rumoured that the great Chief Niqueragua may have been buried, and the village of **Los Angeles**, which has some of the oldest known evidence of ancient settlers on the island, dated at 1500 BC. Between Los Angeles and the next settlement, San José del Sur, a turning leads to the **Numismatic Museum** ⓘ *0800-1730*, which has a collection of bills and coins, some very old. At the fairly developed **San José del Sur**, evacuated in 1998 under threat of massive mudslides from Concepción, the road rises to spectacular views of Volcán Maderas across the lake.

Just past San José del Sur is the rough, narrow access road to **Charco Verde**, a big pond with a popular legend of a wicked sorcerer, Chico Largo, who was said to have shape-shifting powers. Today his discarnate spirit guards the pond, ruling all those who have sold their soul to him. In the rainy season this is one of the most scenic parts of the island. At the end of the road are a petrol storage tank and a twig-covered beach. There is some interesting lodging near the legendary pond (see Sleeping, page 150). Just east is the **Bahía de Sinacapa**, which hides an ancient volcanic cone under its waters, along with an island called **Quiste**. There is a good lookout nearby, **Mirador del Diablo**, where you can breathe in the best sunset on the island. **La Unión** is the highway's closest pass to the active cone and a good place to see howler monkeys. The road then passes through the indigenous village of **Urbaite** where the church's bell tower, typical of a design peculiar to the island, is separate from the church, built alongside it so as to ride out the island's frequent seismic events. After Urbaite, there is a right turn to the isthmus and Maderas volcano (see below). The road to Altagracia then passes the delightful little church at **El Chipote** (this is the entrance to the climb of the eastern face of Volcán Concepción) and enters the south of Altagracia.

Altagracia

This calm, unpretentious town is the most important on the island and it hides its population of around 20,000 well – except at weekends (there is usually dancing on Saturday nights, not to mention the odd fight among the local cowboys) and during festivals and holidays (see page 151). Altagracia predates the arrival of the Spanish and was once home to two tribes who named their villages **Aztagalpa** (egrets' nest) and **Cosonigalpa**. The tribes were divided by what is now the road from Parque Central to the cemetery. Their less than amicable relationship forced the people of Cosonigalpa to flee to what is now San José del Sur and to the bay of Sinacapa. The Spanish renamed the village, but the population remains largely indigenous. In the shade of the trees next to Altagracia's crumbling old church, built in 1924 to replace a much older colonial temple, is a **sculpture park** which contains some of the most famous pre-Columbian statues in Nicaragua. They are estimated to date from AD 800 and represent human forms and their alter egos or animal protectors. The most famous are the eagle and the jaguar, which is believed to have been the symbol of power. West of the plaza, the **Museo de Ometepe** ⓘ *Tue-Sun 0900-1200, 1400-1600, US$2*, has displays of archaeology and covers local ethnographic and environmental themes (in Spanish only).

Playa Santo Domingo

The sweeping sandy beach at Santo Domingo is reached via the southern road from Moyogalpa (see above) or from Altagracia's southern exit. There are signs, which mark the turning on to a dirt road that can be very difficult in sections during the rainy season. The road winds through plantain plantations, past a miniature church, down a steep paved section and across a tiny bridge where women do laundry in the creek. The water is very clean upstream from here and great for swimming at its source, **El Ojo de Agua** ⓘ *0700-1800, USS$1*, where you'll find a small ranch and some gentle

Romeo and Ometepetl – a lake story

Centuries ago, there was no Lake Nicaragua or any islands. Instead, there was a lush valley with fruit-bearing trees, full of deer and the songs of beautiful birds. This was a valley of the gods. Tipotani, the supreme god, sent Coapol to watch over the valley and for that it was called the Valle de Coapolca. Coapol was not alone in his duties; other gods such as Hecaltl, Xochipilli, Oxomogo and Cachilweneye helped tend the garden. But despite all the lush trees, green fields and healthy animal life, there was no source of water in the valley. Its lushness was created and maintained by the gods. Several tribes lived around the edge of the Valle de Coapolca and entered the valley often, to use its forests for hunting, to pick its wild fruits and for romance.

One summer afternoon the beautiful Ometepetl from the Nicaraguas tribe met the brave and handsome warrior Nagrando, from the neighbouring Chorotega tribe, and it was love at first sight. The god Xochipilli sent harmonious breezes across the pastures, while other gods offered gentle rain and singing birds. The gods married them for this life and the afterlife. But Ometepetl and Nagrando had to keep their love secret, as their tribes were rivals and war was possible at any moment. (The tribal chiefs had long since passed laws that their sons and daughters could not mix.) One day when they came to the valley to make love, they were seen by some soldiers and Nagrando was sentenced to death for his insolence. The supreme god Tipotani warned the couple of impending danger and the couple was led to a safe hiding place. Still, they knew that the chief's pronouncement was inexorable and they decided they would rather die together than live apart.

After reciting a prayer to the gods, they held each other tightly, kissed an eternal kiss and slit their wrists. Their blood began to fill the valley; the skies went dark and opened in torrential rains. Thunder clapped across the sky and rain filled with meteorites, as shooting stars ran across the heavens. Nagrando, delirious and writhing in pain, rose to his feet, stumbled and fell away from Ometepetl. The valley filled with water. The gods looked on and Nagrando's body came to rest as the island of Zapatera, while Ometepetl became the island of Ometepe, her breasts rising above the waters of the torrential floods. The instigators of the tragedy, those who put politics above love, were drowned in the floodwaters and the punished bodies from each tribe formed the archipelagos of Las Isletas and Solentiname.

walking trails. The road rises over a pass that allows a view of both cones and then dips into beautiful (and cooler) tropical dry forest and Santo Domingo.

This long sandy coastline is one of the prettiest freshwater beaches in Nicaragua and, with the forest-covered Volcán Maderas looming at the beach's end, it is truly exotic. The warm water, gentle waves and gradual shelf make it a great swimming beach. If you wade out you'll be able to see the cone of Concepción over the forest; a dual volcano swimming experience. The lake here is reminiscent of a sea (visitors are often surprised to see horses going down to drink from its shores, forgetting that it is fresh water). On this side of the island the trade winds blow nearly all year round and keep the heat and insects at bay. At times the wind is so strong that some visitors find it offensive. During the early rainy season there can be many gnats if the wind dies. The width of the beach depends on the time of year: at the end of the dry season there's a broad swathe of sand and at the end of the rainy season bathers are pushed up to the

Mark Twain – "The Nicaragua route forever!"

Samuel Clemens, better known as Mark Twain, first saw the Pacific Coast of Nicaragua on 29 December 1866, after a long boat journey from San Francisco. He described the approach to the bay of San Juan del Sur thus: "…bright green hills never looked so welcome, so enchanting, so altogether lovely, as these do those that lie here within a pistol-shot of us." Travelling on the inter-oceanic steamship line of Cornelius Vanderbilt between the Pacific and the Caribbean, Twain was writing a series of letters to a San Francisco newspaper *Alta California*, letters that were published in book form over 60 years later, in 1940, in a collection called *Travels with Mr Brown*.

He crossed Nicaragua in three days. The first was spent overland in a horse-drawn carriage from San Juan del Sur to the port of La Virgen on Lake Nicaragua. During the only land part of his journey from San Francisco to New York he was amazed at the beauty of the Nicaraguan people and their land. He and his fellow passengers gleefully exclaimed: "the Nicaragua route forever!" It was at the end of that 3½-hour carriage ride that he first saw the great lake and Island of Ometepe. "They look so isolated from the world and its turmoil – so tranquil, so dreamy, so steeped in slumber and eternal repose." He crossed the lake in a steamship to San Carlos and boarded another that would take him down the Río San Juan to El Castillo, where passengers had to walk past the old fort to change boats beyond the rapids there. "About noon we swept gaily around a bend in the beautiful river, and a stately old adobe castle came into view – a relic of the olden time – of the old buccaneering days of Morgan and his merry men."

Back on the river, Twain enjoyed the beauty that today is the Indio-Maíz Biological Reserve: "All gazed in rapt silent admiration for a long time as the exquisite panorama unfolded itself. The character of the vegetation on the banks had changed from a rank jungle to dense, lofty, majestic forests. There were hills, but the thick drapery of the vines spread upwards, terrace upon terrace, and concealed them like a veil. Now and then a rollicking monkey scampered into view or a bird of splendid plumage floated through the sultry air, or the music of some invisible songster welled up out of the forest depths. The changing vistas of the river ever renewed the intoxicating picture; corners and points folding backward revealed new wonders beyond."

edge of the small drop-off that backs the beach. It is not unusual to see a school of freshwater sardines (silversides) bubbling out of the water being chased by a predator. Around the beach there are many magpie jays, parrots, vultures and hawks.

Santo Domingo can be used as a jumping-off point for the ultra-tranquil Maderas side of the island or for climbing either volcano. Facilities in Santo Domingo are limited to the hotels (see page 150), a micro-store and one bar; there is no town. Stock up on water or cookies at the small store in front of the parking lot of the Villa Paraíso.

Balgües and around

The road towards Maderas is sandy and ends at Santa Cruz, a fork leads left to Balgües or right to San Ramón. The road to Balgües is rocky and scenic although the village itself is a little sad in appearance. The people are warm and friendly, however, especially if you are travelling with a local. The feeling that everyone knows everybody on Ometepe is magnified here as most Ometepinos have a relative around every corner. This village is the entrance to the trailhead for the climb to the summit of Maderas (see box, page 143). There are several interesting **organic farms** in the area, including the famous Finca Magdelena, Finca Campestre and Michael's farm, where you can study permaculture techniques (see box, page 144)

Mérida

From the fork at Santa Cruz the road goes south past small homes and ranches and through the towering palms of the attractive village of Mérida, in an area that was once an expansive farm belonging to the Somoza family. The road drops down to lake level and curves east past an old pier where Somoza's coffee production used to be shipped out to the mainland. There are some good places to stay here (see page 151). From the old dock you can kayak the canals of Istián and observe bird and mammal life.

San Ramón

Further along the eastern shores of Maderas is the affluent town San Ramón. Some foreigners and wealthy Nicaraguans have built vacation homes here and there is a private dock for their boats. The 'biological station' is the starting point for a once gorgeous hike up the west face of Maderas Volcano to a lovely 40-m cascade, also called San Ramón. The forest here is home to white face and howler monkeys and many parrots and trogons come to nest. This is a much less athletic climb than the hike to the summit, but sadly it has lost much of its charm thanks to the forest management of the biological station. The path to the cascade has been largely destroyed by the deforestation of the middle slopes that once protected the forest reserve from erosion and landslides. The forest has been cleared in order to plant fruit trees and create grazing land for cattle. What's more, big hissing pipes have been installed that follow the trail all the way up to the cascade. The pipes are used to siphon off water that used to feed a precious mountain stream; it is now channelled to irrigate the biological station's plantain, avocado and other cash crops. The forest is lovely and the cascade is still pretty, but most of the wildlife is now forced to go elsewhere to look for shelter and water. In addition you must pay an entrance fee to an armed guard at the entrance to the biological station, to be able to enter the trail; these fees are said to go towards trail maintenance.

Note that it is sunny and hotter on this side of the mountain with less breeze from the trade winds from the east.

Transport is not as frequent on this side of the island and you may have a long walk if you are not on a tour. Hotels and Moyogalpa tour companies offer packages that are reasonable if you can get together at least two other hikers.

Sleeping

Almost all lodges serve meals.

Moyogalpa *p144*

C American Café and Hotel, muelle municipal, 100 vrs arriba, T645-7193. Excellent value, comfortable, well furnished and immaculately clean rooms, some with a/c, cheaper without (**D**). All have good, new mattresses and hot water. Italian, German, Spanish and English spoken. Recommended.

D Ometepetl, muelle municipal, 10 vrs arriba, T569-4276, ometepetlng@hotmail.com (also reservations for Istián, Santo Domingo, below). This long-standing favourite has rooms with a/c (**E** without) and bath. There's a pool and a popular restaurant attached, vehicle rental and tours on request.

E-G Hospedaje Central, muelle municipal, 1 c sur, 3 c arriba, T569-4262, hospedaje central ometepe@hotmail.com. This brightly coloured Moyogalpa cheapie has dorms (**G**)

For an explanation of the sleeping and eating price codes used in this guide, see inside the front cover. Other relevant information is found in Essentials, see pages 23-27.

and private rooms (**E**), but has seen better days. In the owner's absence there have been reports of theft and other serious offences. Check that these, and related issues, have been reigned in.

F Arenas Negras, opposite Hotel Ometepetl, T883-6167. 10 simple rooms, small but clean, 9 with private bath and fan. Friendly and basic.

F Hotel Bahía, muelle municipal, 120 vrs arriba, T470-3473. Very basic rooms with fan. Nice and breezy upstairs.

Moyogalpa to Altagracia *p145*

B-C Hotel Charco Verde Inn, almost next to the lagoon, San José del Sur, T887-9302, www.charcoverde.com.ni. Pleasant cabañas with private bath, a/c, terrace (**B**), and doubles with private bath and fan (**C**). Good reports.

C-E Finca Playa Venecia, 250 m from the main road, San José del Sur, T872-7668, www.hotelfincavenecia.com.ni. Very chilled out, comfortable lodgings and a lovely lakeside garden. Cabañas overlooking the water are best (**C**), but regular cabañas (**D**) and rooms (**E**) are good too. Recommended.

D El Tesoro del Pirata, Playa Valle Verde, near Charco Verde, Km 15, Carretera a Altagracia, turn towards the lake, T832-2429. Next to a good beach, cabins with private bath and a/c, dorms and rooms with fan and shared bath. Rustic restaurant attached.

E-G Chico Largo Hostel, next to Finca Playa Venecia, T886-4069. Dorms (**G**) and private rooms (**E**), friendly but poor beds.

Altagracia *p146*

E-F Hospedaje Castillo, Parque Central, 1 c sur, ½ c oeste, T552-8744, www.elcastillo.com. Pleasant, friendly hotel with 19 rooms, most have bath outside (**F**). There's a good restaurant, bar and internet facilities attached, credit cards are accepted and TCs changed. They run tours to the volcanoes. Recommended.

E-F Hotel Central, Iglesia, 2 c sur, T552-8770. 19 rooms (**F**) and 6 cabañas (**E**) surround an attractive courtyard, all with private bath and fan. There's a restaurant and bar, bicycle rental, tours and hammocks to rest your weary bones. Friendly and recommended.

F Hospedaje Kencho, Casa Cural, ½ c sur, T820-2246. Basic and scruffy rooms, with or without bath.

Playa Santo Domingo *p146*

B-E Villa Paraíso, beachfront, T563-4675, www.villaparaiso.com.ni. Ometepe's most expensive and luxurious lodging has a beautiful, peaceful setting with 13 stone cabañas (**B**) and 5 rooms (**E**). Most have a/c, private bath, hot water, cable TV, minibar and internet. Some of the rooms have a patio and lake view. The restaurant serves good food, including vegetarian dishes and a fine fruit and pancake breakfast. Various excursions available. Often fully booked, best to reserve in advance.

C Hotel Costa Azul, Villa Paraíso, 50 vrs sur, T644-0327. A new hotel with 7 big, clean rooms. They have a/c, private bath and TV with DVD. There's a restaurant serving *comida típica* and breakfasts. Bike and motorbike rental, tours and guides available.

C-E Finca Santo Domingo, Playa Santo Domingo, north side of Villa Paraíso, T485-6177, www.hotelfincasantodomingo.com. Friendly lakeside hotel with a range of rooms (**D-E**) and bungalows (**C**), all with private bath. There's an artesanía store, bicycle rental and various tours. The restaurant serves *comida típica* and has good views.

E Hotel Buena Vista, Playa Santo Domingo, Villa Paraíso, 150 m norte. Great views, you really feel the lake from here. 10 rooms have private bath and fan, there's a restaurant, a pleasant terrace and hammocks.

E Hotel Istián, Villa Paraíso, 2 km sur, across the road from the beach, T887-9891, reservations through Ometepetl in Moyogalpa. Basic and often seemingly abandoned, friendly, family-run place. Rooms are simple but clean, with fan and bath, cheaper shared (**F**). Nice swimming out front. Restaurant, tours and bike rental.

Balgües and around *p148*

C-G Finca Magdalena, Balgües, T880-2041, www.fincamagdalena.com. Famous co-operative farm run by 26 families, with accommodation in a small cottages, *cabañas* (**C**), doubles (**F**), singles, dorms (**G**) and hammocks. Camping possible. Stunning views across lake and to Concepción. Friendly, basic, and often jammed to the rafters with backpackers. Good meals served for around US$2. You can work in exchange for lodging, 1 month minimum. Locally produced coffee and honey available for sale.

E Albergue Ecológico Porvenir, Santa Cruz, T855-1426. Stunning views at this tranquil, secluded lodge at the foot of Maderas. Rooms are clean, comfortable and tidy, with private bath and fan. Nearby trails run to the crater lake and miradors.

E El Encanto, Santa Cruz, T867-7128, www.goelencanto.com. An experimental 4-ha *finca*. The rooms are good, clean and comfortable, and a there's very pleasant, chilled-out garden. Various tours are available.

F-G Finca Ecológica El Zopilote, about 1 km uphill from Balgües. Funky hostel with dormitory (**G**), hammocks (**G**), camping (**G**) and cabañas (**F**). Full moon parties, use of kitchen and free track up to the volcano.

G Camping Campestre, 500 m east of Balgües, T695-2071, fincacampestre.googlepages.com. English-owned organic farm with camping space near the banana plantation. Lots of opportunities to volunteer, outdoor kitchen and camping equipment provided.

Mérida *p149*

C-G Hacienda Mérida, el Puerto Viejo de Somoza, T868-8973, www.hmerida.com. Popular hostel with a beautiful setting by the lake. Lodgings have wheelchair access and include a mixture of dorms (**G**) and rooms (**D**), some with views (**C**). There's a children's school on-site where you can volunteer, kayak rental, good quality mountain bikes, internet and a range of tours available, including sailing. The restaurant serves fresh, hygienically prepared food – good for vegetarians. Recommended.

San Ramón *p149*

E Ometepe Biological Station, San Ramón, T883-1107. For groups of students only. The station claims to 'manage' 325 ha of conservation land, partly consumed by cash crops. Rooms are simple with shared bath outside. Services include mountain bikes, kayaks, meals (see page 149).

Eating

Moyogalpa *p144*

See also Sleeping, above.

TT Los Ranchitos, muelle municipal, 2 c arriba, ½ c sur, T569-4112. Excellent food, including vegetarian pasta, vegetable soup, chicken in garlic butter. Recommended.

T El Ranchón El Chele, across from Hotel Ometepetl. Coolest place to wait for your boat, good *comida corriente* US$2, relaxed ambience, good fruit juices, dirt floor and thatched roof.

T The American Café, the pier, 100 vrs arriba. Had enough of *gallo pinto*? This is the place for home-made food with flavour, including chilli con carne, pancakes and waffles. They also have a small second-hand book collection.

T Yogi's Café and Bar, Hospedaje Central, ½ c sur. A great place for good American food, beer and big-screen movies. Yogi is an enormous, but gentle, black labrador and not to be confused with the owner, Jerry, who is a very decent fellow and always open to philosophical conversation.

Festivals and events

Moyogalpa *p144*

Jul The town's patron saint festival (**Santa Ana**) is a very lively affair. Processions begin on 23 Jul in the barrio La Paloma and continue for several days. On 25 Jul there is a lovely dance with girls dressed in indigenous costume and on 26 Jul there's a huge party with bullfights at a ring north of the church. Dates for some of the festivities vary according to the solar cycle.

Altagracia *p146*

Oct-Nov The town's patron saint, **San Diego de Alcalá**, is celebrated from 28 Oct to 18 Nov with many dances and traditions, particularly the **Baile del Zompopo** (the dance of the leaf-cutter ant), which is famous throughout the country. The indigenous population celebrate their harvest god, Xolotl, every Nov. The story goes that one year when the harvest was being annihilated by red ants, the tribe shamans practised some ritual sacrifices and instructed the people to do a special dance to drums with branches of various trees. The disaster and starvation were averted and a tradition was born. When the Franciscans arrived in 1613 they brought with them an image of the saint of San Diego whose days coincided with that of the annual celebration for Xolotl and the red-ant dance. Over time, the friars convinced the indigenous locals to substitute one god for another, and the dance is still performed on 17 Nov.

Dec The **Purísima** celebrations to the Virgin Mary on 7 Dec are a marathon affair here of singing to a large, heavily decorated image of Santa María on the back of a pick-up truck in what is truly a Fellini-esque setting.

Activities and tours

Moyogalpa *p144*

Biking and motorbiking

Most hotels offer bicycles for around US$6 per day, some have motorbikes (but not mopeds) for US$30. In Moyogalpa, try **Tyrone's Bar** near the dock. The best mountain bikes are at **Hacienda Mérida** (see page 151), which you should consider if attempting to cross the rough terrain on the north side of Concepción or east side of Maderas.

Canopy tour

Canopy Sendero Los Monos, Playa Santo Domingo. A baby canopy tour, very much for beginners, with 4 cables and 6 platforms, US$10. Suitable for children aged 4 and up.

Kayaking

Hacienda Mérida (see page 151), has kayaks for those wishing to explore the lush Istián canals. Dawn is best, when wildlife is more active and visible.

Organic farming

Bona Fide, Balgües, www.projectbonafide.com. Also known as Michael's farm, Bona Fide offers innovative courses in permaculture as well as volunteer opportunities for those wishing to learn more about the science and work of organic farming. An interesting project (see box, page 144).

Sailing

Hacienda Mérida (see Sleeping, page 151), is the proud owner of a sailing boat that can apparently make it as far as the Corn Islands off the Caribbean Coast. In addition to a sail, it has an onboard motor that makes it ready for the Río San Juan. Trips don't have to be so ambitious, talk to the gregarious owner, Alvaro, about shorter expeditions or whatever you have in mind.

Tour operators

Most of the Managua and Granada tour operators offer Ometepe packages that can be useful if travelling in a group or if you want a tour with bilingual guide service.

Ometepe Expeditions, 75 m from the port in Moyogalpa (in front of Hotel Ometepetl), T664-6910, ometepexpeditions@hotmail.com. A highly reputable agency that worked with the BBC to guide a group of disabled people to the summit of Concepción. They offer a range of tours including half- and full-day hikes to the volcanoes and cloud forests. Experienced, knowledgeable and helpful. English-speaking guides include **Bermán Gómez**, T836-8360 and **Eduardo Manzanares**, T873-7714. Recommended.

Unión Guías de Ometepe, T827-7714, www.ugometepe.com. Formed in 2006, this union of 30 guides offers an interesting range of half and full day tours, including hikes up Maderas and Concepción.

Transport

All times are Mon-Sat; on Sun there are very few buses. All schedules subject to change; always confirm times if planning a long journey involving connections.

Moyogalpa *p144*

Bus

Buses wait for the boats in Moyogalpa and run to **Altagracia** hourly, 0530-1830, US$1, 1 hr. To **San Ramón** 0815, US$1.25, 3 hrs. To **Mérida**, 0830, 1430, 1630, US$2, 2½ hrs. To **Balgües**, 1030, 1530, US$2, 2 hrs. For **Charco Verde**, take any bus to Altagracia that uses the southern route.

Car hire

Toyota Rent a Car, Hotel Ometepetl, T459-4276. A good strong 4WD is a must, US$35-50 for 12 hrs, US$60 for 24 hrs. They can also provide a driver, though advance notice is needed.

Taxi

Pick-up and van taxis wait for the ferry, price is per journey not per person, some have room for 4 passengers, others 2, the rest go in the back, which is the far better view, but dusty in dry season. To **Altagracia** US$12-15, to **Santo Domingo** US$20-25, to **Mérida** US$30. Try **Transporte Ometepe**, T695-9905, robertometeour@yahoo.es.

Altagracia *p146*
Bus
For **Playa Santo Domingo** use any bus to San Ramón, Mérida or Balgües. To **Moyogalpa**, hourly, 0530-1830, US$1, 1hr. To **Balgües**, 0430, 0930, 1140, 1330, 1700, US$1, 1 hr. To **Mérida**, 1030, 1600, 1730, US$1, 2 hrs.

Ferry
The port of Altagracia is called San Antonio and is 2 km north of the town; pick-up trucks meet the boat that passes between Granada and San Carlos. To **San Carlos**, Mon and Thu 1800-1900, US$8, 11 hrs. To **Granada**, Tue and Fri, around 0000, US$4, 3½ hrs.

Lancha
The *Mozorola* departs from San Antonio (Altagracia) Tue, Wed, Fri at 0730; Sat 0530, 2½ hrs, US$2. An apparently scenic journey.

Directory

Moyogalpa *p144*
Banks Banco Procredit, muelle municipal, 3 c arriba, with Visa ATM and dollar changing facility, but best to bring all the cash you need. There's a Western Union attached. You can also change money (but not travellers cheques) in the 2 biggest grocery stores (1 opposite Hotel Bahía) or in hotels. Comercial Hugo Navas also gives cash advances on credit cards (MasterCard and Visa). **Hospital** T569-4247. **Internet** Cyber Ometepe, also known as Museo Ometepe, on main road up from dock, T569-4225. Comercial Arcia (US$2 per hour), very slow. Yogi's Bar (see above) has high-speed Wi-Fi. **Police** T569-4231. **Port Authority** T569-4109. **Post office and telephone** Enitel, T569-4100, from the dock, 2 c arriba, 1½ sur, for both postal and telephone services.

Altagracia *p146*
Internet Hospedaje Castillo, US$2 per hr. They will also change TCs (at a poor rate).

San Juan del Sur and around

→ *Population: 14,621. Altitude: 4 m. Colour map 3, C4.*

Although it has become one of Nicaragua's central tourist destinations, San Juan del Sur has not lost its small town, fishing village feel, with an abundance of little boats anchored just off its rich, golden sands. But the many kilometres of Pacific shoreline north and south of the town's sweeping half-moon bay are even prettier, drawing increasing numbers of visitors to their luxury ecolodges, isolated surfing spots and empty, wave-swept beaches. The real attraction is the olive ridley turtles that have been coming to this stretch of coast for thousands of years – sometimes as many as 20,000 over a four-night period. The dry season along Nicaragua's Pacific Coast is very parched and brown, but most of the year the landscape is fluorescent green, shaded by rows of mango trees and dotted with small, attractive ranches with flower-festooned front gardens. Roadside stalls offer many fruits, such as watermelon, mango, níspero *and some of the biggest papaya you'll see anywhere.*

» *For Sleeping, Eating and other listings, see pages 161-164.*

San Juan del Sur » *pp161-164.*

Not long ago this was a secret place, a tiny coastal paradise on Nicaragua's Pacific Coast. In recent years, however, this little town on a big bay has become very popular, first as an escape from the built-up beaches across the international border in Costa Rica to the south, then as a magnet for real estate developers, US retirees and the international wave hunting crowd. In addition, cruise ships now anchor in its deeper waters and tourists have begun to arrive in quantity. San Juan del Sur is a major destination, increasingly buzzing with activity. And although it has retained its character, it is increasingly starting to resemble Costa Rica, becoming saturated with foreigners looking for (relatively) cheap coastal real estate. Fortunately, the recently elected Sandinista government has put a damper on the land grab, slowing, if not stopping, the destruction of the coast. It's no longer the place to experience a country off the beaten path, but, despite the numerous projects to the north and south of the town, there are still plenty of empty beaches and there is no doubt that the coast here is among the most beautiful in Central America.

Ins and outs

Getting there Most of the buses come from Rivas, though a few leave direct from Managua. If coming from the border with Costa Rica take any bus towards Rivas and step down at the entrance to the Carretera a San Juan del Sur in La Virgen. A taxi is also a possibility from the border with Costa Rica and some hotels will pick you up at the border if you warn them well in advance. If driving, it is very straightforward: look for the turning in La Virgen from the Pan-American Highway (Carretera Panamericana) and head west until the road ends in San Juan del Sur.

Getting around You can get anywhere in San Juan by walking; if you are visiting outlying beaches you can arrange transport with local hotels or the ones at your destination. Additionally, there are many new shuttle services making frequent trips north and south of the town. For the wilder and truly untamed stretches further away from town you will need a decent 4WD or even a boat.

Best time to visit This is one of the driest parts of Nicaragua, with rains coming in late afternoon and blowing over quickly in the wet season and the land looking rather parched half-way through the dry season. Winds from December to March can make exposed beaches uncomfortable with blowing sand and boat excursions a wet experience. For surfing, April to December are the best months. To avoid the crowds don't come at Christmas time or Holy Week; the quietest months are May to June and September to October.

Safety and security Under no circumstances walk to Yankee or Remanso, the beaches north of San Juan del Sur, as this road is a long time haunt of thieves. There have also been reports of unpleasant robberies on the beaches themselves, so check the security situation before heading over. Don't linger on the sand after dark in San Juan del Sur.

Background

Andrés Niño, the first European to navigate the Pacific Coast of Nicaragua, entered the bay of San Juan del Sur in 1523 while looking in vain for a possible passage to Lake Nicaragua or the Caribbean. So San Juan del Sur remained a sleepy fishing village until after Nicaragua's Independence from Spain. It began working as a commercial port in 1827 and in 1830 took the name Puerto Independencia. Its claim to fame came during the California gold rush when thousands of North Americans, anxious to reach California (in the days before the North American railroad was finished), found the shortest route to be by boat from the Caribbean, up the Río San Juan, across Lake Nicaragua, overland for only 18 km from La Virgen (see page 158) and then by boat again from San Juan to California. It is estimated that some 84,880 passengers passed through the town en route to California, and some 75,000 on their way to New York. In 1854 the local lodge, El United

The town of San Juan del Sur is said to have more real estate agents than school children.

States Hotel, charged a whopping US$14 per day for one night's lodging and food of bread, rice, oranges and coffee made from purified water. But as soon as the railway in the USA was completed, the trip through Central America was no longer necessary. The final crossing was made on 8 May 1868 with 541 passengers en route to San Francisco. The steamship was taken over for a while by William Walker to re-supply his invasion forces in the mid-1850s. In 1857, Walker escaped to Panama and later to New Orleans via San Juan. Walker was believed to be attempting another attack on Nicaragua via San Juan del Sur in 1858, but was blocked by the British Navy ship *Vixen*. There was some very tough fighting here during 1979 Revolution in the hills behind San Juan, as Somoza sent his best troops to take on Commandante Zero, Edén Pastora, and his rebel southern front. As victory approached, a ragged group of Somoza's National Guard managed to escape out of San Juan (threatening to burn it down), just as southern Rivas was being taken by Pastora-led rebels. In recent years, San Juan has seen an influx of wealth both from Managua's upper class and foreign capital and there are many expensive homes being built along the low ridge that backs the beach and in the northern part of the bay and beyond.

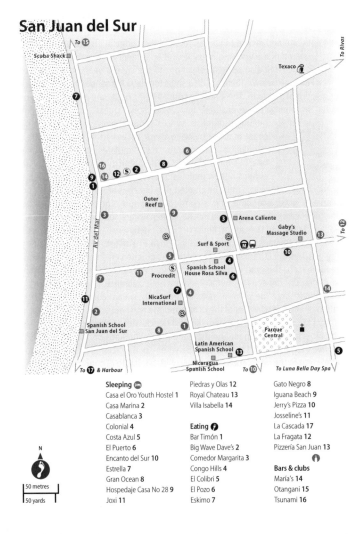

San Juan del Sur

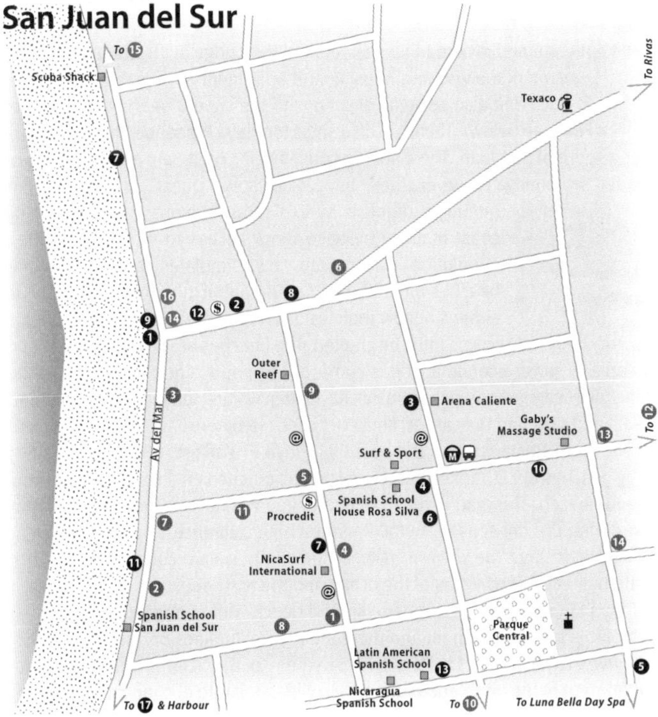

Sleeping
Casa el Oro Youth Hostel **1**
Casa Marina **2**
Casablanca **3**
Colonial **4**
Costa Azul **5**
El Puerto **6**
Encanto del Sur **10**
Estrella **7**
Gran Ocean **8**
Hospedaje Casa No 28 **9**
Joxi **11**
Piedras y Olas **12**
Royal Chateau **13**
Villa Isabella **14**

Eating
Bar Timón **1**
Big Wave Dave's **2**
Comedor Margarita **3**
Congo Hills **4**
El Colibri **5**
El Pozo **6**
Eskimo **7**
Gato Negro **8**
Iguana Beach **9**
Jerry's Pizza **10**
Josseline's **11**
La Cascada **17**
La Fragata **12**
Pizzería San Juan **13**

Bars & clubs
María's **14**
Otangani **15**
Tsunami **16**

N
50 metres
50 yards

Mark Twain described San Juan as "a few tumble-down frame shanties" in 1866, and said the town was "crowded with horses, mules and ambulances (horse carriages) and half-clad yellow natives". Today there are plenty of half-clad people, though less and less are natives and most are enjoying the sun and sea. Most of the horses and all of the mules have been replaced by bicycles, which is the preferred form of transport.

What makes San Juan del Sur different from other Nicaraguan beach towns is the growing ex-patriot crowd that has migrated here from across Europe and North America. San Juan is a natural bay of light brown sand, clear waters and 200 m cliffs that mark its borders. The sunsets are placed perfectly out over the Pacific, framed by the boats bobbing in the bay. The beach is lined by numerous small restaurants that offer the fresh catch of the day, along with lobster and shrimp. Surfers can climb in a boat and find access to very good breaks along the same coastline, one that has a year-round offshore breeze. Deep sea fishing is also possible. Swimming is best at the northern end of the beach. See Activities and tours, page 163.

Pacific Coast south of San Juan del Sur » p162.

If staying in San Juan del Sur most of these beaches are easier reached by boat for a day trip.

A well-kept earth and rock road runs south from the bridge at the entrance to San Juan del Sur. Signs mark the way to a housing and apartment development called Parque Marítimo El Coco and also serve as directions to the superb beach and turtle nesting site of **La Flor** (see below). There are also signs for **Playa Remanso**, the first beach with lodging south of San Juan. There are big houses being built here above a pretty beach good for swimming. However, there have been some questions raised about the treatment of locals by this establishment and others along the coast that are trying to block access to the coast by the local population. Nicaraguan law stipulates that all Nicaraguan beaches must be open to the public (the term 'private beach' is either a hollow promise or they are breaking the law), but the law does not clarify how access must be granted. The beaches are rapidly being shut down to people of lower economic status (90% of the population), creating hard feeling among the Nicaraguans whose families have been visiting these beaches for hundreds of years and now find they are off limits because foreigners have suddenly grown fond of them. Both **Remanso** and the beautiful **Playa El Yankee**, to the south, are good surfing beaches but El Yankee has a hotel project planned on disputed land in front of a gorgeous beach. The road is rough here and you will have to cross streams that are small during the dry season, but will require high-clearance and 4WD vehicles from June to November. The drive is over a beautifully scenic country road with many elevation changes and vistas of the ocean and the northern coast of Costa Rica.

Playa El Coco is a long copper-coloured beach with strong surf most of the year. Much of it is backed by forest and there are several families of howler monkeys that live between here and **La Flor**, two beaches to the south. There is a growing development at the north end of the beach with a mixture of condos, bungalows and homes for rent. This is the closest lodging to La Flor without camping. The housing complex at Playa El Coco is involved in community projects which includes free schooling for local children and the beach is open to the public. Prices for rental range from one night in a one-room apartment for US$85-1900 for one week in a big house.

Refugio de Vida Silvestre La Flor

US$10, US$2.50 student discount, access by 4WD or on foot.

Just past Playa El Coco and 18 km from the highway at San Juan del Sur, the La Flor wildlife refuge protects tropical dry forest, mangroves, estuary and 800 m of beachfront. This beautiful, sweeping cove with light tan sand and many trees is an important site for nesting sea turtles (see box, page 159). The best time to come is between August and November. Rangers protect the multitudinous arrivals during high season and are very happy to explain, in Spanish, about the animals' reproductive habits. Sometimes turtles arrive in their thousands, usually over a period of four days. Even if you don't manage to see the turtles, there is plenty of other wildlife. Many birds live in small, protected mangroves at the south end of the beach and you may witness a sunset migration of hundreds of hermit crabs at the north end, all hobbling back to the beach in their infinitely diverse shells. Camping can be provided (limited amount of tents) during the turtle season, US$25 per night. Bring a hammock and mosquito netting, as insects are vicious at dusk. The ranger station sells soft drinks and will let you use their outhouse; improved facilities are planned.

Pacific Coast north of San Juan del Sur » p162.

There is an unpaved access road to beaches north of San Juan del Sur at the entrance to the town. It is possible to travel the entire length of the Rivas coast to Chacocente from here, though it is quite a trip as the road does not follow the coast but moves inland to **Tola** (west of Rivas) and then back to the ocean, and the surface is changeable from hard pack dirt to sand, stone and mud. Some of the beaches in this part of Rivas are spectacular with white sand and rugged forested hillsides and, like the coastline south of San Juan del Sur, they are being quickly cordoned off. This area is seeing big development and building projects, including gated communities and retirement resorts, and Tola itself has become a service town for the growing numbers of constructions workers.

In the rainy season a 4WD or sturdy horse is needed for these trails.

Playa Marsella has plenty of signs that mark the exit to the beach. It is a slowly growing resort set on a pleasant beach, but not one of the most impressive in the region. North of here, **Los Playones** is playing host to ever-increasing crowds of surfers with a scruffy beer shack and hordes of daily shuttle trucks. The waves are good for beginners, but are often heavily oversubscribed. **Maderas** is the next beach along, where many shuttles claim to take you (they don't, they drop you at the car park at Los Playones). This is a pleasant, tranquil spot, good for swimming and host to some affordable lodgings, best booked in advance. **Bahía Majagual** is the next bay north, a lovely white sand beach tucked into a cove. There was once a famous backpackers lodge here, but this has closed and something new (and no doubt upmarket) is being constructed in its place.

On the road to Majagual before reaching the beach is the private entrance to **Morgan's Rock** a multimillion dollar private nature reserve and reforestation project with tree farming, incorporating more than 800 ha of rare tropical dry coastal forest and the stunningly beautiful Playa Ocotal. Don't even think about dropping by to check it out without first digging deep in your wallet as this is the most expensive place to sleep in Nicaragua and, most reports say, worth every *peso*. While the hotel may not win awards for social consciousness, it is on the progressive edge of conservation and sustainable tourism in ecological terms. If you can afford a few nights here, it is one of the prettiest places on the Central American coast and the cabins are set up high on a bluff wrapped in forest overlooking the ocean and beach (see Sleeping, page 162).

To the north of Morgan's are more pristine beaches, like **Manzanillo** and **El Gigante** and all have development projects. One that has really got off the ground is **Rancho Santana** ⓘ *www.ranchosantana.com*. This is a massive housing and resort project located on the west side of the earthen highway between Tola and Las Salinas, behind a large ostentatious gate and a grimacing armed guard. Rancho Santana is a very organized and well developed project for luxury homes built by foreigner investors and retirees. The popular surf spot Playa Rosada is included in the complex's claim of four 'private' beaches. California-style hilltop luxury homes are being built here with stunning Pacific views and the 'state within a state' ambience includes a slick clubhouse called *Oxford* and a private helipad.

Further north from Rancho Santana is the legendary surf spot **Popoyo**. This place is getting crowded with surfers from around the world and with good reason. The surf here is very big with a good swell and still has waves when the rest of the ocean looks like a swimming pool. There is also lodging at a surf camp here. See www.surf nicaragua.com for information.

One of the prettiest beaches on the northern Rivas coast is **Playa Conejo**, now taken over by **Hotel Punta Teonoste.** It is located near Las Salinas with very funky and creative bungalows along the beach and a memorable circular bar right above the sand. Sadly the land behind the bungalows is completely treeless and the sun and wind are ferocious here in the dry season. Having said that, this is the nearest decent accommodation to Chacocente Wildlife Refuge, 7 km north of the hotel (see below) and access via the highway from Ochomogo is year round.

Refugio de Vida Silvestre Río Escalante Chacocente

ⓘ *www.chacocente.info. There is a US$4 entrance fee to the park. There is no public transport to the park and a 4WD is necessary during the turtle-laying season from Aug to Nov. There are two entrances to the area, one from Santa Teresa south of Jinotepe. Follow that road until the pavement ends and then turn left to the coast and El Astillero. Before you reach the bay of Astillero you will see a turning to the right with a sign for Chacocente. At Km 80 from the Pan-American Highway is the bridge over the Río Ochomogo that separates the province of Granada from Rivas; the Pan-American Highway is in excellent condition here as it continues south to Rivas. On the south side of the bridge a rough dirt road runs west to the Pacific Ocean. This is a 40-km journey through small friendly settlements to the same turning for the reserve.*

Tropical dry forest and beach make up Chacocente Wildlife Refuge. The beach is most famous for the **sea turtles** that come to nest every year. This is one of the four most important sea turtle nesting sites on the entire Pacific seaboard of the American continent (another of the four, the **La Flor Wildlife Refuge**, is further south, see above). The park is also a critical tropical dry forest reserve for the Nicaraguan Pacific and a good place to see giant iguanas and varied bird life during the dry season, when visibility in the forest is at its best. The beach itself is lovely too, with a long open stretch of sand that runs back into the forest, perfect for stringing up a hammock. Camping is permitted – this may be the most beautiful camping spot along the coast – but no facilities are provided and you will need to come well stocked with water and supplies. The Nicaraguan environmental protection agency **MARENA** has built attractive cabins for park rangers and scientists and it is possible that they will rent them to visitors in the future. At the moment the rangers seem surprised to see visitors but they are very sincere in their efforts to protect the wildlife and diversity of the reserve.

La Virgen to the border

La Virgen

At the turning from the Pan-American Highway for the highway to San Juan del Sur, this little windswept village has some less-than-clean beaches and a stunning view of the big lake and Ometepe. If you come early in the morning you may see men fishing in the lake while floating in the inner tube of a truck. This curious sight is particular to this small village. The fishermen arrive at the beach in the early morning and blow up the big tyre tubes, tie bait to a thick nylon cord and wade out, seated in the tubes, as

Sea turtles – the miracle of life

Every year between July and February thousands of beautiful olive ridley turtles (*Lepidochelys olivacea*) arrive at La Flor and Chacocente, two wildlife refuges set aside to aid in their age-old battle against predators with wings, pincers, four legs and two.

The sea turtles, measuring up to 80 cm and weighing more than 90 kg, come in waves. Between August and November as many as 20,000 arrive to nest in a four-night period, just one of many arrivals during the nesting season. Each turtle digs a hole with her rear flippers and patiently lays up to 100 eggs, covers them and returns to the water: mission complete. For 45 days the eggs incubate under the tropical Nicaraguan sand. The temperature in the sand will determine the gender of the turtle: temperatures below 29°C will result in males and 30°C and above will be females, though very high temperatures will kill the hatchlings. After incubation in the sand, they hatch all at once and the little turtles run down to the sea. If they survive they will travel as far as the Galapagos Islands.

The huge leatherback turtle (*Dermochelys coriacea*), which can grow up to 2 m and weigh over 300 kg, is less common than the olive ridley and arrives alone to lay her eggs.

Turtle eggs are a traditional food for the Nicaraguans, and although they are not eaten in large quantities, poaching is always a threat. Park rangers and, during peak times, armed soldiers protect the turtles from animal and human threats in both Chacocente and La Flor wildlife refuges. If you have the chance to witness it, don't miss out and get talking to the rangers who have a great passion for their work. Extreme caution must be exercised during nesting season as, even if you see no turtles on the beach, you are most likely to be walking over nests. Limit flash photography to a minimum and never aim a flash camera at turtles coming out of the water.

Camping is the best way to see the turtles in Chacocente or La Flor, but a pre-dawn trip from either San Juan del Sur or Playa El Coco to La Flor, or from Las Salinas to Chacocente is also possible.

far as 3 km from the coast. When they get out of the water, often fully clothed, the cord can have 15 or more fish hanging from it.

In the 19th century the lake steamships of Cornelius Vanderbilt stopped here (after a journey from New York via the Río San Juan) to let passengers off for an overland journey by horse-drawn carriage to the bay of San Juan del Sur. The North American novelist Mark Twain came here in 1866, doing the trip from west to east (San Francisco–San Juan del Sur–La Virgen–Lake Nicaragua–San Carlos–Río San Juan–San Juan del Norte–New York). He gazed out at the lake and waxed lyrical about the splendour of Lake Nicaragua and Ometepe from his viewpoint in La Virgen (see box, page 148). The dock used by the steamships is no longer visible and there is some debate among the villagers as to where it actually was.

It is here that the distance between the waters of Lake Nicaragua and the Pacific Ocean is shortest, only 18 km blocking a natural passageway between the Atlantic and Pacific oceans. Incredibly the continental divide lies yet further west, just 3 km from the Pacific; the east face of this low coastal mountain ridge drains all the way to the Caribbean Sea via the lake and Río San Juan. The road is paved to San Juan de Sur and follows to a great extent the path used in the 1800s by carriages and ox carts for the inter-oceanic gold rush route of Vanderbilt. What had previously been a full-day's

Border essentials: Peñas Blancas – Costa Rica

The border is your last chance to sell córdobas if leaving or sell colones if arriving.

Crossing by bus or on foot:
When entering Nicaragua (immigration open 0600-2000), show your passport at the border, completing Costa Rican exit formalities, and then walk the 500 m to the Nicaraguan border controls. International bus passengers have to disembark and queue for immigration to stamp their passport. Then you must unload your baggage and wait in line for the customs official to arrive. You will be asked to open your bags, the official will give them a cursory glance and then you reload. Passports and tickets will be checked again back on the bus. For travellers not on a bus, there are plenty of small helpers on hand. Allow 45 minutes to complete the formalities. You will have to pay between US$5-8 to enter Nicaragua plus a US$1 *alcaldía* charge. If you come before 0800 or after 1700 Mon-Fri or at any time at the weekend, you will have to pay US$12 plus the US$1 mayor's charge.

When leaving Nicaragua, pay US$1 mayor's fee to enter the customs area at the border and then complete formalities in the new customs building where you pay US$2 to have your passport checked 0800-1700 or US$4 0600-0800 and after 1700 Mon-Fri or any time on Sat and Sun. Then walk the 500 m to the Costa Rican border and simply have your passport stamped. Buses and taxis are available from the border – hitching is difficult.

Crossing by private vehicle
There is no fuel going into Nicaragua until Rivas (37 km) When entering Nicaragua, go through *Migración* then find an inspector who will fill out the preliminary form to be taken to *Aduana*. At the *Vehículo Entrando* window, the vehicle permit is typed up and the vehicle stamp is put in your passport. Next, go to *Tránsito* to pay for the car permit. Finally, ask the inspector again to give the final check. Fumigation is mandatory, US$1.

When leaving the country, first pay your exit tax at an office at the end of the control station, receipt given. Then come back for your exit stamp, and complete the *Tarjeta de Control Migratorio*. Motorists must then go to *Aduana* to cancel vehicle papers; exit details are typed on to the vehicle permit and the stamp in your passport is cancelled. Find the inspector in Aduana who has to check the details and stamp your permit. If you fail to do this you will not be allowed to leave the country – you will be sent back to Sapoá by the officials at the final Nicaraguan checkpoint. Fumigation is US$0.50 and mandatory.

Transport from Peñas Blancas
Buses to **Rivas**, every ½ hr, 0600-1800, US$0.75, 1 hr. From here buses connect to **Managua**, every ½ hr, 0330-1800, US$2.50, 2¾ hrs or to **Granada**, every 45 mins, 0530-1625, US$1.50, 1¾ hrs, try to board an express bus from Rivas to your destination. Express buses from Peñas Blancas to **Managua**, every 30 mins, 0700-1800, US$3.50, 3½ hrs.

journey through rough terrain became a trip of just under four hours by the construction of this road in earthen form in 1852 by Vanderbilt's company.

La Virgen to Peñas Blancas

The Pan-American Highway continues south from La Virgen to the coastal town of **Sapoá** on the southernmost shores of Lake Nicaragua and **Peñas Blancas,** the one land crossing between Nicaragua and Costa Rica. The landscape changes dramatically as the rainforest ecosystem of the southern shores of Lake Nicaragua meets the tropical dry forest ecosystem of the Pacific Basin, and the stretch of land is rich pasture crossed by numerous streams. It is possible to follow a 4WD track from Sapoá all the way to the town of **Cárdenas**, 17 km away on the shores of Lake Nicaragua and close to the western border of **Los Guatuzos Wildlife Refuge** (see page 173). From here you could try to hire a private boat to Solentiname, Río Papaturro or San Carlos. For information on crossing the border into **Costa Rica**, see box, page 160.

Sleeping

Many hotels in the region of San Juan del Sur double and triple their rates for Semana Santa and around Christmas and New Year.

San Juan del Sur *p153*

LL-AL Piedras y Olas, Parroquia, 1½ c arriba, T568-2110, www.piedrasyolas.com. Beautiful, peaceful, luxurious houses (**LL-L**) and hotel suites with private bath, a/c, cable TV, sitting area, great furnishings and views of the bay. Sailing trips on the *Pelican Eyes* boat can be arranged.

L Casa Marina, Av del Mar, opposite Josselin's, T568-2677. For better or worse, these high-rise timeshare condos are a sign of the times in San Juan del Sur. Apartments have 2 bedrooms, 2 bathrooms, kitchen, living room and unobstructed views of the bay.

A Casablanca, Av del Mar, opposite Bar Timón, T568-2135. Clean, comfortable rooms with a/c, cable TV, private bath, refrigerator and hot water. There's a small pool, parking, free internet and continental breakfast included in the price. Friendly and relaxed.

B Villa Isabella, across from the northeast corner of the church, T568-2568, www.sanjuandelsur.org.ni. This lovely, well-decorated wooden house has 17 clean rooms with private bath, a/c, disabled access, ample windows and light. There's a pool, garage parking, internet, video library and breakfast included in the price. English spoken, very helpful.

B Colonial, Mercado, 1 c al mar, ½ c sur, T568-2539, www.hotel-nicaragua.com. This well-managed hotel has a pleasant, relaxing garden, and 12 comfortable rooms with a/c, cable TV, hot water. Continental breakfast included, bikes and tours can be arranged.

B Gran Ocean, northwest corner of Parque Central, 1 ½ c al mar, T568-2219, www.hotelgranoceano.com.ni. 22 rooms with private bath, a/c and cable TV. The top floor rooms are much more spacious and comfortable, but more expensive. Breakfast included.

B Royal Chateau, Texaco, 300 m sur, T568-2551, www.hotelroyalchateau.com. Motel-style place with a green lawn and 20 clean, unremarkable rooms. They have a/c, cable TV and bath, cheaper with fan (**C**).

D El Puerto, Texaco, 2 c al mar, T823-5729, hotel-el-puerto@gmx.net. Comfortable new rooms with private bath and a/c. Good value and clean.

D Hotel Encanto del Sur, iglesia, 100 m sur, T568-2222. 18 clean, tidy, comfortable rooms with private bath and a/c, cheaper with fan (**E**). Quiet, away from the action and good value.

D-F Costa Azul, mercado, 1 c al mar, T568-2294. Comfortable, cheap rooms with good mattresses and a/c, cheaper with fan (**E**) or shared bath (**F**). There's internet, hammocks, parking and kitchen.

E Hospedaje Casa No 28, mercado, 1c al mar, 1c norte, T568-2441. Good clean budget option with basic rooms and shared bath. Some rooms have private bath, a/c and hot water (**C**).

E Joxi, mercado, 1½ c al mar, T568-2348, casajoxi@ibw.com.ni. Friendly, Norwegian-run place with bunk beds, a/c, cable TV, restaurant and bar.

E-G Casa el Oro Youth Hostel, Hotel Colonial, 20 vrs sur, T568-2415, www.casaeloro.com. Young, popular hostel with dorm beds (**F-G**), private rooms (**E**) and a plethora of services, shuttles, tours and lessons. Good kitchen and garden. Plenty of hammocks.

For an explanation of the sleeping and eating price codes used in this guide, see inside the front cover. Other relevant information is found in Essentials, see pages 23-27.

F Estrella, mercado, 2 c sur, T568-2210. Weathered and fading old cheapie with simple rooms, partitioned walls, good breezes and sea views. Shared bath.

South of San Juan del Sur *p156*

LL-A Parque Marítimo El Coco, 18 km south of San Juan del Sur, T892-0124, www.playaelcoco.com.ni. Differently sized apartments and houses right on the sand and close to La Flor Wildlife refuge. Suits 4-10 people, most have a/c, all have baths, TV and cleaning service included. There's a general store and restaurant in the complex. The beach, back by forest, can have strong waves. Rates vary according to season, weekday nights less expensive. Interesting rural excursions are offered.

North of San Juan del Sur *p157*

LL Morgan's Rock Hacienda & Ecolodge, Playa Ocotal, sales office is in Costa Rica, T506-296-9442, www.morgansrock.com. Famous 'ecolodge' with precious wood bungalows and unrivalled views of the ocean and forest. The cabins are built on a high bluff above the beach and are connected to the restaurant and pool by a suspension bridge. The food, included in the price, has received mixed reviews; the hotel rave reviews. Also included is a night time wake-up call to observe the turtles on the beach. Tours are extra charge. The beach is lovely but the forest much prettier from Jun-Nov. Highly recommended if you've got the dosh.

AL Hotel Punta Teonoste, Playa Conejo, Las Salinas, reservations in Managua at Hotel Los Robles, T267-3008, www.hotellosrobles.com (go to beach link). Charming brick and palm cabins overlooking a lovely beach. The bathroom and shower outside units are in a private open-air area, there's weak water pressure, unique decor, private decks with hammock and circular bar at beach. All meals included. Avoid windy months from Dec-Mar.

B Marsella Beach Resort, Playa Marsella, T887-1337, www.marsellabeachresort.com. Independent cabins with private bath, a/c and great views, restaurant, also house for rent (**L**).

D-G Camping Matilda, Playa Maderas, T456-3461. The best lodgings in the area. They have 8 rooms with private bath (**D**), 2 small dormitories (**F**), and some funny little houses that look just like dog kennels (**G**). Very friendly, relaxed and pleasant. Often full.

E-G Hideout Surf Camp, between Los Playones and Playa Maderas, follow the signs. Perched on a cliff and overlooking the ocean, with 6 dorm beds (**F**), 2 private rooms (**E**) with shared bath, and tent space (**G**). Dinner at sunset, cold beers and guided surf tours. Often full.

G Los Tres Hermanos, Los Playones, T879-5272. Scruffy little shack popular with surfers and budget travellers, conveniently located next to the shuttle drop-off. There's just 10 dorm beds, usually full, and you can pitch a tent for US$2. Beer, water and *comida típica* available.

Eating

San Juan del Sur *p153*

There are many popular, but overpriced, restaurants lining the beach, where your tourist dollars buy excellent sea views and mediocre food. Only the better ones are included below.

TTT-TT Bar Timón, across from Hotel Casablanca, T568-82243. Daily 0800-2200. Probably the best of the beachfront eateries, serving lobster, prawns and a host of other seafood dishes. No plastic furniture. Popular and Nicaraguan.

TTT-TT Big Wave Dave's, Texaco, 200 m al mar, T568-2203, www.bigwavedaves.net. Tue-Sun 0830-0000. Popular with foreigners out to party and hook up with others. Wholesome pub food and a buzzing, boozy atmosphere.

TTT-TT El Colibri, mercado, 1 c este, 2½ sur. The best restaurant in town, with an excellent and eclectic Mediterranean menu, great decor and ambience, fine wines and really good food, much of it organic. Pleasant, hospitable and highly recommended.

TTT-TT El Pozo, mercado, ½ c sur. Smart and stylish, with a robust international menu and an attractive, young clientele. This interesting little restaurant almost belongs in London or New York, not Nicaragua.

TTT-TT La Cascada, Piedras y Olas, parque, 1½ c arriba. One of the best restaurants in town with fine seafood and excellent views overlooking the harbour. Recommended.

TTT-T Pizzería San Juan, southwest corner of Parque Central, ½ c al mar. Tue-Sun 1700-2130. Good pizza and pasta, but a rather plain interior and not much of a dining experience.

TT Iguana Beach, Av del Mar, next door to Timón. Sandwiches, burgers, beer and cheese-drenched nachos, as well as seafood.

Popular with tourists, often buzzing and a good place to drink.

ΨΨ **Josseline's**, on the beach. One of the better beachside eateries, offering the usual seafood fare like shrimps, fillets and lobster. Some limited meat and chicken dishes too.

Ψ **Comedor Margarita**, mercado, ½ c norte. *Comida típica* and other cheap fare.

Ψ **Jerry's Pizza**, mercado, ½ c este. American-owned pizza joint serving reasonable fast-food and breakfasts. A nice, airy, open-front space, good for people-watching.

Ψ **La Fragata**, Texaco, 250 m al mar. The place for cheap and cheerful fast food, including roast chicken.

Cafés and ice cream parlours

Congo Hills, mercado, 15 vrs al sur. Breakfasts and sandwiches, good cappuccinos, espressos, lattes and frappuccinos.

Eskimo, seafront, Hotel Estrella, 2½ c norte. Sweet cold cones, sundaes and banana splits. Another branch just south of Banco Procredit.

Gato Negro, mercado, 1c al mar, 1 c norte. Popular gringo café with good, if overpriced, coffee, a reading space and snacks. This is also one of the best bookshops in the country, with what they claim is the largest collection of English-language books on Nicaragua, in Nicaragua.

Bars and clubs

San Juan del Sur *p153*

The action revolves around **Iguana Beach**, **Maria's** and **Big Wave Dave's**, all located close to each other. You could also try:

Otangani, north on the seafront, next to Gallo de Oro, T878-8384. Thu-Sun 1800-0100. Good fun dancing to techno and salsa. Female travellers should not walk here at night. Catch a cab, especially to return.

Tsunami, seafront, next to María's. Where loud reggae shakes the bamboo walls draped with fairy lights and rasta flags. There's a big screen TV and movies on Mon and Wed night.

Activities and tours

San Juan del Sur *p153*

ATV rental

Moto Rental, mercado, 15 vrs al mar, T568-2439. ATV and motorbike rental including 'Yamaha blasters'.

Canopy tour

Da' Flying Frog, just off road to Marsella, T568-2351, tiguacal@ibw.com.ni. US$25. 17 platforms and great views from the canopy.

Diving

The waters around San Juan del Sur are home to a wrecked Russian trawler and a plethora of sea creatures including rays, turtles and eels.

Scuba Shack, seafront, Hotel Estrella, 3 c norte, T568-2502, www.scubashack-nicaragua.com. This friendly, professional PADI centre offers 1 tank dives (US$46), 2 tank dives (US$86), and open water certification (US$345), including all materials. Training to assistant instructor level, and technical training on request. They also rent out equipment, run snorkelling tours, US$92 for 4 persons, and surfing lessons, US$30 per hr.

Fishing

Many hotels and surf shops offer fishing packages. Otherwise try:

Super Fly Sport Fishing, advance reservation only, T884-8444, www.superflynica.com. Fly fishing and light tackle, deep sea fishing, Captain Gabriel Fernández, fluent in English with lots of experience, also fishes north Pacific Coast and Lake Nicaragua.

Massage and beauty

Gaby's Massage Studio, mercado, ½ este, T568-2654, estrelladeluna@hotmail.com. Professionally trained in Managua, Gaby has 7 years experience and combines techniques from shiatsu, reflexology and aromatherapy. US$25 for 1 hr.

Luna Bella Day Spa, Colibri restaurant, 1 c sur, T803-8196, www.lunabella.org. A range of treatments including massage, beauty, waxing and haircuts. Yoga classes.

Sailing

Pelican Eyes Sailing Adventures, Parroquia 1½ c arriba, T568-2110, sailing@piedrasyolas.com. Sails to the beach at Brasilito, US$70 per person, min 10 people, leaves San Juan at 0900, return 1700.

Surfing

The coast north and south of San Juan del Sur is among the best in Central America for surfing, access to the best areas are by boat or long treks in 4WD. Board rental costs US$10 per day; lessons US$30 per hour.

Arena Caliente, mercado, ½ c norte, T815-3247, www.arenacaliente.com. Friendly surf shop with board rental, surfing lessons (including transport and rash guard) and fishing trips. Also run transport to beaches.

NicaSurf International, mercado, 1 c al mar, ½ c sur, T568-2626, www.nicasurf int.com. Board rental, classes, trips and tons of merchandise.

Outer Reef, mercado, 1 c al mar, ½ c norte. Specialize in supplying the right board for the right person. Tours include a 4-day odyssey to surf hard-to-reach waves to the north.

Surf and Sport, mercado, ½ c al mar, T402-2973. Board rental, fishing equipment, tours, lessons and transportation to the beaches.

Transport

San Juan del Sur *p153*

Bus

To **Managua** express bus 0500, 0530, 0600, 1730, US$3.50, 2½ hrs, ordinary bus every hr 0500-1530, US$2.50, 3½ hrs. Or take a bus/taxi to Rivas and change here. To **Rivas**, every ½ hr, 0500-1700, US$1, 40 mins. For **La Flor** or **Playa El Coco** use bus to **El Ostional**, 1600, 1700, US$ 0.70, 1½ hrs. Return from El Coco at 0600, 0730 and 1630.

Shuttles Several companies run shuttles to the beaches north and south of San Juan del Sur, including **Casa Oro Youth Hostel**, **Arena Caliente** surf shop and **Indian Face Tours**. Each has at least 3 daily departures to **Los Playones**, next to Maderas, US$5.

Boat

Rana Tours, kiosk opposite Hotel Estrella on the seafront. Runs transport to the northern beaches like **Michal**, **Marsella** and **Maderas**. They depart at 1100 and return at 1630, US$10 per person.

4WD

You can usually find a 4WD pick-up to make trips to outlying beaches or to go surfing. You should plan a day in advance and ask for some help from your hotel. Prices range from US$20-US$75 depending on the trip and time. Try also **Servitur Express**, Juan Carlos Silva, T568-2564.

Directory

San Juan del Sur *p153*

Banks Banco Procredit, mercado, 1 c al mar, will change dollars. There is a single ATM in town (Visa only), mercado, 1 c al mar, 1 c norte, ½ c al mar. Some hotels might change dollars too. **Internet** Several places in town (**Casa Joxi** (US$2 per hr, daily 0630-2030), **Leo's** (US$2 per hr, daily 0800-2100) and at **Super-Cyber Internet Service** (US$2 per hr, 0800-2200, internet calls as well). **Language schools** Karla Cruz, Parque Central, 1½ c sur (3rd house to the right after the road turns right), T657-1658, karlacruzsjds@yahoo.com. Private instructor, classes US$5 per hr, discount for longer periods. Additional US$50 for homestay in her house, recommended. **Latin American Spanish School**, southwest corner of Parque Central, ½ c al mar, T820-2252, www.latinamericanspanish school.com. Professionally led, intensive classes, activities and homestay. **Nicaragua Language School**, southwest corner of parque central, ½ c al mar, T568-2142, www.nicaspanish.com. One to one immersion classes, volunteer opportunities and customized classes. Free internet. **Spanish School House Rosa Silva**, mercado, 50 m al mar, T682-2938, www.spanishsilva.com. 20 hrs of 'dynamic' classes cost US$120, student accommodation or homestay are extra. Activities include swimming, hiking and cooking. All teachers are English-speaking. Teaching by the hour, US$7. **Spanish School San Juan del Sur**, T568-2432, www.sjdss panish.com. Regular morning classes, tutoring with flexible hours. **Laundry** Lavandería Gaby, mercado, ½ c arriba, around US$3 for a medium-sized load. **Post office** 150 m left (south) along the seafront from the main junction.

Río San Juan

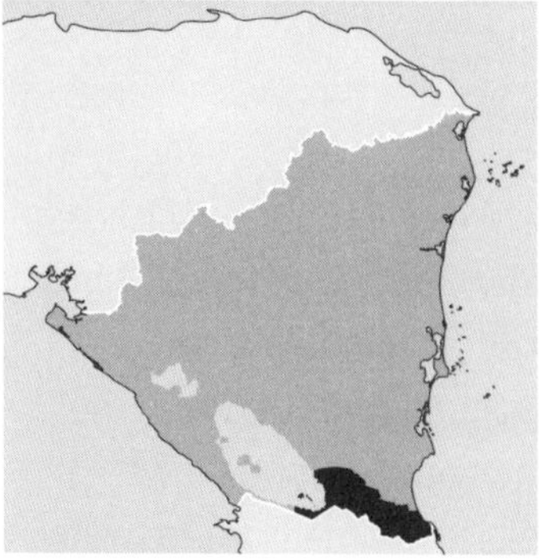

Footprint features

Introduction

The evening symphony of tropical birds, high-pitched cicadas, ardent tree frogs and vociferous howler monkeys merely hints at the multitude of strange creatures inhabiting the darkened rainforests of the San Juan river. A natural canal between the Pacific and Atlantic oceans, this waterway has long drawn enterprising factions keen to exploit its commercial and military potential: the British navy, Napoleon III and the US government among them. Fortunately they all failed, and the river remains one of the great natural attractions of Central America – a mini Amazonas, visited by frequent bouts of life-giving rain, replete with surreal, uniquely adapted biological forms and vigorous plant life. Connected to the outside world by just two unpaved roads, boat is the main form of transport here. From the scattering of upstream ecolodges, downstream to the very heart of the Indio-Maíz rainforest reserve, and beyond, until the Bay of San Juan; travelling this river is an entrancing and unforgettable experience.

Part of this remote region embraces the southeastern sector of Lake Nicaragua, which includes the precious wetlands and rainforest reserve of Los Guatuzos Wildlife Refuge; one of the finest birdwatching locations in the country. On the lake itself lies the Solentiname archipelago, a chain of pretty, drowsy islands that were once the site of an interesting social experiment. In 1965, the poet-priest Ernesto Cardenal came here to preach liberation theology and instruct the locals in artistic methods. His dream was a kind of radical Christian-Communist utopia that combined religion and revolution, spiritual love and community conscience. The result was a school of primitivist art whose output is internationally renowned. Vivid and colourful, this art captures the spiritual essence of rustic life, as well as Nicaragua's scintillating natural world.

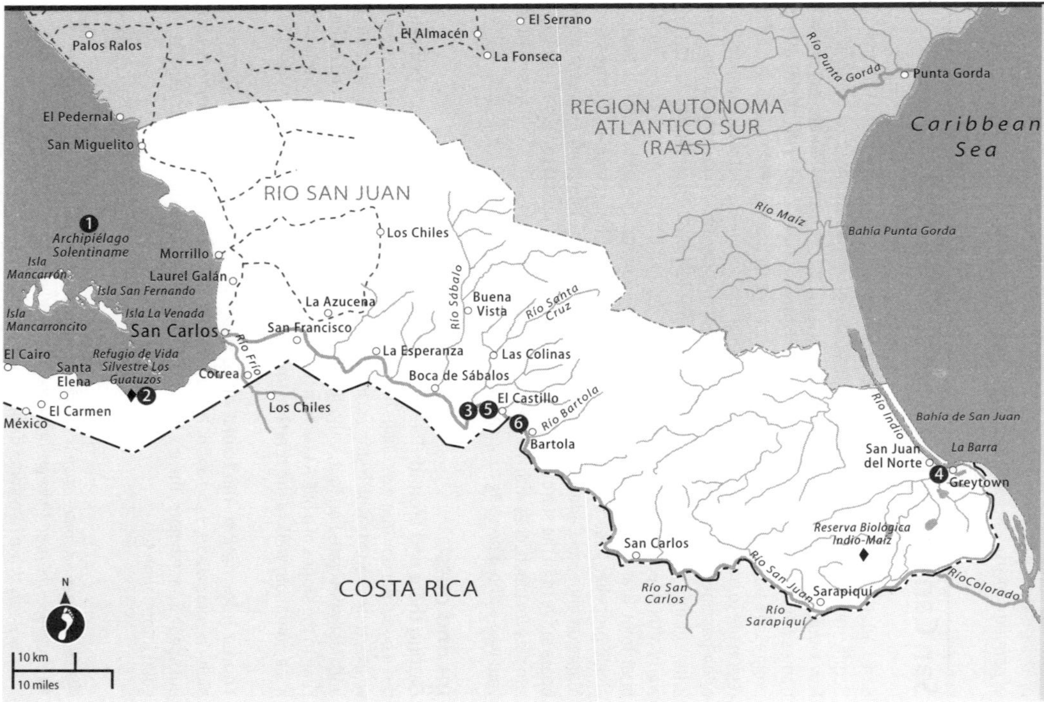

★ Don't miss ...

1. **Rural art** Visit the home of a campesino artist on the Solentiname archipelago, page 172.
2. **Wetlands sunrise** Float down the river in the Los Guatuzos Wildlife Refuge, to an unforgettable symphony of birds, page 173.
3. **Lomas de Nelson** Retrace Nelson's battle at the majestic hilltop fortress at El Castillo, page 180.
4. **Río Indio Lodge** Enjoy an end-of-the-earth ecolodge perched on the banks of the Bahía de San Juan and surrounded by rainforest, page 189.
5. **River prawns** Savour juicy camarones de río grilled in garlic butter sauce at Bar Cofalito, page 189.
6. **River kayaking** Kayak along the Río San Juan's mysterious tributaries, home to prolific wildlife and dense rainforest, page 190.

San Carlos and Archipiélago Solentiname

→ Colour map 3, C6.

Steamy, seedy San Carlos is a major cross-road, regional gateway, border crossing point (with Costa Rica, south along the Río Frío) and unavoidable transport hub. It's also the provincial capital of the isolated Río San Juan department. Most sensible people arrive by plane from Managua, but a single, decrepit, north-bound road also connects it with the capital. For those who don't want to fly, bus or drive, there's always the ferry. West of San Carlos, the waters of Lake Nicaragua stretch away into obscurity, offering connections to tranquil Isla Ometepe, and eventually, the colonial city of Granada. Among the lake's other sublime treasures is the Los Guatuzos Wildlife Reserve, buzzing with nature on its southern shores; and the soporific Solentiname archipelago, a chain of idyllic islands where time unravels and life finds itself in the brush strokes and colours of painted canvases. » *For Sleeping, Eating and other listings, see pages 174-177.*

San Carlos and the border

» pp174-177.

San Carlos stands in contrast to the immense natural beauty that surrounds it. Scruffy, ramshackle and indisputably ugly, the place has a sultry 'last outpost' feel. Few would imagine that the city hides a historic fortress and that elegant colonial homes once lined its cobblestone streets. History has been unkind to the city, though progress is slowly coming to the town where the only bank and hospital in the entire region are to be found. The nearby Costa Rican border means dubious characters are often passing through, but the locals are very friendly and philosophical about the future of this jungle gateway. This is where the last buses arrive from the outside world after a tedious nine-hour journey across rocky paths and muddy bogs. The big boat from Granada docks here after 15 or so hours on the lake. Twice a day the single-propeller Cessna buzzes the rusting tin roofs of the village as it arrives from Managua onto San Carlos' dirt track landing strip. And the long, narrow river and lake boats arrive from the surrounding settlements and wilderness. If you time it right, you can stay for lunch, chat with the friendly locals, pick up necessary supplies and be on your way without needing to spend the night.

Ins and outs

Getting there and around There are 2 daily flights to San Carlos from Managua, three boats per day from Los Chiles in Costa Rica (Monday-Saturday), and boats twice weekly from Granada which stop at Ometepe (see pages 64 and 125). The city is small and easily navigated on foot, although there is a confusing feel to the streets, which cling to the slopes of a hill. A taxi from the airport should cost around US$1, otherwise it's a 30-minute walk to the centre of town. » *For further details, see Transport, page 176.*

Tourist information The **tourist office** ⓘ *on the waterfront malecón T583-0301, Mon-Fri 0800-1200, 1400-1700*, has a selection of maps and flyers. They're helpful, but speak Spanish only. There's a small **CANTUR** kiosk, also on the malecón, that has good information too.

You may see a number of white plastic jugs and two-litre Pepsi and Coca-Cola bottles floating in the river. These are not garbage, but rather markers for shrimp traps. The river is very rich in camarones de río *(freshwater prawns).*

Background and sights

Since the so-called 'discovery' of the Río San Juan by the Spanish Captain Ruy Díaz in 1525, San Carlos has had strategic importance for the successive governments of Nicaragua. Its location at the entrance to the Río San Juan from Lake Nicaragua and at the end of the Río Frío, which originates in Costa Rica, has meant that controlling San Carlos means controlling the water passages from north to south and east to west. The town was first founded in 1526, with the name Nueva Jaén, under the orders of King Carlos V of Spain but it did not officially become a port until 1542. The town (and a fortress that has not survived) were abandoned for an unknown length of time and were re-founded as San Carlos during the 17th century. A new fortress was built but was sacked by pirates in 1670; part of it survives today as a small **museum** ⓘ *0900-1200, 1400-1700, admission free*, and the town's principal tourist attraction. The fort was used for supply backup and troop fallbacks during attacks on the frontline fortress of El Castillo by Dutch and British pirates in the 17th century and British Naval forces in the 18th century. San Carlos was embroiled in the post-Independence struggles between León and Granada. It was a changeover stop for passengers of the Vanderbilt inter-oceanic steamship service and William Walker's forces also occupied the fort during Walker's attempt at a hostile takeover of both the steamship line and Nicaragua.

San Carlos is periodically attacked by plagues of chayules *(green gnats); they are harmless but horribly annoying and can make sleeping here insufferable.*

When Mark Twain visited San Carlos in 1866 on the Vanderbilt line (see box, page 148), he described it simply as Fort San Carlos, making no mention of any town. In 1870 the English naturalist Thomas Belt arrived after the long journey up the Río San Juan when rubber tappers were working in the nearby forests. He spent the night on one of the docked steamships and wrote of skirmishes between the Guatuzo and the rubber-extracting residents of San Carlos.

San Carlos

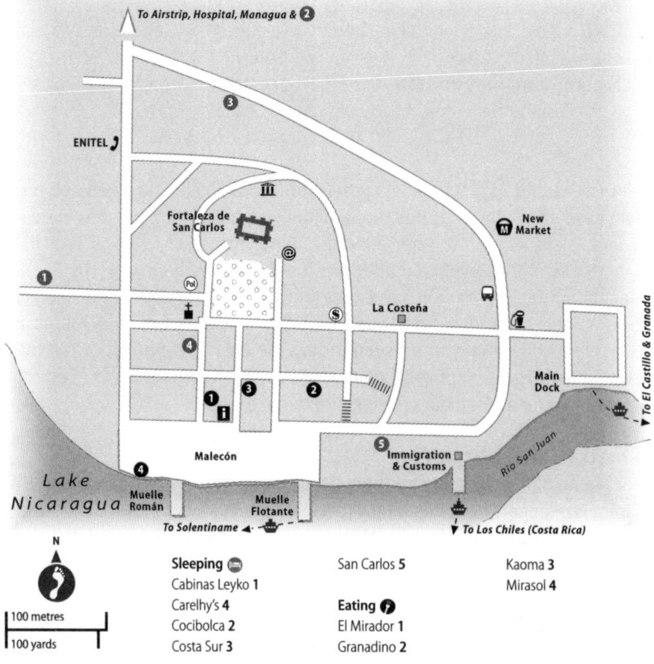

Border essentials: Nicaragua – Costa Rica

The Nicaragua-Costa Rica border runs along the southern bank of the Río San Juan but has been the subject of much government tension and debate. The Costa Rican border reaches the south banks of the Río San Juan 2 km downriver from El Castillo but the river in its length is Nicaraguan territory. Officially Costa Rican boats are only allowed to navigate the river for commercial purposes. It is best to travel in Nicaraguan boats on the river, as Costa Rican ones could be detained or turned back depending on the political climate (see box, page 184).

San Carlos to Los Chiles

This is a frequently used crossing point between Nicaragua and Costa Rica. Crossing from the Río San Juan to other parts of Costa Rica is not legal, though this could change; ask in San Carlos if any other official points of entry or departure have opened up.

Nicaraguan immigration The border is open 7 days a week 0800-1600. Exit stamps, costing US$2, must be obtained in San Carlos Mon-Fri only. Entrance stamps into Costa Rica (US$8) are only available via Los Chiles. Check with the police in advance for the latest situation.

Transport There are 3 boats per day from San Carlos to Los Chiles, 1030, 1300, 1500, US$8, 2 hours.

San Juan del Norte (see page 187)

Crossing to Costa Rica here is not legally permitted at time of printing, nor is entering Nicaragua without passing through San Carlos; the exception are package customers of the Río Indio Lodge, which has special permission for its clients.

Nicaraguan immigration There is no official immigration in San Juan del Norte. Projections suggest that the new San Juan del Norte airport, as yet unbuilt, will include immigrations and customs for international arrivals and departures. Whether this will open up the legality of boat arrivals and departures remains to be seen.

On 13 October 1977 Sandinista rebels from Solentiname attacked and took the military base after a four-day trek through jungle in Costa Rica, but they were forced back into Costa Rica after other attacks around Nicaragua failed. It was the first military victory of the Revolution and after the final triumph in 1979, the Sandinista administration set up a base in San Carlos that was used to fight Contra insurgents in the 1980s. The city's waterfront was burnt down in 1984 and was rebuilt in the ramshackle manner that can be seen today. The town is a trading centre for local goods and used as a jumping-off point for Nicaraguan migrant workers en route to Costa Rica and for a small but growing number of tourists.

Río Frío to the border

This is the river that connects northern Costa Rica with Lake Nicaragua and the Río San Juan. Passengers from Costa Rica pass through customs at San Carlos and then continue to Managua (by bus or plane), or down the Río San Juan towards the Caribbean. Once you pass into Nicaraguan territory, the river enters a reserve, marked

The Guatuzos today are known as the Rama and populate the Rama Cay in Bluefields Bay (see page 279).

by a little green guard house. The reserve is the superb **Refugio de Vida Silvestre Los Guatuzos** (see page 173). The east bank is also home to a small project within the reserve called **Esperanza Verde** (see page 175), a nature reserve with an investigative centre and some basic accommodation. Although the river is used mainly as a commuter route, there is some beautiful wildlife and vegetation and it is rare not to see at least one clan of howler monkeys along the banks or even swimming across the river; while they tend to avoid swimming at all costs, the monkeys can manage a very methodical doggy paddle if necessary.

The indigenous name for the river was Ucubriú.

As late as the 1870s the indigenous **Guatuzo** people (Maleku Indians) inhabited the river banks of this area. The naturalist Thomas Belt recounted battles between the rubber tappers and the Guatuzo people who were fighting to stop the invasion of their land. The Spanish were never able to subjugate the Guatuzos and they gained a reputation for hostility and were left alone for years; the original explorers of the Río Frío are thought to have been attacked and killed by Guatuzo arrows. However, when the India-rubber trade grew and the supply of trees along the Río San Juan was exhausted, the rubbermen were forced to explore the Río Frío. This time they came heavily armed, killing anyone in their path. By 1870, just the sight of a white man's boat along the river sent the indigenous population fleeing into the forest in desperate fear. After that, the end of the culture was quickly accomplished by illegal kidnapping and slave trading with the mines and farms of Chontales.

Archipiélago Solentiname » *pp175-177.*

The Solentiname archipelago is a protected area, designated a Monumento Nacional, and one of the most scenic parts of Lake Nicaragua. It is made up of 36 islands in the lake's southeastern corner which, despite being just one hour in a fast boat from San Carlos, remain remote. The islands are sparsely populated and without roads, telephones, electricity or running water: this is Nicaragua as it was two centuries ago, with only the outboard motorboat as a reminder of the modern world. The islands are home to some of the most industrious and talented artists in the country. The ecosystem is transitional from tropical dry to rainforest and much of the islands' interiors are pasture and agricultural land. About 46 species of fish inhabit the waters around the islands and birdwatching opportunities are good, with many parrots, *oropendulas* and ospreys around. At night you can see the fishing bat, a spectacular and eerie hunter, as it drags its claws through the lake water at night picking off unwary fish near the surface.

Ins and outs

The archipelago has four main islands, from east to west they are: La Venada, San Fernando, Mancarrón and Mancarroncito, which are detailed below. There are many other beautiful islands that can be visited for the day or for a camping trip, but ask for permission from the locals. There is plenty to keep you occupied on the islands, including visits to local artists, boating, swimming and nature walks. The main problem is the lack of public boats. This means you will have to hire a boat or use a tour operator to organize your trip or allow plenty of time to find transport when you're out there. You could probably kayak between some of the islands, if you're strong and experienced enough. » *See also Transport, page 177, for further details.*

Background

The islands are the result of ancient volcanic activity, now heavily eroded and partially submerged. Solentiname has been populated since at least AD 500 and is thought to have been populated up until AD 1000, when historians believe it became a ceremonial site. Today the inhabitants are mostly third and fourth generation migrants from Chontales and Isla de Ometepe.

The islanders make a living from subsistence farming and artistic production. In the early 1960s, 12 local farmers were given painting classes at the initiative of the idealistic and much revered Catholic priest/poet/sculptor Ernesto Cardenal. In addition, the local inhabitants were trained in balsa woodcarving. This small amount of training was passed from family to family; mother to son and father to daughter and soon the entire archipelago was involved in sculpting or painting. The style is *primitivista* and many of the painters have become internationally known and have been invited to study and exhibit as far away as Finland and Japan. The balsa woodcarvings can be found around Central America and the artisans have expanded their themes in recent years. Both the wood and oil arts represent local ecology and legends, with the paintings normally depicting dense tropical landscape and the balsa works recreating individual species of the region.

Ernesto Cardenal ran his church innovatively with participative masses and a call to arms against the oppression of the Somoza government in the 1970s. The islanders, organized by Cardenal and led by local boy Alejandro Guevara, made the first successful rebel attack on a military base at San Carlos in October 1977; one month later Somoza sent helicopters to raze Mancarrón Island. Cardenal, who was defrocked by Pope John Paul II, went on to be the Sandinista Minister of Culture and an international celebrity. The 80-year-old icon still writes poetry, sculpts and visits Solentiname occasionally to stay in his small house on Isla Mancarrón near to his old church, which sadly is no longer in use. Cardenal's glowing (some would say whitewashed) memoir of all that was great about the Revolution and his role at the Ministerio de Cultura was published recently. The 666-page work, called *Revolución Perdida,* reveals some amazing scenes about his life as the international fundraiser for arms for the Sandinista rebel underground. It also documents in detail his administration of Nicaragua's blossoming culture in the 1980s, the biggest success of the Sandinista years. The book is in Spanish only and available at hotels on the islands and in Managua.

Isla La Venada

Named for its once plentiful population of deer, La Venada is a long narrow island that is home to many artists, including Rodolfo Arellano who lives on the southwestern side of the island. He and his wife are among the islands' original painters and his daughters and grandchildren all paint tropical scenes and welcome visitors to see and purchase their work. You can also rent a bed in his house. On the north side of the island is a series of semi-submerged caves with some of the best examples of petroglyphs which are attributed to the Guatuzo people. One of the caves links up with the opposite side of the island and was probably used during low water levels. The cave can be visited by boat, though the entrance is dangerous if the lake is rough.

Isla San Fernando

This island, also known as Elvis Chavarría, is also famous for its artisan work and painting. It has some of the prettiest houses in the archipelago and is home to the famous Pineda artist family. Rosa Pineda is very friendly and will show you her work. Nearby, on a beautiful hill, is a new museum, the **Museo Archipiélago Solentiname** ⓘ *T583-0095 (in San Carlos), US$2*. The museum has a small pre-Columbian collection, with some interesting explanations of local culture and ecology. There is also mural painted by the Arellano family from La Venada. The museum has a fabulous view of the islands and is not to be missed at sunset. If it is closed, ask around to find out who has the key.

Isla Mancarrón

This is the biggest island in the chain and has the highest elevation at 250 m. The famous revolutionary/poet/sculptor/Catholic priest/Minister of Culture, Ernesto Cardenal, made his name here by founding a *primitivista* school of painting, poetry and sculpture, and even decorating the local parish church in naïve art. The church is open and there is a museum just behind the altar (ask permission to visit). It contains the first oil painting ever made on Solentiname, a bird's eye view of the island, and many other curiosities. Next to the church there is a monument to the Sandinistas and the tomb of the deceased rebel commander Alejandro Guevara who was from this island.

Mancarrón is good for walking and it is home to many parrots and Montezuma oropendulas. Ask in the village for a guide to show you the way to the mirador, which has super views of the archipelago. Also at the mirador you can see a coyol palm tree which is used to make a sweet palm wine. The indigenous name for the palm is *mancarrón*, giving the island its name. The village has two small stores and cold drinks, bottled water, crackers and snacks. You can visit the homes of the island's talented artisans.

Isla Mancarroncito

Mancarroncito is a big, wild, mountainous island with primary forest. There is some good hiking in the forest, although the terrain is steep. Ask at your guesthouse for a recommended guide.

Other islands

On the north side of Mancarrón there is a tiny island with an inlet that holds the wreck of a sunken steamship from the inter-oceanic route. Only the chimney, now covered in tropical vegetation, is still visible above the water. On the far west end of the archipelago, just off the west coast of Mancarroncito, is another bird nesting site on a little rock pile island, with hundreds of egret and cormorant nests.

Isla de Zapote, which is in front of the Los Guatuzos river of the same name, is home to over 10,000 bird nests, making it perhaps the richest bird-nesting site in Nicaragua. Most of the nests belong to cormorants or white egrets, although there are other egrets, herons, roseate spoonbills, wood storks and two species of ibis among the other species.

Between San Fernando and Mancarrón is the small forest-covered island of **El Padre**, named after a priest who once lived there. It is the only island with monkeys (howlers), which were introduced only 25 years ago and are now thriving. With a few circles of the island by boat you should be able to find some of them.

Refugio de Vida Silvestre Los Guatuzos » p175.

The Los Guatuzos Wildlife Refuge occupies the southern shores of Lake Nicaragua and the southern banks of the first few kilometres of the Río San Juan. Nicaraguan biologists consider it the cradle of life for the lake, because of its importance as a bird nesting site and its infinite links in the area's complex ecological chain. More than a dozen rivers run through the reserve, the most popular for wildlife viewing being the **Río Papaturro**. The ecosystems are diverse with tropical dry forest, tropical wet forest, rainforest and extensive wetlands. Best of all are the many narrow rivers lined with gallery forest – the ideal setting for viewing wildlife.

Flora and fauna

The vegetation here is stunning with over 315 species of plants, including some primary forest trees over 35 m in height and 130 species of orchid. The quality and sheer quantity of wildlife is the reason most visitors come here; it is astonishing.

This little park is brimming with life, especially at sunrise, and while there are places in Nicaragua and Central America with a longer species list, you can often see as much wildlife in a few hours in Los Guatuzos as you will in several days elsewhere.

Eighty-one amphibious species have been documented so far, along with 136 species of reptile, 42 species of mammal and 389 species of bird. The most noticeable residents of the gallery forest are the **howler monkeys** (*mono congo*), named after the loud growl of the male monkey, which can be heard up to 3 km away. The reserve is loaded with howlers, particularly along the Río Papaturro, where you can see 30-50 monkeys in an average four-hour period. More difficult to spot, but also present, are **white-faced** and **spider monkeys**. Of the reptiles, the easiest to spot are the **caimans, iguanas** and **turtles**, especially if it is sunny. A long way upriver are a number of **Jesus Christ lizards**, famed for their hind-leg dashes across the surface of the water. There are also **sloths, anteaters** and **jaguars**. However, the most impressive aspect of the reserve is the density of its **bird life**. As well as the many elegant egrets and herons, there are five species of kingfishers, countless jacanas, the pretty purple gallinule, wood storks, the roseate spoonbill, jabiru, osprey, laughing falcon, scarlet-rumped tanagers, trogons, bellbirds and six species of parrot.

Background

The original inhabitants of the area that included the Solentiname archipelago were fishermen, hunters and skilled planters with crops of corn, squash, cacao and plantains. They called themselves the **Maleku**. The Maleku language had sprinklings of Náhuatl, as spoken by the Nicaraguas (a root of Aztec Náhuatl), but was basically Chibcha (the language root of the Miskito, Rama and Mayagna). Their name for Lake Nicaragua was Ucurriquitúkara, which means 'where the rivers converge'. The Spanish name for these people was the **Guatuzo** because they painted their faces red, in a colour reminiscent of the large tropical rodent, the *guatuza* (agouti), which is very common to the region. It was the extraction of rubber, which began in 1860, that spelled the beginning of the end for Guatuzo culture. In the 1930s and 1940s the current residents began to move in but you can still see traces of the original Maleku or Guatuzo people in a few residents of Solentiname and the reserve administrators allow them to practise small-scale agriculture and ranching.

Centro Ecológico de Los Guatuzos

Some local residents have become involved in the research and protection of the reserve at the Centro Ecológico de Los Guatuzos run by the Nicaraguan non-profit environmental NGO **Fundación de Amigos del Río San Juan (Fundar)** ① *Managua office T270-5434, www.fundar.org.ni, US$6 including tour of the grounds and projects; canopy bridge US$10 extra*. The ecological centre has over 130 species of orchid on display, a sad butterfly farm (broken into and robbed constantly by local forest animals), a turtle hatchery and a caiman breeding centre. In addition to some short trails with vicious mosquitoes, there is a system of wobbly canopy bridges to allow visitors to observe wildlife from high up in the trees. If you don't suffer from vertigo, this is a wonderful experience allowing you to get right up close to the wildlife. A recommended guide is Armando (Spanish-speaking only), who is a native of the river and an expert on orchids.

Sleeping

San Carlos *p168, map p169*

There is a lack of quality accommodation in San Carlos. Rodents and insects are common; pull your bed away from the wall and don't walk barefoot in the dark.

E Cabinas Leyko, Policía Nacional, 2 c abajo, T583-0354. The best place in town, with clean, comfortable rooms, good mattresses, private bath and a/c. Cheaper with fan and shared bath (**F**).

E Cocibolca, in San Miguelito north of San Carlos, at the end of the jetty, T552-8803. Colonial-style hotel with hard beds; ask for a room with a balcony. Horse riding arranged by the owner, Franklin, as well as day trips to El Boquete and El Morro Islands. The Granada–San Carlos boat stops here.
F Costa Sur, Consejo Supremo Electoral, 50 m sur, T583-0224. 10 rooms with shared or private bath and fan, meals. Some have a/c (**D**).
E Carelhy's Hotel, iglesia católica, ½ c sur, T583-0389. 10 rooms with private bath, fan and cable TV. Can help arrange tours and transport, breakfasts for large groups.
F Hotelito San Carlos, next to Clínica San Lucas, T583-0265. Cleanish rooms are small, basic and cheap; some have private bath.

Isla San Fernando *p172*

C Hotel Cabañas Paraíso, T506-301-8809 (mobile), gsolentiname@ifxnw.com.ni, Managua office in Galería Solentiname, T278-3998. The lack of trees means that the views are spectacular and the sun hot. Rooms are very clean, bright and crowded, with private bath. Feels a bit Miami, but friendly. Excursions in very fine boats are offered.
C-F Hotel Celentiname or **Doña María**, T506-893-1977 (mobile). This laid back place is the most traditional of the hotels here. It has a lovely location facing another island and a lush garden filled with big trees, hummingbirds, iguanas, and at night, fishing bats. The rustic cabins have private bath and nice decks. Sad dorm rooms (**F**) are not much cheaper with shared baths. Generated power, all meals included. Very friendly owners. Recommended.

Isla Mancarrón *p173*

B Hotel Mancarrón, up the hill from the cement dock and church, T583-0083 (in San Carlos), hmancarrun@ibw.com.ni. Great birdwatching around this hotel that has access to the artisan village. Rooms are airy, screened, equipped with mosquito netting and private bath. The managers are personal and friendly. Prices include 3 great home-cooked meals per day. Recommended.
E Hospedaje Reynaldo Ucarte, main village. 4 decent but basic rooms with shared baths. Meals available on request. Friendly, nice area with lots of children and trees.

Refugio de Vida Silvestre Los Guatuzos *p173*

B Esperanza Verde, Río Frío, 4 km from San Carlos, T583-0354 or T277-3482 (in Managua), jtalave@uam.edu.ni. In a beautiful area rich in wildlife, these 280 ha of private reserve inside the Los Guatuzos Wildlife Refuge have good nature trails for birdwatching. There are 20 rooms with single beds, fan, shared bath. Prices include 3 meals per day.
E Centro Ecológico de Los Guatuzos, Río Papaturro, T270-5434 (Managua), www.fundar.org.ni. An attractive wooden research station on the riverfront. 2 rooms have 8 bunk beds in each, shared bath. Meals for guests US$2-3, served in a local house. Guided visits to forest trails, excursions to others rivers in the reserve. Night caiman tours by boat. Private boat to and from San Carlos can be arranged. All tours in Spanish only, some Managua tour operators arrange programmes with an English-speaking guide (see page 64).

Eating

San Carlos *p168, map p169*

Sleeping may be uncomfortable, but if there are no *chayules* (gnats) San Carlos is a good place to have lunch. And if you do have to sleep here, it's probably best to start drinking straight away.
ΨΨ-Ψ Granadino, opposite Alejandro Granja playing field, T583-0386. Daily 0900-0200. Considered the best in town, with a relaxed ambience, good murals, pleasant river views, *Camarones en salsa*, steak and hamburgers.
ΨΨ-Ψ Kaoma, across from Western Union, T583-0293. Daily from 0900 until the last customer collapses in a pool of rum. Funky place, decorated with dozens of oropendula nests, that attracts a friendly, hard-drinking clientele. There's fresh fish caught by the owner, good *camarones de río* (freshwater prawns), and dancing when the locals are inspired. Recommended.
Ψ El Mirador, iglesia católica, 1½ c sur, T583-0377. Daily 0700-2000. Superb view

For an explanation of the sleeping and eating price codes used in this guide, see inside the front cover. Other relevant information is found in Essentials, see pages 23-27.

from patio of Lake Nicaragua, Solentiname, Río Frío and Río San Juan and the jumbled roofs of the city. Decent chicken, fish and beef dishes starting at US$3 with friendly service. Recommended, though it closes if the *chayules* (see post it, page 169) are in town.

Mirasol, next to the Roman lake dock where the river meets the lake. Good grilled meats, fried chicken and decent salads. Good place to sit in the daytime to watch life on the river and lake. Ruthless mosquitoes in the evening.

Shopping

San Carlos *p168, map p169*

Stock up on purified water and food for a long journey. The market is a cramped nightmare, but in front of immigration there are stalls to buy goods. High-top rubber boots or wellingtons are standard equipment in these parts, perfect for jungle treks and cost US$6-9, though large sizes are rarely found.

Transport

San Carlos *p168, map p169*

Air

The flight to Managua is breathtaking. On a clear day you can see Solentiname, Ometepe, Las Isletas, Granada, Volcán Mombacho, Laguna de Apoyo, Volcán Masaya and Lake Managua. **La Costeña** has 2 daily flights from San Carlos to **Managua**, 0925, 1425, US$120 return, US$65 one way (see page 64 for outgoing schedules). There is a maximum weight for flights – you will be asked your body weight. Taxi from airstrip to dock US$1. Arrive 1 hr before departure because the single-prop Cessna Caravan 208B touches down, unloads and takes off again all within five minutes and you must be ready to jump on – also becasue overbooking is common. There are no reserved seats and only 5 seats with a decent view, all on the left. All (relatively) heavy passengers are pushed to the front of the aeroplane for balance reasons. Take out film and camera before arriving in Managua where all bags are X-rayed. Do not lose your little cardboard stub or you will not be able to recover your checked bag in Managua.

Tickets can be bought at **La Costeña** office, 1 block from main dock. The only way to the landing strip (*la pista*) is by walking or taking a taxi up the hill from Enitel.

Taxi

Taxis wait for arriving flights at the landing strip; if you miss them you will have to walk to town (30 mins). To get to the landing strip, taxis can be found in town between the market and *muelle flotante*. All fares are US$1, exact change is essential. Drivers are helpful.

Bus

From San Carlos to **Managua**, daily, 0800, 1145, 1430, 1800, 2000, US$9, 9½ hrs. This is a brutal ride, buses occasionally get stuck in mud bogs during Sep-Nov, but many locals prefer it to the 15-hr Granada ferry odyssey. There are some lovely settlements 2 hrs outside San Carlos, but mostly it is hard going.

Motorboat

Small motor boats are called *pangas*; long, narrow ones are *botes* and big broad ones are known as *planos*.

Public Arrive at least 30 mins in advance to insure a seat on a short ride; allow an hour or more for long trips. To **Solentiname**, Tue, Fri, 1230, US$4, 2½ hrs, stopping at islands **La Venada**, **San Fernando**, **Mancarrón**. To **Los Guatuzos**, stopping at **Papaturro**, Tue, Wed, Fri, 0700, US$5, 3½ hrs. To **Los Chiles**, Costa Rica, daily 1030, 1300, 1500, US$8, 2 hrs. To **El Castillo** (and Sábalos), 0800, 1100 (express), 1300 (slow boat), 1430, 1530, 1630, 1½ hrs (express), 2½ hrs, US$5 (express), US$4, US$2 (slow boat), reduced services on Sun when only first two boats run. Avoid the slow boat if you can, it's a gruelling 6-hr ride. The ferry to **Granada** leaves from main dock in San Carlos, Tue and Fri 1400, 1st class US$7, 2nd class US$3, 15 hrs or more. 1st class has a TV, nicer seats and is usually less crowded. Bring a hammock if you can and expect a challenging journey.

Private Motorboats are available for hire; they are expensive but afford freedom to stop and view wildlife. They are also faster, leave when you want and allow you to check different hotels for space and conditions. Beyond El Castillo downriver there are only 2 boats per week, so private transport is the only other option. Ask at tourism office for recommendations. Average round-trip rates: **El Castillo** US$190-250, **Solentiname** US$100-150, **San Juan del Norte** US$800-950. Some *pangueros* (boatmen) who have been recommended include: Armando Ortiz, Norman Guadamuz, Martín López, Ricardo Henríquez. Packages are available from **Tours Nicaragua** (see page 64) who specialize in this region, providing complete trips with private boat transfers, bilingual naturalist guide and boat tours of wildlife reserves; expensive unless you have a group of at least 4 travellers.

Archipiélago Solentiname *p171*
Boat
Solentiname to **San Carlos**, Tue, Fri 0430, US$4, 2½ hrs. **Los Guatuzos** and **Río Papaturro** to **San Carlos**, Mon, Tue, Thu 0600, US$5, 3½ hrs.

Directory

San Carlos *p168, map p169*
Airline office La Costeña, Fortaleza San Carlos, 1 c sur, 2 c arriba, T583-0271. **Bank** BDF, Fortaleza San Carlos, 1 c sur, 1 c arriba, T583-0144. The only bank, no ATM or TC changes, so bring plenty of cash. Queues can be tremendous on, or near, the 15th or 31st of each month, as this is the only bank on the river. You can also change dollars, córdobas or colones, with the *coyotes* at the entrance to immigration and customs, with fair to poor rates. **Fire** T583-0149. **Hospital** T583-0238. **Police** T583-0350. **Post office** Correos de Nicaragua, across from Los Juzgados de Distritos, T583-0000. **Telephone** Enitel office is on road from landing strip to town, T583-0001.

Along the Río San Juan

→ *Colour map 4, C1-3.*

The vast and extraordinarily beautiful Río San Juan is Lake Nicaragua's sole outlet to the sea. Three major rivers that originate in Costa Rica and more than 17 smaller tributaries also feed this mighty river, which is up to 350 m wide at points. A staggering amount of water flows out of this river to the sea every day. At San Carlos enough water enters the river in a 24-hour period in the dry season to supply water to all of Central America for one year – a gigantic resource that Nicaragua has yet to exploit. For the visitor it is an opportunity to experience the rainforest and to journey from Central America's biggest lake all the way to the thundering surf of Nicaragua's eastern seaboard. From San Carlos, the river passes the easternmost sector of Los Guatuzos Wildlife Refuge before entering a long stretch of cattle ranches that lead to the historic town and fort of El Castillo. Past El Castillo, the Indio-Maíz Biological Reserve runs the remaining length of the river's north bank to the scenic coastal estuaries of the Caribbean Sea. » *For Sleeping, Eating and other listings, see pages 188-190.*

Ins and outs

Getting around Travel is only possible by boat, with a regular daily service to El Castillo and sparse public boat operations downriver. To really explore the river, private boat hire is necessary, though expensive. All travel times between tributaries in this section are estimates based on a private boat with capacity for six to eight passengers and a 45 horse power motor or better, travelling downstream. If you are travelling upstream add 20-35%; for heavy boats, smaller motors and travel at the end of the dry season, add much more time. If travelling in a light boat with a big motor during the rainy season when the rivers are full, travel times can be cut almost in half depending on the bravado of the navigator. » *For further details, see Transport, page 190.*

The river drops an average of 18 cm per km on its 190-km journey from Lake Nicaragua to the Caribbean.

Background

In 1502 Christopher Columbus explored the Caribbean Coast of Nicaragua in search of an inter-oceanic passage. He sailed right past the Río San Juan. The river was populated by Rama Indians, the same people that can be found today on a small island in the Bay of Bluefields. In the 17th century the biggest Rama settlement was estimated at more than 30,000 in the Boca de Sábalo; at the same time, the capital of Nicaragua had some 40,000 residents. Today the Ramas are making a return to the southern forests of Nicaragua, though only in the Río Indio area along the Caribbean Coast.

When Francisco Hernández de Córdoba established the cities of Granada and León, he sent Spanish Captain Ruy Díaz in search of the lake's drainage. Díaz explored the entire lake, reaching the mouth of the river in 1525. He was able to navigate the river as far as the first principal northern tributary, Río Sábalo, but was forced to turn back. Córdoba was unfazed and sent a second expedition led by Captain Hernando de Soto (later the first European to navigate the Mississippi river). Soto managed to sail as far as Díaz and was also forced to turn back due to the rapids.

Explorers were busy looking for gold in Nicaragua's northern mountains and the river was ignored until 1539, when a very serious expedition was put together by the Spanish governor of Nicaragua, Rodrigo de Contreras. This brutally difficult journey was undertaken by foot troops, expert sailors and two brave captains, Alonso Calero and Diego Machuca. Having passed the first set of rapids, they encountered more rapids at El Castillo; Machuca divided the expedition and marched deep into the forest looking for the outlet of the river. Calero continued the length of the river and reached its end at the Caribbean Sea on 24 June 1539. This happened to be Saint John the Baptist's saint's day, so they named the river for him. He then sailed north in search of Machuca as far as the outlet of the Río Coco. However, Machuca had left on foot with his troops and returned all the way to Granada without knowledge of what had happened to the Calero party. The newly discovered passage was exactly what the Spanish had been hoping for. It was quickly put into service for the transport of gold, indigo and other goods from their Pacific holdings to Hispañola (Dominican Republic and Haiti today) and then to Spain. The river was part of the inter-oceanic steam ship service of Cornelius Vanderbilt in the mid-1800s and was used by William Walker for his brief rule in Granada. During the Contra conflict, parts of the river were contested by Edén Pastora's southern front troops in attacks against the Sandinista government army.

San Carlos–Río Sábalo–El Castillo → *Travel time about 2 hrs.*

Outside the limits of San Carlos, the river is lined with wetlands, providing good opportunities for birdwatching. Deforestation in this section of the river (until El Castillo) is getting increasingly worse and, despite numerous reforestation projects, barges can be seen transporting giant trunks of cedar. The Río Sábalo is an important tributary named after the large fish found in this region, the *sábalo* (tarpon). The town at it's mouth, **Boca de Sábalos**, is melancholy, muddy and friendly. There is an earth path that leads to a spooky looking African palm plantation and factory, where palm oil is made. From the road it is possible to connect with the **Río Santa Cruz** and navigate that small and beautiful river to El Castillo. The road in the dry season goes deep into the backcountry and wildlife viewing at the forest edge is very good; you may well see spider, howler and white-faced monkeys, flocks of parrots and many birds of prey. There are decent lodges around the mouth of the Río Sábalo (see Sleeping, page 188) and the people of Sábalo seem happy to see outsiders. There are

A Spanish Jesuit priest warned that opening a passage between the two oceans could lead to the draining of one ocean into the other, creating a massive desert on one side and biblical flooding on the other.

Canal dreams

The dream of making the Río San Juan into part of an inter-oceanic canal was born as early as 1567, when King Phillip II of Spain ordered a feasibility study. By the mid-17th century the English had moved in on Spanish holdings in the Caribbean, wresting the island of Jamaica from them and creating a base for attacks on Central America. Their goal was to conquer the Río San Juan and "divide the Spanish Empire in half". From then on, renowned scientists, engineers, business people and public figures would advocate the canal idea and become directly or indirectly involved in its promotion. The canal dream lived on with none other than Napoleon Bonaparte III, who legally registered a new business venture in London, under the name of the Nicaraguan Canal Company in 1869 (the same year the Suez Canal was inaugurated), after obtaining the canal concession from the Nicaraguan government. He proclaimed that to control the Río San Juan was to control the Gibraltar of the Americas and a guarantee of domination of the new world order. He fell from power the following year and nothing was done. The 19th century also saw aborted projects by the Dutch, Belgians and the US. The US President Ulysses Grant and Ferdinand de Lesseps carried out parallel studies to find the best option for a Central American inter-oceanic canal. Both concluded that the Nicaraguan route was more feasible than Panama or Tehuantepec, Mexico.

In 1885, Aniceto Menocal, an engineer working under the auspices of the US government, estimated that the construction was practicable and that it could be realized in six years at a cost of 75 million dollars. The first dredgers arrived in San Juan del Norte at the mouth of the San Juan river on the Atlantic Coast of Nicaragua in 1891. However, in 1893 the project started by the privately owned US Maritime Canal Company went bankrupt, with only 1 km dredged. The dredger remains in the bay of San Juan del Norte, a rusting monument to broken canal dreams. In 1901 the US House of Representatives passed a bill in favour of the US government building the canal in Nicaragua but, just as the Senate hearings on the proposal were about to begin, a Caribbean volcano erupted, killing thousands. A sharp lobbyist for the Panama Canal project distributed a Nicaraguan postage stamp depicting Volcán Momotombo in eruption to all the senators, with the footnote that a Nicaraguan canal would have to pass by this active volcano. This was not actually true, as it was the active Concepción volcano on the Island of Ometepe that would be passed, but it was convincing enough and, in reality, Panama had a more favourable political climate for the US. The canal project was awarded to Panama.

Several projects are still looking for funding for a canal which would surely destroy the natural splendour of the Río San Juan, which has survived so many invasions, attacks and close calls.

some small rapids just past the river's drainage into the Río San Juan. The fishing for *sábalo real* (giant tarpon) is quite good here. They can reach up to 2½ m and weigh in at 150 kg. *Robalo* (snook) is also a popular sport fish and much better to eat than tarpon. Just downriver from Sábalo is the charming, clean and friendly town of El Castillo, 60 km from San Carlos and home to a famous 17th-century fortress.

The dance of life: an introduction to tropical rainforest ecology

Tropical rainforests are the earth's most biologically diverse places, the visible face of nature's wildest, weirdest fantasies. They're home to such a profusion of plant and animal species that we may never fully identify them all, let alone comprehend their complex interactions. To call the rainforest 'luxuriant' is a cliché. To call it dynamic, ravenous, savage, exuberant and fantastic is only a start. Even the most seasoned naturalist can feel overwhelmed here. The multitude of forms, the sheer scope and intricacy of biological life is unlike anything in the temperate world. Where to begin? With the basics: soil, water and light.

Soil provides the nutrients and physical support necessary for terrestrial plant life, and given the vigour of rainforest flora, it would seem that soil here is exceptionally rich, but it is not. Soil is poor in the tropical rainforest, for there is no 'store' or surplus of energy in this rapidly shifting ecosystem; everything is used and nutrient turnover is high. On the forest floor, dung and dead matter are quickly devoured by fungi who deliver its nutrients to the trees in exchange for photosynthetic energy. This symbiotic trade-off occurs via a vast mat of tangled roots just beneath the thin surface of the soil.

As you'd expect, water is available in prodigious quantities in the rainforest. This abundance is responsible for the evergreen appearance of the vegetation. But water does more than feed the plants, it provides the intense humidity vital for fungi to flourish, and frogs too, who inhabit the rainforest in great numbers, and put on a spectacular nightly chorus.

The energy of sunlight forms the basis of all the earth's ecosystems, but in the tropics it is consistently fierce, beating down 12 hours per day, every day. In spite of such abundance,

El Castillo » pp188-190.

The peaceful little village of El Castillo could well be the most attractive riverfront settlement in Nicaragua. Located in front of the **El Diablo rapids,** El Castillo is a sight to behold: tiny riverfront homes with red tin roofs sit on stilts above the fast-moving river. Behind, on a round grassy green hill, a big, 330-year-old Spanish fort dominates the view of the town. Most people come to see the fort, but the village makes a longer stay worthwhile.

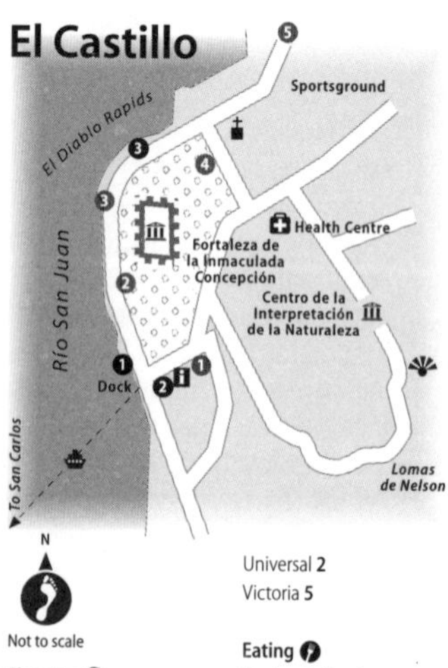

Sleeping
Albergue El Castillo 1
Posada del Río 3
Richardson 4
Universal 2
Victoria 5

Eating
Borders Coffee 2
Cofalito 1
Vanessa's 3

Tourist information Right in front of the town dock is a little office for **INTUR,** often unmanned, but good for advice on hiring boats if it's open.

Fortaleza de la Inmaculada Concepción

When British pirate Henry Morgan made off down the Río San Juan with £500,000 competition for light is particularly intense. A series of canopies filter out this vital energy and many plants have developed creative strategies in response. Vines and creepers germinate on the floor, entwine themselves on tree trunks and drag themselves upwards. Hemiepiphytes germinate up in the canopy and send roots downwards. Meanwhile, the ever-present, spidery epiphytes attach themselves to high branches, utilizing higher levels of light. For this reason the rainforest appears as a multitude of plants clamoring for a glimpse of the sun.

But the most fascinating aspect of rainforest ecology is the complex web of relationships between plant and animal species. Pollination is a vivid example. As there is no wind in the rainforest, plants need animals to pollinate. More than this, they need very specific animals, as their own species tend to be widely dispersed and the right pollen needs to reach the right plant. There can be no randomness here. To that end, flowers proffer up nectar in very specific ways. Orange flowers attract butterflies, trumpet shaped blooms attract hummingbirds, moths and bats are drawn to pale white flowers, and aroid flowers stink of carrion, attracting flesh flies and beetles. But plant-animal relations are usually even more complex than this. For example, there is a certain species of orchid that lures a unique type of bee with a range of different fragrances. The male bees collect these fragrances on their hind legs, one after the other, and when they hit the right combination, they start attracting other males. The males form a swarm, a flashing metallic swirl that attracts females and initiates their own reproductive cycle. Such is the dance of life in the rainforest; intriguing, entrancing and also strangely poetic.

sterling after sacking Granada, the Spanish said *¡Basta!* (enough!). Construction of the fort at El Castillo began in 1673 on the top of a hill that affords long views to the east (the route of attacks) and in front of one of the river's most dangerous rapids. In 1674 French pirates encountered a half-finished fortress, but were warded off. Work was completed in 1675 and today the fort is Nicaragua's oldest standing colonial building (in its original state). Tipped to become a UNESCO World Heritage Site, this was the biggest fortress on the Central American isthmus and the second biggest in all the Spanish American colonial empire when it was finished.

In the 18th century the fort came under siege from the British several times. In 1762 the British Navy came up the Río San Juan to take the fort and control the river. A new national hero was born in El Castillo – a teenage girl called Rafaela Herrera, the daughter of a decorated captain of the Spanish forces who had recently died. The soldiers of the fort were ready to concede defeat, but Rafaela, who had received training in armament, took command of the fortress and troops and fired the first rounds of cannon herself against the British. She is said to have killed a British commander with her third shot. The battle lasted five days. One night, under heavy attack from the boats under cover of darkness, Rafaela ordered sheets to be soaked in alcohol, placed on big branches and set alight upriver. The flaming torches illuminated the enemy for counter fire and the river carried the burning debris downstream toward the enemy's wooden boats. The British were forced to retreat.

In 1779 English chancellor Lord George Germain devised a serious attack on the Río San Juan that was aimed at securing British domination of Lake Nicaragua and control of the province. Seven warships were brought to the mouth of the Río San Juan with a force of 600 British soldiers and 400 Miskito warriors. Also on the mission was a young Captain Horatio Nelson, later to become the British Navy's greatest hero. The fortress at El Castillo had two weaknesses and Nelson's attack exposed both. Firstly, the fort had no water supply, so the Spanish were unable to take water from the river while under siege. Secondly, there is high ground just behind the fort, which allowed the fort attackers to shoot down into the fortress. Nelson brought the troops ashore well before the fort and travelled overland through the forest (legend has it he killed a jaguar on the way and narrowly avoided dying from a snake bite) to attack the fortress from the high hill behind. Today, the hill is a cemetery known as Lomas de Nelson. The British won the battle and took control of the fort, but Matías de Galvez, the captain general of Central America, was every bit as capable as the British generals who masterminded the invasion. Galvez decided to let the jungle do his work for him and, using massive troop reinforcements in San Carlos, kept the British forces bottled up in the fort. Soon the Miskito got tired of waiting and left. Jungle diseases, especially dysentery and malaria, set in and in less than a year the great majority of the invasion forces had died. The British decided to abandon the fort. Many Nicaraguan history books claim Nelson lost his eye in battles at the fort, others say he lost the use of an arm. In fact neither occurred here, but his health was so affected by dysentery that he had to be carried off the boat on a cot when he returned to Jamaica.

A museum and library were built inside the fortress in the 1990s. The **museum** ① *0900-1200, 1400-1700, US$2,* is one of the country's finest with a very complete history of the region (in Spanish) and the views alone are worth the price of admission. There is also an educational museum behind the fortress, **Centro de Interpretación de la Naturaleza**, with displays and explanations of local wildlife and vegetation as well as a butterfly farm.

El Castillo–Río Bartola → *Travel time about 25 mins.*

Travelling downstream from the fortress means riding the small but tricky rapids in front of the town. Locals fish here and Nicaraguan boat drivers have no problems zigzagging through the rapids, though the occasional reckless boatman has flipped over here. Just 2 km downriver, there's a narrow cut through the forest up a hill and a Nicaraguan flag marks the border with Costa Rica, which reaches the southern banks of the river here and follows most of the river to the Caribbean Sea. The confluence of the Río San Juan and Río Bartola marks the beginning of the splendid Indio-Maíz Biological Reserve.

Reserva Biológica Indio-Maíz » pp188-190.

This is Central America and Nicaragua's second largest nature reserve and perhaps its most pristine. Several square kilometres here house more species of birds, trees or insects than the entire European continent. The reserve protects what North American biologists have called "the largest extent of primary rainforest in Central America", its trees reaching up to 50 m in height. Indio-Maíz also has numerous wetland areas and rivers. Its westernmost border is marked by the Río Bartola; at the east is the Caribbean Sea; and the northern and southern limits are marked by the Río Punta Gorda and Río San Juan respectively. There is no accommodation inside the reserve at the time of printing, but the banks of the river have been changed (downgraded in terms of level of protection) from biological reserve to wildlife refuge, in theory allowing for construction of ecolodges along the Nicaraguan bank of the river and opening up the reserve to more tourism.

Background

Inside the reserve's pristine forest are several ancient extinct volcanoes, the highest being **Cerro La Guinea** at 648 m. The reserve is home to over 600 species of bird, 300

Strange bedfellows

Indio-Maíz is home to one of the most industrious and intelligent members of the ant family and one of the most beautiful and deadly of the frog species.

The **leaf-cutter ant**, at 7-10 mm in length, is always at work cutting off little pieces of fresh leaves to carry on his wobbling little body to his colony's underground chamber. The plant matter is used to grow the fungus that is the diet for the subterranean community. Their nests are big, well-protected caverns that the ants defend with zeal – they have been documented chasing off animals as large as armadillos.

Co-existing alongside these ferocious little workaholics is the beautiful and deadly *Dendrobates auratus*, a bright green and black spotted **poison dart frog**. The name is derived from the toxic solution secreted by the frog and used by the indigenous people of the region to coat the tips of their darts and so subdue their prey. While researching in the forest reserve behind the Refugio Bartola, UCLA biology students observed that wherever there was a leaf-cutter ants' nest there also appeared to be a significantly higher population of these deadly frogs.

Several theories were put to the test to discover why they were there. Hunger would be the most obvious reason for the frogs to be at the nest sites, as 70% of their diet is made up of ants, which they must consume in order to maintain their toxicity. However, test frogs left in a bucket with the leaf-cutter ants died of starvation and were actually attacked by the ants. Another possibility is that the frogs use the ant trails as a navigational tool to care for their young. It seems that the male frog carries the tadpoles to a pool of water, usually in a tree hole, and returns daily to feed them. Another theory is that the aggressive nature of the ants' nest soldiers may help protect the frogs from predators.

After several lengthy experiments the students concluded that the frogs stay close to the ants' nests because their skin resembles a large group of leaf-cutter ants or vice versa. These two little characters are part of an intricate forest orchestra that plays a jungle symphony thousands of years old; one of interaction and co-dependence, the song of the chain of life.

species of reptile and amphibian, and 200 species of mammal, including many big cats and howler, white-face and spider monkeys. Rainfall in the park ranges from just under 3000 mm a year in Bartola to 5000 mm in San Juan del Norte. Sadly little research has been done in the reserve and most of its wildlife and vegetation remains a mystery but over the past decade UCLA biologists have been enlisting the help of student volunteers. They report that the density and diversity of the wildlife at the field site (the forest behind Bartola and the MARENA station) is "impressive, even by neotropical standards". As well as the three primate species, the students discovered two bird species previously undocumented in Nicaragua and made a list of birds that include 11 different species of heron, two of ibis and stork, 12 species of hawk, kite and falcon, and eight species of parrot and macaw. They also documented 11 species of hummingbird, six kingfisher, three toucan, seven woodpecker, 19 antbirds and no less than 27 species of flycatcher. The biologists also encountered 28 species of reptile and 16 species of mammal including three-toed sloth, jaguarundi, river otter, tapir, deer, agouti, paca, white-faced,

Costa Rica and Nicaragua: A bridge too far?

They appear on the world map as perfect opposites. The nature- and peace-loving Costa Ricans living happily in their tourist Mecca, the self-proclaimed Switzerland of Central America and darling of international ecotourism. While across the Río San Juan, lies bad-boy Nicaragua, a country synonymous with war and natural disasters, whose inhabitants are always fighting among themselves and daring to defy the United States, driving their own economy into the ground.

It was not always this way, but the tables have been turned over the years, creating bitterness on both sides. During the war against William Walker in 1856, Costa Rica rushed to help Nicaragua fight Walker and occupied southern Lake Nicaragua and the then lucrative inter-oceanic route of the Río San Juan. After Walker was defeated, Costa Rica hoped to annex Granada, Chontales and Rivas, leaving Nicaragua with Río San Juan and Lake Nicaragua. However, they had to settle for Guanacaste, the Nicoya Peninsula and the southern banks of the Río San Juan, sowing the seeds of an animosity that lives on today. The Río San Juan remains the property of Nicaragua, but the Costa Ricans now have rights to its southern shores east of El Castillo after treaty was agreed which allowed Costa Rica limited navigational rights on the Río San Juan, for commercial traffic only.

During the mid-20th century Nicaragua had a booming economy while Costa Rica was at civil war. White-collar Costa Ricans came to stable Nicaragua to find quality employment. Thirty years later, however, Nicaraguans, fed up with a government that was great for business and lousy for personal freedom, rebelled. Arms were shipped from South America, Panama and Cuba to Costa Rica where they were funnelled into Nicaragua and the Sandinista southern front made attacks across the border against the Somoza regime. After the Sandinista victory, disillusioned Nicaraguans, funded by the CIA, mounted Contra attacks against the Sandinista regime, again from Costa Rica. All the while the Costa Ricans were getting a bit tired of being used as a base for rebel operations.

Freedom was finally won after years of war, but Nicaragua's economy was

spider and howler monkey. The sheer beauty of the reserve means that non-enthusiasts will also enjoy the enchantment of a virgin rainforest.

Río Bartola–Río San Carlos → *Travel time about 1 hr.*

This is one of the most scenic sections of the river, in particular the area around the rapids of **Machuca** and just upriver from the mouth of Río San Carlos, which originates in Costa Rica. The forest is in good condition on both sides of the river and the trees are teeming with parrots. As the vegetation rises out of succulent rainforest, it's easy to see why Mark Twain (see box, page 148) and other observers have been so enchanted over time.

At the mouth of the pristine **Río Sarnoso** is a shipwreck from the 19th-century inter-oceanic steam ship service, though the locals like to claim it is a Spanish galleon wreck. Jaguar can be seen here, one of the most difficult jungle animals to spot thanks to their preference for night hunting and large territories (up to 11 sq km). To enter the Río Sarnoso you will need to receive advance permission from MARENA in Managua (see page 44) and show the letter to the guards east or west of the river.

At the confluence of the **Río San Carlos** there is a checkpoint for the Nicaraguan military and MARENA, where passports must be presented. Across the banks in Costa destroyed. With the economy in ruins, much of Nicaragua's uneducated work force left, in an exodus of undocumented workers, for Costa Rica. Social problems in Costa Rica were blamed on Nicaraguan immigrants. Several human rights watch groups documented abuses by the Costa Rican military against Nicaraguan immigrant farm workers and Nicaraguan migrants found little humour in the claim that Costa Rica had no military, a feat achieved by calling their large (larger than the entire Nicaraguan military and police force combined), well-trained troops the 'Civil Guard'. It was the same non-existent Costa Rican military that was caught dressed in battle fatigues patrolling the Río San Juan in a camouflage boat in 1998, with automatic rifles and mounted machine-guns at the ready. The news sent Nicaraguans into outrage. Nicaraguans called for a total ban of Costa Rican boat travel inside its borders. Costa Rica threatened to expel all Nicaraguan immigrant workers and both countries lapsed into uncomfortable diplomatic attempts at repair.

Feelings have calmed and Costa Ricans are once again allowed to navigate the river for commercial purposes, but allowing military patrols inside Nicaragua is a sticking point that remains un-resolved. Though the actual ownership of the river has never been in doubt, Nicaragua has long been suspicious of Costa Rica's desires to incorporate it.

Most people on the Río San Juan in both countries find all this bickering to be counterproductive, as they are commercially interdependent. On the Costa Rican bank of the Río San Juan, at the confluence of the Río Sarapiquí, there is a tiny lodge owned by a kind, aging Nicaraguan woman named Adilia Hernández. Doña Adilia has lived for over 40 years on the Costa Rican side of the San Juan River. Her daughters were all born in Costa Rica and they speak Costa Rican-accented Spanish. Doña Adilia told me one late afternoon, while gazing out at the Nicaraguan river, that she would like to return to live in Nicaragua some day. That night her hotel billiards table was being crowded by both Nicaraguan and Costa Rican border guards, it was pay day and they were playing pool, drinking beer and laughing loudly. I never did find out who won.

Rica there is a general store and a basic eatery. Permission can be obtained from the Costa Rican military to make a quick supply or food stop (córdobas are difficult to use on the Costa Rican side, so keep a supply of small note dollars).

There once was a Spanish fortress on the island that lies at the confluence of the San Carlos and San Juan rivers, which predated the structure at El Castillo. The **Fortaleza San Carlos** (not to be confused with the old fort at San Carlos on the lake) was built in 1667 with room for 70 musketeers and a few artillerymen to operate four cannon. Three years later, pirate Lawrence Prince attacked the little wooden fortress with 200 men. Only 37 Spanish soldiers had survived the climate and insects, but nonetheless put up stout resistance, killing six and wounding eight of the pirates and managing to send a boat up to Granada to ask for reinforcements. They never came and the Spaniards had to surrender. Prince sent his fastest canoe double-manned with Miskito oarsmen to overtake the Spanish messenger. He then went on to sack Granada, prompting the construction of the great structure at El Castillo (see page 180).

Río San Carlos–Río Sarapiquí → *Travel time about 1 hr.*

Past the Río San Carlos the stunning beauty of the Indio-Maíz reserve on the north bank continues, while the south bank is a mixture of forest and ranch settlements, with some clear cutting. There are sandbars and beaches most of the year and slow navigation will allow opportunities to spot crocodiles and turtles, as well as monkeys and toucans in the canopy. The muddy, debris-filled **Río Sarapiquí** drains into the Río San Juan at the second river checkpoint for the military and MARENA. The Sarapiquí is in Costa Rica and there is a small village where basic boat and motor repairs can be made. This was the scene of several significant battles between the Edén Pastora-led southern front Contra forces and the Nicaraguan Sandinista military in the 1980s. At the confluence of the two rivers on the Costa Rican side is **Doña Adilia's** (see page 189), a small friendly lodge and the last chance for a bed before the end of the river.

Río Sarapiquí–Río Colorado → *Travel time about 1 hr.*

Past the drainage of the Sarapiquí, the Río San Juan travels northeast passing some of the river's 300 islands, including the **Isla Nelson**. Petrol is available on the Costa Rican side, which is dotted with sprawling ranches. The Nicaraguan territory (which includes the river and its islands) is pristine rainforest mixed with some secondary growth where land was reclaimed for the biological reserve. At one of the widest parts of the river it branches southeast and northeast. To the southeast is the mighty **Río Colorado** in Costa Rica. To the northeast is the **Río San Juan**. Thanks to sediment build-up in the bay of San Juan since the mid- to late-1800s, the majority of the water now drains out of the Río Colorado to the sea. There is another checkpoint here. Past the intersection of the two rivers, the Río San Juan becomes narrow and runs almost due north.

Río Colorado–Caribbean Sea → *Travel time about 2 hrs.*

As it approaches the sea, the Río San Juan begins to snake wildly. It twists and turns past wetlands and the broad, handsome swamp palms that are common in this area, until it meets the sea at a dark sandbar called simply **La Barra** (the bar). The emerging and submerging sandbar (according to the tides and the force of the San Juan river) has fooled navigators for hundreds of years and has been responsible for many a sailor's death. After hours of dense jungle, the sight of the windswept beach is exhilarating. Here the Caribbean is muddy, filled with sediment from the river and literally teeming with bull sharks that are feeding on the many fish in this rich combination of fresh and salt water. Swimming is only for the suicidal (you could not pay a local to swim here) – strong surf and currents aid the sharks in ripping apart any flesh within its reach.

This section of the Río San Juan is normally quite good for sighting monkeys, toucans, scarlet macaws and king vultures.

Bahía de San Juan » *pp189-190.*

North of the sandbank is a series of connected coastal estuaries known collectively as the Bay of San Juan. If sunny, the bay is glorious, with deep blue water reflecting dense green rainforest and shores lined with flowering waterlilies and grass. This is the end of the earth: a tropical paradise. It is also one of the wettest places in the Americas, with an average annual rainfall of 5000 mm. Sitting forlornly in the bay is the more than 100-year-old dredger that started the canal project to connect the two seas. Today its rusted body is covered with vegetation. There is superb fishing and an ecolodge in front of the dredger.

Greytown

At the edge of one of the lagoons are a small, decaying wooden dock and a tattered Nicaraguan flag which marks the entrance to the historic and now-deserted frontier town of Greytown. This is all that remains of the original San Juan del Norte, known to most as Greytown after the British governor of Jamaica in 1847 when the town was re-baptized by the British. In 1850 the US was flexing its naval muscles in the region and the two powers signed a pact to unify and build a canal in Nicaragua with both British and US Navies controlling its waters. In 1854 the city was destroyed by bombing from a US battleship. It seems the attack was provoked by a boating accident in which the boat of US representative Mr Boland sunk the vessel of a Nicaraguan Indian. The locals demanded that the captain of the US boat be captured and tried. Mr Boland refused, a fight broke out and the honourable Boland was unceremoniously smashed over the head with a beer bottle. The US government fined the Nicaragua government 24,000 pesos for the bump on Boland's head and gave Nicaragua 24 hours to pay up. Nicaragua refused and a hail of 210 cannon balls fell on Greytown, destroying the village but failing to set it alight. That afternoon US troops torched the town house by house.

Twelve years later Mark Twain slept here on his journey from San Francisco to New York and described the town as a "peopled paradise ... composed of 200 old frame houses and some nice vacant lots, and its comeliness is greatly enhanced, I may say is rendered gorgeous, by the cluster of stern-wheel steamboats at the water front. The population is 800 and is mixed – made up of natives (Nicaraguans), Americans, Spaniards, Germans, English and Jamaicans." He added that "the transit business has made every other house a lodging camp and you can get a good bed anywhere for a dollar." Today the only beds are in the town's cemeteries, which are preserved as a national monument. The city was taken over in 1982 by Edén Pastora and his Contra army unit, which provoked further bombardment by the Nicaragua Sandinista government. When Pastora's forces retreated, it was burned down by the Sandinista military and left as it is today. However, Greytown's economic demise had actually come much earlier when the inter-oceanic service was finally discontinued. It was briefly brought back to life by late-19th century canal projects, but then relegated to obscurity in the 20th century and reduced to 300 inhabitants.

After the 1982 burning, the village did not exist at all until it was re-founded upriver in 1990 as San Juan del Norte. The jungle that had taken over Greytown was cut down, ironically, by Edén Pastora in early 2004 so he could land his aeroplane here and get to his new shark fishing business in today's San Juan del Norte. The old village lies just to the north side of the new clearing. There is a quiet often water-filled trail that leads through Catholic, American, Masonic and Anglican cemeteries; the faded tombstones entwined in rainforest. The only other sign of Greytown is the bell from the town church, an old creaking windmill and the front steps of the Pellas family house.

San Juan del Norte

The end-of-the-world feeling is not lost in this little village of winding paths, homes on stilts and flooded yards. Fishing for brown and white lobster are the main sources of income. White lobster (*langosta blanca*), however, is in fact cocaine. The locals comb the beach or coastal waters for big bails of the drug that have been thrown overboard by Colombian speed boats being chased by the coastguard. The ocean currents dictate that a great deal ends up on the coast here. What was once a peaceful little lobster fishing village has become severely corrupted in the last few years thanks to the instant riches available from *langosta blanca*. Nonetheless, the residents of San Juan del Norte are very friendly, a mix of Afro-Caribbeans from Bluefields and El Limón in Costa Rica, Hispanics from the Pacific, and some of the indigenous Rama from Bluefields Bay. The village lines the west bank of the Río Indio, one of Nicaragua's most beautiful rivers, and 200 m wide at this point. There is a road resembling a central avenue with little palms and brightly painted benches and two footpaths. This runs parallel to the river about 50 m inside the village. Across the river is a 400-m wide strip of land full of coconut palms, dense forest and beach that separates the copper-coloured Río Indio from the crashing Caribbean

 Sea. It is a delightfully surreal experience to watch the jungle river flow south as the sun sets over the bright green rainforest that separates the two bodies of water, while being serenaded by the muffled roar of the sea.

Río Indio

If you have chartered a boat, a trip further down the Río Indio is recommended to see wildlife, virgin forest and occasional encounters with the indigenous Rama (please respect their culture and right to privacy), who are returning to the region after centuries of exile. If coming by public boat, Melvin of **Hotel Lost Paradise** (see page 189) can arrange a tour down the river in one of his super-*panga* boats. Upriver is truly spectacular, like a miniature Amazon, with kilometre after kilometre of virgin forest. It is important to leave early to see wildlife, and to bring plenty of petrol and water. You will need permission from the military and MARENA checkpoint at the north end of town on the riverfront. The river provides opportunities for serious adventure, but your budget must be healthy as there is no public transport. The Rama people navigate the river in canoes to buy weekly supplies in San Juan, but will only be able to offer a one-way ride to the jungle. The river goes into the heart of the Indio-Maíz reserve. Ask around locally to see what the current security situation is.

Blue Lagoon

Just past the military checkpoint on the bar that separates the river from the sea is the Blue Lagoon. There can quite a bit of rubbish on its banks, but the water is clean and there are no sharks or crocodiles. Locals swim here because the sea is full of sharks and very rough.

Sleeping

Río Sábalo *p178*

L-C Monte Cristo River Resort, 2 km downriver from Boca de Sábalos, T583-0259, www.montecristoriver.com. Comfortable rooms with private bath. There are also apartments, a swimming pool, dance floor, 'Mark Twain Bar', flexible rates and fishing trips (US$100 per day). Sometimes loud weekend parties arrive from El Castillo to use the dance hall.

B-D Sábalos Lodge, in front of El Toro rapids, just downriver from Río Sábalo, T850-7623, www.sabaloslodge.com. Funky and attractive mix of huts, cabins, shacks, some with bath inside, and hammocks. One nice unit on the river has a sitting room and deck, all open to the outside with mosquito netting. Mixed reports, beautiful grounds but not much forest around.

D Hotel Sábalos, on confluence of San Juan and Sábalo rivers, T894-9377, www.hotelsabalos.com.ni. This simple and friendly wooden hotel has a good location, with views up and down the river, great for watching locals pass in canoes. 12 small rooms have private bath and fan. The best resting spot on upper San Juan. Recommended.

El Castillo *p180, map p180*

Few hotel rooms have private bathrooms.

A Posada del Río, el muelle, 100 vrs arriba, T616-3528. The best place in town, with very comfortable and pleasant rooms, hot water, a/c, private bath and balconies. Breakfast included.

C Hotel Victoria, el muelle, 400 vrs arriba, at the end of the end road, T583-0188, hotelvictoria01@yahoo.es. 9 rooms with fan, private bath and hot water, 3 with a/c and 2 with shared bath (**E**). There are lots of turtles and caimans nearby, but they seem to be feeding on waste from the hotel. Breakfast included.

D Albergue El Castillo, next to fortress above city dock, T583-0195. Comfortable, if simple, wooden rooms and great views from a shared balcony overlooking the river. Only 1 room has a private bath, for extra side

For an explanation of the sleeping and eating price codes used in this guide, see inside the front cover. Other relevant information is found in Essentials, see pages 23-27.

ventilation, the best rooms are Nos 1 and 10, but you have noisy bats for company in 10. Good food; try the *camarones de río* (river shrimp) in garlic butter. Noisy early morning as the public boats warm up (0500) motors. Breakfast included.

D Hotel Richardson, el muelle, 1 c arriba, ½ c sur, T552-8825. Sometimes seems to be abandoned; if the owner isn't there, ask around. The rooms are small and cleanish, and they have private baths (the only place in town that does) with shower curtain doors.

F Universal, el muelle, 50 vrs arriba. Friendly owners, good views and small, clean, wooden rooms. A nice budget choice.

Río Bartola *p184*

B Refugio Bartola, confluence of Río San Juan and Río Bartola, T681-9541, refugiobartola@yahoo.com. Simple wooden rooms with private bath, high ceilings and solid beds. Prices include 3 meals, juice and coffee, bats in roof and frogs in toilet at no extra charge. There's a research station on site, with lots of creepy creatures in jars, including what could be the world's largest cockroach. There's also a private reserve with a labyrinth of trails. You need a guide (US$5, plus tip) as it's easy to get lost, and be sure to ask questions. Snakes, some deadly, are a real danger on a night hike. The pet spider monkey, Daniela, loves men and bites women (she's very jealous).

Camping is also possible in the park. MARENA (the Nicaraguan environmental agency) park rangers at Bartola are very strict, but should let you camp at the guardhouse clearing. Their station is across the Río Bartola from the Refugio Bartola.

Río Sarapiquí *p186*

E Cabinas La Trinidad or **Doña Adilia's**, at confluence of Río San Juan and Río Sarapiquí on Costa Rican bank, mobile T506-391-7120, hurbinacom@yahoo.com. Little rooms (not terribly clean and bring your own mosquito net) with private bath and fan, run by a friendly, kind family. Nice garden with good birdwatching, billiards table, restaurant with decent set meals, US$3. Doña Adilia also has a small store to buy supplies and will accept córdobas. You need to check in with the Costa Rican guard station across from the lodge on the Río Sarapiquí if you just want to pick up something at the store and if you want to spend the night here. Only resting spot on the lower Río San Juan.

Bahía de San Juan *p186*

LL Río Indio Lodge, between Indio and San Juan rivers, near San Juan del Norte, T506-296-0095, www.rioindiolodge.com. Multi-million dollar lodge, designed for upscale fishing packages but excellent for wildlife safaris, birdwatching and rainforest walks. 20 big wooden cabins have screened windows, 2 queen-sized beds, ceiling fans, good ventilation, hot water and a private nature viewing porch. Food is the only weakness: very Americanized buffet-style menu. But this is still Nicaragua's finest rainforest jungle lodge, and recently named one of the top 10 jungle lodges in the world.

San Juan del Norte *p187*

F Hotel Lost Paradise or **Melvin's Place**, on the river at the south end of town. Becoming neglected, this place has rooms with ceiling fan, private bath and screened windows (but bring coils or mosquito netting). Bar, restaurant (order well in advance), night-time generated power, gazebo on the river, bottled water is sometimes for sale.

F Greytown Lodge, no sign, near to Melvin's. Basic and friendly accommodation with cooking facilities.

Eating

El Castillo *p180, map p180*

Eating is good here – the freshwater prawns (*camarones de río*) and snook (*robalo*) are both excellent.

ΨΨ-Ψ Bar Cofalito, on the jetty. Has a great view upstairs overlooking the river and serves excellent *camarones de río*, considered by many the best in town, occasional fresh fish.

Ψ Borders Coffee, next to the dock. Good pasta and fresh organic coffee at this friendly little café. Nice views of the river and a good place to wait for your boat. They can arrange stays at a nearby *finca*.

Ψ Vanessa's, el muelle, 1 c arriba. Great spot by the rapids, with excellent fish and river shrimp.

San Juan del Norte *p187*
Drinks in town consist of Costa Rican beer, Nicaraguan rum and Coca-Cola.
Bar Indio, upriver from Ester's. A big palm ranch and serving cold beer. Friendly, card-playing locals.
Doña Ester's Place, just upriver from Melvin's Place (see Sleeping). The town's only restaurant, average dish costs US$3.

Shopping

El Castillo *p180, map p180*
Just east of the dock is a general store that sells purified water and other basic supplies. If travelling far on the river it may be wise to buy some of the heavy-duty yellow (or orange) plastic bags sold here. Protect all luggage against the rain with a double layer of plastic.

San Juan del Norte *p187*
Near the school sports field are a couple of good shops, one of which has a great variety of supplies including rubber boots or wellingtons (*botas de hule*) in big sizes (not found elsewhere in Nicaragua).

Activities and tours

El Castillo *p180, map p180*
Kayaking and fishing
Most hotels and many restaurants can organize short tours of the river. However, there is a lack of English-speaking guides in town.
Castillo Kayak, inside Cofalito's restaurant, T432-8441. A range of tours including half-day kayak trips and extensive expeditions along the Río San Juan. Miguel is an English-speaking native who has spent 16 years exploring the region. Fun and recommended.

Tour guides
Guías Turísticas Río San Juan, tourist office by the pier. This group of 9 guides offers a range of tours on and off the water; horse rides, kayak excursions and night tours to observe the caimans among them.

Transport

El Castillo *p180, map p180*
To **San Carlos**; 0500 (slow boat), 0520 (express), 0600, 0700, 1100 (express), 1400, US$2.75 (US$3.75 express, US$2 slow boat), 1½-2½ hrs, reduced services on Sun when only first 2 boats run. Avoid the slow boat if you can. To **San Juan del Norte**, Tue, Fri, 0930, US$10, 5 hrs.

San Juan del Norte *p187*
To **San Carlos**, stopping at **El Castillo**, Thu and Sun, 0430, US$15. There's little chance of connecting with **Bluefields**, north on the Caribbean Coast, unless you have lots of patience, cash and a strong, sea-faring stomach. You might hitch a ride on a fishing boat if you're lucky, otherwise expect a challenging trip.

A landing strip has been promised at San Juan del Norte for some time, but was not complete at the time of press. If interested, check with **La Costeña** airline or tour operators in Managua (see page 64) to attain its current status and see if planned flights between San Juan del Norte and **Managua** are now being run.

Directory

El Castillo *p180, map p180*
There are no banks here. Bring all the cash you need before setting out.
Telephone Enitel, T552-6124.

San Juan del Norte *p187*
Banks There are no banks and the most common currency is Costa Rican colones thanks to the (relatively) easy access to El Limón, Costa Rica. You can pay in córdobas or dollars, but expect change in colones. Village locals may be willing to change money at wilderness rates, options are few, ask around.
Nicaraguan immigration There is Nicaraguan customs and immigration at San Juan del Norte, but officially entrance and exit stamps for international travel cannot be obtained here.
Telephone There are 2 shops that offer the use of a mobile telephone, when it is working. The service is via Costa Rica to Nicaragua.

León and El Occidente

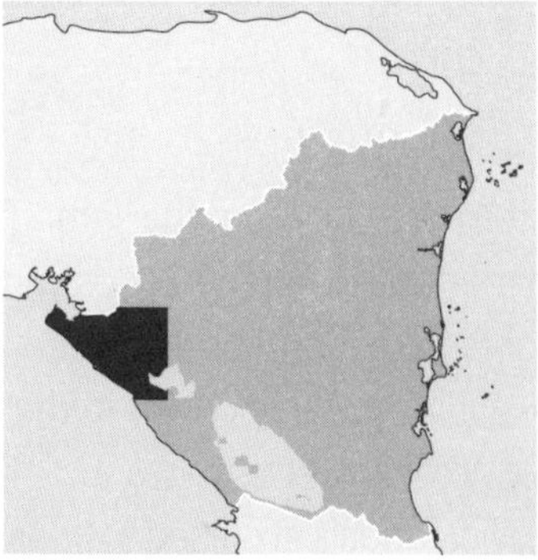

Footprint features

Introduction

Nicaragua's sweltering northwestern provinces are the setting for immense and extraordinary panoramas, scorched skies and violently shifting geological tempers. This a land born of fire, home to one of the most densely active volcanic chains in the world: the Cordillera Los Maribios. Within this tempestuous terrain lie the ruins of León Viejo, Nicaragua's accursed first capital, destroyed by forces of nature and haunted by its notoriously cruel past.

Fortunately, León was rebuilt and today survives as one of Central America's finest colonial cities. The former home Nicaragua's greatest poets, León is the artistic and intellectual heart of the country. As a former hotbed for Sandinista activity, a wealth of satirical murals, commemorative sites, bombed-out ruins and bullet-marked buildings are evidence of the city's turbulent revolutionary history. Today, its student population gives it a vibrant edge and an active nightlife. After a day pounding the colonial streets, you can relax in one of the city's many bars, drink a beer and take in a rousing live music performance.

If you need a break from the heat and chaos of the city, an excursion to the sleepy beaches of Poneloya and Las Peñitas, an hour west, is refreshing and welcome. The departments of León and Chinandega enjoy miles of Pacific coastline accented by beaches, barrier islands and coastal lagoons.

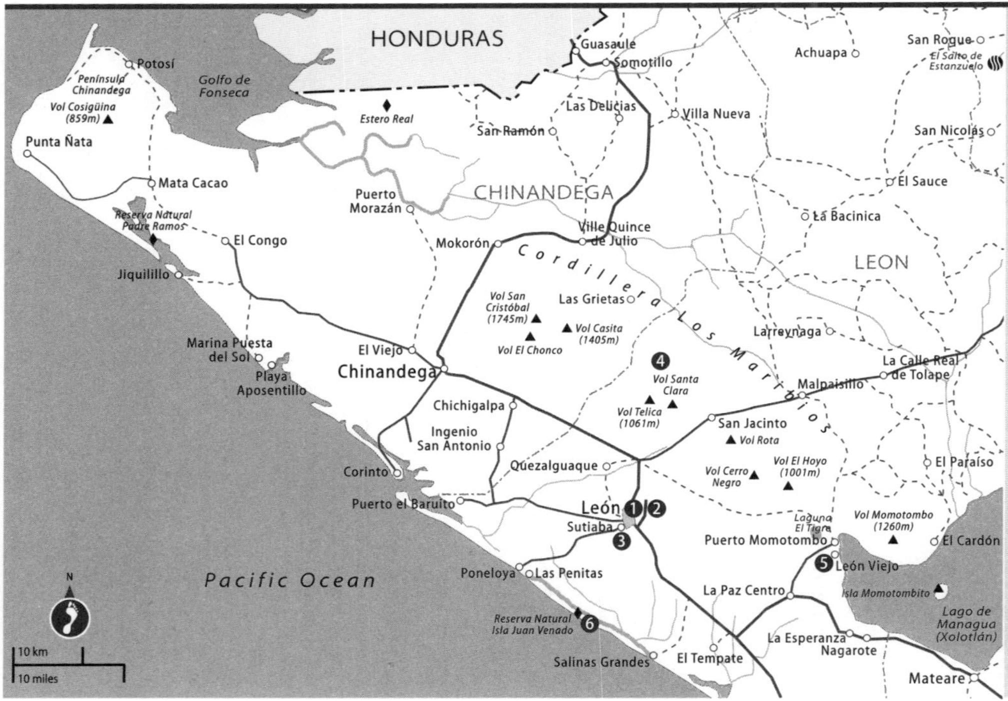

★ Don't miss ...

1 **Adobe temples** Make an early start and wander around León's colonial churches before the sun rises, page 197.

2 **Words of power** Be inspired by the poetry of Rubén Darío, then explore his beloved León, Nicaragua's intellectual heart, page 200.

3 **Good Friday street art** Marvel at the intense colours and emotions of the sawdust street paintings of Sutiava, page 204.

4 **Earth and fire** Trek the violently active Maribios volcano range, an unearthly landscape of smoking craters and fumarolic pools, page 210.

5 **Headless honcho** Explore the UNESCO World Heritage Site of León Viejo and see where country founder Chico Córdoba lost his head, page 214.

6 **Crocodile kayaking** Paddle the brackish waters of the Isla Juan Venado Wildlife Refuge, page 217.

León

→ *Population: 155,000. Altitude: 109 m. Colour map 3, A2.*

The crumbling old Spanish city of León is full of intellectual vitality and artistic tradition; a place to unravel Nicaragua's past and glimpse its future. The colonial capital has fine examples of old Spanish architecture and it is full to the brim with students from all over the country who come to study in its fine secondary schools and universities. With a dozen colonial churches and Central America's largest cathedral, this fervently Catholic city is home to some of Nicaragua's most beautiful religious celebrations and traditions. Despite the sweltering year-round heat of the León valley, the city enjoys an advantageous position set between the ruggedly majestic Maribios Volcanoes to the east and the crashing surf of the warm Pacific Ocean to the west.

›› *For Sleeping, Eating and other listings, see pages 205-210.*

Ins and outs

Getting there

León can be reached by regular bus and microbus services from Managua and Chinandega, and by less frequent services from Estelí and Matagalpa. International buses also stop in León if arriving from Guatemala, Honduras or El Salvador.

Getting around

The city is laid out in the classic Spanish colonial grid system, based around a central plaza. The plaza, named Parque Jérez, is commonly referred to as Parque Central. The majestic León Cathedral faces west and sits on the central park's east side. Roads running east-west are *Calles* and those running north-south *Avenidas*. Calle Rubén Darío runs directly west from Parque Central, through Sutiava and all the way to the Pacific Ocean. Parallel streets to the north of Calle Rubén Darío are Calle 1 NE, Calle 2 NE etc. and on the south side of the park is Calle 1 SE, Calle 2 SE and so on. Avenida Central runs from the cemetery in the extreme south, past the Guadalupe church right into the central plaza and continues north of the plaza past banks, restaurants and the Iglesia La Recolección. Parallel streets to the west and east count up from one, just as with the Calles. There are 10 churches within eight blocks of the centre, with the Sutiava church just a few blocks further away. Though taxis are cheap, León is a terrific city for walking, with each barrio supporting its own unique church and beautiful colonial homes. ›› *For further details, see Transport, page 209.*

Best time to visit

León is hotter and drier than Managua and the rest of the Pacific Basin and daytime temperatures are normally 31-33°C with nights dipping to 24-26°C. The exception is from November to January when the streets are not cooked for quite so long. April is the hottest month. However, despite the searing heat at this time of year, the beauty of León's *Semana Santa* (Holy Week) celebrations makes it one of the best times to visit. The week leading up to Easter is full of endless processions and the extraordinary street paintings in Sutiava during *Viernes Santo* (Good Friday). The countrywide *Gritería* or *La Purísima* celebrations on 7 December were born in León and are very festive. During university vacation times in July and December through to early February the city is comparatively quiet.

Tourist information

The best source of English information is the **Foro** ⓘ *Via Via café, Banco ProCredit ½ c sur, T311-6142, www.viaviacafe.com*, where you'll find lots of useful stuff from bus timetables to details of cultural attractions. The Nicaraguan Institute of Tourism, **INTUR** ⓘ *Parque Rubén Darío, 2½ c norte, T311-3682*, has limited information and flyers; staff speak Spanish only. **UNAN** ⓘ *next to Restaurante El Sesteo, on Parque Central*, is a small office run by the tourism students of the university. They sell a good map of the city and other miscellaneous items. A useful Spanish language website for León and its vicinity is www.leononline.net.

Background

The present city was founded in 1610 after the abandonment of its cursed original location, known today as León Viejo (see page 214). The site was chosen to be close to the large indigenous settlement of Sutiava and to the Pacific, but with a 21-km buffer between it and the sea to protect against pirate attacks. The indigenous people of Sutiava are Maribios Indians, a group distinct from the Nicaraguas and Chorotegas that populated the rest of the Pacific Basin at the time of the arrival of the Spanish. The Maribios are thought to be related to the native inhabitants of southern and Baja California, with whom they share strong linguistic similarities.

Despite its tumultuous beginnings, León was the capital of Nicaragua for 242 years. (In 1852, the Nicaraguan Congress moved the country's capital to Managua as a compromise with Granada, which spent much of the mid-19th century contesting León's capital status.) As the administrative centre of Nicaragua, León was home to the Bishop of Nicaragua, as well as the country's first secondary school and university. Unlike Granada, León was not rich in commerce and therefore not a big target for pirates. The exception to this happened 75 years after the city's relocation, when an unholy alliance of British and French pirates descended upon it. Using the volcano San Cristóbal as a navigational tool, a makeshift army of 520 men entered what is today the port of Corinto and marched overland to León on 9 April 1685. The French pirate William Dampier described the city of 1685: "The homes of León are not tall, but big and solid yes, and with gardens. They have walls of stone and tile roofs. The city has three churches and a cathedral. Our compatriot, Mr Thomas Gage, says that this place is the most pleasant in all of the Americas and so much so that he used the term, 'paradise'. The truth is it exceeds the majority of other places in the Americas in both healthiness and attractiveness." The Spanish agreed to pay the demanded ransom of 300,000 gold pieces and food to sustain 1000 men for four months. The pirates waited, but after realizing the Spanish were stalling while waiting for troop reinforcements, the pirates set fire to the city on 14 April 1685 and retreated to the Pacific.

León produced one of the heroes of the fight for liberation from Spain, Miguel Larreynaga, who helped draft the original Central America constitution and can be seen on the 10 córdoba note today. After independence was declared on 15 September 1821, the Liberal Party of León (which would go on to figure heavily in Nicaragua's future) was pitted against the Conservative Party of Granada in what was to be a violent struggle for power. In 1844, León was invaded and conquered by the Salvadoran General Malespin, with the help of the conservative army of Granada, in a war that damaged the town centre and left the Veracruz Church in Sutiava in ruins.

At the turn of the 20th century, Liberal president José Santos Zelaya (who graces the 20 córdoba note) made radical changes to the country that brought a long occupation by the US Marines. Later, nationalist hero Augusto Sandino, a Liberal Party member, was abducted and assassinated under General Somoza García's orders. Somoza himself had become the country's de facto leader by deposing the

The Maribios people are most famous in Nicaraguan history books for scaring the living daylights out of the Spanish and their horses by dressing in the human skin of a ceremonial victim – worn inside out.

A tour through León and the Revolution (1978-1979)

Most Nicaraguans would like to put the violence of the past behind them for good, but there are still some signs of what passed in the difficult times of the war against Somoza. León was the centre of heavy fighting with brutal attempts at repression by Somoza's National Guard, including a series of air strikes. Revenge was taken on the Guard members after the victory. Visitors can see **El Fortín**, attacked by Somoza García in 1936 to take power of Nicaragua, and defended by Somoza Debayle 43 years later while trying desperately hold on to it. Somoza's guard lost it to the FSLN on July 7, 1979 and a commemorative Sandinista march goes there annually from León. From the cathedral, head west for about 10 blocks, then south; it's best in early morning for great views of León and the Maribios volcano range. It is next to the León city garbage dump; ask the men in hammocks for permission to enter the old fort.

El Veinte Uno, the National Guard's 21st garrison, notorious as the site of torture of Nicaraguan civilians and rebels, is today the Museo de Leyendas. It was taken by rebels from the guard on June 17, 1979. In front is a statue to *El Combatiente Desconocido* (the unknown warrior). Across the street you will see the bombed out ruins of **Iglesia San Sebastián**, destroyed by Somoza's aircraft in the uprising. A statue of Luisa Amanda Espinoza, in Barrio San Felipe, 7-8 blocks north of the market behind the cathedral, remembers the first woman member of the FSLN to die in 1970. The women's organization AMNLAE is named after her.

Opposite the north side of the cathedral is an interesting mural covering the country's history from pre-Columbian times to the Sandinista revolution, completed in 1990. It surrounds a commemorative park, the **Mausoleo Héroes y Mártires**. Across the street from the park are two popular murals on the walls of the old fire station. One illustrates Sandino standing on the head of Somoza, depicted as a pig, and another on the head of Uncle Sam, who is a dog.

Nearby, just 20 m west from the La Merced church park, is the **Galería de Héroes y Mártires** with black and white photographs of the heroes who gave their lives in the insurrection that toppled the final Somoza dictatorship. On the west side of Parque Central is the small exhibition of the **Combatientes Históricos** with various artefacts from the war years.

weak Liberal Party president, Juan Bautista Sacasa, that the US Marines had propped up before they pulled out. When Somoza García was assassinated in León by Rigoberto López in 1956, León's history with the Liberal Party had come full turn.

León became a hotbed for the Frente Sandinista de Liberación Nacional (FSLN) Marxist underground in the 1960s and 1970s and fighting against Somoza Debayle (the son of Somoza García) was fierce in León, with much damage suffered by the old city, some of which can still be seen today. After a final brutal battle which lasted from 3 June to 9 July 1979 and was won by the rebels, the FSLN, led by female Commandante Dora María Tellez, succeeded. The city is still strongly Sandinista, with every mayor since 1979 coming from the FSLN party. The private sector and Spanish government's foreign aid project have invested heavily in restoring the city; although not as thoroughly painted and restored as Granada, León is slowly regaining its visual glory.

Sights

The simplest and richest pleasure in the city is walking its historic streets, noting the infinite variety of colonial doors, ceiling work and window irons as well as sneaking peeks inside the grand houses to see their lush interior gardens. Though damaged in 1685, 1844 and 1979, León has retained much more of its colonial Spanish structural and design flavour than the oft-burned Granada. Reason enough to visit León are its many curious and beautiful churches: the city has more than a dozen of them, including the cathedral, Central America's grandest church.

Cathedral of León

The Cathedral of León, officially the **Basílica de la Asunción**, is the pride of both city and country. This impressive structure is the work of 113 years of labour, but it is not the first cathedral to stand in front of León's central park. Five years after the founding of León in its current location, a simple cathedral made of clay bricks and tiles was consecrated by the first Bishop of new León in 1615. The church was improved by the next Bishop of Nicaragua, with funds from Spain, but it was burned by the pirate invasion of 1685. Another construction was built, bigger still than the first, with three altars and five chapels. This church would survive about 60 years before the construction of the current cathedral began in 1747. Due to the size of the task and constant shortage of funds, it was not open for worship until 1780 and not finished in its current from until 1860. The Atlas figures in the central bell tower were added as a stylistic and structural enhancement in 1905. The Cathedral of León did not receive its pews until 1877 and all masses before that date were celebrated on foot or sitting and kneeling on the floor.

It's possible to climb the cathedral for commanding views of the city and the countryside, US$1.

Legend has it that the plans for the cathedrals of Lima in Peru and León were switched by mistake, but there is no evidence to support that charming excuse for such a big church in such a little country. The plans were drawn by Guatemalan architect Diego de Porres and two Franciscan Friars from Guatemala also worked on the design and layout of the temple, which has been described as 'Central American baroque' with its squat towers and super-thick walls. This design stems from the experience gained from building churches in the seismically active valley of Ciudad Antigua. But there are both gothic and neoclassical elements in this great structure. The fact that the cathedral was built from back to front over more than a century is clearly evident, with the back of the cathedral (the side of the market) exhibiting different design influences from the front (on the plaza). The exterior was painted in the mid-1990s and is in need of a fresh coat, but the interior's white-washed walls and ceiling give the church a peaceful, elegant look. Inside are large oils for the Stations of the Cross; recently restored for the first time since the 19th century.

The cathedral also houses a very fine **ivory Christ**, the consecrated **Altar of Sacrifices** and the **Choir of Córdoba**. The most famous image is called the *Cristo de Pedrarias*. This gothic work of Christ on the cross comes from the old cathedral of León Viejo; the damage on his right foot happened during the pirate attack of 1685. He is celebrated with fireworks every 2 July in León. Most controversial and least admired about the church are the column statues of the **12 Apostles**. At the foot of the Apostle Paul column, guarded by a sorrowing lion, is the **tomb of Rubén Darío**, Nicaragua's greatest poet and one of the greats of the Spanish language. Two of Nicaragua's other great poets are also buried nearby, **Salomón de la Selva** and **Alfonso Cortés** (whose starkly beautiful verses appear above his tomb).

It is said that when the builders ran out of mortar they were forced to use turtle eggs from the nearby coast and locals will tell you that this is the reason it has survived so many earthquakes and tremors.

West of the cathedral

There are several interesting and historic buildings on **Parque Central**. These include the **archbishop's house**, next to the south side of the cathedral, and the historic **Seminario de San Ramón**, founded in 1680, which today houses a primary school. You can ask permission to enter the school; in the eastern hall are the portraits of all the Bishops of Nicaragua and, from post-colonial times, the Bishops of León. The gothic **Colegio de Asunción** (primary and secondary school), just to the west, is often mistaken for a church.

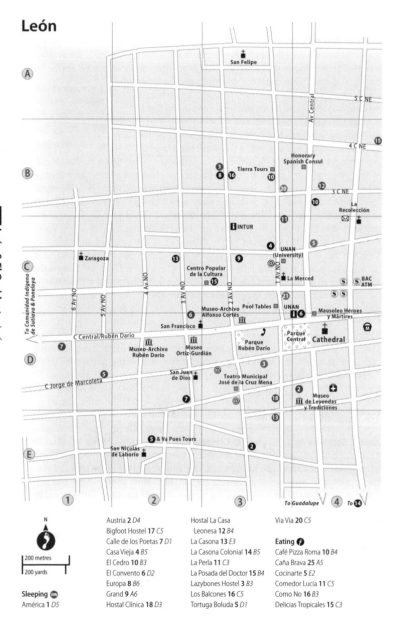

León

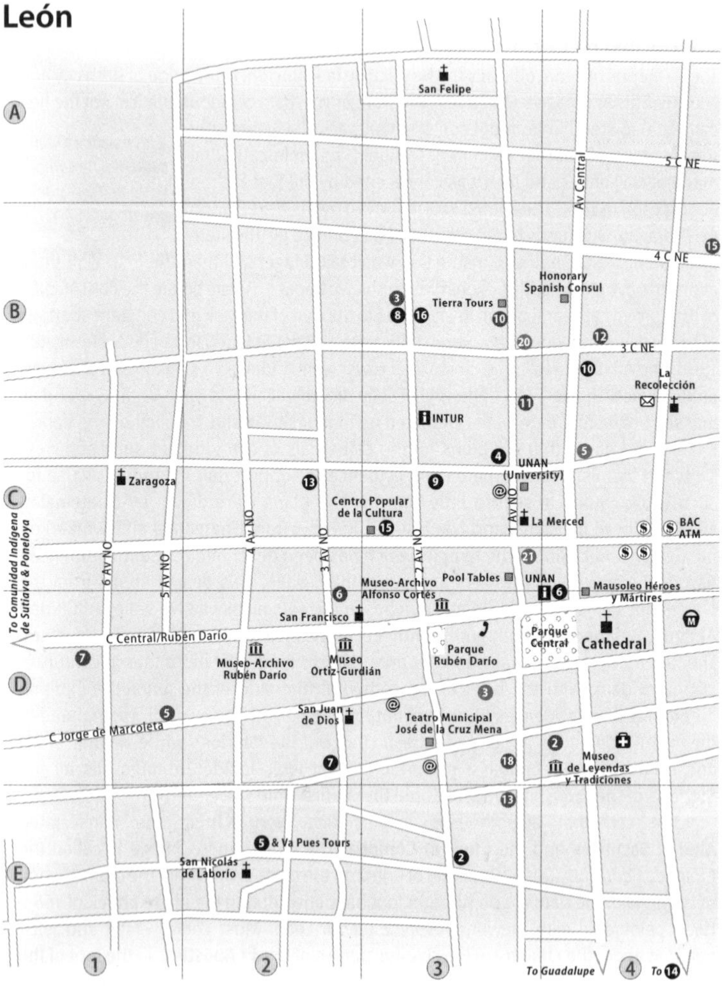

N

200 metres
200 yards

Sleeping
América 1 *D5*
Austria 2 *D4*
Bigfoot Hostel 17 *C5*
Calle de los Poetas 7 *D1*
Casa Vieja 4 *B5*
El Cedro 10 *B3*
El Convento 6 *D2*
Europa 8 *B6*
Grand 9 *A6*
Hostal Clínica 18 *D3*
Hostal La Casa Leonesa 12 *B4*
La Casona 13 *E3*
La Casona Colonial 14 *B5*
La Perla 11 *C3*
La Posada del Doctor 15 *B4*
Lazybones Hostel 3 *B3*
Los Balcones 16 *C5*
Tortuga Boluda 5 *D1*
Via Via 20 *C5*

Eating
Café Pizza Roma 10 *B4*
Caña Brava 25 *A5*
Cocinarte 5 *E2*
Comedor Lucía 11 *C5*
Como No 16 *B3*
Delicias Tropicales 15 *C3*

One block west and south of Parque Central is the beautifully restored **Teatro Municipal José de la Cruz Mena** ⓘ *Mon-Fri 0800-1230 and 1400-1700, plays and concerts from US$1-15*. The theatre was built in the 19th century and was home to many important concerts of touring groups from Europe during the early 20th century. Later the theatre fell into disrepair and was badly burned in 1956. It has now been reopened after more than 40 years of neglect. The theatre is named after León's greatest classical composer (you can see a portrait of him in the El Sesteo Restaurant, see page 207). Maestro Mena suffered from leprosy and for that reason, at the premier of his award-winning composition titled *Ruinas*, he was not allow to enter the theatre to hear its debut performance. Witnesses say that he sat outside on the front steps of the theatre, crying with joy as he listened to the orchestra play his composition inside the elegant theatre. Soon after, he died of leprosy.

The best time to beat the heat and find the churches open is in the morning or late afternoon.

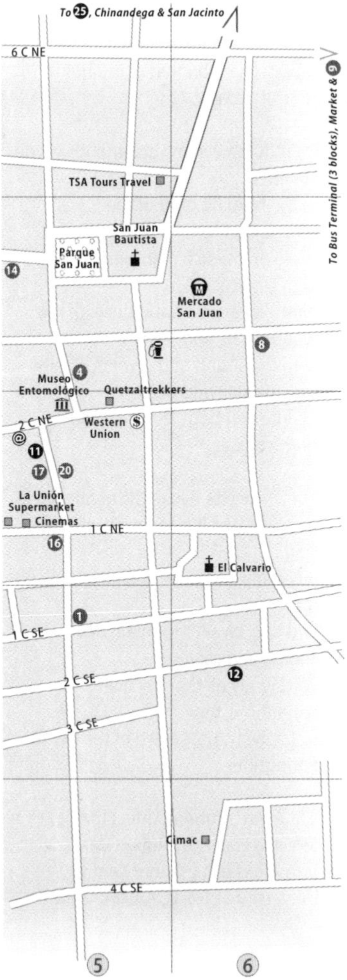

El Mississippi **12** *D6*
El Sesteo **6** *D4*
Flor de Sacuanjoche **9** *C3*
La Buena Cuchara **2** *E3*
La Casa Vieja **13** *C2*
Lacmiel **14** *E4*
Meditterraneo **8** *B3*
Puerto Café Benjamin Linder **4** *C3*
Venivé **7** *D2*

Bars & clubs
Café Taquezal **3** *D3*
Divino Castigo **20** *B3*
Don Señor **21** *C3*
La Pasarela **5** *C4*

Across from the small Parque Rubén Darío on Calle Central is the **Museo-Archivo Alfonso Cortés** ⓘ *Mon-Sat 0800-1200 and 1400-1700, donations appreciated*. The dusty little displays contain the great poet's manuscripts, photographs and other personal objects, but it is often closed due to lack of funding. See also box, page 201. Two blocks west of Parque Central is the **Convento y Iglesia San Francisco**. The church was damaged in 1979 during fighting in the Revolution but maintains much of its ancient charm. It was the city's first convent when founded in 1639. The pillars of the temple and two of its altars remain from the original construction, that of the Sangre de Cristo and of San Antonio de Padua. The façade has been modified greatly over the years, but on the south face of the church the original structure can still be seen. On one of the Virgin Mary altars there are some little wooden model homes that were attached to ask for protection from the destructive Hurricane Mitch in 1998. In 1830, after the expulsion of the Franciscans from Nicaragua, the convent was used by various civic organizations and part of it is now a gallery displaying sombre religious art. The rest has been converted into a new hotel called **El Convento** (see Sleeping, page 207).

The **Museo de Arte Fundación Ortiz-Guardián** ⓘ *opposite Iglesia San*

Rubén Darío: the prince of Spanish letters

The great Chilean poet Pablo Neruda called him "one of the most creative poets in the Spanish language" when, together with the immortal Spanish poet Federico García Lorca, he paid tribute to Rubén Darío in Buenos Aires in 1933. In front of more than 100 Argentine writers, Lorca and Neruda delivered the tribute to the poet they called "then and forever unequalled".

Darío is without a doubt the most famous Nicaraguan. He is one of the greatest poets in the history of the Spanish language and the country's supreme hero. Born Felix Rubén García Sarmiento in Metapa, Nicaragua in 1867, Rubén Darío was raised in León and had learnt to read by the age of four. By the time he was 10, little Rubén had read *Don Quixote*, *The Bible*, *1001 Arabian Nights* and the works of Cicero. When he was 11, he studied the Latin classics in depth with Jesuits at the school of La Iglesia de La Recolección. In 1879, at the age of 12, his first verses were published in the León daily newspaper *El Termómetro*. Two years later he was preparing his first book. Later, he became the founder of the Modernist movement in poetry, which crossed the Atlantic and became popular in Spain. His most noted work, *Azul*, revolutionized Spanish literature, establishing a new mode of poetic expression with innovation in form and content.

As well as being a poet, Darío was a diplomat and a journalist. He wrote for numerous publications in Argentina, the United States, Spain and France. In 1916 he returned to the city of León, and, despite several attempts at surgery, died of cirrhosis on the night of 6 February. After seven days of tributes he was buried in the Cathedral of León. Darío gave Nicaraguan poetry a worldwide projection and solidified it into the national passion that continues to flourish today.

Ox that I saw in my childhood, as you steamed
in the burning gold of the Nicaraguan sun,
there on the rich plantation filled with tropical
harmonies; woodland dove, of the woods that sang
with the sound of the wind, of axes, of birds and wild bulls:
I salute you both, because you are both my life.

You, heavy ox, evoke the gentle dawn
that signaled it was time to milk the cow,
when my existence was all white and rose;
and you, sweet mountain dove, cooing and calling,
you signify all that my own springtime, now
so far away, possessed of the Divine Springtime.

'Far Away', Rubén Darío. From *Selected Poems* by Rubén Darío, translated by Lysander Kemp, University of Texas, Austin, 1988

Francisco, Tue-Sat 1030-1830, Sun 1100-1900, entrance US$2, free on Sun, is a lovely colonial home that doubles as an art museum with works from Europe, Latin America and Nicaragua. It is worth a visit to see a classic example of a colonial period home. Across the street, is an annexe holding more modern art.

Founded in 1964, the **Museo-Archivo Rubén Darío** ⓘ *Calle Central, Iglesia San Francisco, 1 c abajo, T311-2388, www.unanleon.edu.ni/museodario, Tue-Sat 0830-1200, 1400-1700, Sun 0830-1200, entry and guided tour free but donations appreciated*, has an interesting collection of the national hero's personal

Alfonso Cortés: the insanity of genius

None of Nicaragua's poets can match the striking simplicity of the metaphysical poet Alfonso Cortés, who spent most of his life in chains, but who, in an impossibly microscopic script, wrote some of the most beautiful poems the Spanish language has ever seen.

Alfonso Cortés was born in León in 1893. He lived in the very same house that had belonged to Rubén Darío and which today is the Museo-Archivo Rubén Darío. It was in this house that Cortés went mad one February night in 1927. He spent the next 42 years in captivity, tormented most of the time but, for the good fortune of Nicaragua, with lucid moments of incredible productivity. Cortés was kept chained to one of the house's colonial window grilles and it was from that vantage point that he composed what poet-priest Ernesto Cardenal called the most beautiful poem in the Spanish language, *La Ventana* (The Window):

A speck of blue has more intensity
than all the sky; I feel that there
lives, a flower of happy ecstasy,
my longing.
A wind of spirits, passes
so far, from my window
sending a breeze that shatters
the flesh of an angelic awakening.

Later, at the age of 34, Alfonso Cortés was committed to a mental institution in Managua, where he was to live out the rest of his life. In these incredibly adverse conditions, Cortés produced a number of great poetic works, most of which were published with the help of his father. When he was not writing he was tied to his bed, with only his guitar, hanging on the wall, for company.

According to Cardenal, the poet spoke slowly while shaking and stuttering, his face changing from thrilled to horrified, then falling totally expressionless. He used to say, "I am less important than Rubén Darío, but I am more profound". Alfonso Cortés died in February 1969, 53 years later than Darío. Today, just a couple of metres separate these two great Nicaraguan poets, both buried in the Cathedral of León.

possessions, photographs, portraits and a library with a wide range of books of poetry in Spanish, English and French. See also box, page 200. The great metaphysical poet Alfonso Cortés lost his mind in this house and was said to have been chained to the bars that are next to Darío's bed. Cortés died here in 1969 and was buried near to Darío in the cathedral. He has his own museum (see page 199 and box, page 201).

East of the cathedral

On Calle Central, east of the cathedral, is the **Iglesia El Calvario**. Built in the mid-1700s, it was restored in 2000, the towering Momotombo Volcano in the background making for a dramatic setting. Inside are representations of Jesus and the two men he was crucified with. The life-size sculptures are unusual for their stark realism, a rare quality in colonial religious art. Both the interior and the gaily painted exterior of the neo-classical church are attractive and the façade is said to show the stylistic influence of the French in 18th-century Spanish architecture.

North of the cathedral

Two blocks north of Parque Central is the lovely **Iglesia La Merced**. This is León's second most important church and home of the patron saint of León, the Virgen de las

 Mercedes. The first La Merced church was founded in León Viejo in 1528 (see page 214). The present church was founded in 1615, before being burnt down during the pirate raid of 1685. It was rebuilt by a team of architects from Guatemala who came to work on the cathedral. It was demolished and rebuilt once again in the late 1700s. In the early 19th century there was a fire in the main altar that holds the Virgen de las Mercedes. Legend has it that a local black slave rushed into the flames to rescue the Virgen and broke the glass case holding the image with his bare hands. In gratitude for his heroism he was granted his freedom. The current main altar was made out of marble to replace the burnt one. The interior is arguably the most ornately decorated in Nicaragua with fine woodwork and delicately sculpted altars. It is said to be the most representative of León's 18th-century churches. The exterior was restored in 1999, but funds ran short of a paint job.

Next door is Nicaragua's first university, the **Universidad Nacional Autónoma de Nicaragua (UNAN)**. This fine yellow and white building holds the library and dean's office. The rest of the university is made up of less attractive buildings nearby and on the outskirts of the city.

Two blocks north of the cathedral's lions on Avenida Central is the **Iglesia La Recolección**, with a beautiful baroque Mexican façade that tells the entire story of the Passion of Christ. It was built in 1786 and has a neoclassical interior with lovely mahogany woodwork. Two blocks north and one block east of La Recolección is the simple yet handsome **Iglesia San Juan Bautista**, which sits on the east side of the Parque San Juan, otherwise known as the *parquecito*. The church dates from 1739 but was remodelled in the following century. Three blocks west and two blocks north, the **Iglesia San Felipe** was built at the end of the 16th century for the religious services of the black and mulatto population of the city. It was rebuilt in the 18th century in a manner true to its original form, a mixture of baroque and neoclassical.

One and half blocks from the little park, next to La Merced is the **Centro Popular de la Cultura**, which has frequent exhibitions and events (see schedule on bulletin board in front lobby). Three blocks west, the **Iglesia de Zaragoza** was built from 1884 to 1934 and is unique for its two octagonal turrets and arched doorway with tower above. It resembles a fortress more than a church and is unattractive inside.

Museo Entomológico ⓘ *ENEL, 30 varas arriba, opposite Western Union, T311-6586, www.bio-nica.info, Thu-Tue 0900-1200, 1400-1600, US$0.50*, is the amazing collection of Nicaragua's foremost expert on its insect life, Dr Jean-Michel Maes; it includes butterflies from around the world.

South of the cathedral

Three blocks south and half a block west of the cathedral is the **Museo de Leyendas y Tradiciones** ⓘ *Tue-Sat 0800-1200, 1400-1700, Sun 0800-1200, US$3.50*. This project of Doña Carmen Toruño is a physical demonstration of some of the many legends that populate the bedtime stories of Nicaraguan children. León is particularly rich in legends and Doña Carmen has handcrafted life-size models of the characters of these popular beliefs to help bring them to life. Most impressive of the displays is the *carreta nahua* (haunted ox cart) a story symbolic of the harsh labour Spanish masters required of their Indian subjects, so much so that the ox cart became a symbol of literally being worked to death.

One block south of the museum, the **Iglesia de San Nicolás de Laborío**, founded in 1618 for the local Indian population, is the most modest of the León churches. It is constructed of wood and tiles over adobe walls with a simple façade and altar. The interior is dark, cool and charming, with the feel of a village parish more than a city church. The local *padre* is friendly and willing to chat. If the church is closed you can knock on the little door at the back. The celebration for San Nicolás is 10 September.

Comunidad Indígena de Sutiava » pp205-210.

Like Monimbó in Masaya, Sutiava is the one of the last remaining examples of indigenous urban living. The Sutiavans have a fiercely independent culture and a unique language that survived despite being surrounded by the numerically superior Chorotega culture in pre-Columbian times and later by the Spanish. Until the 20th century they managed to maintain a significant level of independence, including the indigenous community's land holdings of more than 72,000 acres, west of León proper. The community finally succumbed to pressure from León elites who had been eyeing the communal lands for centuries and Sutiava was annexed to the city in 1902, making it nothing more than a barrio of the colonial city, and opening up communal lands to non-indigenous ownership. It is no surprise that Sutiava was a major player during the planning and recruitment stages of the Sandinista-led Revolution, as the community has been involved in numerous anti-government rebellions since Nicaragua achieved independence from Spain.

The entrance to the community is marked by the change of Calle Rubén Darío into a two-lane road with a central divider full of plants, including *sacuanjoche* in some unusual colours. Also of note are the neatly presented fruit stands on the street corners and the lack of colonial structures – Sutiava retained its native buildings until long after Spanish rule had ended. The best way to witness the true pride and culture of the barrio is during fiesta time. However, there are also several sites of interest and Sutiava cuisine is superior to León's, so a visit to eat is also worthwhile.

Unlike the secular buildings, the churches of Sutiava date from colonial times and are simple, elegant structures. The **Iglesia Parroquial de San Juan Bautista de Sutiava** was first constructed in 1530 by missionaries, and reconstructed from 1698-1710. The human rights priest Bartolomé de las Casas, known as the 'Apostle of the Indians', preached here on several occasions. The featureless dirt plaza in front of the church was baptized in his name in 1923. The church is one of the most authentic representations of Nicaraguan baroque and thankfully has survived years of invasion and civil war. The indigenous influences, such as the ceiling, saints and other subtle styling clues, are what make the church famous today. The colonial altar was donated by the King of Spain and brought to Sutiava in pieces. There is an interesting representation of the Maribio Sun God, carved in wood in the mid-nave on the ceiling; it has become the definitive icon for indigenous pride along with a certain tamarind tree near by (see below). The church was declared a National Monument in 1944 and was restored in 1992, which is ironic given that this was also the 500th anniversary of the first arrival of Columbus to the Americas, the beginning of the most brutal genocide in the history of the hemisphere.

Inside the handsome **Casa Cural de Sutiava** (1752), on the south side of the plaza in front of the church, is the **Museo de Arte Sacro** ⓘ *Mon-Fri 0800-1100 and 1400-1600, Sat 0800-1000, US$0.50*. The museum contains a display of colonial religious relics, some of which were rescued from León Viejo, with many gold and silver pieces; there is, however, a lack of explanations or qualified guides. Two blocks north of the San Juan church is the **Museo de la Comunidad Indígena de Sutiava** or **Museo Adiac** ⓘ *T311-5371, Mon-Fri 0800-1200 and 1400-1700, Sat 0800-1200, donations greatly appreciated*, marked by a fading mural. This is the indigenous community's museum and the only example in Nicaragua of an indigenous people protecting their cultural patrimony in their very own museum. The tiny rooms are crammed full of statues and ceramics from the Maribios culture. The museum is named after the last great Indian Chief Adiac who was executed after challenging the local Spanish authority. The old tamarind tree where Adiac was hanged by the Spanish remains a vivid symbol of Sutiava's proud but tragic history. The tree, known to all as **El Tamarindón**, is located three blocks south and two blocks west of the San

León festivals

León is famed throughout Nicaragua for the beauty of its religious festivals, particularly during **Semana Santa** (Holy Week). Semana Santa always starts on **Domingo de Ramos** (Palm Sunday) one week before Easter. Upcoming Holy Week dates are: 5-12 April 2009, March 28-April 4 2010, April 17-24 2011, April 1-8 2012. The cathedral has a procession every day of the week and the Parish church of Sutiava has many events (see also below), as do all of the other churches of León. (A program of processions and events can be obtained from the Nicaraguan Institute of Tourism, INTUR.)

The other most famous religious celebration is **La Purísima** or **Gritería** (the Virgin Mary's conception of Jesus), on 7 December and a festival unique to Nicaragua. La Purísima is celebrated throughout the country, like Semana Santa, but León's ceremonies are the best, as this is where the tradition began. Altars are built in front of private residences and outside churches during the day. At 1800, a massive outburst of pyrotechnics opens the proceedings in front of the Cathedral of León, complete with dances, then a roaming Mass visits every makeshift altar yelling: "Who causes so much happiness?" which must be answered by: "The conception of Mary!" Visitors receive small gifts in return, like sugarcane and oranges or more modern snacks. The fireworks end at midnight and the next day is a public holiday when everything is closed.

There is also a **Gritería Chiquita** that was instituted in 1947 to protect León during a violent eruption of the nearby Cerro Negro Volcano; it is still celebrated every 14 August.

In February there are celebrations for the birthday of **Rubén Darío** and the patron saint of León, **La Virgin de la Mercedes**, is celebrated on 24 September.

Juan church. There is a small *tiangue* or indigenous market there every third Sunday in April to celebrate the tree and its importance, with native foods and crafts.

The **Ruinas de la Iglesia de Veracruz** is a sad, crumbling stone relic from the 16th century that was destroyed by an attack from Salvadorian General Malespin in 1844. It is two blocks west from the central plaza of Sutiava and often shut off to visitors by a chain-link fence, though the *comunidad indígena* is doing much to try and make the ruins a cultural focal point. On 7 December, when the Catholic **Purísima** celebration to the Virgin Mary is celebrated, the community mounts a unique semi-pagan altar to the Virgin in the ruins of the old church complete with torch lighting and a replica of the Sun God. Other interesting celebrations include the festival for the second annual planting of corn between 25 July and 15 August. You'll find another ruined 17th-century church one block north of Sutiava's central plaza, **Iglesia Santiago**, which has a small surviving bell tower.

Holy week, or **Semana Santa**, celebrations in Sutiava are the most interesting in Nicaragua. The most spectacular of all events are the sawdust street paintings made on *Viernes Santo* (Good Friday). At the eastern end of Sutiava, marked by a statue of Adiac and a tiny park, two blocks south of the main avenue, the streets leading towards the San Juan church are closed off for the day. Around 1100 you can see the artists framing their sawdust canvas and soaking it in water. Later in the afternoon moist, dyed sawdust is used to make religious paintings, which serve as carpets for the **Santo Entierro** (the funeral procession of the crucified Christ) at around 2100. These short-lived masterpieces are honoured by being trampled by the procession, totally destroying them. Unlike the more famous street paintings of Antigua in Guatemala, no moulds are used for the street in Sutiava, they are created completely freehand. After 1600, when many paintings are complete and others are being finished, a walk up and down the neighbourhood streets is an unforgettable experience. While some of the paintings are amateurish, others are astounding in their detail and scope, especially considering the difficulty of the medium. The leader of the street artist association, Federico Quezada, has invented a new art medium by gluing the coloured sawdust to a wooden 'canvas' to preserve the art of the festival beyond the procession. During Holy Week, Quezada's home is opened as a **gallery** ⓘ *Texaco Guido, 2 c sur, ½ c arriba, T315-3942, fquesadamoran@yahoo.com, Spanish-speaking only*, and he is happy to show his work by appointment. More conventional but equally beautiful examples of Sutiavan art can be found at Don Alejandro Cabrera's brightly painted studio of Primitivist art, **La Ronda Sutiava** ⓘ *BANIC de Sutiava, 25 vrs arriba, www.artecabrera.com.ar.*

Three blocks east of the south side of the San Juan Church is the charming **Iglesia Ermita de San Pedro**. Built in 1706 on top of an even older construct, this church is a fine example of primitive baroque design popular in the 17th century. The adobe and red tile roof temple was refurbished in 1986. Santa Lucia is celebrated in Sutiava throughout most of December, with the focal point being the plaza in front of the parish church; Santa Lucia's day is 13 December. In all celebrations, fireworks are used extensively and the front steps of the parish church can seem more dangerous than the front line of a civil war, with rocket launchers flying horizontally into the crowds and firecrackers set off on the streets – the usual good-natured, life-threatening type of celebration that is so much fun in Nicaragua.

Sleeping

León *p194, map p198*

AL La Perla, Iglesia La Merced, 1 c norte, T311 3125, www.laperlaleon.com. This handsome old colonial building has been carefully remodelled and now boasts a plethora of elegant rooms, some with bath tubs, several suites, a bar, restaurant and pool.

A Hotel El Convento, connected to Iglesia San Francisco, T311-7053, www.hotelelconvento.com.ni. This beautiful, intriguing hotel is decorated with elegant antique art, including an impressive gold leaf altar and sombre religious icons. Rooms are very comfortable, with a/c, bath, hot water and cable TV. There's a very good restaurant (🍴) with excellent coffee and home-made ice cream (try the *níspero sorbete* unique to Nicaragua). León's best hotel. Recommended.

B Hotel Austria, catedral, 1 c sur, T311-1206, www.hotelaustria.com.ni. Very clean and comfortable rooms surrounding a lush central courtyard. They have hot water, a/c, telephone and cable TV. Internet and laundry service available. Continental breakfast is included in the price. Friendly and often fully booked.

B Hostal La Casa Leonesa, catedral, 3 c norte, 15 varas arriba, T311-0551, www.lacasaleonesa.com. This typical León house has a lovely elegant interior, a swimming pool and 10 rooms of varying size, all with private bath, hot water, cable TV, telephone. Breakfast included. Rooms upstairs are cheaper (**C**).

B La Posada del Doctor, Parque San Juan, 25 varas abajo, T311-4343, www.laposadadeldoctor.com. Very clean and nicely furnished rooms with private bath, hot water, cable TV, a/c. Services include laundry, parking and Wi-Fi. Pleasant little patio and relaxed atmosphere. Breakfast included.

B Los Balcones, Esquina de los Bancos, 1 c arriba, T311-0250, www.hotelbalcones.com. A handsome colonial building with an attractive courtyard, bar and restaurant. The 20 rooms have private bath, hot water, a/c and cable TV; some have a have good view. Breakfast included. Tasteful, professional and comfortable.

C Europa, 3 C NE, 4 Av, T311-6040, www.hoteleuropaleon.com. Pleasant patios

For an explanation of the sleeping and eating price codes used in this guide, see inside the front cover. Other relevant information is found in Essentials, see pages 23-27.

and quiet, clean and comfortable rooms with Wi-Fi, safe, telephone, a/c, hot water. Services include restaurant, bar and parking. Cheaper with fan (**D**).

C Grand Hotel, bus terminal, ½ c sur, T311-1327, www.grandhoteldeleon.com. Located in an unattractive area but with good, clean rooms with private bath, hot water, cable TV, telephone, a/c. Cheaper with fan (**D**).

C La Casona Colonial, Parque San Juan, ½ c abajo, T311-3178. This pleasant colonial house has 5 good value, homely rooms with private bath and a/c. Management is friendly and hospitable, and there's a lovely green garden too. Cheaper with fan (**D**).

D América, catedral, 2 c arriba, T311-5533. Plain, comfortable rooms in a friendly old house. There's a pleasant patio and garden, internet, parking and meals on request.

E Calle de los Poetas, Calle Rubén Darío, Museo Darío, 1½ c abajo, T311-3306, rsampson@ibw.com.ni. This comfortable, good value guesthouse has a relaxed home ambience, spacious rooms with private and shared bath, a beautiful garden and friendly hosts. It's also the base for **Sampson Expeditions** (see page 209). Often full, so arrive early. Discounts for longer stays. Recommended.

E El Cedro, T311-4643, northwest corner of parque central, 2½ c norte. 9 clean, comfortable, good value rooms with private bath and cable TV. There's a café and bar attached, and the friendly management speak English. Recommended.

E Hostal Clínica, 1 Av NO, Parque Central, 1½ c sur, T311-2031, marymergalo2000@yahoo.com. Family-run and very Nicaraguan. Single and double rooms have private or shared bathroom, washing facilities, breakfast and drinks available. Very friendly, good reports.

F Casa Vieja, Parque San Juan, 1½ c sur, T311-4235. Sociable Nica hotel with some long-term residents and a family feel. It has 9 large rooms with fan, communal bath and kitchen, cooking on request, laundry service and telephone. Friendly.

F La Casona, Teatro González, 2 c sur, T311-5282, lacasonahostal@hotmail.com. This spacious house has lots of places to relax, a garden with hammocks, pool (sometimes empty), use of kitchen and washing facilities. The rooms have private and shared bath, poor mattresses and fan. Cheap and popular with volunteers. Lovely staff and owners.

D-G Lazybones Hostel, Parque de los Poetas, 2½ c norte, T311-3472, www.lazybones.com. Managed by a friendly English-Colombian couple, this excellent hostel has a refreshing pool and lots of extras including free coffee and tea, pool table, internet, DVD rental and a daily 10-minute long-distance phone call. Clean dorms (**G**) and private rooms; some have private bath (**D**), cheaper without (**E**). Check out the mural by one of Managua's best graffiti artists. Recommended.

D-G Via Via, Banco ProCredit, ½ c sur, T311-6142, www.viaviacafe.com. Part of a worldwide network of Belgian cafés, this excellent and professionally managed hostel offers clean dorm beds (**G**) and a range of private rooms (**D-E**), some with TV. There's a tranquil garden, a well-stocked and socially aware information centre, popular restaurant-bar, community tours and classes. In the manager's words, 'a meeting place for cultures'. Recommended.

G Bigfoot Hostel, Banco ProCredit, ½ c sur, www.bigfootadventure.com. Sociable, buzzing and popular with the whipper-snappers. This Australian-run backpackers' joint has lots of dorm space, a handful of private rooms (**F**), pool, sand-boarding tours, TV, pool table, and a popular restaurant serving everything from real mocaccinos to wholesome Nica fare.

G Tortuga Boluda, Iglesia San Juan de Dios, 1½ c abajo, T311-4653, www.tortugabooluda.com. Pleasant Nica-run hostel with dorms, chill-out spaces, hammocks, kitchen, links to social projects and notice board.

Eating

León *p194, map p198*

₸₸₸-₸₸ Caña Brava, on bypass road, T311-5666. Daily 1100-2200. For many locals the best food in town, with excellent beef dishes, large portions and attentive service. It has very little charm though, and is far from the centre.

₸₸ Café Pizza Roma, catedral, 2½ c norte, T311-3568. 1200-2300, closed Tue. Average pizzas and good meat dishes. Popular with Nicas.

₸₸ Cocinarte, costado norte Iglesia de Laborío, T325-4099. Quality vegetarian restaurant and intriguing international menu of Eastern, Middle Eastern and Nicaraguan cuisine. They use a lot of fresh and organic produce and host a monthly organic market. Fri evenings are music nights and Sun afternoon sees chess matches and free coffee. Recommended.

₸₸ El Sesteo, next to cathedral, on Parque Central, T311-5327. The place for watching the world go by, particularly in the late afternoon. Good pork dishes, *nacatamales*, fruit drinks and *cacao con leche*. Portraits of Nicaraguan cultural greats on the wall. Begging can be frequent if you sit outside.

₸₸ Flor de Sacuanjoche, northwest corner of University UNAN-León, 75 m abajo, T311-1121. Daily 0900-2400. Popular with Nicas. They serve fairly decent meat and veggie dishes, lunch and breakfast.

₸₸ Lacmiel, catedral, 5 c sur. Good meat dishes and onion soup. Occasional live music. Recommended.

₸₸ Meditterráneo, Parque Rubén Darío, 2½ c norte, T895-9392. Tue-Sun 1200-2300. French and Mediterranean cuisine and Italian wines. They have a wide range of meat and chicken dishes, and takeaway pizza too. Popular with foreigners, recommended.

₸₸ Venivé, Iglesia de San Juan de Dios, 1 c sur. León's finest Spanish tapas restaurant. Smart, stylish but neglected by the locals.

₸₸-₸ La Casa Vieja, Iglesia San Francisco, 1½ c norte. Mon-Sat 1600-2300. Lovely, intimate restaurant-bar with a rustic feel. Serves quality meat and chicken dishes, beer and delicious home-made lemonade. Recommended.

₸₸-₸ Via Via, Banco Procredit ½ c sur. A very popular place for breakfast, lunch or dinner. They have a gringo-friendly menu with food glossaries and detailed descriptions of some classic Nicaraguan dishes. They also serve favourites from Mexico and other Central American countries.

₸ Casa Popular de Cultura, Plaza Central, 1 c norte, 2½ c abajo. Friendly little locals' spot, sometimes occupied by passing musicians. They do sandwiches and burgers. Good atmosphere.

₸ Comedor Lucía, Banco Procredit, ½ c sur. Reputable comedor serving good but slightly pricey *comida típica* and buffet food, popular with locals. Lunch only.

₸ El Cedro, northwest corner of Parque Central, 2½ c norte, T311-4643. Good, filling, cheap breakfasts – try the English breakfast for giant portions that will keep you fuelled till dinner time.

₸ El Mississippi, southeast corner of the cathedral, 1 c sur, 2½ c arriba. Also known as, perhaps unfortunately, 'la cucaracha', everyone is raving about the bean soup here. Simple, unpretentious dining at this locals' haunt.

₸ La Buena Cuchara, Parque Rubén Darío, 3½ c sur. Friendly, homely little *comedor* with tasty and cheap buffet food. Lunch only. Recommended.

Cafés, bakeries and juice bars

Como No, Parque Rubén Darío, 3 c norte. Delicious-smelling wholemeal bread, juices, shakes, cheap breakfasts and sandwiches.

Delicias Tropicales, next to the Casa de Cultura. Tasty fresh fruit juices and smoothies, very refreshing after the heat of León's streets.

Puerto Café Benjamín Linder, next to UNAN (northern corner), T311-0548. Daily 0800-2400. Coffee roasted fresh on premises at this café named after a social worker who was killed by Contras in 1980s. Profits go to prosthetic outreach clinic in León. High speed internet access.

Sutiava *p203*

₸₸ Los Pescaditos, Iglesia de San Juan, 1 c sur, 1 c abajo. Daily 1200-2230. Excellent seafood at reasonable prices, go with the waiter to choose your fish from the ice box. Recommended.

₸ El Capote, Billares Lacayo, 3 c sur, ½ c arriba, T315-3918. Mon-Sat 1100-2300, Sun 1000-1700. No frills bar and eatery with very good food, seafood, cow's tail soup, a massive sampler (*surtido*) dish for US$7.

Bars and clubs

León *p194, map p198*

León has a vibrant nightlife, thanks to its large student population. The action moves between different places throughout the week.

Café Taquezal, southwest corner of Parque Central, ½ c abajo, T311-7282. Mon-Sat 1800-0200. Pleasant atmosphere with good live folk music on Thu nights. Classic León decor. Food served.

Discoteca Dilectus, at the southern entrance to the city, Wed-Sun. Inconveniently located, but probably the best disco in town. Upmarket crowd.
Divino Castigo, UNAN, 1 c norte. Daily 1700-0100. Good atmosphere, 'bohemian nights' on Tue and Sat. Look at the *mesa maldita* (cursed table) where old newspaper articles tell you the cruel history of this house. Or ask for Sergio Ramírez's book from which the bar derives its name.
Don Señor, opposite Parque La Merced. Tue-Sun. Popular with students and young Nicas on Fri nights, with liberal doses of karaoke, dancing and beer. A good place to see the locals cut loose.
El Cedro, northwest corner of Parque Central, 2½ c norte, T311-4643. Thu night is rock night in El Cedro, the only place in town to catch some meaty guitar riffs. The friendly management is well travelled and English-speaking. Lots of beer and very popular with Nicas.
La Pasarela, UNAN, 1 c arriba. A great outdoor student venue, best attended in the dry season.
Olla Quemada, Museo Rubén Darío, ½ c abajo. Popular on Wed nights with live music acts and lots of beer. Great, friendly atmosphere.
Salon Estrella, Esquina de los Bancos, ½ c norte. Dark, hot and steamy, with lots of raunchy reggaeton and dance. Definitely a locals' haunt, but gringos are welcome too. On its way down, reportedly.
Via Via, Banco ProCredit, ½ c sur. Good on most nights, but best on Fri when there's live music. Salsa on Sat, free pool on Tue and quiz night on Mon. Good, warm atmosphere. Popular with foreigners and often praised.

Entertainment

León *p194, map p198*

Cinema

There is a cinema next to the La Unión supermarket, Plaza Nuevo Siglo, T311-7080. Modern cinema with 4 screens all showing US movies with Spanish subtitles, US$2.50.

Shopping

León *p194, map p198*

Bookshops

Libro Centro Don Quixote, next to Hotelito, Calle Real. New and second-hand books, a few bad ones in English, the owner is very helpful and knowledgeable about León.

Crafts and markets

León is not a very good place to look for crafts. You could try the **Casa de Cultura**, Parque La Merced, 1½ c abajo, T311-2116, daily from 0800; or **La Esquina del Movimiento**, west side of the cathedral, 3 c norte, T315 3533. The best market is in the pale green building behind the cathedral which sells meat, fruit and veg inside, and shoes, fans and stereos in the street stalls outside. The inside market is a good place to find out what tropical fruits are in season. There are other markets near the Iglesia San Juan, and at the bus terminal, which are dirtier and hotter – the way some people prefer it.

Supermarkets

La Unión supermarket, catedral, 1 c norte, 2 c arriba; there is another supermarket behind Hotel El Convento. There's an inexpensive Palí northeast of the centre, near the bus station and market.

Activities and tours

León *p194, map p198*

Cultural and community tourism

Via Via, Banco ProCredit, ½ c sur, T311-6142, www.viaviacafe.com. Interesting cultural tours include 'Cowboy for a day' where you milk a cow and prepare an ox cart; 'Gallera', where you attend a cockfight; and 'Workshop Cooking', which includes trips to markets and tortilla making.
Casa de Cultura, Iglesia La Merced, 1½ c abajo. Offers a range of courses including traditional and contemporary dance, music and painting. Ask inside for a schedule.
La Esquina del Movimiento, west side of the cathedral, 3 c norte, www.edadeoro.com. This cultural centre and café hosts regular events, and sells organic coffee and locally produced artesanías. Proceeds go to social projects.

Sandboarding

Bigfoot Adventure, Banco ProCredit, ½ c sur, www.bigfootadventure.com. Fancy descending the slopes of an active volcano at high speed? The most professional outfit in town will kit you out with a sandboard and safety gear, and transport you to the top of Cerro Negro. The fastest boards have been clocked at 70 kph.

Sports

Baseball is a huge passion for the Leoneses. They have won many national championships. The stadium is in the far northern part of León. The Nicaraguan bullfight/rodeo happens in Dec in the central plaza of Sutiava for the Santa Lucía festival.

Tour operators

Tierra Tour, La Merced, 1½ c norte, T311-0599, www.tierratour.com. Dutch-owned outfit with good information and affordable tours of León, the Maribios volcanoes and Isla Juan Venado reserve. They run shuttles direct to Granada and other places.

Va Pues, north side of El Laborio Church, inside Cocinarte restaurant, T315-4099, www.vapues.com. Popular tours include Cerro Negro, León Viejo, night turtle tours, kayaking and city tours. English, French and Spanish spoken. They have an office in Granada and can organize trips all over the country.

Trekking

Flavio Parajón, Texaco Guadalupe, 1 c abajo, ½ c sur, T880-8673, fparajon2003@yahoo.es. Good, friendly, honest and experienced mountain guide for Maribios Volcanoes. He has his own 4WD, speaks Spanish and basic English.

Quetzaltrekkers, Iglesia Recolección, 1½ c arriba, T843-7647, www.quetzaltrekkers.com. Non-profit organization, proceeds go to street kids. Multi-day hikes to Los Maribios US$20-US$70 including transport, food, water, camping equipment. Guides are foreign volunteers so check on guide's experience before trip – be sure to climb with at least one local guide who knows the volcanoes well.

Sampson Expeditions, Calle Rubén Darío, 1½ c abajo, inside Hostal Calle de Los Poetas, T311-3306, rsampson@ibw.com.ni. Kayaking in Juan Venado and Laguna El Tigre, volcano expeditions, poetry tours. Rigo Sampson comes from a family of devout hikers and climbers and is Nicaragua's foremost expert on climbing the Los Maribios Volcanoes. He also works closely with educational organizations. Professional and highly recommended.

Transport

León *p194, map p198*

Bus

The bus terminal is in the far eastern part of town, a long walk or short taxi ride from the centre. Small trucks also ferry people between the bus terminal and town for US$0.25. Besides the regular and express buses, small vans (called *compartidos*) go to most places below – often faster than the bus. To **Managua**, express bus, every 30 mins, 0500-1600, US$1.50, 1 hr 45 mins. To **Chinandega**, every 15 mins, 0500-1800, US$1, 1 hr 45 mins. To **Corinto**, every 30 mins, 0500-1800, US$1, 2 hrs. To **Chichigalpa**, every 15 mins, US$0400-1800, US$0.75, 1 hr. To **Estelí**, express bus, 0520, 1245, 1315, 1515, US$2.50, 3 hrs; or go to San Isidro for connections. To **Matagalpa**, express bus, 0400, 0700, 1400, US$2.75, 3 hrs; or go to San Isidro for connections. To **San Isidro**, every 30 mins, 0420-1730, US$1.50, 2½ hrs. To **El Sauce**, every hr, 0800-1600, US$1.50, 2½ hrs. To **El Guasaule**, 0500, US$2, 2½ hrs. To **Salinas Grandes**, 0600,1200, US$0.40, 1½ hrs.

Buses and trucks for **Poneloya** and **Las Peñitas** leave from the terminal in Sutiava, every hr, 0530-1735, US$0.60, 45 mins. Service can be irregular so check to see when last bus will return. There are more buses on weekends.

International buses Contact individual agencies for schedules and costs; **Ticabus**, San Juan church, 2 c norte, in the Viajes Cumbia travel agency, T311-6153, www.ticabus.com. **Transnica**, Colegio Mercantil ½ c abajo, T311-0821, www.transnica.com. **King Quality**, corner of 2a Calle NE and 3a Ave NE, T311-2426, www.kingqualityca.com.

Taxis

There are many taxis in the centre, at the bus terminal and on the bypass road. Average fare is US$$0.50-2. Taxis can also be hired to visit **Poneloya** beach and the fumaroles at **San Jacinto** (see page 212). Rates for longer trips vary greatly, with a trip to **San Jacinto** normally costing US$10-12 plus US$1 for every 15 mins of waiting or a higher flat rate for the taxi to wait as long as you wish. Trips outside must be negotiated in advance. If staying in a **C** level or above hotel ask the front desk to help with the price negotiation and it should be less than looking for one on the street.

Directory

León *p194, map p198*

Banks There are many banks on the 2 roads that lead from the front and back of the cathedral to the north. Next to the La Unión Supermarket is BAC (Banco de América Central) T311-7247, for TCs of any kind and cash from credit cards. Cash can be changed with the *coyotes* 1 block north of the back of the cathedral or at any bank.
Consulates Spain, María Mercedes de Escudero, Av Central 405, T311-4376.
Fire T311-2323. **Hospital** catedral, 1 c sur, T311-6990. **Internet** At nearly every hotel and almost every street in León, best high speed hook-up at **Puerto Café Benjamín Linder**, next to UNAN (northern corner), T311-0548, daily 0800-0000. **Language schools** León Spanish School, Casa de Cultura, Iglesia La Merced, 1½ c abajo, T311-2116, www.apc-spanish schools.com. Flexible weekly or hourly one-on-one tuition with activities, volunteering and homestay options. Pleasant location inside the casa de cultura. **Metropolis Academy**, La Merced, 2 c norte, T875-9325, www.metropolis spanish.com. A range of programmes from simple hourly tuition to full-time courses with daily activities and family homestay. 20 hrs of tuition costs US$115. **Via Via**, Banco ProCredit, ½ c sur, T311-6142, www.viavia cafe.com. This growing cultural centre has good ties to local communities and a popular hostel-restaurant-bar on site. A convenient, sociable option. **Medical services** Laboratories Clínico Galo, Dr Elia Diuna Galo García, Teatro Municipal, 75 m arriba, T311-0437. **Police** T311-3137.
Post office Correos de Nicaragua, Banco Mercantil, 1 c norte, T311-2102. **Red Cross** T311-2627. **Telephone** Enitel, on Parque Central at the west side, T311-7377. Also at bus terminal.

Around León

→ *Colour map 3, A1-2.*

León's rugged volcanoes, windy beaches and hot, sleepy little villages make interesting excursions from the city. Los Maribios Volcanoes are great for climbing and hiking, offering stunning views of the León valley stretching as far as the Pacific Coast. León Viejo is a glimpse of Nicaragua's brutal beginnings as a Spanish colony and a UNESCO World Heritage Site. The little villages that run north and south of León offer glimpses into the lives of local cowboys and farmers, authentic towns cooking under the tropical sun that come to life in the early mornings and late afternoons.
▸▸ *For Sleeping, Eating and other listings, see pages 218-220.*

Los Volcanes Maribios ▸▸ *pp218-220.*

A scintillating landscape of sulphurous craters, steaming black sand slopes, simmering pools and imminent eruptions, Los Maribios are reason enough to visit the hot provinces of León and Chinandega. A rocky 60-km spine made up of 21 volcanoes, five of which are active, the cones rise from just above sea level to an average height of 1000 m, filling every vista with marvellous earthen pyramids. These mountains are bathed in sunlight most of the year and are home to rustic farms and tropical dry forest. The principal volcanoes of Los Maribios are described below from south to north.

Ins and outs

Getting there and around The entire range is an easy day trip from León. Most of the volcanoes have unpaved road access, though some can only be reached on foot or horseback. A 4WD is essential for getting close to the trail heads if a summit climb is planned on the same day. Camping is possible on many of the cones. It is strongly recommended that you bring a guide from León or use someone from the local communities at the base of each volcano. The best option is to use one of the mountaineering outfits in León, like **Sampson Expeditions** (see page 209), that can provide 4WD transfers, camping gear and guide.

Best time to visit It is best to avoid the dry season, because the heat can make hiking and climbing more pain than pleasure. The rainy season showers are normally brief along the mountains and do wonders for both visibility and air quality. During the dry season dust grows worse from February onwards to the first rains of late May or early June; smoke from the farmers burning their fields from March to May mixes with wind-blown dirt to make air conditions miserable. Ideal months are November to January, although even the height of the rainy season (September and October) is preferable to February to May.

Volcán Momotombo → *Altitude: 1260 m.*

In the province of León at the southern tip of the Maribios Volcano range, this symmetrical cone towering over the shores of Lake Managua has been an inspiration to both national and international poets over the centuries. The climb is a long one, normally taking two days, with an overnight camp just below the end of the tree line. Access to the base of the volcano is via the village of **Puerto Momotombo**, the site of León Viejo. *Momotombo* in Náhuatl means 'great boiling summit', though this cone was called *Mamea* 'the fireplace', by the Chorotegas who lived at its base. In many ways, Momotombo is Nicaragua's national symbol and can be seen from as far south as Volcán Masaya. Although only 500 ha of the cone is a forest reserve, there is much nature to see on its lower slopes and its seldom explored lagoons, known as **Laguna Monte Escalante**. The volcano is still active, although it has only produced fumarolic steam and some ash since its last big magma flow in 1905, which can be seen on its eastern face. At the western base of the cone is a geothermal plant, operated by an Israeli company which promises to increase its power output.

There are two principal routes to climb the mountain; the easier one requires permission from the power company. Check with the police in Puerto Momotombo for procedures, or better still use a León tour operator that supplies a guide and camping gear and will take you up via the safest route. The northern ascent is longer and more difficult, but affords a visit to the lagoons. Above the tree line there is a two-hour climb through loose rock that must be done carefully to reach the crater. The view from the smoking summit is breathtaking and one of the most spectacular in Nicaragua.

The forest is full of parrots, iguanas and butterflies.

Volcán El Hoyo and Laguna El Tigre → *Altitude: 1089 m.*

There are some magnificent 1000-m cones northwest of Volcán Momotombo, such as Volcán El Hoyo, an active cone (last major eruption 1954) and part of the **Volcán Las Pilas** complex, which is protected by a 7422-ha nature reserve of tropical dry forest. El Hoyo is a very physical climb and offers a frightening view of a perfectly round 80-m hole in its western face that is a bit of a mystery. Below El Hoyo and the extinct **Volcán Asososca** (818 m) is a pristine crater lake of the same name, but known popularly as Laguna El Tigre, or Jaguar Lagoon. The Spanish misnamed the animals, previously unseen by Europeans: a jaguar is called a 'tiger' (*tigre*) and a puma a 'lion' (*león*). From the 4WD path up to the western rim of the crater, it is an easy 10-minute walk down to the lake shores. This is one of Nicaragua's cleanest crater lakes and is great for swimming. Kayaking can be arranged with **Sampson Expeditions** (see page 208), which brings kayaks from León. The crater lake has an oval shape 1000 m x 1500 m wide. Its waters are 35 m deep and the temperature averages at 29°C. Camping is also possible on the lakeshore. Hikes and camping in this zone should be done with a guide, as much of the land is privately owned.

Volcán Cerro Negro → *Altitude: 675 m.*

This fierce little volcano is the newest in the western hemisphere and the most violent of the marvellous Maribios range. In 1850, what was a flat cornfield came to life with 10 days of violent eruption, leaving a hill 70 m high. In the short period since, it has grown to a height of 450 m above its base, with persistently violent eruptions shooting magma and ashes up to 8000 m in the air. Cerro Negro's most recent eruptions in 1992, 1995 and 1999 have coated León in black ash and put on a spectacular night-time display of fire. The eruption in August 1999 created three new baby craters (named by locals '*Las tres Marías*') at its southern base. The three Marías are simmering quietly, and the main crater is smoking silently as the short, squat mountain keeps everyone nervously waiting for its next hail of rocks, lava and ash. Fortunately, most of the eruptions have come with ample seismic warning. The website www.ineter.gob.ni is worth having a look at before climbing Cerro Negro and you can examine the volcano's daily activity recorded at INETER's seismic station next to the cone. They also have webcams pointed at Cerro Negro and other Nicaraguan volcanoes.

As its name suggests, Cerro Negro is jet-black, made up of black gravel, solidified black lava flows and massive black sand dunes. Hiking on the cone is a surreal experience and quite tiring, for the base is nothing but a giant black sandpit. On the northern fringes of the cone, growing in the volcano's seemingly sterile black sand, is a strange forest full of lizards, birds and flowering trees. This is the only volcano of its kind in Nicaragua and, depending on the route taken, you can choose between a very accessible 4WD drive and hike or a hot day-long excursion.

The most accessible ascent is the partially marked trail that starts at the baby craters near the seismic station and loops around to the east face. The climb is over loose volcanic rock and pebbles, very unstable on the surface, but solid underneath. At the summit, most people traverse the southern lip to reach the west face; the wind can be very strong up here so be careful. The west face descent is great fun but running down can be dangerous. The sunsets from the cone are beautiful – however, with such a perilous mountain, descending in the dark may not be advisable.

San Jacinto fumarolic pools

Further north in the Maribios range is **Volcán Rota**, which overlooks the highway that connects the northern mountains and the Pacific Basin. Known as the Carretera Telica-San Isidro, the highway slices through the heart of the range, at a low point between Volcán Rota and **Volcán Santa Clara**. At the base of Santa Clara is San Jacinto, an extraordinary little village that lives with amazing volcanic activity in its own backyard. Fifteen kilometres from the highway between León and Chinandega is the semi-paved entrance to the town with a big sign that says 'Los Hervideros de San Jacinto'. Follow the road to a stone arch where a US$2 admission is charged. The land drops off behind the village to a field of smoking, bubbling and hissing micro-craters, the Maribios range in miniature. They are the result of the water table leaking onto a magma vein of the nearby Volcán Telica (see below). In an ever-changing landscape, the water is heated and rushes to the surface with a heavy dose of sulphuric gases. Local children act as guides; choose one and heed instructions as to where it is safe

French extreme cyclist Eric Barone set a speed record on the steep gravel slope of Cerro Negro's west face in May 2002, reaching 172 kph before his front forks disintegrated and sent him rolling for 50 m. Very luckily, he survived the crash.

to walk. As a rule it is best to avoid walking on the crystallized white sulphur and to listen for hissing. Increased caution is required after rains, when the ground is particularly soft and prone to collapse. The landscape here is ever-evolving and children show which micro-cones are new and the different minerals that have been brought up to the surface by the superheated water. The kids may well fall upon you when you leave, asking for money; the village is very poor and the best solution is to tip your guide and buy some of the trinkets being offered by the children's mothers on the path back to the arch.

It is possible to climb to the summit of both Volcán Santa Clara and the active Volcán Telica from here. Santa Clara is two hours up and an hour and a half down for those in good shape. Telica is a long haul with an overnight stay on the mountain or a very early departure to do the round-trip in one day. A recommended guide is Arceño Medina who knows both cones well and is reliable and helpful. Rates are negotiable, but you can expect to pay at least US$20 to the guide for Telica and slightly less for Santa Clara, which can be split with other hikers.

Volcán Telica → *Altitude: 1061 m*

This smoking volcano last erupted in January 2007 and is part of a 9088-ha tropical dry forest reserve. Telica's activity creates the spectacle at San Jacinto and the volcano is one of Nicaragua's most active, with recorded eruptions in 1527 and steady activity ever since. This was one of three cones that erupted in the final weeks before the millennium celebrations, which certainly had the prophets of doom wringing their hands in eager anticipation. There is a long but rewarding hike that starts from just off the highway to Chinandega before the entrance to the village of **Quezalguaque**. The walk follows an ox-cart trail up the north shoulder of the cone, around to its east face and then up to the summit. The lip of the active crater affords a breathtaking view of the vertical interior walls of its crater and down to a smaller crater inside that limits the smoke. The hike can take three to five hours for a round trip, or you can continue to San Jacinto next to Volcán Santa Clara. This hike takes six to eight hours and involves three ascents. The climb should be undertaken with a guide; local guides are available if you start the climb from San Jacinto or, for the northeast route, use a León tour operator (see page 208) to allow 4WD access to the trail plus a guide to make the complete hike. Camping is also possible near the summit at a local ranch.

Volcán San Cristóbal → *Altitude: 1745 m*

This is another of Los Maribios' very active volcanoes and the highest in Nicaragua. San Cristóbal has shown almost constant activity since 1999, with the last recorded eruption in March 2006. San Cristóbal shares 17,950 ha of tropical dry forest reserve with **Volcán Casita**. One of the most symmetrical and handsome of the Maribios Volcano range, San Cristóbal is a difficult climb that should only be attempted with a guide and by hikers who are physically fit, though 4WD access to the adjacent Volcán Casita means that lesser athletes can still reach the summit to marvel at its 500 x 600 m wide crater. Some of the ranchers' caretakers are blocking access to the cone so it is critical to have a local with you to ease access and find the best route. Winds are very strong near the summit; avoid the windiest months from November to March if possible.

The owner of the **Hotel Los Balcones** in León (see page 205), Carlos Herdocia, owns a coffee hacienda at 650 m on the slopes of the volcano. He offers hiking tours to the summit of the volcano, coffee tours and nature watching on San Cristóbal and the adjacent Volcán El Chonco, which has primary forest and numerous species of bird, reptile and mammal life including deer, monkeys and ocelots. Guides and transportation to the volcano and its crater can also be found in León with local tour operators and guides, see page 208.

South of León » pp218-220.

León Viejo

ⓘ *The site is open daily from 0800-1700 and costs US$2, which includes parking and a Spanish-speaking guide, usually a native of Puerto Momotombo. A guide will show the ruins and make comments, but ask questions first to gauge the depth of the guide's knowledge. The sun is brutally strong most of the year at the site – avoid 1100-1430, and it is better to visit in the rainy season for the climate, visibility and the lushness of the countryside. Light is better in the late afternoon to photograph the ruins and surrounding volcanoes.*

Inside the quiet lake-side village of Puerto Momotombo, León Viejo or Sitio Histórico Colonial Ruinas de León Viejo, as it is officially known, is a must for anyone interested in colonial history and archaeology. Confirming its historical significance, not just for Nicaragua but for the world, León Viejo was declared a UNESCO World Heritage Site in December 2000 – the first site to receive such status in Nicaragua. It is a very hot and humid place with only the occasional lake breeze. At first sight León Viejo is nothing more than a few old foundations, surrounded by pleasant greenery in the shadow of the imposing Volcán Momotombo, but this unfinished excavation site is all that remains of one of the most tragic of Spanish settlements – one which witnessed some of the most brutal acts of the Conquest and was ultimately destroyed by a series of earthquakes and volcanic eruptions between 1580 and 1610. Nicaraguans will tell you with absolute conviction that León Viejo's destruction was a punishment from God for the crimes committed here.

León Viejo was Nicaragua's first capital, founded in the same year as Granada (1524) by **Francisco Hernández de Córdoba**. The site was selected because of its lakefront location and the existence of an important Chorotega Indian settlement known as **Imabite**. The town was laid out in classic colonial fashion with the cathedral facing west to a central plaza and principal avenues running from the park east-west and north-south. The earliest reports of the town speak of huts made of wood and thatch, and of persistent Indian attacks. León Viejo was the kind of town where if you had money or power you slept with your horse saddled and this first capital set the stage for a long history of unjust rulers, a tradition that would continue almost unbroken for the next 450 years.

The country's original ruler, **Pedrarias Dávila**, was a brutal old man who, before coming to Nicaragua, had run Panama's first settlement like a Mafia boss. When he was declared governor of Nicaragua on 1 July 1527, he was already in his mid-80s. He married a teenage Spanish girl and ordered the country's founder, Captain Hernández de Córdoba, to be beheaded (as he had done with Balboa in Panama). One of Pedrarias Dávila's most famous acts was the theatrically cruel murder of a dozen Indian hostages in 1528 in revenge for the murder of a half-dozen Spanish in the nearby mountains. Dávila devised a little game: he sent the Indians one by one into the Parque Central of León Viejo, in front of the village population, with a stick to protect themselves. First a tiny dog was released, which could be fought off easily. Then real killer dogs (which Pedrarias bred as a hobby) were released, and they tore their victims to bits. Old Pedrarias then insisted on leaving the bodies to rot for four days in the tropical June sun until the population finally convinced him to let them clean them up. Pedrarias died in March of 1531 and was buried in the La Merced Church.

In 1535, Pedrarias' son-in-law, **Rodrigo de Contreras**, was appointed governor. Along with the Crown treasurer, Pedro de los Ríos, and Crown Sheriff, Luis de Guevara, he sacked the country and stole everything he could find for almost ten years. The trio even provoked a rebellion by the highest church authority for continually embezzling the church's tithes. The famous 'Apostle of the Indians', Bartolomé de las Casas, was

“” León Viejo was the kind of town where if you had money or power you slept with your horse saddled ...

run out of Nicaragua after the good priest refused to bless the ill thought-out conquest of the Río San Juan. Casas said from the pulpit in the cathedral, with the Contreras family in attendance, that if the soldiers died on that conquest they would burn in hell. The next day Casas fled Nicaragua for Mexico and Contreras had him prosecuted in absentia. Even after the Spanish Crown ended his political reign and took away some of his slave ranches, Contreras still had control of the country, much in the manner of a tropical Al Capone. In 1550, while Contreras was in Spain to request the return of his land, his wife María de Peñalosa and their two sons, Hernando and Pedro, decided to rebel against the Spanish Crown. They murdered the respected and honest defender of Indian rights, the Bishop of Nicaragua, Fray Antonio de Valdivieso, at his home. They also killed all loyal government officials, stole the Crown's treasury, pirated ships, travelled to Panama and sacked its capital until they were finally defeated. One son, Hernan, may have drowned, but Pedro got away. María de Peñalosa paid her way out of a trial for treason, and went with her husband to enjoy the high life in Lima, Peru.

After the Contreras rebellion, León Viejo never really recovered, and was left to decay before being destroyed in a series of earthquakes and volcanic eruptions from 1580 until 1609. It was finally abandoned for León's current site in 1610.

Nicaragua's first capital was mostly forgotten, though it lived on in legends, including some that said it was located underneath Lake Managua. But after 357 years lying buried under volcanic ash, excavations began in 1967. In 2000, Nicaraguan archaeologist Ramiro García discovered the remains of Nicaragua's founder, Francisco Hernández de Córdoba, in the tomb of the ruins of La Merced church; his bones resting peacefully next to those of his nemesis Pedrarias Dávila. Córdoba's remains were put in a small glass box and paraded around the country, accompanied by a small guard of honour in the back of a big flat-bed truck. To add to the discovery of the tombs of Córdoba and Dávila, archaeologists from the Museo Nacional in Managua excavated and confirmed the remains of the assassinated Fray Antonio de Valdivieso, Bishop of Nicaragua, in the altar tomb of the old cathedral. He lies in a very large and fairly morbid-looking casket in a special roofed exhibit near the park entrance.

La Paz Centro

At Km 54 of the Carretera Nueva a León is the exit for the paved road that leads 12 km to the lakefront village of Puerto Momotombo and León Viejo (see below). Just north of the exit is the friendly, dusty and sad-looking town of La Paz Centro. The survivors of earthquakes, volcanic eruptions and cruel rulers of León Viejo settled here in the early 17th century. The area has a long history of ceramic production as well as many artisan brick and tile factories. The beautiful clay tiles used on the roofs and floors of the colonial homes of León and surrounding villages are made here in big wood-burning ovens utilizing the local soil. To see this centuries-old way of making bricks and tiles it is best to visit before 0900 or after 1700 when the small factories take advantage of relatively cool temperatures to put their ovens to work. The palms used for making the traditional thatched roofs (*ranchos*) are also prevalent in the surrounding countryside.

Few Nicaraguans and increasingly few foreigners pass up the opportunity to eat traditional Nicaraguan food while passing through La Paz and its sister city, Nagarote, to the south (see below). Nagarote is the birthplace of the *quesillo*, the most fattening snack in Nicaragua, but very good if fresh. The *quesillo* consists of a hot corn tortilla stuffed with mild white cheese (similar to mozzarella) and onions, drenched with fresh cream and salted. The most popular place in Nicaragua to eat *quesillos* is the perpetually crowded **Quesillos Guiliguiste** in La Paz Centro, near the entrance to the city. They sell so many here that the ingredients are always fresh and the servings are generous, with fast cafeteria-style service. They are served in tiny open-ended plastic bags, which should keep at least some of the cream off your shirt.

Nagarote

At Km 41 on the Carretera Nueva a León, rising out of the intense heat that bakes the lakeshore plains, Nagarote is a rustic and scenic ranching town and birthplace of a famous dish, *quesillo*, one of Nicaragua's best-loved traditional meals (see La Paz Centro page 215). Nagarote is a good place to savour a cold *tiste* – a traditional Indian drink of corn and *cacao* (raw chocolate bean dried and crushed) served, as it has been for over 1000 years, in the dried and gutted shell of the oval jícaro fruit. The most famous place in Nagarote for a good *quesillo con tiste* is the **Quesillos Acacia**, located at the southern highway entrance to Nagarote. It's a sit-down restaurant, with a waitress, but the only thing on the menu is *quesillo*. Here you can eat them off of a plate with knife and fork (a rare luxury) or you can grab one 'to go' (*para llevar*) in a tiny plastic bag. The eatery can be distinguished from the others by its thatched palm roof; *quesillos* cost US$1 each.

The centre of Nagarote lies well west of the highway, but is worth a visit if you have private transport. During the morning, oxcarts arrive from surrounding farms full of metal milk cans and boys ride into town on bicycles with live chickens dangling from their handlebars. There are many rustic and charming colonial homes and the people of Nagarote are helpful and laid back. Parque Central is sleepy and there's a pretty adobe church with red tile roof; inside, the dining room chandeliers and green curtains give it a homely feel. One block north is the original home of **Silvio Mayorga**, one of the Sandinista party founders who was killed by the National Guard in Pancasán in 1967. One block north and four blocks east of Parque Central an unassuming little park is home to what is believed to be Nicaragua's oldest living tree. This wide, ancient trunk with several surviving branches is the 950-year-old *genízaro* tree (*Pithecellobium saman*). In pre-Columbian times, this same tree gave shade to a *tiangue*, an indigenous market. At the corner of the park is a curious carved wood sculpture depicting a Chorotega chief on the front side and an Indian woman at the back. The monument was carved in 1999 out of a single branch of the ancient tree that watches over it.

Mateare

At Km 25, the highway reaches the sleepy fishing and agricultural town of Mateare, where you'll find the finest fish from Lake Managua. Although not as clean as Lake Nicaragua, this part of the lake is much cleaner than along the shores of Managua and the fish here is safe to eat. The locals say once you eat their *guapote* (large-mouth bass) you will never leave Mateare. Most of the locals who do not fish have small farms in the hills across the highway.

> *Beware of snakes; there are literally hundreds on the island and the guards claim to kill more than five a day just to keep their hut snake-free.*

The village offers rustic access to the seldom-visited **Isla Momotombito**. It is not easy to arrange but, with some asking around (try at the Araica residence on the east side of Parque Central), the fishermen can take you to the small volcanic island. The best time of year to visit is during the rainy season, when the island is green and the swell on the lake is small. Dry (windy) season trips mean a white-knuckle ride and a lot of water in your face. Boats have turned over on occasion during a big swell. It costs around US$60-70 for the day and you may need to drive out of town to fill up the fisherman's petrol tank in Los Brasiles. The ride is up to an hour depending on the lake swell.

The island is situated in the northwest of Lake Managua in the shadow of Volcán Momotombo. **Momotombito** (little Momotombo) has much bird and reptile life and a legendary family of albino crocodiles. There is a small military outpost on the calm side of the island. Stop there to check in if you wish to hike on the islands. Bring drinks or food as gifts for the (non-uniformed) guards, who are very friendly, usually quite bored and thrilled to see visitors. They might take you hiking for a small fee to see what is left of the island's many pre-Columbian statues. Momotombito, like the islands of Lake Nicaragua, is believed to have been a religious ceremonial site for the Chorotega Indians who lived on the lake shore. Most of the basalt idols have been looted or taken to museums. Some examples can be seen at the Museo Nacional in Managua (see page 47). A few kilometres north of Momotombito are several small rock islands where you can see some lake-level petroglyphs and sublime views of the steaming Volcán Momotombo.

West of León » *p219.*

Poneloya and Las Peñitas beaches

The crashing surf of the Nicaraguan Pacific lies only 21 km from León, down a bumpy country road. Past the Estela de los Mares the road forks: to the left is the road to the beaches of Las Peñitas and Poneloya. There is a US$1 entrance fee if you come by car on the weekend or during holidays. A visit during the week means you have most of the beach to yourself with just a few fishermen to chat to, the exception being during Semana Santa when the entire coast turns into the biggest party of the year.

Poneloya, the more popular of the two beaches, lies to the north of Las Peñitas, which tends to be a little cleaner and less crowded. Las Peñitas also has the best hotel and restaurant on the coast, as well as access to the nature reserve of Isla Juan Venado (see below). Both beach towns are passed by a single road lined with a mixture of local houses and luxury holiday homes for the wealthy of León. The locals are very friendly and helpful. The beaches themselves are attractive, with wide swathes of sand, warm water and pelicans. Swimming at either beach must be done with extreme caution; the currents are deceptively strong and foreigners die here every year assuming that strong swimming skills will keep them out of trouble. A good rule is to stay within your depth. You can ask the locals where the best place to swim is, but the truth is you won't see many of them swimming, just wading.

Reserva Natural Isla Juan Venado

This nature reserve is a turtle-nesting site with mangroves, crocodiles, crabs, iguanas and a healthy aquatic bird life. The island is very close to the mainland and is 22 km long and varies from 25 m to 600 m wide. On the ocean side of the island there are sea turtles nesting from August to December. From the beach it is possible to swim across to Salinas Grandes (see below). It is also possible to camp on the island but the mosquitoes are vicious. To explore the entire canal that runs behind the island you should allow about four hours in a motorboat, costing US$50-60, or about US$20 for a short trip. Early morning, late afternoon or at night are the most favourable times to see the reserve, but touring needs to be timed with high tide. Try the fisherman who goes by the name of Toño Ñanga (legal name Antonio González) who lives just 20 m east of the **Bar Comedor El Calamar** in front of an old washed-away pier. Kayaking is also offered here at the hostel **Barca de Oro** and other local tour operators in León, one of which, **Sampson Expeditions** (see page 209), has a house in Salinas Grandes and offers a rewarding circuit with kayaking from Las Peñitas to the beach at Salinas Grandes, traversing the entire wildlife refuge. This journey takes from three to six hours depending on conditions and your level of fitness and includes sea kayaks, a bilingual guide, motorboat for support (and cold drinks), land transfers to Las Peñitas and from

 Salinas Grandes and time relaxing in their beach house. Prices range from US$25-75 per person depending on group size. Night tours are also very interesting and useful for spotting crocodiles and sea turtles laying eggs, but take plenty of insect repellent.

Salinas Grandes

At Km 74 on the Carretera Vieja a León is a scenic dirt track that leads through pleasant pastures to the Nicaraguan Pacific and the long wave-swept Pacific Ocean beach of Salinas Grandes. Past a small settlement, the path drops down through lobster and shrimp farms before arriving at the simple beach with fishermen's homes. South of here, where the main road finishes, is where the fisherman roll their boats out of the sea and on to the beach over logs pushed by half the village. Their catch is normally *pargo rojo* or *negro* (red or black snapper) and you can ask for someone to cook you a fresh *pargo* for US$3. The beach is fairly littered here but is much cleaner to the north and south. About 1 km north is the mouth of a river where the locals like to swim. North of the river outlet is the clean sand of the long barrier **Isla Juan Venado**, a protected nature reserve that runs all the way to Las Peñitas (see above).

North of León » *p218.*

From León, the Carretera a Chinandega runs north along the western slope of the Maribios range. The exit for the only paved highway that connects the Pacific Basin with the northern mountains is at Km 101. This scenic road slices in between the volcano range and connects to the Pan-American Highway at San Isidro.

El Sauce

The Carretera a San Isidro passes the rocky savannah of **Malpaisillo** until the exit at km 150; from here it is 28 km along a paved road in poor condition to the rustic town of El Sauce, a classic colonial ranching village set in a small highland valley. Most of the year not one outsider passes through El Sauce, but every January it comes alive to celebrate *El Señor de Esquipulas*, the black Christ image that was responsible for numerous miracles. One of many stories is about the 18-year-old bride who was being wed in the church of El Sauce around 100 years ago. As she was about to finish her vows she looked above the altar to the Señor de Esquipulas and asked him for the truth. Should she marry, give up her virginity and live a carnal life or should she serve God in heaven? She prayed to the black Christ, asking him for a sign. As the church sat silent waiting for her to say 'I do', she fell to the ground, dying on the steps of the altar. Her virgin death was a sure sign to the people that she was a saint and she is still remembered today in a series of special ceremonies. The celebrations last over a week, but the principal day is 18 January, when people congregate in El Sauce on the culmination of a pilgrimage from as far away as Guatemala. Sadly, the sublimely beautiful church of El Sauce, built in 1594, was damaged in two fires, the first in 1997 and the second in December of 1999. As local firefighters battled the 1999 blaze, back-up fire engines were sent for from León, some three hours away, while the church and its colonial relics burned. The old church has now been completely restored and has maintained much of its former charm.

Sleeping

San Jacinto *p212*

Lodging is available in the town's old cinema, which has been refurbished and made into a hostel (**E**); it sits one block south of the entrance to Los Hervideros with shared bath.

León Viejo *p214*

F La Posada de León Viejo, Centro de Salud, 2 c norte. 3 rooms with shared bath; hotel does not have kitchen, but can arrange meals for customers. This archaeologists' hostel is located just 4 blocks from the excavation site.

Poneloya and Las Peñitas *p217*
Most of the best eating is at the hotels and hostels.

C Posada de Poneloya, Playa Poneloya, from the intersection of Las Peñitas and Poneloya, 150 m to the right, T317-1378. 19 rooms with private bath, hot water, a/c, with room service, parking, not a great part of the beach, but lively on weekends.

C Suyapa Beach Hotel, in Las Peñitas, T885-8345 www.suyapabeach.com. A well-kept and professional hotel with a pool and 20 clean rooms, all with poor beds and private bath, some with a/c. Rooms on 2nd and 3rd floor have ocean views and a breeze. Often full with groups. Cheaper with fan (**D**). The ₸₸-₸ hotel restaurant is very good quality, try *pescado a la suyapa*, fresh snapper in a tomato, sweet pepper and onion sauce.

D El Oasis, Terminal de Buses, 200 varas norte, Las Peñitas, T839-5344, www.oasislaspenitas.com. 7 large rooms with poor mattresses; some have phenomenal views. Lots of chill-out spaces with hammocks. Services include rental of surf boards, horse riding and laundry service. The restaurant has great views but the restrooms are nasty.

D Samaki, overlooking the bay, Las Peñitas, T640-2058, www.LaSamaki.net. 4 tasteful rooms with good mattresses, safes, mosquito nets and private bath. Canadian owned, very relaxed, friendly and hospitable, and home to Nicaragua's only kite-surfing operation. Fresh food made to order, including delicious, real Asian curries. Highly recommended.

D-G Barca de Oro, Las Peñitas, at the end of the beach facing Isla Juan Venado Wildlife Refuge, www.barcadeoro.com.ni. Friendly, funky hotel with dorm beds (**G**) and private rooms (**E**), all with fan and bath, 1 with a/c (**D**). Services include kayaking, horse riding, body boarding, book exchange, hammocks, tours of the area and beauty treatments.

El Sauce *p218*
D Hotel Blanco, alcaldía, 1 c sur, 1 c abajo, T319-2403. 20 rooms around a big tamarind tree with private bath and fan, cooler rooms are on 1st floor, basic, clean and friendly, the best in this region, also good ₸ *comida corriente*.

F Bar y Hospedaje El Viajero, T319-2325. Private bath, fan, clean, friendly, great value. Lunch and dinner on lovely wood tables US$1.50, US$0.80 breakfast.

Eating

San Jacinto *p212*
At the entrance to the fumaroles there is a small ranch that has cheap set meals and offers soft drinks.

Restaurante El Rancho, at the entrance to the village. Greasy food, but very cheap and with cold fruit juices and beer.

La Paz Centro and Nagarote *p215*
For eating options, see in main text, above.

Mateare *p216*
₸ **Bar El Ranchito**, Parque Central. Serves fried chicken, fish and cold beer and offers an up-close glimpse of village personalities (and drinking capacities) along the rural northern lakefront.

₸ **Mirador Momotombo**, Km 31.5, Carretera Nueva a León. Daily 1000-2000. Charming outdoor restaurant with priceless view of Momotombo, Lake Managua and Isla Momotombito, typical beef, pork and chicken dishes at cheap to mid-range prices. The grounds of the restaurant are great for photography and if you don't wish to eat or drink there you can pay US$1.50 to use the grounds to take photographs. Tables are spread out under little palm-roofed huts and it is worth stopping for a drink at least, though a day with no lake breeze will mean lots of insects. Camping is also possible next to the restaurant on an adjacent lakefront field for a small fee, enquire at the restaurant.

Transport

Buses pass through **Mateare**, **Nagarote** and **La Paz Centro** on the Carretera every 15 mins between **León** and **Managua**.

For an explanation of the sleeping and eating price codes used in this guide, see inside the front cover. Other relevant information is found in Essentials, see pages 23-27.

León Viejo *p214*
Buses between Puerto Momotombo (León Viejo) and **La Paz Centro** every 1½ hrs, from 0400-1600, US$0.40. Taxi or hired car can be used as roads are good.

Las Salinas *p218*
Buses to **León** daily at 0900 and 1500.

El Sauce *p218*
Buses to **León**, every 2 hrs, 0800-1600, US$1.40, 2½ hrs. To **Estelí**, 1300, US$1.25, 3 hrs. Express bus to **Managua**, 1200, US$2, 3½ hrs.

Chinandega and Cosigüina Peninsula

The hot plains of Chinandega province were once bursting with thousands of orange trees and caressed by cool breezes. The cotton boom of the mid-20th century brought the local ecosystem to its knees, however, and now the dust and oppressive heat make it a less appealing prospect. That said, the province still boasts forested volcanoes, quiet Pacific beaches and estuary wildlife reserves and is worth a visit in the rainy season when daily showers moderate the sun's fury. The department's modest administrative capital, Chinandega, is a friendly, sleepy place, but no less searing than its surroundings, You'll want to limit your explorations of its colonial churches to the early morning or late afternoon; between 1000 and 1700 temperatures are scorching. *▸▸ For Sleeping, Eating and other listings, see pages 226-228.*

Chinandega ▸▸ *226-228.*

The city of Chinandega sits in the middle of the most extensive plain of volcanic soil in Nicaragua, which some believe to be the most fertile valley in all of Central America. Chinandega is the centre for thousands of hectares of farms that utilize the rich soil to grow sugarcane, bananas and peanuts among many other crops. It is also one of the hottest places in Central America, feeling like an irrigated desert for much of the year.

Ins and outs

Getting there Chinandega is accessed from a good paved highway north of León or another highway that crosses over from Choluteca, Honduras via El Guasaule. Bus services are frequent from Managua, León and the border.

Getting around Inside Chinandega taxis are cheap and friendly, as are the horse-drawn carriages that ply the hot streets. Walking is also a good way to get around if you can stand the infernal sun. Once outside the city, it is best to travel by 4WD, with the exception of El Viejo and Corinto, both of which have easy taxi access and regular bus service. *▸▸ For further details, see Transport, page 228.*

Best time to visit Due to the famously hot days here it is best to visit from between the end of the rainy season to the early dry season (i.e. from September to December and, maybe, early January), when the sun is less aggressive. If using the town to stay overnight as a jumping off point to visit Cosigüina or its beaches, any time of year is fine provided you book a room with air conditioning.

Tourist information **INTUR** ① *Antiguo Banic, 75 vrs sur, T341-1935*, has a selection of flyers and helpful Spanish-speaking staff.

Background

When the Spanish first arrived in Chinandega, it was a large Nicaraguas (as in Rivas) Indian settlement with a rather haughty chief (see El Viejo below). The brutal first governor of Nicaragua, Pedrarias Dávila, found it to be so fertile that he commandeered all of it as one of his own plantations. It was the site of various meetings of Central American states in the 19th century as attempts were made to remake a federation, all of which failed. It used to be known as the 'city of oranges' for its principal crop at the turn of the 20th century, but cotton replaced the orange trees in the 1940s and the heat of the valley began to increase. For decades, cotton was the main export of Nicaragua, until a downturn in the international market prices, combined with exhausted soil, a war of insecticides with local insects and greedy middlemen, ruined the business. Now sugarcane and peanut millionaires utilize the still-fertile soil of the area and there are profitable shrimp farms in the outlying estuaries. Chinandega's patron saint is the grandmother of Jesus, Santa Ana. Her celebrations begin on 17 July and end on 26 July.

Sights

Grungy and super-hot Chinandega will not win any beauty contests but the people who live here are very nice and welcoming and the city has two pretty churches that act as bookends for the city centre. At the east end of the centre is the **Iglesia El Calvario**, with its central bell tower and white-painted wood ceilings with chandeliers that are common in this region. The town's central avenue runs west from the church past one of three markets. Six blocks west of the church is the **Parque Central**, unusual for its north orientation to the church. Inside the park are two pools with crocodiles and plenty of turtles cramped together in the dirty water. It is not unusual to see a big croc sound asleep with locals watching alarmingly close by. The **Iglesia Santa Ana** is attractive with its typical Nicaraguan baroque design and slightly incongruous Wall Street pillars. Inside there are some gold leaf altars and faded frescos.

Around Chinandega » *226-228.*

Chichigalpa

Chichigalpa is a bustling agricultural centre that is best known for the country's oldest sugar mill, the **Ingenio San Antonio**. The French pirate William Dampier noted the factory's existence on his way to sack León in 1685. It is here that the sugar is processed for Nicaragua's superb rum, **Flor de Caña** (flower of the cane). West of the town, the road runs along palm-shaded railroad tracks that connect the village to the sugar mill. This rail line, with the Maribios Volcanoes as a backdrop, is the now famous trademark of *Flor de Caña* and *Toña* beer. There are five trains a day each way from May to November, passengers are taken for US$0.25, or there is a bus for US$0.30. On the edge of Chichigalpa itself is the *Flor de Caña* distillery, the maker of what many believe to be the finest rum in the world, aged up to 21 years and bottled in over 15 flavours. While the installations are not open to the public, the town's *alcaldía* (town hall) may be able to help arrange a special tour.

Corinto

From the roundabout at the entrance to Chinandega, it is 25 km southwest to the only deepwater port in Nicaragua. About 60% of the country's commerce passes through here and Asian cars seem to flow out of the town all year round. (Note that entry to the port is barred to all except those with a permit. There is immigration and customs at the port, but the only way in or out of here is on a container ship.) The town itself is on a sandy island, **Punto Icaco**, connected to the mainland by bridges. Near the port are some tired but graceful old wooden buildings with verandas. The old train station is now a beautiful library. The most popular pastime in Corinto (besides drinking) seems to be riding around the central park at night on bicycles. There is also an unspoken contest to see how many passengers one can fit on a bicycle and still do laps of the park; six appears to be the record.

There are some nice beaches on the north side of town and on the Corinto-Chinandega road is **Paso Caballo** beach. The name comes from the supposed nightly appearance of the Devil on horseback, who is blamed for the many road deaths along this stretch. The sea is also treacherous here and people drown every year.

There are no facilities in Corinto's barrier islands, but they are beautiful with crashing surf on one side and calm and warm swimming water on the other. The longest island (with the lighthouse), **El Cardón**, was a place of inspiration for the poet Rubén Darío. The journey can be negotiated with any fisherman. Bring anything you might need with you to the island. A *panga* can be rented for the whole day for US$60-75 allowing you to explore the numerous islands and mangroves. There is lots of bird life and sandflies, so bring repellent.

El Viejo to the Cosigüina Peninsula » *226-228.*

From El Viejo there is a scenic drive or bumpy bus ride to the Pacific Coast or on to the last of the Maribios Volcanoes, **Volcán Cosigüina** (800 m) and the steamy and beautiful **Golfo de Fonseca** at Potosí. Another interesting trip northeast from El Viejo is to **Puerto Morazán**, which has some simple lodging and some of the friendliest people in Chinandega. The town is on the **Estero Real**, the biggest Pacific Basin nature reserve in Nicaragua at 55,000 ha, an endless labyrinth of estuaries and the biggest mangrove forest in Central America. You can hire a fisherman's boat in Puerto Morazán to explore.

> ! *All routes on the peninsula should be done in public bus or 4WD only. It is essential to buy purified water, and if driving, to fill up with fuel before leaving El Viejo: there are no petrol stations on the peninsula.*

There are some long empty beaches along the west coast of the peninsula that are backed by towering cliffs further north. Despite the close proximity to population centres like Chinandega and León, this region has a forgotten end-of-the-earth feel and is seen by very few foreigners. For those looking to escape the beaten path in Nicaragua (which admittedly is not very beaten), this is one of the most accessible areas to get away from it all – if you can take the heat, which is year-round but more bearable from September to December.

The first section of the highway is paved and passes gigantic ranches, so big and wealthy that this part of the road is nicknamed '*Carretera Millonaria*'. Before the pavement ends there are two turnings that lead to the desolate beaches of the extreme northwest of Nicaragua's Pacific. The first exit leads to **Aposentillo** and the second to **Jiquilillo**. Jiquilillo is one of the dirtiest beaches in Nicaragua, but the highway to the beach leads to the sun-drenched coastal estuary nature reserve of Padre Ramos. Reached by another long winding dirt and rock path off the highway is the marina, hotel and beach resort of Marina Puesta del Sol, located between the sweeping coastline of Aposentillo and the tiny fishing village of **Los Aserradores** on a crystal bay.

El Viejo

Although it is officially a separate city, 5 km from Chinandega, the growth of El Viejo means that it is merging into a single sprawl with Chinandega. This slightly rundown but peaceful place is home to the patron saint of Nicaragua, an ancient church and a large indigenous community. This is one of the most important Catholic sites in a very Catholic country. The 70-cm-tall image in the church of the Immaculate Conception of the Virgin Mary, called **La Virgen del Trono**, is one of the most venerated images in all of Central America. La Virgen del Trono is said to have arrived in Nicaragua on the

Oviedo and Tezoatega

The Spanish chronicler Oviedo visited El Viejo in the early 1500s. At the time it was still known by its original name, Tezoatega, and was ruled by Agateyte, one of the most powerful chiefs of Nicaragua, who had his main plaza where the Basilica of El Viejo stands today. Agateyte ruled at least 20,000 subjects and had a standing army of 6000 warriors. When Oviedo went to Tezoatega, he sent his translator forward to request an interview. When he received the request, the great chief shrugged it off: he was busy and had no idea who this Oviedo was, and anyway he did not have time for peons. Oviedo waited for hours and insisted on an interview, but was denied over and over again. Finally, Oviedo figured out that he needed to show some sign of royal blood, or at least prove he was of a ruling class. He announced that he had a family member who was a governor in Spain to which Agateyte retorted (in Náhuatl): "Why didn't you tell me that in the first place, *chelito* (whitey)?" Oviedo was allowed inside and learned from the chief that Nicaragua's leaders must spend one year in solitary prayer before assuming leadership and were only permitted one daily ration of food. Oviedo also noted that: "The chief wore a thin mantle of white cotton with which he covered himself, and his entire body, arms and legs and neck were painted. He had long hair and a long beard, was over 70 years old, tall, withered and very serious in speech."

back of Alonso Zepeda, the brother of Saint Teresa of Spain, who gave the image to her brother before he left for the New World in the late 16th century. Legend has it that when Alonso Zepeda arrived at the indigenous settlement of Tezoatega, later named El Viejo, he grew tired and rested in the shade of a tree. When he left the comfort of the shade he noticed that the load on his back was much lighter. He wrestled the luggage off his back and found that the Virgen del Trono had somehow escaped his pack and, returning to the resting spot, he found her under the tree where he had taken shade. Alonso packed her once again and headed off, only to find down the road that his load was, once again, strangely lighter. He checked for the image of the Virgin and found that she was missing again. He returned to the same tree and found the Virgin once again in its shade. He decided it was here that she wished to stay and the **Basílica de la Inmaculada Concepción de la Virgen María** was built upon that very spot. She remains there today and La Virgen del Trono was officially named Patron Saint of Nicaragua in May of 2000. The church that houses her received the title of Basilica during Pope John Paul II's visit to El Viejo in February of 1996. The original structure dates from 1562 and it was refurbished in 1884.

One of the most famous religious events in Nicaragua is the **Lavada de la plata** (cleaning the silver). This seemingly innocuous activity is an honour for the devout of the Virgen del Trono, who clean all the silver items associated with the ancient icon every 6 December, before her big day – the huge *Purísima* celebrations that start on 7 December all over Nicaragua in her name. Pilgrims arrive from all over the country and as far away as Guatemala to participate in the cleaning of the icons' silver, stowing away the cotton used to clean her relics for good luck.

Marina Puesta del Sol

This very ambitious project has a world-class marina for the international yachting crowd sailing the Pacific, a heliport and pretty hotel rooms and suites with a view of the bay and northern Maribios range. The marina and hotel are set on a crystal-blue estuary with extensive mangrove forests covering the mainland and barrier islands year-round. Beyond the bay rises the smoking San Cristóbal Volcano and the other cones of the northern range, truly a spectacular place to be on land or in the water. For boaters, this is the only quality marina in Nicaragua with space for 33 boats in slips, end ties and side ties for vessels up to 154 ft in length. The marina's floating dock system is constructed using pressure-treated Nicaraguan pine, roto-moulded watertight floats and heavy-duty hardware, for strength and longevity. The structure rises and falls on fixed piles during average tides of 5-7 ft in the protected harbour. Each slip is provided with a lighted dock box, water service, cable TV, and 110V/30 amp and 220V/50 amp single and three-phase power service. The dock structure also features a high efficiency fire protection system and heavy-duty cleats for secure tie-ups. In addition, the resort provides minor mechanical and electrical repairs, bottom cleaning, expert varnishing, carpentry, and yacht maintenance, as well as a mobile 62 gallon pump-out unit.

For those who don't arrive in their yacht, the resort offers one of the prettiest, cleanest beaches in Central America. Fifteen minutes from the hotel and marina structure on foot or five minutes by car or boat, the stretch of **Playa Aposentillo** opens out on the north side of the barrier islands. The resort has an unusual beach hut, a giant palm frond 'hat', as they call it, that shades a stone floor dining and bar area, next to an infinity swimming pool dug right out of the beach, particularly attractive in the bright morning light.

Reserva Natural Padre Ramos

North of the beautiful Playa Aposentillo is the coastal estuary reserve of Padre Ramos, named after a priest from El Viejo who drowned here. This is the most remote and pristine Pacific Coast estuary in Nicaragua, very wild and unknown to all but a handful of the local population. Most of the reserve must be explored by boat, though several land trails have been cleared. The reserve is protected from the sea by 15 km of beach and low forest that ranges from 200-800 m wide and breaks for a 500 m mouth that opens up to the Pacific Ocean. The reserve is said to protect one of the best preserved mangroves in Nicaragua. More than 150 species of birds have been recorded in Padre Ramos, as well as ocelots, iguanas, three species of sea turtle and crocodiles. The average temperature here is 29°C with an annual rainfall of 1.5 m. Access is best from the highway to Jiquilillo, as the ranger station is located at the southern part of the Pacific mouth that opens up to the estuary. It is possible to camp here and hire a boat and local guide through the park staff's contacts. If you wish to arrange something in advance contact **SELVA** ⓘ *Comanejante del Area Protegida, Mercado Central, 6 c abajo, 1 c sur, ½ c abajo, El Viejo, T884-9156, selvanic@hotmail.com*, the NGO in charge of the reserve.

Volcán Cosigüina → *Altitude: 859 m.*

At the northwestern-most point of Nicaragua, this volcano has some unique wildlife and 13,168 ha of protected tropical dry forest. The forest at the base of the volcano is under threat from farming and burning, and the majority of this part of the peninsula is totally deforested with ground water found below 100 m at some points. The success of the reserve is that it is the last remaining Nicaragua Pacific Coast habitat for the **scarlet macaw**, the star billing in a reserve which has more than 77 bird species as well as 15 species of mammal including the **spider monkey**, not found anywhere else on the Pacific Coast of Nicaragua.

There are two climbs to the summit, **Sendero El Jovo**, which starts just west of Potosí, where there is very simple accommodation, and **Sendero La Guacamaya**, accessed via El Rosario on the north end of the cone and at the Ranger Station located south of El Rosario. It is possible to sleep in the station by prior arrangement with park

Border essentials: Nicaragua – Honduras

Guasaule
The distance between the border posts is 500 m.
Immigration Open 24 hrs. To enter Nicaragua costs are US$7 plus a US$1 alcaldía charge; to exit it is US$2 plus the US$1 immigration charge.
Transport Buses run every 30 mins from the border to Chinandega, US$1. Express Guasaule–Managua, 1130, 1230, 1700, US$3.25, 4 hrs.
Directory Money changers offer the same rates for córdobas to lempiras as on the Honduran side. Bancentro, nextdoor to the immigration office, is recommended: good rates, no commission, and will accept a photocopy of passport if yours is being checked by immigration.

Potosí
Nicaraguan immigration and customs Open 0800-1700, but closed for lunch. Exit is US$2 and Nicaraguan immigration entrance is US$7.
Transport Buses from Potosí-Chinandega, 0230, 0345, 0500, 0620, 0710, 1000, 1500, US$2, 3 hrs. If trying to leave Nicaragua, there is no ferry at the time of printing; try a private boat to El Salvador, from US$100.

managers who have an office in El Viejo, **Lider** ⓘ *Mercado Central, 3 c norte, lider@ibw.com.ni, Thu-Sun*. On the south side of the crater there is a charming lodge, **Hostal Hacienda Cosigüina**, that offers both hiking and 4WD trips to the summit and is by far the most comfortable option (see page 227).

The view from the summit is why most hikers come to Cosigüina, a sweeping panorama that includes the islands in the Gulf of Fonseca and El Salvador to the north and Honduras to the east, not to mention the emerald lagoon 700 m below the summit of the crater, 1½ km in diameter and occupying 90% of the bottom of the crater. The conditions for the crater lake were created by the biggest eruption recorded in Latin American history. During a series of eruptions from 20-26 January 1835, the volcano, which was close to 3000 m at the time, blew its top, sending ash as far away as Jamaica, 1300 km to the east, and Mexico, 1400 km to the north. For local residents in Chinandega, León and even El Salvador, judgement day had arrived. One witness reported the scene in León:

"People groped dumb with horror, through the thick darkness, bearing crosses on their shoulders and vines on their heads, in penitential abasement and dismay, believing the day of doom had come. As a last resort, every saint in León, without exception, lest he be offended, was taken from his niche into the air – but still the ashes fell. People embraced each other saying eternal goodbyes: everywhere, weeping, cries, and lamentations. At last, with superb faith, President Núñez, not knowing the reason for the strange phenomenon, ordered the church bells rung and cannons fired to conjure the calamity away..."

Lava poured out of the volcano in 1852 and then Cosigüina erupted one last time in 1859; by 1938 there was a lake inside the crater. In 1951 a mudslide came down on poor little Potosí destroying it completely. It has been rebuilt since, a tiny town baked to a crust by the fierce sun.

Potosí

Arriving in Potosí is much like arriving at any other end-of-the-world place. Although it is only 60 km from Chinandega, the rocky road, searing heat and chocolate-brown waters of the prehistoric bay of **Golfo de Fonseca** are other-worldly. For those seeking to relax, there are thermal springs inland from the rusty hull of the shipwreck on the east side of the beach. Once woken from their heat-induced trance, the locals are very friendly here and the ocean is calm and good for swimming, though the dark brown sand gives it a less inviting colour. The Golfo de Fonseca is shared by Nicaragua, El Salvador and Honduras and there is constant bickering over fishing right in the waters. From the solitary dock in Potosí, it is only 15 minutes by boat to a commercial shipping port in Honduras and two hours to La Union in El Salvador. There are rumours that the ferry between La Union and Potosí will be resumed, although it is likely they will skip Potosí and head direct to the port at Corinto. At the moment you will have to negotiate a ride in either direction with local boats. To travel from Potosí to El Salvador will cost US$100 or more to make it worthwhile for a fisherman to make the trip. It is reportedly easier coming from El Salvador to Potosí. There is simple accommodation here that gives access to a hike on Volcán Consigüina. Entrance tax to El Salvador is around US$10. The **immigration office** ⓘ *corner of Av General Cabañas and 7a Calle Pte, La Unión, T2604-4375, 0600-2200*, is next to the post office. You will need to stop here whether coming from or going to Nicaragua.

Sleeping

Chinandega *p220*

A Los Volcanes, Km 129.5, Carretera a Chinandega, at southern entrance to city, T341-1000. Very pleasant, comfortable rooms with private bath, hot water, a/c, cable TV. There's a smart restaurant and bar, service is professional.

B Hotel Cosigüina, Esquina de los Bancos, T341-1663, www.hotelcosiguina.com. 20 clean, dark rooms with private bath, warm water, a/c, telephone, cable TV. Facilities include bar, restaurant, casino and internet. Prices include light a breakfast.

C Campestre Terraza, Rotunda entranda a Chinandega, T340-3058, hotelcampesterraza @yahoo.com. This smart new hotel at the entrance to town has comfortable rooms with a/c, cable TV, hot water and internet. There's a pool and private parking.

C Hotel Chinandegano, Esso El Calvario 1½ c arriba, T341-4800. One of the best, with decent rooms, popular bar and restaurant.

C Hotel Pacífico, Iglesia San Antonio, 1½ c sur, T341-1418, hotelpac@ibw.com.ni. Comfortable, friendly hotel with decent, modern rooms, all have a/c, cable TV, private bath and hot water. Recommended.

C Hotel San José, Esquina de los Bancos, 2½ c norte, T341-2723. Clean, comfortable and friendly. 10 small, plain rooms have private bath, a/c, cable TV. Breakfast included. Laundry service and internet available.

E Casa Grande, Frente de Gallo mas Gallo, T341-0325. Management is friendly but the beds are poor. Be sure to get a room with a/c, those without (**F**) can be uncomfortably warm. Tours to the volcanoes and a nearby *finca* are offered.

E Don Mario's, Enitel, 170 vrs norte, T341-4054. Great-value rooms and friendly hosts at this homely lodging. Rooms have a/c, private bath and cable TV. The owners speak excellent English. Recommended.

G Aniram, Shell, 1½ c arriba, T341-4519. Basic rooms, some with smutty, gilt-framed pictures on the walls. Others have TV (**F**) and a/c (**E**). The neighbourhood is run-down and colourful. Take care.

Chichigalpa *p221*

D Hotel La Vista, alcaldía, 1 c arriba, 75 vrs norte, T343-2035. 10 rooms with private bath, a/c, cable TV, includes breakfast, simple rooms with low ceiling, spacious, the best in town.

Corinto *p221*

D-F Puerto Plata, Corinto, Parque Central, 175 m sur, T342-2667. **F** with fan and **D** with a/c, private bath, good.

F Central, in front of Port buildings. Clean rooms with a/c.

For an explanation of the sleeping and eating price codes used in this guide, see inside the front cover. Other relevant information is found in Essentials, see pages 23-27.

El Viejo *p222*
G Casa de Huespedes, near central square. Basic rooms with shared bath.

Marina Puesta del Sol *p223*
LL-L Marina Puesta del Sol, Los Aserradores, T228-7974, www.marinapuestadelsol.com. Set in a unique locale, this hotel has 19 suites overlooking the bay and marina, all spacious and modern with generic decor and patios. Some have Jacuzzi, and the higher level suites have a great view of bay and volcanoes. There's a nice restaurant (𝐘𝐘𝐘) on the dock, but very pricey. Activities include fishing trips in hotel boats, swimming in the bay off island or at nearby Playa Aposentillo where hotel has a great thatched ranch bar restaurant and swimming pool on the region's finest stretch of sand.

Volcán Consigüina *p224*
B-E Hostal Hacienda Cosigüina, Km 60, from Chinandega on highway to Potosí, T341-2872, www.haciendacosiguina.com.ni. One of Nicaragua's most charming rural lodges set on a 3500-acre hacienda where peanuts, corn, sesame seeds and cashews are grown, and cattle are raised. The farm was founded by a Basque migrant in 1775 and still remains under the same family's care, though the original ranch was destroyed in 1835 by the eruption of Volcán Cosigüina. The hacienda offers a variety of tours including horse rides and 4WD excursions up the volcano, visits to Padre Ramos and the cliffs of the coast (Los Farallones) and 𝐘𝐘 home-cooked meals. The 7 homely rooms have private bath, and there are dorms too (**E**).

Potosí *p225*
Contact Héctor for permission to stay in the fishing co-operative (**G**). The fishermen are friendly. You can sling your hammock at the *comedor* 150 m past immigration for US$1.
G Hospedaje Brisas del Golfo, next to the dock. A row of clean, if stark, concrete block rooms with fan inside, toilet and bath outside.

Eating

Chinandega *p220*
𝐘𝐘 Frank's Bar and Grill, southeast corner of Iglesia El Calvario, 1 c sur. One of the best in town, with good beef cuts and fine wine. Smart, clean interior.
𝐘𝐘 Gerry's Seafood, Shell central, 1½ c norte. Reportedly very good fish and seafood.
𝐘 Corona de Oro, Iglesia San Antonio, 1½ c arriba, T341-2539. Chinese food with flavour. The chicken curry and shrimp skewers are especially tasty.
𝐘 El Mondongazo, south side of Colegio San Luis, T341-4255. Traditional Nicaraguan foods like *sopa mondongo* (tripe soup), beef, chicken and meatball soup.
𝐘 El Refugio, Esso, El Calvario, ½ c sur, T341-0834. Great beef specialities, try the breaded tongue.
𝐘 Kingdom's Pizza, Enitel, 1 c arriba, ½ c sur, T341-8911. Burgers, roast chicken and fairly decent, cheap pizza. Delivers.
𝐘 Las Tejitas, Parque Central, 7 c arriba. Cheap and cheerful. They serve buffet food, grilled meats and *comida típica*. Very popular and always packed out. A Chinandega institution.

Bakeries and juice bars
Bambú, BAC, 75 vrs norte. Juices and smoothies from tropical fruits and vegetables.
Panadería Marsella, Shell, 1 c arriba. Sweet rolls, bread and coffee.

Chichigalpa *p221*
𝐘𝐘-𝐘 Rancho Típico, alcaldía, 3½ c sur, T343-1030. Good beef dishes, seafood, traditional Nicaraguan food.

Corinto *p221*
𝐘 El Español, in Corinto, puente Paso Caballos, 100 varas abajo, T851-0677, patipaso@yahoo.com. Good seafood restaurant, also beef, and other meats, pleasant outdoor seating with view of an estuary canal. They are also building hotel rooms planned to open soon. Recommended.

El Viejo *p222*
𝐘𝐘-𝐘 Tezoatega, El Viejo, Basílica 1½ c norte, T344-2436. Daily 1100-2200. Chicken and beef dishes, good value, outdoor seating, friendly.

Potosí *p225*

Bar y Restaurante Gilmari. Fried chicken, steak, fish soup. If you order fish the owner will walk down to the dock, buy one and cook it, usually *pargo* (snapper). Most dishes US$2-3. Pitcher of beer is US$1.75.

Transport

Chinandega *p220*

Bus

Most buses leave from the new market at southeast edge of town. To **Corinto**, every 20 mins, 0600-2100, US$0.40, 30 mins. To **Somotillo**, every 3 hrs, 0900-1500, US$2, 2 hrs. To **Guasaule**, every 2 hrs, 0600-1600, US$2, 2 hrs. To **Managua**, every 30 mins, 0600-1600, US$2.50, 3 hrs. To **León**, every 11 mins, 0600-1700, US$1, 1 hr 45 mins. Buses for **Potosí**, **El Viejo** and **Puerto Morazán** leave from the Mercadito northwest of town. A bus links Terminal, Mercado and Mercadito.

International buses Contact individual agencies for schedules and costs; **Ticabus**, Esquina de los Bancos, 2 c norte, T341-4331, www.ticabus.com. **Transnica**, opposite Colegio Bethelemitas on the Carretera Panamericana, next to Hotel Maribios, T340-1305, www.transnica.com.

Car hire

There are several companies, including: **Avis Rent a Car**, T341-1066, avis@ibw.com.ni; **Toyota Rent a Car**, T341-2303, www.toyotarentacar.com; and **Budget**, T341-3636, www.budget.com.ni.

Taxi

Taxis are very cheap around Chinandega, with fares of US$0.35 for short trips. Longer trips or night-time service can run to US$1.25. Drivers are very friendly and helpful.

Chichigalpa *p221*

Buses to **León** from 0500-1700, every 11 mins, US$0.70, US$1.

Directory

Chinandega *p220*

Banks All banks are between the Hotel Cosigüina and the Parque Central. For cash on Visa cards and all TCs use **BAC**, Texaco Guadalupe, 2 c norte, T341-0078.
Fire T341-3221. **Hospital** T341-4902.
Internet Across the street from Hotel Casa Grande at IBW or at Hotel Cosigüina.
Police T341-3456. **Post office** Correos de Nicaragua BANIC, 125 m norte, T341-0407. **Red Cross** T341-3132.
Telephone Enitel, Central Plaza, 1 c arriba, 25 vrs norte, T341-0002.

Northern Highlands

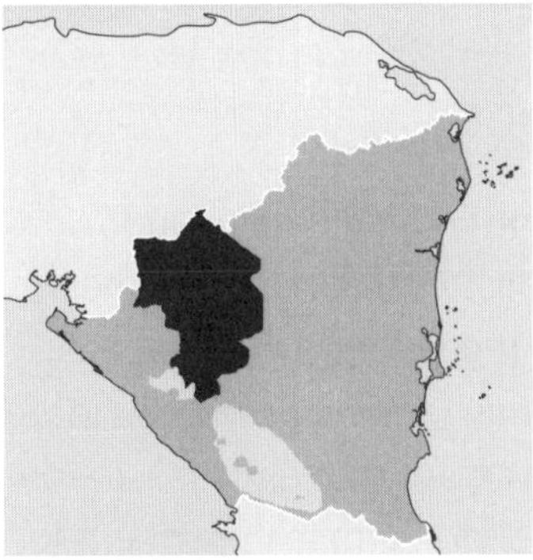

Footprint features

Introduction

Nicaragua's ruggedly beautiful northern mountains and valleys have staged much of the history that has given the country its dubious international reputation. It was here that indigenous cultures attacked Spanish mining operations in the 16th century and, in the 19th century, fought confiscation of communal lands that were to go to German immigrants for coffee growing. This is where nationalist Sandino fought the US Marines' occupation of Nicaragua from 1927 to 1933 and where the rebel Sandinistas launched their first attacks against the Somoza administration in the 1960s. Then, in the 1980s, the Contras waged war against the Sandinista Government in these mountains.

Today, most visitors would be hard pressed to see where all this aggression came from, or that it existed at all. Most of the northern ranges and plains are full of sleepy villages with ancient churches, rustic cowboys and smiling children. This is where the soil and the homes blend into a single palette: the red-brown clay earth reflected in the brown adobe walls and red-tile roofs. Nothing is rushed here and many of the region's villages are evidence that time travel is indeed possible, with the 21st century in no danger of showing itself around here anytime soon, at least not until the 20th century arrives.

In addition to the area's intense history, rustic beauty and kind population, there are precious cloud forest reserves, pine forests and interesting crafts being made using techniques dating back many centuries. The climate is cooler than the rest of the country with elevations rising to 2000 m. As the searing heat of the Pacific Basin gives way to the misty northern villages, you will see people actually wearing sweaters.

★ Don't miss ...

1 **Going green** Sleep, eat and hike in the temperate cloud forest of Esperanza Verde enjoying rich bird life while supporting the local community, page 237.

2 **Smoke rings** Savour some of the world's finest coffee accompanied by the rich aromatic flavours of handmade cigars, pages 238 and 251.

3 **Rebel past** Enjoy the daily street life of San Rafael del Norte and unravel part of Nicaragua's history at the Museo Sandino, page 246.

4 **Rural endeavours** Muck in and discover the joys of agrarian life at UCA Miraflor, Nicaragua's best community tourism project, page 252.

5 **Somoto Canyon** Explore this 13-million-year-old mountain chasm, birthplace of the mighty Río Coco with its crystal clear waters, page 260.

6 **Ciudad Antigua** Travel through time to this colonial village, where a pirate's description of the town from 1685 remains valid, page 264.

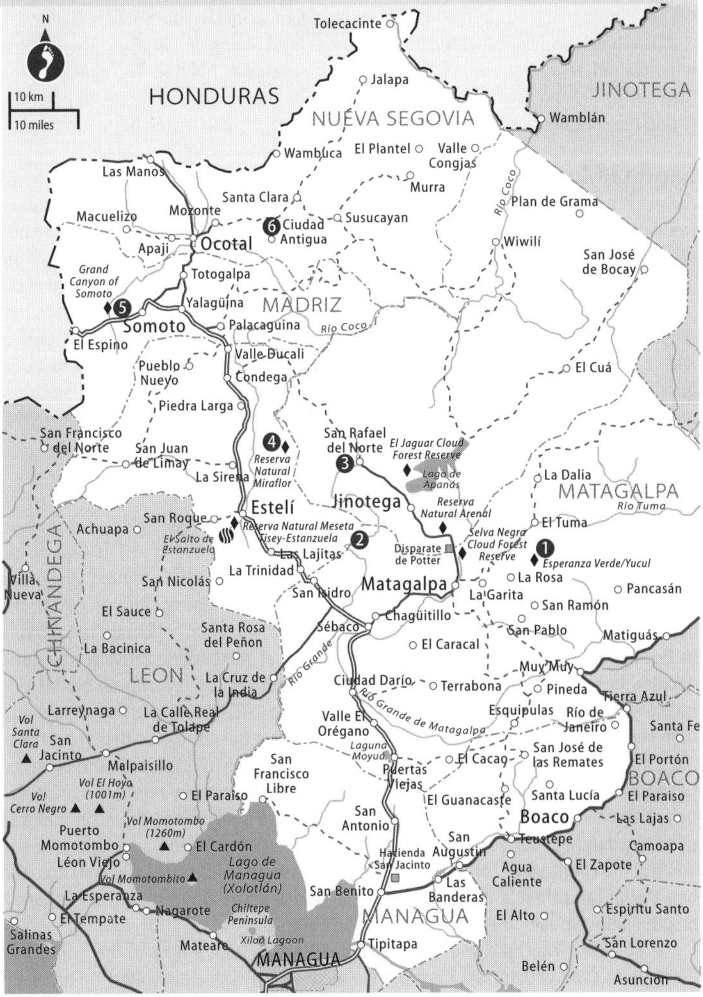

Managua to Matagalpa

The Pan-American Highway leaves Managua just north of the international airport, runs north into Nicaragua's most beautiful non-volcanic mountains and continues all the way to Honduras. There are two interesting routes, one that leads to border crossings through historic villages and another that heads off east near Sébaco to Matagalpa, the heart of coffee-growing country. » *For Sleeping, Eating and other listings, see pages 239-243.*

North of Managua » *pp239-243.*

Hacienda San Jacinto

After Tipitapa, at Km 35 of the Pan-American Highway, is the turning for the cattle ranching departments of Boaco and Chontales (see page 74). Soon after, at Km 39.5 is the short road that leads to the historic ranch of San Jacinto, where William Walker lost a critical battle against rebel Nicaraguan forces from Matagalpa in 1856. The battle is remembered every year on 14 September as a national holiday. The ranch is in a pleasant valley and open as a **museum** ⓘ *Tue-Sun 0900-1600, though it may be hard to find the caretaker on Sun, US$2,* with objects from the celebrated battle on display.

Laguna Moyuá

At Km 57 the remains of a 1000-year-old lake can be seen, in the form of three lagoons: **Las Playitas, Moyuá** and **Tecomapa**, though from the highway they appear to be one calm body of water. During the dry season they recede and disappear from view of the highway, but in the rainy season they form a beautiful contrast to the surrounding dry hills and are full of sandpipers, egrets and ducks. Laguna Moyuá has two islands that show signs of the pre-Columbian populations that inhabited this area and the ruins of what could have been an Indian temple. The lagoons are most famous for their lovely *guapote* and *mojarra* fish, which are offered for sale by children along the roadside. Just north of the fruit stands on the waterfront are several cheap restaurants with fresh *guapote* fish fried daily; worth a stop if you're in a private vehicle.

Ciudad Darío

Near Km 90, on the lefthand side, is the exit for the long three-bridge entrance to Ciudad Darío, a sleepy cowboy settlement set on a hill over the Río Grande de Matagalpa. This is the first of many forgotten villages that dot the northern landscape but one it has found some fame due to a small adobe corner house where the country's national hero, **Rubén Darío** (see page 200), was born in January 1867. Living in Honduras, Rubén's mother was fed up with her husband's abusive ways and decided to return to León to have her child. She only made it as far as her sister's house in the village (then called Metapa), gave birth to Rubén, rested for 40 days and then continued on to León where Darío would receive the education that would help him change Spanish poetry and Nicaragua forever. Today the house is the museum **Casa Natal de Rubén Darío** ⓘ *one block east, two blocks north of bus station, Tue-Sun 0900-1630, US$2,* where you can see the bed he was born on, the china set that was used to wash his mother and a 19th-century kitchen of the kind that is still in use in much of the countryside today. The city centre lies up the hill (one block east) from the bus station and there's an Enitel telephone office across from the museum and a health clinic opposite the church on Parque Central.

A local taxi can take you to the trailhead for an hour's hike to the summit of **Cerro de la Cruz** which has a panoramic view of the city, surrounded by hills and

Community tourism around Matagalpa

The coffee-rich land around Matagalpa is home to several fascinating agricultural co-operatives. The **Unión de Cooperativas Agropecuarias (UCA) San Ramón** is one of the largest and best organized, offering tours, activities and stays in four different communities. **La Pita**, 17 km from Matagalpa, offers rousing guided hikes in the mountains, including a visit to an old gold mine. You can meet a co-operative of women who create paper from organic waste, ride horses, and participate in the coffee production process. The community of **La Corona** boasts two refreshing waterfalls: Yasika and Posa Bruja. They offer courses in natural medicine for US$20 per group, tours of the area, and captivating recitals of their indigenous legends. **La Reina**, 18½ km from Matagalpa, is rich in wildlife and offers guided ecological hikes and horse riding. Two co-operatives comprise the community **El Roblar**: El Privilegio and Daniel Téllez Paz. They're very proud of their organic coffee and offer explanations of the process, great guided hikes with panoramic views, horse riding and lessons in natural medicine. All four communities offer stays with families for US$5 per person per night; additionally, La Corona has two hostels. Meals cost around US$2.50 in all communities, guided hikes are generally US$10 per group.

UCA San Ramón ⓘ *San Ramón, next to the police station, T772-5247.*

rivers. Legend has it that this mountain was growing out of control, skywards at an alarming rate, so a local Franciscan monk hiked to the top and planted a cross on the summit and put an end to the mountain's insolence. No-one can agree how many years it has been there, but every 3 May there is a pilgrimage to the cross with a mass held at the summit. The patron saint, **San Pedro**, is celebrated on 29 July and from 8 to 14 January there are festivities commemorating the birth of Rubén Darío.

Sébaco

Further north along the Pan-American Highway is the dry lakebed valley and agricultural centre of Sébaco. Sébaco is a hot and unattractive town but it has Nicaragua's most colourful vegetables in its **market**. The Pan-American Highway forks here and the market is inside the fork in the highway. The town is the agricultural crossroads of the northern highlands and has been called the capital of onions, as this is where Nicaragua's finest are grown, along with huge quantities of rice and *sorghum*. Also in the market are deep purple beets and bright orange carrots begging to be photographed. Sébaco also has a historic church with a tiny pre-Columbian and colonial period museum inside. To reach the historic **Vieja Iglesia de Sébaco** turn right at the first entrance to the highway after crossing the bridge, go to the back of the new church and head all the way to the top of the hill and turn right.

The Río Grande de Matagalpa flooded its banks here during the hurricane of 1998 and some damage can still be seen when entering the town via the new bridge.

Chagüitillo

From the fork at Sébaco, the highway to the right is the Carretera a Matagalpa which rises gradually past the charming village of Chagüitillo at Km 107, home to some important pre-Columbian sites with petroglyphs and the **Museo Precolombino de Chagüitillo** ⓘ *www.mpch.bravehost.com, US$0.60*. The museum is a simple collection of petroglyphs set against a mural painting depicting pre-Conquest life. There is a mountain stream area called **Salto El Mico**, 1½ km from the town centre, which has an impressive array of petroglyphs, many depicting monkeys, but also one that locals claim to be an Aztec calendar. Look for a guide in the museum or with local children.

The highway continues past massive coffee-processing plants (*beneficios*) and their extensive, concrete platforms used for drying coffee beans under the sun. This area has the highest concentration of *beneficios* in Nicaragua, taking advantage of the drier climate between Chagüitillo and Matagalpa to dry the beans. Harvest time is from November to February.

Matagalpa » *pp239-243.*

→ *Population 98,000. Altitude 682 m.*

Set in a broad valley circled by green mountains, including the handsome Cerro de Apante at 1442 m, Matagalpa appears quite attractive at a distance, though less so up close. This important and bustling café-capital of Nicaragua has a vaguely claustrophobic feel to it. The city streets are narrow, filled with cars and trucks, and a circular sprawl of new homes climb the surrounding hills, threatening to enclose the city in concrete. When it rains, the deforested hills that wrap Matagalpa drain into the quickly overflowing Río Grande de Matagalpa and flood through its barrios. However, Matagalpa sells some interesting crafts in local stores and is an excellent jumping-off point for visiting beautiful scenery and some of the world's best coffee farms.

Ins and outs

Getting there and around There are frequent buses from Managua's Mercado Mayoreo, with regular express services, and lots of buses from Jinotega. Infrequent but direct services exist from Masaya, León and Chinandega and more regular routes from Estelí. Alternatively, get off at Sébaco on any bus passing on the Pan-American Highway and change to a bus heading north to Matagalpa. There are plenty of inexpensive taxis around town. They can also offer transfers to Selva Negra and San Ramón. The centre of town is easy to walk around and safe, but the barrios should not be visited on foot. There are two main streets that run to and from the attractive cathedral south to the little Parque Darío, where it is a bit more peaceful. Along these streets are most of the city's sleeping, dining and entertainment options. The rest of this hilly city is a maze of mixed streets of pavement and mud. » *For further details, see Transport, page 242.*

Best time to visit Due to serious deforestation, Matagalpa dries up like a desert from January to May and fills with dust. It can be misty during the rainy season, but generally it is much prettier at this time. The higher elevations at the ecolodges of Selva Negra and Esperanza Verde can get chilly at night from December to February and stay green year round – a great contrast to the dust and heat of the Pacific Basin.

Tourist information **INTUR** ⓘ *alcaldía, 1 c arriba, ½ c al sur, T772-7060*, has limited, patchy details on local attractions. **Matagalpa tours** ⓘ *Banpro, ½ c arriba, T772-0108, www.matagalpa tours.com*, are an excellent source of information, with a thorough knowledge of the city and the surrounding mountains; they speak Dutch and English. You could also try **CIPTURMAT** next door to Matagalpa tours; and **CANTUR**, in the coffee museum; or **MARENA** ⓘ *T772-3926*.

Background

Matagalpa is the most famous mountain town in Nicaragua. It is in the heart of coffee country, an industry that was started in the 1870s by German and other European immigrants. In 1881, Matagalpa was the scene of the last significant Indian rebellion, which was sparked by a combination of factors: forced labour on telegraph lines between Managua and Matagalpa, attempts to ban *chicha* (fermented corn liquor) and the expulsion by the government of the Jesuits, much loved by the locals, who willingly provided free labour for the construction of Matagalpa's cathedral. The rebellion failed and the government troops' revenge was brutal, moving Matagalpa's indigenous community (which is still quite large) forever to the background in the region's affairs. The German influence in Matagalpa continued until the beginning of the First World War, when the government confiscated German-owned coffee farms but the Germans returned after the war and re-established themselves. The farms were confiscated again in 1941 when Nicaragua declared war on Germany. Many Germans did not return after the end of that war. During the Contra war, Matagalpa was often just behind the front line of battle and many of the residents of the city fought on both sides of the conflict.

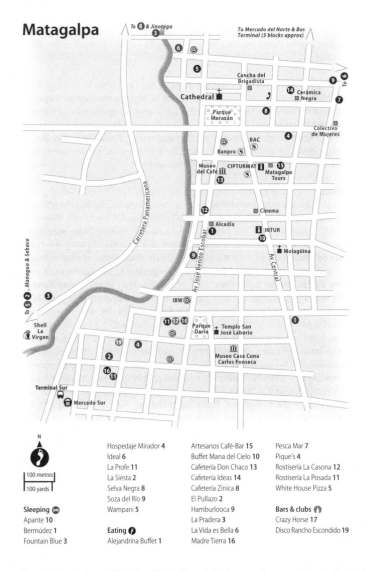

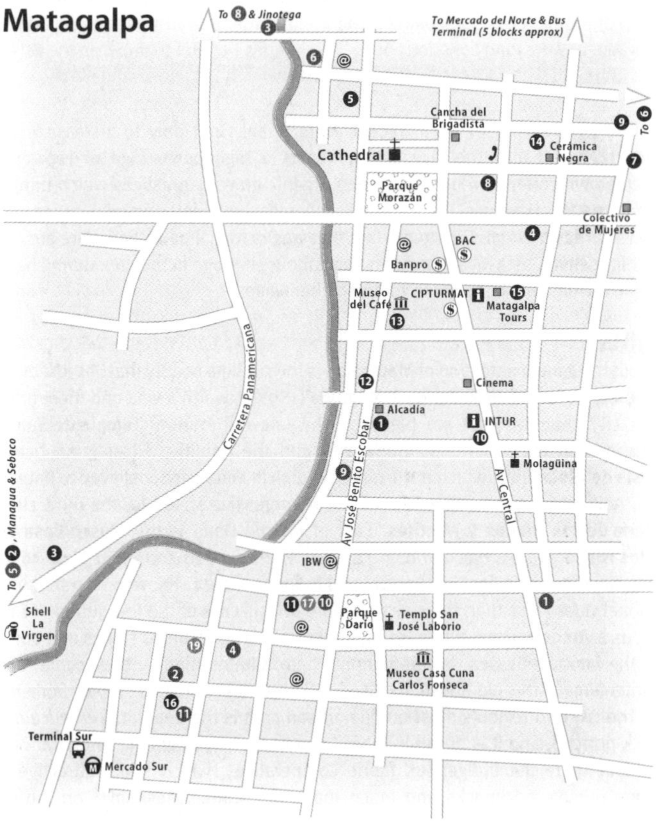

N

100 metres

100 yards

Sleeping
Apante **10**
Bermúdez **1**
Fountain Blue **3**
Hospedaje Mirador **4**
Ideal **6**
La Profe **11**
La Siesta **2**
Selva Negra **8**
Soza del Río **9**
Wampani **5**

Eating
Alejandrina Buffet **1**
Artesanos Café-Bar **15**
Buffet Mana del Cielo **10**
Cafetería Don Chaco **13**
Cafetería Ideas **14**
Cafetería Zinica **8**
El Pullazo **2**
Hamburlooca **9**
La Pradera **3**
La Vida es Bella **6**
Madre Tierra **16**
Pesca Mar **7**
Pique's **4**
Rostisería La Casona **12**
Rostisería La Posada **11**
White House Pizza **5**

Bars & clubs
Crazy Horse **17**
Disco Rancho Escondido **19**

The chocolate castle: A chocoholic's dream

Until recently, chocoholics in Nicaragua were stuck for a good fix, surviving on paltry Snickers and M&Ms. Fortunately a new Dutch initiative, **El Castillo de Cacao**, www.elcastillodelcacao.com, has alleviated this miserable predicament. By utilizing locally produced export-quality cacao beans, this award-winning, environmentally aware enterprise has created a high-quality chocolate bar for the Nicaraguan market. The Aztecs were long conscious of cacao's inherently precious nature, using it as money, and El Castillo's chocolate bars are packed with the stuff. Rich, full of flavor and delivering a noticeable buzz, these are *real* chocolate bars, traditionally produced and 100% organic.

If you would like to visit the factory, tours can be arranged through **Matagalpa Tours** ⓘ *Banpro, ½ c arriba, T772-0108, www.matagalpatours.com.* Long-deprived chocoholics may find themselves transported to euphoric states – try not to drown in the vats.

The city has prospered in recent years, thanks not only to increased coffee production, but also the fact that it boasts a high percentage of high-quality shade-grown coffee and has developed organic growing practices which bring the highest prices. However, the economic rollercoaster of international coffee prices always carries a threat. Due to the fact that wages for coffee pickers here are about half of those in Costa Rica, there can be a labour shortage in the area during harvest season as migrants head south for the higher wages.

Sights

Although the main attraction of Matagalpa is the sublime beauty that lies just outside it, the **Catedral de San Pedro de Matagalpa** (1897) is worth a visit and there are two other city churches that are pleasant: the late-19th-century **Templo de San José de Laborio** in front of the Parque Darío and the primitive Nicaraguan baroque **Iglesia de Molagüina**, which is the oldest church in Matagalpa, believed to date from 1751. Adjacent to the Parque Central is the impressive statue for the (now closed) **Galería de los Héroes y Mártires**. East of Parque Darío is the **Museo Casa Cuna Carlos Fonseca** ⓘ *Parque Darío, 1 c arriba, Mon-Fri 0830-1200 and 1400-1630*, a memorial to the principal intellectual and founder of the FSLN, who was shot by the National Guard less than three years before the success of the Revolution. He lived here as a young boy and the museum houses pictures, writings, stories and objects, like the famous glasses, of this national hero. Contributions are welcome for the maintenance of this old house. If closed, ask next door at the tyre repair workshop.

The city and region's most unique artisan craft is the beautiful *cerámica negra* (black pottery), and it is possible to visit one of the city's ceramic co-operatives. In addition, there are indigenous fabric co-operatives, which make attractive and unique purses, backpacks and much more. The **Coffee Museum** ⓘ *on the main avenue, Parque Morazán, 1½ c sur, 0800-1230, 1400-1900*, houses the town's **cultural centre,** offering music and painting classes and displays on the history of local coffee production. Exhibits include photographs and antique objects used in the early days of coffee production in Matagalpa.

Around Matagalpa » pp240-243.

Apante Hill

Located within the **Reserva Apante** a few kilometres southeast of Matagalpa, this hill offers commanding views of Matagalpa and the surrounding countryside. It takes two hours to reach the summit on the main trail. There is another trail that takes five hours, and another that takes seven hours, concluding in the village of San Ramón. The trails are hard to find and it is recommended that you hire a guide. A guide will be able to lead you to other attractions within the reserve, like streams and waterfalls.

Santa Emilia Waterfall

The thundering waterfall of Santa Emilia, 15 km northeast from Matagalpa, makes a pleasant excursion if you're heading to the **Reserva Peñas Blancas** (see page 247), or just fancy a refreshing dip. Many legends abound here, where there's an enchanted cave occupied by *duendes*, or leprechauns (see box, page 263). To get to the waterfall, take the road to El Tuma-La Dalia. After passing the village of Santa Emilia you will cross two bridges; take a right after the second bridge. You will also see signs to several other waterfalls, including Salto Escondido, a little further ahead.

Esperanza Verde

ⓘ *Office in San Ramón, managed by Giff Laube, from the police station, 1½ c arriba, T772-5003, www.fincaesperanzaverde.org. Buses run to Yucul from Matagalpa's north terminal and there are signs for the reserve from San Ramón.*

East of Matagalpa is the largely indigenous town of **San Ramón** founded by a friar from León, José Ramón de Jesús María, in 1800. Legend has it that the village's small church is built on a thick vein of gold, which almost resulted in the demolition of the church until the villagers campaigned to prevent its destruction.

Beyond San Ramón is **Yucul**, home to a nature reserve designated a *Reserva de Recursos Genéticos*. The pine forest shelters a rare species (*Pino spatula sp tecunmumanii*) that reportedly has the finest seeds of its kind on the American continent. What has made Yucul famous in recent years, however, is the well managed ecolodge and private nature reserve of **Esperanza Verde**. There are few finer places in Nicaragua for birdwatching and enjoying the nature of the northern mountains. The award-winning reserve has a butterfly breeding project, organic shade-grown coffee cultivation, hiking trails and great views to the mountains of the region. The forest has howler monkeys, sloths and more than 150 species of bird, plus numerous orchids and medicinal plants. The reserve came to international attention in 2004, winning a *Smithsonian Magazine* award as the best sustainable new ecolodge project in the world. The lodge has handsome cabins for sleeping in, meals are also available, nature guides (Spanish only) charge US$4 per hour and offer excursions to the nearby **Wabule River National Park**.

Reserva Silvestre Selva Negra

ⓘ *At Km 139.5 on the Carretera a Jinotega an old Somoza-era tank that was destroyed by the rebels serves as an entrance sign to this coffee hacienda and private cloud forest reserve. Any bus heading towards Jinotega will drop you off at the entrance, from where it is a 3-km walk to the hotel; or take a taxi from Matagalpa. US$3 entrance fee if you are not staying in the hotel (but you can use this as a credit in the restaurant).*

The highway rises steeply out of Matagalpa giving panoramic views of the city and the surrounding deforestation. About 7 km beyond Matagalpa, the scenery changes dramatically, with pine trees and oaks draped in bromeliads, in a forest that is green year-round. Eddy and Mausy Kuhl bought this 1470-acre coffee hacienda in 1974 and promptly turned half of it into forest reserve, making them Nicaraguan pioneers in the

Café Nicaragüense: from German to gourmet

Large-scale coffee growing in Nicaragua is directly tied to German immigration, promoted by 19th-century Nicaraguan governments that offered 500 *manzanas* (350 ha) of land to any investor who would plant 25,000 coffee trees, bringing migrant planters from Germany, US, England, France and Italy.

The pioneer of Nicaragua coffee planting was Ludwing Elster, originally from Hanover, and his wife Katharine Braun, from Baden Baden who settled in Matagalpa in 1852. In 1875, Wilhelm Jericho arrived and founded the Hacienda Las Lajas, promising to lure 20 more German families to Nicaragua. When the Nicaraguan government started offering the 500 *manzanas* free to inspire production, more than 200 foreign families settled and began growing coffee in Matagalpa and neighbouring Jinotega.

At the time, Colombia had yet to become a coffee producer and the Nicaraguan product was considered among the world's best, along with coffee from Costa Rica and Guatemala. The international coffee price was US$8 for a 100 pound sack of coffee.

Today Nicaraguan coffee is planted on more than 160,000 *manzanas* by 30,000 different farms with country-leader Jinotega producing around 680,673 one hundred pound bags of coffee a year, followed by Matagalpa at 624,818 bags, and the province of Nueva Segovia with 193,435 bags. The country's best coffee export customers are the USA, Spain, Belgium and France.

The push for high-quality organic shade coffee has lifted Nicaragua to sixth place in the world in gourmet coffee production, with an annual output of organic coffee three times greater than Costa Rica, and Nicaragua's organic coffee now draws frequent international acclaim. In a recent survey by *Coffee Review*, two of the top four ranked brews in the world were Nicaraguan. Matagalpa organic coffee grower Byron Corrales is now charging US$200 for his hundred pound sacks (above an average market price US$75 per sack) after the industry magazine *Coffee Review* gave his coffee 94 out of 100 points ranking it number two in the world. They raved that the Matagalpa grown coffee was a "fruity and richly floral coffee – papaya, lemon, coffee fruit, hints of dusk-blooming flowers and chocolate, all ride a strong, balanced structure: good body, smooth, supple, sweet acidity."

burgeoning practice of setting aside private nature reserves. The 30 creeks within the reserve have benefited greatly from the reforestation of its higher slopes, which were once used for coffee production. Birdwatching is excellent around the property (but best around the shade coffee plantation), with more than 200 species documented so far, including trogons, parrots, flycatchers and the elusive but resplendent quetzal. The property has 14 well-marked paths and the hotel cabins are surrounded by forest and flowers; many even have flowers growing out of their roofs.

What makes Selva Negra really special, however, is the way the hacienda's coffee, vegetable, flower and animal farming is organized and operated. The hacienda is a model for sustainability: everything from coffee husks to chicken blood is recycled. Coffee-processing wastewater (a serious pollutant in coffee-growing regions) is run into two-step pressurizing tanks that create methane or 'bio-gas', which is then used on the farm for cooking and other chores. As many as 250 full-time employees work in flower production, with 10 species grown in greenhouses, all vegetables served at the hotel restaurant are grown organically on the farm and meat served at the hotel is also locally raised. Recommended coffee tours (US$5) are given in the morning when Eddy or Mausy have time.

El Disparate de Potter

Past Selva Negra the forest becomes even thicker as the road leads past lush forest and highland ranches, coffee plantations and flower farms. At Km 143 there is a school and then the Restaurante El Disparate de Potter. Mr Charles Potter, an eccentric English gentleman used to own the land here and had the idea of blowing a hole in the mountain to let the road pass through to Jinotega – you can now climb up the part of the mountain that is left for a good view of the Momotombo and San Cristóbal volcanoes. The border between the provinces of Matagalpa and Jinotega is located here, as well as access to the small but precious Reserva Natural Arenal (see below). The Carretera then passes appetizing fruit and vegetable stands, a great place to stop and enjoy the fresh mountain air, before looping downwards into the broad valley of Jinotega.

Reserva Natural Arenal

ⓘ *At Km 145.5 on the Carretera a Jinotega. Reputable local guides include Pablo Ubeda and his brother Nicho, who are very familiar with the forest. They live near the entrance to the reserve from the highway. You could also telephone the Matagalpa office of MARENA, T772-3926, for their recommendations.*

This is one of the finest cloud forest reserves in Nicaragua that can be accessed by a paved road. The reserve protects **Cerro Picacho** (1650 m) and its surrounding forest which is over 1400 m. There are numerous giant balsa trees, known as *mojagua* (*Heliocarpus appendiculatus*), the favoured nesting sites for the resplendent quetzal, and the forest is also home to giant oak trees, up to 12 m in circumference and 40 m tall, as well as many strangler figs, tree ferns, bromeliads, orchids, mosses, bamboo and even arboreal cacti. The cloud forest has an abundance of the endangered resplendent quetzal (*Pharomachrus mocinno*), considered sacred by the Maya and agreed by all to be one of the most beautiful birds in the world, and the **Sendero Los Quetzales** is one of the best places in Nicaragua to spot it. The path passes plenty of native avocado (*Aguacate canelo*), one of the bird's favourite snacks (the fruit is ripe between March and May). The quetzal shares the forest with 190 documented species, including Amazon parrot, toucans, emerald toucanets, other trogons and numerous colourful hummingbirds, such as the violet sawbrewing hummingbird (*Campylopterus hemileucurus*). The three-wattled bellbird's distinctive song can often be heard, too. There are also 140 documented species of butterfly here, such as the spectacular purple-blue morpho and the almost-invisible, transparent-winged gossamer. Howler monkeys, agoutis and sloths also inhabit this forest.

Sleeping

Ciudad Darío *p232*

G Casa Agricultor, bus station, 1½ c norte, T776-2379. Simple, dark rooms; 3 with bath, 5 without, all have a fan and there's secure parking. The owner, Emma López, is hospitable and friendly.

Sébaco *p233*

F El Valle, on the highway 1½ km south of town, T775-2209. Small, simple rooms with fans and TV at this quiet, motel-style place on the highway. Some have a/c.

Matagalpa *p234, map p235*

B Lomas de San Thomas, Escuela Guanuca 400 m arriba, T772-4189. The most luxurious hotel in the region. 26 spacious rooms have private bath and hot water, cable TV, telephone, mini-bar. Not very central.

C Hotel Campestre Barcelona, Prolacsa 800 m norte. 22 rooms with private bath, a/c, cable TV, secure parking. North of Matagalpa, quiet with nice views and swimming pool.

E Hotel Apante, west side of Parque Darío, T772-6890. Clean rooms with private bath, hot water and cable TV. The management's friendly and there's free coffee 24 hrs.

E Hotel Fountain Blue, catedral, 3 c al norte, 2 c abajo, T772-2733. Comfortable rooms with private bath, cable TV, hot water and fan. A simple breakfast of coffee and bread is included, and laundry service is available.

E Hotel Ideal, catedral, 2 c al norte, 1c abajo, T772-2483. Rooms here have private bath, TV, hot water, a/c or fan. There's also a bar and conference centre.

E Hotel La Siesta, Texaco, 1½ abajo, T772-2476. Clean, tidy, friendly and good value hotel. Rooms have hot water, cable TV and fan. There's internet facilities, international call centre and a café too.

E Hotel Soza del Río, Ava Río Grande, opposite the river, T772-3030. 17 good-value rooms with bath, fan and cable TV. The hotel is also accessible from Restaurante Casa Casea, next to Supermercado Matagalpa. Breakfasts, buffet lunches and dinner served.

E Hotel Wampani, Shell la Virgen, 25 m sur, T772-7154. Reportedly something of a 'love hotel', with large mirrors adjacent to the beds. It has 12 rooms, all with bath, cable TV, a/c and fan. It's far from the centre, so don't walk here at night.

F Hotel la Profe, Shell el Progreso, 20 varas norte, T772-2506. A pleasant, family-run place. Tidy rooms have cable TV, fan, private bath and hot water.

F Hospedaje Mirador, Parque Darío, 1½ c abajo, T772-4084. Simple, bare-bones rooms around a courtyard. Friendly management and a vociferous parrot.

G Bermúdez, Parque Darío, 2 c abajo, T612-9876. Most rooms at this friendly and ramshackle hotel are run-down, some aren't too bad. Dirt cheap for a single traveller too.

Esperanza Verde *p237*

C-F Esperanza Verde lodge, T772-5003, www.fincaesperanzaverde.org. This famous ecolodge has handsome wood and brick cabins with covered patios, solar power, private bath and bunk beds. There's also dorm rooms (**F**) and camping at US$6 per person.

Selva Negra Cloud Forest Reserve *p237*

L-F Selva Negra, T772-3883, www.selvanegra.com. A range of dormitory beds (**F**), rooms (**C**), and Germanic cottages (**L-B**) on the edge of the rainforest.

Eating

Ciudad Darío *p232*

¥ El Buen Gusto, bus station, 3½ c norte. This new, clean comedor serves home-cooked Nicaraguan fare and some good-looking fairy cakes.

¥ El Clementino, Museo, 1 c norte, 10 varas este. Small, simple comedor serving meat, chicken or whatever the Señora has prepared. Look out for the chattering parrots.

Sébaco *p233*

¥¥ El Sesteo, Del BDF, 1½ c abajo. Clean, wonderfully air-conditioned and well-staffed. Their menu boasts a healthy selection of steaks, chicken, soup and shrimp dishes.

¥¥ Los Gemelos, Monumento de la Virgen, 1½ c abajo. Regular buffets and a variety of meat and chicken dishes served. There's a disco on Sat and Sun evenings, playing hip-hop, salsa and dance.

¥ Restaurante Rosario, west side of highway at south entrance to town. Fried chicken or beef dishes, loud music, greasy and friendly.

Matagalpa *p234, map p235*

¥¥ Restaurant La Pradera, Shell la Virgen, 2 c norte, T772-2543. One of the best in town, ideal for 'meat lovers', also good seafood.

¥¥ Restaurante Pesca Mar, Cancha del Brigadista, 3 c arriba, T772-3548. Daily until 2200. Seafood specialities, shrimp in garlic butter, red snapper in onions.

¥¥-¥ La Vida es Bella, Col Lainez, T772-5476. An Italian-run restaurant, which has received strong praise from a couple of readers.

¥¥-¥ Restaurante El Pullazo, on the highway just south of town, T772-3935. Has a famous and tasty dish with the same name as the establishment: a very lean cut of beef cooked in a special oven and smothered with tomatoes and onions, served with fresh corn tortillas, *gallo pinto* and a fruit juice.

For an explanation of the sleeping and eating price codes used in this guide, see inside the front cover. Other relevant information is found in Essentials, see pages 23-27.

¥¥-¥ Rostisería La Posada, Parque Darío, ½ c abajo, T772-2330. Very fine eatery serving roast chicken and fish *à la tipitapa*.
¥¥-¥ Restaurante Pique's, Casa Pellas, 1c arriba, T772-2723. Atmospheric Mexican restaurant serving *tacos*, *tequila*, *tostados* and *chiliquilas*. Popular and friendly.
¥ Alejandrina Buffet, alcadía, ½ c sur. Cheap buffet serving freshly cooked Nica fare. Clean, tasty and friendly.
¥ Buffet Mana del Cielo, cinema, 1 c sur, T772-5686. Daily 0700-2100. Variety of typical Nicaraguan food.
¥ Hamburlooca, La Cancha del Brigadista, 3 c arriba, T772-7402. Rough 'n' ready burger joint. They do home deliveries too.
¥ Rostisería La Casona, Museo del Café, 1½ c sur, T772-3901. Darkened locals' haunt serving a range of chicken and beef dishes, cold beer and refreshments. Not bad and good-value.
¥ White House Pizza, catedral, 1½ c norte, T772-7575. Open daily. Small, locals' pizza place. They do greasy but acceptable pizza by the slice and whole, and deliver locally.

Cafés

Artesanos Café-Bar, Banpro, ½ c arriba. This pleasant café-bar has a wooden, rancho-style interior. They do breakfasts, light lunches, and hot and cold drinks including *licuados*, iced coffee and really excellent cappucinos. Popular with locals and tourists, and a good night spot too.
Cafetería Don Chaco, next to coffee museum. Closed Sat. They do breakfasts and set menus, but are most famous for their fruit and vegetable shakes.
Cafetería Ideas, Cancha del Brigadista 1½ c arriba. Small, good place for a fruit drink, sandwiches or *tacos*.
Cafetería Zinica, across from Enitel office. Cheap, *tacos* and sandwiches.
Madre Tierra, Texaco, 1½ abajo. Adorned with political photos, peace flags and iconic, revolutionary portraits, this new café-bar has an alternative, intellectual feel. They serve tasty home-made burgers, light meals and cold beer. The action hots up at night, with regular live music and documentary films.

El Disparate de Potter *p239*

¥¥ Restaurante El Disparate de Potter, T772-2553. With a bar and food à la carte, good soups and *nacatamales*.

Bars and clubs

Matagalpa *p234, map p235*

Most discos do not start up until after 2100, and all Matagalpa discos serve dinner. You should get a taxi back from any night spot.
Crazy Horse, Parque Darío, 10 varas abajo. Wild West-style drinking hole with log cabin exterior and an inside filled with cart wheels, Stetson hats and other cowboy memorabilia. They serve cold beer and Flor de Caña.
Disco Rancho Escondido, Parque Darío, 2 c abajo. Popular place for dancing and drinking.
La Posada Restaurant and Disco, Parque Darío, ½ c abajo. Another good place for dancing, popular with families.

Shopping

Ciudad Darío *p232*

Ciudad Darío was a big shoe-producing town during the Sandinista years and one can still have a customized pair of cowboy boots made in 3 days, for US$30. If you wear smaller than a size 41, you can pick up boots for US$25 right out of the workshop.

Matagalpa *p234, map p235*

Crafts

Cerámica Negra, Parque Darío. This kiosk, open irregularly, sells black pottery in the northern tradition – a style found only in parts of Chile, Nicaragua and Mexico. There is evidence that this school of ceramics dates back to 1500 BC in this region of Nicaragua. For more information contact Estela Rodríguez, T772-4812.
Colectivos de Mujeres de Matagalpa, Banco Uno, 2½ c arriba, T772-4462. Mon-Fri 0800-1200, 1400-1730, Sat 0800-1200. Native fabrics, leather goods, ceramics and an orange and coffee liquor made by woman's co-operatives in El Chile, Molino Norte and Malinche.
Restaurante La Vida es Bella, see Eating. A good artisan craft store that also sells locally made chocolates *El Castillo de Cacao*.

Around Matagalpa *p237*

Colectivo de Tejidos El Chile, 20 km from Matagalpa off the Carretera a San Dionisio. Founded in 1984 as part of a cultural rescue program, the indigenous community of El Chile makes fabrics,

backpacks, camera cases, purses and wallets out of hand-spun fabrics. Visits to the village can be arranged through **Matagalpa Tours** (see below) or take bus towards San Dionisio and get down at entrance to El Chile.
Colectivo de Tejedoras Entre Hilos, Molino Norte, Km 15, Carretera a Jinotega (take bus towards Jinotega or hire taxi, US$3). Mon-Fri 0800-1600, Sat 0800-1200. This women's co-operative produces hand-spun fabrics elaborated into bags and other small items.

Activities and tours

Matagalpa *p234, map p235*

Coffee tours

The coffee museum, INTUR, or Matagalpa Tours will help you arrange trips to the many coffee *fincas* in the area, including **La Poderosa**, **Shamballa**, **La Leonesa** and **San Antonio**. Other interesting, easily arranged options are:
Finca Esperanza Verde, office in San Ramón, Iglesia Catholica, 1½ c arriba, T772-5003, www.fincaesperanzaverde.org. This award-winning 220-acre certified organic farm has 28 acres of ethically managed, sustainably cultivated arabica coffee. Truly eco-touristic and interesting.
Selva Negra, Km 139.5 Carretera Matagalpa-Jinotega, T772-3883, www.selvanegra.com. At the edge of beautiful rainforest reserve, this famous *finca* offers daily tours of its fascinating, ecologically sound facilities. Call in advance to check times.
UCA San Ramón, next to the police station, San Ramón, T772-5247. This organization can arrange a 'hands-on' experience of coffee production, where you meet farming communities and participate in the process. They also offer more conventional tours of the Solcafe Processing plant outside Matagalpa.

Cultural and community tourism

UCA San Ramón, next to the police station, San Ramón, T772-5247. See box, page 233.

Tour operators

Matagalpa Tours, Banpro, ½ c arriba, T772-0108, www.matagalpatours.com. This reputable agency runs tours to the north and further afield. Trekking, hiking, birdwatching and rural community tours are among their well-established repertoire. Dutch and English-speaking, helpful and friendly. The best agency in town – for all your adventuring needs. Highly recommended.

Transport

Ciudad Darío *p232*

The bus station in Ciudad Darío is at the small park just north of the iron bridge on south side of town. Buses leave 0415-1900 every 15 mins, US$1.20 north to **Matagalpa**, or US$1.10 south to **Managua**.

Sébaco *p233*

Sébaco is a major transportation hub with northbound traffic to **Matagalpa** and **Jinotega** and northwest to **Estelí**, **Ocotal** and **Somoto**.

Buses pass every 15 mins to/from **Estelí** US$1.20, **Matagalpa** US$1.10 and **Managua** US$1.50. Buses between Matagalpa and Sébaco pass the highway just outside **Chagüitillo** every 15 mins.

Matagalpa *p234, map p235*

Bus

Terminal Sur (Cotransur), is near Mercado del Sur and used for all destinations outside the department of Matagalpa.

To **Jinotega**, every half hour, 0500-1900, US$1.40, 1½ hrs. To **Managua**, every half hour, 0335-1805, US$2.20, 3-4 hrs; express buses, every hour, 0520-1720, US$2.75, 2½ hrs.To **Estelí**, every ½ hr, 0515-1745, US$1.40, 2-3 hrs; express buses, 1000, 1630, US$1.50, 1½ hrs. Express bus to **León**, 0600, US$2.75, 3 hrs. Express bus to **Masaya**, 0700, 1400, 1530, US$2.75, 4hrs.

Terminal Norte, by Mercado del Norte (Guanuca), is for all destinations within the province of Matagalpa including **San Ramón** and **El Tuma**. Taxi between terminals US$0.50.

International buses For information on fares and schedules, see individual agencies: **Ticabus**, northeast corner of Parque Darío, ½ c abajo, opposite 'La Posada' Rotisserie, T772-4502, www.ticabus.com; **Transnica**, opposite the Shell Central, T772-2389, www.transnica.com.

Car hire

Budget Rent a Car, Km 131 at Shell station on entrance to city, T772-3041.

Taxi

Matagalpa taxis are helpful and cheap. Average fare inside the city is US$0.35-0.60. Fare to **Selva Negra** US$4-5 per person.

Directory

Matagalpa *p234, map p235*
Banks Banco de America Central (BAC and Credomatic), Parque Morazán, 1 c sur, on Av Central. Change all TCs and cash on Visa and MC and has ATM for most credit and debit cards with Cirrus logo. Banpro, opposite BAC, offers similar services. **Fire** T772-3167. **Hospital** T772-2081. **Internet** There are many places around town, particularly along Av Jose Benito Escobar, most charge US$0.50 per hr. **Language schools** Matagalpa Spanish School, Banpro ½ c arriba, inside Matagalpa Tours, T772-0108, www.matagalpa.info. They offer a range of packages, from hourly tuition to intensive courses of 30 hrs per week. There are options for family homestay, voluntary work and cultural tours. Classes are one-to-one, grammar and exercise books provided. **Police** Parque Central, 1 c sur, T772-2382. **Red Cross** T772-2059. **Telephone** Enitel, catedral, 1 c arriba, daily 0700-1900, T772-4600.

Jinotega

→ *Population 33,000. Altitude 1004 m.*

Nestled in a valley of green mountains and shaded from the tropical sun, Jinotega has a pleasant climate. Like Matagalpa, it is an important area for the nation's coffee industry, though it is considerably more relaxed and friendly; the helpful and charming people of the city are its greatest assets. Jinotega is the capital of a sprawling province that has almost no infrastructure to date and remains one of the poorest and least developed parts of the country. Like Matagalpa, the province is subject to the whims of international coffee prices. ▸▸ *For Sleeping, Eating and other listings, see pages 247-249.*

Ins and outs

Getting there and around Jinotega is served by regular bus services from Matagalpa and a few Express buses from Managua's Mercado Mayoreo. A paved highway between Sébaco and Jinotega was nearing completion, at the time of going to press, which would bypass Matagalpa. Taxis are available and inexpensive inside the city. Jinotega is easy to walk around, but avoid walking after 2200 at the weekend. ▸▸ *For further details, see Transport, page 249.*

Best time to visit Jinotega is pretty all year round, but the rainy season is cooler and dramatically greener. The coffee harvest from November to February is a particularly happy and busy time with lots of work to be had and people coming from the surrounding countryside to the city, loading into big trucks sent by coffee haciendas.

Tourist information **Alianza Turística** ⓘ *alcaldía, 2 c arriba, 1½ c sur, Mon-Fri 1000-1600*, are an alliance of several local organizations including INTUR, CANTUR and the alcaldía; they have good information but speak Spanish only. **INTUR** ⓘ *Texaco, 1 c norte, Mon-Fri, 0800-1200, 1400-1600, T782-2166*, has more limited information on the town and surrounding areas. Also try Tony Robins' www.jinotega.com and www.jinotegalife.com.

Background

Jinotega enjoys the highest elevation of any major city in Nicaragua. A small Indian community in the 17th century, it was sacked by a combination of British and Miskito forces attacking from the east. The US Marines were stationed here during their fight against Sandino who directed his National Sovereignty Army out of nearby San Rafael del Norte much of the time. The city was attacked several times by FSLN rebel groups; one of which cost FSLN rebel hero 'El Danto' Germán Pomares his life. El Danto, who was the most athletic (and seemingly invincible) of the anti-Somoza *guerrilleros* was hit in Jinotega by 'friendly fire', a tragedy that likely inspired the formation of the first Contra groups who suspected that his death had been ordered by FSLN bosses. Jinotega's interior was the site of constant battles and attacks by the Contras on both military and civilian targets.

Sights

Jinotega is not visited by many foreigners, except for those working on international projects. However, it won't be long until its refreshing climes start attracting wealthy North American retirees. The city has grown rapidly to the east of the centre in recent years, which means that the central park is actually now in the west of town. The area around the main plaza and the very attractive cathedral, **El Templo Parroquial** (1805), is full of broad streets and has a tranquil, small-town feel. The gothic cathedral has an interior that reflects the local climate, with a lovely, clean, cool, white-washed simplicity and a very complete collection of imagery imported from Italy and Spain. The pulpit is dramatic, with a life-sized, suffering Christ encased in glass below. The city's symbol is the cross-topped mountain, **Cerro La Peña Cruz**, to the west of central park. The cross was put on the mountain by Fray Margil de la Cruz to stop flooding in the city. The population was suffering from weeks of endless rain and floods and believed the mountain, full of water, was responsible for the inundation. The cross saved the city and every 3 May more than 5000 pilgrims hike to the top to take part in a Mass at the summit at 0900. (The hike to the summit takes just over an hour.)

Around Jinotega

Lago de Apanás

ⓘ *To visit the lake take a bus from Jinotega bound for Austurias-Pantasma (hourly 0700-1500, 1 hr, US$2).*

The beautiful Lago de Apanás, 8 km east of Jinotega, was created by the damming of the Río Tuma in 1964 to form a 54 sq km shiny blue body of water. The lake is full of *guapote* and *tilapia* and good for fishing. Small *ranchos* that lineLa Unión 226 the lake will fry fish for you. There are indigenous communities on the north shore, which is the entrance to the deeply rural towns northeast of here, **El Cuá** and **San José de Bocay**. You can go out on the lake with one of the 87 members of the fishing co-operative **La Unión del Norte** who have three motorboats and many more rowing boats to take people fishing or touring on the glassy waters. They charge US$6 per hour for the motorboat and US$3 per hour in the rowing boats. Ask at El Portillo de Apanás. It is helpful to be able to speak Spanish to avoid misunderstandings, but the locals are very friendly.

Reserva Natural Dantali-El Diablo

ⓘ *The area is managed by the Lina Herrera Cooperative, who can arrange guides and lodging in their wood cabins. For more information, contact Marco García at Aldea Global, a farmers' association of more than 1000 families, mostly indigenous Choretegas, T782-4027. To get to the reserve, take a bus to El Cuá-Bocay, get off at the turning for Venecia and walk 3.5 km to the community of Gobiado.*

Protected since 2002, this easy-to-reach reserve comprises 400 *manzanas* of attractive highlands; roughly a third is cultivated for coffee production. It has rich biodiversity with 79 species of trees, a variety of medicinal plants and many orchids. There's good birdwatching, and the reserve is home to the challenging peak of **El Diablo** (1640 m), offering ample opportunities for hiking, horse riding and breathing in inspiring views.

Reserva Silvestre El Jaguar

ⓘ *Access to this area is only possible in a sturdy 4WD; make sure you get detailed directions and book accommodation well in advance. The entrance fee is $10, and this includes a guide. Food and drinks are available.*

The paved highway from Jinotega to San Rafael del Norte passes through rolling terrain with cabbage and lettuce fields and 'bearded' oak trees (the 'beards' – Spanish moss – are used by the locals for scrubbing during bathing. At the Empalme San Gabriel is an earthen road that leads to towards **Mancotal**. Thirteen kilometres from the paved highway, after several switchbacks and a steady climb, is the organic coffee farm and private cloud forest reserve of El Jaguar. This is one of the most temperate accommodation options in Nicaragua; the reserve is often in the clouds with cool breezes passing over the mountain top, making it an excellent place to visit from February to April when places at sea level are burning hot.

Owners Georges and Liliana Duriaux are lovers of nature, especially birds, and teams of ornithologists can often be spotted here studying the high altitude and (for Nicaragua) upper latitude resident and migratory bird life. The current list for this 200-acre property, is around 180 species. The shade coffee farm produces some of Nicaragua's finest coffee (recently rated 90 by *Coffee Review*), which Georges cooks up at all hours of the day over an open flame. The property has five walking trails, which range from 45 minutes to three hours at a relaxed pace and which pass giant oaks, cedars, prehistoric fern trees, orchids and bromeliads.

San Rafael del Norte

Just 25 km northwest from Jinotega, reached by a paved highway, is the tiny village of San Rafael, a pleasant, authentic mountain town with a gigantic church and a rich history. The dusty streets are a corridor of contrasts, where Franciscan nuns walk smiling past uniformed school children and grizzled cowboys. The population is relaxed and unassuming, with a faith reported to be as big as their magnificent church which, aside from the Sandino museum, is the town's main attraction. **La Iglesia Parroquial** was first built in 1887 with the help of local Franciscan monks from Italy. It was enlarged in 1961 and has grown to be a majestic, beautiful and unique structure. The church sits next to a Franciscan convent and behind a weedy central park where horses graze. Inside are a myriad of bright colours, stained glass and many beautiful icons imported from Italy, including the patron saint of the city. To the left of the main altar is a gigantic altar to the Virgin Mary that reaches from floor to

Coffee with Sandino

US journalist Carlton Beals came to San Rafael del Norte from Tegucigalpa, Honduras after a gruelling, sleepless two-week journey on horseback to meet with Sandino on 3 February 1928. The writer was given an appointment at 0400 with the general, which began with some sweetbread and coffee served by Sandino's wife Blanca. Beals described Sandino: "[He was] short, probably not more than five feet, dressed in a new uniform of almost black khaki, and wore puttees, immaculately polished. A silk red and black handkerchief was knotted about his throat. His broad-brimmed Stetson, low over his forehead, was pinched into a shovel-line shape." Beals described him as "a man utterly without vices, with an unequivocal sense of justice, a keen eye for the welfare of the humblest soldier. 'Death is but one little moment of discomfort; it is not to be taken too seriously', Sandino repeated over and over again to his soldiers."

Beals noted that, "Not once during the four and a half hours during which we talked did he fumble for the form of expression or indicated any hesitancy regarding the themes he intended to discuss. His ideas are precisely epigrammatically ordered." It appears Sandino also had good military intelligence: when Beals asked him where the US Marine bomber aeroplanes were that he had heard so much about, Sandino smiled: "At ten o'clock they will fly over San Rafael". Beals duly noted that at exactly 1000, two US bomber planes "buzzed over the little town, circled lower and lower. Sandino's men were stationed in the doorways, rifles in hand. "Don't fire unless they bomb", were Sandino's orders. On the last approach, the planes roared over the very roof tops, then were gone."

roof, with a built-in waterfall. It is made solely from volcanic rocks taken from a solidified lava flow on Volcán Masaya, more than 200 km to the south. The most famous aspect of the church is a mural next to the entrance on the left depicting the temptation of Christ; the devil's face is said to resemble the Sandinista leader Daniel Ortega. Although it was painted in 1977 before most people even knew who Ortega was, the resemblance is uncanny.

The reason this little village, backed by a clear stream and pine forests, has such a big church is down to Padre Odorico D'Andrea, a Franciscan monk from Abruzzo in Italy, who lived here until his death on 22 March 1990. His memory lives on very much in the hearts of the people of San Rafael and surrounding settlements for the social work he did during his life. Locals are pushing for his sainthood and have constructed a curious chapel on a hill behind San Rafael, with a shrine for his tomb called *Ermita del Tepeyac*. It is a peaceful and pretty place that comes alive on 22 March each year for what the locals already call the celebrations of 'Santo Odorico'.

The **Museo Sandino** (*Casa Museo Ejército Defensor de La Soberanía Nacional*) is where General Augusto C Sandino used to send telegrams to his troops in different parts of the northern hills. The 19-year-old girl to whom he dictated his messages, Blanca Aráuz, married Sandino at the church here on 18 May 1927 and died giving birth to a baby girl in 1933. Blanca Aráuz is buried in the cemetery at the town entrance. When in San Rafael del Norte, Sandino used his father-in-law's house, today's museum, as his rebel base of operations. The museum contains an interesting collection of photographs from the years of Sandino's battles and the country's occupation by US Marines, a famous oil painting of Sandino, some old arms and the original telegraph machine that Blanca used. The museum has recently been restored and although it is often locked, the caretaker (formerly Padre Odorico's driver) lives behind the church and convent.

The festival for San Rafael usually lasts eight days and takes place around 29 September; there are also celebrations for Sandino's wedding on 18 May.

Into the Reserva de Biósfera Bosawás

The Bosawás Biosphere is one of Central America's largest protected areas. Most often accessed from the Atlantic side of the country, details on the reserve's prolific flora and fauna can be found on page 291. The two routes that enter the reserve from Jinotega are neither in particularly good condition, nor easily traversed. On the first route, the **El Cuá-Bocay** road passes the rather stunning **Reserva Natural Peñas Blancas**, on the border of the departments of Jinotega and Matagalpa. Protected as part of the Bosawás Biosphere, this area is home to one of the highest mountains in the country, countless gorgeous waterfalls, misty cloud forests, and some impressive wildlife, including jaguars and resplendent quetzals. Take a bus to **El Cuá** (0400, 1200, three hours, US$2.50, also departures from Matagalpa) and contact the **Cooperativa Guardianes del Bosque**, T829-6544, who offer nature and community tours and rustic lodging within the reserve. Beyond El Cuá, you'll find a ranger's station at **San Juan de Bocay**, as well as access to the **Reserva Natural Cerro Kilambé**, named after the 1750 m mountain within its borders. Beyond San Juan de Bocay the last place of any size is **Tablazo Yulawas**, where the road ends, the Río Bocay begins and the Bosawás biosphere stretches away into obscurity. The Río Bocay also connects with the Río Coco further downstream. The second route into the biosphere leads from Jinotega to **Wiwilí**, directly to the Río Coco and the potential starting point for a great odyssey. If you have the time, resources and seriously adventurous inclination), you could theoretically follow this mighty river all the way to the Caribbean Coast, but most settle for **Waspam**, where flights connect to Managua. Buses depart from Jinotega to Wiwilí at 0430 and 1300, 5 hours, US$3.

The best time for this trip would be at the end of the rainy season, from January to February. The Río Coco skirts the northern border of Bosawás so you will have to leave the river to go into the reserve. A jungle hammock with built-in netting (where you zip yourself inside) for insect protection is a great asset. Also bring a first aid kit, water purification tablets and some kind of portable food. You will need locally hired guides. Allow at least a week for this trip and bring more money than you think you will need, in small bills. For further advice on this and to check the security situation of any area you will visit in the Bosawás area get in touch with **MARENA** in Managua (see page 44).

Sleeping

Jinotega *p243, map p244*

Most hotels and restaurants lock their doors at 2200 on Sat, 2300 Fri-Sun. Only hardy youths are out in the streets after this time.

B Hotel Café and Restaurant Borbon, Texaco, 1 c abajo, ½ c norte, T782 2710. The best hotel in the province has 25 very nice, comfortable rooms with private bath, hot water, a/c, cable TV. Quiet and friendly with a good restaurant attached (🍴) serving traditional dishes.

D Hotel Solentuna Hem, Esso, 1 c arriba, 2½ c norte, T782-2334. Clean, safe, family hotel with 17 rooms. The owner lived in Sweden for many years, and offers a range of beauty treatments including massage and pedicure. Breakfast and dinner are served, and coffee tours are available. Pleasant and professional.

D Las Cabañas del Jinocuba, Km 153 Carretera Matagalpa–Jinotega, T782-2963, chorotegatrekkers@yahoo.com. This lovely wooden hotel, on a steep hill out of town, has received great reports. They have a

For an explanation of the sleeping and eating price codes used in this guide, see inside the front cover. Other relevant information is found in Essentials, see pages 23-27.

range of cabins, a bar and restaurant, and are the base for **Chorotega Trekkers**, who run tours into the surrounding countryside. English and German spoken.

E Hotel Central, catedral, ½ c norte, T782-2063. 20 rooms of varying quality. Rooms upstairs have private bath, cable TV and a great mountain view. Cheaper rooms (**G**) are without bath or view. There's also a communal TV and purified water dispenser downstairs, and a restaurant with very cheap food. Great location, very friendly.

E Hotel La Fuente, Esso, 4 c arriba, T782-2966. 12 rooms with private bath, hot water and cable TV. There's also parking and restaurant. Good value, but away from the centre in a less attractive area. Friendly.

F Hotelito, Esso, 2 c al sur, ½ c arriba. Small but comfortable quarters – clean, tidy and simple. Cheaper without TV (**G**). The owners are helpful and friendly.

F Primavera, Esso station, 4 c norte, T782-2400. This cheap hotel has 28 clean, plain rooms, cheaper without cable TV and bath (**G**). Breakfast is served but not included in the price. Good local atmosphere.

El Jaguar Cloud Forest Reserve *p245*

A-D El Jaguar Cloud Forest Reserve, T279-9219 (Managua), www.jaguarreserve.org. 2 wood cabins **A** at the edge of the forest with spectacular views if clear, private baths, small kitchens and living space and a biological station with dorm rooms **D**.

San Rafael del Norte *p245*

F-G Hotel Rocío, petrol station, 20 vrs sur, T784-2313. Small, intimate and very clean *hospedaje*, with private bath or **G** with shared bath. Serve 3 set meals a day, each US$1.50, good value.

Eating

Jinotega *p243, map p244*

TT Bar y Restaurante La Colmena, Parque Central, 1½ c arriba, T782-2017. Daily 1130-2130. Where the bosses eat, plain decor, attentive service, specializes in beef dishes, moderate price with cheap dishes available, also shrimp, chicken. The best in town.

TT La Perrera, Km 186 Carretera Matagalpa-Jinotega. Oft-praised restaurant just out of town, serving international fare and seafood.

TT Roca Rancho, Esso, 1 c sur, 2½ c arriba. Tue-Sun 1200-0000. This fun, friendly restaurant looks like a beach bar. They serve *comida típica*, shrimps, burgers, *bocas*, beer and liquors. There's live music on Thu.

TT-T Restaurante El Tico, across from La Salle athletic field, T782-2530. Daily 0800-2200. 44-year-old establishment in new, very modern location, popular with couples, moderately priced dishes, try surf and turf (*mar y tierra*) or *pollo a la plancha*, also cheap dishes and sandwiches. Recommended.

TT-T Soda Buffet El Tico, Esso, 2½ c sur. Reputable buffet restaurant serving good Nicaraguan food. Clean, professional and popular with tourists.

T Chaba's Pizza, Esso, 2 c sur, 2½ arriba, T782-2692. When you've had enough of *pollo frito* and *gallo pinto*, try these pizzas.

T Jinocuba No 1, alcaldía, 5 c norte, T782-2607. Daily 1200-1200. Widely recommended Cuban restaurant serving *mojito cubano* and *pollo habanero* among other things.

T Las Marías, Esso, 2½ c sur. Good locals' lunch buffet with pork, chicken and beef-based Nica dishes. Family-run and friendly.

Cafés

Soppexcca, Ferreteria Blandón Moreno, 1 c abajo, www.soppexcca.org/en. The best coffee in town, produced by an environmentally aware and progressive co-operative. Highly recommended.

San Rafael del Norte *p245*

T Bar y Restaurante Los Encuentros, at the exit from town on the highway to Yalí. Outdoor seating overlooking the confluence of hot and cold rivers, backed by pine forests, very pretty and a popular bathing spot. Whole chicken for US$5, beers are US$0.80.

T Comedor Chepita, south of the museum. Offers lunch and dinner, speciality of the day.

Bars and clubs

Jinotega *p243, map p244*

As usual, the action takes place Fri-Sun.

Monkey Jungle, Esso, ½ c al norte. The most popular disco in town, with pumping dance beats, salsa and reggaeton.

Discoteca Jaspe, Esso, 1 c abajo, ½ c al norte. The next most popular place, attracting a similarly youthful, vigorous crowd.

Shopping

Jinotega *p243, map p244*
A new market is planned for Jinotega, at the moment the one next to the bus station is the only one, very muddy and sad.

Activities and tours

Jinotega *p243, map p244*
Coffee tours
UCA Soppexcca, Ferreteria Blandón Moreno, 1 c abajo, www.soppexcca.org/en. This great organization comprises 15 organic coffee co-operatives who operate sustainably and offer tours to see how their award-winning beans are cultivated and prepared for international export.

Cultural and community tourism
Cooperativa Lina Herrera, contact Marco García at Aldea Global, T782-4027. Aside from guided birdwatching, hiking and horse riding within the Reserva Natural Dantali-El Diablo, this co-operative lets you experience rustic communities with cooking, music and story-telling.
Alianza Turística, alcaldía, 2 c arriba, 1½ c sur. This organization can help you organize visits and stays with several different co-operatives and communities around Jinotega, as well as provide general information on the region.

Transport

Jinotega *p243, map p244*
Most destinations will require a change of bus in Matagalpa. To **Matagalpa**, every ½ hr, 0500-1800, US$1.50, 1½ hrs. Express bus to **Managua**, 10 daily, 0400-1600, US$4, 3½ hrs. To **San Rafael del Norte**, 10 daily, 0600-1730 US$1, 1 hr. Taxis in Jinotega are available for local transport, average fare US$.50.

San Rafael del Norte *p245*
Buses to **Jinotega**, 0550, 0615, 0630, 0930, 1000, 1145, 1200, 1345, 1400, 1530, 1730, 1900, US$1, 1 hr. Express bus to **Managua**, Mon-Sat, 0400, US$5, 4 hrs

Directory

Jinotega *p243, map p244*
Banks For cash from cards or TCs there is a BAC, catedral, 2 c norte, T782-4413. **Banpro** and **Bancentro**, catedral, 10 varas al norte, have ATMs and currency change.
Fire T782-2468. **Hospital** Victoria, T782-2626. **Police** T782-2215. **Post office** Correos de Nicaragua, behind Bancentro, T782-2292. **Red Cross** T782-2222.
Telephone Enitel, alcaldía, 1 c arriba, 2½ c sur, T782-2022.

Estelí

→ *Population: 107,458. Altitude: 844 m. Colour map 1, C4.*

Beyond Sébaco, the Pan-American Highway climbs through the villages of San Isidro and La Trinidad before reaching the cigar capital of Central America, Estelí, at Km 148. Estelí appears to be a jumbled, unattractive place, yet this unpretentious town is one of the most lively and industrious in Nicaragua. It is the biggest commercial centre in the north, with an endless array of small family shops and restaurants along its two main boulevards and many side streets. There are also good schools and universities here, which draw students from all over the northern region and, as a result, the population is young and optimistic. The climate, too, is pleasant with average temperatures of 20-23°C. » *For Sleeping, Eating and all other listings, see pages 254-257.*

Estelí remains one of the most Sandinista cities in Nicaragua and the party colours of black and red can be seen all around the town, along with the revolutionary murals that decorate buildings on the Parque Central.

Ins and outs

Getting there and around Estelí is a major transport hub for the north with express bus services from Managua, Matagalpa and León. Regular buses connect it with Somoto and Ocotal, both of which have regular services to the border with Honduras. The city centre lies well to the east of the highway, with the focus of its life and commerce on its two main avenues. The southbound road runs from one block east of Parque Central, 12 blocks south to the south market and bus station. The northbound road passes right in front of the Parque Central and, two blocks north, reaches the central market. Taxis are cheap in the town and walking is safe in the daytime. However, use caution at night, and don't wander around the barrios. ▸▸ *For further details, see Transport, page 256.*

Best time to visit Estelí and the villages in the area enjoy a pleasant year-round climate of about 22°C. It is, of course, greener in the rainy season and much prettier in the countryside. Cigar factories can be visited at any time of year, though December tends to be quieter, as orders must be fulfilled in advance of the holidays. Most of the tobacco leaves are harvested between March and April.

Tourist information INTUR ⓘ *Parque Central, ½ c al sur, on Calle Principal, T713-6799,* has information on local attractions including nature reserves, cigar factories and Spanish schools.

Sights

Estelí was founded in 1711 by Spanish colonists who abruptly left Nueva Segovia, now Ciudad Antigua (see page 264), to escape joint Miskito Indian-British attacks on the old city. Sadly the town was razed in 1978-1979 by Somoza's National Guard, which used aerial bombing and tanks to put down repeated uprisings by the population spurred on by the FSLN. As a result, there is little visual beauty to be found in the city. The **cathedral**, first built in 1823, with upgrades in 1889, was the last to be built in the 'Nicaraguan primitive

Sleeping
Alameda **1**
Alpino **10**
Barlop **2**
Casa Nicarao **7**
El Mesón **3**
Hospedaje Luna **4**
Hospedaje San Francisco **11**
Los Arcos **12**
Miraflor **5**
Moderno **6**
Panorama 1 **8**
Panorama 2 **9**

Eating
Ananda **1**
Café Bar Punto de Encuentro **5**
Café Luz **2**
Cafetería El Rincón Pinareño **7**
Cohifer **3**
Don Pollo 2 **4**
Ixcotelli **6**
Koma Rico **8**
La Carreta **9**
La Casita **10**
Las Brasas **5**
Mocha Nana Café **11**
Café Bar Punto de Encuentro **12**
Repostería Gutiérrez **13**
Soda La Confianza **14**

Bars & clubs
El Chamán **15**
Rincón Legal **19**
Semáforo Rancho **16**
Studio 54 **18**
Zona Zero **17**

baroque' style. However, the façade was altered in 1929 to its current neoclassical appearance. The church is not particularly inspiring inside, but it does have a pretty image of the Virgen del Rosario after which the cathedral is named.

Estelí is known as the capital of **cigars**, with the finest tobacco in Central America grown in the surrounding mountains. The town is full of cigar factories, some of which produce among the best *puros* or *habanos* in the world. Most of the factories were founded by exiled Cubans in the 1960s, who brought their seeds and expertise with them. Many left during the 1980s but they returned in force in the following decade. The complicated and delicate process of making a fine cigar involves 73 stages. However, what interests most people is the final stage, the rolling of the cigars, which is done in male-female pairs. The man prepares the filler and the woman rolls it with wrapper leaf and a touch of glue. Many people visit Estelí to get a glimpse of this process and, although there are no set tours offered by the cigar manufacturers, some factories allow visitors, though you must contact them at least two days prior to your arrival. If you're in a group, you can book a visit with a Managua tour operator and bilingual guide. Most Estelí cigar manufacturers have free-trade tax status for their factories, which means that many cannot (technically) sell cigars locally. Be aware that time spent with visitors is often time lost in production, so remember that you are a privileged guest. For details of tobacco factories, see Activities and tours, page 256.

Around Estelí » *pp254-257.*

Reserva Natural Meseta Tisey-Estanzuela

ⓘ *The reserve is managed by Fundación Fider, Petronic El Carmen, 1½ c abajo, Estelí, T713-3918, fiderest@ibw.com.ni. Accommodation is offered by the Cerrato brothers who have some simple wood cabins, T713-6213, tisey69@latinmail.com.*

This highland nature reserve is home to rugged mountain scenery quite different from the landscape of Nicaragua's Pacific Basin, with its pine and oak forests, moss-covered granite boulders, rivers and cascades, as well as some unique art and horses running free. The biggest attraction is the lovely **Estanzuela waterfall**, accessed by a road just south of Estelí. Nicaragua has few accessible waterfalls and this is perhaps the most beautiful of those that can be reached without an arduous journey. The site is marked by a small sign, just south of the entrance to Estelí and the new hospital, on the highway. A dirt road leads west to the site, 5 km from the highway. Most of the year this road is not passable except in 4WD, but the walk is pleasant, passing small ranches and farms and a small oak forest. After about 4-5 km, turn right down the road to take a smaller road; there used to be a sign marking the turning, but there is now only a post. Keep in touch with the locals and ask them how far you are and where you should turn onto the secondary road. From the smaller road you pass over two crests and then down into the river valley where the beautiful El Salto de la Estanzuela flows into the Río La Pintada. It is a cool place and the pool at the bottom is good for swimming.

The area above the waterfall is best accessed via a dirt road that starts south of Estelí on the Pan-American Highway at the village of **Santa Cruz** and leads to San Nicolás. The park ranger station is 12 km from the highway; from there you can walk in the reserve as well as try some goat's cheese, produced by a co-operative of nuns. Near the Cerro El Quebracho is the farm of **Humberto González**, which has one of the most unusual mountainside art galleries anywhere. Don Humberto started to carve stone to combat alcoholism in 1988. Not only did he win the battle against the bottle, but he found a new passion that keeps him busy to this day. It is a hike from his ranch up to the mountain gallery where he has carved snakes, deer, fox, elephants, clowns and even Augusto Sandino. Ask for directions to his farm at the park ranger station.

Community tourism around Estelí

The beautiful **Miraflor Nature Reserve** is home to Nicaragua's best community tourism project, the Unión de Cooperativas Agropecuarias (UCA) Miraflor. There is so much to see and do here that you should devote at least a few days to exploring it all and soaking up the rural way of life. You could sample the locally produced coffee in the tasting lab, play baseball with the locals on Sunday, ride horses through the hills, hear gripping stories of the revolution, or just relax in a hammock, enjoying the soporific pace. But most people come here to hike. Miraflor has 206 sq km of diverse ecosystems, home to abundant bird life including the resplendent quetzal. In the humid zone, the communities of **El Cebollal**, **La Perla** and **Puertas Azules** provide access to rich cloud forests, Miraflor lagoon (see below), a revolutionary mural, an orchid centre and a modest archaeolgoical site. In the intermediary zone, the friendly community of **Sontule** provides access to a great overlook and the Apaguis cave system, apparently inhabited by *duendes* or leprechauns. **El Coyolito** and **La Pita** in the dry zone lead to bearded oak forests, waterfalls and overlooks.

There are 44 communities in Miraflor and a wide range of mostly rustic accommodation. Private rooms in a family house cost US$8 per person, private cabins are US$10 per person (cheaper for a group) and camping is from US$1.20. Meals cost US$2.50-US$4. Guides are US$10 per group, horses are US$7 per person plus the guide.

ⓘ *Contact the Miraflor office in Estelí, costado sur de cathedral, 2 c arriba, ½ c norte, T713-2971, www.miraflor.org, so you can plan your visit and set up guides and accommodation. Volunteers are always welcome at Miraflor, though Spanish speakers and a 6 month commitment is preferred; speak to Jane at Hospedaje Luna in Estelí, catedral, 1 c al norte, 1 c arriba, T441-8466, www.cafeluzyluna.com.*

Reserva Natural Miraflor

ⓘ *For information on lodging and also different excursion possibilities inside the reserve contact Zepeda Arana who speaks English and is in charge of the superb UCA-Miraflor sustainable conservation project, southeast corner of the cathedral, 2 c este, ½ c norte, Estelí, T713-2971, www.miraflor.org.*

Despite only being 206 sq km, this pristine mountain nature reserve is full of diverse wildlife and vegetation and opportunities to visit and stay in local communities (see box, above). The ecosystem changes with altitude from tropical savanna to tropical dry forest, then to pine forest and finally cloud forest at its highest elevations. The legendary resplendent quetzal lives here, along with trogons, magpie jays, the beautiful national bird – the turquoise browed mot-mot, many birds of prey, howler monkeys, mountain lions, ocelots, deer, sloths, river otters, racoons and tree frogs. The reserve also has some gallery forest, ideal for viewing wildlife, a variety of orchids and a 60-m waterfall that flows during the rainy season.

Laguna de Miraflor is a 1½ ha body of water at an altitude of 1380 m; it has a magical deep-blue colour and an unknown depth. The reserve is shared by the departments of Estelí and Jinotega, but access is much easier from the Estelí side of the mountains. Access is from the Pan-American Highway heading north out of Estelí; at the Texaco petrol station, a dirt road leads towards Yalí and passes the entrance to the reserve. The narrow track (often difficult conditions in rainy season) leads up into the mountains with spectacular views of the valley below. The entrance to the park is beyond the rocky fields of bearded oaks.

San Juan de Limay

North of Estelí, a very poor dirt road runs west to the unique rural village of San Juan de Limay. It can take up to two hours to travel the 44 km, but it's worth it for those who like off-the-beaten-path villages and unique artisan crafts. The village was founded by Chorotega Indians, who escaped the colonial invasions of Estelí (the area is rich in pre-Columbian remains with at least three good petroglyphs sites at **Los Quesos**, **La Bruja** and **El Chorro**) and is famous across Nicaragua for the beautiful soapstone (*marmolina*) carvings produced by more than 50 artisan carvers who work in the area. The material is extracted from the Cerro Tipiscayán and transformed into infinite subjects, varying in size from sculptures smaller than a child's hand (usually tropical birds and reptiles) up to 75 kg sculptures of (mostly) humans, especially large, heavy woman. The workmanship is very good and can be found in markets all over Central America. The locals are happy to receive visitors in their houses, which (as with 99% of Nicaraguan artisans) double as their workshops. The artisans have a **main office** ⓘ *de los Juzgados 3½ c norte, T719-5115*, for sales.

Condega

On the east side of the highway, about 25 km north of Estelí, is the sleepy village of Condega, another vehemently Sandinista town, with a mainly indigenous population. The name Condega means 'land of potters' and the artisans make traditional, red-clay pottery that is both attractive and functional. Condega's central park is a quiet place with an 18th-century church, **Iglesia San Isidro**, that was recently rebuilt. The area around the church comes alive during the week of 15 May to celebrate its patron, the saint of the *campesinos* (peasants), in the hope that he will bring a healthy rainy season for planting.

On the southeastern side of the square is the **Casa de Cultura** ⓘ *Mon-Fri 0800-1200, 1400-1600, Sat 0800-1200*, which produces plays, holds art classes and has a good little pre-Columbian museum. The people of Condega have a love of the *guitarra*, with more than a dozen musical groups in the municipality. You may be able to visit an artisan guitar-maker's shop, located in the back of the cultural centre.

There is a curious **park** at the south end of town above the cemetery, with great views of the surrounding mountains and valleys. The park monument is an old aeroplane from Somoza's National Guard. It was downed by FSLN rebels in 1979 and now sits like the rusting carcass of a dinosaur, staring across the valley, forever grounded but tickled at night by romantic couples and their graffiti.

One kilometre north of Condega, then 3 km west from the highway, is the **Taller Cerámica Ducuale Grande** ⓘ *T715-2418, Mon-Fri 0700-1700*. This co-operative consists of 13 female artisans and was founded in 1990 to help improve the quality and sales of what has been a tradition in this area for thousands of years. The pottery is lovely, burnt-brick red and rustic (no colours are added). Visiting the workshop provides an opportunity to meet with the artists and buy their work, which is not available for sale at many markets in the country. The woman of the co-operative are kind but sombre, working usually in complete silence – quite a contrast from the gregarious indigenous artisans of Masaya. If you show interest in their work they might open up a bit. It's possible to walk here from Condega in about one hour from the town centre.

Sleeping

Estelí *p249, map p250*
For directions, keep in mind that the cathedral faces due west. Directions from the central park start at the street that runs along the other side of the park, opposite the church; directions from the church start at the street that passes directly in front of the church.
B Alameda, Shell Esquipulas, 1 c arriba, 1½ c sur, T713-6292, www.alamedaesteli.com. Clean, large and professionally managed hotel with clean, bright rooms. Services include internet, pool, parking and restaurant. Very comfortable and decent, but far from the centre; use a taxi or car.
B Hotel Los Arcos, catedral, 1 c norte, www.familiasunidas.org/hotelosarcos.htm. This brightly painted, professionally managed and comfortable hotel has 18 rooms with private bath, a/c or fan, and cable TV. The attached restaurant, Vuela Vuela, is also reputable, and profits go to social projects.
B Hotel Panorama 1, Km 147, Carretera Panamericana, T713-3147. Inconveniently located away from the centre, but good if you need to catch an early morning bus. The newer section is brightly painted, and has comfortable rooms with private bath, hot water, a/c and cable TV. The older section is cheaper (**C**) and less attractive, but still quite comfortable.
C-F Alpino, Almacén Sony, ½ c arriba, T713-2828, halpino@hotmail.com. A wide range of lodgings with differing features and prices, from apartments with cable TV and a/c (**C**), to basic, economical rooms with fan (**E-F**)
D Casa Hotel Nicarao, central plaza, 1½ c sur, T713-2490. Clean, comfortable rooms set around a relaxing courtyard filled with plants, paintings and sitting space. Very friendly management and a nice atmosphere, but the walls are a bit thin. There are cheaper rooms without bath (**E**).
D El Mesón, Av Bolívar, central plaza, 1 c norte, T713-2655, barlan@ibw.com.ni. Clean, comfortable rooms at this friendly, helpful hotel, all with hot water and cable TV. There's a travel agency attached, and an *artesanía* shop over the road. Recommended.
E Hotel Miraflor, Parque Central, ½ c norte, T713-2003. 7 rooms with hot water, cable TV and private bath. The attached restaurant serves *comida típica*. Popular with Nicas.
E Hotel Panorama 2, catedral, 1 c sur, ½ c arriba, T713-5023. Same features as number 1 (above), but much quieter at night, with good access to central restaurants, secure parking, rooms upstairs nicer. If leaving on early bus pay in advance, ask for receipt.
E Moderno, catedral, 2½ c sur, T713-2378. Clean and comfortable rooms with a/c, hot water and cable TV. There's a restaurant for guests, where they serve breakfast and dinner.
F Barlop, Parque Central, 6 c norte, T713-2486. 12 rooms, 6 of which are good, 6 basic. The former have showers and cable TV. Parking available.
F Hospedaje Luna, catedral, 1 c al norte, 1 c arriba, T441-8466, www.cafeluzyluna.com. Brand new hostel with 2 dorms and 2 private rooms (**E**). There's hammock space, an activities board, tourist information, DVDs, tours and drinking water. Volunteer work in Miraflor can be arranged here – 3 months commitment and Spanish speakers preferred. Discounts for longer stays and groups.
F Hospedaje San Francisco, next to Parque Infantíl. Just one of a handful of cheapies in this area. Rooms are basic and clean with outside bathroom. The hotel is friendly and pleasant enough. Shabby, but the price is right.

Condega *p253*
E Hotel Restaurante Gualca, T715-2431. 6 rooms with shared baths, clean, noisy at weekends.
F Hospedaje Framar, on main plaza next to Casa de Cultura, T715-2393. 14 very clean and pleasant rooms, cold showers, nice garden, safe, friendly, owner speaks English, excellent value. Safe parking for motorbikes.
F Pensión Baldovinos, opposite the park, T715-2222. Pensión with 20 rooms, cheaper with shared bath. Fan, group discounts, good food.

For an explanation of the sleeping and eating price codes used in this guide, see inside the front cover. Other relevant information is found in Essentials, see pages 23-27.

Eating

Estelí *p249, map p250*

YYY-YY Cohifer, catedral, 1 c arriba, ½ c al sur. A very decent establishment that promises a fulfilling gastronomic experience. They serve a range of excellent steaks, chicken and fish dishes. Well established and recommended.

YY Ixcotelli, Almacén Sony, ½ c arriba, T714-2212. Fine Nicaraguan cuisine in a pleasant, ranch-style setting.

YY La Carreta, catedral, 1 c arriba. This pleasant, ranch-style restaurant is popular with Nicaraguans. They serve tasty meat dishes and *comida típica*. The staff are friendly and attentive.

YY Las Brasas, just off northwest corner of central park, T713-4985. Tue-Sun 1130-2400. Popular, lively place, with stacks of booze and bottles lining the walls. They serve Nicaraguan food and a range of beef dishes, inlcuding steak fillets, *brochetas* and *mixtas*. Try the *cerdo asado*. Recommended.

Y Café Bar Punto de Encuentro, next to Las Brasas just off central park. Good cheap food and beer, giant breakfast upon request, popular.

Y Cafetería El Rincón Pinareño, Enitel, ½ c sur. Cuban and Nicaraguan dishes and home-made pastries, try *vaca frita* (shredded fried beef with onions and bell peppers), *sandwich cubano*, very good service and food, crowded for lunch. Recommended.

Y Don Pollo 2, catedral, 1 c norte, ½ c arriba. This popular roast chicken place is great for a cheap, tasty fill and a bottle or two of cold beer. Mariachis on some evenings.

Y Koma Rico, Enitel, 1 c norte, 1½ c arriba. Some of the best street food in the city. They serve tasty grilled meats and chicken. Very popular with locals.

Y Soda La Confianza, Parque Central, ½ c sur. Cheap, good greasy food and pitchers of Victoria beer. A very male atmosphere.

Y Sopas El Carao, Almacén Sony, 1 c sur, 1 c abajo, T713-3678. Daily 0900-2000. Chicken, crab and iguana soups, grilled meats, bull balls consommé. Authentic and recommended.

Cafés, juice bars and bakeries

Ananda, Enitel, 10 vrs abajo. Chilled out yoga centre with a plethora of happy-looking plants. They serve delicious and healthy fresh fruit *licuados* – the perfect nutrient boost. Highly recommended.

Café Luz, catedral, 1 c al norte, 1 c arriba. This new, English-owned café supports communities in Miraflor. They serve a range of breakfasts, including fruit salads with yogurt and granola, pancakes with honey, and – for those homesick Brits – egg and bacon buttie. They also sell artesanías, light lunches, and have a liquor license for evening entertainment.

La Casita, opposite la Barranca, at south entrance to Estelí on Panamericana, T713-4917, casita@sdnnic.org.ni. Nicaragua's best home-made yogurt in tropical fruit flavours. Very cute place with pleasant outdoor seating underneath trees on back patio. Recommended.

Mocha Nana Café, La Casa de la Mujer, 1½ c abajo. Another friendly, English-owned café. Milkshakes, Irish coffee and English tea are among their tasty beverages. And if you're feeling hungry, there's cakes, brownies, bagels and toasted sandwiches – all home-made.

Repostería Gutiérrez, Parque Infantil, 1 c sur. A good, cheap bakery with bread, *rosquillas* and cakes.

Condega *p253*

Y Bar y Restaurante Linda Vista, on Panamericana just south of Condega. Cheap *comida corriente* dishes and cheap-to- moderate full dishes. They have a few traditional soups and drinks that are very good like *sopa de frijoles* (bean soup) and *leche con banano* (milk and banana), good *gallo pinto*.

Y La Cocina de Virfrank, Km 191, Carretera Panamericana, T715-2391. Daily 0630-2000. Very cute roadside eatery set in a little garden with excellent food, economical prices, traditional Nicaraguan dishes and drinks, also rooms for rent.

Bars and clubs

Estelí *p249, map p250*

There are endless options for dancing in Estelí, Thu-Sun. Otherwise you can dance at many of the restaurants mentioned above.

El Chamán, Hospital San Juan de Dios, 200 m sur. Lively new place that's attracting a young, energetic crowd.

Las Praderas, Km 154, Carretera Pan americana. Decent food, great atmosphere, open-air dance floor, good fun Thu-Sat nights.
Rincón Legal, Textiles Kanan, 1 c abajo. This classic, must-see Sandinista bar is filled with revolutionary memorabilia and managed by an FSLN comrade. They often stage live music and rousing Sandinista tunes.
Semáforo Rancho Bar, Hospital San Juan de Dios, 400 m sur. Don your dancing shoes for Estelí's quintessential night spot. It hosts some of the best live music in the country, with nationally and internationally renowned acts performing regularly.
Studio 54, next to Casa Pellas. A great place for a dance, with bright, young, boisterous crowds descending en-masse.
Zona Zero, opposite Casa Pellas. A hugely popular karaoke spot, if you fancy a drunken croon. Cheesey, but good.

Shopping

Estelí *p249, map p250*
On Calle Principal there is a cheap supermarket, **Palí**; on the same street closer to the centre is **Kodak** for photography supplies.
Artesanía Sorpresa, opposite Enitel. A new shop with locally produced handicrafts.
Casa Estelí, Monumento centenario, 20 m al sur, T713 2584, www.asdenic.org. On the Panamerican highway, this information centre displays arts and crafts by local talent and co-operatives.
La Esquina, costado oeste de catedral, 1 c norte. Owned by Hotel El Méson opposite, they have a decent and interesting stock of crafts.
Mocha Nana Café, La Casa de la Mujer, 1½ c abajo. Has a small selection of English-language books, including Footprint guides.

Activities and tours

Estelí *p249, map p250*

Cigar making

The selection below is a mere taster of Estelí's cigar factories. INTUR has a more comprehensive list, and all visits should be arranged in advanced.
Nicaprosa, Star Mark, 400 m northeast, T713-9373, nicaprosa@alfanumerie.com.ni.
Tabacos Cubanica, SA, de Obispado, 1 c al sur, T713-2383, ileana_06@yahoo.com. Makes the superb *Padron* line, routinely rated in the top 5 in the world.
Tabacalera Cubana García Fernández, opposite the Monumento Centenario, T713-9312, tacubaventas@turbonet.com.ni.
Tabacalera Olivas, CEPAC, 2 c al norte, T713-7376, tacunisa@ibww.com.ni. Excellent cigars and a very professional operation.
Tabacos Puros de Nicaragua, Km 141 Carretera Panamericana, T713-2758, tpn@ibww.com.ni. Mon-Fri 0700-1130, 1400-1630. The oldest of the cigar factories.

Coffee tours

Prodecoop, esquina de los bancos, 75 vrs abajo, T713-3268, www.prodecoop.com. Dedicated to fair trade and sustainable development, this co-operative of 39 groups is a major exporter of quality coffee to Europe, the United States and Japan.
UCA Miraflor, Costado Sur de Catedral, 2 c arriba, ½ c norte, T713-2971, www.miraflor.org. This community tourism project has a processing centre and tasting lab.

Cultural and community tourism

La Garnacha, Reserva Tisey-Estanzuela, contact Yadira Moreno, T713-7785. At the friendly community you can undertake several hikes and witness the production of their famous goats' cheese.
UCA Miraflor, Costado Sur de Catedral, 2 c arriba, ½ c norte, T713-2971, www.miraflor.org. Many have reported wonderful experiences with this organization that arranges visits to the communities of Miraflor nature reserve. See box, page 252.

Condega *p253*

Cultural and community tourism

Communidad Venecia Cantagallo, Condega, Ramón or William Padilla, T621-4573. Located 22 km east of Condega, this rural community offers lodging, rowing on the lagoon and guided tours of the surroundings.

Transport

Estelí *p249, map p250*

Bus

Buses enter and leave Estelí via 2 terminals, both on the Pan-American highway.
The north terminal deals with northern

destinations like Somoto and Ocotal. The south terminal, a short distance away, deals with southern destinations like Managua. A handful of Managua express buses also stop at the Shell station, east of the centre on the Pan-American highway.

North station: to **Somoto**, every hr, 0530-1810, US$1.10, 2½ hrs, use this service to connect to El Espino border bus. To **Ocotal**, every hr, 0600-1730, US$1.40, 2 hrs, use this for bus to Las Manos crossing. To **Jinotega**, every hour, 0445, 0730, 0830, 1330, 1600, US$2.25, 2 hrs. To **El Sauce**, 0900, US$1.25, 3 hrs. To **San Juan de Limay**, 0530, 0700, 1000, 1215, 1400, 1500, US$2.25, 3 hrs. To **Miraflor**, take a bus heading towards **San Sebastián de Yalí** (not one that goes to Condega first), 3 daily 0600, 1200, 1600, US$2, 1½ hrs. Return bus passes at 0700, 1100 and 1620. You can also come in 4WD; there are 2 rental agencies in Estelí (see below).

South station: express bus to **León**, 0645, US$2.75, 3 hrs. To **Managua**, every 30 mins, 0330-1800, US$2, 3 hrs; express buses, roughly 30 mins, 0545-1515, US$2.75, 2 hrs. To **Matagalpa**, every 30 mins, 0520-1650, US$1.40, 2 hrs; express buses, 0805, 1435, US$1.50, 1½ hrs.

International buses For fares and schedules, see individual agencies: **Ticabus**, Esteli Drug Store, ½ norte, T713-7350, www.ticabus.com; **Transnica**, Centro Comercial Estela Módulo 3, T713-6574, www.transnica.com.

Car hire

Budget Rent a Car, catedral, 1 c norte, T713-4030. **Toyota Rent a Car**, Edificio Casa Pellas, Km 148, Carretera Panamericana, T713-2716.

Taxi

Taxis are common on the Carretera Panamericana in Estelí, at the bus stations and in the town proper. Fares per person, inside the city centre US$0.50, from the bus stations to centre US$1. Night fares are higher and trips to the dance clubs on the outskirts should cost US$2-3. As always, agree on fare before long rides; in town just get in.

Condega *p253*

Buses north- and southbound pass through the Parque Central in Condega every half hour. Bus to **Ocotal** or **Somoto**, both 1 hr, both US$0.75 and to **Estelí** US$0.50, 40 mins.

Directory

Estelí *p249, map p250*

Banks Almost every bank in the city is located in 1 city block. BAC, T713-7101, changes all brands of TCs. **Fire** T713-2413. **Hospital** San Juan de Dios, Carretera Panamericana, T713-6300. **Internet** Cafés all over town, try **Computer Soluciones**, northwest corner of Parque Central, US$0.50 per hr. **Immigration** T713-2086. **Language schools** CENAC, Centro Nicaragüense de Aprendizaje y Cultura, Apdo 40, Estelí, T713-5437, cenac@ tmx.com.ni. 2 offices: Texaco, 5 c arriba, ½ c sur; and de los Bancos 1 c sur, T713-2025, ½ c arriba. 20 hrs of Spanish classes, living with a family, full board, trips to countryside, meetings and seminars, opportunities to work on community projects, US$140 per week. Also teaches English to Nicaraguans and others and welcomes volunteer tutors. **Horizonte Nica**, INISER, 2 c arriba, ½ c al norte, T713-4117, www.ibw.com.ni/~horizont. Intensive Spanish courses with a programme of activities and homestay. They offer excursions and voluntary work, and aim to educate you about local communities as well as the language. US$165 for 20 hrs and homestay. **Los Pipitos-Sacuanjoche Escuela de Español**, Costado Noreste Catedral, 1 c norte, ½ c abajo, T713-3830, www.lospipitosesteli.org.ni. Social projects are a part of the course and all profits go to disabled children and their families. Excursions to local co-operatives and homestay available. US$120-170, flexible options. **Police** T713-2615. **Post office** **Correos de Nicaragua**, 75 m east of the banks, T713-2085. **Red Cross** T713-2330. **Telephone** Enitel, catedral, 1 c sur, T713-3280.

Somoto

→ *Population: 14.000. Colour map 1, B3.*

The last major village along the Pan American Highway before Honduras is Somoto, set in a landscape of rugged mountains and pine forests. Despite being the provincial capital of Madriz, everything happens in its own time here, and its peacefulness can be overwhelming. The population is as quiet as the town, with a shy smile often breaking their sombre exterior. Somoto also takes the title of 'donkey capital' of Nicaragua: the animals are everywhere, chomping at grass in the fields, pulling twice their weight as a beast of burden, or waiting patiently for their owners outside a bar in Somoto. It is safe to say that there are certainly more donkeys than tourists in Somoto, but this may change as tourists discover the Canyon of Somoto, just north of the village. Hope reigns supreme that the canyon will make Somoto a destination for foreign visitors and action is being taken to declare it a National Park. Aside from the canyon, there are also many beautiful walks and horse rides in the surrounding mountains, including a municipal forest reserve on a mountain west of the village.
▸▸ *For Sleeping, Eating and all other listings, see pages 260-261.*

Ins and outs

Getting there and around There is a regular bus service from Managua and Estelí using the Pan-American Highway. Somoto is a short drive from the Honduran border at El Espino. Walking is good and very safe in the area. Taxis are available in Somoto for trips near the town, otherwise there are intercity buses or private transport.
▸▸ *For futher details, see Transport, page 261.*

Best time to visit Somoto is very dry from March to May, so the green season from June to November is ideal for a visit. Exploring the Canyon of Somoto is best from December to February as it is too dangerous in the rainy season.

Sights

Somoto is known as one of the safest towns in the country, renowned for its superb *rosquillas* (baked corn and cheese biscuits) – practically a religion – and for its world-famous sons, the folk music artists Carlos and Luis Enrique Mejía Godoy. Their mother, Elsa, has moved back from Managua to the profound peace of the town, and lives across from the INSS office, but the sons are still in Managua and give weekly concerts. The place makes a decent base from which to explore this area and the residents are very welcoming to visitors.

Somoto's church, **La Iglesia Santiago**, was built in 1661 and is an original adobe structure with tile roof, a simple, cool interior and a black Christ above the altar. The Christ figure, *El Señor de los Milagros*, is credited with repelling English pirates in the 17th century. Both this Christ figure and the one in Ciudad Antigua (see page 264) are said to have been brought to Nicaragua in the same year by Spanish missionaries. They left the white icon of Christ in Antigua, where the population was mostly Spanish, and brought the black Christ to Somoto, which is largely indigenous. The old church is charming and must be of very sound construction as it has survived centuries of tremors and earthquakes, including one good shaker in 1954 when General Somoza García was inside attending mass. As elderly locals recall with bemused smiles, the powerful dictator was the first one to sprint outside. Somoto has a small but important pre-Columbian **museum** ⓘ *Parque Central, Tue-Sat, 0900-1300, 1400-1800*, which displays ceramics with unusual iconography and evidence of trade with Honduras.

For those interested in gastronomic tourism, try visiting one of Somoto's 53 *rosquilla* **bakeries**. No-one seems sure when *rosquillas* became a tradition here, but

Border essentials: Nicaragua – Honduras

El Espino / Somoto

There's nowhere to stay in El Espino, 20 km beyond Somoto and 5 km from the Honduran border at La Playa. There's a duty-free shop and a food bar on the Nicaraguan side and several cafés on the Honduran side.

Nicaraguan immigration The Nicaraguan side is open 24 hrs. If you're arriving or leaving Nicaragua you'll have to pay US$7 plus a US$1 *alcaldía* charge.

Crossing by private vehicle Motorists leaving Nicaragua should enquire in Somoto if an exit permit has to be obtained there or at El Espino. This applies to cyclists too.

Transport **Bus** Somoto to El Espino every hr 0615-1710, US$0.50, 40 mins. See Somoto for routes to Managua and other destinations. On the Honduran side, taxis go between the border and the Mi Esperanza bus stops, when totally full, 9-10 people, US$1 for foreigners, less for locals. On the Nicaraguan side taxis wait to take you to Somoto, they may try to overcharge, pay no more than US$8.

Directory **Banks** No money changers on Nicaraguan side but locals will oblige, even with lempiras.

Las Manos / Ocotal

This is recommended as the best route from Tegucigalpa to Managua.

Nicaraguan immigration Open 24 hours. All those arriving must fill in an immigration card, present their luggage to the customs authorities, obtain a receipt, and then present these to immigration authorities along with passport and entry fees. When leaving the country, fill out a card, pay the tax and get your passport stamped.

Crossing by private vehicle After completing immigration procedures, go to *Tránsito* to pay for the vehicle permit, obtain clearance from *Revisión*, and get your vehicle permit from *Aduana* (Customs). Travellers advise that if it is busy, go first to Customs and get your number in the queue. On leaving the country, complete the immigration requirements, then go to *Tránsito* to have the vehicle checked, and to Customs to have the vehicle stamp in the passport cancelled. Surrender the vehicle permit at Customs and take another form back to *Tránsito*; this will be stamped, signed and finally handed over at the exit gate.

Transport Bus Las Manos-Ocotal, every 30 mins or when full, 0615-1730, US$0.80, 45 mins, Taxis also available for US$7-8 set fare before boarding.

Directory Money changers operate on both sides, offering córdobas at a little better than the street market rate in Nicaragua. Rates for cash and TC exchange are usually better in Estelí.

the oldest residents recall that they were already popular in the 1920s. The most famous baker could be **Betty Espinoza** ⓘ *Enitel, 3 c norte, T722-2173, Mon-Sat 0500-1000*, who is happy for visitors to watch the process of butter, corn, eggs, milk, sugar and Nicaraguan feta cheese being made into *rosquillas*; her seven employees and big wood-burning ovens crank out 3000 of them per day. Betty learned from her great-grandmother and 80% of her production is shipped to Managua.

There are also good artisans in Somoto: crafts include white-clay ceramics and rope art. The **Taller de Cerámica Arturo Machado** ⓘ *on the exit to El Espino at Cruz Roja, 2 c norte*, is worth a look. His work can also be seen at the fabulous artisan crafts store in the **Hotel Panamericano** on Parque Central in Somoto, which has a fine selection of northern crafts, with examples from all over Somoto, Condega, Mozonte, Jinotega and more. The owner, Danilo Morazán, knows most of the artists personally so he can tell you where to find them if you're interested in a visit. The artisans in Somoto and San Lucas often work in henequen (*pita*), which is grown in the area and woven into thread and rope to make beautiful mats and other crafts. You can visit the very friendly Ivania Moncada at the **Cooperativa de Henequeneros de Madriz** ⓘ *Profamilia, 5 c arriba, T722-2343.*

If you're in town during the dry season, you may want to check out Nicaraguan Division One soccer at the 2500-seat **Santiago Stadium**, where the local *futból* team *Real Madriz* plays, admission US$1.50. There is also a local version of carnival, which is really a huge block party in Parque Central, with bands coming from all over Central America to perform non-stop from 1800 to 0600; the date changes, but is usually during the last fortnight of November.

Grand Canyon of Somoto

ⓘ *Follow the highway about 15 km north of Somoto, where you'll find a signposted dirt track at the bridge that crosses over the Tapacalí River. The canyon is accessed by a 20-minute walk from here. Follow the track 3 km to the end where you will meet guides with a boat who will ferry you to the canyon. They may also have inner tubes for hire. Once inside the canyon, you don't need a guide to pass over the rocks, but it's recommended because they're slippery. A taxi here will cost around US$5.*

Fifteen kilometres north of Somoto is one of Nicaragua's most impressive canyons, known locally as *Namancambre*. Its jagged walls soar above crystal-clear waters at the source of the great Río Coco – Central America's longest river – which travels more than 750 km to meet the Caribbean Sea. The canyon is at the convergence of the Río Tapacalí and Río Comalí: the former fed by the mountains of Honduras, the latter by the range behind Somoto. The canyon is 3 km long with a depth of 80-100 m and is extremely narrow at some points.

Now protected as part of the **Reserva Tepesomoto-Pataste**, a walk in the canyon is both a contemplative and adventurous experience, requiring careful hiking over slippery shore rocks hugging the sides of the canyon walls. A rest stop reveals trees glimmering in the sun, caressed by gentle winds and the muffled babble of the stream. This is a solitary slot in the earth that a 13-million-year-old knife of water has cut through solid rock. From inside the canyon, with its green water and marvellously-sculpted reddish stone, the sky is but a narrow blue glimmer. You can swim in the waters of the canyon during the dry season, but it can be very dangerous in the rainy season (June to November) even if not swimming, as water levels can change quickly and currents are very strong.

Sleeping

Somoto *p258*

C Hotel Colonial, Iglesia, ½ c sur, T722-2040. An attractive, professionally managed hotel with decent rooms; all have private bath, cable TV and fan. Popular with businessmen and NGOs.

E Hotel Panamericano, on north side of Parque Central, T722-2355. Good value rooms at this interesting hotel, where you'll find an orchid collection, a craft shop and a menagerie of animals. The annexed section, a few roads away, has a lovely garden and

For an explanation of the sleeping and eating price codes used in this guide, see inside the front cover. Other relevant information is found in Essentials, see pages 23-27.

recreation area. They arrange trips to the Canyon and surrounding countryside. Highly recommended.

F Hospedaje La Provedencia, Intel, 2½ c norte, T722-2089. 6 simple rooms with 2 shared baths inside a house. Friendly, family-run and basic.

F El Bambú, Policía Nacional, 2 c norte, T722-2330. 20 simple, cheap rooms with cable TV. Some have bath, some don't. Close to the highway and bus station.

Eating

Somoto *p258*

¥¥-¥ La Llanta, PETRONIC, 1 c abajo, T722-2291. Mon-Fri 1000-2200, Sat-Sun 1000-2400. Good pork dishes, hot pepper steak, *comida corriente*.

¥¥-¥ Restaurante Almendro, Iglesia, ½ c sur. Famous for its steaks, and serves good *comida corriente*. The big tree in the centre gives restaurant its name and is a famous from a Mejía Godoy song.

¥¥-¥ Restaurante Somoteño, Parque Central, 2 c abajo, 75 varas norte, on Carretera Panamericana, T722-2518. Cheery outdoor seating with bamboo walls, great beef grill with friendly service and monumental portions: *corriente* (normal), *semi à la carte* (too big) and *a la carte* (way too big). Sat is karaoke night. Recommended.

¥ Cafetería Bambi, Enitel, 2½ c sur, T722-2231. Tue-Sun 0900-2200. Surprisingly no deer on the menu, just sandwiches, hamburgers, hot dogs, *tacos* and fruit juices.

¥ Comedor Familiar, Iglesia Santiago, 1 c al sur, ½ c al este. Locals' haunt that's good for a cheap meal and discreet people-watching.

Transport

Somoto *p258*

Buses to **El Espino** and the Honduran border, every hour, 0515-1715, US$0.50, 40 mins. To **Estelí**, every hour, 0520-1700, US$1.25, 2½ hrs; express buses are Managua-bound, US$1.65, 1½ hrs, they will drop you off at the Shell station, just east of central Estelí. Express bus to **Managua**, Mon-Sat, 0345, 0500, 0615, 0730, 1400, 1515, Sun 1400, 1515, US$4, 3½ hrs. To **Ocotal**, every 45 mins, 0345-16.35, US$0.75, 1½ hrs.

Directory

Somoto *p258*

Banks Banco de Finanzas (BDF), T722-2240, in front of the alcaldía. **Hospital** West side of Parque Central, T722-2247. **Fire** T722-2776. **Post office** Correos de Nicaragua, southeast corner of park, T722-2437. **Red Cross** T722-2285. **Police** T722-2359. **Telephone** Enitel, behind church, T722-2374.

Nueva Segovia

Along with León and Granada, Nueva Segovia is Nicaragua's oldest Spanish province, founded in the early 16th century for mining purposes. Located in the extreme north of Nicaragua, the province contains the peaceful and historic indigenous communities of Totogalpa and Mozonte, the trading centre of Ocotal, which has decent accommodation, and the ancient forgotten village of Ciudad Antigua. Boasting just two paved roads, the area is deeply rural and a 4WD is a valuable tool because local buses are slow and dusty. This is also an alternative route to Honduras, via the highway to Ocotal and Las Manos. Travelling further from the Pan-American Highway, the Carretera a Ocotal runs north and the landscape changes into jagged hills and pine trees. The bridge just before Ocotal crosses Central America's longest river, the Río Coco, just before which is the historic red-earth indigenous village of Totogalpa.

›› *For Sleeping, Eating and all other listings, see pages 265-266.*

Ins and outs

Getting there and around There are regular buses from Managua and Estelí along the Pan-American Highway. Somoto is a short drive from the Honduran border at Las

 Manos. Walking is not ideal around Ocotal but Totogalpa and Ciudad Antigua offer better hiking opportunities. Taxis are available in Ocotal for trips near to the town, otherwise intercity buses and private transport are available. » *For further details, see Transport, page 266.*

Best time to visit Nueva Segovia is very dry from March to May, so the green season from June to November is ideal. The freshness of December and January evenings is a pleasant contrast to the heat of the Pacific slope.

Comunidad Indígena de Totogalpa » *pp265-266.*

Arriving in Totogalpa, technically in the department of Madriz, feels like arriving at the very end of the earth. This seemingly forgotten town, with its romantic colonial-period churches and ageing population, has seen its youth move to cities and foreign lands in search of work. The bright red clay streets and its crumbling, yet attractive, adobe homes add to the town's rustic other-worldliness. The original settlement dates back more than 1600 years and is located in the community of San José, northeast of the current village, along the banks of the Río Coco. This is now a major archaeological site yet to be excavated at time of printing, but check with the mayor's office if you're interested in a visit. The remains of circular stone houses and ceramics suggest that this was a large settlement from AD 400 to AD 600. Today's indigenous community plans to build a new museum to house the recovered artefacts.

Totogalpa celebrates its patron saint, Virgen de la Merced, from 8 to 23 September. The festival of María Magdalena takes place during the week of 22 July and may afford the opportunity to see an **ancient indigenous dance** that was banned by the church on numerous occasions but is still practised by some indigenous communities in the Northern Highlands – mainly at funerals where they dance with palm fronds around the deceased. During the Magdalena festival the local dance group *Nido de Aves* performs *La Danza de la Palma*.

The British naturalist Thomas Belt visited Totogalpa in 1871, during one of its festival days. He didn't mention which saint the community was celebrating but he did describe the men drinking *chicha liquor* in *jícaro* bowls and the women decorating the interior of Totogalpa's charming parish. "We found a number of the Indian women with great baskets full of the most beautiful and sweet-smelling flowers, making garlands and bouquets to decorate the holy images and church. The beautiful flowers were twined in wreathes, or stuck on prepared stands and shapes, and their fragrance filled the church. At other mestizo towns, where the churches were like dilapidated barns, we heard much of the religious fervour of the Indians of Totogalpa."

Belt explained how the indigenous communities were quite independent in the 19th century – something that indigenous leaders of the region are trying to re-achieve in the 21st century. He observed that: "The central Government interferes but little with the local officials; and the small towns in the interior are almost self-governed. The Indian townships are better managed than those of the Spaniards and mestizos: the plazas are kept freer from weeds and the roads in good order. Probably nowhere but in tropical America can it be said that the introduction of European civilization has caused a retrogression ..."

La Cueva del Duende

In the area surrounding Totogalpa there are opportunities for hiking, caving and rafting along the Río Coco between the Canyon of Somoto and Ocotal. One kilometre

It is said by many that once inside La Cueva del Duende all torches immediately stop working.

Devilish leprechauns: los duendes

The legend of the *Duendes* is prevalent throughout the country but seems to be most popular in the northern and central mountain ranges. The existence of these little people is believed by people of all ages, from young children to their grandparents. *Duendes* are something akin to demonic leprechauns: a race of very small, alien people, dressed usually in red, with pointy hats and, more often than not, sporting beards. The *Duendes* make frequent contact and contracts with the Devil in their homes, the country's hillside caves. Their main purpose, or joy, is to steal babies that are yet to be baptized or unwed young women, though they are also happy to play with the sanity of a farmer or schoolboy. Girls are lured away by hypnotism, little gifts and sweet words, and never seen again. *Duendes* can be heard laughing in the deep forest. They enjoy making life difficult for the country people by putting farm animals in high places where they can't climb down, dropping roof tiles off the house at night, and all the while laughing their little laugh. Local newspapers report of school children who are afraid to attend class because of the *Duendes*, and although they remain totally invisible to most, they are completely visible, both repulsive and enticing, to a select few.

north of Totogalpa is **Cerro de las Rocas** and a trail that leads to a cave inside the mountain, La Cueva del Duende. The name, 'Leprechaun's Cave', relates to a widely held belief in this area (see box, above). Danni Altamirano, at the **Hotel El Camino** in Totogalpa, is brave enough to take visitors to the cave. He, or his brother, can also organize rafting trips along the Río Coco.

Ocotal » *pp265-266.*

This little city with its sprawling suburbs is the financial and trading centre for the region, but has little to offer visitors. The population is more serious and less friendly than in most parts of the country. Ocotal is, however, a useful jumping-off point for visiting some of the beautiful villages in the region, such as Mozonte or Ciudad Antigua, or to rest before or after the border crossing at Las Manos. **INTUR** ⓘ *office, Procredit, ½ c abajo, T732-3429, ocotal@intur.gob.ni*, has brochures of general interest in English, ask about some very interesting farm stays available in the highlands of Dipilto.

Ocotal's main attraction is its Parque Central, which is like no other in Nicaragua. **Parque Las Madres**, as it is called, is a lush tropical garden designed by the ex-mayor of Ocotal and tropical plant expert, Don Fausto Sánchez. It contains a stunning display of plant diversity with its dense tapestry of greens, reds, oranges, yellows and pinks. Set within the relative ugliness of Ocotal, the park is a leafy refuge and a reminder of the stunning fertility of the tropics. If you are fortunate enough to find Don Fausto inside the park caring for his garden, he may take you on an impromptu tour, naming over 100 species and highlighting each plant's special charm. There are more than eight species of rose, as well as magnolias, gardenias, pearls of the orient, birds of paradise, orchids, jupiters, wild ginger, heliotropes and begonias. In addition to the vast displays of flowers, the park is framed by cypress and pine trees that are over 100 years old. The church on the Parque Central is attractive and also worth a look. Founded in 1803, **El Templo Parroquial de Ocotal** was not finished until 1869. Its baroque and neoclassical façade hide a simple and attractive interior with pine (*ocotl*) columns and comfortable curved pews. There are some very pretty icons inside, which are said to have been imported from La Antigua, Guatemala.

The patron saint of Ocotal is the *Virgen de la Asunción* whose day of celebration is 15 August. The festival lasts all week and includes a parade of 22 brightly decorated ox carts, one of which holds the festival queen. On 11 August is the northern Nicaraguan version of Carnival – a sort of a mini-Woodstock held in Parque Central, with an endless flow of bands.

Ocotal, named after the ocotl species of pine tree that once enveloped the town before the arrival of the chainsaw, has the dubious distinction of being the first town in the world to be bombed by a fleet of military aeroplanes in combat circumstances. The co-ordinated bombing raid was courtesy of the US Marines in July 1927. This was a practice that would continue throughout Nicaragua's northern mountains from 1927-1933 as the Marines and newly formed National Guard fought in vain to destroy Sandino's rebel army. In May 1927, Sandino rejected a pact made between liberal generals and the US military. On 11 July the US Marine captain gave Sandino 48 hours to turn over his arms in Ocotal. Sandino waited until 16 July and at 0115 attacked the Marine base, today Ocotal's **Casa de Cultura** ⓘ *Enitel 2 c al sur, T732-2839*. The battle lasted until five Marine biplanes arrived at 1435, dropping over 300 fragmentation bombs during a one-hour period, forcing Sandino's troops to retreat. From then on, Sandino changed his tactics, avoiding face-to-face confrontation whenever possible and moving towards modern guerrilla warfare.

Comunidad Indígena de Mozonte

Four kilometres east of Ocotal is the sleepy, ancient village of Mozonte, renowned for its ceramic artisans. Monzote (often spelt Mosonte) has a special beauty and a proud population that has done much to preserve its indigenous form of government. The system is run by a council of elders and relies on the spirit of community co-operation. This is apparent in the way the ceramic artisans share tools like kilns and shops, while simultaneously keeping independent business ownership. There are several **co-operatives** of over 50 artisans working in ceramics, one of which is located at Km 3.5 on the highway from Ocotal, T732-2810. The most common theme is a floral vase with a country village carved out in relief and painted with bright colours. This is one of the poorest municipalities in Nicaragua, so a good way to support the community is to buy from the talented artisans who are happy to receive visitors.

There are two interesting churches in Mozonte. **Iglesia Mozonte** in the central square dates to 1703 and is one of the oldest parish churches in its original state in the country. The other temple, **Ermita de la Virgen de Guadalupe**, built in 1763, contains several relics dating back to its construction. It is an eerie-looking chapel that sits alone on the summit of the hill to the north of the village. The *Loma Santa* (holy hilltop) chapel is reached by a long flight of steps in the extreme north of the town and affords a fabulous view of the region.

Ciudad Antigua » *pp265-266.*

Nestled in a valley of rolling hills, the Ciudad Antigua of today is truly in the middle of nowhere, but that was not always the case. Originally called *Nueva Ciudad Segovia*, it was founded in 1611 by Spanish colonists who hurriedly abandoned the first Ciudad Segovia settlement (founded between 1541-1543 near current-day Quilalí), as a result of continued attacks by the indigenous populations. In the late 1600s, the city was attacked by pirates and most of the population fled to found Ocotal, or further south to found Estelí at the turn of the 18th century. The economy of Ciudad Antigua was based on pine pitch extraction, which had value as caulking for sailing ships, and also to seal barrels that were used to transport wine from Peru.

The church in Ciudad Antigua is one of the finest examples of *mudéjar* (Spanish Arab influenced) construction and is very similar to the churches of Totogalpa and Sutiava. From the 17th century onwards the town was attacked by English and French pirates, one of whom, Ravenau de Lussan, wrote a description of the church and town that is still accurate today. The British pirate, Charles Morgan, was another pirate who sacked the town and residents of 21st-century Ciudad Antigua claim that these pirates are to blame for their current state of poverty. During the Contra War, 1982-1990, Ciudad Antigua was the scene of heavy fighting between Contra and Sandinista troops and the countryside around the town was a free fire zone.

Sights

The village has not changed much for the last few centuries, providing an excellent opportunity to step back in time. **Parque Central** lies to the left of the road entrance. The park is elegant, inexplicably large and infallibly empty. The lovely **church** was built in 1654 and many of its original 17th-century doors and walls are intact. The interior is whitewashed adobe, with an ornate gold-leaf altar that bears a famous image of Jesus or *El Señor de los Milagros*, donated by an Austrian queen. The image is said to have been brought to Ciudad Antigua, along with the heavy altar, via a Caribbean port in Honduras and transported here by manpower alone. According to local legend, *El Señor de los Milagros* was not willing to be stolen. During the numerous pirate raids, the icon grew so large that it was impossible to extract it through the massive front doors. He is celebrated every 20 January with processions throughout the town.

The **Museo Religioso de Ciudad Antigua** ⓘ *T732-2227, Mon-Fri*, is a small, musty and delightful museum of ancient religious artefacts next to the church. Doña Rosivel (often found in the little crucifix store in front of the church) has the key and is the best guide in town. She can take you into the museum to see rare colonial artefacts (and bats). The talkative Roque Toledo, the official town guide, is a lot of fun, but if your Spanish is not perfect his long-winded explanations can be exhausting, bewildering or both. Roque will also take you to the southern outskirts of town to see the baseball stadium and the ruins of the **Iglesia La Merced**.

Sleeping

Totogalpa *p262*

F Hotel El Camino, along the main entrance road to the village. Private bath, fan, parking, clean, light rooms. Cheap meals are available in the owner's house. Recommended

Ocotal *p263*

Ocotal has a large mosquito population, even in the dry season; bring a mosquito net.

B Hotel Frontera, behind the Shell station on the highway to Las Manos, T732-2668, hosfrosa@turbonett.com. This is the best hotel in town, even if it looks like a prison compound from outside. It has an inviting swimming pool, bar, restaurant and events room. The rooms are clean and comfortable, if uninspiring, and cheaper without a/c (**D**). They also offer internet, laundry service and international call facility.

D Hotel Benmoral, at south entrance to city, opposite FINOSA, T732-2824. 20 dark, clean rooms with a/c or fan (**E**), cable TV and hot water. Food is available, and there's parking space. Friendly and helpful.

E Hotel Belrive, Shell station on the highway, 1 c arriba. This motel-style place has rooms with bath, hot water and cable TV. There's parking and a restaurant. Pleasant and friendly. Cheaper without a/c (**F**).

E Hotel Restaurant Mirador, opposite bus station, T732-2496. 22 rooms with cable TV, private bath and hot water. Some are nicer than others. As the name suggests, there's a small restaurant attached.

For an explanation of the sleeping and eating price codes used in this guide, see inside the front cover. Other relevant information is found in Essentials, see pages 23-27.

F Hotel El Viajero, Esso station, 3½ c abajo, T732-2040. Clean, pleasant, economical place with 15 rooms. All have fan, most with bath. Breakfast and lunch are served, there's internet service and cable TV. Cheaper without bath (**G**).

Eating

Ocotal *p263*

Most restaurants have a mid-range menu with cheap *comida corriente* available.

¥¥-¥ Llamarada del Bosque, south side of Parque Central, T732-2643. Popular locals' joint that serves tasty and cheap buffet food and *comida típica*.

¥¥-¥ Restaurante El Paraíso, at south entrance to Ocotal, T732-3301. Pleasant open-air setting, steak, chicken and pork dishes, moderate prices.

¥¥-¥ Restaurante La Cabaña, next to Hotel Benmoral, T732-2415. Daily 1000-2300. Good steak dishes like *filete a la cabaña* or *jalapeño* steak, moderate prices, avoid the shrimps. Lovely garden setting with banana trees and separate gazebos for the tables.

¥¥-¥ Restaurante La Yunta, Casa Pellas 75 varas al sur, T732-2180. Daily 1100-2300. A range of beef, steak and fillet dishes to delight any carnivore, good sea bass and grilled pork. Recommended.

¥ Comedor la Esquinita, Esso, 1 c al sur. Clean, pleasant *comedor* with tables set around a leafy courtyard. They serve cheap Nica fare.

¥ El Deportivo, Esso ½ c arriba. Daily 1000-2200. Open-air seating in this sport orientated bar where they serve cold *Toña* and *Victoria*. They have rooms for rent too.

Transport

Totogalpa *p262*

Buses pass the village on the highway, every 15 mins for **Ocotal** US$0.40 and **Estelí** US$0.80.

Ocotal *p263*

Bus

The bus station for Ocotal is on the highway, 1 km south of the town centre, 15-20 mins' walk from Parque Central. Buses to **Las Manos/Honduras border** every 30 mins, 0500-1645, US$0.80, 45 mins. To **Somoto**, every 45 mins, 0545-1830, US$0.75, 2½ hrs. Express bus to **Managua**, 10 daily, 0400-1530, US$4.50, 4 hrs. To **Ciudad Antigua**, 0500, 1200, US$1.25, 1½ hrs. To **Estelí**, leaves the city market every hour, 0445-1800, US$1.30, 2½ hrs; express buses are Managua-bound, 2 hrs, US$1.65, they will drop you off at the Shell station, just east of central Estelí.

Taxi

Ocotal taxis are cheap, with rides within town costing about US$0.40. A ride to **Las Manos** and the border with Honduras will cost US$7-9.

Ciudad Antigua *p264*

There is 1 bus per day to **Ocotal** at 1400, 1½ hrs, US$1.50.

Directory

Ocotal *p263*

Bank Bancentro, Parque Central, 1 c norte, 1 c abajo, has a Visa ATM and money-changing facility; as does Banco Procredit, Parque Central, 1 c abajo. **Fire** T732-2390. **Hospital** T732-2491. **Post office** Correos de Nicaragua, Esso, 2c sur, T732-3021. **Red Cross** T732-2485. **Police** T732-2657. **Telephone** Enitel is on the north side of Parque Central, ½ c norte, T732-2321.

Caribbean Coast & Islands

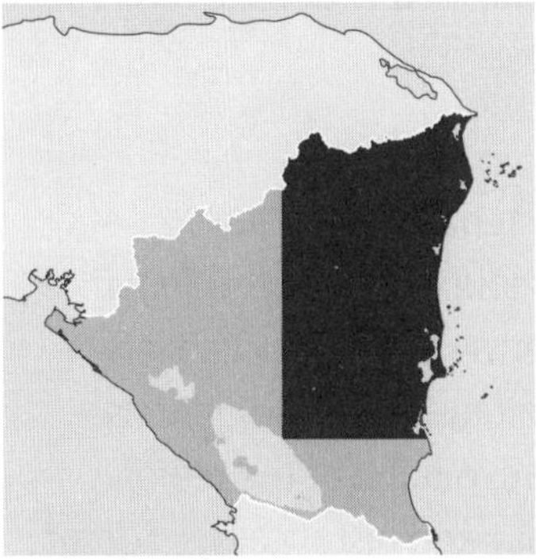

Footprint features

Introduction

A rich cultural melting pot characterizes Nicaragua's Caribbean Coast, where lilting Creole English is the *lingua franca*, lightly peppered with Spanish. British buccaneers, Jamaican labourers, Chinese immigrants and indigenous tribes have all contributed to the evolution of the region's exotic flavours. Politically, culturally and historically, *La Costa Atlántica* is a world apart. Take the single propeller plane over here and you'll soon see why. Vast tracts of virgin rainforest divide Nicaragua from its Caribbean cousin, an unrelenting carpet of green treetops punctuated only by meandering, toffee-coloured rivers and swollen coastal lagoons. Few roads – or Spanish colonists – have ever penetrated this wilderness.

The Corn Islands are the region's principal attraction: two islands with white-sand beaches, scintillating coral reefs and turquoise waters. Little Corn is a low-key dive center, Big Corn is home to diverse fishing communities and a good place to sample authentic Caribbean life while it lasts. On the mainland, Bluefields is the nearest city of any size, a decaying and shambolic spectre, but ripe with all the sights, sounds and smells of any bustling tropical port. This is the place to drink rum and watch the tropical storms roll in.

The coast's isolation has allowed the Miskito peoples to thrive here, asserting their political will through the Yatama political party and controlling municipal governments since 2004. Bilwi is the administrative capital of the Miskito world, but Waspam is its spiritual heart. Located on the banks of the formidable Río Coco, only the truly brave and adventurous will get this far. Surrounded by impenetrable rainforest, a sturdy boat and a trustworthy guide will be necessary to navigate the river, its complex network of tributaries and the many isolated communities that comprise the Miskito nation.

★ Don't miss ...

1. **Swimming with sharks** Snorkel the coral reefs of Little Corn Island with sharks and manta rays, page 273.
2. **Fresh seafood** Taste fresh lobster a la plancha on the patio of Seva's Place on Big Corn Island, page 275.
3. **Cultural tours** Take a tour to Pearl Lagoon to visit Miskito, Creole and Garífuna villages, page 280.
4. **The reggae vibe** Pay a visit to the Four Brothers in Bluefields, for an uncommercialized dance hall experience, page 284.
5. **The Río Coco** Drop in on Waspam, the centre of the Miskito universe and the focus of more than 115 riverside communities, page 288.
6. **Call of the wild** Experience the power and majesty of Bosawás Biosphere Reserve, Central America's largest and least explored area, page 291.

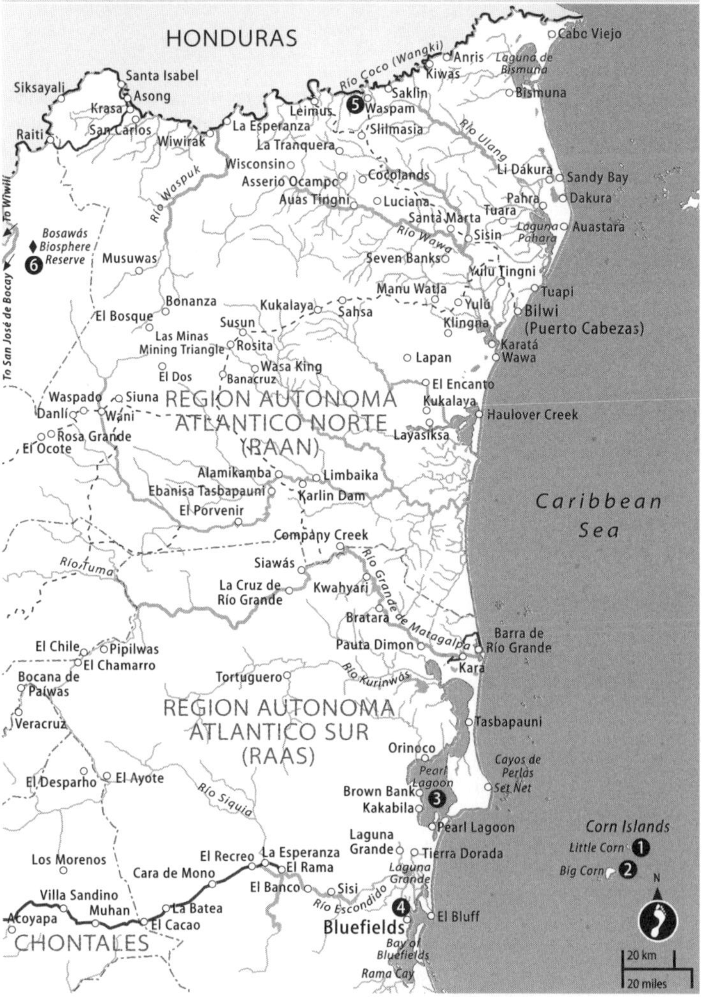

Corn Islands

→ *Population: 6370. Altitude: 4-90 m. Colour map 4, B3.*

The Corn Islands are a portrait of Caribbean indolence with their languid palm trees, colourful clapboard houses and easy, rum-soaked dilapidation. Divorced from the mainland by 70 km of turquoise sea, many islanders are incurable eccentrics. Few, if any, pay much mind to the world outside, concerning themselves only with the friendships, feuds and often entertaining gossip that is the staple diet of island life. But a burgeoning tourist trade and Colombian 'business interests' mean the islands are no longer the place to experience the authentic Caribbean life of days gone by. Outsiders are steadily infiltrating, bringing tourists, foreign-owned hotels and crime. But like everything else here, the pace of change has been slow. For now, the islands remain distinctly low-key, staunchly individualistic, and governed by a handful of families who have been here for generations. Scratch the surface and you'll discover that many things are as they have always been: rains come and go, mangos fall, and waves lap the sugar-white beaches in perpetuity. ⏩ *For Sleeping, Eating and all other listings, see pages 273-276.*

Ins and outs

Getting there The islands are 70 km off the mainland of Nicaragua. The big island is 13 sq km and the little one is 3½ sq km. About 7 km of Caribbean Sea separates them. Two Nicaraguan airlines fly daily to Big Corn and there are boat services three times a week from Bluefields. Transportation to Little Corn is on a twice-daily skiff with two big outboards and good native navigators. The boat has no roofing to protect from rain and sun and it can be a wet ride if it's rough – not for the weak-hearted. ⏩ *For further details, see Transport, page 276.*

Getting around The big island has one paved road that does a lap of the island with two buses and nearly 100 taxis. The small island has no roads; walking or boating are the only way of getting around.

Best time to visit Unlike most of Nicaragua's tourist destinations the dry season is by far the best time to visit the islands, with better visibility in the water and more sunshine. The best and driest months are February to April, or September to October when the waters are normally calm (unless a hurricane passes). Holy Week and Christmas are very crowded, as is 27-28 August when the festival takes place. June and September have the fewest foreigners.

Tourist information There is no tourist office on the Corn Islands, but you could try getting hold of *Right Here!* magazine, www.rightheremagazine.com, which gives a good summary of the attractions; it's available in Bluefields and major tourist offices. A good online source of information is www.bigcornisland.com.

Safety Paradise has a dark side and you should use common sense at all times. On Big Corn, take care at the commercial dock area near Brigg Bay and at Queen's Hill. Avoid walking at night on the island anywhere, always use a taxi to get between bars and your hotel. Theoretically, there is now a police force on Little Corn, but they may be hard to find. It's better not to walk alone in the bush, and don't walk there at night at all. Don't go out with locals unless recommended by your hotel; thieves, known as 'pirates', sometimes pose as informal tour guides.

Both islands are populated by big, menacing-looking land crabs that aren't good for eating whole, but make a very hearty soup.

Learning to dive on the Corn Islands

Home to an array of dazzling tropical sea creatures, the waters off the Corn Islands promise some of the most stunning, cost effective diving in the Caribbean. A dive here will take you to brooding coral reefs, darkened caves and teeming canyons, where weird corals and brightly coloured fish make their home. Sharks are common, with nurse sharks lurking on the ocean floor and hammerheads swarming in great numbers during the months of December and January. Graceful rays also populate the waters, including gorgeous eagle rays, swooping mantas and sting rays. Barracuda and turtles are often spotted, playful dolphins too. If you take a night dive, you're likely to see lots of lobster and octopuses, as well as a shimmering and unforgettable bioluminescent spectacle.

The Corn islands are a good place to get your PADI open water certificate. As an emerging destination, visitor numbers are still low, groups are still small, and prices still reasonable. Little Corn is the more popular dive destination, but Big Corn is good too. Open-water certification takes 3-4 days, depending on experience and aptitude. The training is intensive and covers everything from using equipment to planning a dive. You'll consolidate what you learn with practical exercise and around five open water dives. When you're not in the water, you'll be expected to watch slightly annoying PADI DVDs, study your course book, take tests and a final exam. Be warned: you won't get much beach time. Upon completion, you'll be issued a certificate that qualifies you to dive with a partner ('a buddy' in PADI speak) all over the world.

ⓘ *For more information, see PADI's website, www.padi.com and listings of the islands' dive shops, page 276.*

Background

During his fourth and final exploratory voyage (see box, page 289), Columbus encountered the islands and named them *Islas Limonares*. At the time, they were inhabited by Kukra Indians, of which little is known today except for a reported tendency towards cannibalism. During the 18th century the islands became a haven for pirates resting in between pillages. Eventually they were settled by Afro-Caribbeans, mostly Jamaicans, who arrived from the neighbouring islands of San Andrés. The local economy was based on the production of palm oil until the devastating winds of Hurricane Joan in 1988, which reached over 200 kph and destroyed most of the palm trees on the island. Lobster fishing took over as the biggest industry, but supplies are being depleted rapidly. Tourism and 'white lobster' (cocaine) are taking over as the biggest sources of income for the islanders (see box, page 278). Thanks to their proximity to the San Andrés Islands, which come under Colombian jurisdiction (although located inside Nicaragua's ocean platform), drug traffickers have had a lot of involvement here, using Little Corn as a refuelling stop for many years. Today there's a meagre police presence, frequently rotated to keep hands (and noses) clean. But there is still a lot of drug money on both islands, and parcels of coke are still dumped at sea (albeit less and less frequently), allowing locals to fish for the lucrative 'white lobster'. Meanwhile, there has been a migration of Miskito communities from the mainland to the islands to dive for real lobster, although dwindling supplies have created unemployment in both native and migrant populations, with some desperate people turning to crime. Yet there is a surprising affluence to both islands that can probably only be explained by tourism or drugs. Either way, the Corn Island natives remain some of the most hospitable, polite and welcoming people in Nicaragua; a people with a profound understanding of the word 'relaxed'.

Big Corn » pp273-276.

Big Corn has a good landing strip, airport terminal and quite a few decent hotels. Around Waula Point is **Picnic Centre**, a fine beach for swimming and sunbathing. On the sparsely populated southeastern part of the island is the long and tranquil **Long Beach** in Long Bay. With Queen Hill rising above the western part of the bay it is also very scenic. The most interesting nature is to be found beneath the water, with beautiful reefs and rich marine life. Bird life, however, is disappointing. Snorkelling is best on the northern coast of Big Corn, just west of **Sally Peaches**, in front of the Hotel Bayside. The eastern side of the island is the most rustic and quieter. Facing the Atlantic, it has good waves for most of the year and plenty of rocks. There are numerous estuaries and wetlands all around the island, containing a startling amount of fresh water.

The beaches on the west and southern side of the island are best for swimming. Walking around the island takes about an hour and a half.

Part of the attraction of the place is the locals, who are very friendly and happy to return a smile and a wave. Big Corn does not offer the natural beauty of Little Corn, but

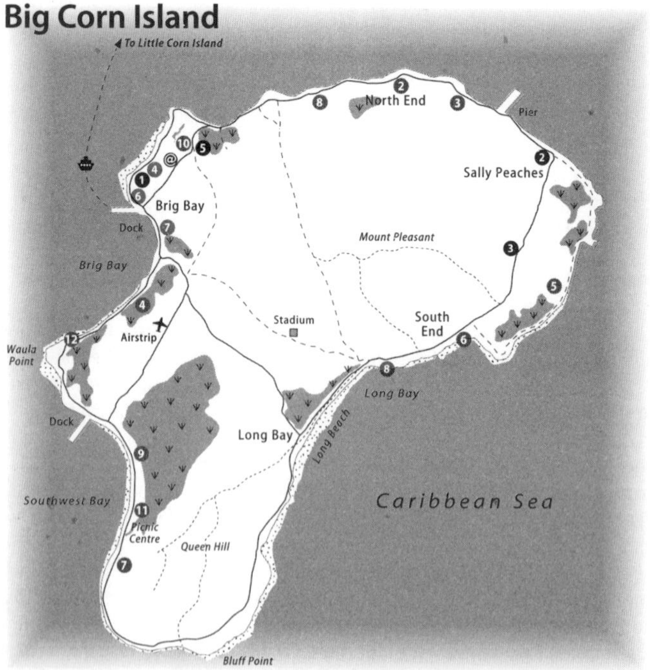

N

500 metres
500 yards

Sleeping
Anastasia's 3
Arenas 9
Casa Canada 6
Martha's Bed & Breakfast 7
Morgan 8
Panorama 10
Paraíso 4
Picnic Centre 11
Princesa de la Isla 12
Silver Sand 5
Vientos del Norte 2

Eating
Fisherman's Cave 1
Nautilus Dive Centre 5
Relax 3
Seva's Place 2

Bars & clubs
Marvin & Myers 6
Nancy's 7
Nico's 8
Reggae Palace 4

it is more lively and those who bore easily or are not into snorkelloing or diving might prefer the big island. The northeastern part of the island has a lovely community called **South End**, the most idyllic example of Afro-Caribbean culture on the islands. There is also some nightlife with a reggae bar and several restaurants. To celebrate the abolition of slavery in 1841, Big Corn holds an annual festival, culminating on the anniversary of the decree on 27 August (book accommodation well in advance for this week) with the **Crab Festival**. Various activities take place, including the election of a Crab Festival Queen, and copious amounts of crab soup are served.

Little Corn » pp273-276.

The small island has some of the finest coral reefs in Nicaragua and is a superb place for snorkelling and diving. *National Geographic Explorer* gave the reefs nine out of ten. Little Corn is more relaxed and less developed than its larger neighbour, although it now suffers from crime. The locals on the island are keenly aware of the beauty of their home and most of the development here is carried out by natives.

The island has good opportunities for walking, with the north end of the island a mixture of scrub forest and grazing land leading down to the brilliant turquoise sea. The prettiest side of the island is also the windward side; visiting during a windy period can be disappointing for snorkellers but helps calm mosquitoes and the heat. The most developed areas are along the western shores of the narrow southern part of the island, separated from the windswept east coast by a large swamp. This is where the boats arrive and there are numerous options for sleeping and eating. The water is calm and good for swimming and there is a good sense of community spirit here.

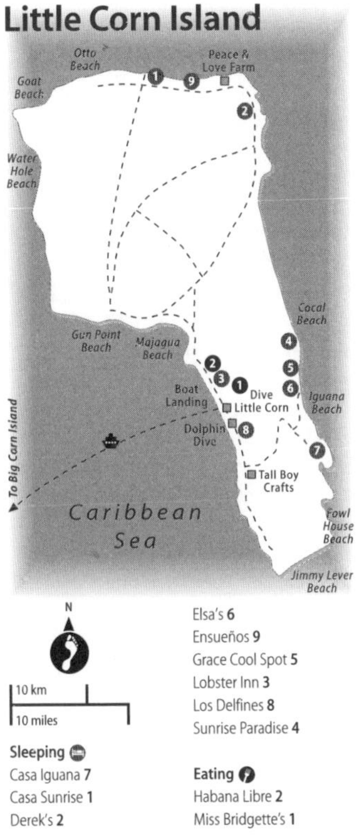

There are lovely highlands at both southern and northern tips of the island. The highlands of the southeast have been cordoned off by the Casa Iguana (see page 274), but the northern ones are open to all and have great beaches and only a few foreign settlers. South of an attractive Southeast Asian-style lodge called Derek's, there is a long spectacular beach that runs the entire length of the island, broken only by some small rocky points. Near the southern end of this beach there are good places to eat right on the sand and simple lodges. All the beaches have sugar-white sand, although it disappears at high tide. There is some very interesting and unique artisan jewellery sold south of Hotel Los Delphines, near the village at the 'bottle house' of Vice Mayor 'Tall Boy' Robert Knight, which also sells shoes, sandals and T-shirts.

Sleeping

Big Corn *p272, map p272*

A Arenas Hotel, Picnic Centre, T546-2220, www.arenasbeachhotel.com. The closest thing Big Corn has to a resort, with modern double rooms, comfortable wooden bungalows and luxury suites (**A**) overlooking the ocean. All have cable TV, hot water, a/c and hammocks. There's a restaurant and conference centre, and a range of other services too.

A Casa Canada, South End, T644-0925, www.casa-canada.com. Sophisticated, luxurious rooms with ocean views. Each is splendidly equipped with a DVD player, mini-bar, coffee-maker, leather chairs and mahogany furniture. A beautiful infinity pool overlooks the waves. Friendly and hospitable management. Recommended.

B Hotel Paraíso, Brig Bay, T575-5111, www.paraisoclub.com. A professional, friendly hotel, managed by two Dutch gentlemen who contribute to local social projects. They offer a range of clean, comfortable cabañas, all with hammocks and mosquito nets. It's right on the beach, and there's good snorkelling at the wreck off-shore. Tours and fishing trips can be arranged; ask Mike about seeing the island in a golf cart. Prices include breakfast. Recommended.

B Martha's Bed & Breakfast, Southwest Bay, just south of Picnic Centre, T835-59320. This hotel has lovely landscaped grounds and 8 clean, unpretentious rooms with private bath, a/c and cable TV. Comfortable enough, but the value isn't great.

B Princesa de la Isla, Waula Point, T854-2403, www.laprincesadelaisla.com. The Princess has seen better days, but her setting on a windswept point is eternally romantic. The bungalow – normally reserved for honeymooners – is much better than the rooms, with lots of character and unique furnishings. The gregarious Italian owner offers Italian food (ŸŸ) and espresso, call ahead to get the pasta cooking. A touch of old Europe.

C Anastasia's, North End, T425-9589. Located by the best snorkelling reef on the island, this hotel offers a marine park with 'snorkel trails'. There's a restaurant on stilts, and all rooms have private bath, cable TV and a/c.

C Hotel Morgan, North Point, T575-5052. 6 cabañas and 4 rooms with hot water, cable TV, a/c and refrigerator. Rooms upstairs have an ocean view.

C Picnic Centre, Picnic Centre Beach, T575-5204. 8 average rooms with private bath, some with a/c. There's a very popular ranch on the beach for eating (ŸŸ-Ÿ) and drinking, and worth a visit if sleeping elsewhere. Good ambience and great location.

C Vientos del Norte, North End, T575-5112, www.bigcornisland.com/vientosdelnorte.html. Comfortable, well equipped quarters overlooking the ocean, with TV, a/c, phone, kitchenette, coffee maker. There's also some new dorm facilities (**E**) – the only dorms on the island.

D Panorama, Iglesia Católica, ½ c al este, T575-5065. Motel-style place by the beach offering simple, economical rooms with mosquito nets. Cheaper without a/c (**E**).

E Silver Sand, Sally Peaches, south of rocky point, T575-5005. Managed by the enigmatic Ira Gomez, who alone makes this place worth a visit. Rustic fishermen's cabins in a gorgeous secluded setting. Ira can organize fishing trips, and cook up the catch in his bar-restaurant on the beach. Look out for the happy neighbours playing reggae through their enormous speakers.

Little Corn *p273, map p273*

The north end is the greenest, wildest area, but somewhat isolated and difficult to reach at night.

A-C Casa Iguana, on southeastern bluff, www.casaiguana.net. This is a famous, popular lodging, beautifully located with stunning views of the beaches. They have 4 cabañas with shared bath (**C**), 9 casitas with private bath (**B**), and 1 'luxury' casita (**A**). They grow their own food in lush, attractive gardens, offer great breakfasts, sociable dining and an expensive internet café (US$10 per hr). An impressive, interesting and professional outfit, even if it is a bit of a gringo summer camp. Book in advance, especially in high season.

B-D Ensueños, Otto Beach, www.ensuenos-littlecornisland.com. Trippy, rustic cabins with sculpted Lord of the Rings-style interiors; some have electricity, some don't. The grounds are wonderfully lush and filled with exuberant fruit trees, and naturalist owner Ramón Gil is an interesting and

For an explanation of the sleeping and eating price codes used in this guide, see inside the front cover. Other relevant information is found in Essentials, see pages 23-27.

friendly host. There are comfortable houses too (**B**), and meals are also available. Recommended.

C Los Delfines, in village just south of boat landing, T820-2242, www.hotellosdelfines.com.ni. Little Corn's most upmarket hotel. The rooms (a/c) are average for the price, comfortable and clean. Hot water is sporadic. The restaurant has nice views, but service is annoyingly slack. Ask about deals if studying at the adjoining dive shop.

D Casa Sunrise, Otto Beach, www.casasunrise.de. Blessed and named in 1997 by the Dalai Lama and officially recognized as an ecological project by the Nicaraguan Tourist Ministry. Simple cabins at a beautiful and isolated location, where the sun can be seen to rise and set. It's seen better days though.

D Derek's, at northernmost point of the east coast, T419-0600, www.dereksplacelittlecorn.com. Southeast Asian-style cabins on stilts, all equipped with renewable energy, mosquito nets, orthopaedic mattresses and hammocks. It's a tranquil, social spot, and the cabins are very clean in spite of the (albeit well-to-do) backpacker clientele. Meals, snorkelling gear and bicycle rental available to guests.

D Lobster Inn, in the village, just north of boat landing, T847-1736. You'll find 13 rooms in this 2-storey, centrally located hotel. They're small but clean, all with private bath and fan. Friendly, and there's a restaurant too.

D-F Sunrise Paradise, on east coast just north of Grace's (see below). Also known as Carlito's, and managed by the head of the island's informal security service, who is a real gentleman. They offer a range of simple cabins all with fan and electricity. There's also food, beer and hammocks, and the grounds are pleasant.

E Grace Cool Spot, just north of Elsa's (see below). Rough and ready backpackers' cabins, all brightly painted and daubed in Jamaican colours. Each has its own hammock, and the sometimes cleanish facilities are outdoors. Breakfast is included for an extra couple of dollars.

F Elsa's, north along beach from Casa Iguana (see above). 9 simple cabins, managed by the lovely Elsa, who is quite possibly the island's best cook. Drop by for a meal in her restaurant (🍴), even if you aren't staying.

Eating

Seafood lovers will be in heaven, others could go hungry, but chicken and coconut bread should sustain the non-fish eaters.

Big Corn *p272, map p272*

🍴🍴-🍴 **Fisherman's Cave**, next to dock. This great little seafood restaurant overlooks the water and fishing boats. A relaxing spot. Check out the pools filled with live fish.

🍴🍴-🍴 **Nautilus Dive Centre**, North Point, T575-5077. Fabulously eclectic menu with Caribbean curry and classic dishes like rondon soup, containing vegetables, coconut milk and seafood. They also do pizza and will deliver.

🍴🍴-🍴 **Seva's Place**, 500 m east of Anastasia's in Sally Peaches, T575-5058. Quite possibly the island's best restaurant. They serve great seafood, meat and chicken from a fine location with rooftop seats and ocean views. Try the lobster *a la plancha*.

🍴 **Relax**, South End. 0800-2000. Also known as Virgil's Place, they do the best ice cream on the island and some light meals too, including fried chicken.

Little Corn *p273, map p273*

See hotels for most of the eating options.

🍴🍴 **Habana Libre**, just north of boat landing, T848-5412. Really tasty, flavourful dishes including succulent veal, fish and lobster served with interesting sauces. There's terraced seating, good music and amiable staff. Cuban specialities are available on request and in advance. Be sure to try a *mojito* – they're outstanding.

🍴 **Miss Bridgette's**, in the village, north of the dock. A lovely little *comedor* serving wholesome, home-cooked fare. Service is very Caribbean, so be prepared to wait.

Bars and clubs

Big Corn *p272, map p272*

After dark, always use taxis to get between your hotel and the bars, even if they're close to each other.

Marvin and Myers bar, next to the dock. Chill out with a beer while waiting for the boat to Little Corn. Good for people-watching.

Nancy's Bar, Brigg Bay. 1900-0200. Head here on a Fri night for cold beer, reggae and raucous dancing.

Nico's, South end, 1900-0200. The action kicks off on Sun, with wall-to-wall drinking and dancing by the waves. They serve beef soup when you need perking up.
Reggae Palace, Brigg Bay. 1900-0200. Sat night is the big night here. As usual, reggae, salsa and rum in heavy doses.

Activities and tours

Big Corn *p272, map p272*

Diving

Nautilus Resort & Dive Centre, North Point, T575-5077, www.divebigcorn.com. Diving and snorkelling tours with Guatemalan NASE-certified training instructor include trips to see the cannon of the old Spanish Galleon, blowing rock, PADI certification from US$275, night dives and 2-tank dives from US$60-90 per person, snorkelling trips and glass-bottom boat tours at US$15 per person.

Fishing

Ira Gómez, Silver Sand hotel, Sally Peaches, south of rocky point, T575-5005. One of those irresistible local characters, Ira is an enthusiastic fishing man and can organize your trip.

Little Corn *p273, map p273*

Diving

Dive Little Corn, boat landing in village, T823-1154, www.divelittlecorn.com. There's a strong PADI ethos at this 5-star, gold palm centre, with training right up to assistant instructor level. They also offer night dives, single and 2-tank dives, snorkelling tours, and 5 or 10 dive packages – trips leave several times daily. Open water training is US$320 including materials, and packages can combine with Casa Iguana stays.
Dolphin Dive, in the village, south of the dock, T690-0225, www.cornislands scubadiving.com. Operated by islander Sandy Herman, a passionate and friendly instructor with many years diving experience. She offers PADI instruction to dive master level, and a range of customized trips for diving, fishing or snorkelling. Open water training is US$320, a 2-tank dive is US$65. Packages are available, including discounts at Delphines. Groups are kept small. Recommended.

Transport

Air

La Costeña flies from Big Corn to **Managua** with a stop in **Bluefields**, daily at 0810 and 1540, US$165 round trip, 90 mins with stop. Re-confirm seats before travelling. **La Costeña** office is on Big Corn, T575-5131.

Boat

Inter-island boats Big Corn to Little Corn, daily 1000, 1630, US$6.50, 40 mins. Little Corn to Big Corn, daily 0700, 1400, US$6.50, 40 mins. Boats leave from main dock, first come, first served. US$0.20 charge to get into the dock area. Buy big blue trash bags to keep luggage dry at shop across from dock entrance, best to sit near the back.

Mainland boats Subject to change, check locally; Corn Islands to **Bluefields** leaves Tue, 0900, US$12, 5-6 hrs; and Fri and Sun 1200. To **Bilwi**, daytime departure, 1 per month, US$30, 3 days.

Bus

2 buses circle the paved island road on Big Corn every 20 mins, US$0.50.

Taxi

Taxis charge US$2 for trips to and from the airport or any trip after 2000. Any other trip is US$1. Hourly taxi rates are US$6 per hr, poor value, as there are many taxis and trip fares are cheap.

Directory

'Bucks' are córdobas in island speak.
Banks The only bank is **BanPro** on southwest bay on Big Corn, T575-5109. No ATM, and credit card advance for VISA only. TCs are not accepted or changed anywhere. Dollars are widely used on the islands; be safe and take all the cash you need with you. If stuck, you might get a credit card advance at the airport. **Hospital** Brig Bay T575-5236. **Internet** Big Corn has a café near Nautilus, US$1.50 per hour. Little Corn has extortionate cafés at **Los Delfines** and **Casa Iguana**, US$10 per hr. **Police** T575-5201. There are few, if any police on the Little Corn – ask around. **Telephone** Enitel, T575-5061.

Bluefields

→ *Population 42,665. Altitude 20 m. Colour map 4, B3.*

Dirty and chaotic but curiously inviting, Bluefields is the heart and soul of Nicaragua's Caribbean world and the capital of Southern Atlantic Autonomous Region, known by its acronym RAAS. It is located at the mouth of the Río Escondido, which opens into Bluefields Bay in front of the city. The majority of the population is Afro-Caribbean, though the other ethnic groups of the region are represented and the main attraction of the town is its ethnic diversity and west Caribbean demeanour. The main church of the city is Moravian, the language is Creole English and the music is calypso and reggae. Bluefields is a good jumping-off point to visit Pearl Lagoon and other less explored areas of the wide-open region. ▸▸ *For Sleeping, Eating and all other listings, see pages 283-285.*

Ins and outs

Getting there and around La Costeña and **Atlantic Airlines** fly twice daily from Managua's domestic terminal and the Corn Islands, and once a day except Sundays from Bilwi. Getting there by land is more complicated. The classic route uses a long-distance bus from Managua to connect with boats at El Rama, from where you travel downstream to the coast. However, an alternative route follows a new road from El Rama to Pearl Lagoon, from where you catch a panga to Bluefields. Most of Bluefields can be seen on foot, though taxis are recommended at night. All visits to surrounding attractions are by boat. ▸▸ *For further details, see Transport, page 284.*

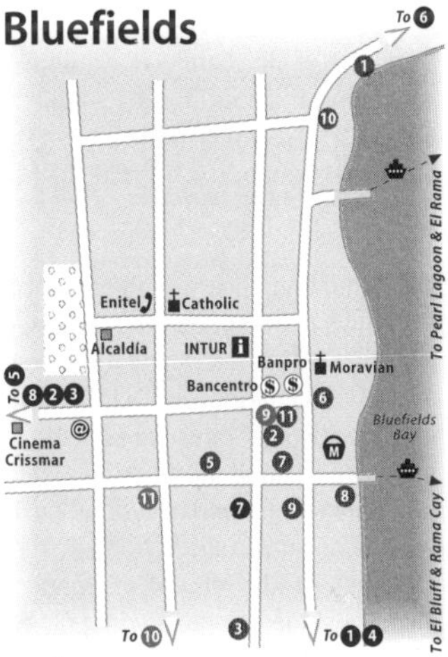

N

200 metres

200 yards

Sleeping
Bluefields Bay **1**
Caribbean Dreams **9**
Costa Sur **2**
El Dorado **3**
Hospedaje Pearl Lagoon **5**
Los Pipitos **7**
Marda Maus **8**
Mini Hotel Central **10**
Oasis **11**
South Atlantic II **6**

Eating
Bella Vista **1**
Chez Marcel **2**
El Flotante **4**
La Loma **5**
Luna Ranch **6**
Pizza Martinuzi **8**
Salmar **3**
Tex Mex House **3**
Twins **7**

Bars & clubs
Cima Club **9**
Four Brothers **10**
Garibaldi **11**

Best time to visit May is the most festive time thanks to Palo de Mayo (maypole) events. Rain is common year-round, but January to April is driest.

Tourist information INTUR ⓘ *opposite Salón Siu, Barrio Central, T572-0221, bluefields@intur.gob.ni*, has friendly staff and some limited information on local sights and activities.

Background

Bluefields is named after the Dutch pirate Henry Bluefeldt (or Blauvedlt) who hid in the bay's waters in 1610. The native Kukra Indians were hired by Dutch and British pirates to help them with boat repairs and small time trade began with the Europeans. The first permanent European settlers arrived at the end of the 18th century and the ethnic mix of the area began to change. The 19th century saw a healthy trade in bananas and an influx of Afro-Caribbeans from Jamaica to work in the plantations and administer the Anglican and Moravian churches. During the 20th century Chinese immigrants also came to Bluefields creating what was

Fishing for white lobster: cocaine and complicity on Nicaragua's Caribbean coast

From sugar and spices to tobacco and alcohol, the human race has always cultivated, consumed and distributed drugs in a big way – for pleasure, profit and power. Cocaine is the one of the most powerful and lucrative drugs of all time, boasting a market value of US$70 billion. Colombian cartels manage the production and distribution of cocaine, processing farm-grown coca leaves into the precious crystalline powder that Westerners like to snort for fun.

Poorly policed and effectively lawless, Nicaragua's Caribbean coast was easily consolidated by the Colombians in the 1990s, where they established a sea route for their traffickers and a network of refuelling bases on the region's isolated islands. Today this route is one of the most frequented and dangerous smuggling lanes in the world. The coast guard, underfunded and under-resourced, is easily outmaneuvered by the sophisticated Colombian speed boats that are equipped with powerful engines, GPS, machine guns and radar. When pursuits do end in capture, the parcels of merchandise are usually dumped at sea before they can be confiscated.

These parcels, often containing many kilos of pure cocaine, wash ashore to be claimed by local fishermen, a new and highly lucrative catch known locally as 'white lobster'. Dealers will typically buy back their stash for US$4000 per kilo – several times less than the US street value, but still an inordinate amount for the region's impoverished inhabitants. In Nicaragua, that kind of cash can buy a lot: a new house, a car, a motorboat – or a ton of bling, and a few months of drinking and dancing. Some church ministers have hailed the white lobster as a gift from God, citing the financial

thought to be the largest Chinese community in Central America. The fighting of the Revolution did not affect the area much, but the Contras of the 1980s used the eastern coast to harass Sandinista positions and many of the Chinese left during these years.

Bluefields was nearly wiped off the map by Hurricane Joan in October 1988. Some 25,000 residents were evacuated and most of the structures were destroyed. An army member arriving the day after the hurricane described the city as appearing trampled by a giant, with nothing left of the buildings but wooden footprints. The famous Bluefields Express boat that worked the 96 km journey from Rama to Bluefields was later found wrecked inside thick forest – 4 km from the riverbanks.

The town, like the entire region, is struggling against the Columbian drug runners. Bluefields is used as a landing and strategic post, and the recent murders of honest local police is a symptom of the Columbians stamping their authority. Most of the merchandise is cocaine and Nicaragua is one of the highways north from the producer, Colombia, to the world's biggest cocaine market, the USA. Local dealers are also getting involved and, although consumption is well below US and European rates, slowly the corruption of the Bluefields/eastern Chontales corridor is being consolidated.

Sights

Within Nicaragua, Bluefields is best known for its dancing and it is the **reggae** capital of the country. The best time to see the locals dance is at the annual **Palo de Mayo** (maypole) celebrations (also known as **¡Mayo Ya!**). The festival is celebrated throughout May and there are countless dance contests between different neighbourhoods. The only rule is to hang on to the ribbon connected to the maypole and move. There is also some interesting local music and poetry in the festival.

miracles it works for their communities (and their donation boxes).

No community knows the value of white lobster better than Little Corn Island. In the days before a regular police force, traffickers fleeing the coast guard would abandon their coke-laden boats on the island's beaches. The locals would promptly loot it, sharing the bounty among themselves and later selling it back for serious profit. Unfortunately, these windfalls became so regular and so profitable that they aroused a good deal of resentment from neighbouring Big Corn island. In retaliation, a gang of islanders from Big Corn landed on Little Corn armed with machetes and baseball bats. They took their share by force, raiding house after house after house.

The continued survival of the cocaine industry demands complicity at all points of the supply chain. The farmers who grow coca, the communities who harbor smugglers, the corrupt customs officials, and the high-ranking politicians who take a share of the pie; all are bought, all turn a blind eye to the violent excesses. And when complicity can't be bought, it can be traded for false promises. Increasingly, a portion of the high grade cocaine that passes through Nicaragua is converted to crack, hooking the poor and disadvantaged who are desperate to escape their problems.

And if complicity can't be traded at all, it is simply taken. In 2004, a gang of Colombians stormed Bluefields police station and cut the throats of four policemen, stamping their authority on the town for all time. The merciless ambitions of the cartels, the woeful ignorance of the recreational user, and the staggering economic realities of this global trade mean that cocaine isn't likely to fade away any time soon.

Although Bluefields is doing its part to pollute the bay that surrounds it, the sheer expanse of water (30 km from north to south and 6 km wide) means that it is still beautiful. If you have some time in Bluefields, a boat excursion to see some of the bay provides a different perspective on the tired city waterfront.

Around Bluefields » *pp283-285.*

Rama Cay

ⓘ *A boat ride to the island will cost US$15-50 depending on the number of passengers. Check at the southern dock next to the market to see if any boats are going; if you hitch a ride, returning could be a problem.*

This island in the Bay of Bluefields, only 20-30 minutes by *panga* from Bluefields, is home to the last tribe of Rama Indians, led by an elderly woman chief. The Rama, calm and friendly people who are renowned for their kindness and generosity, are pretty accustomed to visitors but sadly this is the least studied group of all the indigenous peoples in Nicaragua and the most likely to lose its language. They may have been the dominant group on the coast before the arrival of the Europeans but their reluctance to support the British in their pirate attacks against the Spanish led to the rise of the Miskitos, who allied with the British (and were given muskets, hence their name). With the help of firepower and economic support, the Miskitos eventually took over almost all of the Rama territory and much of the Mayagna, an area comprising the Caribbean coast from Cape Camarón in Honduras to Río Grande in Nicaragua. The exception is the little island of Rama Cay and the Río San Juan, where the Rama are making a comeback.

The Rama are highly skilled at languages, often speaking Rama, Creole English, Spanish and some even Miskito, despite receiving little or no formal schooling. The Rama language is related to that of the northern Amazonian peoples and it is believed they migrated from that area. There is a small **community tourism project** ⓘ *contact Oscar Omier, Martina Thomas or Sonia Omier, T628 1112 (cell), etnoram@yahoo.com, or speak to INTUR in Bluefields,* on the island with accommodation and guides, if you're interested in learning more.

El Bluff

El Bluff is a peninsula that separates the sea from the Bay of Bluefields. In happier days it was a busy port, but now the beach is dirty and not very appealing. There is a good walk to the lighthouse with a fine view of the bay and the sea, and the locals are happy to see visitors. Boats leave from the southern dock in Bluefields next to the market. The boat costs US$3 and leaves when full.

Reserva Silvestre Privada Greenfields

ⓘ *T268-1897, www.greenfields.com.ni. The reserve at Kukra Hill can be reached by a regular panga from Bluefields, or an infrequent bus from El Rama or Pearl Lagoon. One-day entrance is US$15.*

Greenfields is a 284-ha, privately managed nature reserve of mangroves, rivers and forests. There's a botanical park and 30 km of paths snaking through the Swiss-owned wildlife sanctuary, sometimes visited by scientists and home to jaguars, tapirs, monkeys caymans and otters. There are pricey eco-lodgings (US$250 for a two-day all inclusive stay) and camping facilities.

Pearl Lagoon

This oval-shaped coastal lagoon, 80 km north of Bluefields, covers 518 sq km and is one of the most beautiful places on the coast. The lagoon is fed principally by the jungle-lined Río Kurinwás but also by the rivers Wawashán, Patch, Orinoco and Ñari. Pearl Lagoon's shores range from pine forests and mangroves to savanna and rainforest. The cultural diversity is equally broad with Afro-Caribbean, Miskito and Garífuna settlements at different points around the lagoon. To get the most out of a trip, hire a guide or use a tour operator; try Hotelito Casa Blanca (see page 284), who have extensive contacts and offer tours to the wonderfully tranquil Pearl Keys, wildlife viewing on the Wawashán river and fishing trips.

The village of **Pearl Lagoon**, in the far southwest of the estuary, is the most developed and is a good place to start when planning a trip. The village is well-organized, clean and welcoming with an Afro-Caribbean community and interesting Moravian church. All the best accommodation for the lagoon is based here and there are regular boat services to Bluefields.

Between Pearl Lagoon and the Caribbean Sea is the Miskito village of **Tasbapauni**. One hour from the village of Pearl Lagoon, it has around 2000 inhabitants living on a strip of land less than 1 km wide between the sea and the lagoon. Though it can have debris, the beach here is pleasant and the locals have started to clean it up. The village is worth a visit and is also an ideal jumping-off spot to explore the more remote white sand paradise of Pearl Keys.

Also north of the Pearl Lagoon village is **Orinoco**, Nicaragua's most significant population of Garífuna peoples. This group has been studied by anthropologists in Honduras, but went unnoticed in Nicaragua until finally being recognized by the government in 1987 – after more than 150 years of settlement. The language and many of the dances and culinary customs of the Garífuna remain intact, in a curious mixture of old African and Caribbean indigenous influences that has taken on a life of its own. They have an annual cultural festival from 17-19 November.

Grisi siknis: dancing with the devil

Headaches, dizziness, nausea and irrational fear precede an attack of 'grisi sickness', a violent psychotic episode in which the sufferer endures terrifying demonic visions, loss of identity, and eventually, frenzied loss of control. The victim may grab machetes or other weapons to ward off invisible enemies or family members, hurting themselves or anyone else who gets in their way. Also known as 'crazy sickness', grisi siknis is a contagious, culturally bound mental disorder, affecting only the Miskito peoples. Most victims are teenage girls.

Culturally bound syndromes are a real puzzle for western medicine, as they disobey the laws, dogma and classifications that are the lifeblood of psychiatric science. Many contend that the symptoms of grisi siknis closely resemble dissociative fugue, a rare condition in which the sufferer's personality is completely displaced by another. Other commentators argue that such cross-cultural translations are flawed interpretations of complex, culture-specific conditions. For that reason, many have looked to Miskito culture for the answer, speculating that grisi siknis functions as a kind of safety valve for pent up pubescent energies. The sufferer's visions are normally sexual in content, allowing them to transgress social norms of sexual purity and express their sexuality.

Perhaps the most radical and difficult to swallow explanation lies with the Miskito themselves, who contend that grisi siknis is caused by evil spirits and the activities of malicious sorcerers. This would explain the violence of the sufferer's possession, and the generally demonic content of her visions and why Miskito shamans seem to be the most successful at curing the condition, knowing the combination of herbs and prayers to alleviate it.

The **Río Kurinwás** area is a fascinating, largely uninhabited jungle where it is possible to see monkeys and much other wildlife. It might occasionally be possible to get a boat to the town of **Tortuguero** (also called **Nuevo Amanecer**), a mestizo town that will really give you a taste of the frontier. Tortuguero is about a six-hour speedboat ride from Bluefields up Río Kurinwás, or several days by regular boat.

Río Grande is the next river north of Río Kurinwás, connected to the Pearl Lagoon by the Top-Lock Canal. At its mouth are five interesting villages: the four Miskito communities of **Kara**, **Karawala**, **Sandy Bay Sirpi** and **Walpa**, and the Creole village of **La Barra**. Sandy Bay Sirpi is on both the river and the Caribbean, and has a good beach.

Travelling upriver, the Río Grande is a noticeable contrast to the Río Kurinwás; it is much more settled, dotted with farms and cattle grazing. Some distance upriver (about a six-hour speedboat ride from Bluefields, several days by regular boat), you reach the mestizo town of **La Cruz de Río Grande**. It was founded around 1922 by Chinese traders to serve workers from a banana plantation (now defunct). La Cruz has a very pretty church, and there are resident expatriate (US) monks of the Capuchin order in the town. The truly adventurous can walk between La Cruz and Tortuguero; each way takes about 10 hours in the dry season, 12 in the rainy.

Although it may seem appropriate in this tropical climate, the name 'Mosquito' coast is a corruption of Miskito – the name given the indiginous inhabitants after they were armed with muskets by the British.

Nicaragua's British coast: La Miskitia

Although the post-Conquest history of the Pacific coast of Nicaragua began early in the 16th century, that of the Caribbean coast began much later. Throughout the 16th century, the Spaniards were not even close to having a presence on the Caribbean coast, and the first Spanish governor appointed to the area, Diego de Gutiérrez, was eaten by the Miskito Indians in a big barbecue in 1545. By 1610 the Indians had run the Spaniards out of their easternmost town, Nueva Segovia, and forced them to rebuild it 90 km west, at present-day Ciudad Antigua. After that, the Spaniards kept a healthy distance and remained inland.

The first successful European interaction with the coastal communities was when the British set up a colony on the Caribbean island of Providencia (today occupied by Colombia) to begin trading with the Miskito Indians. After some conflicts with Spaniards on Caribbean islands, the British created the hoax of the Miskito Kingdom, complete with a 'Miskito King', to guard their own interests in the mid-1600s. Their interests, along what is now the whole of the east coast of Nicaragua, were a military alliance with the natives, safe harbours for ship repair and resupply, and a profitable trade with the natives, for turtle shells, dye woods, sarsaparilla and vanilla extract.

The headquarters of operations for the British interests was Bluefields. As a result, whenever Great Britain and Spain were at war, Bluefields was used as base for attacks on Nicaragua. The War of Spanish Succession (1700-1713), The War of Jenkins' Ear (1739-1748), The Seven Years' War (1756-1763) and the War Between Great Britain, France, and Spain (1778-1783); all brought British incursions to Spanish Nicaragua from the Caribbean coast. Finally, the Treaty of Paris of 1783 settled the matter for the time being, with Great Britain agreeing to remove all colonists from the Caribbean shore, with the exception of Belize. By 1787 this process was complete.

With the collapse of the Spanish Empire in 1821, helped along by British foreign policy, the British sought to take control of the Miskito coast again. They simply revived the Miskito Kingdom, which demanded British protection as soon as it was resuscitated. In 1850 the United States and Great Britain agreed to divide up control and influence of the Miskito coast, with neither party having complete control of the area. With the Treaty of Managua of 1860, the British agreed to give up all interests in the Miskito coast, but they never got around to actually pulling out. Only when Nicaraguan President José Santos Zelaya sent General Cabezas to take control of the Miskito coast by military force in 1894, did the British control over the Caribbean coast of Nicaragua finally come to an end.

El Rama

There is not much to see in El Rama, a godforsaken transport hub for overland traffic heading between Nicaragua's interior and the central Caribbean coast. The village was an ancient trading centre of Rama Indians and has been settled by Europeans since at least 1747, but there is no surviving evidence of this. El Rama's greatest asset is also its worst: water. The Río Siquia, Río Mico and Río Rama converge on the little port, and the Río Escondido that drains into the Bay of Bluefields. In the last 20 years the village has been erased from the map three times by hurricanes – the worst of which left El Rama beneath 15 m of water. The level was so high that Army rescue boats tangled their propellers on power cables.

Once upon a time, El Rama was literally the end of the road. Apart from a marginal dirt road that allows passage from Managua to Bilwi for a brief part of the dry season, the only reliable way to get to the central and northern Caribbean coast without boarding an aeroplane was via land to El Rama, then by boat to Bluefields. But all that has changed with a new road that connects El Rama to Pearl Lagoon. At present, only a single daily bus plies this modest byway at 1600, the journey time is three hours (you may find trucks that leave sooner). From Pearl Lagoon you can easily catch a panga south along the coast to Bluefields, but not until the next day. This route is longer, but it is far more scenic and interesting, affording the chance to experience the Caribbean warmth and hospitality that is so characteristic of the region's rural stretches. The regular route to Bluefields (from Managua via El Rama) is now a 12- to 13-hour trip with improvements to the highway; the bus from Managua to El Rama takes nine to 10 hours (express bus seven hours), the boat from El Rama to Bluefields takes two hours, as long as you arrive early enough to find a seat. If necessary there is accommodation in El Rama, but most will want to be on their way quickly. See Transport section for boat and bus schedules.

Sleeping

Bluefields *p277, map p277*
Many hotels in Bluefields are quite basic and grim. Check rooms before accepting.
A Hotel Oasis, 150 m from Bluefields Bay, T572-2812, www.oasishotelcasino.net. The best hotel in town with spacious modern rooms, comfortable furnishings and professional service. There's a casino downstairs with a handful of gaming tables, should you fancy a low-key punt. Breakfast included.
C Bluefields Bay Hotel, Barrio Pointeen, T572-2143, www.geocities.com/bluefieldsbay/hotel. Owned by the region's university, this hotel has clean, simple rooms with private bath and hot water. The rooms upstairs are better and less damp. Excursions are offered to surrounding areas.
D Caribbean Dreams, Barrio Punta Fría, opposite market, T572-1943. 27 rooms with private bath, a/c or fan, and cable TV. Services including restaurant with home cooking and à la carte menu, Wi-Fi and laundry. Clean and often booked, call ahead. Owners helpful.
D Mini Hotel Central, Barrio Punta Fría, T572-2362. 9 simple rooms with private bath, a/c, TV. Cheaper with fan (**E**).
D South Atlantic II, Barrio Central, next to petrol station Levy, T572-2265. Clean rooms with reasonable mattresses, private bath, cable TV and a/c. The double rooms (**B**) are much larger and more comfortable. There's a sports bar and restaurant upstairs serving Caribbean dishes. Friendly.
E El Aeropuerto, airport, ½ c norte, T572-2862. 13 rooms with private bath, a/c, some with fan, also has restaurant and disco. Grouchy owner but clean.
E Los Pipitos, Barrio Central, 50 m from Caribbean Dreams (above). 4 rooms with private bath and a/c, cheaper with fan (**F**), simple but good; bakery on premises.
E Marda Maus, pier, 50 m abajo, T572-2429. Rooms are simple, smallish and clean. Not bad for a budget choice, but view the room before accepting it.
F El Dorado, Barrio Punta Fría, T572-2365. Small, grotty rooms, but most have cable TV and private bath. Sketchy atmosphere, but the price is right.
F Hotel Costa Sur, Barrio Central, across from Lotería, T572-2452. Lots of rooms, all with shared bath and fans. Bar and restaurant attached.
F Hotel Kaora View, Entrada a Las Carmelitas, ½ c norte, Barrio Teodoro Martínez, T572-0488. 10 rooms with 1 shared bath, new, very clean, friendly, good service.
G Hospedaje Pearl Lagoon, Barrio Central, across from UNAG, T572-2411. Not very helpful. 9 basic and not terribly pleasant rooms, most with shared bath.

Rama Cay *p282*
G Las Cabinas, T517-0021. Has a/c and garage parking.
G El Viajero. Shared bath, 1 good report.

For an explanation of the sleeping and eating price codes used in this guide, see inside the front cover. Other relevant information is found in Essentials, see pages 23-27.

G Amy, mercado, 1 c abajo, T517-0034. Not too clean, but quiet, shared bath and food prepared.

El Bluff *p280*

F El Bluff. Rooms with bath and fan. Limited water, friendly place with restaurant.

Pearl Lagoon *p280*

D Hotelito Casa Blanca, in May 4 sector, T572-0508, casa_blanca_lp@yahoo.com. The best hotel in town, with clean, light, comfortable rooms; all but 1 have shared bath. The owners are very hospitable and friendly, and offer fishing expeditions, trips to the keys and community tours. They're happy to answer questions by email, and prefer reservations in advance. Good restaurant attached. Recommended.

E Sweet Pearly, from dock, 1c sur, T572-0512. A real locals' hotel, with average, a/c rooms (cheaper with fan, **F**) and an excellent restaurant (**ΨΨ-Ψ**). Sometimes noisy from the church and bar downstairs. A good budget choice, but don't expect too much.

E Las Estrellas, near Enitel tower, T572-0523, rondownleiva@hotmail.com. 12 rooms with shared bath and fan. Basic and friendly.

F Green Lodge, next to Enitel, from dock, 1 c sur, T572-0507. This basic, homely and friendly hotel has 8 tiny, narrow rooms with shared bath. The owner, Wesley, is very knowledgeable about the area, has good contacts and can help arrange tours. They cook cheap grub too.

Eating

Bluefields *p277, map p277*

ΨΨΨ-ΨΨ Chez Marcel, alcaldía, 1 c sur, ½ c abajo, T572-2347. The best place in town, serving *filete mignon*, shrimp in garlic butter and grilled lobster. Often recommended.

ΨΨ Bella Vista, Barrio Punta Fría, T572-2385. Daily 1000-2300. On the water's edge, overlooking the tired old boats and bay, this seafood restaurant serves shrimp, lobster, meat and *comida economica*.

ΨΨ El Flotante, Barrio Punta Fría, T572-2988. Daily 1000-2200. Built over the water at the end of the main street with a great view of the fishing boats and islets. They serve good shrimp and lobster, but service is slow. Dancing at weekends.

ΨΨ Salmar, alcaldía, 1 c sur, ½ c abajo, T572-2128. Daily 1600-2400. This restaurant with a tasteful interior is often recommended as a quality dining establishment. Serves seafood and meat including chicken in wine sauce.

ΨΨ-Ψ La Loma, Barrio San Pedro, opposite University BICU, T572-2875. Open air ranch with a great view from the top of a hill.

ΨΨ-Ψ Tex Mex house, alcaldía, 1 c sur, ½ c abajo. Tex-Mex restaurant above Salmar serving fajitas, tacos, mixed plates, marguerítas, and of course, tequila.

ΨΨ-Ψ Twins, alcaldía, 2 c al mar, 2½ c sur. This seafood restaurant above the 'lobster pot' is one of the better ones.

Ψ Cafetín Central, opposite Bancentro, inside Mini Hotel. Centrally located café serving reliable and cheap fare including breakfasts and chicken dishes.

Ψ Luna Ranch, Santa Matilde opposite URACAN. Fast food and full plates in this interesting cultural centre.

Ψ Pizza Martinuzi, alcaldía, 1 c sur, ½ c abajo. Very reasonable pizza, chicken and burgers.

Bars and clubs

Bluefields *p277, map p277*

Some of the bars are quite shady, but the ones below are safe for gringos.

Cima Club, Banpro, 1 c abajo. It's hard to miss this centrally located dance hall with 2 floors and a large sign. Popular and often recommended by locals.

Garibaldi, alcaldía, 2 c sur, 1 c al mar. Rum, beer and reggae at this darkened joint for dancing and drinking.

Four Brothers, Cotton tree, from alcaldía, 1 c al mar, 4½ c sur. The best reggae spot in Nicaragua, a big ranch full of great dancing. Usually open Tue-Sun, ask around to see what kind of music is playing. Admission US$1.

Transport

Bluefields *p277, map p277*

Air

The airport is 3 km south of the city centre, either walk (30 mins) or take a taxi US$2. **La Costeña** office, T572-2500; also on Managua and the Corn Islands route with similar times and costs is **Atlantic Airlines**, T572-1299.

La Costeña To **Managua**, daily 0710, 0840, 1120, 1610, US$128 return, 1 hr. To

Corn Islands, daily 0740, 1510, US$98 return, 20 mins. To **Bilwi**, daily except Sun 1210, US$148 return, 1 hr.

Boat

Motorboats (*pangas*) depart when full. The early ones are more reliable, and services on Sun are restricted. To **Pearl Lagoon**, from 0830, several daily, US$6, 1½ hrs, continues to **Tasbapauni**, US$12, 2½ hrs. To **El Rama**, 0530-1600, several daily, US$10, 2 hrs. To **Kukra Hill**, from 0830, several daily, US$6, 1 hr. To **Corn Islands**, 0900, every Wed, US$12, 5-6 hrs.

El Rama *p282*

To **Bluefields**, pangas depart when full, several daily, 0530-1600, US$10, 2 hrs. The ferry is slightly cheaper and much slower. It departs Mon, Wed and Fri in the early morning (around 0800 when the bus has arrived), US$8, 8 hrs.

But to **Managua**, every hr, 0300-1100, 1900, 2200, 2300, US$8, 9 hrs. Express bus to **Managua** (recommended) leaves once a day at 0800, US$9.50, 7 hrs. To **Juigalpa**, every hr, 0800-1500, US$6.50, 6 hrs. To **Pearl Lagoon**, 1600, US$7.50, 3 hrs.

Pearl Lagoon *p280*

To **Bluefields**, boat schedules are irregular with boats leaving when full. The first of the day, 0630, US$6, 1½ hrs, is the only one guaranteed, although one usually leaves soon after. Get to the dock at 0600 to get your name on the passenger list. Services are restricted on Sun when it may be quicker to go via Kukra Hill. Bus to **El Rama**, 0600, US$7.50, 3 hrs.

Directory

Bluefields *p277, map p277*

Banks At the moment none of them will change TCs. If desperate try **BanPro** in Barrio Central opposite the Moravian church, T822-2261. As with the Corn Islands and the entire coast, carrying cash is essential. **Fire** T822-2298. **Hospital** T822-2391. **Internet** Several places in town, try a block south of the alcaldía, or along the main road towards the sea. **Police** T822-2448. **Post office** Correos de Nicaragua, Lotería Nacional, 1 c abajo, T822-1784. **Red Cross** T822-2582. **Telephone** Enitel, alcaldía 1 c al mar, T822-2222.

Bilwi (Puerto Cabezas)

→ *Population 50,941. Altitude 10 m.*

Bilwi, or Puerto Cabezas as it has been known for the last century, has now legally changed back to its original name. It is the capital of the RAAN, the North Atlantic Autonomous Region, and it has a distinctly different atmosphere from Bluefields. It is principally a large Miskito village, and although Waspam on the Río Coco is the heart and soul of the Miskito world, it is here that the Miskito political party Yatama became the first indigenous party to have control of a provincial capital in the country's modern history. The town offers an excellent introduction to the Miskito part of the country. There are also significant minorities of Hispanics (referred to as españoles or Spanish) and Afro-Caribbeans (referred to as ingleses or English) here but Spanish is mainly a second language (although most who live in Bilwi speak it well). Outside the town many do not as the municipality is 80% indigenous. ▸▸ *For Sleeping, Eating and all other listings, see pages 291-292.*

Ins and outs

Getting there and around There are two flights daily from Managua's domestic terminal with both **La Costeña** and **Atlantic Airlines** and once a day except Sundays from Bluefields. There is a very bad and not particularly safe road from Siuna that connects to Managua and can be used during the height of the dry season. It is a 560-km drive through some of the most solitary places in Central America (allow at least two days). Bilwi is small and easy to walk round but take a taxi at night. There are seasonal roads around Bilwi, but most visits to surrounding attractions are made by boat. ▸▸ *For futher details, see Transport, page 292.*

 Best time to visit Rain is common year-round, but January to April are driest months and the best time to visit.

Tourist information INTUR ⓘ *corner opposite Carnicería Río Blanco, Barrio Pedro Joaquín Chamorro, puertocabezas@intur.gob.ni*, has limited information on the region. Tourism is generally underdeveloped out here, although some of the locals are working to change that. Hotel owners can be helpful with suggestions, also try **La Asociación de Mujeres Indígenas de la Costa Atlántica (AMICA)** ⓘ *Barrio La Libertad, T792-2219, asociacionamica@ yahoo.es*, whose goal is to promote community tourism and protect the environment. They have extensive contacts with rural communities (see box, page 287).

Background

The name Bilwi is of Mayagna Indian origin. The Mayagna people have traditionally occupied the Río Grande in Matagalpa and northwards but they were forced east by the advances of Hispanic Nicaragua and this brought them into conflict with the Miskitos, who used their alliance with the British in the 17th and 18th centuries to dominate most of the Mayagna land and nearly all of the Rama Indians' territory. The Mayagna, Rama and Miskito are believed to have migrated from South America around 3000 BC. While the Raman language branched off around 2000 years ago, the Miskitos and Mayagna were heavily influenced by Afro-Caribbean migration and intermarriage. The Mayagna and Miskito share some 50% of words and both claim to have originated from the shores of the Río Patuka near its confluence with Río Wampú. It is likely that before the migrations from central Mexico around AD 750, all of Nicaragua, including the Pacific slope, was occupied by variations of these groups.

The first European contact with the region was by Christopher Columbus, who arrived in the midst of a horrible storm and found refuge in the bay at the mouth of the Río Coco. He named it Cabo Gracias a Dios (Cape Thank God) for the protection it afforded his boats from the raging sea (see box). In the early 1600s, the British started trading with people on the coast and eventually made allies out of the Miskitos. Various shipwrecks, from pirates to slave ships, brought new influences to the area, but Bilwi itself is not thought to have been founded until the mid-19th century when Moravian missionaries were landed on the northern coast. More foreign interest arrived in the late 19th and early 20th century in the form of logging and banana-growing

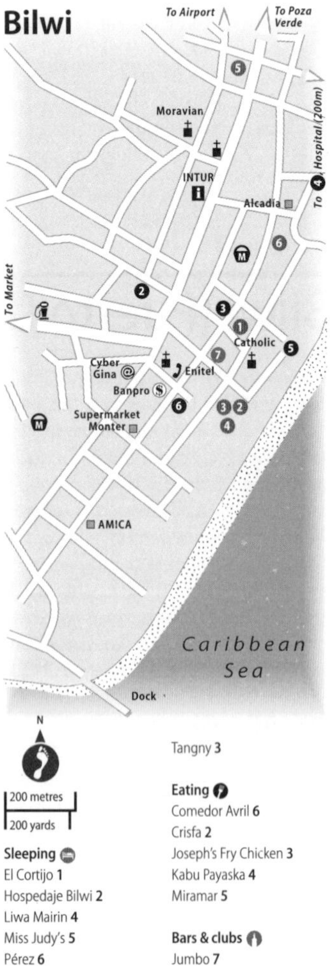

Community tourism around Bilwi

The Miskito communities around Bilwi offer some of the most interesting and adventurous community tourism possibilities in the country. Many of these fishing villages are politically autonomous and have ancient roots in Nicaragua's indigenous past. If you're lucky, you might witness traditional dances, learn about native medicine and discarnate spirits, or hear fading legends of the Miskito nation. Many of these lesser visited communities can only be reached by riverboat, making them the preserve of only the more intrepid travellers. After you've explored the local culture, you can strike out into a wilderness of rainforests and rivers.

Located 18 km south of Bilwi pier on the shores of a large lagoon, the 2000-strong community of **Karatá** is equipped with cabañas and offers fishing, hiking, birdwatching and cultural tours. Nearby, the sandy beach at **Wawa Bar** overlooks the Caribbean. **Haulover** was founded by German missionaries in the 19th century and also has a sand bar, cabañas and large population of migratory birds. West of the village, **Laguna de Huouhnta** backs onto the nature reserves of **Laguna Kukulaya** and **Laguna Layasiska**, easily explored by boat and connected to the outside world by dirt roads. **Tuapi** is a small community of 98 families, just 8 km south of Bilwi and easily reached as a day trip. Consider this if you want a taste of village life but don't have the time, resources or inclination to venture far. **Krukira** is gateway to **Pahara** wildlife reserve, a large lagoon with abundant wildlife. There's little infrastructure out there – this is for adventure tourists who want to get back to nature.

Off the mainland, several wonderfully isolated cays have powder white sand beaches, including **Miskito**, **Wilpin** and **Mahara cays**. Take care though, this is the haunt of drug runners, so check the security situation before heading out and always use a guide.

The **Asociación de Mujeres Indígenas de la Costa Atlántica (AMICA)** ⓘ *Barrio La Libertad, Bilwi, T792-2219, asociacionamica@yahoo.es*, are the people to contact when planning a trip to the communities around Bilwi. It is not advised that you turn up unannounced with a backpack unless you know what you're doing. AMICA offer easy all-inclusive packages which are reasonable for groups of 10, but quite expensive for solo travellers or couples. In such cases you might be better off hitching a ride, organizing your own transport or making enquiries at the pier to see if any public boats are scheduled. AMICA can still help you find guides and lodgings and brief you on what to expect in the community, so don't leave without speaking to them.

operations. After the Caribbean was formally integrated into the rest of Nicaragua in the late 19th century, the name was changed from Bilwi to Puerto Cabezas in honour of the Nicaraguan general who was given the task of integration. The 'Bay of Pigs' invasion of Cuba was launched from here in 1961 and during the Contra war the village grew from 5000 to more than 30,000 residents due to fighting in the region and harshly enforced Sandanista relocation programmes along the Río Coco. The port was important during the Sandinista period for the unloading of Cuban and Soviet military aid. The original name of Bilwi is now legally restored, as a statement of indigenous recognition, and also a sign of frustration with the central government that is seen as selling off resources without any benefit for the local population.

On 4 September 2007, Bilwi was struck by Hurricane Felix, a massive category 5 storm with 260 kph winds. Over 130 people were killed, including 25 Miskito fishermen whose boat was swept away in the chaos. Many thousands more were stranded and displaced by the violent hurricane, which destroyed 9000 houses and caused significant flooding throughout the region.

Sights

The town itself will not win any beauty contests, but does have an end-of-the-earth feel and a 730-m pier that stretches into the Caribbean Sea. The main reasons to visit are to experience Nicaragua's only indigenous-run provincial capital and to meet its friendly population. Bilwi has two main roads which run parallel to each other and to the sea. The airport is at the northern end of the town; the port at the southern end, and a walk along the **pier** at sunset is highly recommended. The main **market** occupies the centre of town and there is a **beach** on the outskirts, but it is dirty. **Poza Verde**, several kilometres to the north, is a good, clean beach with white sand and calm water, although there can be sandflies. Take the road out of town for about 15 minutes and turn right onto the track marked 'SW Tuapi' (SW stands for switch); follow it for a few kilometres to the sea. You can also walk 6 km along the beach from Bilwi, or take a taxi (US$30).

Around RAAN » *pp291-292.*

Waspam and the Río Coco (Wangki)

This is the heart and soul of Miskito country and though some Spanish is spoken in Waspam, only Miskito is spoken in the surrounding villages. For the Miskitos, Waspam is considered the capital of the Río Coco: a trading centre for the 116 communities that line the great waterway. Most travel is by motorized canoes dug out of a single tree (*cayucos*). In the dry season they are punted using long poles. The residents of Waspam and many other communities along the river were seen as allies to the Contra rebels in the 1980s (as many of them were) and evacuated by force as their crops and homes were burned to the ground by government troops. They were allowed to return, but were once again hard hit during Hurricane Mitch in 1998, when the Río Coco's 780 km of water rose to more than 10 m above normal.

The source of the Río Coco is in the mountains near Somoto in northwestern Nicaragua. The river passes through Nueva Segovia before heading north to the border with Honduras and then all the way out to the coastal Laguna de Bismuna (about 80 km downriver from Waspam) and finally out to Caribbean. The river marks the border between Nicaragua and Honduras, but for the Miskitos and Mayagna who live there the divide is hypothetical. Sadly, much of the river's banks have been deforested as a result of logging and agriculture, and by the brutal currents of Hurricanes Mitch and Felix. The riverbanks and tributaries suffer from a major erosion problem and, during the dry season, the Río Coco now has islands of sandbars, making navigation and communication between communities more difficult.

There is a good place to stay in Waspam, though water supply is reported to be unreliable. The road from Bilwi to Waspam is only open during the dry season. It is a 130-km trip that takes at least three hours by 4WD and several hours longer by public bus (see page 292). The bus can be boarded at several points along the road leading out of town. This trip will take you through the pine forests and red plains north of Bilwi towards the Río Coco (also the border with Honduras), and you will pass through two Miskito villages, **Sisin** and **Santa Marta**. Hitching is possible; if you cannot get all

RAAN stands for the Northern Atlantic Autonomous Region. RAAS is the Southern Atlantic Autonomous Region.

Barely afloat: the fourth and final voyage of Columbus

The final voyage of Christopher Columbus was that of a former hero, a once-respected navigator desperate to regain former glory. Colombus had fallen out of favour with the Spanish Crown and found little support while trying to organize what would be his fourth and last exploratory journey. To get him out of the way, the Crown gave him a small fleet of half-rotten boats that could barely float, in the hope that this would dispose of the navigator once and for all. Most thought his boats would not make it past the coast of Africa. Miraculously, however, he managed to cross the Atlantic and reach the eastern coast of Central America in 1502, where he searched for a water passage between the two great oceans.

Columbus sailed the entire isthmus coast including the Caribbean seaboard of Nicaragua and the Corn Islands. Caught in a violent storm, he found refuge at the mouth of the Río Coco and dubbed it *Cabo Gracias a Dios* (Cape Thank God). Somehow the great navigator managed to make it as far as Jamaica, where his disgruntled crew finally abandoned him and his tired ships.

On 7 July 1503, while trying to find a dugout canoe large enough to take him from Jamaica to Santo Domingo, Colombus wrote to the Spanish Crown. The letter shows that the great navigator was barely literate, he heard voices of saints and was unable to state with any clarity what had occurred on the voyage. According to a letter from Diego de Porras, a Columbus crew member and mutineer, most of the crew thought Columbus was crazy and they feared that he would kill them with his dangerous ideas.

Columbus was stranded on Jamaica for a year. He finally found his way back to Spain in 1504 and died two years later.

the way to Waspam, make sure you are left at Sisin, Santa Marta or La Tranquera. You can accepts lifts from the military; never travel at night.

Las Minas mining triangle (Siuna–Rosita–Bonanza)

These three towns are known for their gold and silver mines which are dominated by Canadian mining companies whose employees, along with Evangelist missionaries and US Peace Corps, make up the majority of the foreign population. There is great tourism potential here, but security has always been a big issue. Many locals returned after the war years to face 80% unemployment and subsequently turned to criminal activities. Drug-running, kidnapping and highway robbery were widespread until recently, with most of this lawlessness perpetrated by the Andrés Casto United Front (FUAC), whose mission was to divert funds and attention into the area. This organisation of disenchanted ex-soldiers and mercenaries was effectively broken up by the government in 2001. Still, everyone in this region seems to carry a gun, and land mines may be lurking in the wilderness, despite government assertions to the contrary. Ultimately, any pleasure visits here have to be weighed against potential risks. Tourism is certainly increasing and, despite heavy logging (much of it illegal) and cattle ranching, the area still holds plenty of natural and cultural interest, including more than 50 female medicinal healers, an abundance of pristine forests, wildlife, indigenous communities, and old gold mines. With increased security and environmental protection, this area could be one of the great future areas for travel in Nicaragua. At the moment, however, it is strictly the territory of adventure travel, due to safety concerns and a lack of infrastructure.

Background information is available at www.marena.gob.ni.

The Mesoamerican Biological Corridor

The vast mountains and ancient forests of the Bosawás Biosphere reserve have a beauty and grandeur reminiscent of prehistoric times. This great wilderness is Central America's most vital national park and a major a component in the Mesoamerican Biological Corridor – an exciting conservation project that hopes to link North and South America by a single tract of protected forest.

Central America has always been a bridge between the worlds. About 3 million years ago, geological activity fused the previously disconnected continents of North and South America into a single land mass, initiating a period of intense natural transformation known as 'The Great American Faunal Interchange'. During this time, previously isolated plant and animal species interacted in new and interesting ways, migrated north and south, settled into niches, and evolved together into complex ecosystems. For this reason, Central America is today one of the earth's most biologically diverse places.

The Mesoamerican Biological Corridor is an attempt to protect this biodiversity by preserving Central America's special status as an ancient land bridge. From southern Mexico to Panama, a series of new protected areas are gradually consolidating existing national parks, wildlife refuges and private reserves into a single corridor. Deforested zones are quickly becoming replenished with trees and plantlife, thanks to the rich volcanic soils that permeate the isthmus. This encourages wildlife to move into new areas, combating the problems associated with biological isolation like environmental stresses, inbreeding, loss of fertility and social pressures.

The Mesoamerican Biological Corridor was officially established at a 1997 summit meeting where the Central American countries signed up to its terms and vision. Costa Rica has worked the hardest to realize the project, employing a range of tactics like working closely with NGOs, teaching environmental awareness, offering tax incentives for green enterprises and encouraging eco-tourism. Results elsewhere have been mixed, with the usual difficulties associated with conservation like illegal logging, population displacement and unsympathetic tourist developments. However, the overall impact has been positive, and the political importance of this transnational project should not be underestimated. That eight developing countries can come together and work for the greater benefit of the environment is an admirable and inspirational achievement that the rest of the world should heed.

It is possible to go to the Bosawás Reserve without travelling through the mining triangle, but **Siuna** offers the easiest access to the reserve and local guides are available here. It is the largest of the three towns; the population is predominately mestizo but there is a Creole minority. The surrounding rural areas around **Bonanza** (170 km from Bilwi and reached by seasonal road or plane, see page 292) have a significant Mayagna population, including Musuwas – the capital of the Mayagna world. The alcaldía can help arrange visits to old gold mines, processing plants and panning streams. There's also a lot of jewelry for sale here. **Rosita** used to be entirely owned by the Rosario Mining Company, but the mines were nationalized in 1979 by the Sandinista government, who moved all the mining operations to Siuna and forcibly evacuated the local inhabitants. Today, the **Foundation for Unity and Reconstruction of the Atlantic Coast (FURCA)** ① *T794-1045*, *furca@sdnnic.org.ni*, can arrange tours of the indigenous communities in the area.

Reserva de Biosfera Bosawás

This is the largest forest reserve in Central America. The area is not only the most important swathe of rainforest on the isthmus, but also the most important cloud forest, with numerous isolated mountains and rivers. In addition to all the species mentioned in the Indio-Maíz Reserve (see page 182), the reserve also has altitude-specific wildlife and vegetation. There are seven mountains above 1200 m, the highest of which is Cerro Saslaya at 1650 m. The principal rivers that cross the reserve and feed into the Río Coco are: Río Bocay, Wina, Amaka Río Lakus and Río Waspuk.

Visiting the reserve is still a challenge. The easiest and most organized way to visit is via Siuna (see above), but there are safety concerns and a longer route may be necessary. Ecotourism projects are planned but are a long way off, due to the remoteness of the reserve and the instability of the region. However there is at least one good project, the **Proyecto Ecoturístico Rosa Grande,** supported by Nature Conservancy and the Peace Corps.

The community of **Rosa Grande,** 25 km from Siuna, is near an area of virgin forest with a trail, waterfall on the Río Labú and lots of wildlife including monkeys and big cats. One path leads to a lookout with a view over Cerro Saslaya; a circular path to the northwest goes to the Rancho Alegre falls. Guides can be hired for US$7 a day plus food. Excursions for two or more days cost as little as US$13 per person for a guide, food and camping equipment. You may have to pay for a camp guard while hiking. Clarify what is included in the price and be aware of extras that may be added to the bill. Be certain you have enough supplies for your stay. For information contact Don Trinidad at the *comedor* on arrival in Santa Rosa. In Siuna you can contact the office of the **Proyecto Bosawás** ⓘ *200 m east of the airstrip, Mon-Fri 0800-1700. Groups of 5 or more must reserve in advance, contact is via Amigos de Saslaya, c/o Proyecto Bosawás, Siuna, RAAN, by post or telegram. Large groups are not encouraged.*

There is an alternative way to experience the wilderness of Bosawás without exposing yourself to the risks of the Siuna area mining towns and highwaymen. With a great deal of time, patience and a bit of luck, you can see the great forest of Bosawás and explore a large part of the Río Coco in the process. Access is via **Jinotega** in central Nicaragua (see page 243).

Sleeping

Bilwi *p285, map p286*

C Liwa Mairin, Enitel, 2 c este, 20 vrs norte, T792-2315. The best in town. This new hotel has great big, airy double rooms with lots of light, balconies, sea views, a/c, cable TV and tasteful, comfortable furnishings. Good value and recommended.

D El Cortijo, Barrio Revolución, T792-2340. Big Caribbean house with largish rooms, big TVs, acceptable mattresses and a/c. Some rooms have hot water. There's also internet, laundry, parking. Visa accepted.

D Miss Judy's, next to Centro de Computación Ansell, T792-2225. Also known as Casa Museo, this lovely house has lots of interesting art and artefacts in the attached museum and gallery. Rooms have private bath, cheaper with fan (**E**). Friendly and interesting, with lots of family history. Recommended.

E Hotel Pérez, Calle Central, T792-2362. Friendly, family house with a range of rooms. Some have private bath, some have a/c, some have fan. Some are sweaty, smelly and unpleasant; ask to see before accepting. Meals are available in the little *comedor* downstairs.

E Hospedaje Bilwi, in front of pier. Tucked away from the paved road, this large, basic hotel has 19 rooms, some with fan, some with a/c. Good view of the dock from the back balcony. There's a seafood restaurant downstairs.

F Hotel Tangny, Enitel, 2 c este. Reliable old cheapie with 15 rooms, some have private bath. Family run.

Waspam *p288*

E La Casa de la Rose, roseck@ibw.com.ni. This comfortable wooden hotel has rooms with private bath, hammocks and screened

windows. Home-cooked meals are available, as well as on-site internet access.
F Las Cabañas. Wooden cabins with bath, mosquito netting, fan. Water supply is reported to be unreliable.

Reserva de Biosfera Bosawás *p291*
G BOSAWAS field station, on the Río Labú. Very limited hammocks, clean but simple, locally produced food for US$1.25.

Eating

Bilwi *p285, map p286*
In addition to those below, there are numerous *comedores* in the **San Jerónimo Market**.
₸₸-₸ Crisfa, Enitel, 2½ c norte, 1 c oeste. Tasty *comida típica*, meat and chicken dishes. Not bad, one of the better ones.
₸₸-₸ Kabu Payaska, hospital, 200 vrs al mar. Often recommended by the locals, this restaurant overlooking the water serves some of the best seafood and *comida típica* in town.
₸₸-₸ Miramar, Enitel, 3 c norte, 2 c al mar. At the end of a road leading to the sea, this seafood restaurant overlooks the waves and has a disco at weekends.
₸ Comedor Avril, opposite Banpro. Cheap home-cooked fare, *comida típica* and breakfasts.
₸ Josephy's Fry Chicken, Enitel, 2½ c norte. The place for fried chicken, burgers and beer. Centrally located and reliably greasy.

Reserva de Biosfera Bosawás *p291*
₸ Comedor Melania, Rosa Grande. A meal costs about US$1.

Bars and clubs

Bilwi *p285, map p286*
Jumbo, across from Dragon Chino. The most popular place to dance at weekends.

Transport

Bilwi *p285, map p286*
Air
The airstrip is 3 km north of town. From the airport, taxis charge US$2 to anywhere in Bilwi. To **Bluefields**, **La Costeña**, Mon-Sat, 1110, US$60 1-way, US$110 round-trip. To **Managua**, **La Costeña**, daily 0820, 1220, Mon-Sat 1610, US$96 1-way, US$148 round-trip; **Atlantic Airlines**, daily 1210, US$96 1-way, US$148 round trip. To **Minas**, **La Costeña**, Mon, Wed, Fri, 1315.

Note: Bring your passport as there are immigration checks by the police in Bilwi and sometimes in the waiting lounge in Managua. All bags are x-rayed coming into the domestic terminal from any destination.

Boat
To **Corn Islands**, once a month, night departure, US$30, 3 days. It is recommended that you do not hire a boat with fewer than 2 people.

Indepedent travel to the **Cayos Miskitos** is not recommended due to problems with drug runners from Colombia using the islands as a refuge. Contact an agency like AMICA to arrange a guided visit.

A good boat trip is to **Laguna Bismuna** on the northern coast, reportedly one of the most beautiful in Nicaragua, though easiest access is via Waspam.

Bus
Express bus to **Managua**, Thu and Sat, 0800, US$15 from Enitel, 20 hrs. There are also buses to **Rosita** and **Siuna** that connect to buses to Managua. To **Waspam**, 0700, Mon-Sat, returns from Waspam 1200, US$5.

Las Minas mining triangle *p289*
Bonanza is 170 km from Bilwi, and reached by seasonal road. There is also an air service to **Bilwi** and **Managua**, Mon-Sat at 1030.

Bosawás Biosphere Reserve *p291*
Bus Daily from Siuna market at 0500 and 0730, sometimes another at 1100, US$2.25.

Directory

Bilwi *p285, map p286*
Bank Next to Enitel, **BanPro** has cashed TCs in the past, but do not rely on TCs. Bring as much cash as necessary. **Fire** T792-2255. **Hospital** Nuevo Amanecer, T792-2259. **Post office and telephone** Just south of the park, **Enitel** handles mail during the week and telephone service daily, T792-2237. **Red Cross** T792-2719. **Police** T792-2257.

Background

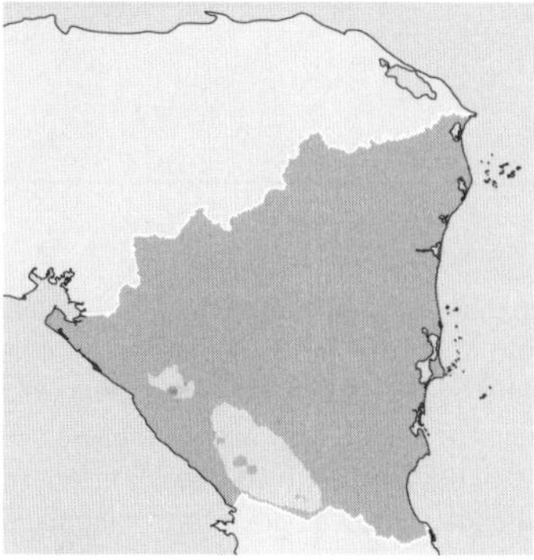

Footprint features

History

Pre-Columbian

Nicaragua was at the crossroads between northern and southern pre-Hispanic cultures for thousands of years. The migration from Asia across the Bering Strait is believed to have reached Nicaragua sometime before 18,000 BC. If migrations did occur from the Polynesian world to South America, as it is now believed, arrivals in South America from the South Pacific might have occurred around 8000 BC. In Museo Las Huellas de Acahualinca in Managua, there are some well-preserved human and animal footprints of what appears to be a family of 10 people leaving the Lake Managua area after a volcanic event in the year 4000 BC. Ceramic evidence of organized settlement in Nicaragua begins around 2500 BC in San Marcos, and by 1500 BC settlements are evident in much of the Pacific area. Nicaragua continued to receive migrations from both north and south until the first arrival of the Spanish explorers in 1523. The best understood culture is that of the **Nicaraguas**, whose final migration to Nicaragua from central Mexico to the shores of Lake Nicaragua occurred just 150-200 years before the arrival of the Spanish. They spoke Náhuat (a rustic version of the Aztec Náhuatl), which became the lingua franca for the indigenous people after the conquest and may have already been widely used for trading in the region before the arrival of the first Europeans.

The Nicaraguas shared the Pacific Basin of Nicaragua with the **Chorotegas** and **Maribios**. The Chorotegas also came from Mexico, though earlier, around AD 800 and were Mangue speakers. The two tribes seemed to have found some common commercial and perhaps religious ground and dominated most of the area west of the lakes. The Maribios, Hokano speakers, and believed to be originally from California and Baja California in Mexico, populated the western slope of what is today the Maribios volcanic range, in northwestern Nicaragua. The Nicaraguas and Chorotegas were a very successful society sitting in the middle of a trade route that stretched from Mexico to Peru.

On the east side of the great lakes of Nicaragua the cultures were of South American origin. The **Chontales** and **Matagalpas** may have used the same language root (Chibcha) as the Caribbean Basin Rama, Mayagna and Miskito (a Mayagna derivative) cultures. In fact it could be that the Mayagna are descendants of the original inhabitants of the Pacific that lost ground to the invading tribes of Chorotegas in the ninth century. The Chontales appear to have been the most developed of the group, though little is known about their culture to date, despite ample and impressive archaeological evidence. Their name means 'barbarian' or 'foreigner' in Náhuatl, and has been applied to many different Mesoamerican groups.

The Conquest

Christopher Columbus sailed the Caribbean shores of Nicaragua in 1502 on his fourth and final voyage and took refuge in the far northern part of today's Nicaragua before sailing to Jamaica. The Spanish explorer Gil González Dávila sailed from Panama to the Gulf of Nicoya and then travelled overland to the western shores of Lake Nicaragua to meet the famous Nicaraguas tribe chief, Niqueragua, in April 1523. After

The only indigenous languages still spoken in Nicaragua are of the Miskito, Mayagna and Rama, with the Rama language now in threat of extinction.

The Conquest of Nicaragua: a business trip

The meeting of the Spanish explorer Gil González and the philosophical Chief Niqueragua is a romantic story filled with fate, adventure and tragedy (see box, page 137). But a brief glimpse at the cold numbers of the original expedition and the conquest that followed paints a very different picture. According to local historian Patrick Werner, Gil González received authorization for the expedition to make Europe's first business trip to the land of Nicaragua. A company was formed with four shareholders: the Spanish Crown 48%, Andrés Niño 28%, Cristóbal de Haro 15% and Gil González with 9% of the shares. The original investment totalled 8000 gold pesos. They even took an accountant with them, Andrés de Cereceda who later reported the returns on the four-month business trip. The bottom line looked a lot better than your average start-up company: 112,524 gold pesos collected on an 8000-peso investment.

Soon after, it was the turn of Pedrarias Dávila to form a new company, especially for Nicaragua. The chief negotiator for this trip, Captain Francisco Hernández de Córdoba, with an army of 229 soldiers, produced spectacular returns on the investment, recovering 158,000 gold pesos while founding the cities of León and Granada. Within one year of the Conquest, the new franchises of León and Granada had collected a further 392,000 gold pesos. It was all the gold the Indians had ever owned; in less than three years, 700-800 years of accumulated gold had been taken.

converting the Nicaragua elite to Christianity, and taking plenty of gold away with him, González Dávila travelled further north before being chased out of the area by a surprise attack of Chorotega warriors led by legendary chieftain, Diriangén. The Spaniards fled to Panama to regroup. In 1524 a stronger army of 229 men was sent and the local populace was overcome by force. The captain of the expedition, Francisco Hernández de Córdoba, founded the cities of Granada and León (Viejo) on the shores of Lake Nicaragua and Lake Managua respectively. A little is known about the actual battles of the conquest, thanks to a lost letter from Córdoba to the country's first governor describing the events. Nueva Segovia was founded as third city in 1543 to try and capitalize on mineral resources in the northern mountains. The famously cruel Pedrarias Dávila (see page 214) was given the first governor's post in Nicaragua, a position he used as a licence to run a personal empire. His rule set the stage for a tradition of *caudillos* (rulers of personality and favouritism, rather than of constitution and law) that would run and ruin Nicaragua, almost without exception, until the 21st century.

Colonial era

By the middle of the 16th century, the Spanish had realized that Nicaragua was not going to produce the same kind of mineral riches as Mexico and Peru. Gold reserves of the indigenous population had been robbed blind in the first three years of occupation and mines in the north did not seem to be as productive as was hoped. What Nicaragua did have was a solid population base and this was exploited to its maximum. There are no accurate figures for slave trade in early to mid-16th century Nicaragua as it was not an approved activity and was made officially illegal by the Spanish Crown in 1542. However, it is estimated that somewhere between 200,000 to

 500,000 Nicaraguans were exported as slaves to work in Panama and Peru or forced to work in the gold mines near Nueva Segovia. The Consejo de Indias (Indian council) and the Casa de Contratación (legal office) in Seville managed affairs in Spain for Nicaragua. These administrative bodies controlled immigration to the Americas, acted as a court for disputes, and provided nominees for local rulers to the Spanish Crown. On a local level the province of Nicaragua belonged to the Reino de Guatemala (Kingdom of Guatemala) and was administered by a Spanish governor in León. While the *conquistadores* were busy pillaging the New World, there were serious discussions in Spain as to the legality of Spanish action in the Americas. Thanks in part to some tough lobbying by the humanist priest, Fray Bartolomé de Las Casas, laws were passed in 1542 to protect the rights of the Indians, outlawing slavery and granting them (in theory) equal rights. Sadly, enforcement of these laws was nearly impossible due to local resistance, communication obstacles and the sheer distance of the colony from Spain. The estimated indigenous population of the Pacific Basin on the arrival of the Spanish was at least 500,000. Within 40 years the total population was no more than 50,000 people, and by 1610 the indigenous residents of the Pacific slope had been reduced to around 12,000. (It wasn't until the 20th century that the population of Nicaragua returned to match pre-Conquest numbers.)

Due to the exhaustion of the Indian population and mineral resources, many of the Spanish left Nicaragua looking for greener pastures. The ones who stayed on became involved in agriculture. Cattle were introduced and they took over cacao production, which was already very big, upon their arrival. Indigo was the other principal crop, along with some trade in wood. The beef, leather and indigo were exported to Guatemala, the cacao to El Salvador. The exports were traded for other goods, such as food and clothing, and the local population lived primarily off locally grown corn and beans. There was also a busy commercial route between Granada and the Caribbean colonial states via the Río San Juan and trade between Nicaragua and Peru. Granada became much wealthier thanks to its advantageous position along the international trade routes (although this made it a target for attacks from Dutch, French and British pirates during the 17th century), but administrative and church authority remained in León, creating a rivalry that would explode after Independence from Spain.

Independence from Spain

After 297 years as a colony of Spain, Nicaragua achieved independence. It was not a hard fought independence, but it was one that would release built-up tensions and rivalries into an open and bloody playing field. What followed was the least stable period in the history of the country: a general anarchy that only an outside invader would stop, by uniting Nicaraguans in a common cause, against a common enemy.

In 1808 Spain was invaded by French troops and Fernando VII King of Spain was held in captivity. Since the American colonies of Spain recognized Fernando as the legitimate ruler of Spain and its colonies (a ruler with zero effective power), the foundation was laid for the collapse of the world's greatest empire. The greatest impulse for the demise of Spanish rule came from a new social class created during the colonial period, known locally as *criollos*, the descendants of Spaniards born in Nicaragua. At the beginning of the 19th century they still only represented 5% of the population, but they were the owners of great agricultural empires, wealthy and increasingly powerful, a class only the Spanish Crown could rival. The *criollos* did not openly oppose the colonial system, but rather chipped away at its control, in search of the power that they knew would be theirs without colonial rule.

They continued to organize and institutionalize power until 5 November 1811 when El Salvador moved to replace all the Spaniards in its local government with *criollos*. One week later, in León, the local population rebelled. The people of León took to the streets demanding the creation of a new government, new judges, and abolition of the government monopoly to produce liquor, lower prices for tobacco and an end to taxes on beef, paper and general sales. All the demands were granted. There were also demonstrations in Masaya, Rivas and Granada.

In September 1821 Mexico declared Independence from Spain. A meeting was called in Guatemala City on 15 September 1821. At the meeting were the representatives of the central government in Spain, Spanish representatives from every country in Central America, the heads of the Catholic Church from each province, the archbishop of Guatemala and the local senators of the provinces. Independence from Spain was declared; yet in Nicaragua the wars had just begun.

León versus Granada

In October 1821 the authorities in León declared that Nicaragua would become part of the Mexican Empire, while the Guatemalan office of Central America created a local Central American government office in Granada, increasing sentiments of separatism in Granada. Regardless, Nicaragua remained more or less part of the federation of Mexico and Central America until 1823 when the United Provinces of Central America met and declared themselves free of Mexican domain and any other foreign power. The five members – Guatemala, El Salvador, Honduras, Nicaragua and Costa Rica – were a federation free to administer their own countries and in November 1824 a new constitution for the Central America Federation was decreed. Nicaraguans, however, were already fighting among themselves.

In April 1824 León and Granada had both proclaimed themselves capital of the country. Other cities chose sides with one or the other, while Managua created a third 'government', proclaiming Managua as Nicaragua's capital. The in-fighting continued until, in 1827, civil war erupted. It was not until Guatemala sent another general that peace was achieved and a new chief of state named in 1834. The civilian head of state was Dr José Núñez, but the military chiefs were not pleased and he was soon thrown out. In 1835 José Zepeda was named head of state but still more violence followed. In 1836 Zepeda was thrown in prison, put against a wall and shot. By this time, the federal government in Guatemala was increasingly helpless and impotent and, as the power vacuum of 300 years of colonial rule wreaked havoc upon the isthmus, the state of anarchy in Nicaragua was common across Central America.

On 30 April 1838 the legislative assembly of Nicaragua, in a rare moment of relevance, declared Nicaragua independent of any other power and the Central American Federation collapsed, with the other states also declaring the Federation to be history. A new constitution was written for Nicaragua, but it was one that would have little effect on the constant power struggle.

In 1853 Granada General Fruto Chamorro took over the post of Director of State, with hope of establishing something that resembled peace. Informed of an armed uprising being planned in León, he ordered the capture of the principal perpetrators, but most escaped to Honduras. In 1854 yet another new constitution was written. This one changed the post of Director of State to 'President' which meant that Conservative General Fruto Chamorro was technically no longer in power. However the assembly, going against the constitution they had just approved, named him as president anyway. The Liberal León generals in Honduras had seen enough and decided to attack. Máximo Jérez led the attack against the Conservatives and Chamorro, the León contingent hiring US mercenary Byron Cole to give them a hand against Granada. He signed a contract and returned to the US where he gave the job to the man every single Nicaraguan (but not a single North American) school child has heard of.

William Walker and the Guerra Nacional

On 13 June 1855, North American William Walker and his 55 hired guns set sail for Nicaragua. The group was armed with the latest in firepower and a very well-planned scheme to create a new slave state in Nicaragua. His idea was for a new colony to be settled by North American Anglos (to own the lands and slaves) and blacks (to do all the work). William Walker planned to conquer and colonize not only Nicaragua, but all of Central America, isolating what remained of Mexico, which had just lost one-third of its territory to the US in the Mexican-American War. Key to the success would be the ready-made inter-oceanic transportation of Cornelius Vanderbilt's steamship service from San Francisco to New York via San Juan del Sur, La Virgen, the Río San Juan and San Juan del Norte.

In September of the same year, Walker and his little battalion landed in San Juan del Sur, confronted Granada's Conservative Party army in La Virgen and won easily. On 13 October 1855 he travelled north, attacked and took Granada with the local generals escaping to Masaya and later signing a peace pact. As per prior agreement, Patricio Rivas of León's Liberal Party was named President of the Republic and Walker as the head of the military. Rivas, following Walker's wishes, confiscated the steamship line of Vanderbilt, which Walker then used to ship in more arms, ammunitions and mercenary soldiers from the US. Soon he had the best-equipped and most modern fighting force in Central America.

On 6 June 1856, Walker appeared in León, demanding that he be allowed to confiscate the properties of the León elite. President Patricio Rivas and his ministers refused and after numerous meetings and no agreements William Walker left León for Granada. The people with power in León had finally realised what they were up against and contacted generals in El Salvador and Guatemala for help. Soon all of Central America would be united against the army of William Walker.

From 22-24 June 1856 farcical elections were held and William Walker was named President of the Republic. On 12 July, Walker officially took office with a pompous parade through Granada, while flying his new flag for the country. A series of decrees were proclaimed during that month, including the legalization of slavery, and the immediate confiscation of all properties of all 'enemies of the state'. English was made the official language of business (to ensure that North American colonists would receive all the land confiscated). Walker's government was recognized by the pre-civil war US government as legitimate. What would follow is known to Nicaraguans as the *Guerra Nacional* (National War) and its victory is celebrated today with decidedly more vigour than the anniversary of Nicaragua's independence from Spain.

The turning point in William Walker's troops' apparent invincibility came at the little ranch north of Tipitapa called San Jacinto. It is a museum today and a mandatory visit for all Nicaraguan primary school children. Walker had never been able to control Matagalpa and a division of the rebel Nicaraguan army was sent south from Matagalpa to try and stop the confiscation of cattle ranches in the area of San Jacinto. The two forces met. The Nicaraguan division used the little house in San Jacinto, with its thick adobe walls, as their fort and it provided great protection. A battle on 5 September was a slight victory for the Nicaraguans, but both sent for reinforcements and on 14 September (the national holiday now celebrated annually), 200 of Walker's troops lost a bloody and difficult battle to 160 Nicaraguan troops. The Nicaraguan battalion included a contingent of 60 *flecheros* – Matagalpa Indians fighting with bow and arrow and legendary marksmanship. The indigenous warriors may have been the key to the victory. The tide had turned and battles in Masaya, Rivas and Granada would prove victorious for the combined Central American forces. William Walker escaped to a steamship from where he watched the final grisly actions of his troops in Granada, who, completely drunk, proceeded to rape and kill the fleeing natives and then burned the city to the ground. Walker's administrators mounted a mock

“” The Guerra Nacional and its victory against William Walker's government is celebrated today with decidedly more vigour than the anniversary of Nicaragua's independence from Spain.

procession in Granada, burying a coffin in Central Park with a sign above it that said, “Here was Granada”.

Walker would later return to Nicaragua, before just escaping with his life. He then tried his luck in Honduras where he was taken prisoner by Captain Salmon of the British navy and handed over to the Honduran authorities. He was tried, put against a wall and shot by the Honduran armed forces on 12 September 1860.

General José Santos Zelaya

For the next 30-plus years, the wealthy families of Granada would control the government (now based in Managua), thanks partly to a law stating that, to have the right to vote, you must have 100 pesos, and in order to be a presidential candidate, over 4000 pesos. But, in 1893, the Conservative president was overthrown by a movement led by Liberal Party General José Santos Zelaya.

General Zelaya did much to modernize Nicaragua. A new constitution was written in 1893 and put into effect the following year. The separation of church and state was instituted, with ideas of equality and liberty for all, respect for private property, civil marriage, divorce, mandatory schooling for all, the death penalty abolished and debtors' prison banned and freedom of expression guaranteed. Construction was rampant, with new roads, docks, postal offices, shipping routes and electricity installed in Managua and Chinandega. A whole raft of new laws were passed to facilitate business, proper police and military codes, and a Supreme Court was created. The Caribbean Coast was finally officially incorporated into the country in 1894. Despite all of this, however, Zelaya did not endear himself to the US. With the canal project close at hand in either Panama or Nicaragua, Zelaya insisted that no single country would be permitted to finance a canal project in Nicaragua and, what's more, only Nicaragua could have sovereignty over a canal inside its country. The project went to Panama. In 1909 as Zelaya was flirting with Japan to build a rival canal, he was pushed out of power with the help of the US Marines.

US Marines – Augusto C Sandino

In 1909 there was an uprising in Bluefields against Zelaya. Led by General Juan Estrada, with the support of the Granada Conservative Party, two American mercenaries were caught and executed during the battles. The US Marines entered in May 1910 to secure power for Estrada who took control of the east coast in what they termed a ‘neutral zone’. General Estrada marched into Managua to install himself as the new president of Nicaragua. Stuck with debts from European creditors, Juan Estrada was forced to borrow from the North American banks. He then gave the US control over collection of duties, as a guarantee for those loans. The Nicaraguan National Bank and a new monetary unit called the *córdoba* were established in 1912.

 The Granada aristocrats were not happy with General Estrada and a new round of fighting between León Liberals and Granada Conservatives erupted.

On 4 August the US Marines entered Managua to secure order and establish their choice, Adolfo Díaz, as president of the country. Two years later, under occupation of the Marines, Nicaragua signed the Chamorro-Bryan Treaty, with Nicaragua conceding perpetual rights of any Nicaraguan canal project to the US, in exchange for US$3 million, which went to pay US banks for outstanding debts. There was no intention to build a canal in Nicaragua; the deal was rather to keep Nicaragua from building a competing one.

In 1917, with Emiliano Chamorro in control of the presidency, more problems followed. Díaz, still fighting to regain the presidency, called for more Marines to be sent from the US. Over 2000 troops arrived and Díaz was put back into the presidency, but nothing could be done to bring together the various factions.

In what were then considered to be fair elections (albeit under occupation) in 1924, moderate Conservative Carlos Solórzano was elected to the presidency with Liberal Party physician Dr Juan Sacasa his VP. In 1925 the Marines withdrew from Nicaragua. Two and a half months later a revolt broke out led by hard-line Conservative Emiliano Chamorro. Solórzano fled with his Liberal VP Sacasa to Honduras. Chamorro purged congress and was declared president in 1926. The Liberals rebelled, but the US Marines returned to prop up the president.

In May 1927, the US State Department agreed a plan with the Nicaraguan authorities to organize a non-political army, disarm both the Liberal and Conservative armies and hold new elections. The new army would be called the *Guardia Nacional* (National Guard). Most parties agreed to the solution, with the exception of General Augusto Sandino, who had been fighting under the command of Liberal General José María Moncada. Sandino returned to the northern mountains determined to fight against the government of Adolfo Díaz, whom he panned as a US puppet president, and the occupation of the Marines, something the nationalist Sandino found unacceptable. Several months after the agreement Sandino attacked a Marine post in Ocotal and the war between Sandino's troops and the US Marines began.

In 1928, José María Moncada won the elections under supervision of the US government. Despite the fact that a Liberal was now president, Sandino refused to lay down his arms as long as Nicaragua was under occupation. Fighting side by side with the Marines, to exterminate Augusto Sandino's rebel army, was the newly created Guardia Nacional. The Marines thought they would defeat General Sandino's rebel forces quickly, in particular because of their vastly superior artillery and advantage of air power. While trying to take out Sandino and his men in Nicaragua's northern mountains, the US practised formation air to ground bomb attacks for the first time. However, the charismatic general had widespread support in the north and was not defeated. He relentlessly attacked US Marine positions with what some say was the first use of modern guerrilla warfare. Finally, with elections approaching in 1933, and with the National Guard under the command of General Anastasio Somoza García, the US announced that the Marines would pull out when the new president took power. Juan Bautista Sacasa was elected, and the day he took power, 1 January 1933, the last regiment of Marines left Nicaragua by boat from Corinto. Twenty-four years of intervention had ended.

The Somoza family

With the US Marines gone, General Augusto Sandino went to the presidential palace (today the Parque Loma de Tiscapa) and signed a peace and disarmament treaty with President Sacasa. The treaty stipulated that the rebel army would gradually turn over their weapons and receive amnesty, with ample job opportunities for ex-rebel fighters. One year later, on 21 February 1934, when Sandino returned to the presidential palace for dinner with President Sacasa, the commander of the Guardia Nacional, Anastasio Somoza García plotted the abduction and death of Sandino, which was carried out while Somoza was enjoying a concert. After Sandino left the dinner party he was stopped at a road block, sent to a rural part of Managua, shot and buried. With the death of Sandino the Liberal Party was divided into two camps, one that supported Somoza and the other President Sacasa. Somoza attacked the fort above León in May 1936 and the Guardia Nacional demanded Sacasa's resignation. A month later Sacasa resigned and new elections were won by Somoza García. Yet again, a leader of Nicaragua's military took state office. The history of the 19th and early 20th century was to be repeated, only now the opposition was no longer able to mount military challenges, thanks to the unity and sweeping efficiency of the Guardia Nacional. Various 'presidents' were elected from 1937-1979, but there was never any doubt who was running the show. Anastasio Somoza García and later his son Anastasio Somoza Debayle maintained effective power as the head of the National Guard.

Nicaragua enjoyed a period of relative stability and economic growth. The relationship between the US and Nicaragua had never been better, with close co-operation, including the use of Nicaragua as a training and launching ground for the Bay of Pigs invasion in Cuba. Somoza used the Guardia Nacional to keep the populace at bay and the technique of *pactos* (political pacts) to keep Conservative political opponents in on some of the Somoza family's ever-increasing riches and power. During the Second World War, Nicaragua entered on the side of the US and Somoza García used the war to confiscate as much property from German nationals as possible (including what is today Montelimar Beach Resort, see page 73). This formed a basis for building a business empire that used state money to grow.

After accepting the Liberal Party nomination for the election of 1956, Somoza García was shot and killed by a young León poet named Rigoberto López Pérez. Despite his death, the family dynasty continued with Somoza García's sons, Luis and Anastasio. Together they lasted 42 years in power, one of the longest dictatorships in Latin American history. By the time his son, Somoza Debayle, was kicked out in 1979, the family owned more than 50% of all arable land and controlled an estimated 65% of the GDP.

Sandinista National Liberation Front

The birth of the Sandinista Liberation Front was preceded by moments of resistance that were quashed with relative ease by the national guard. In 1954 a Conservative Party rebellion led by old Conservative Party *caudillo* Emiliano Chamorro, National Guard officers, poet Ernesto Cardenal and newspaper man Pedro Joaquin Chamorro, failed. In May 1959 an armed excursion into Nicaragua from Costa Rica by Chamorro was easily defeated by the National Guard. A student demonstration in León, to protest the National Guard massacre one month earlier of a pre-FSLN rebel group inside Honduras, was broken up by National Guard by firing into the crowd in July 1959, killing six and wounding nearly one hundred. In 1961-1963 the **Frente Sandinista de Liberación Nacional** or FSLN was founded, originally named after Algerian resistance fighters (Front de Libération nationale, FLN); around 1963 Sandino's name was adopted at the insistence of party founder Carlos Fonseca.

The first attack of the FSLN was along the Río Coco in 1963 in which Tomas Borge and ageing Sandino fighter Santos López participated; they were routed. More than 200 civilians died in January 1967 when the National Guard broke up a 60,000-person opposition rally in Managua by firing into the crowd. The FSLN rebels regrouped and carried out a number of urban bank robberies and minor rural attacks, but later that year they were attacked at Pancasán, Matagalpa, and many founding members of the party were killed. In the same year one of the bank robbers, **Daniel Ortega**, was thrown in jail and Tomas Borge escaped to Cuba, leaving the FSLN almost completely disbanded or in exile. Founder Carlos Fonseca was jailed in Costa Rica in 1969 and Somoza made one of many public blunders by broadcasting the National Guard attack of a FSLN safe house. As the house was being shelled into ruins, rebel Julio Buitrago defended it alone, against tanks, troops and helicopters, inspiring the Nicaraguan public. An aeroplane hijacking achieved the release of Carlos Fonseca and Humberto Ortega from a Costa Rican jail in 1970 and the next year rebels regrouped in the northern mountains, including flamboyant rebel Edén Pastora.

In 1972 a massive earthquake destroyed Managua, killing 5000-15,000 people and leaving some 200,000 homeless. The millions of dollars of aid and reconstruction money were funnelled through Somoza's companies or went straight into his bank accounts and the Nicaraguan elite started to loose patience with the final Somoza dictator.

Somoza was elected to yet another term as president in September 1974, but on December of the same year, a FSLN commando unit led by Germán Pomares raided a Managua party of Somoza politicians, gaining sweeping concessions from the Somoza government including US$6 million in cash, a rise in the national minimum wage, the release of 14 prisoners including Daniel Ortega on a flight to Cuba, and the broadcast of a 12,000-word FSLN communiqué.

The FSLN was at a crossroads in 1975, with the three principal Sandinista ideological factions at odds on how to win the war against Somoza, and FSLN General Secretary Carlos Fonseca returned from five years of exile in Cuba to try and unify the forces. The most pragmatic of the three factions, led by the Ortega brothers Daniel and Humberto, proposed a strategy of combining select assassinations and the creation of broad alliances with non-Marxist groups and a whole range of ideologies. Too conveniently for some, party founder and devout Marxist Carlos Fonseca, who was in the mountains of Matagalpa expecting a reunion of the leaders of the three bickering factions, was ambushed and killed by the National Guard on 8 November 1976, one week before the three faction summit. Early the following year the Ortega faction came out with a highly detailed 60-page plan on how to defeat Somoza; they also quickly solidified their domination of FSLN leadership, an iron grip that Daniel Ortega has held until today. In 1977 the Revolution stalled, despite a successful attack on the National Guard barracks in San Carlos on 13 October by the Solentiname FSLN rebel group; it was not until January 1978 that the general uprising really began in force.

1978-1979 Revolution

Since 1821, the watchdog for either the Conservatives or the Liberals hanging on to power for too long was the guaranteed opposition, the inevitable revolution, and the overthrow of one party or the other. During the Somoza family reign, control of the military was critical, but so was the weakness of the Conservative Party (today almost defunct), which was continually bought out by the Somozas whenever they made too much noise. The exception was *La Prensa* newspaper publisher Pedro Joaquín Chamorro. A man who could not be purchased and who was the most vocal opposition to Somoza rule in Nicaragua, PJ Chamorro was the Conservative Party's great hope, a natural to take over leadership of the country if the Liberal dictator could be disposed of. For the FSLN the timing (once again) could not have been better for a political assassination, and who better a martyr than their only competition as legitimate opposition to Somoza, someone immensely popular and part of the upper-class (still not yet committed to the struggle)? On 10 January 1978 Pedro Joaquín Chamorro was riddled with bullets in Managua on his way to the office, a murder attributed to the

National Guard. The country erupted. Over the following days rioters set fire to Somoza businesses, 30,000 people attended the funeral and the entire country went on strike (including the Central Bank employees) as demonstrations broke out around Nicaragua. The National Guard attacked many of the public gatherings in Managua; the FSLN went into action with Edén Pastora leading an attack on Rivas barracks; and Germán Pomares led attacks in Nueva Segovia in early February. The Catholic Church published a letter in *La Prensa* approving of armed resistance and one week later the indigenous community of Monimbó was tear-gassed by the National Guard at a Mass for Pedro Joaquín Chamorro and took over their town in a spontaneous rebellion that surprised even the FSLN. Somoza, after one week of defiance by citizens armed with hunting rifles and machetes, had to use tanks and planes to retake Monimbó, killing more than 200. The indigenous community of Sutiava also rebelled, as did the largely Indian city of Diriamba in the same month. Monimbó rioted again in March 1978, and between April and August there were many rebellions and skirmishes, but the insurrection was beginning once again to stall, until the most famous act of the revolution brought it back to life: the attack by FSLN commandos on Nicaragua's parliament in session that lasted from 22-24 August. The rebels held the Congressmen hostage, along with more than 1000 state employees in the National Palace, until demands were met. The strike, led by Edén Pastora and female Comandante Dora María Tellez, won the release of 58 prisoners and US$500,000 in cash and a plane ride for the prisoners (including Tomas Borge) and commandos to Panama. The National Palace raid was followed by more strikes and a spontaneous uprising in Matagalpa, squashed by bombing from Somoza's air force killing more than 80.

In September 1978, the FSLN launched their most ambitious series of attacks ever, winning National Guard posts in east Managua, Masaya, León, Chinandega and Estelí, though the National Guard with air and tank support took back each city one by one causing hundreds of deaths. The National Guard was overrun again in Monimbó one week later and fighting broke out along the border with Costa Rica, while in Diriamba more than 4000 died in uprisings. The public and the rebels, sometimes together, sometimes working apart, continued harassing the National Guard for the next eight months, as international pressure was stepped up on Somoza. He in turn accused Venezuela, Panama, Cuba and Costa Rica of supporting the FSLN (which they were). The US, in a very late effort to effect damage control, tried to convince Somoza to resign, cut off aid and searched for a way to salvage the National Guard without Somoza but Somoza would have nothing of it. From February to May 1979, rebels attacked Nicaraguan cities at will, spreading out the National Guard's defences with raids on Diriamba, Granada, León, Masaya, Managua barrios, Nueva Segovia, San Carlos, San Juan del Norte, Rivas, El Sauce, Condega, Estelí and Jinotega. In the Jinotega raid, FSLN party founder and dynamic warrior Germán Pomares was shot by his own regiment; he died two days later on 24 May.

In June the attacks became more prolonged, the forces of the FSLN swelling with new recruits as the general public became part of the rebellion and doing even more fighting than the FSLN. There was total insurrection around the Pacific, central and northern regions, with Edén Pastora forces occupying Somoza's elite troops in a frontal battle in southern Rivas. On 20 June American news reporter Bill Stewart from ABC was put on the ground and executed by the National Guard in front of his own cameraman who captured the scene, which was broadcasted across the USA.

By the end of June, Masaya, Diriamba, eastern Managua, Chontales and other rural areas were liberated by the FSLN and under their control. By 6 July, Jinotepe, San Marcos, Masatepe and Sébaco had fallen, cutting off supply routes for the National Guard north and south. León was finally liberated on 9 July; four days later Somoza flew to Guatemala looking for military aid which was denied. At 0100 on 17 July Somoza finally resigned and his National Guard disintegrated, some escaping out of

 San Juan del Sur on commandeered shrimp boats, while others fled to Miami, Honduras and Guatemala.

At the huge cost of more than 50,000 Nicaraguan lives, Somoza Debayle and the Guardia National were finally defeated. Nicaragua was in ruins, but free. A huge party was held in front of the Old Cathedral and National Palace on 20 July. Somoza escaped to Miami and later to Paraguay, where he was blown to bits by an Argentine hit squad on 17 September 1980.

Sandinista Government and the Contra War

A national reconstruction committee assumed power of Nicaragua on 20 July 1979. It was made up of five members: FSLN leader Daniel Ortega, novelist Sergio Ramírez, physics professor Dr Moisés Hassan, widow of the slain *La Prensa* publisher Violeta Barrios de Chamorro and businessman Alfonso Robelo. It looked to be a well balanced group, but what the public did not know at the time was that Ramírez and Hassan were both sworn secret members of the FSLN, giving them three to two control of the ruling board. Within a year both Doña Violeta and Alfonso Robelo would resign.

The committee abolished the old constitution and confiscated all property belonging to Somoza and his 'allies'. A new legislative body was organized to write a new constitution. Several key bodies were created by the Sandinistas that helped them to consolidate power quickly, like the Comités de Defensa Sandinista (CDS) that was organized in the barrios of Managua and the countryside to be the 'eyes and ears of the Revolution'. The unions were put under Sandinista control with the creation of the Central Sandinista de Trabajadores (CST) and FETSALUD for the health workers. The police force and military were both put under party control, with the military being renamed the Ejército Popular Sandinista (EPS). The EPS and Policía Sandinista were both put under control of key party members. Any idea of shared power among other groups led by Violeta Barrios de Chamorro, or the non-Marxist forces of Edén Pastora, were quickly dashed. Much of the Nicaraguan public who fought had believed that the Revolution was about getting rid of Somoza (and not much beyond that) while many also hoped to establish a democratic system based on the Costa Rican model. However, the Sandinistas' aim was to change society as a whole, installing a semi-Marxist system and, in theory, reversing over four centuries of social injustice.

The peace in Nicaragua was short lived. Thanks to the pre-victory death of legendary non-Marxist FSLN rebel leader Germán Pomares in Jinotega in May 1979 – by what was at first said to be a National Guard sniper, then revised as a 'stray bullet' – the first anti-Sandinista rebel units formed in Nueva Segovia. Four days after the first anniversary of the victory over Somoza, a group of ex-Sandinista rebels attacked Sandinista Government troops, overrunning the local military base in Quilalí. The Contra War had begun. By August 1980, ex-National Guard members were also forming groups in Honduras and, thanks to organization by CIA, at first directed via Argentine generals, and then with direct control from ex-Guard members, the movement began to formalize rebel groups. The first planned CIA attack was carried out in March 1982 with bombs planted to destroy key bridges in the north. Although the original Contras and the majority of the Contra fighters had nothing to do with the National Guard, the Resistencia Nicaragüense (better known as the Contras – short for counter-revolutionary in Spanish) was to be commanded in Honduras by former Guard members and funded by the US government under Ronald Reagan. The war waged by the Contras was one of harassment and guerrilla warfare like Sandino had used against the US Marines. But, unlike Sandino, the Contra bands attacked freely 'soft (civilian) targets' and country infrastructure as part of their strategy. A southern front against the Sandinista administration was

The Contra War

Then US President Ronald Reagan labelled the Contras the 'Freedom Fighters', and on one occasion even sported a T-shirt that read, 'I'm a Contra too'. His administration lobbied to maintain and increase military aid to the Nicaraguan Contras fighting the Sandinista Revolution during the 1980s. The first bands of Contras were organized shortly after the Sandinistas took power in 1979. The leaders were mainly ex-officials and soldiers loyal to the overthrown general Anastasio Somoza Debayle. Thanks to the United States, the Contras grew quickly and became the largest guerrilla army in Latin America. When they demobilized in May 1990, they had 15,000 troops.

The Contras divided Nicaragua in two: war zones and zones that were not at war. They also divided United States public opinion between those who supported President Reagan's policy and those who opposed it. The US House of Representatives and the Senate were likewise divided. The Contras are also associated with one of the biggest political scandals in the US after Watergate. The so-called 'Iran-Contra Affair' broke at the end of 1986, when a C-123 supply plane with a US flight crew was shot down over Nicaraguan territory. The scandal that followed caused some US government officials to resign, including Lieutenant Colonel Oliver North. The intellectual authors of the affair remained unscathed.

The most famous Contra leader was former Guardia Nacional Colonel Enrique Bermúdez, known in the war as 'Commander 3-80'. In February 1991, Bermúdez was shot dead in the parking lot of Managua's Intercontinental Hotel. The 'strange circumstances' surrounding his death were never clarified, and the killers were never apprehended. After agreeing to disarm in 1990, the majority of the Contra troops returned to a normal civilian life. However, most of them never received the land, credit, work implements, etc. they had been promised. The Contras live on today as the political party Partido Resistencia Nicaragüense (Nicaraguan Resistance Party), which has been ineffective due to internal disputes and divisions.

opened up by ex-FSLN hero Edén Pastora who was disillusioned with the new Sandinista government and the meaningless roles he was given to play in it. By introducing mandatory military service the Sandinista army swelled to over 120,000 to fight the combined Contra forces of an estimated 10-20,000 soldiers. The national monetary reserves were increasingly taxed, with more than half the national budget going on military spending, and a US economic embargo that sent inflation spinning out of control, annihilating the already beleaguered economy that was finally killed by the collapse of partner states in the Soviet bloc. Massive migration to avoid the war zones changed the face of Nicaragua, with exiles choosing departmental capitals, Managua or Costa Rica, while those who could afford it fled to Miami. Indigenous groups suffered greatly during this period with the Mayagna in the heart of the Contra War and the Miskitos being forced to live in internment camps while their village homes and crops were razed by government troops. The Miskitos formed their own rebel Contra groups who attacked from the Caribbean side and the Río Coco. Human rights violations were common on both sides, though the Contras' ineffectual command structure and corrupt leaders meant that the Contra rebels were greatly feared by the civilian populace in war zones, where frequent atrocities were well documented.

The Sandinistas are credited with numerous important socio-political achievements including the **Literacy Crusade**, a fresh sense of nationalism, giant cultural advances, improved infrastructure, yet the Contra War, US economic embargo, a thoroughly disastrous FSLN agriculture reform program, human rights abuses and dictatorial style of running the government would spell their doom. Progress in education and culture was undeniably impressive during the Sandinista years, especially considering the circumstances, but the cost was too high for the majority of the Nicaraguan people. Personal freedoms were the same or worse (especially regarding freedom of speech and press) as they had been in the time of Somoza's rule, and fatigue from the death and poverty caused by the Contra War was extreme. Hundreds of studies have been written on what happened in the 1980s in Nicaragua and defenders of the FSLN rule point out that they never had a chance to rule in peace. Their detractors, on the other hand, highlight that democracy was never on the agenda for the party.

A peace agreement was reached in Sapoá, Rivas and elections were held in 1990. Daniel Ortega (40.8%) lost to Violeta Chamorro (55.2%). After losing the elections the Sandinistas bravely handed over power to Doña Violeta. Then they proceeded frantically to divide and distribute state-held assets (which included hundreds of confiscated properties and businesses) among leading party members in the two months between the election loss and handing over power, in what has since been known simply since as *la piñata* (a *piñata* is a papier-mâché sculpture that you bash with a stick during a fiesta; it's filled with sweets and when it breaks they spill everywhere).

Violeta Barrios de Chamorro

After an entire century (and in many ways 450 years) of limited personal freedoms and military backed governments, most Nicaraguans considered the election of Doña Violeta as the beginning of true democracy in Nicaragua. Violeta Barrios de Chamorro had her sons on both sides of the fence in the 1980s: the elder, Pedro Joaquín junior, was with the Contras while the younger, Carlos Fernando, was with the Sandinistas. As she brought together her family, she brought together the country. Doña Violeta was forced to compromise on many issues and at times the country looked set to collapse back into war, but Nicaragua's first woman president spent the next six years trying to repair the damage and unite the country. The Nicaraguan military was de-politicized, put under civilian rule and reduced from over 120,000 to less than 18,000. Uprisings were common with small groups taking up arms or demonstrations meant to destabilize the government. Despite claims that her son-in-law, Antonio Lacayo, was actually running the country and that some of her administration was financially corrupt, by the time Doña Violeta handed over the presidency in 1997, Nicaragua was fully at peace and beginning to recover economically. Inflation had been controlled and foreign investment was starting to trickle in, along with capital from middle and upper class returnees. Doña Violeta left office with a miserable public rating, but is now one of Nicaragua's most beloved figures, thanks principally to her personal charm and that fact that she has stayed out of politics ever since her term ended.

Arnoldo Alemán

In 1996 Liberal Party candidate Arnoldo Alemán won 51% of the vote against the 37.7% garnered by his opponent Daniel Ortega, with the rest divided among 21 different presidential candidates. The Sandinistas maintained pressure on the Alemán government with strikes, protests and intermittent negotiations. Another in

Cuba and Nicaragua: love hurts

Over the years, Cuba and Nicaragua have had a love-hate relationship. The Bay of Pigs invasion to overthrow the government of Fidel Castro embarked from Bilwi (Puerto Cabezas) on the North Atlantic Region of Nicaragua. As they left Nicaragua, Anastasio Somoza Debayle requested that they bring him "a piece of hair from Castro's beard". The adventure ended in defeat for the anti-Castro invaders. Later, ironically, Castro's Cuba was one of the first countries to send humanitarian aid to Nicaragua after the violent earthquake that destroyed most of Managua in December 1972. Somoza Debayle had no choice but to accept the aid and to accept Cuban doctors. Cuba also played a very important role in the Sandinista victory of July 1979. The Caribbean nation became Nicaragua's main ally, especially in the areas of military assistance, health care and education. By the mid-1980s, around 9000 Cuban advisers were in Nicaragua, 3000 of whom were working with the country's security forces. At the same time, thousands of Nicaraguans, especially those from poor families, went to Cuba to finish secondary school or to study in the vocational schools and universities. Likewise, thousands went to Cuba for free medical attention they couldn't receive in Nicaragua due to a lack of specialists, hospitals and modern equipment. While many Nicaraguans were grateful to the Cubans for their assistance, others didn't want them in the country. In the South Atlantic Region, the population publicly demanded that the Cubans leave the area at the beginning of the 1980s.

Today, official relations between Cuba and Nicaragua have cooled. Both countries have low-level diplomats in their respective capitals and there is almost no commercial interchange between them. Nonetheless, hundreds of Nicaraguans are still attending medical school in Havana with scholarships granted by the Cuban government after Hurricane Mitch struck Central America in October 1998.

the historical parade of Nicaraguan closed-door pacts between seemingly opposed political parties, this time between the Liberals and the Sandinistas, created compromised and politicized government institutions and much controversy. Sandinista objectors to the pact were tossed out of the party. Alemán made great strides in increasing economic growth and foreign investment in Nicaragua and improved education and road infrastructure. He also managed to buy up huge tracts of land and build expensive highways that led to his multiplying properties, while stealing more than US$100 million of state funds from the poorest Spanish speaking country in the world. Alemán left office with an approval rating of less than 25%. The 1998 hurricane disaster encouraged foreign countries to consider cancelling Nicaragua's debt and in 2004, the World Bank agreed to clear 80% of what was owed to them. The country must still jump through IMF hoops to receive aid though.

Enrique Bolaños

In 2001 the candidate-for-life Daniel Ortega held a pre-election poll lead and the world's media took note, with press excitement building for a possible Sandinista comeback in the time of George W. Bush and growing potential for new conflict. However, the electorate once again voted for the Liberals, or more precisely against

 Ortega, electing Liberal Party candidate Enrique Bolaños in a record turnout in the polls of some 96% of the registered voters. Bolaños promised to attack the corruption of his party leader Arnoldo Alemán, something very few believed, although he did exactly that. At great political cost to Nicaragua's executive branch, Bolaños had Alemán tried, convicted and sentenced to 20 years in prison on corruption charges.

The Liberal congressmen, all purchased by Alemán, in an astonishing display of total disregard for public opinion, refused to abandon their leader and still insist on amnesty for Alemán, who continues to rule the Liberal party from his luxury ranch, enjoying full movement about the country while he serves his sentence. Despite the great victory against state thievery, Bolaños' administration has been largely ineffectual; the war against corruption left him without support in the Nicaraguan congress, controlled by the pact players, Liberal and FSLN senators loyal to Alemán and Ortega. At the time of printing Alemán and Ortega have entered into a new pact that promises freedom for Alemán after Liberal parliamentary members vote the Sandinistas into power at all levels of non-Federal government, from Parliament to the Supreme Court, and a modification of the Nicaraguan constitution that makes the country's presidency mere window dressing. It looks like the time of Somoza all over again, although now the former rebel Sandinistas are calling the shots, using their control over the country's court system to manipulate the proven corrupt Liberals at will. During Bolaños' term, Nicaragua has continued to progress economically and infrastructure has also improved, though most of the Nicaraguans view the president as ineffectual and insensitive to the daily toil of Nicaragua's poor majority.

Daniel Ortega and the future

Daniel Ortega returned to the run the Executive Branch in 2007 after winning 38% of the vote. The Nicaraguan people started the year with great hope, and Ortega still carried favourable ratings into mid-year. However, the CAFTA free trade agreement finally took hold (singed by the last president, but approved by FSLN Parliament members under Ortega's orders) and speculation on such critical food staples as beans, cheese and milk (caused by more fluid exports and dwindling supply) created record local market prices for what 80% of the poor majority lives on. This has caused widespread discontent and Ortega's approval rating now hovers below 30%. Even some of his most loyal supporters are losing patience. Many had hoped for a more pragmatic Daniel Ortega once in power, but there have been few signs of this. Despite ample promises of help from new allies such as Venezuela and Iran, little has changed in Nicaragua's daily reality, with the rising cost of living continuing to outpace mandated salary adjustments. More than this, Ortega is employing the same neo-liberal policies of the last 17 years. The *Economist* called it "Ortega's Crab Walk"; tough revolutionary, anti-Imperialist rhetoric combined with a textbook IMF economic policy.

Most Nicaraguans are well aware that the FSLN is a skeleton of its past glory with Ortega having made space for only himself and his wife. Still, they are remarkably patient and the general feeling is to wait out the rest of his term. But if Ortega attempts to realise his political ambition of eternal re-election, or a parliamentary system where he could rule as Prime Minister ad infinitum, then Nicaraguans are likely to snap. A storm is brewing on the horizon.

Culture

People

Ethnicity

The origin of the Nicaraguan, as with much of the Americas' population, is typically diverse. The pre-conquest cultures of the central and western sections of the countries mixed with small waves of European immigration, beginning in the 16th century and continuing today. The eastern section of Nicaragua remained in relative isolation for the first several centuries and fairly well defined indigenous ethnic cultures are still present in the communities of Miskito, Rama and Mayagna as well as Afro-Caribbeans from Jamaica (Creole) and San Vincent (Garífuna) Islands. Ultimately, however, the Hispanic *mestizo* culture of the western two thirds of the country dominate the ethnic profile of the Nicaraguan. Recent surveys suggest a country 96% *mestizo*, with 3% indigenous and 1% Afro-Caribbean. Among the peoples classified as *mestizo* are many of close to pure indigenous roots who have lost their distinguishing language, but retained many cultural traits of pre-Columbian times. There is also a very small, nearly pure European sector that has traditionally controlled the country's economic and land assets. Massive movements of population during the troubled years of the 1980s has also blurred these once well defined lines, although you can still see some definite ethnic tendencies in each province of the country.

Population

Population density varies wildly from department to department with the obvious concentration of people on Managua and vicinity and the traditionally (since pre-Conquest times) populous cities of the Pacific Basin where 83% of Nicaragua's people live. On a national level, population density is 42 people per sq km, making Nicaragua the least densely populated country in Central America (the other extreme being El Salvador at more than 300 per sq km).

The estimated population, at the time of the first arrival of the Europeans in 1523, for the area that is Nicaragua today ranges from 350,00 to one million. Thanks to imported illnesses, forced labour, murder and a short-lived, but devastating, export of indigenous Nicaraguans to work as slaves abroad, the population of Nicaragua was estimated at 50,000 less than 50 years later. Estimated population for the country in a 1778 census was 100,000. In 1900 it had grown to 480,000, which took a full 50 years to double to 1,097,916 in 1950. Twenty years later it had doubled again with 1970 figures at 2,052,544. Current population growth is pegged at 3.2% annually (the average in Latin America is 1.9%). Nonetheless, the average size of the Nicaraguan family is diminishing with the 1950 average of 7.3 children per mother being lowered to 4.7 today.

In 1971 the ratio of male to female in Nicaragua was 97.5 men for every 100 women. Thanks to the revolution, Contra war and fleeing of young men to escape military service, the ratio was down to 91.4 men to every 100 women in 1990. The 1995 census showed a total of 2,147,105 male and 2,209,994 female inhabitants. The country is also very young with 45% of the population being under the age of 15. Only 3% of the population are over the age of 65. The average life span of the Nicaraguan has risen since 1950, when it was 42 to 63 years old. Infant mortality is at 50 per 1000.

Religion

By 1585, the majority of the local population had been converted to Christianity. Recent surveys suggest that now only 59% of the population is Roman Catholic. Evangelical groups have made great strides in recent years in attracting worshippers, and Baptist, Methodist, Church of Christ, Assembly of God, Seventh Day Adventists, Jehovah's Witness, Mormon and other churches now account for 29% of the population, with the remainder claiming no church affiliation. Religion and spirituality in general are very important parts of Nicaraguan life. The combined forces of the Evangelist churches have their own political party in Camino Christiano (who joined in alliance with the Liberal party for the elections in 2001) and won the third largest tally of votes in the 1996 campaign. The Catholic Church has no official political wing, but plays heavily the political scene, although the retirement of the legendary Cardinal Miguel Obando y Bravo in April 2005, a priest who was at the centre of Nicaragua's political conflicts for 30 years, will no doubt change that.

Dance

During the early years of Spanish colonization, dance as a discipline did not have a defined style. Indigenous dances were considered heretical due to the ceremonial nature of some of them (although many were danced for pure pleasure) and therefore discouraged or banned. The dances considered folkloric or traditional in Nicaragua today are a mixture of African, indigenous and European dances and cultures. In the colonial period, celebrations of religious festivities saw the performance by the upper class Spanish of European dances that were in fashion back home. The manner of dancing and behaviour of the upper class was observed by the native, African and mestizo populations and then mixed with each culture's respective dances.

The terms *el son* or *los sones* are used to define the dances that first appeared in the 1700s, such as the **Jarabe, Jaranas** and **Huapangos**. These dances are the local adaptations of the Fandango and Spanish tap dance. In Nicaragua the dances or *sones Jarabe Chichón* and *Jarabe Repicado* are still performed today in the festivals of Masaya and its *pueblos*. Many traditional dances have a love message; a good example is the flirtatious **Dance of the Indian Girls** (*Baile de las Inditas*) or the entertaining physical satire on relationships known as the **Dance of the Old Man and Lady** (*El Baile del Viejo y la Vieja*).

Other well-known dances are the **Dance of the Black Girls** (*Danza de las Negritas*), another dance performed by men in drag, and a spectacular and colourful traditional dance **The Little Demons** (*Los Diablitos*). This is a native mock-up of an Iberian masquerade ball, danced in the streets and with performer's costumes consisting of every possible character from Mr Death to a tiger, or a giant parrot or the Devil. One of the most traditional dances from Masaya is **El Torovenado**, which follows the rhythm of *marimbas* and *chicheros*. The participants are all male and dress in costumes representing both male and female politicians and members of the upper class. Their handmade masks and costumes are created to satirize important events happening in the country or behaviour of the moneyed class. The Torovenado is a street performance-protest against social injustice and government corruption. This tradition was brought to national attention recently, when a native of Masaya appeared at a Managua Sandinista rally for the 2001 elections, dressed as Nicaragua's Cardinal Miguel Obando y Bravo, causing outrage. Another of the many traditional Nicaraguan dances is the **Dance of the Hungarians** (*Danza de la Húngaras*), which developed from early 20th century immigration of eastern European gypsies to Nicaragua.

Dances and regions

Masaya is far from unique in its local dances, for Nicaraguan regional dance is rich and impressive across the board. The most famous of all, **El Guegüence** (see box, page 103), has disputed origins – it is either from the highland village of Diriamba or from Masaya. The small, but historic village of Nindirí is home to many unique dances like **The Black Chinese** (*Los Chinegros*), **El Ensartado** and **Las Canas**. León is the origin of the spectacular joke on the early colonisers called **El Baile de La Gigantona y el Enano Cabezón**, in which a three metre tall blond women spins and dances in circles around an old dwarf with a big bald head. León is also home to **Los Mantudos** and **El Baile del Toro**. Managua has **La Danza de la Vaca** and Boaco has the **Dance of the Moors and the Christians** (*Los Moros y Cristianos*). Very unique inside Nicaragua is the dance only performed on the Island of Ometepe in the village of Altagracia (see page 146) called the **Dance of the Leaf-Cutter Ants** (*El Baile de Los Zompopos*).

In the northern cities of Matagalpa and Jinotega, the coffee immigrants from Germany and other parts of northern Europe in the late 19th century had violin and guitar-driven polkas, *jamaquellos* and *mazurkas*.

The Caribbean coast is home to some little-known Garífuna dances that are now being performed in Managua and some native Miskito dances that have also been recognized and performed by dance troupes on the Pacific side. The favourite of both coasts for its raw energy may be the **Palo de Mayo** (maypole) dances, a hybrid of English Maypole traditions and Afro-Caribbean rain and fertility dances.

Aside from the tradition of dancing in festivals, the dances of Nicaragua have been brought to the stage and are performed regularly in Managua and Masaya with less frequent performances all over Nicaragua. Of all stage performances of any kind in Nicaragua, there is no doubt that folkloric dance shows are the most popular. There are numerous groups in Masaya and Managua, as well as many others around the country. An opportunity to see one of the professional companies is not to be missed. Masaya often has dance groups performing on Thursday nights at the artisan's market and the **Centro Cultural Managua** and **Teatro Rubén Darío** also have regular shows.

Literature

Early Nicaraguan poetry and narrative, influenced from the beginning by the chronicles of the West Indies, uses a straightforward descriptive style to depict the life of the indigenous people and the Spanish conquest through colourful narratives. This type of **native literature** was the most prevalent during the pre-Hispanic era. One of the original works was *Canto al sol de los Nicaraguas*, dedicated to the principal cultures to inhabit this remote region, the Nicaraguas and Chorotega tribes. The writing of the indigenous peoples, generally pictographs, called *books* by Fernandez de Oviedo for their manuscript form, is largely anonymous. While the native languages would later become mixed with Spanish, a series of primitive dialects were conserved, so that later it was possible to recover and compile different works, including **Sumu poetry**, **Miskito songs**, **Sutiavan poems**, **Carib music** and **native myths** f rom different regions of Nicaragua. These were songs related to the Spanish conquest or religion – a product of the colonization process – sayings, riddles, ballads and children's games that would later reappear in different narratives and poetic forms. The first book attributed to Nicaraguan-born Spanish descendants was *Relaciones verdaderas de la deducción de los indios infieles, de la provincia de Teguzgalpa* (True Revelations about the Pagan Indians from the Province of Teguzgalpa) by Francisco Fernández Espino, which appeared in 1674. The work was little known. In 1876, according to literary critic Ricardo Llopesa, the first literary group *La Montaña*, was founded in Granada. Two years later the first anthology titled *Lira Nicaragüense* was published.

Rubén Darío

The Father of Modernism Rubén Darío (1867-1916) overshadowed everyone with his proposals for innovation in the Spanish language through the Modernist movement, which he himself founded. The modernist school advocated aestheticism, the search for sensory and even sensual values, and the artistic effects of colour, sound, voice and synthesis. His first verses were published in 1879. In 1881 he edited his first complete work, *Poesías y artículos en prosa*, which was published after his death, and *Epítolas y poemas* in 1888. That same year, *Azul*, one of the fundamental works for understanding modernism, was published. In 1896, he published *Los Raros y Prosas Profanas*, in Buenos Aires. In 1901 a second edition of this work was published. Upon returning to Valparaiso, Chile, he published *Abrojos* (1887) and his novel *Emelina*. Other Darío narratives include *El Fardo*, *Invernal*, *El Rey Burgues*, and *La Ninfa*. Darío's works had a significant impact on the Spanish language, especially his literary production, personal letters and stories. In 1916, after many years of absence, Darío returned to the city of Leon, Nicaragua, where he died on 6 February. See also box, page 200.

The Vanguard

A significant group of poets were followers of Darío, but with very individual styles. These included **Father Azarias H Pallais** (1884-1959), **Alfonso Cortés** (1893-1969) and **Salomon de la Selva** (1893-1959). These world-class poets were known for their innovation and experimentation. Literature, and especially poetry, has always been attractive to Nicaraguan youth. For that reason the Vanguard movement was born. Founded by **Luis Alberto Cabrales** (1901-1974) and **José Coronel Urtecho** (1906-1994) this movement exerted an important renovating influence on Nicaraguan literature. Coronel Urtecho's work *Oda a Rubén Darío* (1927) contains the essence of the new style and marks the transition from the Darío school of Modernism to the Vanguard movement. **Pablo Antonio Cuadra** (1912-2002), the movement's principal author, wrote a declaration reaffirming the national identity, which was later incorporated into his first book *Poemas Nicaraguenses* (1934). Cuadra, together with Coronel Urtecho as the movement's chief promoter, Luis Cabrales, and **Joaquín Pasos** (1914-1947) author of the dramatic poem *Canto de Guerra de las Cosas*, summarized their programme and released the *Anti-Academia de la Lengua* declaration. Another member of the Vanguard was **Manolo Cuadra** (1907-1957) who became known for his poems, *Perfil* and *La palabra que no te dije*, published in *Tres Amores* (1955). Aside from Coronel Urtecho, the most outstanding Vanguard writer is **Pablo Antonio Cuadra**, with a truly prolific literary production, including *Libro de horas* (1964), a collection of *Náhuatl myths El Jaguar y la Luna* (1959). He wrote about the life of the mammal in *Cantos de Cifar* and *Al mar dulce* (1926); his excellent treatise against dictatorships in *Siete arboles contra el atardecer* (1982) and *Poemas para un calendario* (1988). Cuadra's work has been translated into several languages. For more than a decade he was the general director of the *La Prensa* daily newspaper.

The 1940s

The main themes of the generation of the 1940s were love and freedom, reflected in the poetry of **Francisco Pérez Estrada** (1917-1982), **Enrique Fernández Morales** (1918-1982), and **Julio Ycaza Tigerino** (1919-2001). However, this period is especially known for the emergence of two great poets. **Ernesto Mejia Sánchez** (1923-1985) cultivated a style marked by brevity and precision in his most important works *Ensalmos y conjuros* (1947) and *La Carne contigua* (1948). **Carlos Martínez Rivas** (1924-1999) used a modern rhythm, making his ideas felt through quick turns of phrase and ruptures of his own language. *El paraiso recobrado* (1948) was a revelation and the publication of *Insurreccion solitaria* (1953) even more so. He published a series of poems titled *Allegro rato*, in 1989, which continued a very experimental line.

Sergio Ramírez: revolutionary novelist

Former Vice-President (1984-1990) Sergio Ramírez Mercado, tired of political setbacks, has now returned to his literary roots forever. His last incursion into politics was made in 1996 as the presidential candidate for the Sandinista breakaway party Movimiento Renovador Sandinista (MRS), but he received a very low percentage of votes, barely enough for one party seat in the 92-member legislature.

Putting the political life behind him, Ramírez returned to what he does best, write. His novel *Margarita está Linda la Mar* won a prestigious award for fiction from the Alfaguara Spanish publishing house. That same year another one of his novels, *Baile de Máscaras*, won a French award.

Ramírez is back to writing full-time. He calls it "the best job in the world". Besides novels, he writes articles for important international newspapers such as the Madrid daily *El País*, and does stints as a guest professor at several universities in the US, Germany and Latin America.

Sergio Ramírez, who was born in 1942, graduated with a degree in law and had his first book published in Managua in 1963 under the title *Cuentos*. He was living in Costa Rica when he was asked to participate in the struggle against Somoza and in 1977 he was a very active member of the Sandinista underground. Following the 1979 victory of the Sandinista Revolution, Ramírez became a member of the first Junta de Gobierno de Reconstrucción Nacional (JGRN), made up of five prominent Nicaraguans. Later, in November 1984, he was elected vice-president as part of the ticket headed by Daniel Ortega. They both sought re-election in 1990, but were defeated by Violeta Barrios de Chamorro. In 1999, 20 years after the violent overthrow of the Somoza dictatorship, Ramírez Mercado published *Adiós Muchachos*, his personal memoirs of the Sandinista Revolution.

Expressionist poetry

The poetry of **Ernesto Cardenal**, born 20 January 1925, reflects spoken language and contains simple expressions. He is the founder of the expressionist poetry current, which opposed the subjectivity of lyrical poetry. Through his poetry he attacked the Somoza family dictatorship for over four decades. Also a priest, he founded the Christian community of Solentiname on a group of islands in Lake Nicaragua. His extensive work has been translated into several languages. *La ciudad deshabitada* (1946), *Hora o* (1960), *Oracion por Marylin Monroe y otras poemas* (1966), are poems reflecting religious, historical and Christian themes as well as the topic of social commitment.

The 1950s and 1960s

In the 1950s, **Guillermo Rothschuh Tablada** (1926) and **Fernando Silva** (1927) stand out. Rothschuh wrote *Poemas Chontaleños* (1960), while Silva follows the traditional-regional approach, reflecting the spoken language of the rural areas. His work *Barro de Sangre* represents a vernacular renewal in the authenticity of its theme and language. In the 1960s, the left-leaning *Grupo Ventana* (Windows Group) emerged led by students at the Autonomous National University of Leon, including **Fernando Gordillo** (1940-1967), who left only a scattered poetic work, and **Sergio Ramírez Mercado** (1942). Other poets of this generation include

 Octavio Robleto (1935), **Francisco Valle** (1942), a surrealist and a writer of prose. **Beltrán Morales** (1945-1986) is the most outstanding poet of this generation for his synthesis and irony, reflected in *Agua Regia* (1972). Other groups emerging in this period were the *La Generación Traicionada* (The Betrayed Generations) and *Grupo M*, both from Managua, *Grupo U* from Boaco, and *Los Bandeleros* (The Bandoliers) from Granada. **Mario Cajina-Vega**, a poet and thoughtful but comic narrator, published *Breve Tribu* in 1962. **Julio Valle-Castillo**, poet, narrator and critic, published one of his first books *Materia Jubilosa* in 1953. Along with **Jorge Eduardo Arellano** (1946), Julio Valle is one of Nicaragua's most respected researchers.

The 1970s

In the 1970s, the modern short story was born in Nicaragua with **Lisandro Chávez Alfaro**'s *Los Monos de San Telmo* (1963), known for its innovative technique and themes. Chronicles from poor Managua neighbourhoods are found in *Se Alquilan Cuartos* (1975), by Juan Aburto (1918-1988). **Sergio Ramírez Mercado** (see box, page 313) is one of the best internationally known writers to have ever come out of Nicaragua. The ex-vice president of Nicaragua under Daniel Ortega has published novels and books of short stories including *De Tropeles y Tropelias* (1972), and *Charles Atlas también muere* (1976). In 1998 he won the International Prize for Fiction of the Alfagura publishing house of Spain who also published his later works: *Margarita está linda la mar* (1998), *Adiós muchachos* (1999), and his most recent work *Mentiras Verdaderas* (2000). He is considered among the finest novelists in Latin America today.

Poetic revelations

The revelation of the 1970s was **Gioconda Belli**. Her first book *Sobre La Grama* (1974) is a sensual work of poems that broke ground with its frank femininity. *De La Costilla De Eva* (1987) speaks of free love at the service of revolutionary transformation. Her novels, *La mujer habitada*, *Memorias de amor y de guerra* and *El país bajo mi piel*, among others, have been published in more than twenty languages. Along with Belli, other writers emerging in this period included **Vidaluz Meneses**, **Daisy Zamora**, **Ana Ilce Gómez**, **Rosario Murillo**, and **Christian Santos**.

Exteriorism

In the 1980s, a new literary phenomenon called Exteriorism became popular. Founded by **Ernesto Cardenal**, who at the time was the Sandinista government's Minister of Culture, this movement advocated political poetry, and promoted what he called "objective poetry: using fragments of narrative, anecdotes, and employing proper nouns with imprecise details and exact statistics." This style was taught in widespread poetry workshops where members of the army, the recently literate farming population and other sectors of the country were encouraged to write. The use of a unified style for the workshops was later criticized and with the end of the Sandinista government the poetry workshops disappeared.

Modern trends

From the 1990s onwards, a more intimate poetry emerged. The traditional literary topics are prevalent: death, existentialism and love, along with new themes including homosexuality, women's rights and the environment. New writers have emerged: poets like **Blanca Castellón**, **Erick Aguirre**, **Pedro Xavier Solís**, **Juan Sobalvarro**, **Isolda Hurtado**, **Marta Leonor González** and **Ariel Montoya**; there are also new literary groups and magazines such as *400 Elefantes*, *Decenio* and *Cultura de Paz*.

Music

Music is a very integral part of Nicaraguan life with everything from traditional festivals to political rallies using music as its driving backbone. Rock, pop, folk, regional, romantic and protest music are all a part of the national offering.

Marimba

The Marimba is the most traditional among these varieties of rhythms. The instrument is known as Nicaragua's 'national piano' and although its origin has never been well defined, most believe it has its roots in Africa. In musical terms it is a complex instrument: shaped in the form of a triangle and comprising 22 wood keys. The marimba player uses two sticks with rubber heads called *bolillos*. The instrument has very clear and sonorous tonalities. In the past the marimba was used to play folk pieces and typical music of the countryside, but today it has been diversified, *marimberos* performing anything from salsa to *merengue* and *cumbia*. The country's best *marimberos* are from the indigenous barrio of Masaya, Monimbó, which has a generations-long tradition of marimba playing.

Classical music

Classical music was the music of *criollos* in Nicaragua and the original European-influenced music of the country. The classical symphony music of the Nicaraguan artists in the 19th century was played by orchestras in León. Key names like **Juan Bautista Prado**, **Manuel Ibarra**, **Alfonso Zelaya**, **Salvador Martínez**, **Santos Cermeño**, **Alfonso Solórzano** and **Lizandro Ramírez** dominated the classical music scene of Nicaragua that survives today, although original compositions have diminished greatly since the end of the 1800s. The greatest of all Nicaraguan classical composers was the León artist **José de la Cruz Mena**, who received international recognition before dying of leprosy (see León, page 199). The poet **Salomón Ibarra Mayorga** wrote the Nicaraguan national anthem. The short piece was written on 16 December 1910 and performed by the greatest musicians of the time, the masters **Abraham Delgadillo Rivas** and **Carlos Alberto Ramírez Velásquez**.

Folk music

Folk music also has its roots in Masaya, with many artists known as *orejeros* (those who learn to play by ear). Nicaraguan rhythms such as *Mamá Ramona* come from the city. The *orejeros* are famous for their deft guitar playing. One of the most important creators of the Nicaraguan song is **Víctor M Leiva** who wrote the song *El Caballo Cimarrón* (The Untamed Horse) in 1948, the first Nicaraguan song recorded in the country. During his more than 50 years of performing and composing he painted portraits of the Nicaraguan's daily life, landscape and labour. Some of his most famous compositions include *Santo Domingo de Guzmán*, *Tata Chombo*, *Coffee Season*, *El Toro Huaco* and *La Chapandonga*. He received a Gold Palm award in United States, as the second greatest folkloric composer in Latin America. Another important folk singer songwriter is **Camilo Zapata**, known as 'The Master of Regionalism'. Born in 1917 and still performing today, he wrote his first song *Caballito Chontaleno* (Little Horse from Chontales) at the age of 14. His songs are nourished by culture and Nicaraguan critics have crowned him as the face and heart of Nicaraguan regionalism. In 1948 Zapata came to national fame with songs like *El Nandaimeno*, *El Ganado Colorado* (The Pink Cattle), *El Solar de Monimbó* (The Backyard of Monimbó), *Flor de Mi Colina* (Flower from my Hill), *Minga Rosa Pineda*, *El Arriero* (The Muleteer) and some other romantic ones such as *Facing the sun*, *Cariño*. El Maestro Zapata, even now in his eighties, continues to compose beautiful melodies sprinkled with regionalist stamps.

Chicheros

Chicheros are an integral part of any festival or traditional party. The Chichero band consists of six to eight amateur musicians who play snare drums, bass drum, cymbal, trumpet, flute, clarinet and trombone. Their music ranges from energetic dance tunes to solemn funeral marches.

La Misa Campesina

With marimbas, guitars, *atabales* (Indian drums), violins and mazurcas and Nicaraguan rhythm, a new style in popular religious music was born with *La Misa Campesina* or the Peasant Mass. The Mass is composed of 10 songs, written by legendary folk singer Carlos Mejía Godoy and recorded in the 1980s by the Popular Sound Workshop. It was composed in Solentiname, where Ernesto Cardenal was preaching, and was later extended to all the 'peoples' churches and even to Spain. For Carlos Mejía this body of work is his dearest one. The Catholic Church in Nicaragua prohibited the work on orders from Pope John Paul II. The lack of acceptance by the church did little to diminish the worldwide acceptance of the music. *La Misa Campesina* has been translated into numerous languages and is even sung by Anglicans, Mormons and Baptists in the United States. Among the most loved are the *Welcome Song*, *The Creed*, *The Meditation song*, *Kirye*, *Saint* and *Communion*. The music has also been chosen as one of the hundred hymns of the Mennonite Church in the United States.

Protest music

Protest music had its glory days during the years leading up to the Revolution. This music of pop and folkloric rhythms brought to fame such bands as Engel Ortega, Norma Elena Gadea and Eduardo Araica, the Pancasan Band, Duo Guardabarranco formed by Katia and Salvador Cardenal, Keyla Rodríguez and Luis Enrique Mejía Godoy.

Palo de Mayo

Palo de Mayo is a collection of native music from the Caribbean Coast of Nicaragua. The music is characterized by its vibrant rhythm. The songs that are a joy hymn for the Afro-Caribbean Nicaraguans include *Tululu Pass Under*, *Oh Nancy, Oh*, *Simón Canta Simón*, *Mayaya Oh*. To perform the unique Caribbean rhythms, local musicians incorporate numerous unique instruments such as cow and donkey jawbones, combs, pots, as well as more common instruments like drums and guitars.

Land and environment

Geography

Nicaragua is located between the Tropic of Cancer and the Equator, ranging from 11°-15° north and between 83°-88° longitude. The 530-km northern border of Nicaragua runs from the Golfo de Fonseca to Cabo Gracias a Dios, much of it marked by the Río Coco. The Caribbean Coast from Gracias a Dios to just south of the mouth of the Río San Juan is 509 km. From the Caribbean outlet of the Río San Juan to the Bay of Salinas is the 313-km border with Costa Rica. The Pacific Coast is 325 km from Salinas to the Golfo de Fonseca. The total surface area of the country is 131,812 sq km; 10,384 sq km of this is covered by lakes and coastal lagoons. Despite losing more than 40,000 sq km of territory over the last two centuries to Honduras in the north, to Costa Rica in the south and to Colombia in the Caribbean, Nicaragua is still the biggest of the Central American republics.

The land can be divided into three principal sections. The **Caribbean lowlands,** which include pine savannas in the north and, further south, the largest remaining expanse of rainforest on the Central American isthmus are crossed by numerous rivers that drain the central mountain range to the emerald sea. The **central and northern mountains and plains** are geologically the oldest in the country, with many long-extinct volcanoes. The mountains are low, ranging from 500 m in the far south of the zone to 2000 m as they reach the border with Honduras in the north. This is a mineral-rich area that has been prospected for centuries. The diversity of the ecosystem is immense, with rainforest giving way to tropical dry forest in the south, and cloud forest to pines in the north.

The third division is the **Pacific Basin**, which is marked by numerous crater lakes, the two great lakes of Managua and Nicaragua and the lumpy spine of volcanoes, the Cordillera Los Maribios, that run from the extreme northwest at Volcán Cosigüina to the dual volcano island of Ometepe in Lake Nicaragua. The area is a mixture of tropical dry forest and savanna with two cloud forests on Volcán Mombacho and Volcán Maderas, and a pine forest on the Volcán Casita.

Lakes and rivers

In the Pacific Basin plain are 15 crater lakes and the two largest expanses of water in Central America. The capital, Managua, lies on the shores of **Lake Managua** (also known as *Xolotlán*), which is 52 km long, 15-25 km wide, and sits 39 m above sea level. Its maximum depth is only 30 m and it has a surface area of 1025 sq km. The Peninsula of Chiltepe juts out into Lake Managua and holds two crater lakes, Xiloá and Apoyeque. Managua also houses four small crater lakes. Lake Managua drains to Lake Nicaragua via the Río Tipitapa just east of the capital. The mighty **Lake Nicaragua**, often called by one of its pre-Conquest names, *Cocibolca*, is 160 km long, 65 km at its widest, and 32 m above the level of the sea. This massive sheet of water averages 20 m in depth with a maximum depth of 60 m. Lake Nicaragua covers a total of 8264 sq km. Just 18 km separates the big lake from the Pacific Ocean on the southern part of its western shores. But Lake Nicaragua drains 190 km to the Caribbean Sea via the **Río San Juan**, the second longest river in Central America behind the 680 km Río Coco in Nicaragua's north. In total there are 96 principal rivers, most lying east of the great lakes.

Volcanoes

Nicaragua is one of the most geologically active countries in the world. It lies at the intersection of the Coco and Caribe continental plates. Subduction of the Coco plate underneath the Caribe plate is at a rate of 8-9 cm per year, the fastest rate of plate collision in the hemisphere. The newest of the countries in the Americas in geological terms (8-9 million years old), its constant subterranean movement results in over 300 low level tremors per day in the region, with the majority occurring on the Pacific shelf. Another result of the land in upheaval is a line of more than 40 beautiful volcanoes, six of which have been active within the last 100 years. The volcanoes run 300 km from north to south along a fault line that is full of magma 10 km below the topsoil.

The northernmost is **Volcán Cosigüina** (800 m), overlooking the Golfo de Fonseca, with a lake in its crater. Its final eruption was in 1835, in what is believed to have been the most violent in recorded history in the Americas, with ash being thrown as far as Mexico and the ground shaking as far south as Colombia. To the southeast continues the Maribios volcanic chain, with the now-extinct **Volcán Chonco** (1105 m) and the country's highest, the cone of **Volcán San Cristóbal** (1745 m). San Cristóbal began erupting again in 1971 after a long period of inactivity after the highly explosive years of 1684-1885. Since 1999 it has been throwing up a lot of ash, its last activity was in 2006.

Just south rises the extinct cone of **Volcán Casita**, which is notable for its pine forest, the southernmost of its kind in the American continent's northern hemisphere. One side of Casita collapsed during the torrential rains of Hurricane Mitch in 1998, burying numerous villages in the municipality of Posoltega and killing more than 2000 people. Further south, just before León, is the very active **Volcán Telica** (1061 m) with eruptions occurring often in the 1990s and the last one in 2007. It was recorded erupting in 1529, 1685 and between 1965-1968 with more activity in 1971. It seems to erupt in unison with San Cristóbal. Next to the bald, eroding summit of Telica are the dormant cones of little **Volcán Santa Clara** (or **Volcán San Jacinto**) and **Volcán Rota** or **Volcán Orata** (836 m), which is believed to be the oldest in the chain.

Just south of León is one of the youngest volcanoes on the planet, **Cerro Negro**; born in 1850, it has risen from just above sea level to 450 m in this short period. Major eruptions have occurred 12 times since 1867, including three times since 1990. This is the most dangerous of the volcanoes with violent eruptions and lava flows, and the eruption in August 1999 opened new craters at its southern base.

Volcán Pilas is formed of various craters, the highest of which rises 1001 m and contains one active crater known as *El Hoyo*, which last erupted from 1952-1955, though it is still smoking. Other extinct cones lie between Pilas and the majestic **Volcán Momotombo** (1300 m), which overlooks the shores of Lake Managua. Momotombo's eruptions in the late 1500s convinced the residents of León Viejo to leave. It erupted with force in 1764, regularly erupted from 1858 to 1866, and had its most recent significant eruption in 1905 with a large lava flow to its east side. Today a geothermal plant on the base of its west side utilizes its considerable fumarolic energy on a daily basis. The chain ends with little extinct **Volcán Momotombito**, which forms an island in Lake Managua. Managua's volcanoes are all extinct and six contain crater lakes.

The **Dirianes** volcanic chain begins just north of Masaya with the complex of **Volcán Masaya**, including the smoking, lava-filled **Santiago** crater as well as four extinct craters and a lagoon. Masaya is the only volcano on the American continent, and one of four in the world, with a constant pool of lava. During its very active recent history there have been noteworthy eruptions in 1670, 1772, 1858-1859, 1902-1905, 1924, 1946, 1965 and 1970-1972. It fell dormant for two decades before coming alive again with up to 400 tonnes per day of sulphur output from 1995 until today. It had a small, but nasty little eruption on 23 April 2001, with more expected.

South between Masaya and Granada is the extinct **Apoyo**, which died very violently 20,000 years ago, leaving the deep blue Laguna de Apoyo, 6 km in diameter. Along the shores of Lake Nicaragua and shadowing Granada is dormant and mildly fumarolic **Volcán Mombacho** (1345 m), wrapped in cloud forest. Mombacho had a major structural collapse in 1570 that wiped out a Chorotega village at its base. Fall-out and lava flows from a prehistoric eruption (around 6000 BC) of the Mombacho cone created Las Isletas in Lake Nicaragua.

The **volcanoes of Lake Nicaragua** include the extinct and heavily eroded cone that forms the **Isla de Zapatera** (600 m), a national park and a very important pre-Columbian site. The last two volcanoes in the Nicaraguan chain of fire make up the stunning Isla de Ometepe. The symmetrical and active cone of **Volcán Concepción** (1610 m) became very active in 1883-1887, 1908-1910, 1921 and 1948; the last major lava flow was in 1957 and has had ash emissions as recently as 2007. The cloud forest covered **Volcán Maderas** (1394 m), believed to be extinct, holds a lake in its misty summit.

In reality there are many, many more volcanoes; some are so heavily eroded that they merge with the landscape, but Nicaragua, in essence, is one string of volcanoes from west to east varying in age from eight million to 160 years.

Climate

Nicaragua's location between the Tropic of Cancer and the Equator (11-15° north) dictates a well defined annual wet and dry season, which the Nicaraguans refer to as winter and summer respectively, despite the fact that the rainy season is in the northern hemisphere's summer. Bands of high pressure areas arrive from the South Pacific and collide with Caribbean low pressure areas in the rainy season from May to November in most of the country. During the dry season, Pacific low pressure heads south pushed by bands of high pressure from the northeast, creating rains in the southern hemisphere tropics and dry winds in Nicaragua.

The trade winds from the Caribbean modify the pattern, creating a longer rainy season directly proportional to the proximity to the Caribbean Sea. The rain-soaked Caribbean Coast receives up to 5000 mm of rain annually at San Juan del Norte with inland jungle and northern Caribbean coastal areas soaking in 2500 to 4000 mm annually. The dry season is between two and three months long depending on position, with San Juan del Norte receiving a break from the rains only from mid-March to the end of April. The central and northern highlands between 500 and 1500 m have their own weather profile, with rainfall averaging between 1500 to 2500 mm annually. The rainy season is shorter than it is on the Caribbean Coast and jungles, but still longer than the Pacific lowlands with seven to eight months of rain and a January to April dry season. The Pacific Basin is classic dry tropical with 700 to 1500 mm of rain annually, coming almost exclusively during the six-month wet season from mid-May to mid-November followed by a very dry six-month period.

Monthly profile

Temperatures are directly related to altitude in Nicaragua. In essence, every 140 m of altitude above sea level translates into a 1°C lower temperature. This means that it can be 32°C in Managua and in the mid-20s in the mountain regions. The forest also has a cooling effect with trapped moisture after rains keeping the mercury from shooting back up. World weather irregularities due to global warming have also been felt in Nicaragua with rain in the dry season, dry during the rainy season and hurricanes of record force. Even the usually infallible weather rhythms of the tropics have been fouled. However, in a typical year, January and February are dry windy months, night time temperatures are cool, dropping down to 18-20°C. The landscape is beginning to turn brown though many tropical trees are beginning to flower on the savannas. March and April means much higher temperature, the landscape now very dry and dusty with the added smoke of farmers burning brush and sugar cane refuse. Jungle trees come into full bloom during this period. May and June starts the rainy season, humidity can be very high, above 85%, during these months as the weather changes. Rains are in the afternoon and at night, though some storms will bring two or three days of rain. The landscape transforms into a spectacular green after the third good rain, a green that builds all the way to November. July and August are rainy with a two-week break in the rain known locally as *veranillo* (little summer). The forest is now in full swing and green is the dominant colour. September and October are very rainy months with high hurricane risk and tropical depressions bringing two or three blocks of rainy days. The landscape is lush and the temperature is moderate. November and December are transitional months with rain tapering off and warm, clear days.

Flora and fauna

Like all neotropical countries, Nicaragua is blessed with rich biodiversity and, thanks to its relatively low population, economic underdevelopment and many nature reserves, much of the country's native wildlife and vegetation have been preserved. Some species endangered in neighbouring countries are prevalent here, like the **howler monkey**, which enjoys many habitats and a population of thousands. Nonetheless, Nicaragua has not been immune to the world crisis of deforestation, most of which has occurred to clear land for farming, along with limited logging. Forest coverage has been reduced from 7,000,000 ha in 1950 to under 4,000,000 ha in the 21st century. Compounding the problem is the dominant use of wood for energy, with kindling wood (*leña*) still the main fuel for cooking. *Leña* represents 57% of the national consumption of energy, while petroleum is only at 30%. The development of responsible tourism to Nicaragua's outstanding natural areas provides hope for economic viability and nature conservation.

Principal ecosystems

The Pacific Basin is dominated by **savannah** and **tropical dry forest**. There are several significant **mangrove forests** and major areas of **wetlands** in diverse parts of the country. The biggest expanse of **cloud forest** in Central America is present on Pacific volcanoes and northern mountain ranges, especially within the Bosawás reserve. **Pine forests** run along the northern territories all the way to the Caribbean with the central-northern mountains home to extensive, but dwindling numbers. Transitional **tropical wet forests** are present on the east side of the great lakes and Lake Nicaragua's southern coast. The most extensive growth of **primary rainforest** on the isthmus dominates the Río San Juan's Indio-Maíz reserve and much of the northeastern and Caribbean lowlands. **Plant species** are, of course, diverse with 350 species of tree, part of some 12,000 species of flora that have been classified so far, with at least another 5000 yet to be documented. Those classified include more than 600 species of orchid alone. **Animal species** are equally impressive, most of all the insect life, with an estimated 250,000 species, although only about 10,000 of those have been documented to date. Mammals include some 251 species along with 234 different variations of reptile and amphibian. Bird diversity is particularly impressive with the ever-growing list of species currently totalling 714.

National parks and reserves

Ministro de Medio Ambiente y Recursos Naturales (Ministry of Environment and Natural Resources) better known as MARENA is responsible for the administration of Nicaragua's 83 protected areas, which cover more than 18% of its land. The organization is gravely under-funded and understaffed, but tries hard to overcome these shortcomings to preserve Nicaragua's spectacular natural resources. The ministry is open to tourism, but has yet to fathom how to utilize visitors as a means of financing preservation. The exceptions are the well-organized parks where the non-profit Cocibolca Foundation has joined forces with MARENA to offer a viable ecological experience for foreign and national visitors. If you have some grasp of Spanish you will find the *guardabosques* (park guards) to be very friendly and helpful in any natural reserve. It is important to realize that the MARENA park guards are very well intentioned, earnest and serious about their responsibility, despite being considerably underpaid. They will ask for proof of permission for entrance into some areas and should be treated with respect and appreciation for the critical role they play in preservation of reserves and parks. Check with MARENA before setting out to visit one of the lesser known reserves. Parks and reserves that charge admission (see individual destinations) are prepared and welcome visitors, but many areas, like the remote reaches of the Indio-Maíz Biological Reserve, cannot be entered without prior consent from **MARENA** ⓘ *Km 12.5, Carretera Norte, Managua, T233-1278, www.marena.gob.ni.*

Volcanic parks and reserves

Along with the flagship Parque Nacional Volcán Masaya, many of Nicaragua's volcanoes have forests set aside as a reserve. Ancient volcanoes in the central and eastern regions all have forest reserves on them, critical for the local climate and water tables. In many parts of the country they are covered in rain and cloud forest and there are more than 28 such reserves set aside as protected areas, including the following Pacific Basin volcanoes: **Momotombo, El Hoyo, San Cristóbal, Casita, Telica, Rota, Concepción, Maderas, Cosigüina** and **Mombacho**. Volcanic crater lakes and their forests are also set aside as protected areas, such as **Laguna de Apoyo, Laguna de Asososca, Laguna de Nejapa, Laguna de Tiscapa** and the two crater lakes of Península de Chiltepe, **Laguna Apoyeque** and **Laguna Xiloá**.

Turtle nesting sites and mangroves

Some of the most rewarding of all parks to visit are the wildlife refuges set aside for the arrival of egg-laying sea turtles. Along the central Pacific Coast is **Chacocente** and its tropical dry forest reserve. More accessible is the beach at **La Flor**, south of San Juan del Sur. **Isla Juan Venado** is also a place to see turtles, not in the quantity of the other reserves, but with the added attraction of accessible mangroves and their wildlife.

Cloud forest reserves

Given the the great challenges of visiting the hard-to-reach protected cloud forests of the Bosawás Reserve, the best place to enjoy the wildlife of the cloud forest is on the **Volcán Mombacho**, just outside Granada, and **Volcán Maderas** on Ometepe Island. In Matagalpa, the **Selva Negra Reserve** is also easy to access, as is the **Arenal Reserve** on the border of Jinotega and Matagalpa, and **El Jaguar** in Jinotega; another good option is the **Miraflor Reserve** in Estelí.

Rainforest reserves

With the two biggest rainforest reserves in Central America, Nicaragua is the place for the rainforest enthusiast who does not need luxury lodging. The best, for its access and reliable lodging, is **Indio-Maíz**. **Bosawás** is the biggest area of forest on the isthmus, accessible from the Northern Highlands or Caribbean side of the country. Travel safety is an issue in the region (see page 291 for details), and although it is improving, this vast wilderness is generally the preserve of hardened adventure travellers. If you are planning to visit Bosawás, always check with MARENA in Managua to see which entrance to the park is most advisable. They can put you in contact with guides too, as well as supply maps.

Wetland reserves

Nothing can match the natural splendour of the wetlands in **Los Guatuzos**, which one US environmental writer called "one of the most beautiful places on earth". This wildlife refuge has only basic and rustic lodging, but it is well worth the effort to see its fauna.

National monument parks

Archipiélago Solentiname is great for culture lovers as well as birders. Solentiname's 36 islands are teeming with bird life and are home to a very interesting community of rural artists. The fortress at **El Castillo** is an important historic landmark set on a beautiful hill above the majestic Río San Juan.

Books and films

Books

Anthropology

Field, LW *The Grimace of Macho Ratón* (Duke University, 1999). A cultural anthropological look at Nicaragua's national play, *El Güegüence*, and how it relates to Nicaraguan identity, in particular its effect on definitions of indigenous and *mestizo* in Pacific Nicaragua. This curious wandering work also focuses on Nicaragua's ceramic artisans as a model for understanding Nicaraguan social-behavioural traits, and on occasion slips into being a travel diary.

Gould, JL *To Die in this Way, Nicaraguan Indians and the Myth of Mestizaje 1880-1965* (Duke University Press, 1998). A fascinating, though academic, study of the tragic trajectory of Nicaragua's Pacific and central indigenous communities and the resulting effect on the definitions of the country's ethnic make-up. A very important work for anthropology and also for the history of Nicaragua and its injustice to its most vulnerable citizens. Despite the breadth and quality of the research, readers are still left wondering about the 'myth of *mestizaje*', how should we define 'indigenous' in today's Nicaragua?

Lange, FW *Archaeology of Pacific Nicaragua* (University of New Mexico, 1992). Dr Lange is one of the foremost experts on Nicaraguan archaeology. Though not meant as an introduction for the layman, this book is very interesting in its descriptions and observations about Nicaraguan archaeology in the extraordinarily ceramic-rich Pacific region.

Fiction

Belli, G *The Inhabited Women* (translated by Kathleen March, Warner Books, 1994). One of Nicaragua's most famous writer/poets, her work is famously sensual and this story is no exception. A yuppie turns revolutionary after being inspired by a native Indian spirits tale. The hero joins an underground rebel group for a story based partially upon historic events. It works well, at least until its action-film ending, and is an enjoyable read, with some beautiful and magical prose.

Ramírez, S *To Bury Our Fathers* (translated by Nick Caistor, Readers International, 1993). Nicaragua's finest living author recounts life in the Somoza García period of Nicaragua, from the viewpoint of exiled rebels in Guatemala. Sergio Ramírez paints a detailed picture of the Nicaraguan character and humour. Vice-President of Nicaragua during the Sandinista period, Ramírez is recognized as one of Latin America's finest writers and this is one of his best-known works. Translations of other classic works, and his newest award-winning novels, can only be hoped for.

Narratives and travelogues

Beals, C *Banana Gold* (JB Lippincott Company, 1932). A true jewel. Although half of the book gripes about the life of a journalist travelling through southern Mexico and Central America, the half that deals with Beals' harrowing trip on horseback from Tegucigalpa to Sébaco during the war between Sandino and the US Marines is fascinating, humorous, tragic and beautiful. Beals' poetic prose further adds to the thrill as we ride along on his unrelenting quest to meet with August C. Sandino and interview him. At once both a brilliant travel and political history work.

Cabezas, O *Fire from the Mountain* (translated by Kathleen Weaver, Crown Publishers, 1985). This first-hand account of a revolutionary rebel in the making, and later in action, was dictated into a tape recorder and reads like a long, tragic and often hilarious confession. If read in its original Spanish, it's a study on Nicaraguan use of the language. This very honest book is a must for those who wish to get the feel of this time in Nicaraguan history and the irreverent Nicaraguan humour.

Rushdie, S *The Jaguar Smile* (Penguin Books, 1988). This diary of sorts, is a detailed and entertaining account of this famous writer's visit to Nicaragua during the volatile Sandinista years. Salmon Rushdie's attention to detail and power of observation are a pleasure to enjoy but, sadly, the book serves as an apology for the Sandinista government, while claiming objectivity. With a grain of salt, a very interesting read.

Twain, M *Travels with Mr Brown* (Alfred A. Knopf, 1940). Although his observations on Nicaragua make up only a small part of this book, Twain's irrepressible humour and use of language make this memoir an enjoyable read. Twain describes in detail the Nicaraguan inter-oceanic steamship route from San Francisco to New York, using the Río San Juan and Lake Nicaragua as a crossing from ocean to sea, which was so popular with gold-rushers at that time. This book is only available in its original edition.

Walker, W *The War in Nicaragua* (University of Arizona Press, 1985). A reproduction of the 1860 original by the walking evil empire himself, General William Walker, the brilliant racist who tried to annex Nicaragua to the USA in 1856. Walker wrote the book at rest in the USA while planning his final attack on Central America that would spell his doom. There is an eerie feeling that Walker loves the country he is trying to torture and destroy and a twisted love-hate attempt at justification of his actions and failure.

Nature

Belt, T *The Naturalist in Nicaragua* (University of Chicago, 1985). Reprint of a 1874 classic. Very enlightening in its observations of insect life and acute observations of 19th-century Nicaragua. Calleld by Charles Darwin, "the best of all natural history journals which have ever been published", this book by a mining engineer also sheds light on the mentality of a naturalist 130 years ago. Alongside brilliant and sensitive analytical observation, Belt freely admits beating his pet monkey and shooting dozens of birds and laments not bagging a giant jaguar he encounters in the forest.

Poetry

Darío, R *Selected Poems* (translated by Lysander Kemp, Prologue by Octavio Paz, University of Texas, 1988). Darío is one of the great poets of the Spanish language, a founder of the Modernist movement and Nicaragua's supreme national hero. This attractive collection of some of his best-known poems has the original Spanish and English translations on facing pages and an enlightening introduction by the great Mexican poet/essayist Octavio Paz.

Gullette, DG, *!Gaspar! A Spanish Poet/Priest in the Nicaraguan Revolution* (Bilingual Press, 1993). A sentimental but balanced look at the Spanish Jesuit rebel-priest, Gaspar García Laviana, who died in action during the Revolution. A great hero among the poor of Nicaragua's southern Pacific Coast during the 1970s, Gaspar was one of many unusual heroes the Nicaraguan revolution produced. This thin volume includes many of his very compassionate poems about the plight of the Nicaraguan *campesino* in the original Spanish with English translations, as well as a biographical sketch and some humorous accounts of early botched battles.

Political history

Brody, R *Contra Terror in Nicaragua* (South End Press, 1985). A book with a political purpose written at the height of the Contra War to demonstrate to the US Congress what was happening to the Nicaraguan public during the conflict. Although unabashedly one-sided, it is a graphic and convincing condemnation of the methods used by the Contra rebels during the war, often horrifying and tragic. A strong message directed at Ronald Reagan's many fans who must consider the full ramifications of his statement that the Contra's were, "the moral equivalent of our founding fathers".

Brown, TC *The Real Contra War* (University of Oklahoma Press, 2001). Written by a former 'Senior Liaison to the Contras for the US State Department' one would expect an apology for the Contras and that is exactly what one gets. However, the book grinds its axe with great elegance and brings to light some very little known aspects of the grass-roots origins of the Contra rebellion. Well researched and a valuable counterweight to the numerous books batting on the other side of the fence. A necessary companion.

Dickey, C *With the Contras* (Simon and Schuster, 1985). This is a mixture of journalism and sensationalist reporting, with the theme of the Contra insurgency and the US government's role in the war. Despite being too colourful for its own prose at times, the book manages to highlight many key characters in the conflict and exposes the difficulty of defining good and bad guys in real life war dramas. When Dickey enters the battlefield his self-satisfied irreverence cools off and he starts reporting. A valuable first-hand account.

Hodges, DC *Intellectual Foundations of the Nicaraguan Revolution* (University of Texas, 1986). An in-depth study of Nicaragua's 20th-century political players and the lead up to the Revolution of 1978-1979. A very good account of the Sandinista's namesake, the nationalist hero Augusto Sandino. Written with a rare combination of balance and eloquence, this book is a must for those who wish to understand 20th-century Nicaraguan politics.

Kinzer, S *Blood of Brothers, Life and War in Nicaragua* (Doubleday, 1991). A landmark book on the Revolution and its aftermath. Kinzer spent many years in Nicaragua working for the *Boston Globe* and *New York Times* and aside from occasional fits of arrogance has written one of the most interesting, informative and perceptive books ever written by a foreigner about Nicaragua on any subject. A must-read for anyone interested in what happened to Nicaragua in the 20th century; great power of observation, research and writing.

Mulligan, J *The Nicaraguan Church and the Revolution* (Sheep and Ward, 1991). This subject deserves better treatment, for it is undoubtedly a fascinating one. Mulligan's book deals with liberation theology and its direct effect on the Nicaraguan Revolution and the local Catholic Church. Unfortunately the book doubles as a platform for defending any and all that was Sandinista. Interesting reading, but difficult to take seriously among all the gushing.

Pezzullo, L and R *At the Fall of Somoza* (University of Pittsburgh Press, 1993). Written by the last US Ambassador to Somoza's Nicaragua with the help of his son, this is a riveting book that is much more balanced and sympathetic to the Revolution than most would expect. Great writing on heroism during the rebellion and the head games of the US government and Somoza, with first-hand accounts and solid research. Another must-read.

Zimmermann, M *Sandinista, Carlos Fonseca and the Nicaraguan Revolution* (Duke University Press, 2000). A very detailed biography of the founder of the FSLN who died before the final victory. Though sympathetic, it is fairly even-handed in its use of historical analysis. A very well researched and interesting work for those already familiar with the history of the struggle, though sadly the book finishes with a lopsided view of what occurred after Fonseca's death, discrediting some of the work's painstakingly balanced approach, as a selective prelude to an apology.

Films

Loach, Ken *Carla's Song* (Scotland, 1996). With big points for originality, this film ends up playing like a Sandinista party film. Aside from political axes being ground, however, the picture shows some great elements of Nicaraguan life in the 1980s. The film also features Nicaragua's unique use of the Spanish language (which at the film's opening in Managua had the audience in tears of laughter) and many other fine details. The obligatory love story is between a Glasgow bus driver and a Nicaraguan immigrant who lives by begging, performing folkloric dancing in the streets for coins. The fact that a Nicaraguan woman who spoke English (and even understood the Scots) would be begging was particularly offensive to many Nicaraguan women but, nevertheless, the film is the best yet made using Nicaragua as an authentic stage for drama.

Meiselas, Susan, Roberts, Richard and Guzetti, Alfred *Pictures from a Revolution – A Memoir of the Nicaraguan Conflict* (USA, 1991). In 1978, the 30-year-old Susan Meiselas was an inexperienced documentary photographer with a degree in education from Harvard who had never covered a major political story. After just being admitted to the most prestigious photo agency in the world, Magnum, she read about the assassination of the *La Prensa* editor Pedro Joaquín Chamorro and soon found herself in Managua with no knowledge of Spanish

and doubts about what she was even to photograph there. When she returned from shooting the Nicaraguan Revolution, she had became a world-famous, award-winning war photographer and her images stand today as some of the defining ones of the struggle. In this film she returns 10 years later to Nicaragua, with a film crew in tow, to find out what happened to her photo subjects.

Spottiswoode, Roger *Under Fire* (USA, 1983). Hollywood does the Nicaraguan Revolution. This film starring Nick Nolte and Gene Hackman is a hearty attempt at historical drama, with a lot of factual events being massaged to keep the necessary love story plot thumping along. Some interesting details in the film like authentic Nicaraguan beer and street signs of obscure villages are made all the more impressive by the sad fact that not one scene was actually shot in Nicaragua. The murder by the Somoza's army of a US journalist is factual, if twisted, and gives the movie a surprise element.

Footnotes

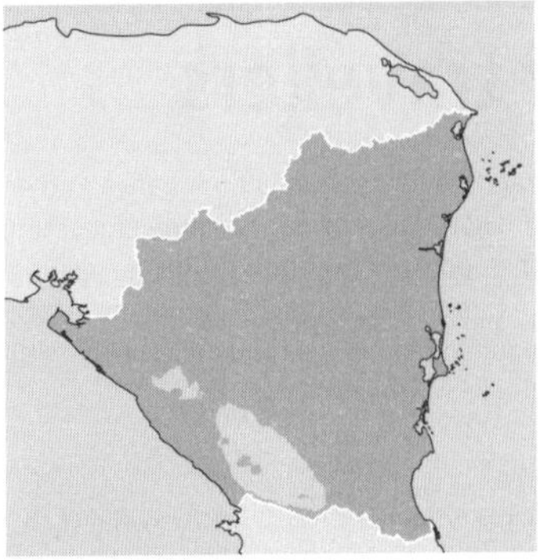

Basic Spanish for travellers

Learning Spanish is a useful part of the preparation for a trip to Latin America and no volumes of dictionaries, phrase books or word lists will provide the same enjoyment as being able to communicate directly with the people of the country you are visiting. It is a good idea to make an effort to grasp the basics before you go. As you travel you will pick up more of the language and the more you know, the more you will benefit from your stay.

General pronunciation

Whether you have been taught the 'Castilian' pronounciation (*z* and *c* followed by *i* or *e* are pronounced as the *th* in think) or the 'American' pronounciation (they are pronounced as *s*), you will encounter little difficulty in understanding either. Regional accents and usages vary, but the basic language is essentially the same everywhere.

Vowels

a	as in English *cat*
e	as in English *best*
i	as the *ee* in English *feet*
o	as in English *shop*
u	as the *oo* in English *food*
ai	as the *i* in English *ride*
ei	as *ey* in English *they*
oi	as *oy* in English *toy*

Consonants

Most consonants can be pronounced more or less as they are in English. The exceptions are:

g	before *e* or *i* is the same as *j*
h	is always silent (except in *ch* as in *chair*)
j	as the *ch* in Scottish *loch*
ll	as the *y* in *yellow*
ñ	as the *ni* in English *onion*
rr	trilled much more than in English
x	depending on its location, pronounced *x*, *s*, *sh* or *j*

Spanish words and phrases

Greetings, courtesies

hello	*hola*
good morning	*buenos días*
good afternoon/evening/night	*buenas tardes/noches*
goodbye	*adiós/chao*
pleased to meet you	*mucho gusto*
see you later	*hasta luego*
how are you?	*¿cómo está? ¿cómo estás?*
I'm fine, thanks	*estoy muy bien, gracias*
I'm called...	*me llamo...*
what is your name?	*¿cómo se llama? ¿cómo te llamas?*
yes/no	*sí/no*
please	*por favor*
thank you (very much)	*(muchas) gracias*
I speak Spanish	*hablo español*
I don't speak Spanish	*no hablo español*
do you speak English?	*¿habla inglés?*
I don't understand	*no entiendo/ no comprendo*
please speak slowly	*hable despacio por favor*
I am very sorry	*lo siento mucho/ disculpe*
what do you want?	*¿qué quiere? ¿qué quieres?*
I want	*quiero*
I don't want it	*no lo quiero*
leave me alone	*déjeme en paz/ no me moleste*
good/bad	*bueno/malo*

Questions and requests

Have you got a room for two people?
¿Tiene una habitación para dos personas?
How do I get to_?
¿Cómo llego a_?
How much does it cost?
¿Cuánto cuesta? ¿cuánto es?
I'd like to make a long-distance phone call
Quisiera hacer una llamada de larga distancia
Is service included?
¿Está incluido el servicio?
Is tax included?
¿Están incluidos los impuestos?
When does the bus leave (arrive)?
¿A qué hora sale (llega) el autobús?
When? *¿cuándo?*
Where is_? *¿dónde está_?*
Where can I buy tickets?
¿Dónde puedo comprar boletos?
Where is the nearest petrol station?
¿Dónde está la gasolinera más cercana?
Why? *¿por qué?*

Basics

bank	*el banco*
bathroom/toilet	*el baño*
bill	*la factura/la cuenta*
cash	*el efectivo*
cheap	*barato/a*
credit card	*la tarjeta de crédito*
exchange house	*la casa de cambio*
exchange rate	*el tipo de cambio*
expensive	*caro/a*
market	*el mercado*
note/coin	*le billete/la moneda*
police (policeman)	*la policía (el policía)*
post office	*el correo*
public telephone	*el teléfono público*
supermarket	*el supermercado*
ticket office	*la taquilla*
traveller's cheques	*los cheques de viajero/ los travelers*

Getting around

aeroplane	*el avión*
airport	*el aeropuerto*
arrival/departure	*la llegada/salida*
avenue	*la avenida*
block	*la cuadra*
border	*la frontera*
bus station	*la terminal de autobuses/camiones*
bus	*el bus/el autobús/ el camión*
collective/fixed-route taxi	*el colectivo*
corner	*la esquina*
customs	*la aduana*
first/second class	*primera/segunda clase*
left/right	*izquierda/derecha*
ticket	*el boleto*
empty/full	*vacío/lleno*
highway, main road	*la carretera*
immigration	*la inmigración*
insurance	*el seguro*
insured person	*el/la asegurado/a*
to insure yourself against	*asegurarse contra*
luggage	*el equipaje*
motorway, freeway	*el autopista/la carretera*
north, south, west, east	*norte, sur, oeste (occidente), este (oriente)*
oil	*el aceite*
to park	*estacionarse*
passport	*el pasaporte*
petrol/gasoline	*la gasolina*
puncture	*el pinchazo/ la ponchadura*
street	*la calle*
that way	*por allí/por allá*
this way	*por aquí/por acá*
tourist card/visa	*la tarjeta de turista/visa*
tyre	*la llanta*
unleaded	*sin plomo*
waiting room	*la sala de espera*
to walk	*caminar/andar*

Accommodation

air conditioning	*el aire acondicionado*
all-inclusive	*todo incluido*
bathroom, private	*el baño privado*
bed, double/single	*la cama matrimonial/ sencilla*
blankets	*las cobijas/mantas*
to clean	*limpiar*
dining room	*el comedor*
guesthouse	*la casa de huéspedes*
hotel	*el hotel*

noisy	*ruidoso*	soap	*el jabón*
pillows	*las almohadas*	toilet	*el sanitario/excusado*
power cut	*el apagón/corte*	toilet paper	*el papel higiénico*
restaurant	*el restaurante*	towels, clean/dirty	*las toallas limpias/ sucias*
room/bedroom	*el cuarto/la habitación*		
sheets	*las sábanas*	water, hot/cold	*el agua caliente/fría*
shower	*la ducha/regadera*		

Health

aspirin	*la aspirina*	diarrhoea	*la diarrea*
blood	*la sangre*	doctor	*el médico*
chemist	*la farmacia*	fever/sweat	*la fiebre/el sudor*
condoms	*los preservativos, los condones*	pain	*el dolor*
		head	*la cabeza*
contact lenses	*los lentes de contacto*	period/sanitary towels	*la regla/ las toallas femeninas*
contraceptives	*los anticonceptivos*		
contraceptive pill	*la píldora anti-conceptiva*	stomach	*el estómago*
		altitude sickness	*el soroche*

Family

family	*la familia*	boyfriend/girlfriend	*el novio/la novia*
brother/sister	*el hermano/la hermana*	friend	*el amigo/la amiga*
daughter/son	*la hija/el hijo*	married	*casado/a*
father/mother	*el padre/la madre*	single/unmarried	*soltero/a*
husband/wife	*el esposo (marido)/ la esposa*		

Months, days and time

January	*enero*	Friday	*viernes*
February	*febrero*	Saturday	*sábado*
March	*marzo*	Sunday	*domingo*
April	*abril*		
May	*mayo*	at one o'clock	*a la una*
June	*junio*	at half past two	*a las dos y media*
July	*julio*	at a quarter to three	*a cuarto para las tres/ a las tres menos quince*
August	*agosto*		
September	*septiembre*	it's one o'clock	*es la una*
October	*octubre*	it's seven o'clock	*son las siete*
November	*noviembre*	it's six twenty	*son las seis y veinte*
December	*diciembre*	it's five to nine	*son cinco para las nueve/las nueve menos cinco*
Monday	*lunes*		
Tuesday	*martes*	in ten minutes	*en diez minutos*
Wednesday	*miércoles*	five hours	*cinco horas*
Thursday	*jueves*	does it take long?	*¿tarda mucho?*

Numbers

one	*uno/una*	six	*seis*
two	*dos*	seven	*siete*
three	*tres*	eight	*ocho*
four	*cuatro*	nine	*nueve*
five	*cinco*	ten	*diez*

eleven	*once*	twenty-one	*veintiuno*
twelve	*doce*	thirty	*treinta*
thirteen	*trece*	forty	*cuarenta*
fourteen	*catorce*	fifty	*cincuenta*
fifteen	*quince*	sixty	*sesenta*
sixteen	*dieciséis*	seventy	*setenta*
seventeen	*diecisiete*	eighty	*ochenta*
eighteen	*dieciocho*	ninety	*noventa*
nineteen	*diecinueve*	hundred	*cien/ciento*
twenty	*veinte*	thousand	*mil*

Food

avocado	*el aguacate*	lime	*el limón*
baked	*al horno*	lobster	*la langosta*
bakery	*la panadería*	lunch	*el almuerzo/la comida*
banana	*el plátano*	meal	*la comida*
beans	*los frijoles/ las habichuelas*	meat	*la carne*
		minced meat	*el picadillo*
beef	*la carne de res*	onion	*la cebolla*
beef steak or pork fillet	*el bistec*	orange	*la naranja*
boiled rice	*el arroz blanco*	pepper	*el pimiento*
bread	*el pan*	pasty, turnover	*la empanada/ el pastelito*
breakfast	*el desayuno*		
butter	*la mantequilla*	pork	*el cerdo*
cake	*el pastel*	potato	*la papa*
chewing gum	*el chicle*	prawns	*los camarones*
chicken	*el pollo*	raw	*crudo*
chilli pepper or green pepper	*el ají/pimiento*	restaurant	*el restaurante*
clear soup, stock	*el caldo*	salad	*la ensalada*
cooked	*cocido*	salt	*la sal*
dining room	*el comedor*	sandwich	*el bocadillo*
egg	*el huevo*	sauce	*la salsa*
fish	*el pescado*	sausage	*la longaniza/el chorizo*
fork	*el tenedor*	scrambled eggs	*los huevos revueltos*
fried	*frito*	seafood	*los mariscos*
garlic	*el ajo*	soup	*la sopa*
goat	*el chivo*	spoon	*la cuchara*
grapefruit	*la toronja/el pomelo*	squash	*la calabaza*
grill	*la parrilla*	squid	*los calamares*
grilled/griddled	*a la plancha*	supper	*la cena*
guava	*la guayaba*	sweet	*dulce*
ham	*el jamón*	to eat	*comer*
hamburger	*la hamburguesa*	toasted	*tostado*
hot, spicy	*picante*	turkey	*el pavo*
ice cream	*el helado*	vegetables	*los legumbres/vegetales*
jam	*la mermelada*	without meat	*sin carne*
knife	*el cuchillo*	yam	*el camote*

Drink

beer	*la cerveza*	coffee	*el café*
boiled	*hervido/a*	coffee, white	*el café con leche*
bottled	*en botella*	cold	*frío*
camomile tea	*la manzanilla*	cup	*la taza*
canned	*en lata*	drink	*la bebida*

drunk	*borracho/a*
firewater	*el aguardiente*
fruit milkshake	*el batido/licuado*
glass	*el vaso*
hot	*caliente*
ice/without ice	*el hielo/sin hielo*
juice	*el jugo*
lemonade	*la limonada*
milk	*la leche*
mint	*la menta*
rum	*el ron*
soft drink	*el refresco*
sugar	*el azúcar*
tea	*el té*
to drink	*beber/tomar*
water	*el agua*
water, carbonated	*el agua mineral con gas*
water, still mineral	*el agua mineral sin gas*
wine, red	*el vino tinto*
wine, white	*el vino blanco*

Key verbs

to go	**ir**
I go	*voy*
you go (familiar)	*vas*
he, she, it goes, you (formal) go	*va*
we go	*vamos*
they, you (plural) go	*van*

to have (possess)	**tener**
I have	*tengo*
you (familiar) have	*tienes*
he, she, it, you (formal) have	*tiene*
we have	*tenemos*
they, you (plural) have	*tienen*
(also used in 'I am hungry'	*tengo hambre*)

there is/are	*hay*
there isn't/aren't	*no hay*

to be **ser** (permanent state) **estar** (positional or temporary state)

I am	soy	estoy
you are	eres	estás
he, she, it is, you (formal) are	es	está
we are	somos	estamos
they, you (plural) are	son	están

This section has been assembled on the basis of glossaries compiled by André de Mendonça and David Gilmour of South American Experience, London, and the Latin American Travel Advisor, No 9, March 1996

Nicaraguan Spanish

Hablando Nica – Nicaraguan Spanish

You've done your Spanish course and you're ready to chat up the Nicaraguan people. But wait, what's that? *¿Cómo, perdón? Err…¿Qué dice?* It seems all that hard work in class has yet to pay off. Nicaraguans (Nicas) are famous for their creativity and humour and this carries over to their use of the Spanish language, nothing is sacred. In fact the Nicaraguans are credited with hundreds of words unique to their inventive, heavily indigenous-influenced version of Spanish. Here are some essentials for a head start, *¡dale pues!* (just do it!):

Nica-speak	Meaning
boludo	lazy
chele	white person
chapín	barefoot
charula	worthless thing
chiringo	old clothes
cipote	little boy
fachento	arrogant
jaña	girlfriend
palmado	broke, penniless
pinche	stingy
tapudo	big-mouth
tuanis	cool
turcazo	hard punch

When and when not to say ¡Hola!

Nicaraguans are renowned for their friendliness and, compared with many Latin Americans, are very informal people. To get the most out of your visit, it's a good idea to learn at least some basic greetings in Spanish and to heed local customs and culture.

The traditional greeting for complete strangers is *Mucho gusto* (my pleasure) which will be followed by a handshake or a nod and a smile. One kiss to the right cheek (to the air, as the two right cheeks meet) is also common if you are being introduced – although never between men. In the countryside children often reach up to kiss someone they are being introduced to; this is a polite way to greet an adult. If a child cups his hands together as if in prayer and presents them to you, it is a sign of great respect (normally reserved for family members). If you encounter this you should cover the child's hands with yours very briefly and say *Dios te bendiga* (God bless you) with a smile. The time of day greeting (*Buenos días, Buenas tardes* or *Buenas noches*) is the polite norm when entering a shop, restaurant, hotel or place where you don't know anyone. If you are in a shop or corner store (*pulpería*) and there appears to be no-one around to attend you, call out ¡*Buenas*! to receive service. *Hola* (hello) is reserved for people who know each other well and should not be used to greet strangers, unless they are children. If in Nicaragua on business, try not to get down to business right away; even if just placing a business call, see how his or her day is going first.

Food glossary

A

aguacate canelo native avocado
ajillo garlic butter sauce
a la plancha food cooked on a sizzling plate or flat grill
asado roasted or grilled meat or fish

B

bistec encebollado steak bathed in onions
boa en salsa boa constrictor in tomato sauce
¡buen provecho! enjoy your meal
burrito flour tortilla stuffed with meat, rice and vegetables

C

cacao raw cocoa bean, ground and mixed with milk, rice, cinnamon, vanilla, ice and sugar
café de palo home-roasted coffee
café percolado percolated coffee
cajetas traditional sweets, candied fruit
cajeta de leche milk sweet
cajeta de zapoyol cooked zapote seeds and sugar
caliente hot
camarones de río freshwater prawns
carne asada grilled beef
cerdo asado grilled pork
ceviche raw fish marinated in onions and lime juice
chicha corn-based drink, sometimes fermented to alcohol
chimichangas fried burritos
churrasco steak grilled steak in garlic and parsley sauce
comidas meals
comida corriente/comida casera set menu
comida económica cheap food/menu
cocktail de pulpo octopus
cuajada lightly salted, soft feta-type cheese
curvina sea bass
curvina a la plancha grilled sea bass
cuzuco armadillo
cuzuco en salsa armadillo in tomato sauce

D

dorado a la parilla grilled dorado fish

E

empanadas pastries filled with meat or chicken
enchilada meat or chicken wrapped in flour tortilla

F

fritanga street food

G

gallo pinto fried white rice and kidney beans, with onions and sweet pepper
garbanzos chick peas
garrobo black iguana
garrobo en caldillo black iguana soup
gaseosas fizzy drinks
guardatinaja large nocturnal rodent
guapote local, large-mouthed bass

H

huevo de toro asado grilled bull's testicles

I

indio viejo cornmeal and shredded beef porridge with garlic and spices

J

jugo pure fruit juice

L

langosta *lobster*
langosta blanca 'white lobster' ie cocaine
lomo relleno stuffed beef

M

mahi mahi grilled dorado fish
mar y tierra surf and turf
mariscos seafood
melocotón star fruit/peach
mojarra carp
mole chocolate, chilli sauce

N

nacatamales cornmeal, pork or chicken and rice, achote (similar to paprika), peppers, peppermint leafs, potatoes, onions and cooking oil, all wrapped in a big green banana leaf and boiled
níspero brown sugar fruit

P

paca large, nocturnal rodent
pargo al vapor steamed snapper
pargo rojo/blanco red/white snapper
para llevar to take away
parrillada Argentine-style grill
pescado fish
pescado a la suyapa fresh snapper in a tomato, sweet pepper and onion sauce
piniona thin strips of candied green papaya
Pío V corn cake topped with light cream and bathed in rum sauce
pitaya cactus fruit, blended with lime and sugar
plátano plantain
plato típico typical Nicaraguan food
pollo chicken
pollo asado grilled chicken
posol grainy indigenous drink served in an original *jícaro* gourd cup
pupusas tortillas filled with beans, cheese and/or pork

Q

quesadillas fried tortilla with cheese, chilli and peppers
quesillos mozzarella cheese in a hot tortilla with salt and bathed in cream
queso crema moist bland cheese, good fried
queso seco slightly bitter dry cheese

R

refresco/fresco fruit juice or grains and spices mixed with water and sugar
robalo snook
rosquillas baked corn and cheese biscuits

S

sábalo/sábalo real tarpon/giant tarpon
sopa de albóndiga soup with meatballs made of chicken, eggs, garlic and cornmeal
sopa de mondongo tripe soup
sopa de tortilla soup of corn tortilla and spices
sopa huevos de toro bull testicle soup
sopa levanta muerto literally 'return from the dead' soup
sorbete ice cream
surtido sampler or mixed dish

T

tacos fried tortilla stuffed with chicken, beef or pork
tacos chinos egg rolls
tres leches very sweet cake made with three kinds of milk (fresh and tinned)
tamales cornmeal bars boiled
tilapia African lake fish introduced to Nicaragua
tiste grainy indigenous drinks served in an original *jícaro* gourd cup
tipitapa tomato sauce
tostones con queso flat plantain sections fried with cheese

V

vigorón banana leaf filled with fried pork rind, cabbage salad, yucca, tomato, hot chilli and lemon juice

Index

→ *Entries in bold refer to maps.*

D

E

F

G

H

I

J

K

L

M

N

Acknowledgements

So many people were kind and helpful on the road in Nicaragua. Without their hospitality, conversation, help and insights, none of it would have made any sense. In Managua, a special thanks to Richard Leonardi for all the good work he did on the first and second editions of this book, and for stashing my luggage and paperwork all those weeks. In Granada, thanks to Roger Ramírez, Ilich, Alejo, Olga and Erik for their instruction in Nicaraguan grammar and conversation, and to Marlon. In Apoyo, thanks to Donna and Ann for their hospitality. In Estelí, thanks to Jane and Melissa for the coffee, conversation and community tourism tip-offs. In Jinotega, thanks to Tony Robins, architect of jinotega.com. In San Juan del Sur, thanks to Mary for the excellent steak and much-appreciated company. In Ometepe, thanks to Alvaro Molina for his kind hospitality and useful information, and to Gerry, and to Michael Judd. In El Castillo, thanks to Miguel for the river kayaking. In León, thanks to Bart and Veronie for their hospitality and insights. In Las Peñitas, thanks to Gordon and Pita. On Big Corn, thanks to Mike for the eye-opening tour by golf cart. On Little Corn, thanks to Sandy Herman for her diving instruction. Thanks also to various writers, editors and Footprint folk; they include Alan Murphy, Sarah Thorowgood and Peter Hutchison, particularly, for his helpful correspondence and words of experience. At home, thanks to Jennifer Kennedy, Terri Wright, Alan Peacock Johns and Peter McCallan for their continued love and support. In New York, thanks to Jo, Dan, Frankie and Ruby.

Credits

Footprint credits
Editor: Sarah Thorowgood
Map editor: Sarah Sorensen
Picture editor: Kevin Feeney

Managing Director: Andy Riddle
Publisher: Patrick Dawson
Editorial: Alan Murphy, Felicity Laughton, Nicola Gibbs, Jo Williams, Sara Chare, Ria Gane, Emma Bryant
Cartography: Robert Lunn, Kevin Feeney, Emma Bryant
Cover design: Robert Lunn
Design: Mytton Williams
Sales and marketing: Zoë Jackson, Hannah Bonnell
Advertising sales manager: Renu Sibal
Finance and administration: Elizabeth Taylor

Photography credits
Front cover: Los Guatuzos Wildlife Refuge, Richard Leonardi
Back cover: Granada market, Robert Francis/South American Pictures
Inside colour section: Richard Leonardi, Robert Francis, Fabienne Fossez/South American Pictures, age fotostock/Superstock

Print
Manufactured in India by Nutech
Pulp from sustainable forests

Footprint feedback
We try as hard as we can to make each Footprint guide as up to date as possible but, of course, things always change. If you want to let us know about your experiences – good, bad or ugly – then don't delay, go to **www.footprintbooks.com** and send in your comments.

Publishing information
Footprint Nicaragua
3rd edition

ISBN 978 1 906098 292
CIP DATA: A catalogue record for this book is available from the British Library

Published by Footprint
6 Riverside Court
Lower Bristol Road
Bath BA2 3DZ, UK
T +44 (0)1225 469141
F +44 (0)1225 469461
discover@footprintbooks.com
www.footprintbooks.com

Distributed in the USA by Globe Pequot Press, Guilford, Connecticut

Every effort has been made to ensure that the facts in this guidebook are accurate. However, travellers should still obtain advice from consulates, airlines etc about travel and visa requirements before travelling. The authors and publishers cannot accept responsibility for any loss, injury or inconvenience however caused.

Map symbols

Administration

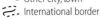

- Capital city
- Other city, town
- International border
- Regional border

Roads and travel

- Motorway
- Main road (National highway)
- Minor road
- Track
- Footpath
- Railway
- Railway with station
- Airport
- Bus station
- Metro station
- Cable car
- Funicular
- Ferry

Water features

- River, canal
- Lake, ocean
- Seasonal marshland
- Beach, sandbank
- Waterfall
- Reef

Topographical features

- Contours (approx)
- Mountain, volcano
- Mountain pass
- Escarpment
- Gorge
- Glacier
- Salt flat
- Rocks

Cities and towns

- Main through route
- Main street
- Minor street
- Pedestrianized street
- Tunnel
- Track
- Footpath
- One way-street
- Steps
- Bridge
- Fortified wall
- Park, garden, stadium
- Sleeping
- Eating
- Bars & clubs
- Building
- Sight
- Cathedral, church
- Chinese temple
- Hindu temple
- Meru
- Mosque
- Stupa
- Synagogue
- Tourist office
- Museum
- Post office
- Police
- Bank
- Internet
- Telephone
- Market
- Medical services
- Parking
- Petrol
- Golf
- A Detail map
- A Related map

Other symbols

- Archaeological site
- National park, wildlife reserve
- Viewing point
- Campsite
- Refuge, lodge
- Castle, fort
- Diving
- Deciduous, coniferous, palm trees
- Hide
- Vineyard, winery
- Distillery
- Shipwreck
- Historic battlefield

Map 1

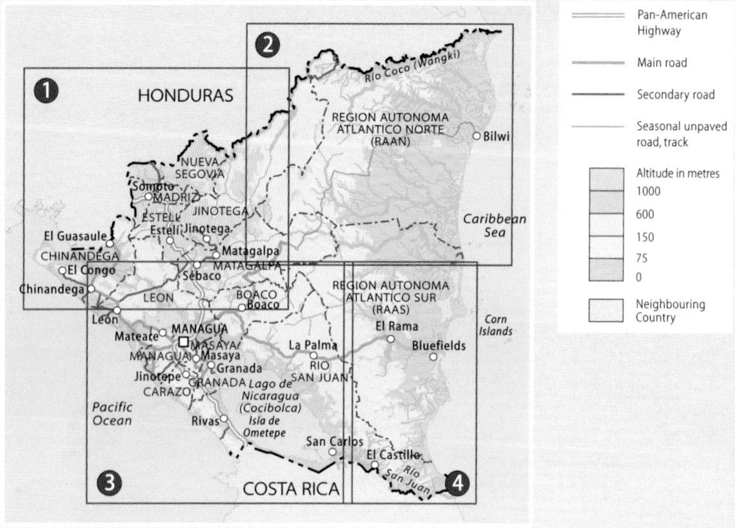

1
2
3
4
HONDURAS
Río Coco (Wangki)
REGION AUTONOMA ATLANTICO NORTE (RAAN)
Bilwi
NUEVA SEGOVIA
Somoto
MADRIZ
JINOTEGA
ESTELI
Estelí
Jinotega
Caribbean Sea
El Guasaule
Matagalpa
CHINANDEGA
MATAGALPA
El Congo
Sébaco
Chinandega
LEON
BOACO
Boaco
REGION AUTONOMA ATLANTICO SUR (RAAS)
León
Corn Islands
Mateare
MANAGUA
El Rama
MASAYA
La Palma
Bluefields
MANAGUA
Masaya
Granada
RIO SAN JUAN
Jinotepe
GRANADA
Lago de Nicaragua (Cocibolca)
CARAZO
Pacific Ocean
Isla de Ometepe
Rivas
San Carlos
El Castillo
Río San Juan
COSTA RICA
Pan-American Highway
Main road
Secondary road
Seasonal unpaved road, track
Altitude in metres
1000
600
150
75
0
Neighbouring Country

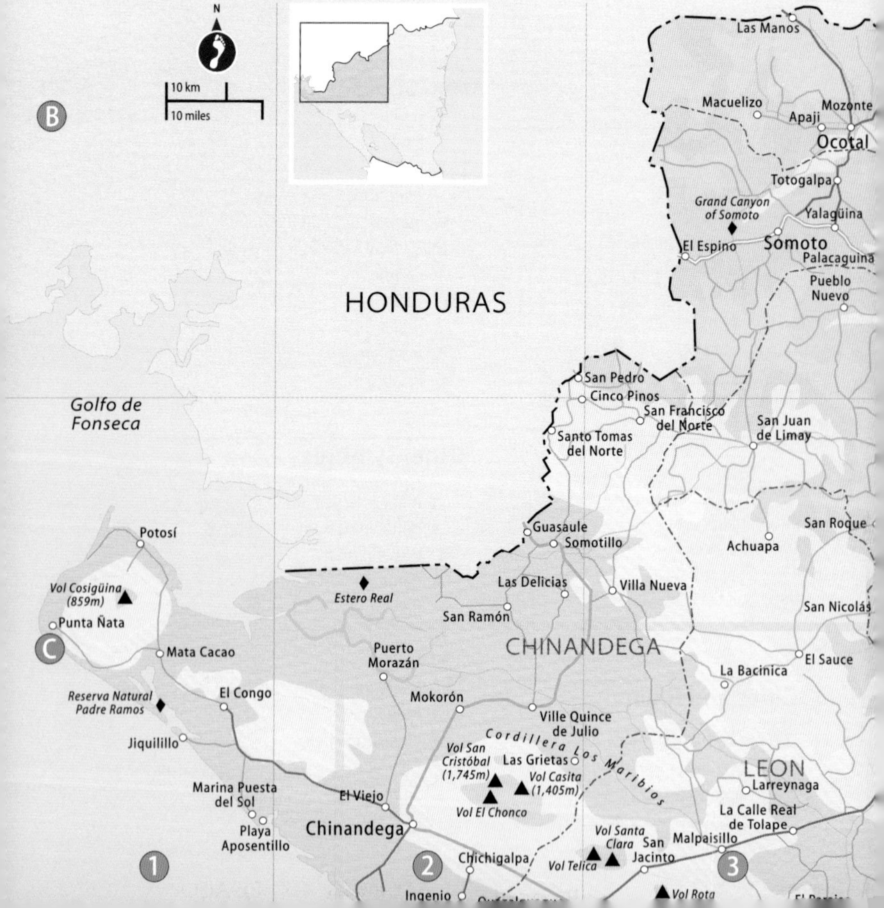

N
10 km
10 miles
B
C
1
2
3
HONDURAS
Las Manos
Macuelizo
Mozonte
Apaji
Ocotal
Totogalpa
Grand Canyon of Somoto
Yalagüina
El Espino
Somoto
Palacaguina
Pueblo Nuevo
San Pedro
Cinco Pinos
San Francisco del Norte
San Juan de Limay
Santo Tomas del Norte
Golfo de Fonseca
Guasaule
Somotillo
San Roque
Achuapa
Potosí
Estero Real
Las Delicias
Villa Nueva
Vol Cosigüina (859m)
San Ramón
San Nicolás
Punta Ñata
CHINANDEGA
Mata Cacao
Puerto Morazán
El Sauce
La Bacinica
Reserva Natural Padre Ramos
El Congo
Mokorón
Ville Quince de Julio
Jiquilillo
Cordillera Los Maribios
Vol San Cristóbal (1,745m)
Las Grietas
Vol Casita (1,405m)
LEON
Larreynaga
Marina Puesta del Sol
El Viejo
Vol El Chonco
La Calle Real de Tolape
Playa Aposentillo
Chinandega
Vol Santa Clara
San Jacinto
Malpaisillo
Chichigalpa
Vol Telica
Ingenio
Vol Rota

Bosawa
Biosphe
Reserv
Río Bocay
Map 2
Tolecacinte
Jalapa
NUEVA SEGOVIA
Wamblán
Valle Congjas
El Plantel
Wambuca
JINOTEGA
Murra
Río Coco
Santa Clara
San Fernando
Susucayan
Plan de Grama
Ciudad Antigua
Wiwilí
El Oco
San José de Bocay
El Naranja
Puerto Viejo
MADRIZ
Río Coco
Valle Ducali
Condega
El Cuá
Piedra Larga
Reserva Natural Miraflor
San Rafael del Norte
El Jaguar Cloud Forest Reserve
La Sirena
Lago de Apanás
La Dalia
Estelí
Jinotega
Reserva Natural Meseta Tisey Estanzuela
Reserva Natural Arenal
Río Tuma
El Salto de Estanzuelo
El Tuma
Disparate de Potter
Selva Negra Cloud Forest Reserve
Esperanza Verde/Yucul
MATAGALPA
Las Lajitas
Monte Grande
La Trinidad
San Isidro
La Rosa
Santa Elsa
Matagalpa
Pancasán
Río Blanco
La Garita
Map 3
San Ramón
Cordillera Dariense
Chagüitillo
Güilique
San Pablo
Sébaco
El Caracal
Matiguás
Río Grande
Santa Rosa del Peñon
Río Matagalpa
Bocana de Paiwas
Muy Muy
La Cruz de la India
Pineda
El Trapichito
Ciudad Darío
Terrabona
Santa María (1,210m)
Río Grande de Matagalpa
Tierra Azul
Veracruz
Valle El Orégano
Esquipulas
Santa Fe
Río de Janeiro
San José de las Remates
Laguna Moyuá
El Cacao
El Portón
Puertas Viejas
San Francisco
El Guanacaste
El Paraiso
BOACO
A
B
C
4
5
6

Map 2

Santa Isabel
Anris Tara
Siksayali
Asong
Krasa
A
Sang Sang
San Carlos
Umbra
Nasma Almuk
Krin Krin
Wiwirak
La Esperanza
Santa Fe
San Jerónimo
Leimus
Kisalaya
Slilmasia
Raiti
Miguel Bikan
La Tranquera
Wisconsin
Asserio Ocampo
Río Waspuk
Auas Tingni
Bosawás Biosphere Reserve
Río Bocay
Map 1
Musuwas
Sahsa
Bonanza
Kukalaya
Españolina
Wasminona
El Bosque
B
Susun
Rosita
Las Minas Mining Triangle
El Dos
Wasa King
Banacruz
REGION AUTONOMA ATLANTICO NORTE (RAAN)
Siuna
Waspado
Yaoya Central
Danlí
Wani
El Empalme
El Ocote
Rosa Grande
El Naranja
Puerto Viejo
Alamikamba
Limbaika
Karlin Dam
Ebanisa Tasbapauni
El Porvenir
Company Creek
Makantaca
C
Siawás
Río Tuma
La Cruz de Río Grande
Río Blanco
Pipilwas
Map 3
Map 4
El Chile
Güilique
1
2
3
El Chamarro

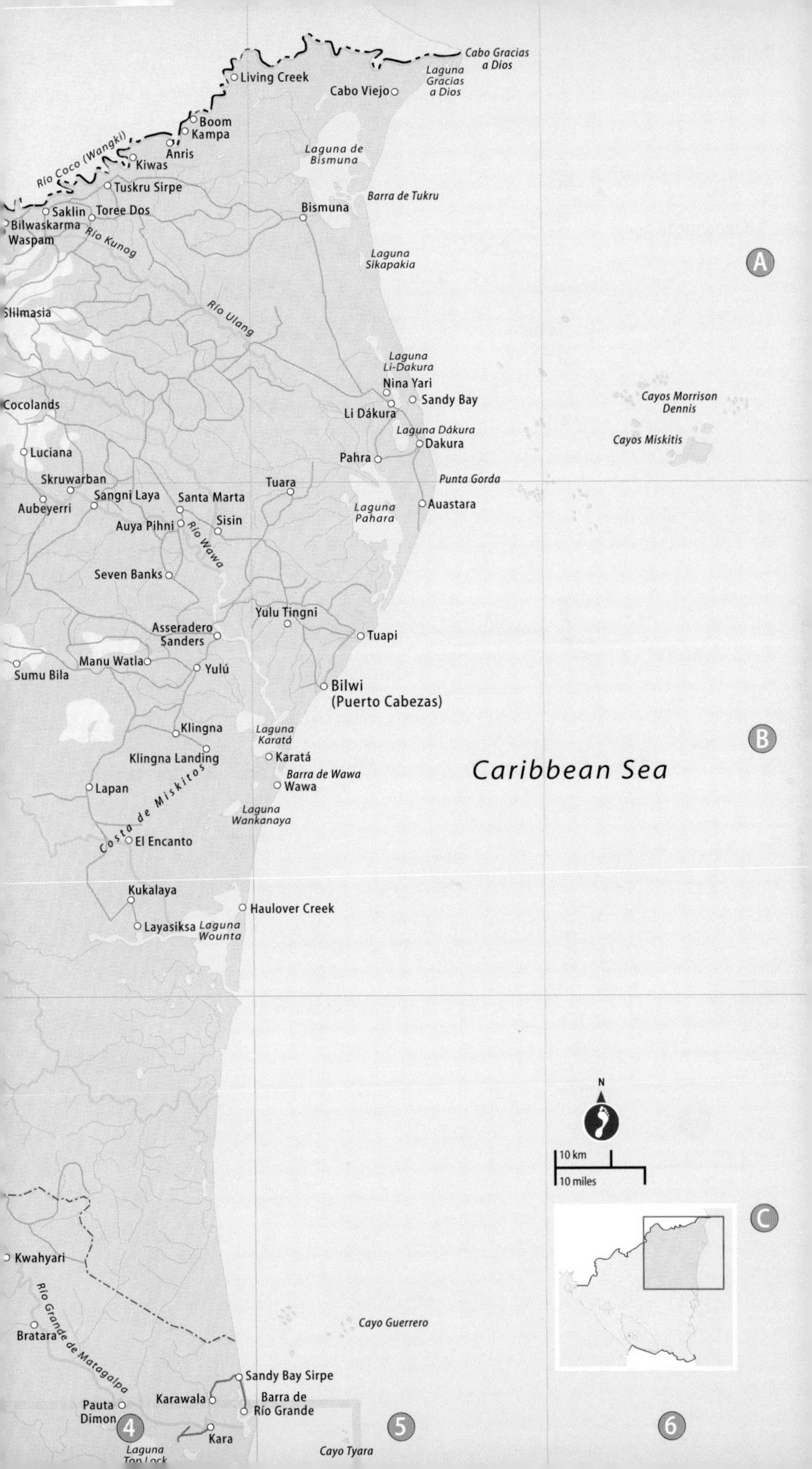

Cabo Gracias a Dios
Laguna Gracias a Dios
Living Creek
Cabo Viejo
Boom
Kampa
Anris
Kiwas
Río Coco (Wangki)
Laguna de Bismuna
Tuskru Sirpe
Barra de Tukru
Saklin
Toree Dos
Bismuna
Bilwaskarma
Waspam
Río Kunog
Laguna Sikapakia
A
Slilmasia
Río Ulang
Laguna Li-Dakura
Nina Yari
Sandy Bay
Cayos Morrison Dennis
Cocolands
Li Dákura
Laguna Dákura
Dakura
Cayos Miskitis
Luciana
Pahra
Punta Gorda
Skruwarban
Tuara
Sangni Laya
Santa Marta
Auastara
Aubeyerri
Laguna Pahara
Auya Pihni
Sisin
Río Wawa
Seven Banks
Yulu Tingni
Asseradero Sanders
Tuapi
Manu Watla
Yulú
Sumu Bila
Bilwi (Puerto Cabezas)
Klingna
Laguna Karatá
B
Klingna Landing
Karatá
Caribbean Sea
Barra de Wawa
Lapan
Wawa
Costa de Miskitos
Laguna Wankanaya
El Encanto
Kukalaya
Haulover Creek
Layasiksa
Laguna Wounta
N
10 km
10 miles
C
Kwahyari
Río Grande de Matagalpa
Bratara
Cayo Guerrero
Sandy Bay Sirpe
Karawala
Barra de Río Grande
Pauta Dimon
Kara
4
5
6
Laguna
Cayo Tyara

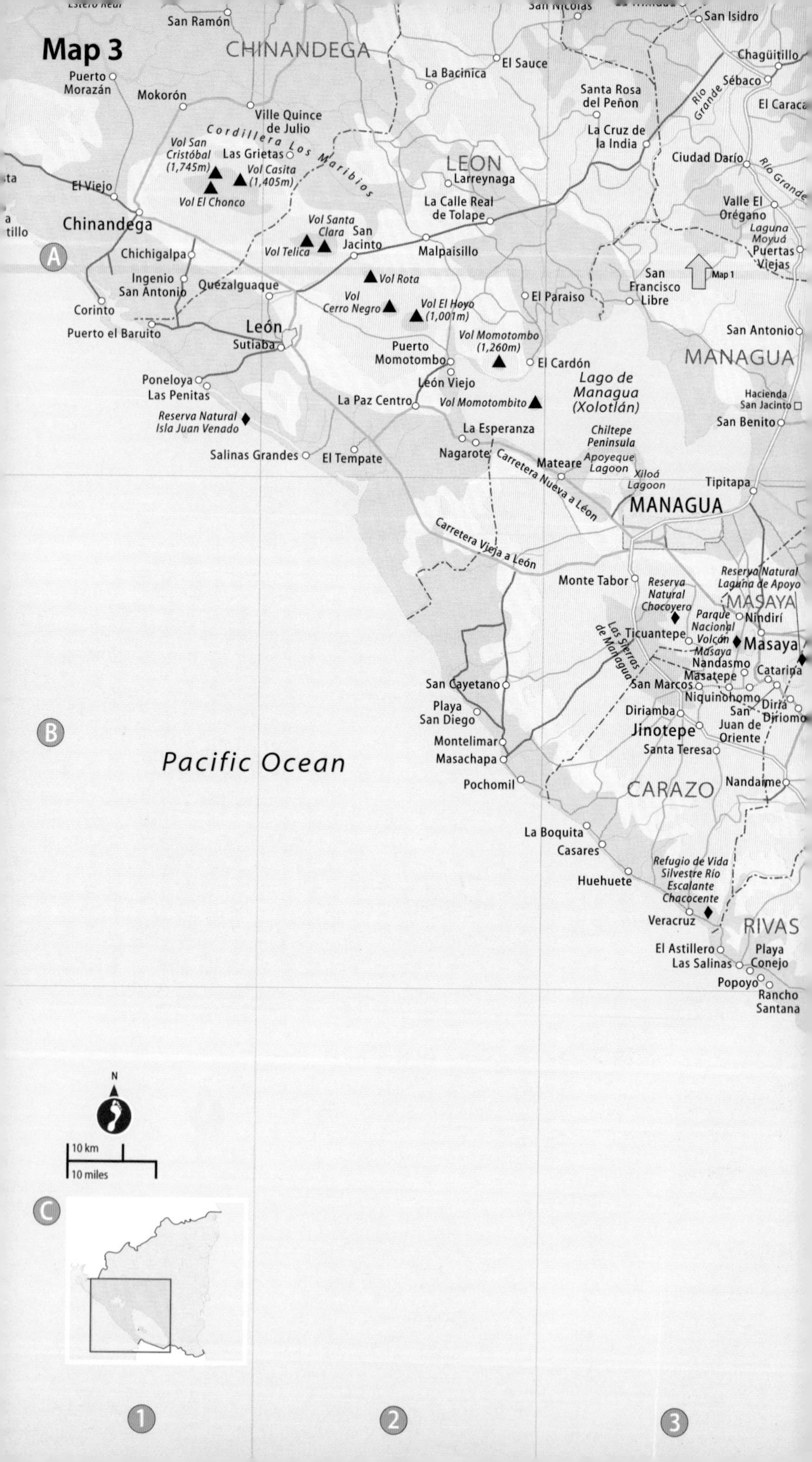

Map 3
CHINANDEGA
San Ramón
Puerto Morazán
Mokorón
Ville Quince de Julio
Cordillera Los Maribios
Vol San Cristóbal (1,745m)
Las Grietas
Vol Casita (1,405m)
Vol El Chonco
El Viejo
Chinandega
Chichigalpa
Ingenio San Antonio
Corinto
Puerto el Baruito
Quezalguaque
León
Sutiaba
Poneloya
Las Penitas
Reserva Natural Isla Juan Venado
Salinas Grandes
El Tempate
Vol Santa Clara
San Jacinto
Vol Telica
Vol Rota
Vol Cerro Negro
Vol El Hoyo (1,001m)
Puerto Momotombo
León Viejo
La Paz Centro
Vol Momotombo (1,260m)
Vol Momotombito
El Cardón
La Esperanza
Nagarote
Mateare
Carretera Nueva a León
Carretera Vieja a León
LEON
Larreynaga
La Calle Real de Tolape
Malpaisillo
El Paraiso
La Bacinica
El Sauce
San Nicolás
San Isidro
Chagüitillo
Sébaco
El Caraca
Río Grande
Santa Rosa del Peñon
La Cruz de la India
Ciudad Darío
Valle El Orégano
Laguna Moyuá
Puertas Viejas
San Francisco Libre
Map 1
San Antonio
MANAGUA
Lago de Managua (Xolotlán)
Hacienda San Jacinto
San Benito
Chiltepe Peninsula
Apoyeque Lagoon
Xiloá Lagoon
Tipitapa
MANAGUA
Monte Tabor
Reserva Natural Chocoyero
Reserva Natural Laguna de Apoyo
MASAYA
Parque Nacional Volcán Masaya
Nindirí
Masaya
Ticuantepe
Las Sierras de Managua
Nandasmo
Catarina
Masatepe
San Marcos
Niquinohomo
Diriá
Diriomo
San Juan de Oriente
Diriamba
Jinotepe
Santa Teresa
San Cayetano
Playa San Diego
Montelimar
Masachapa
Pochomil
CARAZO
Nandaime
La Boquita
Casares
Huehuete
Refugio de Vida Silvestre Río Escalante Chacocente
Veracruz
RIVAS
El Astillero
Las Salinas
Playa Conejo
Popoyo
Rancho Santana
Pacific Ocean
N
10 km
10 miles
A
B
C
1
2
3

Reserve
La Rosa
Santa Elsa
La Garita
Pancasán
MATAGALPA
Río Blanco
Pipilwas
Matagalpa
San Ramón
El Chile
Cordillera Dariense
Güilique
Map 2
San Pablo
El Chamarro
Matiguás
Río Matagalpa
Bocana de Paíwas
Muy Muy
Terrabona
Pineda
El Trapichito
Santa María (1,210m)
Veracruz
Esquipulas
Tierra Azul
de Matagalpa
Río de Janeiro
Santa Fe
San José de las Remates
El Cacao
El Portón
A
BOACO
El Guanacaste
El Paraiso
El Desparho
Santa Lucía
El Ayote
Boaco
Las Lajas
Villa Revolución
Teustepe
Las Canoas Dam
Agua Caliente
Camoapa
Río Siquia
San Augustin
El Zapote
Las Banderas
Espiritu Santo
El Alto
Cuapa
Map 4
La Libertad
Río Malacatoya
CHONTALES
San Lorenzo
El Naranjal
Belén
Asunción
Los Morenos
Paso de Panaloya
Juigalpa
La Calabeza Island
La Pelona
La Palma
Villa Sandino
El Chilamate
El Cacao
San Blas
Isla Grande
Puerto Díaz
Acoyapa
Muhan
La Gateada
Isla Redonda
Granada
Isla el Muerto
Colonia Río Rama
El Coral
Archipiélago Las Isletas
Asese
San Ubaldo
Reserva Natural Volcán Mombacho
Sabano de Flores
GRANADA
B
Reserva Silvestre Privada Domitila
El Carmen
Islas El Nancil
Fátima
Parque Nacional Archipiélago Zapatera
Río Ochomogo
Ochomogo
Lago de Nicaragua (Cocibolca)
Laguna Nocarime
Isla de Ometepe
Altagracia
Las Viejitos
Vol Concepción (1,610m)
Palos Ralos
Moyogalpa
Playa Santo Domingo
Esquípulas
Balgües
Belén
San Jorge
El Corozal
Tola
Vol Maderas (1,394m)
El Pedernal
Rivas
Mérida
San Ramón
San Miguelito
La Virgen
Brito
Morgan's Rock
Bahía Mahagual
La Boca de la Montaña
Cañas Gordas
Playa Marsella
San Juan del Sur
Sapoá
Archipiélago Solentiname
Morrillo
Playa Remanso
Peñas Blancas
Cárdenas
Isla Mancarrón
Laurel Galán
Isla San Fernando
Refugio de Vida Silvestre La Flor
Isla Mancarroncito
El Tigre
Isla La Venada
San Carlos
Playa El Coco
Colón
Río Frío
El Ostional
El Cairo
C
Santa Elena
Correa
El Carmen
Los Chiles
Refugio de Vida Silvestre Los Guatuzos
COSTA RICA
4
5
6

Map 4
Pauta Dimon
Karawala
Barra de Río Grande
Kara
Cayo Tyara
Map 2
Tortuguero
Laguna Top Lock
Río Kurinwás
Cayo King Pequeño
Tasbapauni
REGION AUTONOMA ATLANTICO SUR (RAAS)
A
Wawasang
Marshall Point
Orinoco
Punta Set Net
La Fe
Pearl Lagoon/ Laguna de Perlas
Cayos de Perlas
Set Net
Brown Bank
Río Siquia
Map 3
Kakabila
Pearl Lagoon
Corn Islands (70km east of Tierra Dorada)
Little Corn
Big Corn
Laguna Grande
Tierra Dorada
El Recreo
La Esperanza
El Rama
Laguna Grande
Cara de Mono
Río Escondido
El Banco
Muelle de los Bueyes
Sisi
Laguna Smokey Lane
San Antonio
Krisimbila
La Batea
El Bluff
El Cacao
Bluefields
El Coral
Bay of Bluefields
Rama Cay
Caribbean Sea
B
El Almendro
Nuevo Guinea
La Esperanza
Verdún
Yolaina
La Letra
El Serrano
El Almacén
La Fonseca
Río Punta Gorda
Punta Gorda
N
RIO SAN JUAN
10 km
10 miles
Río Maíz
Bahía Punta Gorda
Los Chiles
Río Sábalo
Buena Vista
Río Santa Cruz
La Azucena
San Francisco
C
La Esperanza
Las Colinas
Boca de Sábalos
Los Chiles
El Castillo
Río Bartola
Río Indio
Bahía de San Juan
Bartola
San Juan del Norte
La Barra
Greytown
COSTA RICA
Reserva Biológica Indio-Maíz
San Carlos
1
2
3
Río San Juan
Río Colorado
Río San Carlos
Sarapiquí